Internet

Information Server™ 4

Administrator's

Guide

Internet

Information Server™ 4

Administrator's

Guide

Allen L. Wyatt
with
Garrett Pease

Prima Publishing

ISBN: 0-7615-1387-6

Library of Congress Catalog Card Number: 97-75919

Printed in the United States of America

98 99 00 01 HH 10 9 8 7 6 5 4 3 2 1

Publisher:
Matthew H. Carleson

Managing Editor:
Dan J. Foster

Acquisitions Editor:
Jenny L. Watson

Senior Editor:
Kelli R. Crump

Project Editor:
Susan Christophersen

Editorial Assistant:
Kim Benbow

Technical Reviewers:
Richard Cravens and Allen L. Wyatt

Copy Editor:
June Waldman

Interior Layout:
Jimmie Young

Cover Design:
Prima Design Team

Indexer:
Sharon Hilgenberg

Acknowledgments

I thought about putting together a fancy set of acknowledgments, but figured I could never do justice to all those I have to thank. Then I thought about putting together a blanket acknowledgment, but that almost seems too trite. (You know the type—I would like to thank the thousands of people who make the Internet what it is today—yuck!) Then I thought about just making it simple and stating what I really feel as this book comes to press, and this seemed like a sane course to follow in what can be an insane business.

Writing a book is hard—very hard. There is a lot of sweat and hard work that goes into it. It is virtually impossible for those who have not written a book to understand what it takes to do so. It is particularly difficult when you are writing about something as nebulous as the Internet, which seems as fast-changing as the morning dew. Going into the project, you know that your work will only have meaning to someone for a short period, and then everything will change and the frontier of knowledge will move on to other areas.

Because it is so difficult, there are many people who help. There are those who post messages on the various newsgroups or send e-mail with little tidbits of information. There are those at Microsoft who send out software for you to work with. There are those at the publisher who coax and cajole to help get the manuscript in on time in some semblance of order. And then there are those who provide moral support behind the scenes as patience frays and tempers flare.

These last people are the real strength behind getting a book such as this to market. They are the ones who must put up with late hours, detached stares, infrequent paychecks, empty food closets, and missed family outings. They are the ones who hear your fears and frustrations as you talk about your struggles and efforts. They are the ones that tell you everything will be all right, and then believe in you to make it that way. Others don't and cannot fill that role, so I would like to acknowledge my family and all they do to help me carve out my little corner of the world. Lee, Eric, Jeremy, Andrew, and most of all Debbie, thank you for your love, support, and encouragement. It is never wasted and always appreciated.

About the Authors

Allen L. Wyatt, an internationally recognized expert in small computer systems, has been working in the computer and publishing industries for almost two decades. He has written more than 35 books explaining many different facets of working with computers, as well as numerous magazine articles. His books have covered topics ranging from programming languages to using application software to using operating systems. Through the written word, Allen has helped millions of readers learn how to better use computers.

Allen is the president of Discovery Computing Inc. (**http://www.dcomp.com**), a computer and publishing services company located in Sundance, Wyoming. Besides writing books, he helps further the computer book industry by providing consulting and technical services. With his wife and three children, he lives on a 390-acre ranch just outside of town on the edge of the Black Hills. In his spare time he tends to his animals, has fun with his family, and participates in church and community events. If you would like to know more about Allen, visit his Web page at **http://www.decomp.com/DCI/AboutAllen.htm**.

Garrett Pease is a freelance computer consultant specializing in finding solutions, whether it be creating new programs or spare parts. He is currently located in Sundance, Wyoming where he spends a lot of time at Discovery Computing, Inc. , a local computer and publishing services company. Sundance is a small, out-of-the way community where independence is a necessity because the only reliable constants are odd weather and computer breakdowns. Garrett has recently come to understand the importance of taking some time out while appreciating the beauty of blizzards.

Contents at a Glance

Contents

Introduction

Welcome to *Internet Information Server 4 Administrator's Guide*. Internet Information Server (IIS) is one of the most exciting Web servers on the market today. It enables you to publish information in two different formats immediately (Web and FTP). It also provides a foundation to which you can add other components to tailor your site for the information your users need, including an e-mail and NNTP server.

Why Write This Book?

The world in which we live, and especially the computer industry, has become a very fast-paced place. The popular press talks about "Internet time." Software development is moving so quickly that it is virtually impossible for developers to produce the sort of in-house support materials necessary to effectively use their products. With the emphasis on the Internet, most product support is available only online. IIS doesn't come with a printed manual.

Filling this void is where third-party books (such as this one) come into play. More and more software vendors (Microsoft included) are either unwilling or unable to provide the necessary documentation and are relying on independent authors to pick up the slack. I don't claim to be on any of the Microsoft development teams, although I have been a daily user of IIS since before its first official release. I have worked with it, cursed at it, and found ways to make it perform the way that it needs to. Thus the need for this book: if I can pass just a little of that information on to you, then your purchase of this book has served its purpose.

Why Read This Book?

The stores are full of computer books these days. Some hit the shelves one day, only to be removed the next week. Changes in technology challenge authors and publishers to deliver quality information in a timely fashion.

The feature that sets *IIS 4 Administrator's Guide* apart from the competition is that this book is designed to last. You will use it not only as you are setting up IIS but also as your site develops and matures. Later, you will use the book to help you make management decisions and implement changes in structure or features.

I have made every effort to provide a well-rounded treatise on how to use IIS. Here you find information on the basic services included in IIS, as well as some of the technically advanced features needed to run a dynamic Web site. Here you learn how to put these tools to work one at a time or all together. *IIS 4 Administrator's Guide* provides a wealth of information that you simply cannot find in any other single place.

Who Are You?

In my opinion, most people who want to use IIS are doing so because they have information they want to disseminate to the world or to an in-house audience via an intranet. You are looking for practical answers to real-world problems. In some instances, you may be at a point where you would be happy if you could "just get the darn thing to work."

If you are in this boat, then you are in luck. *IIS 4 Administrator's Guide* can help you get your Internet (or intranet) site up and running as quickly as possible. Unfortunately, it is impossible to provide in one place every piece of knowledge you need to run IIS. With that said, you, as reader, should understand the following points before starting to use this book:

◆ **What the Internet is.** Many books provide a quick history of the Internet, providing you with information that is interesting, but not relevant to the task at hand—making IIS work. I assume that you already know a bit about the Internet, including what it is and how you can establish a connection to it.

◆ **How to use HTML.** The basis of any Web document is HTML. Understanding what HTML is, how it works, and how a browser interprets it is very beneficial to piecing together how your site should be designed.

◆ **How to use Windows NT.** IIS functions within the Windows NT environment. Because IIS works very closely with Windows NT, you need to understand the environment before you can understand how to use the full capabilities of IIS. During the course of this book, some Windows NT features are described and discussed in passing, but it is best to leave the full discussion of NT to another book entirely.

◆ **How to use non-IIS tools.** Many tools are available to help you manage your Internet or intranet site, including these provided by Windows NT: the Registry Editor, Performance Monitor, Event Viewer, and almost every applet from the Control Panel. It is beyond the scope of this book to explain each of these non-IIS tools in detail.

Instead, you should learn how to use them from other sources and bring that knowledge with you when you start this book.

If you need help in any of these areas, check your bookstore or library for any number of good books. In addition, some excellent resources are available online.

How to Use This Book

In many respects, a book can be viewed as a tool you use to create something. This book is no different; it has been crafted to convey information you will find invaluable in learning how to use IIS. As with any tool, it is most productive to those who use it properly. So, how should you use this book? A good first step is to examine the structure and content of the book, as well as some design elements that you will definitely find helpful.

Structure Is Everything

Computer book authors and publishing houses spend quite a bit of time at the start of a project developing an outline. This outline serves as a road map for the author writing the book, and functions as a framework for the reader. *IIS 4 Administrator's Guide* is divided into seven major parts:

◆ Part I, "Planning and Creating Your Site," lays the groundwork for setting up your site. Here you learn how to intelligently decide which services to offer, how to select the proper hardware and software, how to use the Internet Service Manager, how to configure your services, and how to set up virtual servers and directories.

◆ Part II, "Developing Basic Web Site Content," covers how you can start creating the information you offer on your Web site. Here you learn not only how to plan the content but also how to develop it using FrontPage. Other chapters cover linking your Web site, developing forms, and using various IIS extensions to HTML.

◆ Part III, "Developing Dynamic Web Site Content," focuses on the more advanced ways you can create content. Here you learn about CGI, different scripting languages, Dynamic HTML, Active Server Pages, ISAPI (the IIS programming interface), and team development tools.

◆ Part IV, "Database Publishing with IIS," discusses how you can use various IIS tools to dynamically access information in your databases. You learn how to use the Internet Database Connector, how you can use Microsoft Transaction Server, and how to link your pages to databases external to your site.

◆ Part V, "Establishing and Maintaining Security," covers the basics of securing your IIS site. You learn how IIS bases its security on the security model used by Windows NT, how to utilize IIS in a secure network environment, and how to implement Secure Sockets Layer (SSL) at your site (perhaps for commerce transactions).

◆ Part VI, "Issues for Serious Site Management," provides the information you need to make your site really shine from a management perspective. Here you learn how to perform remote administration, develop a wide-area intranet through PPTP, make the most of your log files, maximize the performance of your site, and understand how IIS uses the Registry.

◆ Part VII, "Additional Content Considerations," provides the information you can use to work with other types of information. Here you learn how to index your site, manage an FTP site, and work with the e-mail and NNTP services included with IIS.

Finally, three appendixes provide information related to setting up your site. You learn how to install IIS and how to troubleshoot your site; in addition, you will find answers to some frequently asked questions.

If you are still in doubt as to whether you can get your questions answered in *IIS 4 Administrator's Guide*, take a look at the Table of Contents and then review the index at the back of the book. Both are very descriptive and very complete, and they should help you locate the information you need right away.

Signposts Along the Way

As you read through this book, you will discover specific design features that point out helpful information. These nuggets stand out because of the way the book design presents the information. Please pay special attention to the following elements as you are reading:

NOTE

Notes identify information that is related to the discussion at hand, but may need special attention. Many notes refer you to places where you can find additional information.

> ### TIP
>
> Generally, tips call out information that you can use to make a task easier. Applying these tips can speed up your use of IIS and make you more productive.

> ### CAUTION
>
> Cautions mark critical information. Some steps or information can be dangerous to your site if used improperly; the icon draws your attention to information you should be aware of before proceeding.

 This icon identifies a place on the Web or elsewhere on the Internet where you can locate more information about the topic. It is also used to signal where you can locate tools or other programs being discussed.

 This icon identifies information that is available in a sample file. These files are available online, as described in the following section.

 This icon identifies Intranet-related material.

Put these elements to work to help you zero in on ways you can derive even more information from *IIS 4 Administrator's Guide.*

Examples and More Examples

IIS 4 Administrator's Guide includes quite a few hands-on examples that let you experience first-hand how to publish your information. Many of the chapters in the second section of the book refer to sample files and source code that it is helpful to use as you work through the chapter.

If you are like most people, you hate to type. That means you might not want to enter each example—particularly those that are quite long or detailed. (Some examples refer to databases that you cannot reconstruct from the information in the chapter alone.) Fortunately for you, the examples in this book are available online. If you like, you can download the appropriate files from one of the following locations:

- ◆ **http://www.dcomp.com/DCI/Books/iis4ag/iis.htm**
- ◆ **ftp://ftp.dcomp.com/pub/books/iis4ag/examples.zip**
- ◆ **http://www.primapublishing.com/iis4supportfiles**

Before you start reading through the book, you may want to take the time to download the examples so that you have them at hand. The Discovery Computing Web site (**HTTP://www.dcomp.com**) is particularly helpful. You should feel free to browse and examine the information provided there. If any errors or corrections come to my attention, I will be sure to post them at this site so you can access them as well.

Contacting the Author

I believe that any computer book effectively represents a meeting of the minds between the author (me) and the reader (you). In writing this book, I have attempted to clearly, concisely, and completely describe how to use Internet Information Server. I believe I have succeeded, but you are the ultimate judge. Did I succeed? I would like to hear from you. Your feedback can help to improve future editions of this book, as well as any other books I may write. Feel free to send your comments to **gpease@dcomp.com**.

As you can imagine, an open invitation to e-mail me can lead to a tremendous amount of e-mail. In fact, keeping up with it all can be a bit difficult at times. For this reason, I cannot promise that I will respond to every message, but I can say that I will read every one. I read my own e-mail; I don't have other people do it for me. If I like a message, I print it out and keep a copy so I can use it for future projects. I especially appreciate constructive criticism and messages that point out errors and omissions that may have made it into the final book. If a reader has a particular problem, I will try to help if I can and if time allows.

PART I

I

Planning and Creating
Your Site

Chapter 1

Understanding and
Choosing Internet
Services

In This Chapter

◆ The Internet Revisited

◆ Internet versus Intranet

◆ Client-Server Essentials and the Internet

◆ Picking Your Services

The Internet (and closely related intranets) is the hottest area in computing these days. You may have been charged with developing services and content to distribute on the Internet, or you may be examining how you can set up an intranet for your company. In either case, you need to understand the implications of what you are doing before you actually set about doing it. This task is analogous to creating a building or some other structure. You must decide what you want to include in your building, determine how you want the building to be used, select the proper tools, put the building together, and finally make sure it is used for the purpose originally intended.

This chapter introduces the services that you can use to make information available on either the Internet or an intranet. In addition, you will learn the basic information necessary to understand how to make those services available. If you already have a firm grasp of these services and the foundation technologies on which they rely, you can safely skip this introductory chapter. If not, or if you find yourself having trouble with the information presented later in the book, then use this chapter to learn or review the fundamentals. In either case, make sure that you understand the foundation before trying to create the rest of the building.

The Internet Revisited

So, exactly what is the Internet? Unfortunately, an exact, concise description is very difficult to craft. Perhaps the best description is that the Internet is a loose, volunteer connection of millions of computers and networks around the world. Despite their differences, these individual computers can exchange information using a common language, or protocol. Because computer connections and protocols are involved, the Internet is, by definition, a computer network. It is not a centrally controlled network, however. Instead, each computer or organization connected to the Internet is responsible for its portion of the whole.

Internet protocols and policies are described in Request for Comment (RFC) documents and can be found online at places such as **http://www.isi.edu/rfc-editor/**.

This is where you come into the picture. Each computer connected to the Internet has the potential to provide information to other computers connected to the Internet. Because people like you, with a unique focus and interest, control the different computers and determine what information is made available, the breadth and depth of information available on the Internet is absolutely astounding. The vast wealth of information that is available means that the Internet becomes more than a simple connection between computers—it becomes a tool that you can access through your computer. You can find and distribute information about virtually anything on the Internet. People are connecting to the Internet in astounding numbers and making their own information available.

If you are interested in the latest growth statistics about the Internet, one good source is **http://www.mids.org/**, where you can find both charts and graphs about this fascinating topic.

The Roots of the Internet

The Internet started in the mid-1960s when researchers, experimenting with computer communications, developed a fast and reliable method of sharing information over ordinary phone lines. This communication method, known as *packet switching*, involved breaking down a message (regardless of its size) into small packets that were sent individually over the communications channel. These packets have three primary components:

- ◆ **Header** Contains information about the intended recipient of the packet, along with an indication of where, in the message sequence, the packet belongs.
- ◆ **Body** Contains the main information being conveyed. This portion can be either an entire message (if the message is very short) or a part of the larger message.
- ◆ **Trailer** Indicates when the end of the packet has been reached.

As information is broken down into packets, it is transmitted over the network. Each computer that encounters a packet examines the header to determine whether the packet is intended for that node. If not, the computer passes on the packet in a direction closer to the ultimate destination. Eventually, all the packets arrive at their destination and are reassembled in order. The use of packets provides three primary benefits over other connection technologies:

- ◆ Easier sharing
- ◆ Easier error detection and correction
- ◆ Easier routing

Easier sharing means that multiple users can share the same communications link with each user's packets intertwined with the packets of other users. This condition is analogous to a busy interstate. Thousands of cars belonging to thousands of drivers and headed to thousands of destinations can share the same roadway. If one large vehicle destined for one location replaces all the cars, then the use of the highway becomes much less flexible.

Being able to detect and correct errors easily is another benefit of using packet switching. The receiving program checks each packet for errors. If the receiving program detects an error, it can request that only a single packet be retransmitted. Other communication methods might require the resending of an entire message. Even though errors may not happen often, the secondary transmission of a single packet is much more efficient than the rebroadcast of an entire message.

Finally, packet switching is, by design, very dynamic; that is, the packets in a single message can take multiple routes to the same destination. This dynamic approach to networking means that even if one route between two nodes on the network goes down, the packets can travel a different route to their destination. The result is less potential for downtime.

Over the years, packet switching has been used in networks of all sizes. In the early days of the technology, only computers at a single location were connected. As local networks grew at individual research facilities and universities, connecting these networks to share information between facilities became desirable. These interconnections were treated as extensions of the original, individual networks. In 1969, the Department of Defense, through its Advanced Research Projects Agency (ARPA), created an experimental packet-switched network called ARPANET, an early forerunner of the Internet. In 1982, ARPANET joined with the military network (MILNET) and a few other networks, and the Internet was created from this consolidation. The term *Internet* is a shortened version of *internet work system*.

Today, millions of networks and individual computers are connected to the Internet, and the result is very exciting to watch. You have probably felt this excitement as well, or you would not be considering offering your own services over the Internet.

TCP/IP and the Internet

The transfer of information over networks always follows a *protocol*, which is nothing more than a set of rules used in orderly communication. The basic protocol of the Internet is *Internet Protocol*, or *IP* for short, which is responsible for transmitting packets of information to the proper address. IP isn't very reliable, so a second protocol is generally added to enhance IP's reliability and functionality. Most Internet programs add the transmission control protocol (TCP) to IP. The result, known as

TCP/IP, provides a reliable way to communicate information between computers—even if the computers are fundamentally different platforms and are separated by great distances.

In some operating systems, TCP/IP is built in. For example, UNIX uses TCP/IP as its native networking protocol. In contrast, to use TCP/IP with other operating systems, including Windows NT, you need to install the proper network drivers and configure them properly for your system. With all the interest in the Internet, Microsoft is making TCP/IP a more integral part of Windows, but it still needs to be configured properly.

Internet Addressing

Everything you do on the Internet involves the use of an address in some way. In reality, the Internet uses two types of addresses, both of which are intrinsic to the TCP/IP protocols discussed in the previous section.

Internet addresses perform the function that their names suggest—they uniquely identify either an area of the Internet or a user accessible through the Internet. The truest (and most accurate) analogy is to your home address. This address, when provided fully, uniquely identifies where you live. If someone wants to send you a package or visit you, he or she must know your address. Similarly, on the Internet, if someone wants to send you something, such as e-mail, the sender must know your address. If someone wants to retrieve something from a computer on the Internet, such as a Web site or FTP site, that person must know the address of the site.

As with physical home addresses, an Internet address goes from the more general to the more specific. Take a look at a typical physical address:

Allen L. Wyatt
Discovery Computing Inc.
20101 U.S. Highway 14
Sundance, WY 82729

This address indicates that I can be found at a place called Discovery Computing Inc. Because more than one company in the world could have that name, more details are necessary. The next line indicates that the company is located at a particular place on a particular road, whereas the final line indicates the town and state in which that road is located. Each addition to the address makes it more specific.

Now take a look at the following address, this one for someone on the Internet:

awyatt@dcomp.com

The preceding address is a real address—mine. It functions in much the same way as my physical address. The part of the address before the @ sign is the *user ID*, in this case awyatt. The portion of the address after the @ sign is the *domain*, with periods between each level of the domain. Domains are simply different organizational levels. These levels are increasingly general, from left to right. This address contains both a user ID and a domain, thus introducing the first type of addressing on the Internet—*domain addressing*.

Internet Domains

The Internet addressing scheme employs the *domain naming system*, which provides a method of uniquely identifying different organizations, computer systems, and individuals on the Internet. The system allows an address to include multiple domain levels, so at times the domains can appear rather complex. For example, take a look at the following fictional address:

jclark@cis.ubc.yitl.edu

This domain has four levels. If you start at the end of the domain and work backward, you can get a more specific idea of the domain's location. The *edu* level indicates that this address belongs to an educational institution. The domain that appears at the very right side of a domain address is referred to as a *top-level domain*, as discussed shortly. The next domain level, *yitl*, probably indicates the specific educational institution, and *ubc* may be a department within that institution. Finally, *cis* identifies a specific computer within that department—a computer that is used to link to the Internet. Each level of the domain may have other subdivisions. For example, the ubc department may have more than one computer, and yitl is more than likely to have more than one department.

The preceding explanation uses terms such as *probably* or *may* because the domain naming system doesn't have hard and fast rules. The important thing for you to remember is that domains help to identify the location of a computer or network. This information is essential for accessing resources and directing information across the Net.

Top-level domains can be either organizational or geographical. Table 1-1 describes the seven possible organizational domains.

Table 1-1 Organizational Domains

Domain	Purpose
com	Commercial entities, such as businesses
edu	Educational institutions
gov	Nonmilitary U.S. government institutions
int	International institutions, such as NATO
mil	U.S. military institutions
net	Network resources, including Internet service providers
org	Nonprofit organizations

NOTE

With the tremendous growth on the Internet, there is some cause for concern that a limited number of names is available. One solution to this problem is to increase the number of top-level domain names available for use. For more information about new top-level domain names, you can check out **http://www.iahc.org/press/press-final.html.**

ONLINE

For the most part, you can assume that any domain name ending with an organizational domain is physically located within the United States. For domains outside the United States and for state and local governments within the United States, the top-level domain is geographical in nature. This top-level domain consists of two letters that indicate the country in which the domain is located. At last count, more than 240 geographical domains existed. Table 1-2 shows the available geographical domains as of this writing.

Table 1-2 Sample Geographical Domains

Domain	Country	Domain	Country
ad	Andorra	aq	Antarctica
ae	United Arab Emirates	ar	Argentina
af	Afghanistan	as	American Samoa
ag	Antigua and Barbuda	at	Austria
ai	Anguilla	au	Australia
al	Albania	aw	Aruba
am	Armenia	az	Azerbaijan
an	Netherlands Antilles	ba	Bosnia-Herzegovina
ao	Angola	bb	Barbados

Table 1-2 Sample Geographical Domains *(continued)*

Domain	Country	Domain	Country
bd	Bangladesh	dm	Dominica
be	Belgium	do	Dominican Republic
bf	Burkina Faso	dz	Algeria
bg	Bulgaria	ec	Ecuador
bh	Bahrain	ee	Estonia
bi	Burundi	eg	Egypt
bj	Benin	eh	Western Sahara
bm	Bermuda	es	Spain
bn	Brunei Darussalam	et	Ethiopia
bo	Bolivia	fi	Finland
br	Brazil	fj	Fiji
bs	Bahamas	fk	Falkland Islands
bt	Bhutan	fm	Micronesia
bv	Bouvet Island	fo	Faroe Islands
bw	Botswana	fr	France
by	Belarus	fx	France (European Territory)
bz	Belize	ga	Gabon
ca	Canada	gb	Great Britain
cc	Cocos (Keeling) Islands	gd	Grenada
cf	Central African Republic	ge	Georgia
cg	Congo	gf	French Guyana
ch	Switzerland	gh	Ghana
ci	Ivory Coast (Cote D'Ivoire)	gi	Gibraltar
ck	Cook Islands	gl	Greenland
cl	Chile	gm	Gambia
cm	Cameroon	gn	Guinea
cn	China	gp	Guadeloupe (French)
co	Colombia	gq	Equatorial Guinea
cr	Costa Rica	gr	Greece
cs	Former Czechoslovakia	gs	South Georgia & South
cu	Cuba		Sandwich Islands
cv	Cape Verde	gt	Guatemala
cx	Christmas Island	gu	Guam (USA)
cy	Cyprus	gw	Guinea Bissau
cz	Czech Republic	gy	Guyana
de	Germany	hk	Hong Kong
dj	Djibouti	hm	Heard and McDonald Islands
dk	Denmark	hn	Honduras

Table 1-2 Sample Geographical Domains (continued)

Domain	Country	Domain	Country
hr	Croatia	mc	Monaco
ht	Haiti	md	Moldavia
hu	Hungary	mg	Madagascar
id	Indonesia	mh	Marshall Islands
ie	Ireland	mk	Macedonia
il	Israel	ml	Mali
in	India	mm	Myanmar
io	British Indian Ocean Territory	mn	Mongolia
iq	Iraq	mo	Macau
ir	Iran	mp	Northern Mariana Islands
is	Iceland	mq	Martinique (French)
it	Italy	mr	Mauritania
jm	Jamaica	ms	Montserrat
jo	Jordan	mt	Malta
jp	Japan	mu	Mauritius
ke	Kenya	mv	Maldives
kg	Kyrgyzstan	mw	Malawi
kh	Cambodia	mx	Mexico
ki	Kiribati	my	Malaysia
km	Comoros	mz	Mozambique
kn	Saint Kitts & Nevis Anguilla	na	Namibia
kp	North Korea	nc	New Caledonia (French)
kr	South Korea	ne	Niger
kw	Kuwait	nf	Norfolk Island
ky	Cayman Islands	ng	Nigeria
kz	Kazakhstan	ni	Nicaragua
la	Laos	nl	Netherlands
lb	Lebanon	no	Norway
lc	Saint Lucia	np	Nepal
li	Liechtenstein	nr	Nauru
lk	Sri Lanka	nt	Neutral Zone
lr	Liberia	nu	Niue
ls	Lesotho	nz	New Zealand
lt	Lithuania	om	Oman
lu	Luxembourg	pa	Panama
lv	Latvia	pe	Peru
ly	Libya	pf	Polynesia (French)
ma	Morocco	pg	Papua New Guinea

Table 1-2 Sample Geographical Domains *(continued)*

Domain	Country	Domain	Country
ph	Philippines	th	Thailand
pk	Pakistan	tj	Tadjikistan
pl	Poland	tk	Tokelau
pm	Saint Pierre and Miquelon	tm	Turkmenistan
pn	Pitcairn Island	tn	Tunisia
pr	Puerto Rico	to	Tonga
pt	Portugal	tp	East Timor
pw	Palau	tr	Turkey
py	Paraguay	tt	Trinidad and Tobago
qa	Qatar	tv	Tuvalu
re	Reunion (French)	tw	Taiwan
ro	Romania	tz	Tanzania
ru	Russian Federation	ua	Ukraine
rw	Rwanda	ug	Uganda
sa	Saudi Arabia	uk	United Kingdom
sb	Solomon Islands	um	USA Minor Outlying
sc	Seychelles		Islands
sd	Sudan	us	United States
se	Sweden	uy	Uruguay
sg	Singapore	uz	Uzbekistan
sh	Saint Helena	va	Vatican City State
si	Slovenia	vc	Saint Vincent &
sj	Svalbard and Jan Mayen Islands		Grenadines
sk	Slovak Republic	ve	Venezuela
sl	Sierra Leone	vg	Virgin Islands (British)
sm	San Marino	vi	Virgin Islands (USA)
sn	Senegal	vn	Vietnam
so	Somalia	vu	Vanuatu
sr	Suriname	wf	Wallis and Futuna Islands
st	Saint Tome and Principe	ws	Samoa
su	Former USSR	ye	Yemen
sv	El Salvador	yt	Mayotte
sy	Syria	yu	Yugoslavia
sz	Swaziland	za	South Africa
tc	Turks and Caicos Islands	zm	Zambia
td	Chad	zr	Zaire
tf	French Southern Territories	zw	Zimbabwe
tg	Togo		

Note that the United States also has a geographic domain code. Typically, this code is used only when someone wants an address to be complete. An Internet address without a geographic code is assumed to be located within the United States.

The Internet Protocol Address

By now, virtually everyone knows that computers understand numbers, but not the letters or symbols that humans use to communicate. Thus, every host (a computer linked to the Internet) on the Internet has a unique host number, which is called the *Internet Protocol address*, or *IP address*. Each IP address is unique; it identifies a single location on the Internet. These IP addresses consist of four 8-bit numbers, represented in decimal notation but separated by periods. The following is an example of an IP address:

205.163.44.2

This notation for an IP address is sometimes called a *dotted-decimal notation*, or *dotted-quad notation*. Each of the four numbers in this IP address is called an *octet* and represents 1 byte of the full 32-bit address. Thus no octet can have a value above 255, which means that the lowest possible IP address is 0.0.0.0 and the highest is 255.255.255.255 (although this is misleading because the network uses some IP addresses for overhead). An IP address refers to an individual host on the Internet, meaning an individual computer system that is responsible for distributing mail or messages. No two hosts on the network will ever have the same IP address.

IP addresses are assigned to networks based on the size of the network. Only three classifications of networks exist: A, B, and C:

♦ *Class A networks* are very large, and few IP addresses are available for these types of networks—only 126 possible class A addresses exist in the world. Each class A network can have in excess of 16 million computers in its individual network. For class A networks, the first octet of its IP address is between 1 and 126, and all the remaining octets are used to identify members of that network.

♦ *Class B networks* are a bit smaller; they can have up to approximately 65,000 workstations. For these types of networks, the first octet of the IP address is a number between 128 and 191, and the second octet further denotes the network address. Thus, approximately 16,000 class B networks can exist in the world. The last two octets of the IP address denote individual workstations.

♦ *Class C networks* are the smallest. These networks can include up to about 250 workstations per network. The first octet of the IP address has a value between 192 and 223, and the second and third octets further define the network. The final octet identifies the workstation on the network. Several million class C networks are available under the current addressing scheme.

The breakdown of IP addresses into different classes is simply a way of allocating addresses among the various networks that access the Internet. Table 1-3 summarizes IP address network classifications.

Table 1-3 IP Address Network Classification

	Class A	Class B	Class C
First octet values	1–126	128–191	191–223
Net ID octets	1	1–2	1–3
Host ID octets	2–4	3–4	4
Nets in class	126	16,384	2,097,151
Hosts per net	16,777,214	65,534	254

As you can see, many IP addresses are available. However, some people are concerned that the current growth rate may require a change in the IP addressing scheme to allow for more addresses. IPng, or the Next Generation Internet Protocol, is being developed to handle future growth. For more information, check out

`ONLINE` **http://playground.sun.com/pub/ipng/html/ipng-main.html**.

Internet versus Intranet

As the Internet has grown, and particularly in the past few years, a number of computing tools have emerged that were designed specifically for use on the Net. These tools were developed to take advantage of the TCP/IP protocol that you learned about earlier in this chapter. Because the TCP/IP protocol can be used on both local networks and on the Internet as a whole, you can use the same tools in both environments.

This points out the similarity between the Internet and an intranet. The only real difference is that the Internet is a network connection with computers *outside* your organization, and an intranet provides similar connections and services for use *within* your organization, as illustrated in Figure 1-1.

Many large companies are using the tools originally developed for publishing information over the Internet but limiting those tools to use within the company. For example, Eli Lilly and Company, a large pharmaceuticals corporation based in Indianapolis, has established a Web site that isn't open to everyone on the Internet.

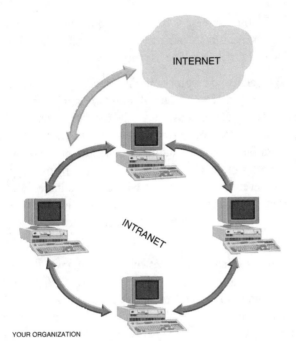

FIGURE 1-1

The relationship between the Internet and an intranet.

Instead, it is used on Lilly's internal network to disseminate information quickly and easily to a group of authorized users.

Intranets are not limited to large companies, however. Indeed, companies of all sizes are developing internal networks to share information necessary to the successful growth of the organization. Other companies are seeking to improve their internal communications by using common networking protocols and tools.

From a technical standpoint, the Internet and an intranet are very similar. Indeed, they use the same networking concepts, and the same tools come into play. As you work through this book, remember that everything discussed about the Internet can also be adapted for use on your own private intranet.

Client-Server Essentials and the Internet

In traditional computer processing, information presented to a computer user is transferred across a network in a straightforward manner. The user begins by requesting information from a program running on his or her computer. This program accesses a remote database and requests the information it needs to fulfill the user's request. The information in the database is transferred to the user's computer where it is processed, and the answer is finally provided to the user. Under this processing model, the raw data is actually transferred across the network to the user's computer.

In most respects, this approach to data processing is unnecessarily wasteful of computer resources. The problem is that a precious commodity—time—is used to transmit large amounts of raw data over the network. While the data requested by the user is being transmitted, no other data can be transmitted over the network. This problem may not be significant when only a handful of users are on the network, but it quickly becomes significant as more and more users enter the picture. For example, imagine a network with several hundred users who are simultaneously trying to retrieve information from a centralized source. Bottlenecks can quickly develop as large amounts of raw information are transferred from the centralized source to the various nodes on the network.

To overcome this problem, the client-server networking model was developed. This model breaks the program doing the processing into two parts: a client and a server. The client portion of the program runs on the user's computer, and the server portion runs on the centralized computer where the database is located. The client doesn't request raw information; instead, it requests final answers, and the server at the remote database is responsible for processing the information. In this way, only the answer is transmitted across the network, thereby requiring less time and network resources.

This client-server relationship between two programs provides most of the information on the Internet. The site that publishes information establishes a server; the site that wants to access the information uses a client. The client software communicates with the server software, and the requested information is transferred over the Internet between the two systems. Figure 1-2 illustrates this process.

Thousands of client-server applications have been developed for use on the Internet. Perhaps the most prevalent is the common e-mail program. The client program (which allows you to read and manage your own e-mail) runs on your local computer. The server program, which is analogous to a post office, runs on a computer elsewhere on your network or a computer to which you have access. This server program manages e-mail messages until your local client program is ready to receive them. The server also takes care of communicating with and transferring information to other mail servers on the network.

Client-server technology also implements other well-known Internet tools. These tools include the World Wide Web, FTP, Usenet, e-mail, and Gopher, and each one requires a server component and a client component. The servers for these tools are

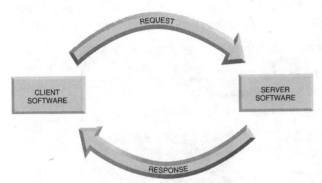

FIGURE 1-2

Client and server programs work with each other to provide information on the Internet.

part of Internet Information Server (IIS). You can implement any or all of the tools at your site. The following sections describe each type of server so that you can make a decision as to which tools to implement.

NOTE

Information on how to install IIS appears in Appendix A.

Understanding a Web Server

The World Wide Web enables you to publish and/or view all sorts of information. In many respects, the Web is the multimedia portion of the Internet. You can publish text, graphics, sounds, full-motion video, and programs, to name a few types of information.

The interaction between Web servers and Web clients makes the World Wide Web possible. (The client portion is referred to as a *Web browser.*) The client and the server communicate by using a protocol called *HTTP*, which stands for *HyperText Transport Protocol.* Using HTTP, the client issues a command to the server. The server then responds to the command, providing information to the client. The client can use that information as desired. In most instances, the client displays the information on the browser screen or processes it in some other way (such as playing a sound or downloading a file).

Information on the Web is published as a series of pages. Be careful not to confuse a page on the Web with a physical page, such as the page of this book. Although the two items have some similarities, there are many differences as well. The biggest difference is that a Web page can be as big as the designer chooses to make it. The page can contain any of the resource types already discussed, along with links to other pages on the Web. Figure 1-3 shows an example of a Web page, as seen within a browser. (A Web browser is the client portion of the client-server model.)

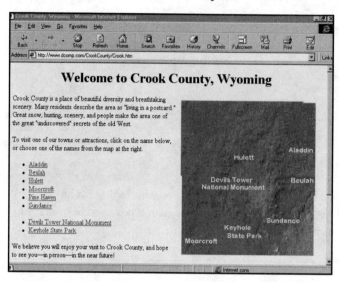

FIGURE 1-3

A Web page can contain many different elements.

The underlined text that appears on the Web page denotes a link to related information elsewhere on the Web. As the person using the browser moves the mouse pointer over the link, the status bar indicates the link's address. When the user clicks on the link, the server at a remote location is contacted, a page is transferred over the Internet, and the new page is displayed in the user's browser.

Estimates on actual growth of the Web are hard to come by, but all reports indicate that millions and millions of people are actively using the Web on a daily basis.

Understanding an FTP Server

FTP is the name of a program used to transfer files from one system to another. In reality, FTP is an acronym for File Transfer Protocol. This protocol (and program) has its roots in the UNIX environment and is a very handy tool. As you might surmise, the FTP program uses the FTP protocol to accomplish its work. From a user's standpoint, the FTP program accomplishes several tasks:

◆ Enables you to establish a connection between your machine and a remote site

◆ Enables you to perform limited directory-related operations at that site

◆ Enables you to transfer files between the remote site and your machine, or vice versa

Because FTP allows files to be transferred, it is one of the most popular programs used on the Internet. This statement is particularly true for people who have been using the Internet for a while. (Many newer users think the Web and the Internet are synonymous; therefore, they don't try additional programs such as FTP.)

The Internet has thousands of FTP sites, which are particularly well suited for file-related materials. For example, if you publish a magazine, you may want to make the files referenced in your publication available to subscribers. Or, if you produce a computer peripheral, you may want to make the appropriate drivers available on the Internet. These needs (and hundreds of similar scenarios) lend themselves to a solution involving FTP.

Understanding an E-mail Server

E-mail is unquestionably the single largest use of the Internet. This statement makes sense because the Internet is a medium for communication, and e-mail is the standard way of communicating electronically. If you are responsible for your own domain, you may want to set up a mail server for your site.

You may be familiar with e-mail from the user side of the fence: when you need your mail, you fire up your e-mail program (such as Eudora, MS Mail, or E-Mail Connection) and manage your messages. These programs are called *user agents*; they enable you (the user) to manage your mail by using an interface with which you are comfortable.

User agents don't take care of all the behind-the-scenes tasks related to e-mail, however, because they are the client portion of a client-server software pair. This situation is very common on the Internet; all of the Internet services described in this chapter use a combination of client and server software. You may remember that when you first set up your e-mail program, you provided the name of an e-mail server with which the program should connect. From the network administrator's viewpoint, this server (called a *Message Transfer Agent*, or *MTA*) is the key program required for e-mail. If you manage your own domain, you may want to install your own MTA program or e-mail server.

Understanding a Usenet Server

Usenet news is another popular method for communicating ideas. In contrast to e-mail, which is sent to specific recipients, news is sent to a server using Network News Transport Protocol (NNTP), which anyone can access. Usenet news is similar to an electronic bulletin board on which you post a message for everyone to see.

A Usenet server is a good place to hold a discussion. People can ask questions about your products and services and get responses from specialists at your site or from other users. Microsoft, Borland, and a few other companies have public Usenet newsgroups that provide support and information for their products. Newsgroup sites may be either moderated or unmoderated. A moderated newsgroup has a moderator who reviews all of the posts—generally to make sure they are related to the topic—before posting them to the newsgroup.

Understanding a Gopher Server

Like FTP, Gopher predates the emergence of the World Wide Web. Developed in early 1991 by the University of Minnesota's Microcomputer, Workstation, and Networks Center, the software has been widely accepted and implemented over much of the Net, particularly in the educational and government arenas. Gopher is a tool that enables a user to retrieve information that has been stored in Gopher servers at various sites across the Net.

The main reason for Gopher's success is that finding information on the Internet can be difficult. Prior to the creation of Gopher, locating an uncommon file or resource was more of a chore than a learning adventure; people often spent hours tracking down the information they needed. Although finding obscure information can still take considerable time, Gopher makes the job easier. Gopher allows information providers to organize the information at their site and create links to similar information elsewhere.

In a nutshell, Gopher is a program that enables you to access databases from all around the Internet. More specifically, as its name implies, it will "go for" the data or topic that you specify. But rather than force you to blindly search a database for your desired topic, Gopher always presents a series of menus from which you can make choices. Each choice represents a resource that you can use. These resources can be on a local computer system or from virtually anywhere on the Internet.

If you need to publish information that is predominately text oriented, using Gopher can be a better choice for Net publishing than using the Web. The drawback is that most novice computer users are using the Web, not Gopher. Depending on your audience, however, this situation may not be a drawback at all.

NOTE

Gopher has almost disappeared from the scene of popular Internet services. As a sign of its decline, IIS 4 no longer includes a Gopher server. Most of the use of Gopher has been taken up with Web-based search engines.

Picking Your Services

Now that you have learned the basics of how the Internet works, as well as what you can do on the Internet, you are ready to decide which services you want to offer. IIS includes several services that you can use to transmit information on the Internet. The services you pick are up to you, but you need to be concerned with the following issues:

◆ **Content.** What type of content are you making available on your site? What is the best way to present that content to your user?

◆ **Development effort.** How much work will it take to develop and maintain your site? How much time can you devote to these efforts?

◆ **Type of user.** What type of user are you trying to reach? How can you best meet that user's needs?

◆ **User interaction.** How much user interaction do you want at your site? What is the user expected to do?

Each of these items is important in your decision, and you will need to do some strategic planning to make sure that you cover all your bases. In your decision-making process, you may want to talk with others at your company and perhaps discuss your options with other people in your industry who have built their own Internet sites. Examining other Internet sites is a great way to learn techniques that you can use to make your site the best it can be.

CAUTION

The services you use at your site can affect the security of both the computer on which the services are running and your entire network. Make sure that you understand the security issues, as discussed in Part VI of this book.

The information in Table 1-4 can help you decide which Internet services to offer. Although some of the specifics may depend on how you decide to implement a site, Table 1-4 provides good, general guidance on which services may be right for your needs. In the case of an e-mail server, you may already have an existing server that you don't want to change.

Fortunately, the site that you develop with IIS does not have to be "all or nothing." You can install any number of services up front and then add or remove services as your needs change.

Table 1-4 Decision Points in Picking Internet Services

	Web	FTP	E-mail	Usenet	Gopher
Content					
Lots of text	X			X	X
Lots of graphics	X				
Looking for "pizzazz"	X				
File based		X			
Stored in database	X				
Highly structured	X	X		X	X
Dynamic	X			X	X
Static	X	X			X
Development Effort					
Very little work		X		X	
Moderate work	X		X	X	X
Lots of work	X				
Type of User					
Consumer	X		X	X	
Technical		X	X	X	
Professional	X	X	X	X	
Educational	X		X	X	X
Government			X	X	X
User Interaction					
Easy to use	X		X	X	X
Read-only	X	X	X	X	
Download special programs		X			
Upload information	X	X		X	

Chapter 2

Selecting the Right
Hardware and Software

In This Chapter

◆ Hardware You Need to Run IIS

◆ Software You Need to Run IIS

◆ Other Services for Your Site

◆ Windows NT Tools

The foundation of any successful Internet or intranet site is the computer hardware and software that you use to put the site together. If any component is not up to par, then you cannot expect to operate a successful site. In addition, if you match your hardware to the needs of your software, and fit your software to the demands of your users, you will have far fewer problems. Indeed, the performance of your site will enhance the user's experience and your management efforts rather than serving as a drawback.

This chapter focuses on both the hardware and software that you should use at your site. The information presented here will help you make the most appropriate selections.

NOTE

If you already have IIS installed on your server, then the hardware issues surrounding your site may be a moot point. However, if you are experiencing hardware-based performance issues or if you are thinking of upgrading your hardware, this chapter is a must.

Hardware You Need to Run IIS

As you learned in Chapter 1, when you connect to the Internet or develop your own intranet, you are establishing a network environment. Even if your site uses a single computer, it becomes part of the Internet. By definition, the Internet is a network of computers that can share information using a common set of protocols. The same is true of all Internet services; they operate within and take advantage of a networked environment.

When you use IIS to publish information on the Internet or an intranet, you are running server software. This server software runs within the environment created by the operating system—Windows NT Server. The operating system, in turn, is running on a hardware platform (your computer), which is also often referred to as a *server*.

Three levels of "servers" may sound a bit confusing. Don't let the terminology throw you; *server* (in this context) tends to be rather all encompassing. The important thing to remember is that you are running server software (IIS), a server operating system (Windows NT Server) and a high-powered computer system (your hardware server). This relationship is depicted in Figure 2-1.

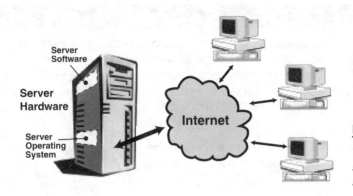

FIGURE 2-1

The relationship between server software, operating systems, and hardware.

Because IIS is running within the environment established by Windows NT Server, your hardware must conform to the requirements of both IIS and Windows NT Server. Unless you plan on running a site that has a large number of simultaneous visitors, the difference between server hardware and any other high-powered computer system is minimal; if you purchase a high-powered computer system, you generally can use it as a server. You can, however, find many computers that are marketed specifically as servers. These computers are typically optimized in some manner—at a hardware level—to make them particularly well suited for use as a server. Purchasing such systems, although not essential to the use of IIS, may offer performance advantages if you are running a heavily used site. You should understand, however, that specialized server systems typically carry a premium price tag.

NOTE

If you are running an older version of Windows NT (prior to NT 4.0), you can also run older versions of IIS; you can use the same CPUs in both instances. However, I highly recommend that you upgrade your system to take advantage of the new features and interface of Windows NT, as well as the new features of IIS 4.0.

The hardware requirements for establishing a server using IIS are very specific. Your system requires items in the following categories:

- ◆ **Computer.** You can run IIS on any system that can run Windows NT Server 4.0, including an 80486 system running at 25 MHz or higher, a DEC Alpha AXP, the MIPS Rx400, and the PowerPC. Most small- to medium-sized businesses are probably using the Intel platform for Windows NT.

> **CAUTION**
>
> Microsoft has announced that it is no longer planning products for the MIPS and PowerPC environments. Although Windows NT 4.0 is available on MIPS and PowerPC, future versions of the operating system will not be. For this reason, you may want to consider a different platform for your Windows NT system. IIS 4.0 will not run on these platforms.

♦ **Hard drive.** The amount of disk space that you need for IIS depends on the platform on which you are installing the software. On an Intel system, IIS does not take that much space, but with all the other requirements (including the operating system), you need at least a 150MB hard drive. This size should not present a problem, as most new systems are being sold with at least a 1GB hard drive.

♦ **Memory.** Your system needs at least 16MB of RAM for the server to work properly. With this relatively small amount of memory installed, you will notice slow response times, however. If you are using additional server software on your server, you should increase the RAM for each service.

♦ **CD-ROM drive.** Microsoft supplies Windows NT Server 4.0 only on CD-ROM. Thus you need a CD-ROM drive in order to install the operating system. Any single-speed CD-ROM drive will suffice, although you will be happier with a faster model.

♦ **Video system.** The video system within a computer comprises a video card and a monitor. Unless you actually plan on doing development work on your server, the size and type of monitor that you get is not particularly important. If you are doing development work on the system, you will want a good graphics accelerator and at least a 17-inch monitor.

Remember that these system requirements are *minimums*. Anyone who has used computers for any length of time realizes that adequate system performance calls for more robust hardware. In fact, looking at the requirements, you may believe that you could use some hand-me-down system that has been lying around the office for a few years. Although you can try this approach, I can guarantee that you won't be happy with the results. The performance of your system will limit your productivity, and even low demands for information from your site will face long delays.

If you expect to create a new system, you may want to look at a few companies that sell bundled hardware and software. Compaq Computer Corp. and Digital Equipment Corp. (DEC) offer core servers that run Windows NT with IIS and a few other Internet services bundled together. These companies don't currently offer IIS 4.0, but that situation may have changed by the time you read this book.

Workstations

You don't *need* a workstation to establish your Internet site. You will quickly find, however, that having a workstation separate from your server is advantageous. The workstation enables you to do development work without taxing the server. In effect, you can develop resources for your server without slowing the response time of your server, which should be handling requests from remote clients.

The workstations that you use can run any variety of operating systems and therefore can have any number of hardware requirements. Most often, however, you will want a workstation that can use the tools available. Currently, you'll find the largest selection of tools for Windows NT 4.0 and Windows 95.

The minimum system requirements for these systems are quite small. Remember, again, that you want a workstation that will perform well with the available tools. If you want only to create HTML pages, you can get by with just about anything; even an old 286 running a simple text editor can create HTML pages. However, to create a multimedia experience or develop clever Web applications, you should have a fast Pentium-class machine with at least 16MB of RAM, a quality graphics accelerator, and a good monitor.

Network Hardware

The type and complexity of network hardware that you need depends on two main items: your network topology and the number of nodes in your network. The topic of network configuration can be quite complex and is definitely beyond the scope of this book. If you have a network already in place, information in relation to network hardware is probably pointless, anyway—you must work with what you have.

If you haven't set up a local area network, you need the following items:

◆ A *network interface card* for each computer connected to the network. All these cards must use the same protocols. For example, if you are establishing an Ethernet network, all the interface cards must use Ethernet.

◆ A *hub* or *concentrator*. This device provides a central, localized connection for each computer on the network. Hubs and concentrators do essentially the same thing, but different network protocols refer to them by different names. In general, you need a hub or concentrator only if you are connecting more than two computers in your network.

To use your network hardware effectively and efficiently, you should refer to a good book on network basics, such as *Windows NT Server 4 Administrator's Guide* by Paul Robichaux, published by Prima. You also may want to employ the services of a knowledgeable network technician. The time savings alone can more than justify the cost of paying for professional help.

INTRANET

If you are establishing an intranet, all you need is your internal network. If you are setting up an Internet site, you also need specialized networking hardware that makes your Internet connection possible. Typically, a connection requires two pieces of equipment:

◆ **Router.** This device inspects data packets to determine where they should be sent. In layman's terms, a router acts as a "traffic cop" to determine what information gets sent where. A router is essential to direct information between your network and the Internet at large (and vice versa).

◆ **DSU/CSU.** Between the router and the phone line is a device known as a data service unit/channel service unit (DSU/CSU). The DSU/CPU used to be two separate units: the DSU serviced the data terminal equipment (the router) and the CSU serviced the digital data service (the phone line). Today, however, the DSU/CSU is typically a single device about the size of an external modem. In technical terms, the CSU portion of the device terminates the digital phone circuit through line conditioning and equalization. The DSU then converts the signaling protocol from the phone company's format to the router's format.

You can purchase the specialized networking hardware required to connect to the Internet either from a specialized vendor (or the manufacturer) or from your Internet service provider.

Software You Need to Run IIS

So far, this chapter has covered the computer hardware you need to set up your own Internet or intranet site using IIS. Hardware is only part of the story, however. You also need to meet certain software requirements. The requirements depend on the version of IIS you are using. If you are using version 2.0 (which came with Windows NT Server 4.0), the requirements are very simple: as long as you can run Windows NT Server 4.0, you can use IIS. If you are using IIS version 4.0 (which can be downloaded from the Microsoft Web site), then you also need service pack 3 for Windows NT Server 4.0.

Periodically, Microsoft issues service packs for its operating systems. These service packs contain minor upgrades to correct problems, bugs, and errors. Microsoft also creates service packs to update features, which is the main reason that some of its products require service packs. The service packs aren't widely publicized, but they come out fairly regularly.

CAUTION

The operating system requirements for IIS are very specific; you must be using Windows NT Server 4.0. If you try to run IIS under an earlier version of NT or under an entirely different operating system (such as Windows 95 or Windows NT Workstation 4.0), the services will not work properly.

You should always check whether you need a service pack by looking at the release notes before using the latest one for your version of NT. Sometimes Microsoft releases a service pack that is only a bug fix or is for developers. This limited type of release is likely to happen more often as Microsoft changes its strategy for handling updates. Currently, service packs can be quite large—service pack 3 for Windows NT is almost 18MB to download. In the future, Microsoft expects to issue smaller updates.

NOTE

For any given version of Windows NT, service packs are cumulative. Thus, service pack 3 includes everything in service packs 1 and 2, as well as new material. Eventually, this policy will change as Microsoft makes smaller updates available.

Remember that if you are using IIS version 2.0 with Windows NT 4.0, you don't need a service pack. If you are using IIS 4.0, then you need service pack 3 at least. It is good practice, however, to check whether a service pack is available and install it if you find one.

You can download the latest service pack from the Microsoft Web site. The following Uniform Resource Locator (URL) lists the service packs that are available for download:

http://www.microsoft.com/windows/NTW/info/ntupdates.htm

Other Services for Your Site

In addition to the services provided with IIS (Web, FTP, NNTP, and SMTP, all of which are described shortly), you can install other services on your system. Some of these services are basically mandatory; others provide a more rounded collection of services for your site.

DNS Server

In Chapter 1, you learned that the Internet uses two types of addresses: domain name addresses and IP addresses. A *Domain Name System (DNS) server* is a program that translates between these two types of addresses. The translation is necessary because computers cannot understand domain addresses directly; they can understand only the numeric IP addresses.

When you provide an address for an Internet operation, you can use either the domain name address or the IP address; most programs don't care in the least. Most people use domain name addresses because they are easier to read and understand. The DNS server converts the domain name to the IP address completely behind the scenes.

When You Need a DNS Server

If you are setting up an Internet service and have reserved your own domain name, you are entirely responsible for that domain and you should have your own DNS server.

For example, my company has a reserved domain name of **dcomp.com**, and that domain has a class C address range assigned to it. Therefore, my company is responsible for everything that happens within that domain. If we add servers, we assign the fourth octet number of the IP address to the machine. However, for the rest of the Internet to be aware of this new addition, we need a DNS server to handle the resolution from the domain name (such as **www.dcomp.com**) to the IP address (such as **205.163.44.2**).

In some circumstances, you will not need your own DNS server. These circumstances include the following:

◆ You are not responsible for your own domain; for example, your Internet service provider provides domain management functions for you.

◆ You have arranged with a different server, somewhere else on the Internet, to act as your DNS server

In both of these instances, you need to work very closely with your DNS services provider. Remember that the purpose of the DNS server is to convert IP to domain addressing, and vice versa. Thus, you need to tell the person or company managing the DNS server when you add new hosts to your network and when you assign different IP addresses to those hosts.

If you are establishing an intranet, you may need to install a DNS server. This requirement depends on the type of network you have. For example, we use a

INTRANET

Windows NT network and can access any computer on the network simply by using the computer's name. If your intranet uses a variety of networks or has many different types of computers connected to it, you may want a DNS server.

Where to Get a DNS Server

You can get a DNS server in many places. Some are free, and others cost money. In general, you can use the DNS server that is provided with Windows NT 4.0, or you can use a DNS server provided by any number of sources.

Microsoft's DNS Server

Microsoft has been kind enough to provide a DNS server with Windows NT Server 4.0. You can determine whether the DNS server is installed by following these steps:

1. Open the Control Panel.
2. Double-click on the Services icon to display the Services dialog box.
3. Scroll through the list of services. If the DNS server is installed, you should see the following entry: Microsoft DNS Server.
4. Close the Services dialog box.

If the Microsoft DNS server is not installed and you want to install it, you can do so by following these steps:

1. Open the Control Panel.
2. Double-click on the Network icon to display the Network dialog box.
3. Click on the Services tab to display the network services currently installed on your system.
4. Click on the Add button to display the Select Network Service dialog box.
5. Scroll through the list of network services and select the Microsoft DNS Server item.
6. Click on OK.

At this point, the system may prompt you for the location of your Windows NT Server CD-ROM. Windows NT then copies the appropriate files to your system, and the Microsoft DNS Server appears in the list of installed services in the Network dialog box. When you close the dialog box, Windows NT prompts you to shut down your server and restart your system. The DNS server is now fully functional and ready to use. Information on configuring DNS servers can be found in Chapter 5, "Working with Virtual Servers and Directories."

Other DNS Servers

You can download several DNS servers from the Internet. Some of these are free or shareware, whereas others are demo versions of commercial software. The best (and most stable) freeware DNS server for Windows NT is a port of BIND, the standard DNS server for the UNIX environment. (BIND is an acronym for Berkeley Internet Name Domain.) You can download this program by connecting to **http://www.software.com/prod/bindnt/bindnt.html** or by e-mailing Larry Kahn at **access@drcoffsite.com.** These two sources provide different ports of BIND, but both are excellent. (We use the version from Software.com at our site and have been very pleased.) Several commercial DNS products are also available for Windows NT. If you want more information about commercial versions, contact either of the following vendors:

> MetaInfo
> (206) 523-0484
> **http://www.metainfo.com**
>
> FBLI
> (514) 349-0455
> **http://www.fbli.com**

Managing Your DNS Server

When you have a DNS server at your site, you are responsible for managing it. DNS, in and of itself, is quite complex. Although some vendors have done an excellent job of making their DNS servers as user friendly as possible, quite a bit of activity is still going on behind the scenes. To manage your server effectively, you need to become familiar with exactly what a DNS server does and how it does it.

Setting up and managing a DNS server can be frustrating and complicated; you must follow the DNS server software instructions *exactly* as they appear. (Instructions vary from server to server.) Getting additional explanatory material also is helpful. A good book on the subject, recommended by many sites on the Internet, is *DNS and BIND* by Paul Albitz and Cricket Liu, published by O'Reilly and Associates.

If you already have access to the Internet, you can get more information on DNS theory and management from the following sites:

- ◆ **ftp://ftp.njit.edu/pub/dns/cptd.faq**
- ◆ **http://www.telemark.net/~randallg/ntdns.htm**

E-mail Server

In Chapter 1, you learned about the importance of an e-mail server. IIS includes an e-mail server. However, this simple e-mail server may not fit all your needs. It handles only the Simple Mail Transport Protocol, or SMTP, and is very limited compared with other e-mail servers.

Several e-mail servers are available for Windows NT, and new products are coming out all the time. Some are shareware and others are available as commercial products. On the shareware side, you may want to look at the following programs:

- ◆ **EMWAC.** This free version of a mail server also includes the capacity to run your own mailing list. You can get additional information on the software at **http://www.emwac.ed.ac.uk**.

ONLINE

- ◆ **Internet Shopper.** This new shareware product by Brian Dorricott is packed with features. You also can get several add-on utilities that provide special management features. Prices vary depending on the capabilities of the program, but useful systems start at about $200. You can get more information at **http://www.ntmail.co.uk/**.

Commercial vendors also offer several programs that provide server capabilities. When you contact the following companies, be sure to ask for their server products. (I am most fond of post.office from Software.com.)

- ◆ **IRISoft.** A relative newcomer to the market, Mi'Server appears to be a very good value for commercial mail servers; the cost is only $99 for a full version. You can download a test version and use it for 30 days before making your final decision. For more information, connect to **http://www.irisoft.be/frame.htm** (notice that IRISoft is located in Belgium).

ONLINE

- ◆ **Lotus.** cc:Mail includes both a user interface (the user agent discussed earlier) and a server that runs in the background 24 hours a day. This product comes in several configurations, based on the number of users. Prices start at $825 for your local network, with an additional fee in excess of $3,400 to provide gateway access to the Internet. You can find out more at **http://www.ccmail.com/**.

- ◆ **Microsoft.** The BackOffice products available from Microsoft include the Exchange Server 5.5. This server is Microsoft's mail server. You can learn more about this product at **http://www.microsoft.com/exchange/**.

- ◆ **Software.com.** This company's post.office product retails for $495, but you can download a fully functional copy from the Web for a 30-day trial. Installation is easy, and configuration is done using a Web page (really cool!). Information is available at **http://www.software.com**.

> **NOTE**
>
> To find more servers as well as some good client software, you can check out **http://www.email-software.com/**. This site is devoted to keeping up with e-mail servers and clients.

News (NNTP) Server

Newsgroups are another popular way to communicate on the Internet. This approach is a good way to get feedback from customers, especially if you want others to be able to access the information. IIS now comes with a news server. This server works great for handling internal needs, but if you want to provide access to other feeds or simply want more advanced features, you need to look elsewhere.

The best way to start looking for another news server is to contact the makers of e-mail servers. Many of them also provide news servers. More advanced news servers are available from companies such as Internet Shopper, IRISoft, and Microsoft.

Proxy Server

A *proxy* is essentially a piece of software that allows multiple clients to connect through it to the Internet. For example, suppose you have 15 or 20 computers in your local network. If you don't have a full-time connection to the Internet for your entire network, then each computer needs its own dial-up connection. Using a proxy server, you can connect a single computer to the Internet, and then (in turn) each of the other computers on the network can access the Internet through that single proxy. This scenario requires only a single IP address for the proxy server; all other computers use software that can communicate with the proxy server to retrieve message packets destined for them. The result is lower hardware costs because you are sharing a single hardware connection.

Reduced cost is not the only benefit of a proxy server, however. Proxy servers are also typically used in some security installations. The proxy server acts as a barrier to the free flow of information, and it can filter out information packets that do not meet specific criteria. The proxy server, which is typically run on a special gateway server, helps protect your entire network from unauthorized access.

The following sites offer more information about proxy servers:

◆ **NetProxy**. Multiple-protocol proxy and firewall shareware. This proxy enables you to connect your entire corporate LAN to the Internet using an existing dial-up modem or ISDN connection to an Internet service provider. For more information, visit **http://www.grok.co.uk/netproxy/**.

- ◆ **WinGate.** Another proxy for connecting multiple systems through a single server. Fees vary according to the number of systems being connected. For more information, visit Qbik Software at **http://www.creative.co.nz/special/sam/home.htm.**
- ◆ **WinProxy.** A low-cost ($299) proxy server designed for connecting an unlimited number of systems through a single proxy server. For more information, contact Ositis Software at Sales@Ositis.com or visit **http://www.winproxy.com.**

Remote Access Server

Remote Access Service (RAS) is provided with Windows NT Server. It supports dial-in access to your network from any computer using a modem. Access is account and password protected, and you can control the information that dial-in users can access. Dial-up is easiest from other systems using Windows, particularly Windows 95 and Windows NT Workstation, where Dial-Up Networking (the client portion of RAS) can be used.

A remote user who connects to your system by using RAS has access to all network resources for which you have provided permission. These resources include access to the Internet, as RAS connections are established using Point-to-Point Protocol (PPP) or Serial Line Internet Protocol (SLIP). RAS is a great way for employees on the road to stay in touch, and you can also start your own Internet access service for other people.

NOTE

Explaining how to use RAS effectively is beyond the scope of this book. However, I suggest that before you try to enable RAS, you have a firm understanding of how it works and what it implies for your system. RAS, if implemented improperly, can compromise the security of your entire network. Get yourself a good book on the subject of remote networking specifically for Windows NT networks.

Windows NT Tools

If you have been working with a Windows NT network for some time, you may already be familiar with many of the administrative tools built in to the operating system. If your background lies in other areas, however (for example, managing Internet services on a UNIX-based system), you may not yet be familiar with the Windows NT tools.

Windows NT provides many tools that may at first seem esoteric or hard to find, but they are nonetheless beneficial to administering an Internet site. The following tools, in particular, are helpful:

♦ Control Panel

♦ Windows NT Explorer

♦ User Manager

♦ Event Viewer

♦ Performance Monitor

♦ Registry Editor

This chapter is not intended to provide detailed information on how to use each of these tools. That being said, the following sections do provide some introductory material that you may find helpful in getting started with the tools. The best way to learn how to use the tools, quite honestly, is to start using them and studying the online help provided with each tool.

The Control Panel

The Control Panel is the heart of how you configure Windows NT. The way in which you access the Control Panel depends on your version of Windows NT. In Windows NT 4.0, you access the Control Panel by clicking on the Start button, selecting the Settings option, and then choosing Control Panel.

When the Control Panel opens, it looks just like any other program group window, as shown in Figure 2-2. Not all the icons within the Control Panel (called *applets*) are useful for an Internet site, but four of them can be critical. These applets—Network, Services, Internet, and ODBC—are described in the following sections.

FIGURE 2-2

The Control Panel contains various configuration elements for a Windows NT system.

The Network Applet

If you double-click on the Network applet within the Control Panel, you have an opportunity to change the configuration of your network (see Figure 2-3). Chances are good that you had this set up when you first installed your local area network, but you will undoubtedly be visiting it again as you configure your Internet services.

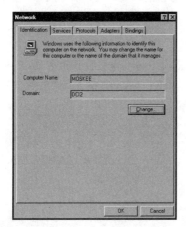

FIGURE 2-3

The Network applet enables you to modify your network configuration.

NOTE

If you haven't already configured your network for the TCP/IP protocol, you need to do so. The Internet uses TCP/IP for all communications, and you use the Network applet to make your changes for TCP/IP.

As you decide to add various servers to your Internet site, you are, in effect, adding network services. Many of these services end up in the Network applet, and you need to return here from time to time to configure the services.

The Services Applet

In the Windows NT environment, services are programs that run in the background and provide functionality that can be called on by other programs. If you are familiar with the UNIX environment, you know services as *daemons*. An example of a service is the Microsoft DNS Server, which you learned about earlier in the chapter.

When you double-click on the Services applet, Windows NT displays the Services dialog box shown in Figure 2-4.

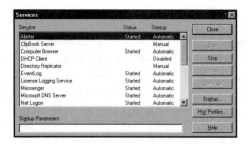

FIGURE 2-4

The Services applet provides a way to control all the services installed as part of Windows NT.

Notice that the Services dialog box lists each service alphabetically, along with an indication of the service's condition (running, stopped, or paused) and how the service initially starts. You can modify a service by double-clicking on the service name.

Internet services are designed to run around the clock. To do so, they must run as Windows NT services. After you successfully install a service (such as your Web server), it appears in the Services dialog box. By using this dialog box, you can control whether the service runs or modify how the service is started.

TIP

You also can start, stop, and configure the Internet services provided with IIS by using the Internet Services Manager. You don't necessarily need to use the Services applet. See Chapter 3 for more information on starting and stopping services.

The Internet Applet

The Internet applet is a new addition to Windows NT Server 4.0. When you double-click on this applet, the Internet Properties dialog box opens, as shown in Figure 2-5.

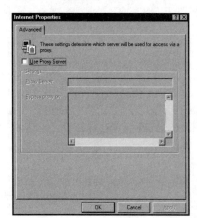

FIGURE 2-5

The Internet Properties dialog box controls how your server interacts with any proxy servers you may have installed at your site.

The only settings in the Internet Properties dialog box are for your proxy server. You may recall from earlier in the chapter that proxy servers provide hardware sharing and security in a network connected to the Internet. The settings in the dialog box enable you to tell the system to use a proxy server and to specify its location.

The ODBC Applet

ODBC is an acronym for *Open Database Connectivity*, which is a standard developed by Microsoft for transferring data between database applications. If you use the Internet Database Connector (covered in Chapter 20), you need to be concerned with how ODBC handles the transfer of data between your Web server and your ODBC-compliant database (such as Access or SQL Server).

The ODBC applet enables you to modify the data sources and drivers used by ODBC. When you double-click on the applet, Windows NT displays the Data Sources dialog box, as shown in Figure 2-6.

Using the ODBC applet is covered in Chapter 20.

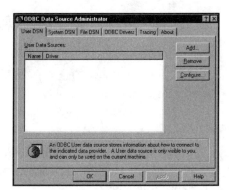

FIGURE 2-6

The ODBC applet enables you to manage various data sources in your system.

Windows NT Explorer

Windows NT Explorer enables you to effectively and easily manage the files on your disk drives. As you are setting up your site, you use this program to create directories, move files, and assign permissions for directories and files.

To start Explorer, click on the Start button, choose the Programs option, and finally choose Windows NT Explorer. The Explorer window appears, similar to that shown in Figure 2-7.

The left pane of each window in Explorer displays the directory structure of a drive, and the right pane shows the contents of whatever directory is selected in the left pane. The menus and toolbar at the top of the Explorer window enable you to manipulate the files.

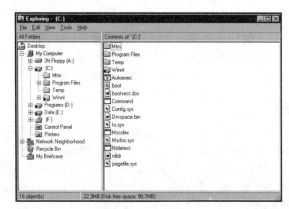

FIGURE 2-7

Windows NT Explorer displays the organization of your drives and directories.

TIP

Explorer is so essential to the work I do as an administrator that I added a copy of the Explorer icon to my Startup folder. That way, Explorer starts every time I log on to Windows NT.

The User Manager

The User Manager is where you control who has access to your network. When you first install IIS, it adds user information to your domain user database. You should know how to use the User Manager to modify account access rights because you may need to do so.

To start the User Manager, choose Programs from the Start menu, then Administrative Tools (Common), and finally User Manager for Domains. Windows NT opens the User Manager window, as shown in Figure 2-8.

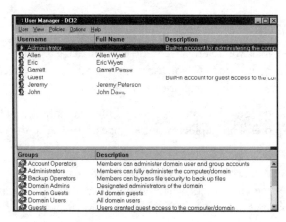

FIGURE 2-8

The User Manager displays a list of your defined user accounts and groups.

At the top of the User Manager window are the user accounts that have been defined for your domain. At the bottom of the window are the user groups that you have set up. If you want to change user account information, double-click on the user's name. Likewise, if you want to change a group, double-click on the group name.

> **NOTE**
>
> The menus at the top of the User Manager window manage the various users and groups on your system. Perhaps the most important menu options are under the Policies menu. Here you set the default rules for using your network. To fully understand the implications and importance of these settings, get a good book on Windows NT network management, such as *The Essential Windows NT 4 Book* by Richard Cravens—you'll find it well worth the investment.

The Event Viewer

While Windows NT runs, events crop up from time to time. These events may be triggered by a software program or by the operating system itself. If desired, you can record these events in a log file so that you can review them as you deem necessary. When you want to review the events, you use the Event Viewer.

To start Event Viewer, choose Programs from the Start menu, then Administrative Tools (Common), and finally Event Viewer. Windows NT displays the Event Viewer window, as shown in Figure 2-9.

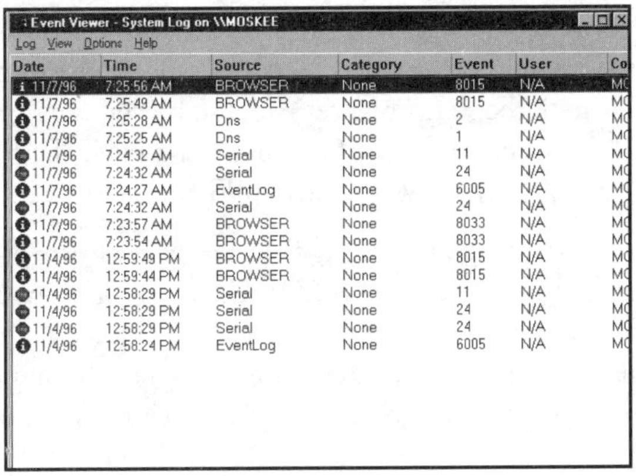

FIGURE 2-9

The Event Viewer enables you to review and manage the event log files.

You can use the Event Viewer to review any of the three log files maintained by Windows NT. The three log files and their purposes are as follows:

◆ **System.** The system log file records events that occur in managing the operating system. For example, a device not responding as expected by Windows NT might be a recordable event.

◆ **Security.** The security log file records events generated by the security system of Windows NT. For example, if someone tries to log on to the system by using a bad password, this event is recorded in the security log.

◆ **Application.** The application log file records events generated by your programs. Different programs can generate different types of events, such as a word processor indicating when it got an unexpected result from a system query.

You select which log file is displayed in the Event Viewer from the File menu. You can see more information about a specific event by double-clicking on the event in question.

After you install your Internet servers, they behave like a part of your system. (Remember that the servers run as services on your system.) The servers log events as they occur, and you may need to review those events from time to time.

The Performance Monitor

The performance of a computer system is always of interest to some users. In reality, it should be of great interest to all network administrators. If your network slows down in any way, it can affect every user on the network.

Windows NT includes a tool to help experienced users evaluate the performance of their system. You access this tool, the Performance Monitor, by choosing Programs from the Start menu, then Administrative Tools (Common), and finally Performance Monitor. The Performance Monitor window is shown in Figure 2-10.

You can use the Performance Monitor to monitor different system objects or subsystems by adding them to the window (select the Add to Chart option from the Edit menu). You can also specify how often you want to sample these objects, and then the Performance Monitor displays the results of its monitoring. By thoughtful use of the Performance Monitor, you can find ways to tweak your system to improve throughput.

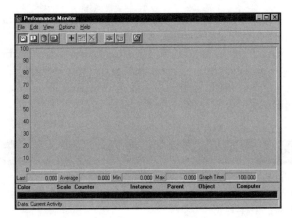

FIGURE 2-10

The Performance Monitor enables you to see how different parts of your system are responding over time.

When you add portions of IIS to your system, IIS automatically adds objects that can be monitored for performance. You then can select these objects in the Performance Monitor window. More information on using the Performance Monitor with your Internet services appears in Chapter 29.

The Registry Editor

The Registry is a centralized database of configuration information used by all areas of Windows NT, as well as by applications written expressly for Windows NT. Normally, the Registry changes automatically when you install applications or services on your system, removing the need to manually modify the Registry. If you need to modify the Registry, however, you do so by using the Registry Editor. You start this tool by choosing Run from the Start menu and then typing in the program name **regedit**. When running, the Registry Editor appears as shown in Figure 2-11.

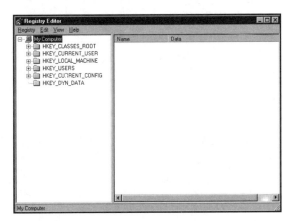

FIGURE 2-11

You can use the Registry Editor to change information stored in the Windows NT Registry.

Using some features of IIS isn't as automatic as Microsoft would have you believe. Sometimes you actually need to configure options by making changes to the Registry. In those instances, your only choice is to use the Registry Editor. Some sections in this book walk you through making configuration changes in this manner. Chapter 28, "Customizing IIS," is a good start for additional information about using the Registry Editor to customize IIS.

CAUTION

Always be careful when changing the Registry. Windows NT does not check your changes, and changing some values in the Registry could render your system unstable or unusable.

Chapter 3

Managing Your Server Locally

In This Chapter

◆ What Is the Internet Service Manager?

◆ Starting and Stopping the Servers

◆ Using the Internet Service Manager over the Network

IIS provides two different ways for you to manage the services at your site. The most common method is to use the Internet Service Manager. The other method is to use the HTML version of the Internet Service Manager, which is described in Chapter 26. This chapter focuses on how to use the traditional Internet Service Manager for the everyday management of your various Internet services.

What Is the Internet Service Manager?

The command center for working with IIS is the Internet Service Manager. This tool, which is installed automatically whenever you install any part of IIS, enables you to quickly and easily configure and control any portion of IIS.

As the name implies, you use the Internet Service Manager for managing your Internet services. In reality, it is always used for managing IIS, regardless of which services you are offering. These services may include your Web server, your FTP server, and any other Internet or intranet services you may have installed on your system. The Internet Service Manager can be used not only for services running on your local hardware server but also for services running on remote hardware servers.

The Internet Service Manager, shown in Figure 3-1, is actually a tool used by the Microsoft Management Console (MMC). The MMC, a program that Microsoft is adding to its operating systems, uses components called *snap-ins* to manage applications. The MMC will be part of Windows NT 5.0. One of the benefits of using the MMC is that you can have access to all of your site management tools in one place.

When you installed IIS, you also created an MMC console file called IIS.MSC. This file, or tool—the Internet Service Manager—is a collection of snap-ins that you can use to manage your Internet site. When you select Internet Service Manager from the Start menu, you are actually starting the MMC and loading the IIS console. Throughout this book, all references to the Internet Service Manager mean the MMC with the IIS.MSC file is loaded.

Starting the Internet Service Manager

Because the Internet Service Manager is installed when you first install IIS, the program is added to the same menu structure as your other IIS-related programs. You start the Internet Service Manager by choosing Programs from the Start menu,

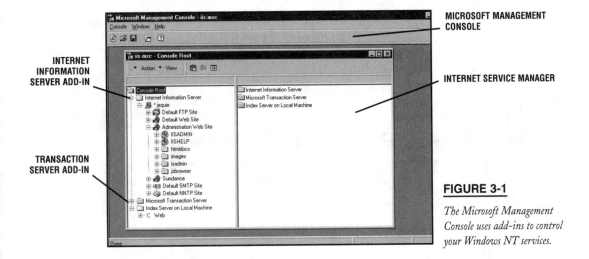

MICROSOFT MANAGEMENT CONSOLE

INTERNET SERVICE MANAGER

INTERNET INFORMATION SERVER ADD-IN

TRANSACTION SERVER ADD-IN

FIGURE 3-1

The Microsoft Management Console uses add-ins to control your Windows NT services.

selecting Microsoft Internet Server (Common), and finally choosing Internet Service Manager. This sequence opens the Microsoft Management Console window with a tip of the day displayed at the top. After looking at the tip of the day, you can close the dialog box and get to work with the Internet Service Manager, as shown in Figure 3-2.

When you first open this program, all you see is a Console Root with two subfolders: Internet Information Server and Microsoft Transaction Server. At first glance, the console doesn't look like much more than a modified Windows NT Explorer, but many site-management tools are hidden in the Internet Service Manager.

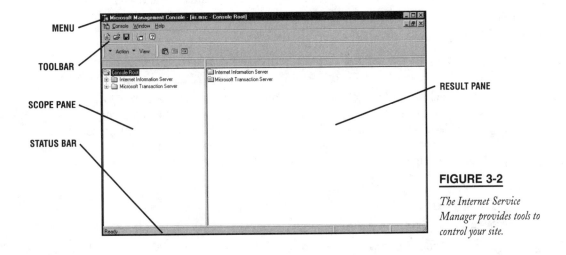

MENU

TOOLBAR

SCOPE PANE

STATUS BAR

RESULT PANE

FIGURE 3-2

The Internet Service Manager provides tools to control your site.

Because you will be working predominantly with IIS in this book, click on the box with a plus next to its folder. The folder displays a list of computers that you are set up to manage. The default installation displays only the local machine. Click on the plus sign next to the computer name to get a list of services, or sites, that are installed on the computer, as shown in Figure 3-3.

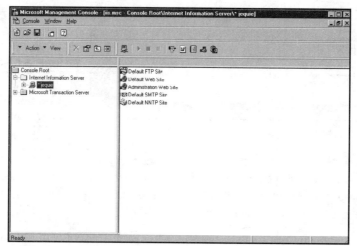

FIGURE 3-3

The Internet Information Server snap-in provides access to all your Internet sites.

Understanding the Interface

The Internet Service Manager user interface, which is very similar to the Windows Explorer interface, consists of a menu, two toolbars, a status bar, and a split window in the middle. The two parts of the main window display information about your services.

> **TIP**
>
> When you close the Internet Service Manager, it asks whether you want to save the console settings. If you do, the next time you work with the Internet Service Manager, the console will look the same as it did when you last worked on it—you won't have to reopen the Internet Information Server folder, or other folders that you use, every time you want to work with the Internet services.

The Menus

The menu at the top of the program window is part of the Microsoft Management Console and contains three choices: Console, Window, and Help. Most of the choices available from the menus are for use with the MMC, and a few are in the top toolbar.

The following choices are available from the Console menu:

- **New** Creates a new console with an empty Console Root.
- **Open** Opens a previously saved console.
- **Save** Saves the console you are using.
- **Save As** Saves the console you are using with a new name.
- **Send To** Sends the console to someone via e-mail (a variation of saving).
- **Add/Remove Snap-in** Allows you to configure your tool by adding or removing snap-ins.
- **Status Bar** Displays the status bar.
- **Toolbar** Displays the toolbar.
- **Navigate** Opens a dialog box for a URL that you want to visit.
- **Exit** Exits the program.

The choices available from the Window menu are similar to those in any other multiple-document program, such as Microsoft Word. You can open a new window, cascade or tile the windows, or arrange the window's icons.

The third menu, Help, contains the options you would expect: help options for IIS and the MMC, as well as the tip of the day. From the Help menu you can also connect to Microsoft on the Web, which includes a link to a site containing more snap-ins.

Exactly how you use the various options available from the menus is covered either elsewhere in this chapter or in other chapters throughout this book.

The Microsoft Management Console Toolbar

The Microsoft Management Console also includes a toolbar at the top of the program window. Another toolbar is part of the Internet Service Manager tools. Because the upper toolbar is part of the MMC, you can turn it on and off by choosing Toolbar from the Console menu. You cannot turn the Internet Service Manager toolbar on or off. The various tools on the MMC toolbar enable you to perform many of the same functions that you can select from the MMC menus.

The five tools on the MMC toolbar enable you to create a new console, open a console, save the console, create a new window, or look at the About dialog box.

The Internet Service Manager Toolbar

The second toolbar contains the most useful commands for controlling your Internet services. The Internet Service Manager toolbar has three sections. These sections can be moved to add more space between the sections, or they can be rearranged or stacked.

The first section includes two drop-down options that act like menus. The Action menu has the following choices:

- **Explore** Opens the selected directory in Windows NT Explorer.
- **Open** Opens the selected site or page in its associated program, generally your Web browser.
- **Browse** Opens the selected site or page in your Web browser.
- **Start** Starts the selected service.
- **Stop** Stops the selected service.
- **Pause** Pauses the selected service.
- **New** Creates a new site or virtual directory.
- **Task** Is generally disabled.
- **New Window from Home** Opens a new window with the currently selected item as the root in the Scope pane.
- **Properties** Displays the Properties dialog box for whatever you have selected.
- **Scope Pane** Displays the Scope pane.
- **Description Bar** Displays a bar just below the toolbar that is similar to a status bar.

The View menu has options for viewing information in the Result pane. You can display the items with large icons, small icons, in a list, or with full detail as in Windows NT Explorer. The option for a Web view is rarely available.

Selecting an object in the scope or result pane changes the tool available in the second toolbar section, but generally includes the following items:

- **Delete** Deletes the selected item.
- **Properties** Displays the property sheet for the selected item.
- **Up One Level** Moves the selection from the currently selected item up one level of the hierarchy.
- **Hide/Show Scope** Controls whether or not the Scope pane is displayed.

The tools in the third toolbar section access other Windows NT features, such as the following:

- **Connect to a Computer** Enables you to connect to a specific server through your network.
- **Start** Starts the selected service.
- **Stop** Stops the selected service.

- ◆ **Pause** Pauses the selected service.
- ◆ **Key Manager** Opens the Key Manager program, which is discussed in Chapter 25.
- ◆ **Performance Monitor** Opens the Performance Monitor, which is used in Chapter 29.
- ◆ **Server Manager** Opens the Server Manager.
- ◆ **User Manager** Opens the User Manager.

The Status Bar

The status bar at the bottom of the program window is a standard Windows-program status bar. Its primary purpose is informational, but it is almost repetitive. If you look at the information in the status bar, you will find that it closely duplicates the information in the main body of the program window.

To turn the status bar on or off, choose Status Bar from the Console menu. If a check mark appears next to the option, the status bar is on; otherwise, it is off.

Understanding Property Sheets

One of the primary uses of the Internet Service Manager is to manage the various services you offer at your site. Most of the time, you will be using property sheets to make changes on your site. Regardless of which service you are configuring, the property sheets have some similar features. Property sheets are available for all the items in the Internet Information Server folder including services, directories, and content. The proper use of each property sheet is covered elsewhere in this book.

Starting and Stopping the Servers

You already know that the various Internet servers that make up IIS run as services under Windows NT. Consequently, the servers are available all the time, even when you are not logged on to the system. At times, however, you may need to stop and restart a server, which means stopping and starting the service. You can do so either from the Internet Service Manager (which is easiest) or from the Services applet. The following sections cover both methods.

From the Internet Service Manager

If you have spent any time working with the Internet Service Manager, you may already have discovered how to start and stop a server. You can change the state of a server by following these steps:

CAUTION

When a service has been stopped, that server is no longer operational. People can't connect to your server until you restart the service. If they try, they get an error indicating that a connection was not possible. This situation makes sense, because it takes both the server and client to publish and view information on the Internet.

1. Start the Internet Service Manager as described earlier in this chapter.

2. Highlight the service located under the computer name of the server whose state you want to change. (Don't double-click on the computer name; that opens the Properties dialog box for the server.)

3. Select the Stop Service tool from the toolbar to stop the service; select the Pause Service tool to pause the service.

At this point, the service is stopped (or paused); no dialog box appears to ask for confirmation. You can accomplish anything you need to do before restarting the service. To restart, repeat these steps, but select the Start Service tool from the toolbar.

From the Services Applet

To stop the Web server service from the Services applet, follow these steps:

1. Open the Control Panel.

2. Double-click on the Services applet to display the Services dialog box shown in Figure 3-4.

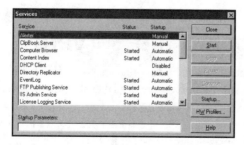

FIGURE 3-4

The Services dialog box controls the execution of system services in Windows NT.

3. In the Service list, highlight the name of the service that you want to stop. The service names used for different servers are shown in Table 3-1.

4. Click on the Stop button.

5. Click on the Yes button when asked to confirm your action. The service is then stopped, and the services list is updated.

6. Click on the Close button to close the Services dialog box.

To restart the server, follow steps 1 through 3; then in step 4, click on the Start button.

Table 3-1 Service Names Used in the Services Dialog Box

Server	Service Name
Web	World Wide Web Publishing Service
ftp	FTP Publishing Service
NetShow	Microsoft NetShow On-Demand Server Service
Index	Content Index
NNTP	Microsoft NNTP Service
SMTP	Microsoft SMTP Service

Using the Internet Service Manager over the Network

The Internet Service Manager is most often used for controlling the services on your local server, but you can also use it to control IIS over a network. From the manager's perspective, remote management is transparent; that is, when you are connected to a server, all the functions and features of the Internet Service Manager act the same whether it is a local or remote server.

TIP

Even though the Internet Service Manager enables you to control remote servers, IIS 4.0 provides a more flexible method for accomplishing the same task. This alternative method is mandatory when you want to manage sites over the Internet—sites that are not connected to your local network. For more information, refer to Chapter 26.

You can install the Microsoft Management Console on any system running either Windows NT Workstation 4.0 or Windows NT Server 4.0. When you try to connect to another computer, the attempt will fail if the remote computer doesn't have services managed by MMC components. Of course, after installing MMC on another computer, you need a copy of IIS.MSC to use the Internet Service Manager tools.

If you know the address of the server you want to manage, you can simply choose Connect to Server from the Properties menu. Alternatively, you can click on the Connect to Server tool on the toolbar to open the Connect to Computer dialog box, shown in Figure 3-5.

FIGURE 3-5

The Internet Service Manager enables you to specify a server name to connect with.

NOTE

Regardless of how you are connecting to the remote server, you must have Administrator privileges on that server. If you don't, you won't be able to make changes to the information on the remote server.

All you need to do now is provide the address of the remote server. You can specify the address in one of four ways:

- ◆ **UNC.** If you know the UNC naming convention for the server, you can use it.
- ◆ **DNS.** You can use the domain name for the server, provided that it has a DNS entry in your DNS server.
- ◆ **IP address.** If you know the IP address of the server, you can use it.
- ◆ **Machine name.** If the machine is defined either by WINS or in your LMHOSTS file, you can use the machine name.

After you supply a name, the Internet Service Manager attempts to connect to the server. When you are connected, you can manage the services on the server the same as you would manage services on your local network.

TIP

If you get an error when trying to connect, you may have entered an incorrect address. Check your spelling or use one of the other naming methods.

Chapter 4

Configuring Internet
Information Server

———

In This Chapter

◆ General Server Configuration

◆ Web Server-Specific Configuration

◆ FTP Server-Specific Configuration

◆ SMTP Server-Specific Configuration

◆ NNTP Server-Specific Configuration

After IIS is installed properly, you are ready to configure your common Internet services. The Internet Service Manager, which you learned about in Chapter 3, is the tool you use to configure servers. As used in the context of this chapter, a server is considered a copy of one of the IIS services running on a server computer. Most of the configuration settings control how your servers react to requests from the outside world or how those external clients react with your Windows NT Server system.

This chapter focuses on how to configure the operational side of your common Internet services. You learn which configuration information is applicable to each of the servers and which configuration information is specific to individual servers. The configuration settings are specified by changing individual controls on the various Properties dialog boxes in the Internet Service Manager. This chapter discusses only controls that affect the general operation of the server, not every possible control. Some individual configuration parameters are discussed in other, more appropriate chapters of this book.

General Server Configuration

Some common configuration parameters are very similar for all servers. Granted, they are set individually for each server, but they are common in concept and implementation. In general, these configuration settings affect how a connection is made between the external client and your server. Each configuration area is discussed in the following sections.

> **NOTE**
>
> Unlike earlier versions of IIS, you rarely have to restart a server or your computer when changing a server's configuration in IIS version 4.

Changing the Description of Your Server

After working with the Internet Service Manager for a while, you may get tired of seeing all your sites listed as Default Web Site or Default FTP Site. You can change the names or descriptions of all the sites you are managing. Perhaps you are even managing several sites and need descriptive names for them.

To change the site name that appears in the Internet Service Manager:

1. Open the Internet Service Manager.

2. Select the name of the server whose description you want to change, and click on the Properties tool. The Properties dialog box for the server opens. (The Properties dialog box for the Default FTP Site is shown in Figure 4-1.)

FIGURE 4-1

You can easily change the TCP port used by your servers.

3. Make sure that the Site tab is selected. (This tab should be selected by default; its name varies from server to server.)

4. Change the text in the Description field to a more meaningful name, such as Main FTP Site. This field is always the first field on the Site tab of the server Properties dialog box.

5. Click on OK to close the Properties dialog box, and you will see the new name of your server.

6. Close the Internet Service Manager.

Changing the Default Port Settings

You already know that both the Internet and intranets rely on tools that use the TCP/IP protocol. This networking protocol defines how communication is to occur between different parts of a network. When a TCP-based message is sent to a server, it is directed to a specific port. This port, which is a simple integer number, is contained in each packet transmitted. The purpose of the port number is to allow proper handling of the packet at your site. Different software servers on the physical server listen to different ports. In this way, you can run multiple services on a single machine, using a single TCP/IP connection, and each service listens only to the appropriate messages.

Each server has its own default TCP port settings. The common port settings include the following:

- **Web.** Clients, by default, send HTTP commands (understood by Web servers) to port 80.
- **FTP.** Clients, by default, send FTP commands to port 21.
- **SMTP.** Clients, by default, send SMTP commands to port 25.
- **NNTP.** Clients, by default, send NNTP commands to port 119.

When first installed, your IIS services listen to their respective default ports, but you can change the port settings if desired. You might want to change the port settings for any of the following reasons:

- You are running a different service on the default port.
- You want to increase security a bit by using a port that only authorized users know about.
- You are running more than one server in your system. For example, you already have a Web server using port 80, and you want to set up a secondary server on a different port.
- You hate following conventions and want to be different.

NOTE

A few products, such as the e-mail server that my company uses, include a Web interface for managing configuration settings. These programs work by running a simple HTTP server that listens to a typically unused port.

In most cases, you don't need to worry about the port setting. After all, the common port numbers are those used and understood around the Internet, and if you want to maximize visits to your site, you should use the common ports. If you are determined to change the port, however, you can easily do so. To change the port being used by a server, follow these steps:

1. Open the Internet Service Manager.
2. Select the name of the server whose port you want to change.

3. Click on the Properties tool to display the Properties dialog box for the server.

4. Make sure that the Site tab is selected. (This tab should be selected by default; its name varies from server to server.)

5. Change the value in the TCP Port field to the desired port.

6. Click on OK to close the Properties dialog box.

7. Close the Internet Service Manager.

Setting the Connection Timeout

When a communications channel is established between a client and a server, system resources are set aside on your server to manage that connection. System resources, particularly memory, tend to be very precious, especially at a busy site. The more simultaneous connections that are established, the more resources that are necessary.

This scenario does not present a problem unless inactive communications channels start cropping up. Inactive channels occur when a connection is established, and then nothing is done with the connection. For example, a user may establish a connection and then leave for lunch without shutting down the client program. The result is that resources are consumed for no reason, and your site is less able to meet the demands of active clients who need the resources.

To overcome this problem, IIS allows you to establish connection timeouts. These values, specified in seconds, enable you to indicate how long an inactive connection remains established. After that specified period of inactivity, IIS would automatically terminate the channel. The default connection timeout for FTP and Web servers is 900 seconds, or 15 minutes. If you are considering changing the values, the following guidelines can help you make your determination:

◆ **Web.** Normally the default timeout is fine because Web clients automatically close connections after each transaction is completed. If a client fails to close a connection, however, the timeout value comes into play. You can safely set a lower value, such as 300 seconds.

◆ **FTP.** When an FTP connection is established, it stays established until the remote client explicitly issues a command to break the connection. If an abnormal occurrence terminates the connection (loss of power at the remote site, for example), the connection remains open until the timeout is reached. For this reason, you may want to set the timeout lower, such as to 300 seconds. You should not set it lower than 100 seconds, though, as it can easily take this long for people to make decisions about files or directories.

◆ **SMTP.** When an e-mail client connects to a server, it is generally connected only long enough to send messages and to retrieve any waiting messages. The default 600 seconds provides more than enough time to handle any lag, and you should feel free to change this value. Another consideration for the SMTP is that it allows you to have a different value for incoming connections and outgoing connections.

◆ **NNTP.** NNTP servers generally have a lot of text. To give someone enough time to read the posting, you may want to leave the timeout at 600 seconds. If most of your postings are short, then you can set the value lower.

You can set the connection timeout value to anything between 0 and 32,767. To change the connection timeout values, follow these steps:

1. Open the Internet Service Manager.
2. Select the name of the server whose timeout value you want to change.
3. Click on the Properties tool to display the Properties dialog box for the server.
4. Make sure that the Site tab is selected (the default tab named after the type of site you are editing).
5. Change the value in the Connection Timeout field as desired. This field is always the second field on the Services tab of the server Properties dialog box.
6. Click on OK to close the Properties dialog box.

CAUTION

Stopping and restarting a server disconnects any currently active sessions. In addition, anyone trying to connect between the time you stop the server and restart it will not be able to establish a connection with your site.

7. Close the Internet Service Manager.

Specifying Simultaneous Connections

More than one remote client can connect to your site at any given time. Therefore, because of the popularity of some sites, site managers have had to limit the number of simultaneous connections to their site.

The reason for limiting simultaneous users has to do with bandwidth. If you are running any Internet services, you already know that bandwidth, as specified by the type of data line you are leasing, determines how much information can be transmitted to and from your site at any given time. The more users you have at one time, the less information you can ship within a given period of time to any given user. If you get too many users, the response time at your site can slow to a crawl.

To get around this problem, IIS allows you to limit the number of simultaneous users you can have. Because Web connections don't stay open for long time periods, there isn't a default limit for connections. However, FTP and NNTP servers rely on extended connections. The FTP server has a default of 1,000 connections, whereas the NNTP server has a default of 5,000 connections. The SMTP server allows you to control the number of incoming connections (the default is not limited), as well as the number of outgoing connections, with a default limit of 500. Theoretically, 6,000 people could be maintaining connections to your site at any time, with an unlimited number connecting and disconnecting all the time.

If your data connection is a 56Kb line and you need to reserve part of the channel for outgoing communications (internal personnel who need to connect to the rest of the Internet), then you should limit the number of simultaneous connections. The numbers you set are up to you, but you may need to come up with your limit by a process of trial and error. You can use log reports, discussed in Chapter 28, to help determine the number of connections your servers are making.

To change the simultaneous connections limit, follow these steps:

1. Open the Internet Service Manager.
2. Select the name of the server whose connection limit you want to change.
3. Click on the Properties tool to display the Properties dialog box for the server.
4. Make sure that the Site tab is selected.
5. Select the Limited To option if necessary. (This option is already selected for an FTP or NNTP site.)
6. Set a value in the Connections field to indicate the number of connections that can occur at the same time. You can set any value between 1 and 32,767. (You may need to adjust this setting after some trial and error.)
7. Click on OK to close the Properties dialog box.
8. Close the Internet Service Manager.

Changing Logon Information

If you have used Windows NT for any length of time, you already know that it has a robust security system. Only people who have accounts on your system can gain access to the information stored there. IIS, operating under the Windows NT security system, is no exception; anyone who wants to gain access to the information you publish on your server must have an account.

Does this security scheme mean that every person connecting to your server must have an individual account? No, not really. Because all access for a particular server is lumped together under a default account, all users of your site (no matter how many) access your system through the same account name. When IIS is first installed, it creates a user account for your servers to use. This account has the name IUSR_*server*, where *server* is replaced with the name of the hardware server on which the Web, FTP, SMTP, or NNTP server is running. For example, if the name of the hardware server were MOSKEE, the default user account would be IUSR_MOSKEE. This user account is automatically created in the User Manager and is also specified in the Internet Service Manager.

The default user account is automatically added to the GUESTS user group, which means that the account inherits all the rights and privileges assigned to the GUESTS group. This approach obviously has security implications, and you should think through them to ensure that the rights are appropriate for your Internet or intranet users. If they are not, you have two choices: you can change the rights of the GUESTS group, but doing so may adversely affect any other accounts that also belong to the group; or you can create a new group strictly for site users, and then assign the IIS user accounts to that group.

TIP

Changing the IIS accounts and the group to which they belong is actually a good idea from a security standpoint. It helps you to later track security problems that may occur, and attribute them to a particular service.

To change the logon information for IIS, the steps are slightly different for each server. The following general steps are for the NNTP and FTP servers:

1. Use the User Manager to create a new user group for your site visitors. Grant the group at least read-only rights to the root directories used by your services, as well as any other directories that are appropriate.

2. Create a new user account for each IIS service that you offer. Thus, if you are running the FTP and NNTP services, you would create two accounts, one for each service.

3. Remember the account name and password that you used for the new accounts; you will need them shortly.

4. Assign each of the new accounts to the user group that you created in step 1.

5. Close the User Manager.

6. Open the Internet Service Manager.

7. Select the name of the server whose logon information you want to change. Click on the Properties tool to displays the Properties dialog box for the server.

8. On an FTP or NNTP server, make sure that the Directory Security tab is selected.

9. Enter the exact name of the user account that you set up for this particular service in the Username field or click on the Browse button to select the name from a list.

10. Enter the exact password of the user account that you set up for this particular service in the Password field.

11. Click on OK to close the Properties dialog box.

12. Repeat steps 7 through 11 for each of the other services you are running at your site.

13. Close the Internet Service Manager.

Changing logon information for the Web and SMTP servers is only slightly different from the preceding sequence. On the Directory Security tab of the server's Properties dialog box, click on the Edit button in Anonymous Access and Authentication Control section. The Authentication Methods dialog box opens. Clicking on the Edit button for the Account Used for Anonymous Access opens a dialog box similar to the one used in step 9.

Setting the Home Directory

A home directory is the root directory for a server. It is the directory whose contents are first "served up" by the server when someone connects to your site. For example, the address of my company's Web site is **http://www.dcomp.com**. When someone uses this address as the URL, the contents of the default file in the home directory are displayed. (Default files for Web servers are discussed later in this chapter.)

In addition, your home directory serves as the base point for all other directories accessible from the server. As an example, suppose that the home directory for your FTP server is the default C:\InetPub\ftproot. When someone connects to the FTP server, this physical directory on your drive appears as the root directory to them; the user is not aware of the physical location of the directory. If the user then changes to the products/info/ directory on the FTP server, in reality he or she is accessing files in the C:\InetPub\ftproot\products\info directory on your system.

> ### NOTE
>
> Home directories do not have to be on the same machine as the server. Your home directory can be on a shared directory on another machine, and Web servers can even use URL redirection to have the home directory be a URL pointing to another server.

When you first installed IIS, you were prompted for the name of the root directory for each service you installed. If you later want to change a server's home directory, you can do so by following these steps:

1. Open the Internet Service Manager.

2. Right-click and select Properties on the computer name of the server whose home directory you want to change. The Properties dialog box for the server opens.

3. Click on the Home Directory tab. (A sample Properties dialog box for an FTP server is shown in Figure 4-2.)

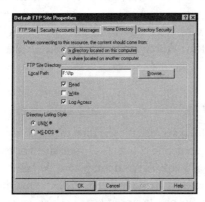

FIGURE 4-2

You can use the Home Directory tab to modify how the server interacts with your disk drives.

4. Select the option that describes whether the home directory is on the local machine or on another machine.

5. Change the directory field to the full pathname of the subdirectory on your system, or use the Uniform Naming Convention (UNC) to connect to a networked path server. This directory will be used as the home directory for your site. You can use the button next to the field to browse for the directory.

6. Click on OK to close the Properties dialog box. The Properties dialog box for the server is again displayed, and the path in the list of directories should be updated.

7. Click on OK to close the Properties dialog box.

8. Close the Internet Service Manager.

> **NOTE**
>
> IIS also supports virtual directories and virtual servers. These topics are discussed fully in Chapter 5.

Web Server-Specific Configuration

As you might suspect, some configuration settings are specific to your Web server. Using the Properties dialog box for the Web server, you can easily make the changes necessary to customize the way your Web server operates.

Setting the Default File

When a client connects to your Web site and does not specify an actual file in the URL, one of two things can happen. First, IIS checks whether you have specified a default file or files for your site. The default file is loaded and displayed whenever the client does not specify a file.

> **NOTE**
>
> IIS enables you to have different files listed for your site. This feature is great when you start using ASP files and want to have IIS load either the default HTML or ASP file

If a default file cannot be located, IIS checks to see whether directory browsing is turned on. If directory browsing is enabled, IIS displays the contents of the directory to the client. If directory browsing is disabled and no default file is available, the user receives an error. (How you control directory browsing and error messages is discussed later in the chapter.)

Using IIS, you can specify any file as your default. This filename is valid for all directories on your server. Suppose that you have the following directory structure for your site:

```
WWWRoot
    Artwork
    Hulett
```

```
Moorcroft

Newcastle

Sundance
```

If someone points a URL at the Hulett directory (using a URL, of course), the file with the default filename in that directory will be returned. Likewise, if someone points a URL at the Newcastle directory, the file with the default filename from that directory would be returned.

When you first install IIS, the default filename is set to default.htm. To change the default filename to something else, follow these steps:

1. Open the Internet Service Manager.

2. Select the Web server whose default file you want to change and click on the Properties tool. The Properties dialog box for the server opens.

3. Click on the Documents tab. The Properties dialog box now appears, as shown in Figure 4-3.

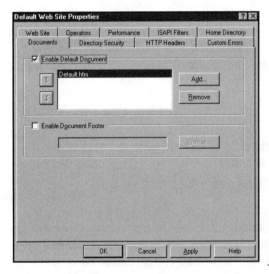

FIGURE 4-3

You can change the name of the default file used by your Web server.

4. Make sure that the Enable Default Document check box is checked.

5. To add a new default file, such as default.asp, simply click on the Add button. A new dialog box pops up to accept the name of the file. When you click on OK to close the dialog box, the new file is added to the list of default files.

6. To remove a default file, select the file and click on the Remove button.

7. To change the search order that IIS uses to determine which type of file to use, click on the arrow buttons located to the left of the file list.

8. Click on OK to close the Properties dialog box.

9. Close the Internet Service Manager.

Controlling Directory Browsing

Earlier in this chapter, you learned that when someone tries to contact your server and access a directory (without specifying a particular filename), the server returns the default file from that directory. This statement is true as long as a feature called directory browsing isn't enabled. If directory browsing is disabled and no default file exists in the directory, the server generates an error indicating that the user entered a bad URL. (Error messages are described in the next section.)

Directory browsing enables remote users to view the contents of your Web site directories. For example, Figure 4-4 shows what a browser would display with directory browsing enabled at a site.

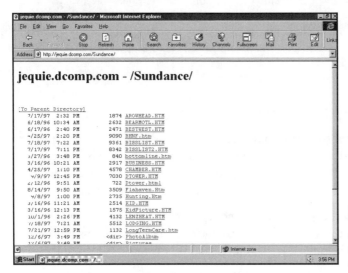

FIGURE 4-4

Directory browsing enables users to view the contents of a directory.

The following list describes a few instances when directory browsing may be advantageous:

◆ You have a lot of non-HTML files for people to download.

◆ The files available in a directory change rapidly and often.

◆ The users of your site are comfortable working with directory listings.

◆ You want others to see how neat your directories look.

By default, IIS turns off directory browsing. To change the default file, follow these steps:

1. Open the Internet Service Manager.
2. Select the name of the Web server that you want to change and click on the Properties tool. The Properties dialog box for the server opens.
3. Click on the Home Directory tab. The Properties dialog box resembles the dialog box shown earlier in Figure 4-3.
4. Select the Directory Browsing Allowed check box.
5. Click on OK to save your changes.
6. Close the Internet Service Manager window.

NOTE

You can turn directory browsing on or off only for the entire site, not by directory. If you want people to be able to browse one directory but not another, you should turn on both default files and directory browsing. For those directories you don't want people to browse, simply make sure that you have a default file in the directory.

Changing Error Messages

Whenever a visitor to your Web site tries to get the Web server to do something that it can't do, the server sends an error message to the visitor's Web browser. While surfing the Web, you have probably run into a few of these. For example, when you try to access a file that has been moved or deleted, you get an error message.

You may want to change the default messages generated by the server and displayed by a Web browser. For example, you can include an e-mail address to someone who might be able to help the user, or you can add your company's logo to the page.

By default, IIS displays an HTML file for every type of error that it encounters. These HTML files are found in a folder with other files for your NT operating system—C:\WINNT\Help\Common\ if NT is installed on your C drive. If you want to change these messages, you can either edit these files or create new ones.

To change the error message used by IIS, follow these steps:

1. Open the Internet Service Manager.
2. Select the name of the Web server that you want to change, and click on the Properties tool. The Properties dialog box for the server opens.
3. Click on the Custom Errors tab. The Properties dialog box now appears, as shown in Figure 4-5.

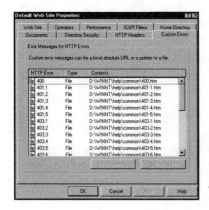

FIGURE 4-5

The Custom Errors tab enables you to change the error messages that IIS displays.

4. Select an HTTP error from the list.

5. Click on Edit Properties to change the error message that IIS uses. An Error Mappings dialog box displays the current settings and describes the error.

6. Select the proper Message Type. IIS enables you to use a file, a default message, or a URL for an error message.

7. If you choose a file or URL, you have to enter the location of the desired error message in the second text box.

8. Click on OK to return to the Custom Errors tab.

9. Continue changing error messages by repeating steps 4 to 8 until you are finished. Then click on OK to close the Properties dialog box.

10. Close the Internet Service Manager window.

Changing Password Authentication

Your IIS Web site supports three different types of password authentication; that is, the server has three ways to verify that a user is allowed to access the site. The three types of authentication are the following:

◆ **Allow Anonymous.** This authentication method effectively means that anyone can access your site. It is also the default of most Web browsers and Web sites.

◆ **Basic.** This type of authentication is often used in connection with Secure Sockets Layer (SSL) sites to send encoded usernames and passwords. When not used with SSL, basic authentication sends the information as clear text (unencoded and available for interception—not very secure).

INTRANET

◆ **Windows NT Challenge/Response.** This method of authentication is used within Windows NT networks and is supported by current versions of Microsoft's Internet Explorer. This method encrypts every authentication session.

When you install the IIS Web server, only Anonymous and Windows NT challenge/response authentication methods are selected, which provides a wide latitude for connecting to your site. However, you may want to limit the authentication acceptable at your site for some reason—particularly if you are developing a secure intranet. In this case, you will probably want to at least disable Anonymous access. Doing so ensures that only those with the proper user ID and password can gain access to your site.

To change the password authentication methods used at your site, follow these steps:

1. Open the Internet Service Manager.
2. Select the name of the Web server that you want to change, and click on the Properties tool. The Properties dialog box for the server opens.
3. Make sure that the Directory Security tab is selected.
4. Click on the Edit button in the Anonymous Access and Authentication Control area of the dialog box. This step opens the Authentication Methods dialog box shown in Figure 4-6.

FIGURE 4-6

IIS allows you use up to three types of password authentication.

5. Make sure that only the authentication methods desired are selected.
6. Click on OK to save your changes; click on OK again to close the Properties dialog box.
7. Close the Internet Service Manager window.

FTP Server-Specific Configuration

Although FTP is very simplistic by design, the IIS implementation of FTP allows you some latitude on configuration, as discussed in the following sections.

Setting the Types of Connections

When you set up an FTP site, you can configure it to reflect how you want users to connect to your site. Users can log on using their user IDs and passwords, or they can log on as anonymous users.

By default, IIS is configured so that only anonymous FTP connections are allowed at the site. You can change the types of connections allowed at your site by following these steps:

1. Open the Internet Service Manager.
2. Select the name of the FTP server that you want to change and click on the Properties tool. The Properties dialog box for the server opens.
3. Select the Security Accounts tab, as shown in Figure 4-7.

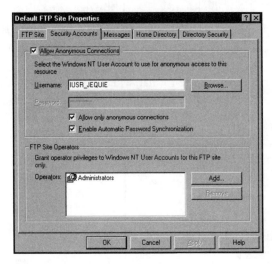

FIGURE 4-7

The FTP Service Properties dialog box contains the various configuration settings for the FTP server

4. To allow only nonanonymous connections to your site, clear the All\underline{o}w Anonymous Connections check box. When you clear the box, IIS warns you about the security implications of sending plain-text passwords across the Internet.
5. To allow both anonymous FTP connections and nonanonymous connections, select the All\underline{o}w Anonymous Connections check box and clear the A\underline{l}low Only Anonymous Connections check box.
6. To allow only anonymous connections, select the A\underline{l}low Only Anonymous Connections check box.
7. Click on OK to save your changes.
8. Close the Internet Service Manager.

Picking a Directory Listing Style

The IIS FTP server can display directory listings in two formats. The default method is to display them as they would appear under the UNIX environment. Because the vast majority of systems offering FTP sites are UNIX based, the majority of FTP users are familiar with the UNIX-style directory listings. Figure 4-8 shows a UNIX-style directory listing.

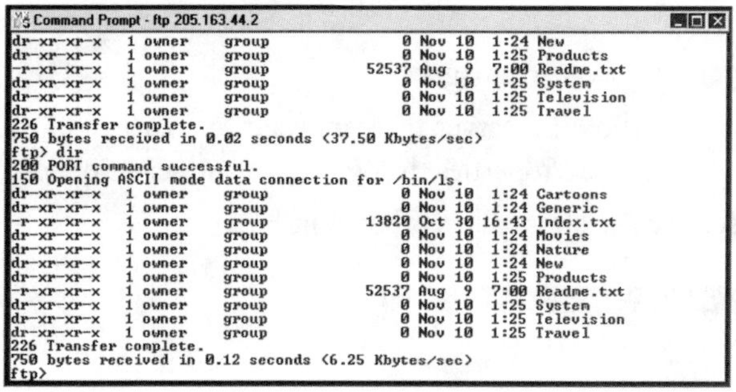

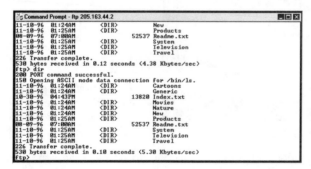

FIGURE 4-8

The FTP server displays directory listings in UNIX format by default.

You also can display directories in MS-DOS format, which is familiar to many long-time Windows and DOS users. Figure 4-9 shows the same directory as Figure 4-8, this time displayed in MS-DOS format.

FIGURE 4-9

A MS-DOS listing format is the same as that produced by a DOS DIR command.

NOTE

The default setting for the directory listing style is the MS-DOS format. This default setting seems to change with each version of IIS.

To change the FTP directory listing style used at your site, follow these steps:

1. Open the Internet Service Manager.

2. Select the name of the FTP server that you want to change and click on the Properties tool. The Properties dialog box for the server opens.

3. Click on the Home Directory tab. The Properties dialog box appears, as shown in Figure 4-10.

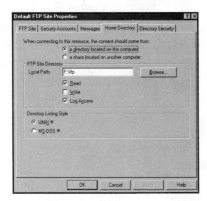

FIGURE 4-10

You have complete control over how a directory listing is displayed during an FTP session.

4. Select the radio button from the bottom of the dialog box that indicates how you want to format the directory listings.

5. Click on OK to save your changes.

6. Close the Internet Service Manager.

SMTP Server-Specific Configuration

An SMTP server can be viewed as a very simple server, just like the post office. For most people, the post office is a place to drop off and pick up mail. However, when you are responsible for managing the post office, it appears to be a much more complex operation.

The SMTP server works in much the same way. It is a very simple server—and, left to itself, works fine. You can, however, go behind the scenes and configure the server to best serve your needs with the two additional tabs—Messages and Delivery—on the Properties dialog box.

One of the main tasks of a mail server is handling the mail. The SMTP server does a good job of receiving mail and sending it to the correct destination. As the administrator, you will really have only two main concerns. One relates to the size of the load that is handled, and the other relates to undeliverable mail.

Limiting Message Sizes

All mail that goes through your SMTP server stops on that machine. If the number of e-mail addresses is small, you don't have much to worry about. However, you may manage a site that sees a great deal of mail. Active mailing lists can send a lot of mail your way, or you may have to deal with large messages.

The SMTP server has two settings that control the size of the messages that are sent. One setting, the Maximum Message Size, sets the preferred limit of an e-mail message; the default is 2MB. If a message larger than 2MB is sent, the server will still try to process the message. The second setting is the Maximum Session Size, and its default is 10MB. When a message is larger than this size, the server will close the connection and will not route the mail.

To change the limits on message sizes, follow these steps:

1. Open the Internet Service Manager.

2. Select the name of the SMTP server that you want to change, and click on the Properties tool. The Properties dialog box for the server opens.

3. Click on the Messages tab. The Properties dialog box appears, as shown in Figure 4-11.

FIGURE 4-11

You can limit the size of messages sent through your SMTP server.

4. Select the Limit Messages option at the top of the dialog box.

5. Enter the preferred size limit for a message in the Maximum Message Size box.

6. Enter the maximum size for a message in the Maximum Session Size box.

7. Click on OK to save your changes.

8. Close the Internet Service Manager.

Handling Dead Letters

Occasionally, the post office gets letters that can't be sent as addressed or returned to the sender. These letters are called *dead letters*. As with the real post office, you can expect some dead letters to go through your SMTP server. What happens to the dead letters is up to you. By default, all the messages are sent to a Badmail directory—a dead letter office. The path of this subdirectory of your main directory is probably something like F:\Mailroot\Badmail.

You will probably want to know about any mail that is being stored in the Badmail directory. The SMTP server has two ways of notifying you of bad mail. It can send a copy of the bad mail to a specific address, or it can send you a report of all the messages that weren't delivered.

To change the way your SMTP server handles undeliverable mail, follow these steps:

1. Open the Internet Service Manager.
2. Select the name of the SMTP server that you want to change, and click on the Properties tool. The Properties dialog box for the server opens.
3. Click on the Messages tab.
4. To receive a report of all the undeliverable mail, enter an e-mail address in the Send a Copy of Non-delivery Report To text box.
5. To receive a copy of all the bad mail, enter an e-mail address in the Send a Copy of Badmail To text box.
6. To change the directory that stores the bad mail, enter a new directory in the Badmail Directory text box.
7. Click on OK to save your changes.
8. Close the Internet Service Manager.

NNTP Server-Specific Configuration

An NNTP Server hosts two types of newsgroups. One group allows anyone to post messages. The other group is moderated, and only the moderator can post messages for everyone to see. As the administrator of the NNTP server, you must set up the site properly (as explained in more detail in Chapter 34). This section covers a few default settings that enable you to control your NNTP server.

Limiting Postings

The default setting for your NNTP server is to allow newsreader clients to post messages to your newsgroups. You may need to limit the size of the messages posted or limit the amount of space that these messages take up on your hard disk. These two settings are easy to change with the following steps:

1. Open the Internet Service Manager.

2. Select the name of the NNTP server that you want to change and click on the Properties tool. The Properties dialog box for the server opens.

3. Click on the NNTP Settings tab. The Properties dialog box appears, as shown in Figure 4-12.

FIGURE 4-12

You can control the posting limits of your newsgroups.

4. Select the Allow Client Posting option at the top of the dialog box.

5. Enter the size limit for a posting in the Limit Post Size box.

6. Enter the maximum amount of storage space that can be used by a message posted from a news client in the Limit Connection Size box.

7. Click on OK to save your changes.

8. Close the Internet Service Manager.

Configuring Moderated Newsgroups

When you operate moderated newsgroups, messages are automatically sent to an SMTP server for the moderator to review. If these messages are undeliverable, a report is sent to an administrator's e-mail account.

To setup NNTP for moderated groups, follow these steps:

1. Open the Internet Service Manager.

2. Select the name of the NNTP server that you want to change, and click on the Properties tool. The Properties dialog box for the server opens.

3. Click on the NNTP Settings tab.
4. In the SMTP Server for Moderated Groups text box, enter the SMTP server that will send messages to the group's moderator.
5. In the Administrator Email Account text box, enter the e-mail address of the administrator who will receive the error reports.
6. Click on OK to save your changes.
7. Close the Internet Service Manager.

Chapter 5

Working with Virtual
Servers and Directories

In This Chapter

♦ Understanding Virtual Servers

♦ Understanding Virtual Directories

In the first Web and FTP servers that hit the market years ago, you could use only a single directory tree for the data you planned on publishing. IIS 4.0 is more versatile and provides more flexibility through its support of both virtual servers and virtual directories.

Although FTP servers do not support either of these technologies, they can greatly increase the value of your site when applied properly. When applied improperly, however, they can cause a management headache and might open security holes at your site. This chapter focuses on how you can effectively implement both virtual servers and directories.

Understanding Virtual Servers

Most organizations are interested in running only a single Web site, but you may have a special need for more than one server. Your options are to get additional servers (other computers running IIS) or to use *virtual servers*. IIS enables you to set up virtual servers on a single physical server. To the outside world, you appear to be running multiple hardware servers, when in fact, IIS is taking care of all the "detail work" associated with managing the different appearances.

Two methods are available for creating multiple Web sites, or virtual servers, on one machine. One method is to have one of the servers listen to a different port. The HTML version of the Internet Service Manager is an example of this type of virtual server. This server was installed with IIS and is running on the same machine as your Web site. However, instead of listening to port 80, which is the default port for a Web site, it is listening to another port.

The second option is to use multiple IP addresses. As an example of the second type of virtual server, my company provides Internet services for several domains. The first domain, dcomp.com, is for Discovery Computing, Inc. Another domain, wyowriters.org, is for Wyoming Writers, Inc., a nonprofit organization that promotes writers within the state of Wyoming. A single instance of IIS can easily handle both organizations. The key is to set up a regular home directory for one of the domains (dcomp.com) and a virtual server for the other.

 You can also use virtual servers when setting up intranets within an organization. Suppose that you are running a company that has multiple divisions. Your company, Wally's Widgets, has the domain address widget.com. When it comes time to set up your intranet, your industrial division wants to run a Web server, as does the electronics division. Your options are to set up a single intranet Web server for the entire company or to set up a virtual server for each division. In the latter case, you might use a URL of industrial.widget.com for the industrial division, and electronic.widget.com for the electrical division.

Setting Up Virtual Servers

When you decide to set up virtual servers for your site, IIS makes the process quite easy. From a high-level perspective, you need to accomplish only the following tasks if you are going to set up your virtual servers by assigning individual IP addresses:

- ◆ Decide on an IP address for each Web server that you want IIS to handle.
- ◆ Bind each IP address to the network card in your server.
- ◆ Change your DNS server so that it knows how to route the addresses of the virtual servers.
- ◆ Set up IIS to handle the directories properly.

If you are going to set up your virtual servers by assigning different ports for each server, then you need to accomplish only the last task in the list, not the first three. You also have the added task of assigning the proper port to the proper server.

Each step is covered in the following sections.

Selecting IP Addresses

When you set up your original Internet site, you should have been assigned at least a class C IP address range by your Internet service provider. This range provides you with 255 unique IP addresses, which you can assign to the machines in your network. Using a feature of Windows NT known as *multihoming*, you can also assign multiple IP addresses to the same physical machine.

INTRANET

If you are running an intranet site and it is not connected to the Internet in any way, you don't need to worry about conflicts with IP addresses outside your organization. Because you are not connected to the Internet, no IP address conflicts can arise with the outside world. In this case, you can decide on which IP addresses you want to use for the servers in your network.

If you think that you might someday connect your intranet to the Internet, you should probably use IP addresses that won't conflict with addresses already in use. A few IP addresses have been set aside for this kind of local use. They are described in RFC 1918 and include the following blocks of IP addresses:

10.0.0.0 – 10.255.255.255

172.16.0.0 – 172.31.255.255

192.168.0.0 – 192.168.255.255

For each virtual server you want to set up, you need a unique IP address. Returning to the examples started in the previous section, if you have a class C network with the first three octets as 212.15.312, you could assign 212.15.312.11 to industrial.widget.com and 212.15.312.12 to electronic.widget.com. In the case of our company server, the class C network uses the first three octets of 205.163.44. Using this address range, we set up dcomp.com as 205.163.44.2 and wyowriters.org as 205.163.44.30.

Binding to the Network Card

With Windows NT Server, you can bind multiple IP addresses to a single physical network card as an alternative to adding multiple network cards. Binding the IP addresses used by your servers to the network card is necessary so that the network drivers know which informational packets are destined for the server. To bind multiple IP addresses to a single network card, follow these steps:

1. Open the Control Panel.
2. Double-click on the Network icon to open the Network dialog box.
3. Click on the Protocols tab. The Network dialog box appears, as shown in Figure 5-1. (You may have different protocols listed in the dialog box, but you should at least have the TCP/IP protocol.)

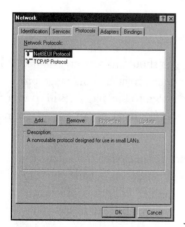

FIGURE 5-1

The Network dialog box enables you to change the configuration of your network

4. Double-click on the entry for TCP/IP Protocol in the Network Protocols box. The Microsoft TCP/IP Properties dialog box opens.
5. Click on the Advanced button to display the Advanced IP Addressing dialog box, as shown in Figure 5-2.

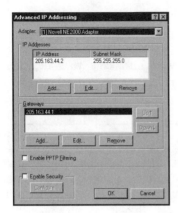

FIGURE 5-2

In the Advanced IP Addressing dialog box, you specify IP addresses for your network card.

6. Click on the Add button (in the IP Addresses area) to add an IP address for the network adapter in your system. A small dialog box opens in which you can enter both the IP address and the subnet mask.

7. Move to the IP Address field. Enter the IP address that should be bound to your network card.

8. Move to the Subnet Mask field. Enter the subnet mask for the IP address you are entering. (If you administer an entire class C IP address range, your subnet mask is 255.255.255.0.)

9. Click on the Add button. The new IP address appears in the list of IP addresses.

10. Repeat steps 6 through 9 for each IP address that you are using for your virtual servers.

11. Click on the OK button to close the Advanced IP Addressing dialog box and save your changes.

12. Click on OK twice to close the remaining dialog boxes.

At this point, a message box may tell you to restart your system for the changes to take effect. Go ahead and restart. (Even if the message box does not appear, you should restart your system.) When your system has been restarted, any IP packets directed to the IP addresses that you used are routed to your system.

NOTE

Prior to Windows NT 4.0, Windows NT would allow you only a maximum of five IP addresses per network card. Some of the online help still mentions this limit, but Windows NT 4.0 no longer has the limit of five IP addresses per card.

Changing the DNS Server

In Chapter 2, you learned that a DNS server provides address resolution between domain names and IP addresses. If a DNS server is installed at your site, you need to modify the DNS server configuration files to reflect the new virtual servers that you are setting up.

NOTE

If you don't have a DNS server at your site, somebody somewhere must have one for your domain. Chances are good that it will be either your Internet service provider or a different hardware server on your intranet. Make sure that whoever is responsible for the DNS server is aware of the domain address changes you are instituting with your new virtual servers.

Several DNS server implementations are available for Windows NT, and the exact steps that you go through vary for each implementation. In general, you need to create server definitions to be associated with your new IP addresses. In the case of one of the examples provided earlier, you need to define industrial.widget.com and associate it with 212.15.312.11, and define electronics.widget.com and associate it with 212.15.312.12.

On our DNS server, we do this step by changing the forward-referencing file, which defines names used in our domain. (Our forward-referencing file is called named.zoneinfo; yours will probably differ.) Such a file for the widget.com domain could look like this, after the new changes:

```
;   File:      named.zoneinfo
;   Purpose:   This file establishes the name/address information
;              for this zone.
;
@        IN SOA    web-server.widget.com. root.widget.com. (
             970201    ; serial number
             43200     ; refresh every 12 hours
             7200      ; retry after 2 hours
             1209600   ; expire after 2 weeks
             172800)   ; default ttl is 2 days
;
         IN NS     web-server.widget.com.
localhost               IN   A    127.0.0.1
web-server.widget.com.  IN   A    212.15.312.2
```

```
widget.com.            IN   A   212.15.312.2
;
;    Mail Exchange Records
;
widget.com.        IN MX   10     web-server.widget.com.
;
;    Define local hosts
;
industrial   IN A   212.15.312.11
             IN MX 10 web-server.widget.com.


electronic   IN A   212.15.312.12
             IN MX 10 web-server.widget.com.
;
; CNames
;
www.widget.com.               IN    CNAME    web-server.widget.com.
www.industrial.widget.com.   IN    CNAME    industrial.widget.com.
www.electronic.widget.com.   IN    CNAME    electronic.widget.com.
;
```

In addition to changing the forward-referencing file, you may also need to change the reverse-lookup file, which is used to translate from the IP address back to domain addresses. You should check your DNS documentation for instructions.

TIP

If your DNS server uses configuration files, be sure to also change the version number at the start of each file you modify. If you don't change the version number, the information isn't propagated correctly through the Internet.

If you are setting up a new domain entirely (as was done with the wyowriters.org domain discussed earlier), you need to do more extensive alterations to your DNS configuration files. In our server, we needed to perform three steps:

◆ Create a new forward-referencing file for the new wyowriters.org domain.

- ◆ Modify the existing reverse-lookup file to include information about the IP address assigned to wyowriters.org.
- ◆ Change the DNS boot file to contain a pointer to the new forward-referencing file for wyowriters.org.

Again, how you make the changes depends on your DNS server. Regardless of the server you are using, however, when you are done making changes, you should stop the DNS service and then restart it. This step causes the configuration files to reload, which is necessary for your change to be effective. To stop and start the DNS server, follow these steps:

1. Open the Control Panel.
2. Double-click on the Services icon to open the Services dialog box, as shown in Figure 5-3.

FIGURE 5-3

The Services dialog box controls the execution of system services in Windows NT.

3. Highlight the service name for your DNS server in the Service list box. (This name varies, depending on the vendor that created your DNS server.)
4. Click on the Stop button.
5. Click on the Yes button to confirm your action. The service is stopped and the services list is updated.
6. Click on the Start button. (The DNS server service name should still be selected in the Service list box). This action starts the service again and forces the modified configuration files to reload.
7. Click on the Close button to close the Services dialog box.

With your DNS server configured properly, you are almost done. However, exactly what you do next depends on what you are setting up. If you are setting up a brand new domain (as was the case with wyowriters.org), you must register the new domain with InterNIC. InterNIC is the network organization responsible for registering domain names so that conflicts do not occur. You can find out how to register a domain name at **http://rs.internic.net/rs-internic.html.**

ONLINE

If you are not setting up a new domain, but you are simply setting up a new virtual server within your existing domain (as in the case of industrial.widget.com), you don't need to register anything else with InterNIC; you are ready to proceed to the final step (assuming, of course, that you previously registered widget.com with InterNIC).

Creating a New Web Site

Setting up IIS for your new virtual servers is perhaps the easiest step of all. In essence, you are simply creating a new Web site. To configure IIS for virtual servers after you bind the new IP addresses to the network card and make your DNS changes, follow these steps:

1. Open the Internet Service Manager.

2. Select the computer name of your Web server.

3. Select New from the Action toolbar menu and then click on Web Site, as shown in Figure 5-4. The New Web Site Wizard starts.

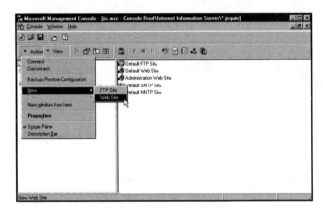

FIGURE 5-4

The Action menu is used to start the New Web Site Wizard.

4. Enter a description in the Web Site Description field. This name will appear in the Internet Service Manager. Then click on Next to move to the next step of the Wizard, shown in Figure 5-5.

5. Select the IP address for this Web site from the drop-down box for a local machine, or enter the IP address for a remote machine. (You assigned this address to your new Web site with your DNS server.)

6. You may also assign a new port now, but most of the time, you will use the default port of 80. Note that you will need to assign a different port number if you are setting up virtual servers by using different port numbers. You do not need to assign a different port if you are using different IP addresses.

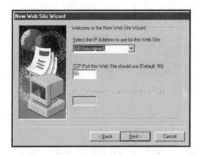

FIGURE 5-5

Use a different IP address and/or port for every virtual server.

NOTE

Notice that as far as IIS is concerned, domain names don't enter into the configuration at all—everything is done with IP addresses. For the virtual server to function as you intend, be sure to select the proper IP address (associated with a particular domain address) for the proper home directory. The domain names are handled entirely by the DNS server, as you configured them in the previous section.

---

7. Specify the home directory for your site: either enter the path of the directory or use the browse button to find the directory you want to use. You may also decide whether to allow anonymous connections before clicking <u>N</u>ext to move on to the final step shown in Figure 5-6.

NOTE

When using remote administration, it is important to note that the path is dependent on the machine running IIS. It is extremely important to make sure that the Web server machine has the rights to access any network drives that you may wish to use as a home directory.

---

8. Select the permissions for the new home directory. If you are using basic HTML or ASP content, then the default selections will work fine. For more on access permissions, look at Chapter 21.

9. Click on Finish when done.

10. You are returned to the Internet Service Manager. To start your new site, simply select the site and click on the Start tool.

11. Close the Internet Service Manager window.

FIGURE 5-6

*The new Web site
needs a base directory.*

How Does It Work?

Now that your virtual servers are up and running (and without any extra hardware expenditure), you may be wondering how people can find your new virtual server. The process is quite simple, really. Here's a look at it from the perspective of someone who knows the URL of the wyowriters.org site on my company's Web server.

ONLINE ▶ First of all, the user is running a browser and puts in the **http://wyowriters.org** URL. The browser's requested URL is passed to the TCP/IP networking system of the computer. TCP/IP uses the DNS server to resolve the domain address to an IP address. If someone else using the same DNS server had recently visited the site (meaning that the address had been resolved), the DNS server would be able to perform the resolution.

If the main DNS server cannot perform the resolution, then any secondary DNS servers are used to find an IP address for the browser. (Secondary DNS servers are specified when a system is configured for the TCP/IP protocol.) If the secondary DNS servers cannot resolve the address, then one of the top-level DNS servers in the world is automatically checked. These servers can then direct the local DNS server to the DNS server that is responsible for the wyowriters.org domain—in this case, the DNS server maintained by DCI (my company).

My DNS server then sends the IP address information for wyowriters.org (205.163.44.30) to the user's local DNS server to store in its cache. The information is cached so that the next time someone wants to contact wyowriters.org, the local DNS server will have the information.

Now the domain address has been resolved, and a Web session can be initiated between the user's browser and a particular IP address. The communication packets are routed to 205.163.44.30, which arrives at the same network card that also receives packets destined for several other IP addresses (thanks to the multihoming feature of Windows NT). The packets are marked for port 80, which is the port for the Web server. The IIS Web server examines the packets. It then compares the IP address on the packets with the IP address of the virtual servers that have been set up. If the IP address matches a virtual server IP address, the information in the home directory of that virtual server is "served up" to the user (as would happen with wyowriters.org). If the IP address does not match any of the virtual servers, then the default server (in this case, dcomp.com) serves the information requested.

If you created a virtual server by simply adding a different port, then the process used by the Web server to resolve the address is quite similar. The packet is routed to the same machine and IP address as your primary Web server but is marked for a different port. IIS matches up this port number with the virtual server that is running on your machine and returns the requested information.

> **NOTE**
>
> You should note that if the user's browser URL does not include the port designation (as in www.dcomp.com:432), then the connection is made to the default port of 80. Thus, the intended server is never accessed.

Understanding Virtual Directories

If you were working with computers in the early days of DOS, you may remember the **JOIN** command. It allowed you to treat a different disk as if it were a directory on the current drive. Virtual directories under IIS operate pretty much the same way. When you set up a virtual directory, in effect you provide an alias for a path and that alias appears to remote users as a subdirectory on your server. IIS supports virtual directories for Web and FTP servers, and various IIS components make extensive use of these directories.

When you first specify the home directory of a server, all other directories accessible through the server must be subdirectories to the home directory. Virtual directories enable you to get around this limitation. As an example, suppose that your main Web directories are on drive D, but you have a directory on drive F that you want to make available from the Web. Instead of copying the contents of the directory to drive D, you can create a virtual directory that points to the original information on drive F. As far as visitors at your site are concerned, the directory is part of your Web site.

> **NOTE**
>
> When users are looking through your site, they won't see the virtual directories in any directory listing. Instead, they need to know the proper path to change to the virtual directory.

Creating a Virtual Directory

You can use either the Internet Service Manager or Windows NT Explorer when you are ready to create a virtual directory. To create a virtual directory with the Internet Service Manager, follow these steps:

1. Open the Internet Service Manager.

2. Select the server, in the scope pane, on which you want to create a virtual directory. The contents of your Web site, including any virtual directories, appear in the results pane, as shown in Figure 5-7.

3. From the Action menu, select <u>N</u>ew and then select Virtual Directory. The New Virtual Directory Wizard, shown in Figure 5-8, opens.

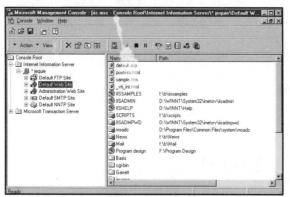

FIGURE 5-7

A server's virtual directories are listed in the Results pane.

FIGURE 5-8

The New Virtual Directory Wizard makes adding a virtual directory a snap.

4. Enter an alias for your virtual directory and select <u>N</u>ext. (This alias is the name of the directory that will be used in URLs.)

5. Enter the physical path of the directory you are adding and click on <u>N</u>ext.

6. Click on Finish. This step enables you to set up access permissions on this directory, but the default permissions are probably fine.

7. The Wizard closes, and your new virtual directory appears in the scope pane of the Internet Service Manager.

8. Close the Internet Service Manger.

Internet Information Server's integration with Windows NT makes adding a virtual directory even easier on a local machine using Windows NT Explorer. To create a virtual directory with Windows NT Explorer, follow these steps:

1. Open Windows NT Explorer and find the folder that you want to use as a virtual directory.

2. Right-click on the folder and select Properties from the shortcut menu.

3. Select the Web Sharing tab in the Property sheet. This tab, shown in Figure 5-9, was added when IIS 4 was installed on the system, and provides easy access to virtual directory information.

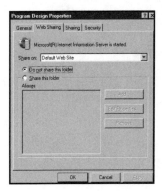

FIGURE 5-9

The Property sheet eases the creation of a virtual directory on a local machine.

4. Choose the Web site that will use this directory from the Share On drop-down list. This list includes all the virtual Web servers running on your machine.

5. Select the Share This Folder option. An Edit Alias dialog box, shown in Figure 5-10, pops up. This dialog box enables you to enter an alias name for the directory and to set privileges. (The default settings are generally fine.)

FIGURE 5-10

The new virtual directory starts with the same name as the folder.

6. Click on OK to close the Edit Alias dialog box, and the new alias appears in the folder's Property sheet (see Figure 5-11).

7. Click on OK to close the Property sheet.

FIGURE 5-11

A folder can have any number of virtual directory aliases.

Default Virtual Directories

When you install IIS 4.0, it creates quite a few virtual directories on your system. Although these directories provide useful services, such as help, they can present a bit of a security nuisance. Notice that I didn't say "security problem." Indeed, the nuisance is that because default directories are created using standard names, they are available to the rest of the company or the rest of the Internet as well. Thus other people can access them. If you doubt this statement, try accessing someone's Web site and then accessing the /IISHelp directory. Remember that this element is a virtual directory, so it will not show up if directory browsing is turned on. Instead, you need to type in the entire directory name. For example, if the site is **www.bigcompany.com**, you could try the following URL:

ONLINE ▶

http://www.bigcompany.com/IISHelp/default.htm

If the site is running a standard installation of IIS 4.0, you should see the help files for IIS 4.0. This same documentation is on your system, but you are accessing it from someone else's. In the spirit of fair play, you should understand that a visitor can do the same thing on your site.

TIP

You can often find sites that use IIS by looking at two things. First, the site might have a Microsoft BackOffice logo. Second, the default filename for the site is often default.htm.

Although the permissions on the automatic virtual directories are read-only, the mere fact that others can access the directories means that someone outside the organization can "poke around" in directories set up by IIS. At a minimum, this situation raises the potential of wasted resources on your server. As your server is responding to the poking-around requests, it cannot respond to other more relevant requests.

The only server for which IIS sets up automatic virtual directories is the Web server. The virtual directories set up by IIS depend on the components that you have installed. Table 5-1 lists the possible directories. Additional virtual directories will be created if you install the SMTP and NNTP servers.

Table 5-1 Virtual Directories Automatically Created by IIS

Directory	Alias
C:\Inetpub\iissamples	IISSAMPLES
C:\WINNT\System32\inetsrv\iisadmin	IISADMIN
C:\InetPub\scripts	SCRIPTS
C:\Program Files\Common Files\System\MSADC	MSADC
C:\WINNT\Help	IISHelp
C:\WINNT\System32\inetsrv\iisadmpwd	IISADMPWD

If you don't want people tampering with these directories, you can always remove them. However, doing so also removes some of the capabilities of IIS. Another solution is to rename the aliases that IIS uses for these directories, but even this approach may make some IIS 4.0 samples nonfunctional. Make your changes carefully and then fully test those changes. Understand, however, that some changes are necessary to fully secure your site.

PART II

Developing Basic Web Site Content

Chapter 6

Planning Basic Content

In This Chapter

◆ Planning Your Site

◆ Establishing a Directory Structure

◆ Establishing Content

◆ Liability for Content

Any discussion on setting up a Web site requires at least some mention of content. After all, the entire purpose of a site is to publish content that others may find valuable. The importance of content must be balanced, however, with the fact that this book is about how to run IIS, not about how to create a whiz-bang Web site.

Like any other tool, IIS can work either for you or against you. For example, if you are working with a desktop publishing program, you can make better use of the tool (the DTP program) by understanding the type of content with which you are working. IIS is no different; if you understand the content of your site, you can better understand how to use IIS to accomplish your goals. This chapter focuses strictly on putting content together for use within IIS. By understanding the information presented here, you can make IIS work in the best way possible for your needs.

Planning Your Site

Long before you actually open the doors of your Web site, you should sit down and plan what information you want it to offer. Even though the Web is a dynamic place and your Web site may change weekly or daily, you still need some idea of what your initial offering is going to look like.

Your plans should cover not only the appearance of your site but also the goals that you have for your site. Goals? For a Web site? Absolutely! Without goals, you cannot know whether your site has succeeded. Your goal-setting process can be informal or relatively structured; that is up to you. The important thing, however, is to plan your site with an eye toward a specific goal.

Many organizations go through extensive testing, focus groups, or planning before they release a new product. If you think of your Web site as a product—an informational product—then you can begin to understand why it requires planning. At a minimum, your plan should include the following information:

INTRANET

◆ Who will do the work

◆ When they will do it

◆ What you expect from the site

♦ When you expect it

♦ How you will measure the results

♦ What you will do if your site falls short

Essentially, these six items are the crux of a business plan. A detailed examination of each area is thus beyond the scope of this book, but you should approach your Web site as if it were a real business. If you use the same business skills that you have learned in your other endeavors, you will be better prepared to take advantage of the opportunities and recognize the problems that may arise. In addition, you won't be as likely to lose your shirt if the business really goes south.

Establishing a Directory Structure

Sooner or later, you will need to think about the organization of your Web site. Ideally, you should do so before making your Web server operational. It is not unusual, however, to reorganize your site from time to time. The structure of your site affects how users access your site, as well as how you create the content pages that you publish on the Web. How you put your directories together is entirely up to you, but you should keep in mind that, unlike with your personal computer, many people will need to work through your directories. Therefore, you should always keep your users in mind as you establish any structure or make any changes.

NOTE

The biggest reason for planning your directory structure before going online is that robots wander around the Web, gathering information to appear in high-powered search engines such as Lycos or Alta Vista. Many people use those search engines to locate the information at your site. If you change your directory structure after the robots have cataloged your site, you run the risk of having bad URLs in the search engines. This situation can frustrate users and signal missed opportunities.

If you are running a very small Web site, with a single purpose, the organization of your site is quite easy. In fact, you may be able to get by with only a single directory—the root directory—for your server. If your content is quite diverse, you should set out an organization up front.

ONLINE ▶ As an example, my company (Discovery Computing Inc. at **http://www.dcomp.com**) provides Internet advertising services for businesses in northeastern Wyoming and adjoining states. The natural way for these businesses to be organized is by town.

Thus, the directory structure appears as follows:

```
Home
    Aladdin
        Pictures
    Art
    BelleFourche
        Pictures
    Class
    CrookCounty
        Pictures
    DCI
    DevilsTower
        Pictures
    Hulett
        Pictures
    Misc
    Newcastle
        Pictures
    Spearfish
        Pictures
    Sundance
        Pictures
```

The Home directory, of course, is the root directory set up in IIS for the Web site. This home directory contains top-level documents, such as the default page for the site. Most of the next level of directories represents a town or geographical area in the region. These directories contain HTML files that advertise businesses within those communities. Town directories have a Pictures subdirectory that contains pictures used by the HTML files within the town directory. This hierarchy creates a relationship between the HTML files and graphics files that comes in handy if we ever need to move the files.

Several other directories do not represent towns or geographical areas. These other directories have the following contents:

◆ **Art** Contains common graphics files: icons, buttons, wallpaper, and the like. If a file is used in more than one place on the site, it is stored here for easy access.

- ◆ **Class** Contains files for the company's Internet classified service.
- ◆ **DCI** Contains documents related directly to the company.
- ◆ **Misc** Contains documents that don't fit into any of the other directories.

The advantage of this type of organization is that it is clear. Site administrators and visitors can easily understand exactly what is in each directory. I have seen some sites that use numeric codes or what appears to be random gibberish for their directories. Although this structure works without a hitch—as far as the computer is concerned—it is not very friendly to the human visitors at the site.

Another site with which we are acquainted is the Web site for the Independent Motels of America, which is an association of approximately 130 small, independent motels. This association's Web site **http://www.imalodging.com** is much simpler in concept. Each member lodge has its own page, including pictures and maps that tell how to get to the motel. The straightforward structure is almost self-explanatory:

```
Home
    Lodges
    Maps
    Pictures
```

The Lodges subdirectory contains the pages for the individual motels, Maps contains the maps that explain how to get to the lodges, and Pictures contains the pictures for each motel. Higher-level pages, such as the main page and individual state pages, reside within the Home directory.

These suggested directory structures are not the only (or even the best) way to organize your Web site, but this method works for many sites. The key is to think through how to organize your site before you start publishing documents. If you plan carefully and allow for growth, you will have fewer problems as you work on the Web.

Establishing Content

If you have ever visited a busy Web site, you probably noticed all sorts of documents, graphics, sounds, files, and so on. Amassing huge amounts of information isn't particularly difficult; it just takes time. To manage the information at your site, you need to understand both your site and the information you are providing.

Focus, Focus, Focus

The low cost of disk space these days might encourage you to believe that you can create and store huge documents at your site and then make them available to the world. The problem with this theory is that although disk space might be cheap, your Internet pipeline is not. The more people using your site, the greater the opportunity for creating a bottleneck.

To get around this problem, you should try not to publish every piece of neat information you run across. Instead, focus on the unique topic (or topics) you want to provide. As an example, you may want to become the ultimate Web site for information related to the U.S. Civil War. Although this topic is still broad, it's much more focused than simply publishing everything about warfare in general.

Of course, if the primary reason for the existence of your site is to sustain your company's marketing and support efforts, then you already have a built-in focus for the information you make available. Realizing your purpose enables you to define which information is acceptable and which isn't.

Copyrighted Information

If you are providing information on your server in which your company has a proprietary interest, you need to make that interest known to everyone who visits your site. For example, if your product documentation is available at your site, you should make sure that copyright notices exist within the documentation pages or files (if you allow complete files to be downloaded).

Conversely, if you are running a general-interest Web site (for example, the U.S. Civil War site mentioned in the previous section), you need to be sure that you have the right to post and publish the information you're including at your site. In many respects, the area of reusing information electronically is still quite gray, and you need to be as conservative as your insurance agent and lawyer suggest that you be. For example, if you have posted electronic copies of textbooks about the U.S. Civil War, you are probably violating U.S. copyright law.

CAUTION

If you are in doubt about what you can safely publish at your Web site, you should definitely check with a qualified legal advisor.

Compressed Files

If your site includes files that visitors can download, you should consider compressing the files so that they can be transferred more quickly. Both you and your visitors benefit. Compressed files take less disk space and travel over the Internet faster. Consequently, your visitors receive their files faster, and you free up bandwidth sooner.

Many compression programs and standards are in use around the world. Typically, compression standards crop up around various operating systems. As you browse various Internet sites, you can tell which compression programs are being used by looking at the filename extension for a file. Table 6-1 lists some of the most common file compression standards that you'll run into on the Internet.

Table 6-1 Common File Name Extensions for Compressed Files

Extension	Platform	Program
.arc	DOS	ARC
.lh	DOS	Lharc
.lzh	DOS	Lharc
.sit	Macintosh	Stuffit
.tar	UNIX	Tar
.Z	UNIX	Compress
.z	UNIX	Pack
.zip	DOS/Windows	PKZIP; WinZip
.zoo	DOS/UNIX	zoo210

Even though the information in Table 6-1 indicates a platform for the various file extensions, programs are available on the Internet that allow you to decompress (or compress) files using any given compression standard on virtually any type of computer system.

Which compression standard should you use for the files available through your site? That depends on the type of files you are compressing and who your typical user is. If the file that you want to make available at your site is an executable program for a UNIX system, for example, you should use the TAR standard. However, if the files are transportable to a wide variety of platforms (as is typically the case with audio, graphics, text, or video files), you may want to keep several different compressed versions of the files.

TIP

Compressing single files doesn't make much sense unless the single file is quite large. If you can, compress entire collections of related files.

File Formats

One of the issues that you need to be concerned with when publishing information on the Web is the format in which your information will be stored. Clearly, most of your documents will be in HTML format—the format used for Web pages. Beyond this, however, is quite a bit of latitude and even more confusion.

If you are creating a corporate Web site, most of the information you want to present to the world may be on your computer already. However, this information probably isn't in HTML or text format. It is more likely to be in a desktop publishing, word processor, spreadsheet, database, or some other program that has its own file type. Perhaps you even have graphics, video clips, or audio clips that you want to make accessible.

In many cases, you can easily transfer this information to the Web. The excitement over the Internet in the past few years has caused many software companies to add Internet capabilities to their software. For example, in new versions of popular programs such as Microsoft Word and Corel's WordPerfect, you can save a file in HTML format. And for many years, programs have enabled you to save files in a plain-text format. Check to see whether your software can quickly translate information to Internet-friendly file types.

The real confusion arrives when you want to publish multimedia information. Various types of files are available for graphics and sounds, and they all have unique strengths and weaknesses. The following sections discuss your options when publishing these types of files.

Graphics Files

Even though the Web originally began as a text-only Internet service, these days almost all Web pages include graphics. If you have been around computers for any length of time, you know that you can format and store a graphics file in dozens of ways. Table 6-2 lists some of the most common graphics file formats.

Even though you can create graphics in any of the formats shown in Table 6-2, you shouldn't necessarily do so. Not all browsers can display all graphics file formats. Although your visitors could download helpers, or browser add-ons, that would enable them to view virtually any type of graphics file, why put them through that trouble?

The most common graphics file formats used on the Web are GIF (pronounced either with a hard *G* or as "jiff") and JPG (pronounced "jay-peg"). Every popular browser understands these formats, so it's a fair bet that your graphics will not go unappreciated if they're in one of these formats.

Table 6-2 Common Filename Extensions for Graphics Files

Extension	Format
.bmp	Windows or OS/2 bitmap
.cdr	CorelDraw
.cgm	Computer graphics metafile
.gif	Graphics interchange format
.jpg, jpeg	JPEG format
.mac	MacPaint
.msp	Microsoft Paint
.pct, .pict	Macintosh PICT
.pcx	ZSoft Paintbrush
.psd	Adobe Photoshop
.ras	Sun raster image
.tga	Truevision Targa
.tif, .tiff	Tagged image file format
.wmf	Windows metafile
.wpg	WordPerfect graphic

The GIF format was developed years ago by CompuServe, the large online service. Typically, GIFs are used for small, low-color (256 or less colors) images. Thus they are great for icons and small artwork. The strengths of GIF files are as follows:

◆ **Small file size.** GIF files are saved using automatic compression, which means that they consume fewer bytes than many formats and can be transmitted quickly.

◆ **Interlacing.** When working with large graphics, you can direct the image to be saved in an interlaced format. Interlacing makes visitors think that an image is loading quickly because it is loaded in multiple passes.

◆ **Transparency.** You can direct some GIF variations to treat a specific color in the image as "transparent." When a browser encounters a transparent color, the existing browser background appears in place of the color.

These benefits do not mean that you should always choose GIF files. If you need higher-quality graphics, try the high-resolution, high-color capabilities of JPG files. Images saved in JPG format are highly realistic, although saving a JPG file with many colors and a high resolution can create a very large file.

NOTE

All else being equal, one of the biggest advantages of GIF as opposed to JPG is that GIF files can be decompressed more quickly. Thus, choosing GIF files means a speed advantage for the site visitor.

In my experience, GIFs are used as inline graphics mainly because of the speed of decompression and the advantage of transparency. However, I don't want to leave you with the impression that JPG is only for high-quality rendition or that JPG encoding has to produce larger file sizes. You can adjust image quality and color palette depth during JPG compression to yield file sizes that compare favorably with GIF files. JPEG is therefore perfectly suitable for a large variety of content, although the files are relatively slow to decompress. A site administrator with little graphics experience may need a short primer on this.

Your job as a site administrator is to select the image format that is best for your intended uses. Think about your images, your desired effect, and your visitors; then, pick the format that is best for you (and them).

Audio Files

The number of audio file formats is almost as large as the number of graphics file formats. Audio files are making great inroads into the Web, although they are not as widespread as graphics. The reason is that your visitor must have a sound card and speakers in order to appreciate your audio selections. If you decide to include audio clips at your site, however, you can save them in many different ways. The most common audio file formats are WAV and AU, both so-named because of the file extensions (.WAV and .AU, respectively) used for sounds saved in those formats.

The WAV format is typically used on Windows-based systems. The format was originally designed by Microsoft but now can be played on various hardware platforms. The AU format is widely accepted in the UNIX environment and is making large strides into the Windows world. The format originated on Sun and NeXT systems. WAV and AU files have similar file sizes and produce similar sound quality on the Internet. Most browsers understand the WAV format automatically, and a fair number of new browsers understand the AU format. Thus, you can base your decision about which format to use on whether you expect your visitors to be UNIX or Windows users.

> **TIP**
>
> If you want additional information on audio file formats, check out some of the search engines on the Internet, such as Alta Vista. Use the search words *audio file formats*.

Other Multimedia Files

Along with graphics and sound files, you will probably be using video files and files for multimedia presentations. Video files, like graphics and sound files, come in many varieties, and some are supported by the various browsers. Internet Explorer, for example, shows its Microsoft roots by displaying AVI files—a video file format used by Windows.

So many different types of multimedia files are in use that no one browser can possibly display them all. One solution is to have extensible browsers. Both Netscape Navigator and Internet Explorer support extensions that enable them to display new and different file types.

When looking at the various types of content that you want to make accessible to Web surfers, you need to ask two main questions. First, is this type of file supported by the different browsers? Second, can you provide an add-on to enable a browser to show this type of file?

Standard Information

When you surf the Web, you will find that most pages at any given site have many common elements. For example, a common masthead may appear at the top of each page, or a common footer may appear at the bottom. The reason is simple: consistency and familiarity. Common elements enable a user to quickly begin to use the Web site.

> **NOTE**
>
> Web pages are not the only place where common design elements are used. Take a look at the pages of a book, even this book. Common elements include the headers and footers on each page and the icons used in the margins. The use of common elements to Web documents reflects the comfort that both designers and users feel with these elements.

As you develop your Web pages, you will probably also want to strive for a consistent look. You can do so by simply thinking about how you want your pages to appear and the impression you want them to leave.

Good candidates for common elements are a navigational aid or address information. Figure 6-1 shows an example of such elements at the bottom of a Web page.

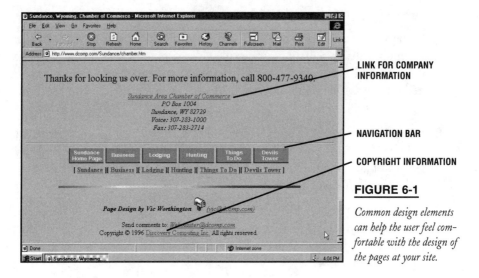

LINK FOR COMPANY INFORMATION

NAVIGATION BAR

COPYRIGHT INFORMATION

FIGURE 6-1

Common design elements can help the user feel comfortable with the design of the pages at your site.

These elements are designed to be used repeatedly on other pages. The code is the same, the icons are the same, and the effect is the same: ease of use on behalf of the user.

TIP

Make sure to include full address information somewhere on your Web site. I cannot tell you how frustrated I have been at many Web sites because I could not find a simple address or phone number. These elements are easy to forget, but you can quickly miss business opportunities by not including them at your site.

Liability for Content

The Web is, for many people, an uncharted and new territory. Unfortunately, we live in a litigious society. This fact, coupled with the type of person who thinks that providers (such as Webmasters) are responsible for everything on their sites, means that whenever you publish any information, you open yourself to liability for the content of that information.

The concept of being liable for content is nothing new. Publishers have operated under that concept for years, as have product developers. The concept is new, however, to those in the transmission end of the business. For example, phone companies have historically not been liable for the content that is transmitted over their lines. The service instigating the transmission (the publisher) is liable, however.

In the following two sections, you will learn about two particular areas where you may want to pay close attention to content and your potential liability.

Rating Your Content

The consumer, home, and political arenas have been engaging in quite a bit of discussion about the suitability of information on the Internet for users of all ages. Although most people agree that not everything on the Internet is suitable for young children or for those with "thin skins," few people agree on how to handle the situation. Librarians and school officials are calling for censorship to protect themselves from their perceived liability for what they allow students to view. Politicians, trying to make points with certain types of voters and operating in knee-jerk mode, have tried to pass laws that would outlaw "indecent" material (without providing any guidelines for defining the term *indecent*).

The upshot is that Webmasters need to be concerned with the content of their sites. One way to provide guidance to viewers is to rate your content. Browsers can then automatically recognize the rating and block out your site if it falls above a user-set threshold.

Several suggested rating systems are currently on the table. The one that is most widely accepted (but not yet widely implemented at Web sites) is the PICS standard. PICS is an acronym for Platform for Internet Content Selection. This rating system, maintained by the World Wide Web Consortium, is supported by the Internet Explorer browser (beginning with version 3.0). The PICS system does not work in a void, however. It relies on rating information embedded in the header of your HTML documents. The following portion of an HTML file header shows PICS-compliant coding:

```
<HTML><HEAD>
<TITLE>David's Web Page</TITLE>
<META http-equiv="PICS-Label" content='(PICS-1.1
"http://www.rateservice.org/v1.0"
  labels on "1996.10.05T05:15-0500"
  for "http://www.my.org/etc/mypage.html"
```

```
ratings (s 0 v 0 g 0)
)'>
</HEAD>
```

When Internet Explorer encounters this heading, it retrieves the ratings file from www.rateservice.org where *www.rateservice.org* is the URL of the site that stores ratings information used by your site. This may be your site or a remote site. The browser then compares the ratings information with the user's threshold. If the rating is higher than the threshold, the page is not displayed.

The PICS standard (or any other rating standard) can work only if content publishers (that's you), tool developers, and other interested parties work together. Otherwise, we may all be destined for a long series of political and legal solutions to a sticky situation.

TIP

It may be well worth your effort to look at the PICS standard and decide how best to implement it at your site. This issue is particularly important if you are publishing material that is more suitable for a mature audience.

A complete description of PICS is obviously beyond the scope of this book. For more information on PICS, visit the informational site at **http://www.w3.org/pub/WWW/PICS/**. You can also find helpful information at **http://vancouve webpages.com/PICS/HOWTO.html.** Software filters (or Internet Explorer, which has the filter built-in) work with independent ratings systems that such as those at **http://www.rsac.org/**.

Viruses in Your Content

We all know what viruses are and how they can affect a computer user. From the standpoint of running an Internet or intranet site, you need to be aware of two things:

- ◆ The content that you publish for others
- ◆ The items that you allow to be uploaded to your site

Fortunately, from a protection perspective, IIS does not support Web-site uploading. Thus, the second point is most applicable to an IIS FTP site. The first area, however, is more problematic because in some jurisdictions you may be liable for any viruses transmitted from your site to a user.

If you offer files for downloading from your Web site, you should strongly consider taking the following actions. These measures will help your users protect themselves and help you minimize your liability.

◆ **Educate users.** If you have an extensive library of software that users can download, you should consider adding some pages that educate your users about the dangers of viruses. These pages, rather than simply issue dire warnings that may scare people away from your site, can explain what steps you have gone through, what the risks are, and how users can protect themselves.

◆ **Test software.** If possible, you should test any software that you download through your site, including any shareware or freeware from other authors that you may distribute.

◆ **Provide tools.** Give users the weapons they need to protect themselves. You can provide either links to antivirus tools or the actual tools on your site.

◆ **Use disclaimers.** Include a legal disclaimer to indicate that you don't warrant the merchantability or fitness of any programs that you offer at your site. These disclaimers are fairly common in the software world, but you still may want to have yours reviewed by your legal counsel.

◆ **Use an upload directory.** Establish a write-only directory especially for uploads from users. You, as administrator, can then review the files in the directory and check them for viruses before making them available to other visitors.

ONLINE ▶ If you want more information about computer viruses and what you can do about them, check the site at **http://www-dcd.fnal.gov/dcd/virus/**. In addition, McAfee Associates was the premiere site for antivirus information and protection. They have now merged with a few other companies to form Network Associates, which you can find at **http://www.nai.com/**.

Chapter 7

Creating Content with FrontPage

———

In This Chapter

- ◆ A Word on HTML
- ◆ What Is FrontPage 98?
- ◆ Starting FrontPage Editor
- ◆ Formatting Your Document
- ◆ Adding Graphics to Your Document
- ◆ Working with Tables

Every Webmaster needs to be concerned with creating and developing content for his or her Web site. Fortunately, Microsoft includes with IIS 4.0 a powerful Web development and management system called FrontPage 98. This chapter focuses on how you can use the FrontPage system to develop the content for your site.

A Word on HTML

At the heart of publishing on the Web are plain ASCII text files that have special tags inserted throughout the text. The syntax of these tags is collectively known as *Hypertext Markup Language* (HTML). HTML was created specifically for use on the Web, but it is related to an older and much more complex standard known as *Standard Generalized Markup Language* (SGML).

This book assumes that you already know, in general, how to code a document in HTML. This means that you understand what HTML is and how it works, you can figure out what the various codes mean, and you have a grip on the structure of an HTML document. The purpose of this chapter is not to teach HTML coding or to provide an end-all reference on the subject. If you need such a book (or books), plenty are on the market.

TIP

For a dynamic look at HTML from a reference standpoint, check out **http://www.wilcam.com/cmat/html/crossref.html.** For content, this site is better than most HTML reference books I've seen.

What Is FrontPage 98?

FrontPage 98 is Microsoft's latest version of its HTML authoring and Web site management tool. The first version of the product was released a few years ago under the name FrontPage version 1.1. Microsoft then decided to position FrontPage as part of its Office suite of products and released FrontPage 97 as a companion to Office 97. Now it has released FrontPage 98, which is the latest and greatest version of this product.

With FrontPage 98, you can develop single Web pages or entire Webs. In FrontPage terminology, a *Web* is an entire Web site—a collection of related HTML documents that are interrelated. FrontPage Editor edits Web documents, and FrontPage Explorer manages the relationships of those documents or manages entire Web sites.

Using the creative aspects of FrontPage, you can perform the following tasks:

◆ Create Web pages without knowing HTML

◆ Use templates and wizards to create a single page or an entire Web

◆ Edit HTML source code

◆ Perform spell checking on documents

◆ Verify and correct hyperlinks automatically

◆ Add and manage graphics with ease

◆ Create tables on-screen

◆ Add extra components to your Web pages, such as those in JavaScript, VBScript, or Java

◆ Add predesigned programming features called FrontPage components

This list is just the tip of the iceberg, however, because FrontPage 98 also includes management functions that enable a single person or a team to engage in easy on-going development and management of Web projects. This chapter focuses on the development of content using FrontPage 98, which means predominantly the use of FrontPage Editor. Very few management aspects of the product (as implemented in FrontPage Explorer) are covered.

NOTE

Entire books have been written about how to use FrontPage 98. If you are interested in using the product to manage your Web site, you should get hold of such a book or dive right in and use those features until you are comfortable with them.

Client-Server Technology

Like so many tools on the Internet, FrontPage 98 relies on client-server technology and has both a client and a server portion. The FrontPage client runs on either Windows 95 or Windows NT. You can run it on a development workstation, remote from the server on which IIS is installed, or on the IIS server itself. The client uses a graphical user interface to handle the development and management functions.

The client communicates with the FrontPage server, which is officially called FrontPage Server Extensions. This group of software extensions adds to the capabilities of IIS and enables the FrontPage client to operate. FrontPage Server Extensions also implement the interactive features of the Web as seen by a Web browser.

NOTE

Because FrontPage 98 is sold as a stand-alone product and not just with IIS 4.0, the server extensions can be used with a number of different Web servers in addition to IIS. For example, FrontPage 98 can also be used with Web servers from Netscape, NCSA, CERN, Apache, and O'Reilly.

FrontPage server extensions do their work behind the scenes and effectively enable two different aspects of FrontPage. First, the server extensions enable the Web site management tools provided with FrontPage. For example, you can develop and test a Web site on a remote Windows 95 system and then automatically copy the entire site to the system on which IIS is installed. The server extensions automatically copy the entire site and modify all links within the site to adjust to the new server location.

The other primary purpose of the server extensions is to support FrontPage components, which can be used in a FrontPage Web document. *FrontPage components* are self-contained tools that implement features that would otherwise require extensive programming on the part of the Web page developer. For example, a FrontPage component might be used to develop a form, gather information from a site user, and store that information in a file on the server for later processing by the Webmaster. FrontPage 98 includes about a dozen FrontPage components that you can use in your development efforts. When you place the FrontPage component and then publish your pages, the server extensions recognize the component and generate the appropriate HTML or related code to implement the desired function. All this activity happens behind the scenes, of course, so that neither the developer nor the site user needs to be concerned with the nitty-gritty details of how the function was developed.

NOTE

Those who have followed Microsoft's product strategies for some time already realize that terminology often changes from one version of a product to another. FrontPage is no exception. The feature of FrontPage 98 now known as FrontPage components was previously known (in FrontPage 97) as WebBots. The only real difference between FrontPage components and WebBots is the name.

Installing FrontPage 98

When you install IIS, FrontPage 98 is not installed automatically. You need to explicitly install the product in order to use it. Fortunately, installation is a rather easy step. In this section, you learn how to install FrontPage 98 on your server. This process installs both the client and server portion of the product. If you were installing the product on a remote workstation instead of on the IIS server, you would follow very similar steps.

Microsoft has officially positioned FrontPage 98 as a stand-alone product, a part of its Microsoft Office line. FrontPage 98 is different from the version of FrontPage provided with some versions of Windows NT Server. There are several ways to obtain FrontPage 98, including the following:

◆ Purchase the stand-alone FrontPage 98 product or an upgrade either directly from Microsoft or from a software dealer

◆ Purchase the IIS 4.0 CD-ROM directly from Microsoft (**http://www.microsoft.com/iis/**)

◆ Download the FrontPage 98 files from the Microsoft Web site (**http://www.microsoft.com/frontpage/wpp/exts.htm**)

Not all of these methods deliver the same package, however. Although the last two provide the FrontPage 98 server extensions (which you need in order to use FrontPage 98 with IIS), they do not provide the commercial FrontPage 98 product. The only way you can get that product is to purchase it from Microsoft or from a software dealer.

The exact steps that you use to start the FrontPage 98 installation depends on which of these three formats you use for the program. If you are installing FrontPage 98 (the commercial version), then you should simply insert the CD-ROM in your drive and follow the instructions that appear on your screen. The directions in the balance of this section assume that you have downloaded the fp98ext_x86_enu.exe program from Microsoft's Web site and that you are installing the server extensions for use with IIS. If you are installing the server extensions from a different source, then you may need to take these instructions with a grain of salt and adapt them to your specific needs.

TIP

Installation requires you to stop your Web server, which makes your site content unavailable to the rest of the world. For this reason, you may want to install the server extensions at a time of traditionally low site activity.

To start the installation process, double-click on the fp98ext_x86_enu.exe program file. This compressed file is self-extracting, and by running the program, you start the decompression process. After the installation files are extracted, the Setup program is run and the screen shown in Figure 7-1 appears.

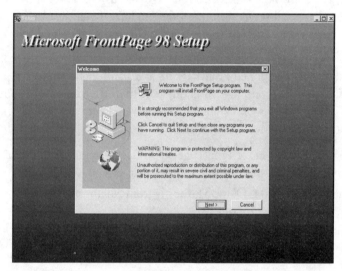

FIGURE 7-1

FrontPage 98 server extensions use a standard Microsoft Setup program.

To continue with the installation, click on the <u>N</u>ext button. You can accept the standard Microsoft end-user license agreement by clicking on <u>Y</u>es. Setup then begins copying program and configuration files to your system. If your system has multiple Web servers, then you will see shortly the dialog box shown in Figure 7-2.

Here you should make sure that you select the servers for which you want to install the FrontPage extensions. When you are satisfied with your selections, click on OK to continue. After a short pause, you will see a dialog box similar to the one shown in Figure 7-3.

FIGURE 7-2

You can install the server extensions on any of your Web servers.

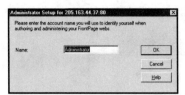

FIGURE 7-3

You must provide a user ID to use when managing your Webs.

Enter the name that you want to use to identify yourself when administering FrontPage for the particular server being installed. The default name is Administrator, but you can change it to any name that you desire. When you are ready to proceed, click on the OK button. The FrontPage server extensions are then installed on IIS; this portion of installation can take a while, depending on the speed of your computer. If you are asked to restart the server when the installation process is finished, click on Yes to stop and restart the server. Otherwise, a dialog box informs you that the installation is complete. In this case, click on the Finish button to conclude the installation.

Starting FrontPage Editor

You use FrontPage Editor to create individual Web pages. To start the program, from the Start menu choose Programs and then choose Microsoft FrontPage. This sequence actually starts FrontPage Explorer, not the editor. However, to access the editor, you need to start from Frontpage Explorer.

NOTE

The first time you run FrontPage 98, you may be led through some configuration steps. These are necessary so that FrontPage Explorer knows how to work with your network.

By default, when FrontPage Explorer starts, a wizard begins to guide you through creating your Webs. If your system displays a wizard screen, you can click on Cancel to close it; you will not need it for this chapter. The FrontPage Explorer window then appears, as shown in Figure 7-4.

With FrontPage Explorer displayed, you can start FrontPage Editor by choosing Show FrontPage Editor from the Tools menu. The FrontPage Editor program window is shown in Figure 7-5.

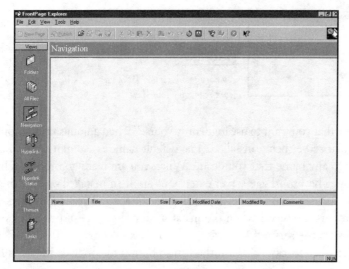

FIGURE 7-4

FrontPage Explorer is the default starting place when working with FrontPage 98.

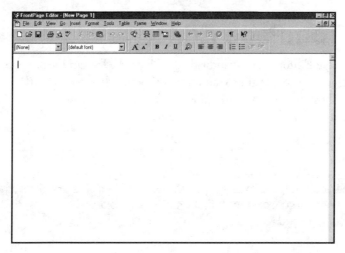

FIGURE 7-5

FrontPage Editor looks similar to many other Microsoft applications.

When you start FrontPage Editor, it may look rather boring. Remember, however, that this empty screen is only the beginning; no Web pages are yet loaded into the editor, nor have you started developing any Web pages. The rest of this chapter shows you how to use FrontPage Editor to create the exact look you desire for your pages.

The User Interface

If you are familiar with other Microsoft applications, such as Word or Excel, the FrontPage Editor program interface should look very familiar. Because the product is designed to work as part of the Microsoft Office family of products, it uses the standard Office interface. As you begin to work with the product, you will undoubtedly discover many additional similarities between FrontPage and the other Office programs.

At the top of the editor window, you can see three elements: the menu and two toolbars. The first toolbar row contains the Standard toolbar, and the next row contains the Format toolbar.

You can turn on or off any element on the program window by using the View menu. To turn off an element, click on the item from the menu to remove the check mark. When the option has a check mark, beside it, it is displayed; without a check mark, the option is not displayed.

How FrontPage Editor Creates Web Pages

Just a little later in this chapter, you learn how to use FrontPage Editor to edit and manipulate Web pages. Before doing so, however, you should understand the many ways in which you can use FrontPage to create Web pages.

FrontPage Editor provides at least four ways for you to create a new Web document. The method that you choose is up to you and depends on what you want to do. The following sections describe these methods.

Blank Pages

If you want to start a document from scratch, you can open a new, blank document by clicking on the New Document tool at the left side of the Standard toolbar. (You can also choose New from the File menu and then choose Normal Page.) Your screen displays a blank document, similar to a blank document in a word processing program. Now you can add text, images, and other objects as desired.

Using a Template

FrontPage includes quite a few different templates that you can use to create your Web pages. Templates in FrontPage are the same as templates used in Microsoft Word; they provide a starting place for your page. To see the various FrontPage templates, choose New from the File menu. The Page tab of the New dialog box is shown in Figure 7-6.

The Page tab lists all the templates and wizards that you can use to create a new Web page. (Wizards are discussed in the following section.) The first item on the list is Normal Page, which was discussed in the previous section. The other options in the list are templates and wizards. You can tell them apart because the templates are the items that do not end with the word *Wizard*.

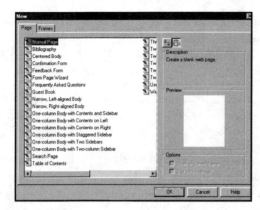

FIGURE 7-6

You can use a template to create a new Web page.

FrontPage 98 also includes templates to create Web pages that use frames. You can display these templates by clicking on the Frames tab in the New dialog box. Between the Page and the Frames tabs, FrontPage 98 has 34 templates. The templates available on the Page tab are detailed in Table 7-1. Those contained on the Frames tab are listed in Table 7-2.

Table 7-1 Standard Page Templates Provided with FrontPage 98

Template Name	Purpose
Bibliography	Creates a document for references to printed or online works.
Centered Body	Creates a page in which all the text is centered at the middle of the screen.
Confirmation Form	Creates a page that confirms user input to other standard FrontPage documents.
Feedback Form	Creates a page to gather input from users.
Frequently Asked Questions	Creates a page that displays common information about a topic.
Guest Book	Creates a page that serves as a public guest log, including comments from users.
Narrow, Left-aligned Body	Creates a page that pushes all the text to the left side of the page. The right side can then be used for other purposes, such as graphics.
Narrow, Right-aligned Body	Same as the previous template, but all the text is right-aligned.

Table 7-1 Standard Page Templates Provided with FrontPage 98 (continued)

Template Name	Purpose
One-column Body with Contents and Sidebar	Creates what is essentially a three-column page, but the sidebar at the right is intended for graphics.
One-column Body with Contents on Left	Creates a two-column format, with a small contents area at the left of the page.
One-column Body with Contents on Right	Same as the previous template, but reverses the positions of the contents and body text.
One-column Body with Staggered Sidebar	Creates a page with the body to the right and a two-column staggered (checkerboard) sidebar at the left.
One-column Body with Two Sidebars	Same as the previous template with an added sidebar at the right of the page.
One-column Body with Two-column Sidebar	Creates a page with the body to the left and a two-column sidebar at the right.
Search Page	Creates a page that enables users to search your site by keyword.
Table of Contents	Creates a page that provides a table of contents for your entire site.
Three-column Body	Creates a newspaper-style page with a main heading across three columns of text.
Two-column Body	Same as the previous template, but the body has only two columns.
Two-column Body with Contents on Left	Creates a two-column layout with a contents column added to the left.
Two-column Body with Two Sidebars	Creates a two-column body layout with a sidebar on the left and right.
Two-column Staggered Body	Creates a modified two-column body in which groups of text are staggered for a checkerboard effect.
Two-column Staggered Body with Contents and Sidebar	Same as the previous template with a contents column on the left and a sidebar on the right.
User Registration	Creates a page for users to register for access to your site.
Wide Body with Headings	Creates a layout that uses a single wide text column, but also uses subheadings.

Table 7-2 Standard Frame Templates Provided with FrontPage 98

Template Name	Purpose
Banner and Contents	Creates a document that uses three frames. A narrow banner frame is at the top, and a narrow contents frame is at the left. Links in the banner frame change what is displayed in the main frame.
Contents	Creates a two-frame document. The narrow contents frame appears at the left. Links in the contents frame change what is displayed in the other frame.
Footer	Creates a two-frame document. The narrow footer frame appears at the bottom. Links in the footer frame change what is displayed in the other frame.
Footnotes	Creates a two-frame document. The smaller footnote frame appears at the bottom. Links in the main frame change what is displayed in the footnote frame.
Header	The opposite of the footer template, with the narrow area appearing at the top.
Header, Footer, and Contents	Creates narrow header and footer frames at the top and bottom and a contents frame at the left. Links in the header and footer change what is displayed in the main frame.
Horizontal Split	Creates two equally sized independent frames, one over the other.
Nested Hierarchy	Creates a document with three frames. The full-height contents frame at the left controls what is displayed in the other two frames.
Top-Down Hierarchy	Creates a document with three stacked frames. The top frame controls the contents in the other two.
Vertical Split	Creates two equally sized independent frames, one beside the other.

To use one of the templates in the New dialog box, simply highlight the template and click on OK. The template then appears in the FrontPage Editor as a document that you can edit.

TIP

If you are developing a large Web site, you may want to create your own templates. To do so, simply develop a Web page and then save it as a template (using the Save As option from the File menu). Make sure that you use the Hypertext Templates file type when you save.

Using a Wizard

Wizards have been very popular since the introduction of Windows 95 and Windows NT 4.0. A wizard is a series of steps that walk you through what might otherwise be a complicated task. FrontPage 98 comes with one wizard. The Form Page Wizard (which helps you create a page that contains forms) is available from the Page tab of the New dialog box, shown earlier in Figure 7-6. You learn more about forms in Chapter 9.

Working with an Existing Page

There would be little purpose to using FrontPage Editor if it didn't provide a way for you to save pages and work on them later. FrontPage Editor gives you three ways to edit an existing page: you can load it from disk, grab it from your site, or grab it from the Web. You access all of these methods by choosing Open from the File menu. The Open dialog box is shown in Figure 7-7.

FIGURE 7-7

The Open dialog box loads an existing Web page from a variety of sources.

NOTE

If you haven't used FrontPage to edit Web pages before, then it automatically assumes that you want to load a document from your disk. In this case, it displays the Select File dialog box over the top of the Open dialog box. You can use the Select File dialog box to locate the disk file that you want to load. If you don't want to load from disk, simply click on the Close button to display the Open dialog box, as shown in Figure 7-7.

The Open dialog box lists any Web pages defined in the currently open Web. (Remember, you can use FrontPage to manage an entire Web site.) If you want to open a Web page that is not listed, you can do so by entering a URL at the bottom of the dialog box or by clicking on the file folder button in the lower-right corner.

> **TIP**
>
> Remember that U.S. copyright protection extends to much of what is available on the Web. Taking what you find there, without regard for whom it belongs to, is infringing on the intellectual property of others. Make sure that you have permission to use someone else's page before doing so.

Select the Web page that you want to work with and click on the OK button.

Formatting Your Document

In the previous sections, you learned how you can create new Web pages with FrontPage Editor. After a Web page is created (or loaded), you are ready to begin the process of making the page appear exactly as you want it to appear.

In the sections that follow, you learn how to format the content of a page. To prepare for this step, you should use FrontPage Editor to load the file \Chap07\RawPage.txt from the support files for this book. To load and then save the file, follow these steps:

1. Choose Open from the File menu. The Open dialog box opens.
2. If the Select File dialog does not automatically appear, click on the file folder icon at the lower-right corner of the Open dialog box.
3. Locate and select the RawPage.txt file from the support files and then click on Open. The Convert Text dialog box opens , as shown in Figure 7-8.

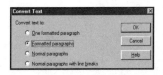

FIGURE 7-8

FrontPage can convert a text file as it is loaded.

4. Choose Normal paragraphs and then OK. The file is loaded.
5. Choose Save As from the File menu to display the Save As dialog box
6. If the Save as File dialog box also appears, click on Cancel. The Save As dialog box is shown in Figure 7-9.
7. Change the URL for the page to **Overview.htm**.
8. Enter **Overview of DCI** in the Page Title field at the bottom of the dialog box.
9. Click on the file folder button at the bottom right of the dialog box. This step displays the Save as File dialog box, which is similar to most other file dialog boxes in Windows applications.

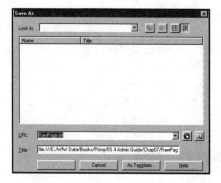

FIGURE 7-9

To save a page, you need a title and URL.

10. Save the file on your hard drive, using the name **Overview.htm**.

The unformatted Web page is now loaded, converted, and saved on disk. Your screen should now appear as shown in Figure 7-10. Notice that everything appears as plain, normal text..

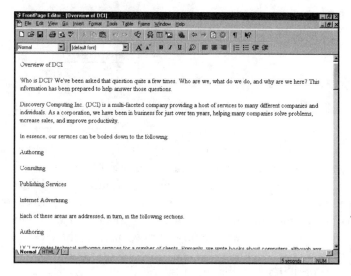

FIGURE 7-10

With raw text loaded, you are ready to begin formatting and editing

Applying Paragraph Formatting

When you first open a file in the Editor window or when you first type text into the editor, it is plain text. That is, the text is formatted as normal paragraphs, in regular type, and without the font being enlarged or reduced. The easiest way to change the format of your text is to use the tools on the Format toolbar.

If you examine the first line of the text you just loaded, you can see that it should be formatted as the major heading for the page. To do so, all you need to do is change the formatting of the paragraph. Simply position the cursor somewhere within the paragraph and then choose Heading 1 from the pull-down Format list at the left side of the Format toolbar. You can then center the paragraph by clicking on the Center tool, also on the Format toolbar. Figure 7-13 shows the results of these formatting actions.

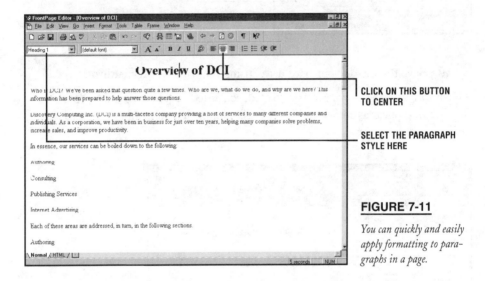

CLICK ON THIS BUTTON
TO CENTER

SELECT THE PARAGRAPH
STYLE HERE

FIGURE 7-11

You can quickly and easily apply formatting to paragraphs in a page.

Notice that you didn't need to know the relevant HTML codes in order to format the paragraph; FrontPage Editor takes care of this for you. What you just did highlights exactly how you format anything in FrontPage Editor: you select what you want to format, and then use one of the tools or menu commands to perform the formatting. When you position the cursor within a paragraph, FrontPage Editor understands that the actions you want to take (in this case, applying the Heading 1 style and centering) pertain to the entire paragraph. Thus, FrontPage Editor applies your actions to the paragraph in which the cursor is located.

You can apply several predefined formatting styles to your paragraphs. These styles correspond to the HTML styles that you may already be familiar with. Table 7-3 details the different styles and their corresponding HTML codes.

A common way to format information is in lists. As an example, the four paragraphs that list the services DCI offers can be formatted as a bulleted list. All you need to do is select the four paragraphs and then either choose Bulleted List from the pull-down format style list or click on the Bulleted List tool near the right side of the Format toolbar. The result, with the text still selected, is shown in Figure 7-12.

Table 7-3 Predefined Web Page Styles in FrontPage Editor

Style	HTML Codes
Address	<ADDRESS></ADDRESS>
Bulleted List	<UL><LI></LI></UL>
Defined Term	<DL><DT></DT></DL>
Definition	<DL><DD></DD></DL>
Directory List	<DIR><LI></LI></DIR>
Formatted	<PRE></PRE>
Heading 1	<H1></H1>
Heading 2	<H2></H2>
Heading 3	<H3></H3>
Heading 4	<H4></H4>
Heading 5	<H5></H5>
Heading 6	<H6></H6>
Menu List	<MENU><LI></LI></MENU>
Normal	<P></P>
Numbered List	<OL><LI></LI></OL>

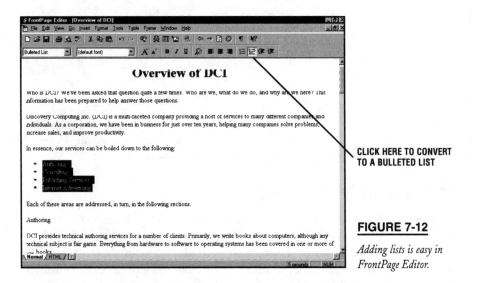

CLICK HERE TO CONVERT
TO A BULLETED LIST

FIGURE 7-12

*Adding lists is easy in
FrontPage Editor.*

By default, a normal Web page paragraph ends with an extra blank line. This convention is great for regular text, because it facilitates reading. If you scroll down to the end of the overview file, you will notice that some lines (the address of Discovery Computing Inc.) have too much space between them. Here the extra space is distracting and almost makes the information seem as though it doesn't belong together.

In this case, the address would probably look much better without the extra line between each paragraph. This situation is where line breaks come in handy. You add line breaks in FrontPage Editor the same way that you do in Microsoft Word—by pressing Shift+Enter. In the case of the address, delete the paragraph breaks currently at the end of each line and then break the lines at the proper place by pressing Shift+Enter. When you do so, the lines appear next to each other.

As you are working in FrontPage, you might want to turn on some of the format codes so they appear on the screen. The codes show you where paragraphs end and line breaks occur. You can display this information by choosing the Format Marks option from the View menu. When this option is on, you can see where formatting has been applied, as shown in Figure 7-13. (In this figure, the address has also been centered and formatted with the Address style.)

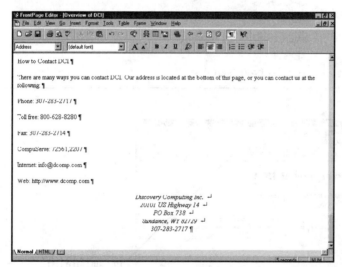

FIGURE 7-13

Line breaks don't show an extra blank line after each paragraph.

Applying Character Formatting

Paragraphs aren't the only part of your document that you can format. As you might be able to tell by looking at the Format toolbar, you can also format individual characters. FrontPage Editor provides quite a few different ways to format characters, but if you are used to working with a full-featured word processor or desktop publishing program, you may find these effects somewhat limited.

You can set some character formats with the Format toolbar, but the widest array of formats is available from the Font dialog box. You display this dialog box by selecting the characters that you want to format and then choosing Font from the Format menu. The Font dialog box is shown in Figure 7-14.

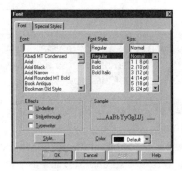

FIGURE 7-14

You can change many character attributes in the Font dialog box.

You can also access special formatting styles by clicking on the Special Styles tab at the top of the Font dialog box. The different styles and their meanings are detailed in Table 7-4.

Table 7-4 Character Formatting Styles Used by FrontPage Editor

Style	HTML Codes	Purpose
Bold	<STRONG></STRONG>	Used for strong text, usually displayed in **bold**
Italic	<EM></EM>	Used for emphasis, usually displayed in *italic*
Underline	<U></U>	Used for underlined text
Typewriter	<TT></TT>	Used for fixed-width (monospace) text
Citation (<cite>)	<CITE></CITE>	Used for citations, usually displayed in *italic*
Sample (<samp>)	<SAMP></SAMP>	Used to specify a sequence of literal characters
Definition (<dfn>)	<DFN></DFN>	Used to define a term the first time it appears; typically displayed as **bold** or ***bold and italic***
Blink (<blink>)	<BLINK></BLINK>	Used to make text blink (very annoying)
Code (<code>)	<CODE></CODE>	Used for program code, usually displayed in a monospace typeface
Variable (<var>)	<VAR></VAR>	Used to define a variable, as in programming code
Bold (<b>)	<B></B>	Used for **bold** text
Italic (<i>)	<I></I>	Used for *italic* text
Keyboard (<kbd>)	<KBD></KBD>	Used to designate keystrokes that a user should type

> **NOTE**
>
> Although you can format characters any way you want, what the user actually sees depends on the browser he or she is using. You may want to experiment to make sure that your desired effect is achieved under the browsers most likely to access your site.

You can also use the Font dialog box to set the size, color, and position of text. The character size is always relative to other characters, not an absolute size as you might expect in your word processor or desktop publishing program. The reason is that the rendition of text is left to the browser, and implementations can vary quite widely. The default size is 3 (approximately 12 points), but you can pick any size between 1 and 7. You can also pick Normal, which makes the user's browser responsible for picking a type size.

You can pick any character color you want, subject to the limits of your video card. You should remember, however, that the exact shade of chartreuse that you spent hours testing and setting probably will not display exactly the same way on the user's browser. Two factors can cause this discrepancy: the user may not use the same browser you do, and he or she probably doesn't have the same video card that you do. When picking colors, you're best off settling on a few standard colors.

You can also set the vertical position of your text (on the Special Styles tab), which is most often used to set superscripts and subscripts. To get the desired effect from these types of characters, you also need to experiment with different type sizes. For instance, you will probably want to shrink the type size if you are creating a superscript.

As an example of how you can format individual characters, suppose that you want to emphasize the company name (Discovery Computing Inc.) at the beginning of the second paragraph of the page. You then want to increase the point size on the first letter of each word. You do so by first selecting the text and clicking on the Bold tool; then select each first letter, in turn, and increase the point size by one or two notches. Figure 7-15 shows the results of such formatting.

Setting the Page Colors

FrontPage Editor enables you to easily control the colors used in your page. You can set the colors for the background and for several other items. Because the colors are used for the page as a whole, you make your changes by selecting Page Properties from the File menu and then by clicking on the Background tab. The Background tab of the Page Properties dialog box appears in Figure 7-16.

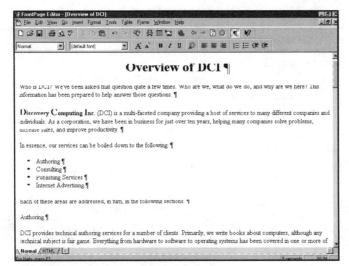

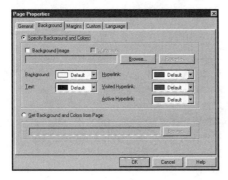

As you can tell, most of the items in the Page Properties dialog box are set to their default value. (You can tell because the word *Default* appears on each color field.) The options are turned off because the default condition of any page is to use the browser's default colors. For many users, the browser defaults are more than acceptable; in fact, leaving control up to the browser enables visitors to control what your pages look like on their computers. If you don't want to leave anything to chance, however, you can explicitly specify colors to use for the various parts of your page. You can select any color desired for a background color, link color, text color, visited link color, and active link color. These five color settings are translated by FrontPage Editor to various attributes of the HTML <BODY> tag, as indicated in Table 7-5.

The most common color to change is the background color. As with the other colors, you can select any color desired. For this example, set the background color to white. This option gives the appearance of black text on a white background. When you are done making changes, click on OK to close the dialog box.

Table 7-5 Color Setting Translation to HTML Code

Color Property	HTML <BODY> Attribute
Background	BGCOLOR
Hyperlink	LINK
Text	TEXT
Visited hyperlink	VLINK
Active hyperlink	ALINK

NOTE

The Background tab of the Page Properties dialog box also enables you to specify a background image for your page. Background images are discussed a little later in this chapter.

NOTE

You can continue formatting the sample DCI Web page using the techniques you have already learned, or you can save your work and load a page that is already formatted from the support files. If you want to use these files, load the file \Chap07\Overvu1.htm and then save it to your hard drive under the same name. You are ready to continue with the examples in this chapter.

Adding Graphics to Your Document

Because the Web is the multimedia portion of the Internet, you may want to include graphics in your Web pages. FrontPage Editor enables you to add graphics as well as horizontal rules to your documents. The latter feature helps break up the length of the document.

Adding Graphics Images

To insert a graphics image, simply position the cursor where you want the image to be placed and then choose Image from the Insert menu. For example, suppose you want to add a company logo to the beginning of the Web page developed thus far in the chapter. Simply position the cursor at the beginning of the document and then choose Image from the Insert menu. The Image dialog box opens. If the Select File dialog box is not displayed in front of the Image dialog box, click on the file folder icon in the lower-right corner of the screen. The dialog boxes should now appear as shown in Figure 7-17.

FIGURE 7-17

You can insert an image from either the Web or from a file.

SUPPORT FILE

As with other items, FrontPage Editor is quite flexible when it comes to inserting images. If you play around with the Image dialog box, you discover that FrontPage Editor enables you to insert images from a number of sources. For this example, use the Select File dialog box to select the file \Chap07\DCILogo.gif from the support files. Then click on <u>O</u>pen to add the image to the document. You see the results in Figure 7-18.

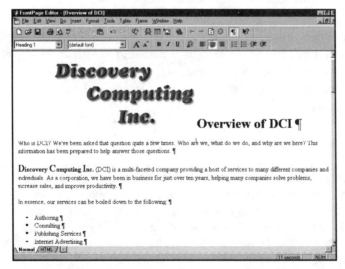

FIGURE 7-18

Images can be placed anywhere in a Web page.

NOTE

Remember that graphics, depending on the type, resolution, and size, can take considerable space on your server's hard disk. The larger or more complicated the graphic, the longer it takes to transfer from your Internet site. If your graphics are too big, you can alienate some people who visit your site.

Obviously, this Web page still needs some more work. Either the heading (Overview of DCI) must be moved to the next line, or it must be removed altogether. For the sake of simplicity, remove the heading by simply selecting it and pressing the Delete key. Now the logo appears centered, with text beginning just below it.

That is all there is to inserting a graphic in your Web page. With the graphic inserted, you can modify its properties by right-clicking on it and then choosing Image Properties. Doing so displays the Image Properties dialog box, similar to what is shown in Figure 7-19.

FIGURE 7-19

You control the properties associated with an image.

The Image Properties dialog box enables you to define exactly how FrontPage Editor should save and treat the image you have placed. You specify how you want FrontPage Editor to save the image—either in the GIF or in the JPEG format—in the Type area near the top of the dialog box. (You learned about these graphics formats in Chapter 6.)

NOTE

If saving in the GIF format, you can instruct FrontPage Editor to make the image interlaced or transparent (which you also learned about in Chapter 6). The Interlaced attribute means that the image is loaded in stages. For example, first the even pixel rows load, and then the odd pixel rows load. This feature enables the image to slowly come into focus when the user is connected to the Internet over a slow link.

The Alternative Representations area is where you will probably want to make a couple of changes. The fields in this area control alternative information sent to the remote browser if it cannot display your image. For example, any information you place in the Text field is displayed in the remote browser if that browser cannot handle graphics—or if the user has turned off the browser's graphics display capabilities. Notice that FrontPage 98 automatically places some default information in this field.

The Default Hyperlink area defines imagemap information that you may want to associate with your graphics file. Imagemaps are discussed in Chapter 8. When you finish setting the properties for your image, click on the OK button and the Image Properties dialog box disappears. Any changes you made are reflected in the FrontPage Editor window.

Adding Horizontal Rules

Horizontal rules, if used judiciously, can enhance the presentation of information. These rules automatically extend across the browser window, regardless of the window's width. You can add a horizontal rule by positioning the cursor at the beginning of the paragraph where you want to insert the rule and then choosing Horizontal Line from the Insert menu. Figure 7-20 shows an example of a horizontal line placed near the end of the page, just before the company address.

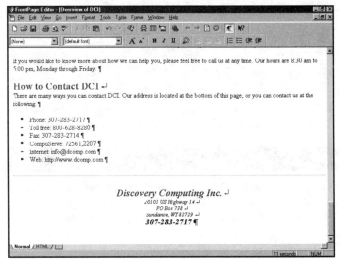

FIGURE 7-20

You can use horizontal rules to break up sections of your document.

Adding Background Images

Sometimes you may find the standard background colors of a Web page to be a little less than interesting. To overcome this problem, you can add a background image to the page. Background images are the same as wallpaper in Windows. When you specify the image, it is repeated over and over again, over the entire width and length of the page.

To specify a background image, simply select the Page Properties option from the File menu and then click on the Background tab. The Page Properties dialog box appears as shown earlier in Figure 7-16. Select the Background Image check box and then click on Browse. The Select Background Image dialog box (similar to the dialog box displayed in Figure 7-17) opens. If the Select File dialog box does not appear as well, click on the file folder icon in the lower-right corner of the dialog box. You can then specify the \Chap07\DCIBack.gif file from the support files. Click on the OK button, close the Page Properties dialog box, and the background image is displayed on your document. Figure 7-21 shows what your document should look like.

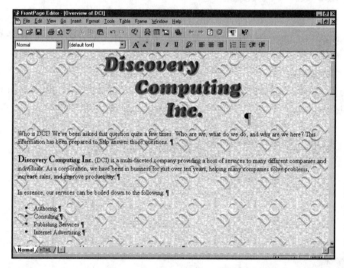

FIGURE 7-21

Background images can add character to a Web page, but sometimes they can be overpowering.

CAUTION

Be careful to keep your background images from overpowering the message you are trying to convey at your page. If you don't have enough contrast between the background and the text on the page, your information might be hard to read.

Working with Tables

Another common element in a Web page is a table. Tables enable you to organize information so that it looks much more structured on-screen. Tables are quite flexible in nature; they can have as many rows or columns as you want.

Because tables are a special element in documents, FrontPage Editor devotes a special menu entirely to tables. The menu choices enable you to create and manipulate the various parts of your table. To create a table, all you need to do is position the cursor where you want the table to appear and then use the proper menu commands to create the table. As an example, take a look back at Figure 7-20. Suppose that you want to place the contact information (just above the horizontal line) within a table so that the information can be lined up and easier to understood.

The first step is to position the cursor at the beginning of the horizontal line. Then choose the Insert Table option from the Table menu to open the Insert Table dialog box, shown in Figure 7-22.

FIGURE 7-22

You can insert any size table in your Web page.

At the top of the dialog box, you specify the size of the table that you want to create. In this instance, you want six rows and two columns. (You know these numbers from examining the information you are placing in the table—the contact information.)

NOTE

You can have as many rows and columns in a table as you desire. From a design standpoint, however, you probably want to have only a few columns. If you have too many columns, the result is a table that's wider than your display area. In this instance, the remote browser displays what it can and then provides a horizontal scroll bar so that the user can move his or her screen left and right.

With the rows and columns specified, click on OK. The table should appear as shown in Figure 7-23. The cursor is blinking in the first cell of the table, awaiting your input.

Go ahead and enter the contact information in the table. In the left column, enter the contact type (phone, toll free, and so on); in the right column, enter the phone numbers or address. When you are done, you can delete the original contact information.

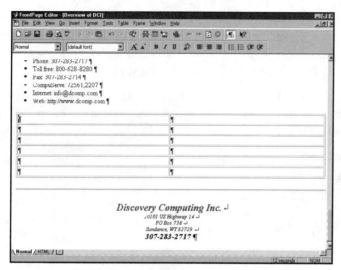

FIGURE 7-23

Tables appear at the position you specify in your Web page.

Borders and Other Table Properties

When you create a table, it has a standard border. You can modify the way in which the borders appear by changing the table properties. To change the borders for your table, right-click anywhere within the table and choose the Table Properties option from the Context menu. The Table Properties dialog box, shown in Figure 7-24, opens.

By modifying the information in the Border Size field, you can change the border used for your table. You can specify a border width anywhere from 0 (no border) to 100. You should experiment with different border sizes, clicking on the Apply button to see the effects of different sizes.

As you test different border widths, you may notice that the border affects only the outside of the table, not the spacing between or within the cells. If you want to affect

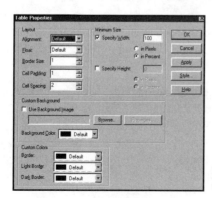

FIGURE 7-24

You can quickly modify the properties of your table.

the inside cell dividers, use the Cell Spacing property. This attribute accepts values just as the Border Size property does but defines the thickness of the cell walls.

The final common property that affects an entire table is the Cell Padding property, which defines the space between the contents of the cell and the cell dividers. The default value for this attribute is 1, but you can set it to any value you like, just as with the other table attributes. The larger the value you set, the more space within your cells.

To pick good-looking table properties, set the Border Size to 8, the Cell Padding to 2, and the Cell Spacing to 3. Then close the Table Properties dialog box. Figure 7-25 shows the result of these changes.

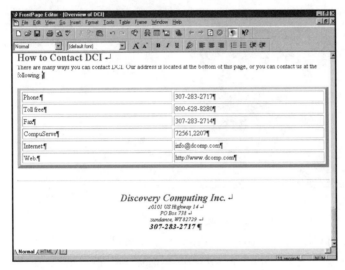

FIGURE 7-25

A proper mix of table properties can greatly enhance the appearance of your table.

Adjusting Column Widths

In Figure 7-24, you can see that the Table Properties dialog box enables you to set the minimum width for the table. The problem with this option is that the width you specify (in pixels or a percentage of the page width) affects each column within the table equally. This feature is great if your data can be represented in equal-size columns, but it is not so great if your data does not lend itself to this format.

To adjust individual column widths, you need to jump through a couple of hoops. First, you turn off the minimum width specification for the table as a whole; then, you adjust the width of each column individually. You can use the following technique to adjust column widths for any table.

1. Right-click on somewhere within the table to display a context menu.

2. Choose Table Properties from the context menu. The Table Properties dialog box opens.

3. Clear the Specify Width check box.

4. Click on OK to close the Table Properties dialog box. The table automatically reformats to a narrow width.

5. Place the cursor in one of the cells in the first column and choose Select Column from the Table menu. The first column is highlighted.

6. Choose Cell Properties from the Table menu. The Cell Properties dialog box opens, as shown in Figure 7-26.

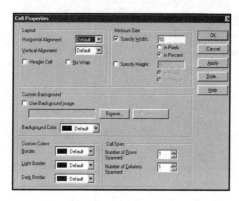

FIGURE 7-26

The Cell Properties dialog box enables you to change properties of a single cell or a group of cells.

7. Clear the Specify Width check box.

8. Click on OK to close the Cell Properties dialog box.

9. Repeat steps 5 through 8 but this time place the cursor in the second column of the table.

SUPPORT FILE

The result of this procedure is a table in which the width of each column better matches the type of data it contains. If you like, you can adjust the column widths to wider or narrower based on how you want to present your information. To adjust the column widths, position the mouse pointer over the column dividers. When the pointer changes shape, you can drag the divider and drop it when the column is the width you want. When you are done, save the Web page and close it.

TIP

After your table columns are sized to your liking, you may want to center the table on the screen. Use the Table Properties dialog box and then set the Alignment to Center.

Spanning Columns

To understand the other ways in which you can present information in a table, you need to open a new page that contains some tabular information. Use FrontPage Editor to load the file \Chap07\Schools.htm from the support files. Your screen should then appear as shown in Figure 7-27. (You should save the file on your hard drive, using the same filename of **Schools.htm**.)

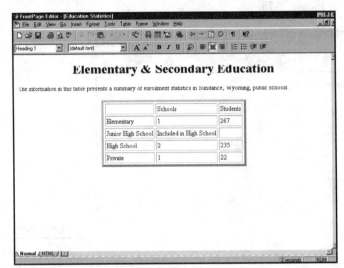

FIGURE 7-27

You may have to span information across several columns.

TIP

Notice that the formatting marks are not visible in Figure 7-27. They were turned off by selecting Format Marks from the View menu. Sometimes working with tables is easier when the marks are not visible.

The rather common table in Figure 7-27 is not presented as clearly as it could be. It has only three columns, but some of the data in the body of the table needs to span more than one column. Notice the information in the Junior High School row. This information, for better presentation, should be spread across two columns. Merging cells to span columns is easy to implement in FrontPage Editor. Simply select the cells you want to affect and then perform a merge.

1. Click and hold down the mouse pointer anywhere within the cell that contains the following text: Included in High School.

2. Drag the mouse into the cell just to the right. The two cells should now be entirely highlighted.

3. Choose Merge Cells from the Table menu. The cells are merged, and the table is reformatted.

The third row of the table now contains only two cells, with the second cell spanning what would otherwise be the second and third columns of the table. This format provides a much better presentation of the data in the table. When you are done viewing the information, save your data on your disk and close the page.

Spanning columns is particularly useful in the headings of some tables. For example, load the file \Chap07\Widget.htm from the support files. The information in this table is shown in Figure 7-28.

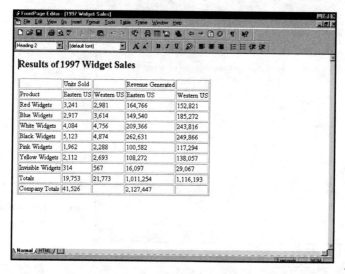

FIGURE 7-28

Tabular information often uses multiple rows for headings.

In this example, the Units Sold heading should actually extend over the cell just below it and to the right of that. Likewise, the Revenue Generated heading should extend to the cell to its right. At the bottom of the table, the two company totals could also span two columns each. Use the same techniques that you learned earlier in this section to make the table adjustments and then save your modified page to your hard drive. The resulting page appears in Figure 7-29.

Designating Headings

Even though the information in Figure 7-29 is understandable, the presentation still isn't optimal. You can specify headers within your tables, which means that the contents of a heading cell are automatically shown in bold and the cell contents are centered. Headings are often located along the top rows or left-most column of a table.

To designate a heading, select the cell or cells in the heading and then use the Cell Properties dialog box to make the designation. In the instance of the Widget Sales table, you can specify headings by following these steps:

1. Select the top two rows of the Widget Sales table.

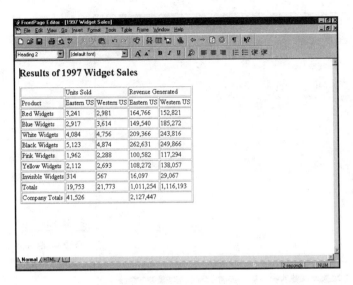

FIGURE 7-29

Column spanning is commonly used in table headings and other areas, such as the company totals.

2. Choose the Cell Properties option from the Table menu. The Cell Properties dialog box appears, as shown earlier in Figure 7-26.

3. Select the Header Cell check box.

4. Click on OK to close the Cell Properties dialog box. The selected headers are now shown in bold type and the text is centered within each cell.

5. Select the left-most column of the Widget Sales table.

6. Repeat steps 2 through 4.

Headings are useful in differentiating "overhead information" from the meat and potatoes of the table. Figure 7-30 shows what the table looks like with its newly designated headings.

Spanning Rows

Just as you can span columns in tables, you can also span rows. This method is commonly used for the same reasons as spanning columns—to make the information in the table more meaningful. For example, take a look at the table shown in Figure 7-31. This table presents enrollment figures over the course of several years, and you can see that several cells span multiple rows. (This table is stored in the support files as \Chap07\Enroll.htm.)

The spanned rows were created in the same way as you earlier learned to create spanned columns. First, the cells to be combined were selected, and then Merge Cells was selected from the Table menu.

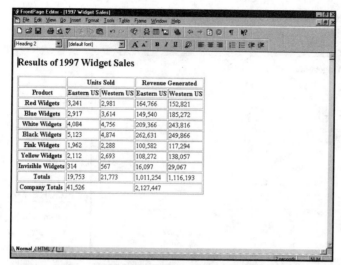

FIGURE 7-30

Table headings are automatically shown in bold.

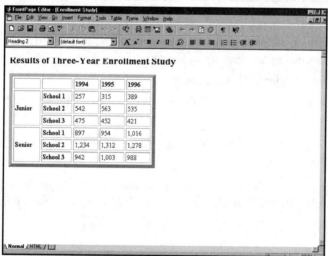

FIGURE 7-31

You can merge cells so that a cell spans multiple rows.

Aligning Cell Contents

You may have noticed that the cell contents in the last few examples didn't look as good as they could because the information in the cells wasn't aligned properly. Aligning the contents of cells can make them more readable.

Three types of cell alignment are available: left, center, and right. If you don't specify an alignment, the default is left alignment (except for headings, where center is the default). To specify another alignment, select the cells whose alignment you want to change and then use the Cell Properties dialog box to make your alignment change. Alternatively, click on the alignment tools on the Format toolbar.

Judicious use of cell alignment can make your table much more readable, particularly when displaying numbers. Figure 7-32 shows the Widget Sales table presented earlier, but this time with the contents of the cells aligned for better readability. (Compare the table in this figure with the table in Figure 7-30. The updated page is stored in the support files as \Chap07\Widget2.htm.)

Graphics in Tables

You may have realized after working through the graphics section earlier in this chapter that FrontPage Editor really has no provisions for displaying text and graphics side by side. This limitation is a product of the way in which HTML (the underlying mark-up language) is designed, not a limitation of the software. The way around this problem is to use a table to display the text and graphic. Typically, you would use a simple two- or three-cell table.

As an example, Figure 7-33 shows a modified version of one of DCI's Web pages for a popular natural attraction in the area. (If you want to see the real page, it's at **http://www.dcomp.com/sundance/dtower.htm**.) This page is also available in the support files as \Chap07\dtower.htm.

Notice how the text and picture were handled at the beginning of the page. A two-column table was used, with the first cell in the first row spanning two columns. The result is three cells in which information can be placed. The top-most row contains the heading for the page. The bottom-left cell contains the graphics image of Devils Tower, and the bottom-right cell contains the introductory text.

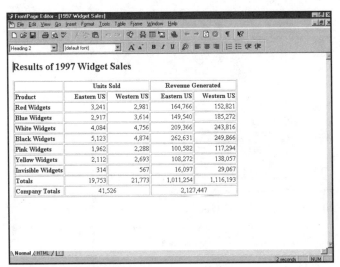

FIGURE 7-32

Aligning information in cells makes the information more readable.

Results of 1997 Widget Sales

Product	Units Sold		Revenue Generated	
	Eastern US	Western US	Eastern US	Western US
Red Widgets	3,241	2,981	164,766	152,821
Blue Widgets	2,917	3,614	149,540	185,272
White Widgets	4,084	4,756	209,366	243,816
Black Widgets	5,123	4,874	262,631	249,866
Pink Widgets	1,962	2,288	100,582	117,294
Yellow Widgets	2,112	2,693	108,272	138,057
Invisible Widgets	314	567	16,097	29,067
Totals	19,753	21,773	1,011,254	1,116,193
Company Totals	41,526		2,127,447	

SUPPORT
FILE

Because you put a graphic into a table, you also can combine the other table attributes to make the graphic look any way you desire. One effect that I've seen adds a nice touch and is a unique use of the border attribute for tables. Figure 7-34 shows the Devils Tower page with a significant change in how the graphic is handled. (This page is stored with the support files as \Chap07\dtower2.htm.)

Here the graphic has been enclosed in a nested table; the two outer tables are included only to use their borders. The border of each table layer is progressively narrower, producing the effect of a compound border. In addition, the heading for the page, along with the introductory text, has been moved outside the table and placed just beneath it.

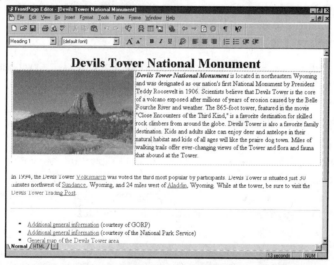

FIGURE 7-33

You can insert graphics into table cells to create a more professional look.

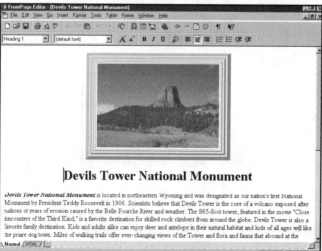

FIGURE 7-34

Graphics and tables can be used together to create special effects.

Chapter 8

Linking Your Web Site

The key to the success of the World Wide Web is the capability to link one Web page to another, which enables users to point and click to their heart's content. Adding links to the content in your pages is necessary so that you can remain connected to the rest of the Web or to other locations on your intranet.

One or two of the sample files that you worked with at the end of the previous chapter included some links in them. This chapter shows how you can add links of many different kinds to your own pages. From simple text-based links to more complex graphics links and imagemaps, you learn how to add them all. In addition, you learn how to establish links to FTP and Gopher sites, as well as to e-mail addresses. As in Chapter 7, the techniques in this chapter focus on using FrontPage Editor to establish your links.

Creating Text-Based Links

When you use FrontPage Editor, adding text-based links is simply a matter of selecting the text that you want to serve as the link (the text the user clicks) and then clicking on the Create or Edit Hyperlink tool on the toolbar. To understand this process, start FrontPage Editor and then load the file \Chap08\overvu2.htm from the support files. (This file is very similar to one of the pages you worked on in Chapter 7.)

You can create two types of links in your Web pages: external and local. Both types of links are explored in the following sections.

Creating External Links

An *external link* is a link from your current Web page to a page at a different Web site. You can tell when an external link is being used because the entire URL is used in the link specification.

To create an external link, start by highlighting the text you want as the link. With the overvu2.htm page loaded, scroll through the content until you see the Authoring section. In the last paragraph of the section, highlight the words *commercial books*. Then click on the Create or Edit Hyperlink tool on the toolbar. (This tool is just to the right of center in the top row of toolbars; it contains the links of a chain and the globe.) This action immediately displays the Create Hyperlink dialog box, as shown in Figure 8-1.

Notice that the cursor is blinking in the <u>U</u>RL field near the bottom of the dialog box.

FIGURE 8-1

You use the Create Hyperlink dialog box to add a link to your page.

All you need to do is provide the URL that you want to use for a link. For this example, enter the **URL http://www.dcomp.com/dci/books/** and click on OK. The link is added to your document, and the Create Link dialog box is closed.

Creating Internal Links

An internal link is a link between your current Web page and another Web page at your site. When specifying internal links, you don't need to use the entire URL for the link.

Creating an internal link is done in much the same manner as creating an external link. The only difference is that FrontPage Editor can help you browse and find the page you want to use as the target for the link. In Figure 8-1, the Create Hyperlink dialog box includes a list of open pages. These pages are currently open in FrontPage Editor; you can establish links with any of them simply by picking the page and then clicking on OK. If you have not opened the page, you can use the Look In field at the top of the dialog box to select one of the Webs you are managing with FrontPage.

Using Bookmarks in Links

When you establish a link, you normally create the link with an entire page. Thus when you jump to the link, the beginning of the page is displayed in your browser. It is possible, however, to establish links to named positions within a page. In FrontPage Editor, you can use bookmarks to do so.

NOTE

The term *bookmark* seems to be used many different ways, depending on the program that you are using at the time. Microsoft Word uses bookmarks to designate places or text in a document that you want to designate for some special referential purpose. In Netscape Navigator, bookmarks are used to denote Web pages that you want to remember for future reference. These other uses of bookmarks should not be confused with the FrontPage 98 usage of the term. To avoid any ambiguity, many other HTML editing programs refer to named positions with a page as *anchors*.

To see how this process works, you can establish a few bookmarks in the overvu2.htm file. You can use the same technique that you use to create bookmarks in Microsoft Word: select the text you want to use as the bookmark and then use the <u>B</u>ookmark option from the <u>E</u>dit menu. For example, select (highlight) the Authoring section heading and then choose <u>B</u>ookmark from the <u>E</u>dit menu. The Bookmark dialog box is displayed, as shown in Figure 8-2.

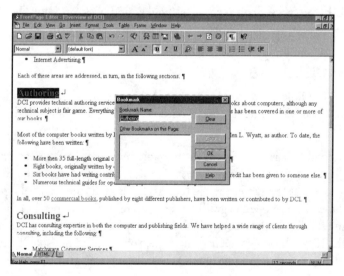

FIGURE 8-2

Bookmarks indicate a named position in a page.

The suggested bookmark name appears at the top of the dialog box. Although you can change the name, it is probably acceptable as is. Click on OK, and FrontPage Editor adds the bookmark. In your Web page, the bookmark location is underlined with a dashed line. For the current example, you should continue to add bookmarks to your page. In turn, select each of the first four section headers and mark them as bookmarks. When done, you should have bookmarks for Authoring, Consulting, Publishing Services, and Internet Advertising.

CAUTION

Just because FrontPage Editor underlines both bookmarks and links on your screen, make sure that you don't confuse the two. The dashed underline used to note bookmarks appears only within FrontPage Editor; it is for your convenience in creating your page. The underline for links appears both in FrontPage Editor and in the user's browser.

With your bookmarks created, you are ready to establish links to them. You can create the four new links to bookmarks by following these steps:

1. Move to the beginning of the Web page, displaying the bulleted list near the top of the page.

2. Select the first word in the bulleted list (Authoring).

3. Click on the Create or Edit Hyperlink tool. The Create Hyperlink dialog box is displayed, as shown earlier in Figure 8-1.

4. Select Overview of DCI (the current page) in the list of open pages because the link you are going to establish is within the current document.

5. Use the pull-down Bookmark list to select the bookmark you want to add to the link. In this case, select Authoring. (You want users to jump to the Authoring section when they click on the link.)

6. Click on OK. The link is added to your page.

7. Repeat steps 2 through 6 for each of the other three links. Make sure that you select the appropriate link text and the appropriate bookmark for each link.

You can use these techniques to establish links to bookmarks for either local links (as done here) or external links.

Using Graphics Images as Links

It is becoming more and more common to use graphics as links, and you can find such usage on a wide array of sites. For example, the Web site in Figure 8-3 uses graphics as links. This particular site (**http://www.imalodging.com**) is for IMA, the Independent Motels of America. The page depicted in Figure 8-3 is for one of the motels in the chain, and the images at the top of the page are termed a *facilities key* (this terminology is used by the motel chain). By clicking on one of the icons, the user can see an explanation of it.

ONLINE

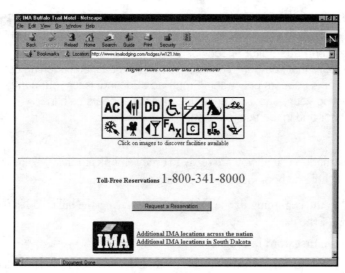

FIGURE 8-3

Images can be used as links on a Web page.

NOTE

If you plan to use only part of a graphic image as a link or to associate multiple links with a single graphic image, then you want to create an imagemap. Imagemaps are discussed later in this chapter.

The process of creating a graphic link is essentially the same as creating a text link. The links that you make can be local or external, and they can use bookmarks if desired. To use a graphic as a link, simply select the graphic (by clicking on it) and then click on the Create or Edit Hyperlink tool. FrontPage Editor knows that you want to use the graphic as the link, and you can specify the link itself using the steps described earlier in the chapter.

After you create a link, no visual indicator tells you that the link is associated with a graphic. You can, however, right-click on a graphic that you suspect is used as a link and examine its context menu. If a link exists, then the menu contains a Follow Hyperlink option; if there is no link, then this option is not shown.

A user will know that a graphic is an active link under the following conditions:

- ◆ You add text near the graphic that explains it is a link.
- ◆ The user moves the mouse pointer over the graphic and notices that the pointer changes shape.
- ◆ You add a border to the graphic.

The first two methods are fairly self-explanatory. The final method may need a bit more discussion, however. When you place a graphic in your document, by default it does not include a border. This approach is good, because sometimes a border around an image can look a bit "boxy." When you make the image a link, you might want to add the border. The border is displayed using the same color as you have assigned to an active link (normally blue by default).

To add a border to a graphic image, follow these steps:

1. Right-click on the graphic to which you want to add a border. This action displays a context menu for the image.

2. Choose Image Properties from the context menu. The Image Properties dialog box opens.

3. Click on the Appearance tab. The Image Properties dialog box now appears as shown in Figure 8-4.

FIGURE 8-4

FrontPage Editor enables you to control the appearance of your images.

4. Change the value in the Border Thickness field in the Layout section. The value represents a number of pixels (0 means no border).

5. Click on OK to close the Image Properties dialog box and add the border.

Using Imagemaps

If you have spent any time on the Web, you've seen imagemaps. An *imagemap* is a graphic that has different clickable on regions. When users click on the image, the location they clicked on is translated to a link that is associated with that location. Two types of imagemaps are in use: server side and client side. FrontPage Editor enables you to create both types, as discussed in the following sections.

Server-Side Imagemaps

A server-side imagemap is (oddly enough) managed by the server and has two parts: a graphic image and a map file. When the user clicks on a part of the image, the server compares the coordinates of where he or she clicked with the information in the map file. The contents of the map file define the URL to be associated with different coordinate regions on the graphic. The URL corresponding to the point where the user clicked is then returned to the browser, and a jump is made to the target URL.

Because a server-side imagemap consists of two parts, you need to have both parts available when you are ready to add the map to your Web page in FrontPage Editor. Creating the graphic is easy; there is nothing special about it at all. You can use any graphics editing program that you desire to create the image. The map file, on the other hand, is a different story entirely.

Creating a Map File

A map file is an ASCII file that essentially contains a series of coordinates and URLs associated with those coordinates. The coordinates refer to different pixel ranges within the graphic file. Coordinates are specified in an X,Y system with the upper-left corner of the graphic being 0,0. In addition, the file contains a designation of a default URL, which is used if the user clicks on a portion of the map outside a defined area.

Two types of map files are in wide use on the Internet: CERN and NCSA. Each of these map file types deserves a little examination.

The CERN Format

The CERN map file format features the default URL on the first line, followed by *shape definitions*. Each shape definition includes an indicator of the shape type (rectangle, circle, or polygon), followed by pairs of coordinates that define the limits of the shape. The last thing included in each shape definition is the URL associated with that region of the map. For example, the following is a map file in the CERN format:

```
default http://www.dcomp.com/crookcounty/crookcounty.htm

rect (266,114) (331,143) http://www.dcomp.com/crookcounty/crookcounty.htm#aladdin

rect (216,267) (300,297) http://www.dcomp.com/crookcounty/crookcounty.htm#sundance

circle (57,176) 25 http://www.dcomp.com/Sundance/Dtower.htm

rect (113,285) (208,332) http://www.llbean.com/parksearch/parks/195LLN90LL.html

rect (134,131) (190,160) http://www.dcomp.com/crookcounty/crookcounty.htm#hulett
```

Notice that each rectangular area (those lines beginning with `rect`) includes two pairs of coordinates. These identify two opposing corners of the rectangle. The circular areas (the line beginning with *circle*) includes not only a coordinate (which is the center of the circle) but also a radius. In this case, the number **25** means that the radius of the circle is 25 pixels.

The NCSA Format

The NCSA map file format contains much the same information as the CERN format. The difference is that the URL is included in each shape definition right after the shape type, instead of at the end of the line. Also, the coordinate syntax for the circle shape is a little different. Here's the same map file shown in the preceding section, but now in the NCSA format:

```
default http://www.dcomp.com/crookcounty/crookcounty.htm

rect http://www.dcomp.com/crookcounty/crookcounty.htm#aladdin 266,114 331,143

rect http://www.dcomp.com/crookcounty/crookcounty.htm#sundance 216,267 300,297

circle http://www.dcomp.com/Sundance/Dtower.htm 57,176 82,176

rect http://www.llbean.com/parksearch/parks/195LLN90LL.html 113,285 208,332

rect http://www.dcomp.com/crookcounty/crookcounty.htm#hulett 134,131 190,160
```

Notice that the coordinates do not have parentheses on them, and the coordinates are now at the end of each line. In addition, the circle designation in this example includes two pairs of coordinates. The first is the center of the circle again, whereas the second is a point somewhere on the circumference of the circle.

IIS Map Files

The IIS Web server can use both the CERN and NCSA format for imagemaps. Unfortunately, neither the server nor FrontPage Editor includes a map file utility. Instead, you must turn to third-party products that enable you to create your map file. One such program that is very helpful (and very good) is MapEdit. This program is available as shareware from **http://www.boutell.com/mapedit/**.

When creating a map file, you can define three different types of shapes:

◆ *Rectangles* are defined by two sets of coordinates that define the two opposite corners of the rectangle.

◆ *Circles* are defined by a coordinate pair for the centerpoint, along with a radius for the circle or a point on the circumference (depending on your map file type).

◆ *Polygons* are defined as a series of coordinates that define the outline of the shape.

You create the shapes (with MapEdit) by simply outlining the corners of each shape with the mouse, directly on the graphic image. The mouse clicks are then translated to the proper coordinates and stored in a map file. Other map file utilities should work in much the same way, although you will undoubtedly find some differences between them and MapEdit.

Server-Side Imagemaps in FrontPage Editor

After you have your graphic image and map file, you are ready to use FrontPage Editor to add the imagemap to your Web page. First, make sure to place both the image and the map file in the directory where you want to do your work. For this example, you should copy three files from the support files to your hard drive: \Chap08\toolbar.gif, \Chap08\toolbar.map, and \Chap08\Home1.htm. Then follow these steps to add the server-side imagemap:

1. Use FrontPage Editor and load the file home1.htm.

2. Scroll to the bottom of the page where you see a two-cell table. (The left cell of the table is empty.)

3. Position the cursor in the left cell of the table.

4. Choose Image from the Insert menu. This action displays the Image dialog box.

5. If the Select File dialog box does not automatically appear, click on the file folder icon near the lower-right corner of the Image dialog box.

6. Insert the toolbar.gif graphic image.

7. Right-click on the image you just placed in your document. A context menu for the image appears.

8. Choose Image Properties from the context menu to display the Image Properties dialog box.

9. Enter the specification **toolbar.map** in the Location field of the Default Hyperlink area. (Do not click on Browse; you will not be able to select the file in this manner.)

10. Click on OK to close the Image Properties dialog box.

11. With the graphic image still selected, click on the HTML tab at the bottom of the screen. This action displays the HTML source code for your Web page, as shown in Figure 8-5.

12. Notice that the code responsible for the graphic image is selected. Position the insertion point right after the closing quote mark of the SRC attribute and just before the Width attribute.

13. Type the letters **ISMAP**. This required entry tells the server and browser that this graphic is an imagemap.

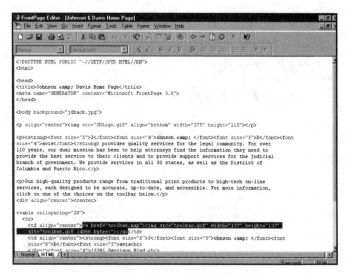

FIGURE 8-5

You need to edit the source code slightly to add a server-side imagemap.

14. Click on the Normal tab at the bottom of the screen. Your Web page reappears.

15. Save your updated page under the name **home.htm**.

NOTE

FrontPage 98 does not allow you to add the ISMAP attribute using the graphical interface, as you could if you used FrontPage 97. However, if you forget to include the attribute, your server-side imagemaps will not work.

Now, viewers of the page will see the page shown in Figure 8-6. When they click one of the tools, the server returns the address associated with the region specified in the map file.

Client-Side Imagemaps

A client-side imagemap is similar to a server-side imagemap except that the former does not need two files. Instead, the contents of the map file are effectively stored in the Web document itself. Because it is part of the HTML file, the imagemap can be interpreted and used directly by the browser—the client; thus, it is a client-side imagemap.

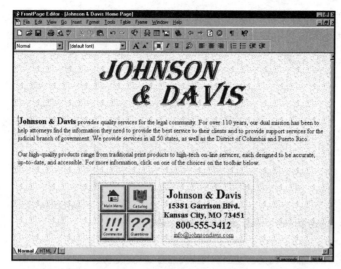

FIGURE 8-6

Map files are often used for icon toolbars.

CAUTION

Client-side imagemaps are easy to make, and they remove a small amount of burden from your server. However, not all browsers support client-side imagemaps. Older browsers (several generations old)do not understand what to do with the map and will effectively ignore it.

For this example, you work with two of the three files you used in the previous section. Follow these steps to create a client-side imagemap:

1. Use FrontPage Editor and load the file home1.htm. Save it under the name **home2.htm**.

2. Scroll to the bottom of the page where you see a two-cell table. (The left cell of the table is empty.)

3. Position the cursor in the left cell of the table.

4. Choose Image from the Insert menu. This action displays the Image dialog box.

5. If the Select File dialog box does not automatically appear, click on the file folder icon near the lower-right corner of the Image dialog box.

6. Insert the toolbar.gif graphic image.

7. Click on the image that you just inserted into the page. The Image toolbar appears on the screen.

8. Click on the Rectangle tool on the Image toolbar.

9. Move the mouse pointer over the selected image; the pointer turns into a pencil.

10. Outline the Main Menu icon by clicking on the lower-right corner of the icon and then dragging the mouse to the upper-left corner. When you release the mouse button, the Create Hyperlink dialog box appears.

11. Choose the Johnson & Davis Home Page from the list of open pages. The URL (hyperlink) at the bottom of the dialog box changes to reflect your selection.

12. Click on OK to close the dialog box.

13. Use the Rectangle tool on the Image toolbar to outline the Catalog icon. When you release the mouse button, the Create Hyperlink dialog box appears.

14. Enter a name such as **http:\\JohnsonDavis.com\catlog.htm** in the URL field. (This URL is fictitious. If you were developing your own Web, you would use a URL for a real Web page or a disk file.)

15. Click on OK to close the dialog box.

16. Use the Rectangle tool on the Image toolbar to outline the Comments icon. When you release the mouse button, the Create Hyperlink dialog box appears.

17. Enter a name such as **http:\\JohnsonDavis.com\comments.htm** in the URL field. (Again, this URL is fictitious.)

18. Click on OK to close the dialog box.

19. Use the Rectangle tool on the Image toolbar to outline the Questions icon. When you release the mouse button, the Create Hyperlink dialog box appears.

20. Enter a name such as **http:\\JohnsonDavis.com\help.htm** in the URL field. (Again, this URL is fictitious.)

21. Click on OK to close the dialog box.

When you create a client-side imagemap with FrontPage Editor, it uses one of the built-in FrontPage components that you learned about in Chapter 7. Therefore, the page you create must belong to a Web that you are managing with the FrontPage Explorer, and you must turn on the client-side imagemap capability for the Web to which the page belongs. Although explaining how to manage a Web with FrontPage Explorer is beyond the scope of this book, you should understand how to enable client-side imagemaps. To practice enabling client-side imagemaps, follow these steps:

1. Open FrontPage Explorer and then open the Web to which your new page belongs.

2. Choose Web Settings from the Tools menu. This action displays the FrontPage Web Settings dialog box.

3. Click on the Advanced tab. The FrontPage Web Settings dialog box now appears, as shown in Figure 8-7.

FIGURE 8-7

You must enable client-side imagemaps in FrontPage Explorer.

4. Select the Generate Client-Side Image Maps check box.

5. Click on OK to close the dialog box. If you actually made a change, you are asked whether you want to refresh the Web. (You should do so.)

6. Close the FrontPage Explorer and use your new Web page.

Linking with Other Services

Although HTML files (Web pages) form the majority of resources accessible with a Web browser, most browsers have become rather adept at accessing other kinds of information as well. The key to accessing different types of information is in the URL that is used in a link on your page. The uniform resource locator, or URL, got its name because it provides a way to designate not only the address of a resource but also the type of resource at the address. For example, the following simple URL designates a Web site:

```
http://www.dcomp.com
```

You know that this URL is a Web site because it starts with the letters *http*. This indicator designates the server at the address www.dcomp.com as an http server (a Web server). To access a different type of resource, simply provide the appropriate resource type at the beginning of the URL along with the address of the server. Most Web browsers can understand and handle all the resource types indicated in Table 8-1.

Table 8-1 URL Resource Types

Type	Meaning
ftp://	FTP server
gopher://	Gopher server
http://	http (Web) server
https://	Secure Web server
mailto:	E-mail location
news:	News server
telnet://	Telnet
wais://	Wide Area Information server

The different resource types supported by a URL mean that you can provide links from your Web site to resources located on different types of servers. These may be servers that you maintain, or they may be servers located in a different department of your company or around the world.

The biggest benefit to providing links to other types of resources is that this approach expands the value of your Web site. If you provide a common starting point for many resources, people will want to visit your site more often. In addition, if the information is located somewhere else, you don't need to maintain the information—only the link.

Besides the Web, the three most popular resources to which you can provide links are FTP, Gopher, and e-mail. The following sections describe how to establish links to each of these resource types.

Accessing FTP Files from Your Web Site

Many FTP files are accessible from the Web. Providing Web-to-FTP access can be done in one of two ways. I refer to the first method as a *directory link* and the other as a *file link*.

Establishing a Directory Link

Establishing a directory link to your FTP site doesn't take a lot of work. All you need to do is provide a link from one of your Web pages to the home directory of an FTP site. For example, use FrontPage Editor to load the file \Chap08\Ajax.htm from the support files. This page is shown in Figure 8-8.

This Web page is fairly straightforward; it probably looks similar to some pages that you have created. It is not complete, however, because it does not yet contain the actual link to an FTP site. To add the proper FTP link, follow these steps:

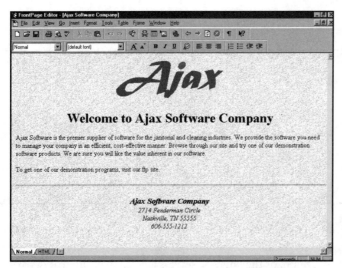

FIGURE 8-8

The Ajax Software Company uses a link to an FTP site.

1. Highlight the words *ftp site* at the end of the second paragraph. (This phrase serves as the text link to the site.)

2. Click on the Create or Edit Hyperlink tool on the toolbar. The Create Hyperlink dialog box is displayed, as shown in Figure 8-9.

FIGURE 8-9

You can establish FTP links with the Create Hyperlink dialog box.

3. Erase the default information in the <u>U</u>RL field and replace it with the full URL of the FTP server. In this case, enter **ftp://ftp.ajax.com**.

4. Click on OK to close the Create Hyperlink dialog box. The link is added to the Web page.

Because the URL you used in the link points to an FTP server, the Web browser references and displays the FTP home directory. The information displayed is similar to what users see if they use FTP to visit the site—basically, just a listing of files and directories. Users can navigate the directories by double-clicking on folders, or they can download a file by right-clicking on the filename and choosing to download.

Establishing directory links provides several advantages:

◆ It's easy to do—much easier than establishing the file links discussed in the next section.

◆ It gives the user full access to everything at your FTP site.

◆ If the contents of your FTP site change quite often, directory links provide the most stable way to link from your Web site.

On the negative side, a directory link does not provide much descriptive information; users usually needs to figure out the purpose of the files on their own. (This process can be quite frustrating to some users.)

SUPPORT FILE

You are not limited to linking to the root of an FTP site. You can also establish links with subdirectories to provide greater focus on your Web page. For instance, Figure 8-10 shows the Ajax Software Web page with three links that, in turn, reference individual directories at the company's FTP site.

NOTE

The Web page in Figure 8-10 is stored with the support files as Ajax2.htm.

FIGURE 8-10

You can provide more focused links to FTP directories at your site by linking to subdirectories.

Establishing a File Link

Many Web sites use the files at their FTP site by establishing direct file links. This strategy provides the most user-friendly method of accessing your FTP files. In this type of link, the reference is directly to a filename on the FTP site, rather than to a directory. To create this type of link, use FrontPage Editor to load the \Chap08\Ajax3.htm file from the support files, as shown in Figure 8-11.

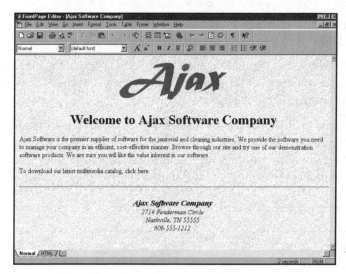

FIGURE 8-11

You can add links to specific files at your FTP site to your Web pages.

To create a link to a file at your FTP site, follow these steps:

1. Highlight the words *click here* at the end of the second paragraph. (This phrase serves as the text link to the site.)

2. Click on the Create or Edit Hyperlink tool on the toolbar. The Create Hyperlink dialog box is displayed, as shown earlier in Figure 8-9.

3. Erase the default information in the URL field and replace it with the full URL of the file to download. In this case, enter **ftp://ftp.ajax.com/marketing/catalog.zip.**

4. Click on OK to close the Create Hyperlink dialog box. The link is added to the Web page.

Notice that the link in this example points directly to a ZIP file on the FTP server. When users click on the link, the file is accessed; they can then download the file to a local drive. (The user's browser determines exactly how this process is handled on the user's part.)

Using file links in this manner requires no navigation on the user's part, and he or she can directly access the needed file. How elaborate you get with this access method is up to you. The support file \Chap08\Ajax4.htm (Figure 8-12), which is a variation on previous examples in this chapter, provides a great deal of information on products available at the Ajax Software Company.

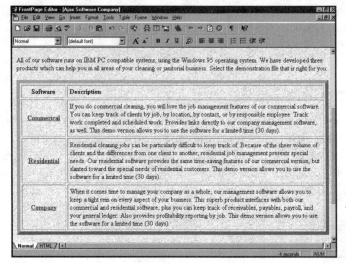

FIGURE 8-12

FTP file linking enables you to create pages that contain quite a bit of descriptive text.

In this example, the user clicks on the appropriate choice and then directly downloads the desired file. Although establishing file links is definitely the most user-friendly approach to sharing FTP content, it does have a drawback. Suppose your company runs both a Web site and an FTP site. You are in charge of the Web site, and another department is in charge of the FTP site. In this type of arrangement, the contents of the FTP site can change frequently or without warning to you. Consequently, you might need to update your Web pages quite often to point to the proper files or to provide complete links to the FTP files. If you instead establish a directory link, the contents can change all they want and you won't need to change the Web link. The latter setup shifts the burden to your site visitors to figure out what they need from the FTP site.

Accessing Gopher Files from Your Web Site

Before the advent of the World Wide Web, Gopher was the hottest method of accessing widely distributed information. If you have established a Gopher site or if you know of unique information available through a remote Gopher site, you can make the content directly available to your Web visitors. You accomplish this goal by establishing a link from your Web page to the Gopher server. The procedure is exactly the same as the procedure for establishing links to an FTP site except that you use the Gopher protocol specification (gopher:) at the beginning of your URL link.

NOTE

Typically, Gopher access is handled as just that—access to a Gopher server itself. Links are sometimes established to directories within a Gopher server, but seldom are links established to specific files at Gopher sites, as they often are for FTP sites.

Sending Electronic Mail

Perhaps the most common type of external resource referenced in Web pages is an e-mail account. Many pages contain at least one e-mail reference, typically at the bottom of the Web page. For example, earlier in this chapter, you worked with the overvu2.htm file. Load that file again and move to the contact information table at the end of the file. Your screen should now look like the screen in Figure 8-13.

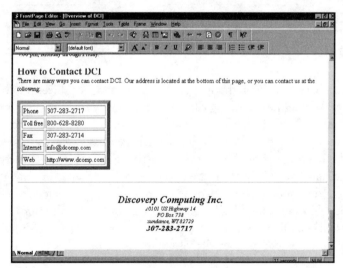

FIGURE 8-13

Many Web pages include e-mail contact information.

To add an e-mail link, follow these steps:

1. Highlight the e-mail address shown in the fifth row of the table (info@dcomp.com).

2. Press Ctrl+C to copy the address to the Clipboard.

3. Click on the Create or Edit Hyperlink tool on the toolbar. The Create Hyperlink dialog box is displayed, as shown earlier in Figure 8-9.

4. Click on the icon that looks like an envelope in the lower-right corner of the dialog box. This action displays the Create E-mail Hyperlink dialog box, as shown in Figure 8-14.

5. Press Ctrl+V to paste the contents of the Clipboard (the e-mail address) into the dialog box.

6. Click on OK to close the Create E-mail Hyperlink dialog box.

7. Click on OK to close the Create Hyperlink dialog box. The link is added to the Web page.

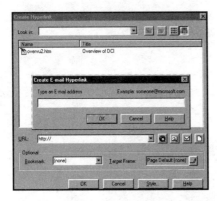

FIGURE 8-14

You can easily specify an e-mail address for a link.

To the user, this link appears just like any other link. The difference (as far as the browser is concerned) is denoted by the mailto: resource type at the beginning of the URL. When someone clicks on this type of link, the e-mail program used by the browser is opened and the user can enter an e-mail message. The message then is sent to the address specified in the link.

TIP

Including an e-mail address at the bottom of your pages enables readers to send you messages automatically. Some of these messages may help you improve the content at your site.

Chapter 9

Working with Forms

———

In This Chapter

◆ Creating a Simple Form

◆ Adding On/Off Controls

◆ Using Pull-Down Lists

◆ Using Text Boxes

It's hard to use the Web these days without running into forms. If you've used popular search engines such as Yahoo or Alta Vista, you've seen simple forms. A form is the basic method by which a user communicates with a Web server. The user's information can either be manipulated using a script by the browser or be transmitted to your Web server, where it's passed to a specified script. The script then uses the information to do whatever is required. (Client-side scripts are covered in Chapter 11, and server-side scripts are covered in more detail in Chapter 13.)

FrontPage 98 includes some great features that enable you to quickly and easily incorporate forms into your Web pages. This chapter focuses on how you can put forms to work in your Web pages and how you can make them work the best with IIS.

Creating a Simple Form

SUPPORT FILE

You can use simple forms for many different purposes. To understand how easy it is to create a form in FrontPage Editor, start FrontPage Editor and load the file \Chap09\mail.htm from the support files. As shown in Figure 9-1, this file is Web page just waiting for you to add form information.

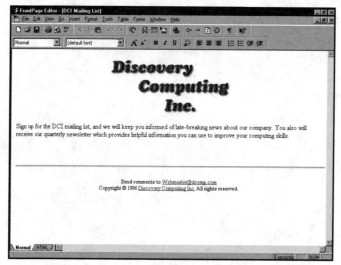

FIGURE 9-1

You can add forms to any regular Web page.

.This page collects names and e-mail addresses for a newsletter. Collecting information is a great use for a form, and one that is very common on the Web. The only thing that is missing on the page is the form with its input boxes and buttons that are used to actually enter information. To add input boxes for the form, follow these steps:

1. Position the cursor at the beginning of the blank line just before the horizontal line and just after the first paragraph of text.

2. Choose Form Field from the Insert menu and then choose One-Line Text Box. This action inserts a generic input text box and two buttons, as shown in Figure 9-2.

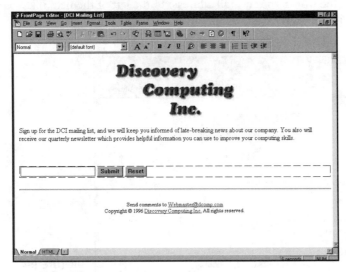

FIGURE 9-2

Forms are indicated in FrontPage Editor with a dashed line.

3. Right-click on the form field text box. This action displays a context menu.

4. Select the Form Field Properties option from the context menu. The Text Box Properties dialog box, shown in Figure 9-3, opens.

5. Enter **UserName** in the Name field.

6. Leave the other dialog box fields as they are and click on OK.

7. Enter the words **Your name:** to the left of the field that you just added.

8. Position the cursor right after the text box but before the buttons.

9. Press Shift+Enter to add a line break.

10. Choose Form Field from the Insert menu and then choose One-Line Text Box. Another text box field is added to your form.

11. Right-click on the form field text box. This action displays a context menu.

FIGURE 9-3

You use the Text Box Properties dialog box to modify the appearance and behavior of a text input field.

12. Select the Form Field Properties option from the Context menu. The Text Box Properties dialog box opens again.

13. Enter **UserAddress** in the Name field and then click on OK.

14. Enter the words **Your e-mail address:** to the left of the field that you just added. The Web page now appears as shown in Figure 9-4.

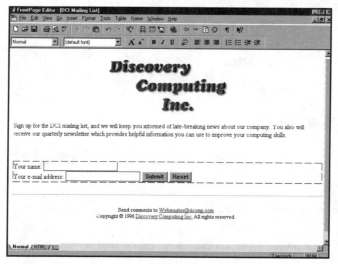

FIGURE 9-4

Text boxes are easy to add in FrontPage Editor.

When you added the two input fields to your form, you also provided a name for each field. There was nothing special about the names that you used (UserName and UserAddress); they simply identify the information entered into the field by the user. For example, suppose that someone using your form entered his name, Don Johnson, in the first field. This text (Don Johnson) is stored internally under the name UserName. If you have a programming background, you can liken the field names to variable names that you would use in developing a program.

Input Field Settings

The Text Box Properties dialog box (refer to Figure 9-3) also enables you to specify an initial value, field width, and tab order for the input field and whether the purpose of the field is to gather a password from the user. For many instances (such as this example), the default settings are just fine. You can, however, change the settings to change the way in which your input field functions.

> **NOTE**
>
> While working with your forms, a quick way to access a form field's property sheet is to select the field and then press Alt+Enter, or double-click on the form field.

Initial Value

The first setting you can change is the Initial Value field. Whatever you place in this field becomes the default for your input field. The user can change it, of course, but it is a way for you to suggest a value, which may make the user's job of inputting information just a bit faster.

Field Width

The second setting you can change is the Width in Characters field, which limits the width of the input box used in your form. You can specify any width (size) between 1 and whatever limit you desire. The default width is 20 characters. Because the exact size of a "character" is left up to the user's browser, the results of this setting are very imprecise—especially because each character can be a different width. In the Windows environment, the Width in Characters setting is really a relative value. For example, a setting of 10 would be a certain width, 20 would be twice that size, and 40 would again be twice as large.

Tab Order

If you have ever used one of Microsoft's visual programming languages, you may already be familiar with the concept of tab orders. This setting is nothing more than a designation of the order in which fields should be selected when the user is in the form and presses the Tab key.

You can enter a value between 1 and 999 to specify the order in which the fields should be selected. If you enter a value of -1, then the field is not selectable by pressing the Tab key.

> **CAUTION**
>
> The Tab Order setting is supported only by Microsoft's Internet Explorer, and then only beginning with version 4. Browsers from any other vendor and any earlier version of Internet Explorer do not support the feature.

Passwords

The final setting on the Text Box Properties dialog box is the Password Field setting. Here you can specify whether the purpose of your field is to gather a password from the user (Yes or No). The default is No, but if you change it to Yes, the user's browser changes how input is gathered. On most browsers, the text the user types in a password field appears as asterisks on-screen. This feature provides a small amount of protection for what is being typed by the user.

CAUTION

Although a password may be displayed on the screen as asterisks, it is still transferred from the browser to the server as plain text. Thus a password field on your form does not provide a high degree of security.

Submitting a Form

The process of sending information from a form to a server is called *submission*. The user's browser takes care of actually submitting the information, and then your Web server decides what to do with the information. The form you have developed so far in this chapter is very simple—it contains only two input fields and two default buttons. FrontPage 98 recognizes the need to enable a user to explicitly signify that he or she has completed and is ready to submit information. For this reason, FrontPage automatically added two default buttons to your form.

These buttons are two of the most common types of buttons used in a form: a Submit button and a Reset button. Both have a specific purpose, and both are extremely helpful to the user. The Submit button enables the user to send the information on the form to your server. The Reset button clears the form and restores it to its unchanged condition.

NOTE

The Reset button is similar in purpose to the Reload button at the top of a Web browser. The difference is that the Reset button is faster because all processing occurs at the browser itself; there is no need to request the entire Web page again from the server.

The default names used with the buttons automatically added by FrontPage 98 (Reset and Submit) are very generic in nature. You may want to change the button names to more accurately describe their functions. To work with the buttons on your form, follow these steps:

1. Position the cursor at the end of the second input field in your form, just before the Submit button, and press Enter. The cursor and buttons should be on the next line of the form.

2. Right-click on the Submit button. This actions displays a context menu.

3. Select the Form Field Properties option from the context menu. The Push Button Properties dialog box, shown in Figure 9-5, opens.

FIGURE 9-5

You can use the Push Button Properties dialog box to modify Submit and Reset buttons.

4. Leave the <u>N</u>ame field unchanged. You don't need to change the default value because a name is not that important for a button.

5. Enter **Join List** in the <u>V</u>alue/Label field. This text will appear on the face of the button (instead of Submit).

6. Click on OK. The button is updated on your form.

7. Right-click on the Reset button. This action displays a context menu.

8. Select the Form Field Properties option from the context menu. The Push Button Properties dialog box opens again.

9. Leave the <u>N</u>ame field unchanged.

10. Enter **Clear Form** in the <u>V</u>alue/Label field.

11. Click on OK. The button is updated on your form, which now appears as shown in Figure 9-6.

NOTE

Regardless of how the buttons appear in FrontPage Editor, the actual appearance of the buttons is handled exclusively by the user's browser.

You have now created a very simple form, which you can save to disk if you desire. The balance of this chapter discusses other types of controls that you can add to your form.

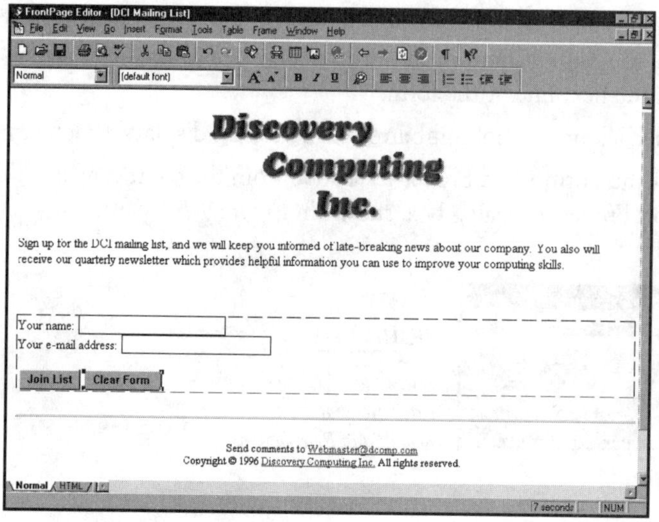

FIGURE 9-6

Pushbuttons enable the user to control a form.

Adding On/Off Controls

If you have used Windows for any length of time, you are already familiar with two types of controls: check boxes and radio buttons. These controls are considered on/off controls because they can be either selected or not selected. You can add both types to your forms, as described in the following sections.

Using Check Boxes

Check boxes select or deselect an option. On a Web form, they are a great help in narrowing down exactly what a user wants. As an example of how to use this type of control, load the \Chap09\mail2.htm file from the support files. This page, shown in Figure 9-7, is very similar to the page on which you were working in the previous section.

The only thing missing from this version of the form is two check boxes that enable users to specify which type of information they want to receive from the mailing list. To add check boxes to the form, follow these steps:

1. Position the cursor on the blank line just before the two push buttons. This location is where the check boxes will be placed.

2. Choose Form Fie<u>l</u>d from the <u>I</u>nsert menu and then choose <u>C</u>heck Box. This action adds a check box to your form.

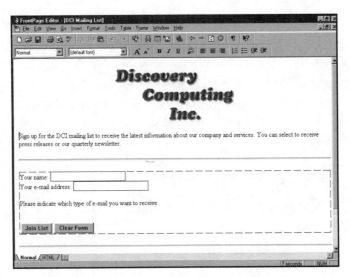

FIGURE 9-7

You can add check boxes to this Web form.

3. Right-click on the check box you just placed to open a context menu.

4. Select the Form Field Properties option from the context menu. The Check Box Properties dialog box, shown in Figure 9-8, opens.

5. Enter the name **Newsletter** in the Name field.

6. Leave the Value field unchanged (ON).

7. Change the Initial State to Checked. This setting means that the check box is selected when the form is first loaded.

8. Click on OK. The check box is updated in your form.

9. Move the cursor to the right of the check box and type the word **Newsletter**; then, press Shift+Enter.

10. Choose Form Field again from the Insert menu and then choose Check Box. This action inserts a second check box in your form.

11. Right-click on the check box you just placed to open a context menu.

12. Select the Form Field Properties option from the Context menu. The Check Box Properties dialog box opens again.

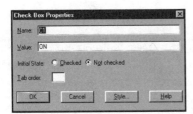

FIGURE 9-8

You can use the Check Box Properties dialog box to change the characteristics of check boxes.

13. Enter **PressRelease** in the Name field box. This entry is the name of the field (notice that you must use a single word with no spaces).

14. Leave both the Value field and Initial State unchanged.

15. Click on OK. The Check Box Properties dialog box closes.

16. Move the cursor to the right of the check box and type the words **Press releases.** The finished form (which you should save) now appears as shown in Figure 9-9.

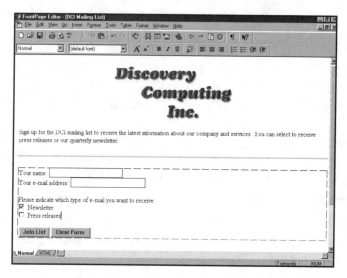

FIGURE 9-9

Check boxes enable users to make a selection.

When someone clicks on a check box, its state changes. If it was previously checked, it becomes unchecked, and vice versa. When a user clicks on the Submit button (the one that says *Join List*), the value of the variable associated with the check box is set to *on* if it was selected. The value (ON) is then passed back to your server. If the check box wasn't selected, no information is sent to your server. Thus your script (which acts upon the information passed from the form) can assume that all check boxes are unchecked unless it receives other information from the browser. Your script can then take the appropriate action based on the settings.

Using Radio Buttons

Another type of input that you can add to a form is a radio button. A radio button enables the user to select one (and only one) option from a group. You specify the group to which a radio button belongs when you place it in the document. All radio buttons belonging to the same group have the same group name.

You can use radio buttons in the Web page on which you have been working to enable users to specify their position with the company and their decision-making authority. Such marketing information is very helpful in developing content of other Web pages and in reaching the right people in a mailing list. Because you follow the same general process to place each radio button, the steps can be a bit repetitive. Follow these steps to place a total of eight radio buttons in your form:

1. Position the cursor at the end of the last line that you added in the previous section (Press releases) and then press Enter.

2. Type the words **How would you best describe your position in your company:**; then, press Shift+Enter to add a line break.

3. Choose Form Field from the Insert menu and then choose Radio Button. This action adds a radio button to your form.

4. Right-click on the radio button you just placed to open a context menu.

5. Select the Form Field Properties option from the context menu. The Radio Button Properties dialog box, shown in Figure 9-10, opens.

FIGURE 9-10

You can use the Radio Button Properties dialog box to change the behavior of radio buttons in your form.

6. Enter the name **Position** in the Group Name field.

7. Enter the name **President** in the Value field.

8. Change the Initial State to Not Selected.

9. Click on OK. The radio button is updated on your form.

10. Move the cursor to the right of the radio button, type the word **President**, and then press Shift+Enter. This label appears to the right of the radio button.

11. Add another radio button, loosely following steps 3 through 10. The Group Name field should be **Position** (the same name you used in step 6), the Value field should be **Officer**, and you should set the Initial State to Not Selected.

12. Type the words **Company officer** to the right of the radio button and then press Shift+Enter. This label appears to the right of the radio button.

13. Add a third radio button. The Group Name field should again be **Position**, the Value field should be **Manager**, and you should set the Initial State to Not Selected.

14. Type the word **Manager** to the right of the radio button and then press Shift+Enter. This label appears to the right of the radio button.

15. Add a fourth radio button. The Group Name field should again be **Position**, the Value field should be **Employee**, and you should change the Initial State to Selected. (This item is the default choice in the Position radio button group.)

16. Type the words **Regular employee** after the radio button and then press Shift+Enter. This label appears to the right of the radio button.

17. Add a fifth (and final) radio button for the Position group. The Group Name field should be **Position**, the Value field should be **None**, and you should make sure that the Initial State is Selected.

18. Type the words **None of the above** to the right of the radio button and then press Enter. You are done adding the first radio button group (Position), which is used to specify the position the user holds with his or her company.

19. Type the words **Please select the statement which best describes your decision-making authority:**; then, press Shift+Enter to add a line break.

20. Add the first radio button in this group. The Group Name field should be **Power**, the Value field should be **Full**, and you should leave the Initial State unchanged.

21. Type the sentence **I can make any decision necessary to further the needs of my company or department** just after the radio button. Press Shift+Enter to add a line break.

22. Add the next radio button. The Group Name field should again be **Power**, the Value field should be **Partial**, and you should leave the Initial State unchanged.

23. Type the sentence **I must clear my decisions with my boss** just after the radio button. Press Shift+Enter to add a line break.

24. Add the final radio button. The Group Name field should again be **Power**, the Value field should be **None**, and you should leave the Initial State unchanged.

25. Type the sentence **I provide input to the appropriate committees or individuals, and they make the final decisions** just after the radio button.

Now you have successfully added two groups of radio buttons—a total of eight buttons. The first group has a default choice selected, and the second group has no default selected. The radio buttons appear as shown in Figure 9-11.

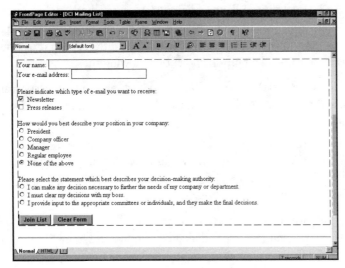

FIGURE 9-11

Radio buttons enable users select one option out of a group.

The first radio button group you added is named Position, and the second is named Power. Remember that when radio button groups have the same name, selecting one radio button deselects the others of the same name. The first group has a default radio button selected (Regular employee). If the user selects a different option in the Position group, the default is deselected. The second group, which does not have a default option set, functions in the same way—the user can pick one (and only one) option from the group, but is not required to do so.

From the perspective of your server, only one variable exists for each radio button group, and that variable can have different values. When the user clicks on the Submit button (Join List), the value specified by the properties of the selected radio button is assigned to the variable name for the radio button group. This procedure may sound confusing, but it isn't really. As an example, in the form shown in Figure 9-11, if the user clicks on President as his or her position, the variable named `Position` (this is the name of the group itself) will have the value of `President` assigned to it. If, instead, the user clicks on Manager as his or her position, the `Position` variable will have the value `Manager` assigned to it. Your script can then take action based on the information returned by the form.

Using Pull-Down Lists

In the Windows environment, pull-down lists are used all the time. You can also create pull-down lists in your forms. In FrontPage Editor, however, pull-down lists are called *drop-down menus*. Using pull-down lists makes sense when you have more than a couple of options from which the user can select. For example, a natural place to make a change in your form is to replace the first radio button group (Position) with a pull-down list. You can add a pull-down list by following these steps:

1. Select all the first-section (Position) radio buttons and their accompanying labels, and then press Delete. (You should have deleted five lines from your form.)

2. Choose Form Field from the Insert menu and then choose Drop-Down Menu. This action inserts an empty pull-down list in your form.

3. Right-click on the pull-down list that you just placed. This action displays a Context menu.

4. Select the Form Field Properties option from the context menu. The Drop-Down Menu Properties dialog box, shown in Figure 9-12, opens.

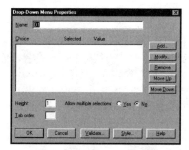

FIGURE 9-12

You can use the Drop-Down Menu Properties dialog box to create a pull-down list.

5. Enter the name **Position** in the Name field.

6. Click on the Add button. This action displays the Add Choice dialog box, as shown in Figure 9-13.

7. Enter the name **President** in the Choice field, but leave the rest of the options unchanged.

8. Click on OK. The new choice now appears in the Drop-Down Menu Properties dialog box.

9. Add each of the other position choices (**Officer, Manager, Regular employee**, and **None of the above**) in the same manner. The only change is that when you add **Regular employee**, you should specify a Value of Regular and change the Initial State to Selected. Also, when you add **None**

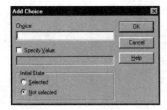

FIGURE 9-13

You can add any items that you like to your pull-down list.

> **of the above,** you should select the Specify Value check box and change the value to None. When you are done, the Drop-Down Menu Properties dialog box appears, as shown in Figure 9-14.
>
> **10.** Click on OK to close the Drop-Down Menu Properties dialog box and add the pull-down list to your form.

Using pull-down lists allows your form to take less space vertically than using lists of options, but it also means that users can't see all the options simultaneously. Pull-down lists are particularly useful if you have lots of options. On the Web, pull-down lists frequently appear on forms in which the user must select a state or a country. The result of adding the pull-down list to your form is shown in Figure 9-15.

The server treats information returned by a pull-down list and information returned by a radio button group the same way. In either case, the server assigns the value selected from the list or the group to the variable specified by the name you gave the control. In the case of the pull-down list, if the user selects None of the Above, then the server assigns the value None to the variable Position.

Using Text Boxes

Earlier in this chapter you learned how to add one-line text boxes to your form. Although these are useful for getting limited information from a user, text boxes aren't necessarily a good way to obtain large amounts of information. In these instances, you can use a scrolling text box instead. This control is particularly useful for comment fields and larger blocks of text, such as an address.

FIGURE 9-14

You can quickly add choices to your pull-down list.

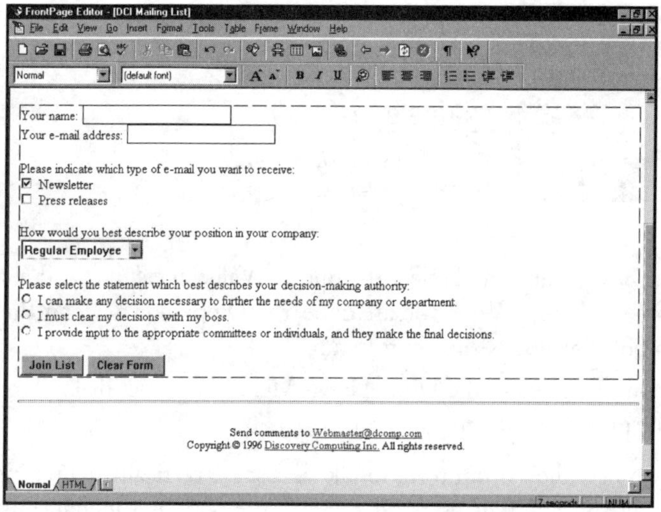

FIGURE 9-15

Pull-down lists are familiar control devices in a form.

As an example, suppose you want to add a Comments field to the Web page you have been developing throughout this chapter. The purpose of the field is to solicit ideas for your newsletter. To add a scrolling text box to a Web page, follow these steps:

1. Position the cursor at the beginning of the line containing the two buttons (Join List and Clear Form) and then press Enter. Position the cursor on the blank line you just created.

2. Type the sentence **What type of topics would you like covered in our newsletter?** and then press Shift+Enter to add a line break.

3. Choose Form Field from the Insert menu and then choose Scrolling Text Box. This action adds a large text box to your form.

4. Right-click on the text box you just placed to display a context menu.

5. Select the Form Field Properties option from the context menu. The Scrolling Text Box Properties dialog box, shown in Figure 9-16, opens.

6. Enter **Ideas** in the Name field.

7. Change the Width in Characters field to 50; this value determines the width of the text box.

FIGURE 9-16

You can use the Scrolling Text Box Properties dialog box to add larger text input areas to your form.

8. Change the Number of <u>L</u>ines field to 4; this value determines the height of the text box.

9. Click on OK to save the changes to the text box. Figure 9-17 shows the results.

Notice that there were three settings described in the previous steps. The purpose of the first, <u>N</u>ame, should be obvious—this setting is the variable name that the browser uses when returning the contents of the text box to your server. The second setting, <u>W</u>idth in Characters, indicates the width of the text box. (This setting is similar to the width setting you used for the single-line text box earlier in the chapter.) The final setting, Number of <u>L</u>ines, indicates the number of vertical rows the text box should occupy.

The biggest drawback to using a text box is that you can't limit the length of its contents. Your user could type a novel in the box, and it would be passed to your server. The result, besides sucking up bandwidth on your Internet connection, is that your script could possibly reject the information and die. The result is a crashed server, which is not good. Chapter 13 explains how you can program your script to avoid this potential problem.

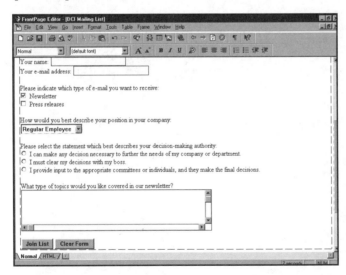

FIGURE 9-17

A text box accepts input of unlimited length in your form

NOTE

Even though you can program a script so that it doesn't crash when its input is too long, you can't avoid the drain on your bandwidth. The only way around this problem is to not use the scrolling text box. Thus, unless you have a real need to enable users to enter lots of text, you may want to avoid scrolling text boxes.

Chapter 10

Examining IIS HTML Extensions

In This Chapter

◆ Using Server-Side Includes

◆ Using FrontPage 98 Components

◆ Using Themes

Although you may not have known it, in the past several chapters you have learned how to build HTML-based Web pages. Granted, you were using FrontPage Editor, which does a fantastic job of hiding the intricacies of HTML, but nonetheless, the HTML code is lurking behind every page you have created or edited.

HTML is a specification for a series of tags and attributes that define how information should be displayed. The specification is maintained by a consortium of industry representatives, and therefore represents a "least-common denominator" approach to the topic.

IIS, while fully supporting the HTML standards, goes one step farther with additional bells and whistles that you can use in your Web pages. In this chapter, you learn how to take advantage of the two types of HTML extensions that you can use with IIS: a native IIS extension and FrontPage components.

> **NOTE**
>
> Parts of this chapter discuss HTML coding directly. If you do not understand HTML coding, you may want to refer to a good reference on the subject (such as Prima Publishing's *Learn HTML in a Weekend* by Steven E. Callihan). Chapter 7 of this book is a good place to start.

Using Server-Side Includes

The IIS Web server features special instructions that are extensions to regular HTML. These instructions are called server-side include (SSI) directives, or just server-side includes.

The syntax of the directives is as follows:

```
<!—#directive [additional information]—>
```

This syntax isn't unique to IIS, but the *use* of this syntax is unique. This tag, using a bang (!) followed by two dashes (hyphens), some text, and ending with two dashes, is technically an HTML comment tag. You can place comments anywhere in your document. Microsoft has built on this comment concept and uses it to signify a server-side include directive. The # sign at the start of the comment text indicates that this text is a directive to the server. Additional information may be used in conjunction with the directive. When the server encounters a directive, the server processes the directive before sending the HTML file to the client.

Adding Server-Side Include Directives

In the previous section, you learned that you can add server-side include statements to a regular HTML file to enhance how you use your Web pages. You can add the statement in one of two ways: using a text editor or using an HTML editor, such as FrontPage 98. Both methods are discussed in the following sections.

Using a Text Editor

HTML files are simply ASCII text files, which means that you can use any text editor, for example, Notepad, to load and edit them. You can also use Notepad to add the `include` statement to your HTML files, following the syntax already introduced.

NOTE

You should not use a word processor to load your HTML files unless you are absolutely sure they are saved back to disk as ASCII files. Some word processors convert ASCII files to their own internal format so that special characters and formatting attributes can be displayed. If these special attributes are saved on disk with the HTML file, then only that word processor can subsequently understand them. Consequently, the files will be inaccessible to remote browsers or to programs such as FrontPage 98. The safest approach is to use a plain-text editor—such as Notepad—to display and edit your HTML files.

Using an HTML Editor

Many HTML editors are on the market, and some do a fantastic job of "protecting" you from the HTML code behind the scenes. (Actually, I think it may be a case of protecting the HTML code from the person using the program.) FrontPage 98 is not one of those programs; it enables you to quickly and easily see and change the HTML code that makes up a Web page. This feature is one of the improvements in FrontPage 98. You can use FrontPage 98 to add HTML code to a Web page by following these steps:

1. Load or create the base Web page you want to use.
2. Position the cursor at the point in the file where you want the included file to appear.

3. Click on the HTML tab at the bottom of the editor. This action changes the view mode so that you can enter HTML directly.

4. Enter the `include` statement using the exact syntax discussed earlier in this chapter.

5. Click on the Normal tab to return to the normal FrontPage Editor view.

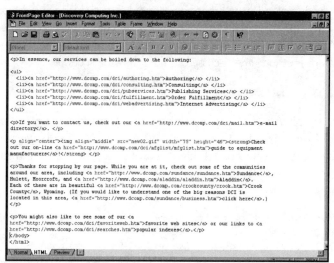

FIGURE 10-1

You can add HTML codes as desired in FrontPage Editor.

Saving the Files

Besides using the special syntax for the server-side `include` directives, IIS also requires that you use a special filename extension when you save the file. Instead of using the regular htm or html extension, you should use the extension stm. To use the sample files mentioned earlier in this chapter, you must first save home.htm as home.stm; the other file (footer.htm) can use the same filename, with the htm extension.

> **NOTE**
>
> The `include` statement also works in ASP files. While processing the scripts in an ASP file, IIS will also look for the `include` statement and process it correctly.

The stm extension tells IIS that the file contains a directive to be processed. Figure 10-2 shows what happens when you use the proper extension. In this case, the page home.stm uses the `#include` directive to include the footer.htm file at the end of the page.

FIGURE 10-2

The same file named with the proper extension includes the footer.htm contents.

If you don't use the stm extension, then IIS doesn't "gear up" to look for the `include` statement, and indeed ignores it if it is there. Figure 10-3 shows what a page using the same `#include` directive looks like in a browser if the page is saved using an htm extension. The six server-side `include` directives are as follows:

◆ `#config`—Changes the format used for error messages, dates, and file sizes sent to the Web browser

◆ `#echo`—Sends environment variable information to a browser

◆ `#exec`—Executes a program or command and returns the output in the HTML page

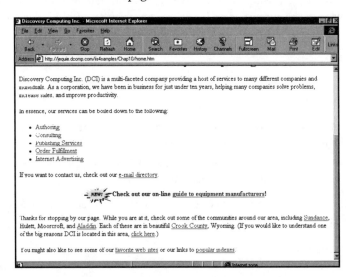

FIGURE 10-3

An improper base filename can defeat the purpose of having an included file.

NOTE

If you use default documents with IIS (see Chapter 4), you should not use an `include` file in the default document unless you have set your default document to use the stm filename extension. For example, if your default file is set to default.htm and you rename it on your server to default.stm (because it uses an `include` file), IIS won't make the htm-to-stm transition automatically and the server will not display the default file.

♦ `#flastmod`—Inserts the HTML page's last modification time

♦ `#fsize`—Inserts the HTML page's files size

♦ `#include`—Inserts another file into the HTML page

These commands are described in some detail in the following sections.

The `Config` Directive

The `Config` directive determines the type of format for error messages, dates, and file sizes in the current HTML page. You need to use one of the following three options:

```
<!- #config errmsg="An error has occurred." ->
```

```
<!- #config timefmt="%A the %m of %B, %Y" ->
```

```
<!- #config sizefmt="bytes" ->
```

These changes modify the way that the server formats different information being sent to the browser in the current page. If an error occurs, instead of displaying a useful diagnostic error, the browser displays the following message: An error has occurred.

The `Echo` Directive

The `Echo` directive enables you to send the value of an environment variable to the user. Several environment variables are used with IIS to describe the version of the server and the hardware platform that it is being run on. Table 10-1 lists several environment variables that you can use with this directive.

To use the `Echo` directive, simply select the environment variable that you wish to use and then add the command to your stm file, as shown in the example:

```
<!-#echo var="SERVER_SOFTWARE" ->
```

Table 10-1 Environment Variables

Environment Variable	Purpose
ALL_HTTP	Obtains all the HTTP headers not included in other variables listed in this table
AUTH_TYPE	Contains the type of authentication currently being used, which may be Basic for a basic authentication or NTLM if you are using a challenge/response authentication
AUTH_PASSWORD	Returns the user's password, if you are using Basic authentication
AUTH_USER	Returns the user's name, if you are using Basic authentication
DOCUMENT_NAME	Names of the current file
DOCUMENT_URL	Returns the current file's virtual path
DATE_GMT	Obtains the current date in Greenwich Mean Time (GMT)
DATE_LOCAL	Obtains the current date in the local time zone
GATEWAY_INTERFACE	Returns the revision number of the CGI specification that IIS is using
LAST_MODIFIED	Obtains the date of the current file's last modification
REMOTE_ADDR	Returns the client's IP address requesting this file
REMOTE_HOST	Returns the client's host name of client requesting this file
REMOTE_USER	Returns an empty string for an anonymous user, or the name used by the client when authenticated by the server
REQUEST_METHOD	Returns the HTTP request method
SERVER_NAME	Returns the server's name or IP address
SERVER_PORT	Obtains the TCP/IP port receiving the HTTP request
SERVER_PORT_SECURE	Returns a 1 for a request made on a secure port or 0 for a non secure port
SERVER_PROTOCOL	Returns the protocol and version being used, which is typically HTTP/1.0
SERVER_SOFTWARE	Returns the name and version of the Web server—Microsoft-IIS/4.0

The Exec Directive

The Exec directive tells the server to run a program and to include the program's output in the current HTML page.

This directive allows you run only two types of programs. You can run CGI scripts, which are explained in Chapter 13, or console applications such as the FINGER command. The following example shows the two uses:

```
<!—#exec cgi="/scripts/guestbook.exe?firstname+lastname" —>
<!—#exec cmd="d:\Winnt\System32\finger.exe gpease@dcomp.com"—>
```

In the first example, the Exec directive runs a CGI program. The second example runs the Finger program provided with Windows NT. The fact that a foreign user is running a program on your computer may present a security risk, and you may not want to use this command.

NOTE

You cannot use the Exec directive inside ASP files. It can be used only in regular HTML files.

The Flastmod Directive

The Flastmod directive tells the server to insert the date on which a file was last modified. When you have links to FAQ files or other frequently updated files, you can use this directive to show when a link was last updated. The following example shows the syntax:

```
<!—#flastmod file = "LatestNews.htm" —>
```

This example tells IIS to look for the LatestNews.htm file and display the date when the file was last modified. You can use the Config directive to change the format used for displaying the date and time.

The Fsize Directive

The Fsize directive enables you to include a file's size in the source. At first glance, this feature may not seem very useful. However, if you have files at your site for download, it may come in handy, especially if the file may change over time to become larger or smaller. Instead of manually editing an HTML page to tell the user how big the file is, you can use the Fsize directive, as shown in the following example:

```
<!—#fsize file = "download.htm" —>
```

This example tells IIS to look for the download.htm file and display its size in the HTML file being sent to the browser.

NOTE

You cannot use the Flastmod directive inside ASP files. You can use it only in a regular HTML file.

The `Include` **Directive**

The `include` directive enables you to load a specified file and send it to a browser as if it were a part of the original HTML file. The syntax of the statement is as follows:

```
<!—#include file="boilerplate.htm"—>
```

In this example, the boilerplate.htm file will be included as part of the Web page. What makes this strategy so handy is that common text—address, contact information, copyright information, and the like—often appears at the bottom of each of your Web pages. You can simply put this common information into its own file and then easily include it in every one of your other pages.

The HTML file that is included with the `include` statement doesn't have any special features. It is an ASCII file, like any other HTML file, but it doesn't use the full structure of an HTML document. You don't need to include a document head or body unless you want to include those elements in the `include` file.

As an example of how to use the `include` statement, use the Notepad accessory to load the file \Chap10\home.htm from the support files. This file is a home page for DCI, similar to pages that you have reviewed in other chapters. The code should appear as follows in Notepad:

```
<html>
<head>
<title>Discovery Computing Inc.</TITLE>
</head>

<body>
<center>
<img src = "DCILogo.gif">
<h1>Welcome to Discovery Computing Inc.</h1>
</center>

Discovery Computing Inc. (DCI) is a multi-faceted company providing a host of ser-
vices to many different companies and individuals. As a corporation, we have been
in business for just under ten years, helping many companies solve problems,
increase sales, and improve productivity.

<p>In essence, our services can be boiled down to the following:
```

```html
<ul>
<li><a href="http://www.dcomp.com/dci/authoring.htm">Authoring</a>
<li><a href="http://www.dcomp.com/dci/consulting.htm">Consulting</a>
<li><a href="http://www.dcomp.com/dci/pubservices.htm">Publishing Services</a>
<li><a href="http://www.dcomp.com/dci/fulfillment.htm">Order Fulfillment</a>
<li><a href="http://www.dcomp.com/dci/webadvertising.htm">Internet Advertising</a>
</ul>

<p>If you want to contact us, check out our <a
href="http://www.dcomp.com/dci/mail.htm">e-mail directory</a>.

<p>
<center>
<img align="middle" src="new02.gif"><strong>Check out our on-line <a
href="http://www.dcomp.com/dci/mfglist/mfglist.htm">guide to equipment manufactur-
ers</a>!</strong>
</center>

<p>Thanks for stopping by our page. While you are at it, check out some of the
communities around our area, including
<a href="http://www.dcomp.com/sundance/sundance.htm">Sundance</a>,
Hulett,
Moorcroft, and
<a href="http://www.dcomp.com/aladdin/aladdin.htm">Aladdin</a>.
Each of these are in beautiful
<a href="http://www.dcomp.com/crookcounty/crook.htm">Crook County</a>, Wyoming.
(If you would like to understand one of the big reasons DCI is located in this
area, <a href="http://www.dcomp.com/sundance/business.htm">click here</a>.)
<p>You might also like to see some of our <a
href="http://www.dcomp.com/dci/favoriteweb.htm">favorite web sites</a> or our links
to <a href="http://www.dcomp.com/dci/searches.htm">popular indexes</a>.

<!--#include file="footer.htm"-->

</body>
</html>
```

Notice the `include` statement near the end of the file. This instruction directs the server to load a file called footer.htm. If you use Notepad to load this file from the support files, it appears as follows:

```
<p>
<center>
<img src = "rainban.gif">
<address>
Discovery Computing Inc.<br>
20101 US Highway 14<br>
PO Box 738<br>
Sundance, WY  82729<br>
800-628-8280<br>
307-283-2714 (fax)
<p>Send comments to: <a href =
"mailto:webmaster@dcomp.com"><em>Webmaster@dcomp.com</em></a>
<p>Copyright &copy 1996 Discovery Computing Inc. All rights reserved.
</address>
</center>
```

The beauty of the `include` statement is that common information such as this need be stored only once. If you need to make changes, you change just the address.htm file, not all the files that reference it.

Using FrontPage 98 Components

In Chapter 7, you learned a little about components, sometimes referred to as FrontPage Components. FrontPage 98 includes a collection of components, formerly called WebBots, which you can use to add features to your Web pages that otherwise would require programming on your part. These objects can be placed anywhere within your pages and represent an add-on or an extension to the basic HTML coding that you normally use.

Some components are made possible by the use of the FrontPage 98 Server Extensions. These extensions, which were installed when you first installed IIS, examine the HTML code in a Web page as it is served to the rest of the world and substitute the elements necessary to support the components.

FrontPage 98 includes many different components. Several are discussed in the following sections.

CAUTION

Although components can provide many great extensions for your HTML pages, they do tie you down to using FrontPage 98. If you think that your pages will be used from a server that does not have the FrontPage 98 extensions, or you plan on removing the extensions from your server in the future, using the components now may entail extensive reworking of your HTML pages at a later date.

The Confirmation Field Component

In Chapter 9, you learned how to add forms to your Web pages. One of the forms you developed was a registration form from which users could sign up for company publications. With sign-up or registration forms, you may want to create a confirmation page that is displayed right after the user clicks on the Submit button. The purpose of the page is to provide a document that the user can view or print out to confirm his or her registration at your site.

The Confirmation Field component displays the contents of a form field within a confirmation page. Follow these steps to add the Confirmation Field component:

1. Use FrontPage Editor to develop everything about your confirmation page except the actual fields to be displayed.

2. Position the cursor at the point on the page where you want to display the contents of a field.

3. Choose the FrontPage Component option from the Insert menu. The Insert FrontPage Component dialog box appears, which provides a list of available components.

4. Highlight the Confirmation Field option and then click on OK. The Confirmation Field Properties dialog box appears, as shown in Figure 10-4.

5. Enter the name of the field whose contents you want to appear at the cursor position. The spelling should be exactly the same as that used to name the field when you placed it in your page.

6. Click on OK to close the Confirmation Field Properties dialog box. FrontPage Editor inserts the name of the field (within brackets) at the cursor location. (The field contents replace the field name when the page is actually viewed with a browser.)

The Include Page Component

Earlier in this chapter, you learned how you can use the IIS `include` statement to extend your use of HTML. FrontPage allows you to use the Include Page component

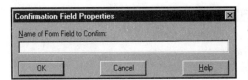

FIGURE 10-4

You can display the contents of any field with the Confirmation Field component.

to accomplish the same purpose. There are several differences between the two methods, however:

◆ The IIS `include` statement is parsed by the IIS Web server itself, whereas the Include Page component is handled by the FrontPage server extensions.

◆ IIS requires you to rename the files that contain the `include` statement with the stm filename extension; the Include Page component may be used with standard htm and html filename extensions.

◆ The IIS `include` statement is not directly supported by FrontPage Editor, but the Include Page component is.

To add the Include Page component to your Web page, follow these steps:

1. Position the FrontPage Editor cursor at the point in your page where you want to include the other HTML file.

2. Choose the FrontPage Component option from the Insert menu. The Insert FrontPage Component dialog box appears, which provides a list of available components.

3. Highlight the Include Page option and then click on OK. The Include Page Component Properties dialog box appears, as shown in Figure 10-5.

4. Enter the URL for the page you want to include at the cursor position.

5. Click on OK to close the Include Page Component Properties dialog box. FrontPage Editor inserts the URL as italics text (within brackets) at the cursor position. The actual file replace this annotation when the page is viewed with a browser.

The Scheduled Image Component

The Scheduled Image component enables you to display an image for a limited duration. For example, suppose that you run a Web site that promotes your company's products from July 1 to July 15. You can use the Scheduled Image component to display a specified image during this time range. To use the Scheduled Image component, follow these steps:

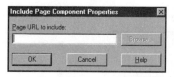

FIGURE 10-5

To include another HTML file in your document, you simply need to specify the URL.

1. Position the FrontPage Editor cursor at the point in your page where you want the image to appear.

2. Choose the FrontPage Component option from the Insert menu. The Insert FrontPage Component dialog box appears, which provides a list of available components.

3. Highlight the Scheduled Image option and then click on OK. The Scheduled Image Properties dialog box appears, as shown in Figure 10-6.

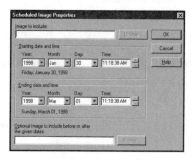

FIGURE 10-6

You can add an image to your page for a specified period of time.

4. Specify the name of the image you want to display in the Image to Include field.

5. Specify when the image should first be displayed in the Starting Date and Time field.

6. Specify when the image should no longer be displayed in the Ending Date and Time field.

7. Specify the name of the image to be used at all other times in the Optional Image field. (Leave this field blank if you don't want any image displayed.)

8. Click on OK to close the Scheduled Image Properties dialog box. FrontPage Editor inserts the image specification as italics text (within brackets) at the cursor position.

The Scheduled Include Page Component

The Scheduled Include Page component is similar in purpose to the Include Page component except that the former includes the specified page only during a specific

NOTE

The Scheduled Image component is suited only for displaying an image for a set range of time. If you have more complex insertion needs, you need to program your own script to handle them (for example, if you want to display an image to every third visitor or only on Mondays and Thursdays). Refer to a good Web programming book for help with these types of insertion needs.

time range. (With its scheduling capabilities, it is also similar to the Scheduled Image component.) For example, you can use the Scheduled Include Page component to display a particular advertisement or offer only between 1:00 a.m. and 6:00 a.m. next Tuesday.

To add the Scheduled Include Page component to your page, follow these steps:

1. Position the FrontPage Editor cursor at the point in your page where you want the included file to appear.

2. Choose the FrontPage Component option from the Insert menu. The Insert Component dialog box appears, which provides a list of available components.

3. Highlight the Scheduled Include Page option and then click on OK. The Scheduled Include Page Component Properties dialog box appears, as shown in Figure 10-7. (This dialog box looks very similar to the Scheduled Image Component Properties dialog box shown in Figure 10-6.)

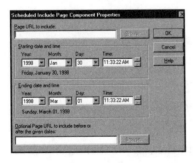

FIGURE 10-7

You can include another page in your current page during a particular time range.

4. Specify the URL for the page to be included in the Page URL to Include field.

5. Specify when the file should first be included in the Starting Date and Time field.

6. Specify when the file should no longer be included in the Ending Date and Time field.

7. Specify the name of a page to be included at all other times (if desired) in the Optional Page field.

8. Click on OK to close the Scheduled Include Page Component Properties dialog box. FrontPage Editor inserts the URL as italics text (within brackets) at the cursor position.

The Search Component

The Search component creates a form that enables page users to search through all the pages at a Web site. Users can search for any word or combinations of words. The results are then displayed with optional information that you can specify, and the user can then jump to any of the matches.

To add the Search component to your page, follow these steps:

1. Use FrontPage Editor to design your search page. You should include everything except the actual search form.

2. Position the cursor at the point in your page where you want to include the search form.

3. Choose the Search Form option from the Active Elements submenu in the Insert menu. The Search Form Properties dialog box appears, as shown in Figure 10-8

FIGURE 10-8

You have complete control over the Search form.

4. In the Label for Input field, indicate the text you want to appear beside the field where users enter what they want to search for.

5. In the Width field, specify how many characters you want the user to be able to input in the search string.

6. In the Label for "Start Search" Button field, specify the text to appear on the Submit button within the form.

7. In the Label for "Clear" Button field, specify the text to appear on the Reset button within the form.

8. Click on the Search Results tab to specify other options, shown in Figure 10-9.

9. Specify any additional information that you want to include in the output with the search results.

10. Click on OK to close the Search Form Properties dialog box. FrontPage Editor creates and inserts a form, as shown in Figure 10-10.

FIGURE 10-9

The Search Results tab controls the results of your search.

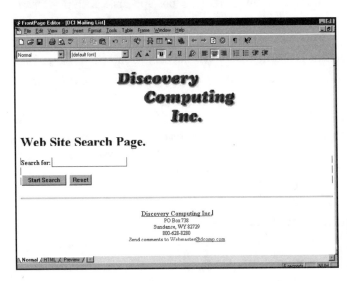

FIGURE 10-10

The Search component adds a search form to your page.

The Substitution Component

The Substitution component is really handy for displaying common system information. You can use the component to add the values of configuration variables set in FrontPage Explorer. The standard configuration variables that you can use are specified in the page properties maintained by FrontPage Explorer and include the following:

- ◆ **Author.** The name of the person who created the page, as specified in the Created By field of the page properties.
- ◆ **Modified By.** The name of the person who most recently changed the page, as specified in the Modified By field of the page properties.
- ◆ **Description.** The description of the current page, as specified in the Comments field of the page properties.
- ◆ **Page URL.** The URL of the current page.

In addition, you can use FrontPage Explorer to define other system variables, which you can then display in your pages using the Substitution component. To use the Substitution component, follow these steps:

1. Position the FrontPage Editor cursor at the point in your page where you want to place the Substitution component.
2. Choose the FrontPage Component option from the Insert menu. The Insert FrontPage Component dialog box appears, which provides a list of available components.
3. Highlight the Substitution option and then click on OK. The Substitution Component Properties dialog box appears, as shown in Figure 10-11.
4. Pull-down the Substitute With list and select the FrontPage variable whose contents you want to display in your page.
5. Click on OK to close the Substitution Component Properties dialog box. FrontPage Editor inserts the system variable name (within brackets) at the current cursor location. (The actual value of the system variable is used when the page is viewed by a browser.)

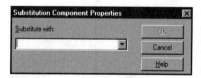

FIGURE 10-11

You can display the contents of any system variable with the Substitution component.

The Table of Contents Component

If you have a large or complex Web site, you might want to create a table of contents for the site. The Table of Contents component makes this task a snap. The purpose of this component is to look through your Web site, create a table of contents for each page, and then present that information in a meaningful manner.

NOTE

The Table of Contents component works only with a Web that you manage with FrontPage Explorer. If you are not using FrontPage Explorer to manage your site, don't try to use the Table of Contents component.

To use the Table of Contents component, follow these steps:

1. Use FrontPage Editor to design your table of contents page. You should include everything except the actual table of contents links.

2. Position the cursor at the point in your page where you want the table of contents to appear.

3. Choose the Table of Contents option from the Insert menu. The Table of Contents Properties dialog box appears, as shown in Figure 10-12.

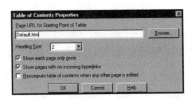

FIGURE 10-12

You can create a table of contents for your Web site.

4. Enter the highest level page within your site in the Page URL field. Typically, this value is your default page or your index page. This page serves as the root for everything done by the Table of Contents component.

5. Enter the heading level to use for the table of contents heading in the Heading Size field.

6. Use the check boxes at the bottom of the dialog box to indicate how you want the table of contents to appear.

7. Click on OK to close the Table of Contents Properties dialog box. FrontPage Editor creates and inserts a series of placeholder links, as shown in Figure 10-13. The actual table of contents replaces these placeholders when the page is viewed by a browser.

The Timestamp Component

The Timestamp component adds a date and time to your Web page. The date and time can represent either when the page was last edited or when it was last automatically updated. To add the Timestamp component to your page, follow these steps:

1. Position the FrontPage Editor cursor at the point in your page where you want the timestamp to appear.

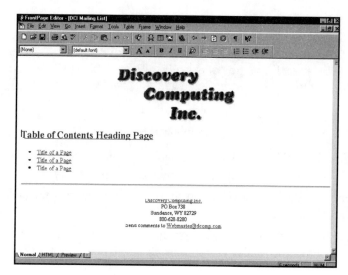

FIGURE 10-13

The Table of Contents component automatically creates a table of contents according to your specifications.

2. Choose the <u>T</u>imestamp option from the <u>I</u>nsert menu. The Timestamp Properties dialog box appears, as shown in Figure 10-14.

3. Pick the type of timestamp in the Display area that you want added to your page.

4. Use the Date <u>F</u>ormat pull-down list to select the way in which you want the date displayed.

5. Optionally, use the <u>T</u>ime Format pull-down list to select how you want to time displayed.

6. Click on OK to close the Timestamp Properties dialog box. FrontPage Editor adds the date to the page.

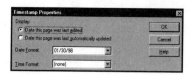

FIGURE 10-14

You can add different types of timestamps to your Web page.

NOTE

You may have seen Web pages that display the current local time. The Timestamp component is not used for this type of display. If you want to display the time of day, you must program a script yourself.

Using Themes

The final extension described in this chapter enables you to add themes to your Web site. A *theme* is essentially a template that is applied to a Web page. You can use a theme to give all your pages a standard look. FrontPage 98 includes more than 50 themes.

You can apply themes either to a single page, using FrontPage Editor, or to an entire site, using FrontPage Explorer. After you apply a theme, all the affected pages use the same background image and fonts, as well as images for bullets and other visual elements. The following sections describe how to add themes to your Web site.

Adding a Theme to a Page

Using the FrontPage Editor, you can apply a theme to a single HTML page. Even if you want to apply a theme to your entire site, you should start with a one-page sample to see how adding the theme will affect your pages. To add a theme with FrontPage Editor, follow these steps:

1. Open an existing page in the FrontPage Editor. You can start with a blank page; however, it is often best to see how the theme will affect your existing pages.

2. Right-click anywhere on the page and select Theme from the shortcut menu. This action displays the Choose Theme dialog box, as shown in Figure 10-15.

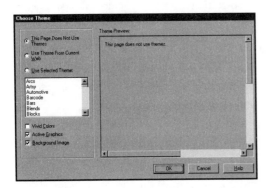

FIGURE 10-15

The Choose Theme dialog box manages the themes at your Web site.

3. Select the Use Selected Theme option to display the available themes.

4. Choose a theme from the list box, and a sample page will appear in the Theme Preview area.

5. Select a theme and click on OK to add the theme to your page. Changing themes may require changing some of your existing graphics, as shown in Figure 10-16.

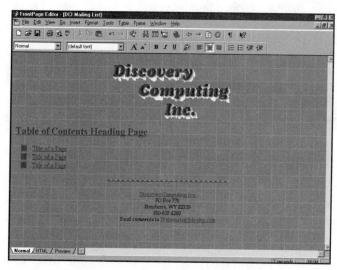

FIGURE 10-16

You can use themes to quickly change the appearance of your page.

Adding a Theme to a Web Site

You can use FrontPage Explorer to apply a theme to an entire Web site in much the same way that the FrontPage Editor adds a theme to a Web page. This feature enables you to quickly change all of the pages of your existing site so that they have the same background images, colors, and fonts. To add a theme to your Web site with FrontPage Explorer, follow these steps:

1. Open a Web site in FrontPage Explorer.
2. Select Themes from the View panel, or select Themes from the View menu if you have closed the View panel. This action displays the properties for using themes in your Web site, as shown in Figure 10-17.
3. Select the Use Selected Theme option to display the available themes.
4. Choose a theme from the list box, and a sample page will appear in the Theme Preview area.
5. Select from the options below the list box control for even more control over the type of graphics used in the theme.
6. Select a theme and the graphics options you want; then, click on Apply to add the theme to all the pages at your Web site. FrontPage Explorer uploads the graphics to your Web site and edits your HTML files. (This process may take a few minutes.)

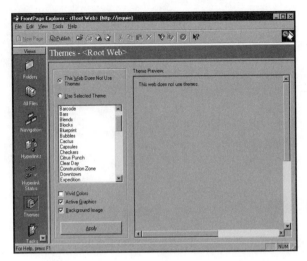

FIGURE 10-17

Themes view controls the theme properties of your entire Web site.

NOTE

To remove themes from the pages at your site, open Themes view and select the This Web Does Not Use Themes option.

PART III

III

Developing Dynamic Web Site Content

Chapter 11

Working with
Client-Side Scripts

In This Chapter

◆ The Big Picture

◆ Web Scripting Languages

◆ Web-Distributed Technology

To add a degree of interactivity at your Web site, you can include scripting in your HTML code. Scripting enables you to add interactivity and functionality to your Web site in much the same way that macros enable you to extend an application.

In this chapter, you learn about some of the technologies that you can use to make your Web site dynamic. Here you learn about JavaScript, VBScript, Java, and ActiveX. The information presented in this chapter is introductory, with a focus on how you can make these technologies work from the IIS environment. For more detailed information, check a good reference book on the technology in question.

The Big Picture

Every month or so, a new Web-based development technology seems to make its way into the news. Some of the technologies even make their way into the browser and server marketplace—particularly if they are developed or backed by Microsoft or Netscape.

With all of these different technologies available, you may be wondering how everything fits together. The technologies can be divided into two broad categories, which I like to call *Web scripting languages* and *Web-distributed technologies*. Figure 11-1 shows this categorization scheme.

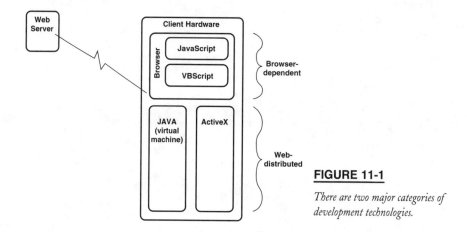

FIGURE 11-1

There are two major categories of development technologies.

In essence, the difference between Web scripting languages and Web-distributed technologies is that the former are typically included as part of the HTML file and are run within the browser itself. Web-distributed languages are normally downloaded as files, stored on a local hard drive, and then executed within either their own memory space or a separate area of the browser.

Web Scripting Languages

Web scripting languages are also referred to as *browser-dependent languages*. They are full-fledged programming languages that cannot create stand-alone applications. These languages require a *host application*, in this case a Web browser, to provide functionality to the scripting language. For example, a scripting language can add 2 + 2, but it requires the Web browser to display the result in a page or dialog box.

The major Web scripting languages are JavaScript and VBScript. Both have been around for a while, but JavaScript is the oldest. Each language is described in the following sections.

What Is JavaScript?

For lack of a better description, JavaScript is a scripting language developed by Netscape and Sun Microsystems in late 1995. Because Sun was involved in the development, you might be tempted to think that JavaScript and Java are related to each other. (Java is discussed later in this chapter.) This hunch isn't true; even though their names are similar, JavaScript and Java are unrelated.

JavaScript is a scripting language and in many ways can be viewed as an extension to HTML. Java, on the other hand, is a full-blown programming language separate from HTML. For JavaScript to work properly, the browser must be capable of understanding the scripting language.

NOTE

If you include JavaScript in your Web pages, not all browsers will be able to take advantage of your enhancements because not all browsers understand JavaScript. Although most users have a browser capable of using JavaScript, some do not.

JavaScript typically runs more quickly than other forms of scripting, such as CGI. The reason is quite simple: much of the burden of interpreting the script is transferred to the browser, rather than remaining solely up to the server. When you use CGI scripts with forms, the browser displays the form, but processing form information remains the duty of the server. Therefore, the data must be transferred to the server, verified, processed, and returned in a meaningful form to the browser. Under JavaScript, your programs can do at least some data verification on the browser before transmitting data to the server for final processing. Depending on the script, this approach can have a dramatic effect on the dynamic nature of your Web site.

As you might expect, Netscape Navigator 2 supported the first version of JavaScript, JavaScript 1.0. Currently, Netscape Navigator supports JavaScript 1.2. Microsoft Internet Explorer 3.0 was the first Microsoft Web browser to support JavaScript.

Using JavaScript Objects

JavaScript is an object-based language. JavaScript relies on the browser to be truly useful, and it accesses the browser's usefulness through objects. An object is simply something that you want to use in your program. For example, an HTML page is an object—a document object, to be exact.

When dealing with JavaScript, you will typically use two main objects: windows and documents. The *window object* refers to a program window (browsers can typically have more than one window open at a time). This object enables you to create dialog boxes and window controls. The *document object* is typically used to modify HTML pages and process information in forms.

Adding JavaScript to Your Pages

You can easily add JavaScript code to your current HTML pages by using the `<SCRIPT>` and `</SCRIPT>` tag pair. Everything between these two tags is assumed to be JavaScript. For example, take a look at the file \Chap11\JSExample.htm, which is available in the support files. It contains the following simple HTML page with an even simpler script embedded in it:

```
<html>
<head>
<title>Sample Page Using JavaScript</title>
<script language="JavaScript">
    var name = window.prompt("What is your name?", "John Doe");
    document.write("<p>Hello, " + name + ".</p>");
</script>
```

Understanding Different Versions of JavaScript

As with many of the other technologies used on the Web, JavaScript has gone to an independent organization for standardization. ECMA, an international association based in Europe, has created a standardization for ECMAScript, called ECMA-262. The actual JavaScript language is a variant of the standard. Microsoft's Internet Explorer supports another implementation of ECMAScript called JScript. Both JScript and JavaScript include a few features not yet found in the ECMA standard. To avoid confusion, this book uses the original name, JavaScript.

Because JScript and JavaScript are not entirely compatible, you have three choices when it comes to creating your scripts:

◆ **Develop scripts for a single browser.** When only a single browser supported JavaScript, this solution was, of course, the default choice; it was also a choice with no consequences. Now, however, if you develop implementation-dependent scripts, you may severely limit your audience. Thus, this choice becomes a nonviable option. The only time to develop scripts for a single browser is when you are creating an intranet in which only one type of browser is in use.

◆ **Develop standards-based scripts.** This option may be the most viable. If you can meet your demands using the ECMA-262 standard, you have no real problem. If you really must use a nonstandard feature, then this option becomes untenable.

◆ **Develop code in tandem.** This alternative may be the most viable long-term solution. Developing code in tandem means that you add code to your pages for both JavaScript and JScript, which obviously entails longer development and testing cycles. The result is that your pages work with the greatest number of browsers out there. Of course, this option may not remain viable if more implementations of JavaScript become available.

```
</head>

<body>

<p>The following line is created by a JavaScript script:</p>

<script language="JavaScript">
    document.write("<p>Welcome to JavaScript</p>");
```

```
</script>

<p>Now we are back at regular HTML.</p>

</body>
</html>
```

Notice that the page consists of two sets of `<SCRIPT>` and `</SCRIPT>` tags. The first set of tags appears in the HEAD of the page. All scripts in the HEAD are run before the page is displayed by the browser. This code has two lines. The first line uses the window object to create a dialog box, or prompt. This dialog box prompts the user for a name and even offers a default name of John Doe.

The second line uses the document object. The document object includes a write function used to put information in the HTML page being displayed. In this case, the document.write function displays a welcome message. This message appears at the top of the document in the browser before any of the standard HTML.

The second script appears in the **BODY** section of the page. It also uses the `docu-ment.write` function. This time the message appears in the middle of the HTML.

When you open this page on a JavaScript-capable browser, a dialog box immediately asks for your name. You may want to change the name from John Doe to your name, or you may prefer to leave the anonymous name there. After you click on OK, the HTML page appears as four lines (see Figure 11-2). Granted, this example is very simple; however, the important point is the construction of this Web page, which shows how you can embed a script in a document.

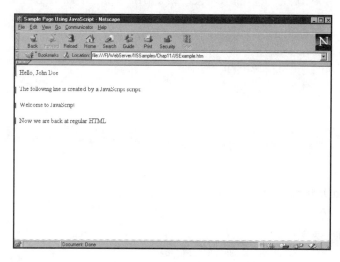

FIGURE 11-2

The browser interprets JavaScript scripts after the page is loaded.

If you look back at the code for this page, you will notice that the <SCRIPT> tag uses the LANGUAGE attribute. This attribute, although optional, is a good feature to use. It indicates which scripting language is being used in the page. JavaScript used to be the only language on the block, but with the appearance of VBScript, some browsers may get confused if you don't include the LANGUAGE attribute. If you use the LANGUAGE attribute as shown in this example, the browser assumes that you are using JavaScript based on the ECMA-262 standard. If you want to use code that is specific to JavaScript 1.2, you can change the LANGUAGE attribute to the following:

```
<script language="JavaScript1.2">
```

As new versions of JavaScript are released, the version number on the end of the LANGUAGE attribute will probably also be changed.

Hiding the JavaScript Code

As you already know, not all browsers understand JavaScript. As an example, Microsoft Internet Explorer 2.0 does not understand JavaScript, and if you try to use that version of Internet Explorer to view the page developed in the previous section, the result is unsatisfactory. If a browser supports the <SCRIPT> tag but not the LANGUAGE you are using, the script will be ignored, so you don't have to worry about hiding it.

To avoid the problem of a script showing up in browsers that don't support the <SCRIPT> tag, JavaScript enables you to embed the entire script in an HTML comment tag. This approach is handy because it means that older browsers will ignore the embedded script but newer browsers will pick it up. For instance, the file \Chap11\JSExample2.htm, available in the support files, is a slightly modified version of the sample page. This time, however, the script is placed within a comment tag:

SUPPORT FILE

```
<html>

<head>

<title>Sample Page Using JavaScript</title>

<script language="JavaScript">

<!— Begin JavaScript

    var name = window.prompt("What is your name?", "John Doe");

    document.write("<p>Hello, " + name + ".</p>");

// End JavaScript —>

</script>

</head>
```

```
<body>

<p>The following line is created by a JavaScript script:</p>

<script language="JavaScript">
<!— Begin JavaScript
    document.write("<p>Welcome to JavaScript</p>");
// End JavaScript —>
</script>

<p>Now we are back at regular HTML.</p>

</body>
</html>
```

The information placed at the beginning of the comment (in this case, `Begin JavaScript`) or at the end of the comment (`End JavaScript`) is unimportant. What matters is the inclusion on the comment start (`<!— `) and end (`—>`). You could use the lead-in information to help document your script, if desired.

CAUTION

Make sure that you place your <SCRIPT> tag before you start the HTML comment block and the </SCRIPT> tag after you end the HTML comment block. The HTML parsers in older browsers will ignore the <SCRIPT> tag pair, but the JavaScript interpreter in newer browsers needs to find the start of the script *before* it sees the start of the HTML comment block. If you don't place the lines in this order, the browser will never see your script.

When an older browser displays this page, the information in the comment tag (the script) is ignored. Although this result may not be the best of all worlds, it's better than displaying "garbage" in the old browsers, which makes your pages seem to contain errors. Browsers that understand JavaScript display the embedded script as intended. With the popularity of JavaScript-enabled browsers, you may not need to comment out the JavaScript. However, it is a good practice if users of older browsers may be visiting your site.

Additional JavaScript Resources

Many excellent resources can teach you how to program effectively in JavaScript. For example, *JavaScript* by Paul Kooros and Michele DeWolfe (Prima Publishing, ISBN 0-7615-0685-3) is a good hands-on guide to using JavaScript at your site.

If you would like an online resource, check out the following sites:

ONLINE

- ◆ **http://www.ecma.ch/stand/ecma-262.htm** ECMA maintains the standards for implementing JavaScript among the different Web browsers.
- ◆ **http://developer.netscape.com/library/documentation/communicator/jsref/index.htm** Perhaps the definitive JavaScript site, from the creators at Netscape Communications.
- ◆ **http://www.inquiry.com/techtips/js_pro/** Online answers about JavaScript from professional Web page developers.
- ◆ **http://jrc.livesoftware.com/** An impressive online resource for JavaScript examples and information.

A few other sites provide JScript-specific help. For the most part, the two languages are quite similar, and one reference is as good as another. If you get a good JavaScript book, you may want to reference one of the online sources and mark your book according to what you discover there.

You can find JScript information, which is best viewed with Internet Explorer 4.01, in the online documentation installed with IIS listed here:

ONLINE

- ◆ **http://localhost/iishelp/JScript/htm/Jstutor.htm** An online JScript tutorial with information and examples.
- ◆ **http://localhost/iishelp/jscript/htm/js430.htm** A listing of JScript features that aren't part of the ECMA standard.
- ◆ **http://localhost/iishelp/jscript/htm/jstoc.htm** An online JScript quick reference with easy access to information about a JScript function or object.

Configuring IIS for JavaScript

You don't have to do anything special to configure IIS for JavaScript. Remember that JavaScript is a browser-dependent language, which means that the JavaScript code embedded within the HTML pages is sent to the user's browser and translated there. The rest is up to the browser to handle.

The upshot is that you can use your JavaScript code directly with IIS without any need for additional configuration or without any delay. If you have developed pages that contain JavaScript for use on a different server, you should have no problems at all.

What Is VBScript?

If you have ever done any programming or if you are familiar with different programming environments, you have undoubtedly heard of Visual Basic. VBScript is essentially a subset of Visual Basic, designed to work within an HTML document in much the same way that JavaScript works.

> **CAUTION**
>
> Very few browsers can take advantage of the enhancements made possible by VBScript.

Like JavaScript, VBScript can process information on forms more quickly than comparable forms written using CGI. This is because the burden of running the code is transferred from your server to the remote browser, which means that your server is free to process other requests.

Adding VBScript to Your Pages

You can easily add VBScript code to your current HTML pages by using the `<SCRIPT>` and `</SCRIPT>` tag pair, along with the **LANGUAGE** attribute set to `"VBScript"`. Everything between the tags is assumed to be VBScript. For example, load the file \Chap11\VBSExample.htm from the support files. It contains the following simple HTML page that shows a sample VBScript script:

```
<html>

<head>

<title>Sample Page Using VBScript</title>

</head>


<body>


<p>The following lines are created by a VBScript script:</p>


<script language="VBScript">

    document.write "<p>Running VBScript<br>"

    document.write "Current time is " & Time() & " on " & Date() + "</p>"

</script>
```

```
<p>Now we are back at regular HTML.</p>


</body>
</html>
```

Notice that the script consists of two lines within the `<SCRIPT>` and `</SCRIPT>` tags. The script uses the `document.write` function to write information to the document being viewed. When you view this page on a VBScript-capable browser, the output is very simple and should appear as shown in Figure 11-3.

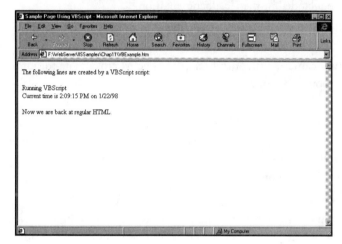

FIGURE 11-3

VBScript scripts enable you to create dynamic output.

This simple exercise may appear contrived (and it is), but it begins to show what you can do with VBScript. Notice the use of the `Time()` and `Date()` functions in the second VBScript line. These functions may look very familiar to Visual Basic programmers; they return, respectively, the current time and current date, according to the system on which the program is running. Because the script is running on the user's browser, the time returned is based on the user's system. Such on-the-fly capability is not possible with normal HTML.

NOTE

You can hide your VBScript code within HTML comments, the same as with JavaScript.

Additional VBScript Resources

Because VBScript has not been around as long as JavaScript, the resources available for learning more about the language are a little harder to find. Resources are beginning to pop up, however, and persistence pays off in this area.

A number of books on the market deal with VBScript. Check your local computer bookstore, or you can check out **amazon.com.** Other online resources for VBScript that are best viewed with a browser supporting VBScript include the following:

- **http://localhost/iishelp/vbscript/htm/vbstoc.htm**   VBScript quick reference included in the IIS documentation.
- **http://localhost/iishelp/VBScript/htm/vbstutor.htm**   Tutorial for VBScript included with the IIS documentation.
- **http://www.microsoft.com/vbscript/**   The Microsoft site for information about VBScript.

Configuring IIS for VBScript

No special server configuration is necessary to use VBScript. When you include VBScript code within your HTML files, the user's browser takes care of interpreting the information and acting on it.

If your VBScript sends information back to your server, you need to make sure that your server is set up to handle the information. For example, you might have to write a custom script or obtain some other server add-on that can deal with the information. Such considerations, however, are way beyond the scope of this book. Detailed Web programming references would be of more help in this area.

Web-Distributed Technologies

The two contenders in the area of Web-distributed technologies are Java and ActiveX. Java is most prevalent, but ActiveX has the muscle of Microsoft behind it. The following section describe these technologies.

What Is Java?

If you have been browsing the Web for a while or have been keeping tabs on the Internet in the popular media, you probably have heard about Java; it is very popular among Internet developers. Java is a programming language first developed by Sun Microsystems in 1990 under the name of Oak. The language was originally intended for use in embedded systems. (*Embedded systems* are applications stored on computer chips in devices such as automobiles, home electronics, and appliances.) When that use of the language did not pan out, Java was released on the Internet, and the excitement and spread of the language has been phenomenal. As a result of its new popularity, Java is now being used as it was originally intended—in embedded systems.

The Java language is a simplified version of C++, so many programmers feel right at home using it. Java is object-oriented, interpreted, secure, portable, and multithreaded. Applets written in Java for Web pages are generally stored on the server, downloaded to the browser on demand, and executed within a "virtual machine" on the remote system. The benefit to the developer is that you need to develop a program only once. The virtual machine on each platform takes care of running your applet, so you don't need to develop a new version for each disparate system such as Windows, UNIX, and Macintosh as long as the system has a Java-capable browser.

NOTE

Some network computers (NCs) on the market utilize Java as their operating environment.

Earlier in this chapter, you learned about JavaScript, a scripting language developed by Netscape and Sun. JavaScript was originally called LiveWire. The name was changed to JavaScript when the popularity of Java became evident. Although much of the syntax and programming procedure in JavaScript is similar to Java, the two languages are not the same.

The Virtual Machine Concept

As mentioned in the previous section, Java relies on a concept referred to as a *virtual machine.* Typically, a computer program is written with instructions that the CPU will understand. In contrast, Java programs are not created for a specific type of CPU. Instead, a program called the virtual machine runs the program and translates the instructions into something that the CPU can use. These days, the virtual Java machine is created by the browser you are using. Many of the newer browsers understand Java, which simply means that they create an environment (a virtual machine) in which a Java program can be executed.

To a programmer, the biggest advantage of the virtual machine concept is that he or she needs to develop only a single version of the program—one designed to run on the virtual machine. This single version can be executed on a universal virtual machine, even though that virtual machine may be contained within widely different hardware platforms. Consequently, Java is platform independent.

If you have used a programming language before, you might be familiar with the traditional write/compile/link/execute cycle. As you develop a program, you must first write it, then compile it, then link it, and, finally, you can execute it. Each step in the cycle is necessary to produce a program that can be used on the target machine. Java changes this development cycle slightly. Now the cycle is write/compile/download/execute. The download and execute phases are handled by the server and browser, whereas the programmer needs only to write and compile the program (no linking is necessary).

Another advantage of the virtual machine is that it makes it harder for unruly programs and viruses to be transmitted to a host system. Because everything runs within a virtual machine created by software, the added buffer between application and hardware makes spreading viruses much more difficult. In the case of the Java-enabled browsers, the virtual machine does not allow the program access to files on the host's computer.

The virtual machine used as a basis for Java supports quite a bit of flexibility but does have a few drawbacks. The biggest drawback is that programs downloaded from the Internet are not executed directly on hardware. Java is stored in an intermediate code format that the virtual machine must translate into something that can be run on the host system. This translation phase means that Java programs run slower—much slower—than programs compiled and linked to the native format of the host. Although this drawback makes huge, monolithic programs impractical in Java, it does not present an insurmountable barrier for most of the smaller programs now surfacing on the Internet.

To speed up the execution of Java programs, several Java virtual machines include a JIT, or just in time, compiler. This compiler changes the Java program into machine-specific code. This approach allows the program to run faster, but it takes a little longer to start the program.

Applications versus Applets

You can use Java to develop two types of programs. The first is called an application; the second is called an applet. *Applications* are full-blown, Internet-aware programs that run within the virtual machine on your system. For example, you might develop a Java application that is used as a word processor or as a spreadsheet program. Most of the currently available Java applications are Internet related, such as Web browsers and development tools.

Applets are smaller programs designed to perform limited tasks or to add flavor to a Web page. For example, a Java applet might add animation to a Web page or check information before it's transmitted back to your server. Applets are stored at your Web site just as any other resource (such as a graphics file or sound clip) is. When the applet is referenced in a Web page, it's downloaded to the browser without intervention by the Web server. If a Java environment exists on the remote system, then the applet is executed.

Server Side versus Client Side

As you read about Java programs, you often see references to server-side and client-side programs. *Server side* simply means that the Java program is executed on the server, with some amount of interfacing going on with the client. A *client-side* program is the opposite: all processing taking place on the client's machine. In today's Internet environment, most Java programs are applets, and all applets are client based. Most Webmasters want to offload processing from their server and thus choose Java programs that place the computing burden on the client.

An exception to this rule occurs when developers are building intranets. In an intranet, where the community of users is smaller and more homogenous, there are advantages to creating server-side applications—they allow a certain amount of centralized control over processing. On a high-speed local network, the greater control can be a huge benefit, particularly without a great slowdown in processing speed.

Additional Java Resources

Both on the shelves and about to be released, there are many good books about Java and its use. In addition, many online resources are available. Perhaps the premier site is at **http://java.sun.com.** This is the site at Sun, where Java was first developed. Other sites of note include the following:

ONLINE

◆ **http://www.mindq.com/java/javaintro.html** This site provides products that help you learn how to program in Java on your own system.

◆ **http://www.developer.com/directories/pages/dir.java.html** The Gamelan Java Directory provides good examples of Java programs.

◆ **http://www.MageLang.com/** This is another company that provides tutorials in how to develop programs in the Java environment.

Configuring IIS for Java

If your site offers Java applets, you don't have to do anything special to configure IIS to use them. When you reference them in your pages, they are downloaded automatically to the remote browser, where it is up to the browser to provide the environment needed to host the applet.

In contrast, if you are developing Java applications, you may need to make quite a few changes in how IIS works. If the applications are designed to be downloaded and run on a remote system, you can either download them as files and allow the user to run them or you can develop them as programs that automatically download and execute. Setting up IIS for this configuration is beyond the scope of this book. For further information, you should refer to the Sun Microsystems Web site (**http://java.sun.com**).

To use Java to any extent, you need the Java Developer's Kit (JDK). The JDK is available on the Sun Microsystems Web site at **http://java.sun.com/nav/read/products.html.** Make sure that you have ample time to work with the JDK the first time. Getting used to the environment and configuring your machine for the development tools can take a while.

What Is ActiveX?

ActiveX is a set of technologies, created by Microsoft, that enable programmers to extend the uses of the Internet. The ActiveX programmer creates programs, or program parts called *components*, which can be used to create applications that are run across the Web. ActiveX is essentially a descendent of OCX, an older technology that was not network aware and that most programmers agree never worked quite right. Many ActiveX components have been developed specifically for the Internet. As of this writing, ActiveX consists of the following components:

- ◆ **ActiveX Controls.** These components are the interactive objects that appear on a Web page.
- ◆ **ActiveX Documents.** These components enable users to view non-HTML documents through a Web browser without the need for plug-in modules, as is done on Netscape Navigator.
- ◆ **Active Scripting.** This component is the scripting language that controls the behavior of several ActiveX controls or Java Applets from the browser or the server.
- ◆ **Java Virtual Machine.** This component is the code necessary to enable Java applets to run together with ActiveX controls on an ActiveX-compatible browser.
- ◆ **ActiveX Server Framework.** This component provides Web server-based functions such as security and database access.

From a programmer's perspective, the portions of the technology that you use most often are the ActiveX controls and scripts to link the controls. You use a programming language, such as C++, to develop the controls and then use a scripting language to add them to a Web page.

Cross-Platform Development

Earlier in this chapter, you learned that Java is a platform-independent environment. You provide this environment by creating a virtual machine on each system where you want Java programs to run. ActiveX is a cross-platform development tool, which means that programmers create ActiveX controls in a similar fashion for different environments. Unlike Java, a control created for one platform will not run on another platform. For example, an animation control created for the Macintosh will not run on a Windows NT machine. However, you can quickly create a different control, using almost the same code, for the Windows NT environment. Right now, ActiveX is available only for use under Windows and Macintosh systems.

NOTE

If your programs must work on many platforms, you should invest the time to learn how to program in Java. Java currently works on a wide variety of platforms and will continue to do so into the future.

The feature that makes ActiveX so popular right now (even though it is predominantly a Windows-based product) is that it is targeted toward a community of programmers who have quite a bit invested in the technology on which ActiveX was originally based. For example, if you have spent years developing OCX controls, converting your controls to ActiveX will be far easier than learning Java from scratch and re-creating your controls in that environment.

Setting a Standard

Because Microsoft was the developer and chief advocate of ActiveX, many people worried that ActiveX would be a proprietary set of tools. Although this consideration is not a big problem on desktop PCs, with Microsoft essentially monopolizing the environment of every PC in the world, it can be a problem in the networked environment. One of the advantages of the Internet is that it is ideal for a heterogeneous computing environment (that is, all sorts of computers can be connected to the Internet). If a proprietary standard is adopted, then the Internet becomes less heterogeneous and more tied to a single vendor's products.

To avoid this situation, Microsoft has announced that it will transfer control of ActiveX to an "appropriate industry standards body." Exactly what this promise means is still up in the air; the actual transition has not occurred as of this writing. Some evidence suggests that Microsoft, despite its announcement, is hesitant to release control of the standards it has developed to date. If the transition occurs soon, ActiveX may have a bright future on many different computing platforms.

Security Concerns

When an ActiveX control is downloaded to a browser on the Internet, the control is actually cached on the user's hard drive. This situation is both good and bad. It is good because it means that once downloaded, the control is available for use over and over again. The result is faster response for repeat visits to the same Web site.

On the down side, if a control is written to disk, it has the potential to cause security problems. It is a relatively easy task to create virus and Trojan horse programs that hide inside ActiveX controls. In fact, this security risk is perhaps the biggest advantage of Java applets over ActiveX controls. With Java, the applet is not stored on disk, but must be downloaded from the Web server each time it is needed. Thus, applets are less likely to cause security problems.

To address security concerns, Microsoft has started a *code-signing standard*. Under this standard, the author of a program must "sign" the software he or she creates and distributes over the Internet. Theoretically, code-signing means that any problem programs could always be traced to their source. Critics argue that such a scheme could be circumvented in the same way that anonymous "remailers" bypass the origination information in e-mail messages.

Configuring IIS for ActiveX

By default, IIS is configured to work properly with ActiveX. All you need to do is start including ActiveX controls and scripting in your Web pages, and they are automatically handled properly by the server. The rub, however is that you need to get the controls into your Web pages.

Including an ActiveX control in your Web pages is more difficult than including a Java applet. The HTML code for an ActiveX control includes quite a bit of "baggage," which indicates how the control should be loaded and executed by the browser. For instance, the following snippet of HTML code loads and runs an ActiveX control:

```
<OBJECT ID="Slider1" WIDTH=137 HEIGHT=43
 CLASSID="CLSID:373FF7F0-EB8B-11CD-8820-08002B2F4F5A"
 CODEBASE="/scripts/">
    <PARAM NAME="_Version" VALUE="65536">
    <PARAM NAME="_ExtentX" VALUE="3625">
    <PARAM NAME="_ExtentY" VALUE="1111">
    <PARAM NAME="_StockProps" VALUE="64">
    <PARAM NAME="Max" VALUE="20">
</OBJECT>
```

Notice the number of lines necessary to use an ActiveX control. These lines specify the location, identity, and initial properties (characteristics) of the control. Creating the proper HTML code for your Web page can be taxing, particularly if you are trying to do it by hand. Fortunately, Microsoft has provided a tool that you can use to automatically create the HTML code.

Understanding the ActiveX Control Pad

Microsoft has developed a program which enables you to automate the way in which you use ActiveX controls in your Web pages. The ActiveX Control Pad, as it is called, consists of the following items:

- ◆ **Text editor** Enables you to modify HTML documents (like a glorified version of Notepad).

- ◆ **Object editor** Enables you to place ActiveX controls directly into an HTML document and change their properties.

- ◆ **Script Wizard** Helps generate VBScript or JavaScript code for working with ActiveX controls.

- ◆ **Page editor** Helps you create 2-D–style layout regions in an HTML document. This capability conforms with a draft specification for HTML style sheets, as submitted to the World Wide Web Consortium.

- ◆ **ActiveX controls** Includes a wide selection of generic ActiveX controls that you can use in your Web pages.

The complete use of all of these components is beyond the scope of this book, but it is certainly appropriate to discuss how you would use the ActiveX Control Pad to generate the proper HTML code for using controls in your pages.

NOTE

Don't confuse the ActiveX Control Pad with other HTML editors; it is not meant to replace products such as FrontPage 98 Editor. Instead, it is used to quickly determine the proper code necessary to include ActiveX controls in your documents.

ONLINE You can download the ActiveX Control Pad from the Microsoft Web site at **http://www.microsoft.com/workshop/author/cpad/download.htm.** If you have not done so already, you may also want to download Internet Explorer 4.0, which includes built-in support of the ActiveX Control Pad.

The file is downloaded as a self-extracting compressed file. Once it is downloaded, you can run the file to decompress it and install the ActiveX Control Pad.

Using the Text Editor

The ActiveX Control Pad text editor is essentially a glorified version of NotePad. When you start the ActiveX Control Pad, the interface appears as shown in Figure 11-4.

Notice that the first thing opened when you start the program is a blank HTML document. You can begin editing the default document, or you can load an existing HTML document by choosing Open from the File menu. The tools and menus across the top of the program window offer different options for working with your HTML file.

Inserting ActiveX Controls

The object editor is the tool that you use to add ActiveX controls to your HTML document. Without the object editor, adding ActiveX controls can be very difficult and laborious because each ActiveX control requires the following elements:

◆ A unique 128-bit code, which is used to identify the control in the Registry

◆ A series of properties for the control

Although the list is short, to manually discern and transcribe the proper information for these items is a cumbersome task. The object editor automatically derives this information and includes it in your HTML file. To insert an ActiveX control in your HTML file, follow these steps:

1. Position the cursor at the point in the file where you want to place the control.

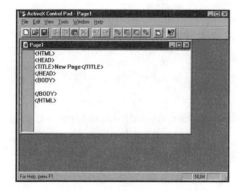

FIGURE 11-4

The ActiveX Control Pad uses a simple Windows interface.

2. Choose the Insert ActiveX Control option from the Edit menu. This action displays the Insert ActiveX Control dialog box, as shown in Figure 11-5.

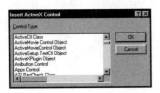

FIGURE 11-5

You can select from a number of ActiveX controls to insert.

3. Select the control that you want to include in your HTML document from the list of available controls. (The list reflects controls installed on your system and may vary from one computer to another.)

4. Click on OK to insert the control in your document.

Exactly what happens next depends on the nature of the control that you placed in your document. Two windows appear: one for the object editor and the other for the properties of the control. You can use the Object Editor window to change the size of the actual control that will appear on your page.

The Properties window enables you to change the properties of the control. If you are familiar with programming environments such as Visual Basic or Visual C++, setting properties through the use of a dialog box in this manner should seem almost second nature. Figure 11-6 shows an example of a typical Properties window. The properties that are actually available vary from control to control. To change a property, simply select it from the list of available properties and then change the value for that property at the top of the window.

FIGURE 11-6

You can change the properties of an ActiveX control.

TIP

If you prefer to use a different HTML editor, you can always use the ActiveX Control Pad to generate the HTML for your control, copy the code to the Clipboard, and then paste it in your preferred HTML editor.

When you are done sizing and changing the properties of your control, all you need to do is close the object editor. This action causes the ActiveX Control Pad to place the proper HTML code for the object in your document. As shown in Figure 11-7, an icon is also placed in the margin to the left of the control block. This icon indicates, first of all, that the element is an ActiveX control. You can also double-click on the icon to invoke the object editor for that control again.

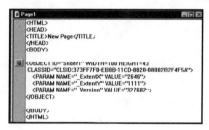

FIGURE 11-7

ActiveX controls are marked in the text editor with an icon in the left margin.

Using FrontPage for ActiveX

The ActiveX Control Pad is a good start for inserting ActiveX controls into your HTML pages. However, if you are already using FrontPage 98, you can use this editor for all your ActiveX needs as well. You can use the following steps to add ActiveX controls to an HTML page using FrontPage 98.

1. Position the cursor at the point in the file where you want to place the control.

2. Click on the Insert menu; then, select ActiveX Control from the Advanced submenu. This action displays the ActiveX Control Properties dialog box, as shown in Figure 11-8.

3. From the Pick a Control drop-down list, select the control that you want to include in your HTML document. (The controls listed reflect those installed on your system and may vary from one computer to another.) After you select the control, the dialog box changes, allowing you to edit the properties of the ActiveX control.

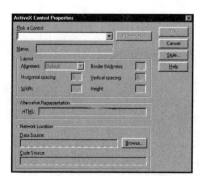

FIGURE 11-8

Select an ActiveX control to insert.

4. Change the properties of the control.

5. Click on OK to insert the control in your document.

Downloading ActiveX Controls

When a browser is connected to your site and accesses a page containing an ActiveX control, it first checks in the Registry on the client machine to see whether the control is already installed. If so, then it is loaded from the local machine. If not, then the browser attempts to download the control from the location specified in your HTML code. This location is specified in the <CODEBASE> tag, which in turn is set as a property within the ActiveX Control Pad. If you don't provide a <CODEBASE> tag, then the browser cannot download and subsequently display the control.

At your site, you should place your downloadable ActiveX controls into your /Scripts directory. You can then provide, as the CODEBASE property for the item, the URL to the control. This technique allows a browser to easily locate the control and download it if necessary.

When a control is downloaded to the user's machine, it is stored in the special ActiveX control cache located in the \windows\occache directory. Depending on the security settings that the user has specified within his or her browser, the user also has the opportunity to accept or reject the downloading of the control before it actually happens.

Additional ActiveX Resources

Because ActiveX represents a new version of older technology, many resources are available. In fact, new books are coming out almost every day. One good candidate is *ActiveX* by Bud Aaron (Prima Publishing, ISBN 0-76150801-5).

You'll also find quite a few online resources for information about ActiveX. The following are a few highlights. (You can also check your favorite Web search engine for more sites.)

ONLINE

◆ **http://www.microsoft.com/activex/** The Microsoft site for ActiveX information.

◆ **http://www.techweb.com/tools/developers/** A site providing lots of information about ActiveX development and tools.

◆ **http://activex.adsp.or.jp/Public/default.asp** This Japan-based site includes both English and Japanese informational documents on how to use ActiveX as a development tool.

◆ **http://www.activex.com/** A source for ActiveX controls that you can download and use at your site.

Chapter 12

Developing Dynamic
Content

—

In This Chapter

◆ Understanding HTML Styles

◆ Understanding Dynamic HTML

Chapter 11 explained how to use scripting languages to create browser-dependent dynamic content. Scripting has been available for quite some time on Web browsers, and a few advances have been put forth to create more dynamic content using existing technologies. This chapter describes additional types of dynamic content that can be used with browser scripting languages.

Understanding HTML Styles

One of the initial complaints about HTML was that the standard allowed the browser to decide how documents where displayed. The first tags were simply ideas of what the author wanted displayed. For example, the header tags, <H1></H1>, tell the browser to display the text between the tags using a level-one heading style. However, the browser's programmer decides how to display a level-one head. The text generally appears with a large font, but it could also be bold or italicized, or simply use a different color. Early HTML didn't provide any way for the author to describe how to display the level-one heading style.

Later revisions of the HTML standard, however, enabled the HTML author to describe the style of a particular tag and added more tags that could be used to change the style of the text. The current HTML specification allows the author to specify the font, color, alignment, and other attributes of a particular selection of text. The only problem with this method is that authors must repeat the attribute instructions every time they use a particular tag. For example, HTML still doesn't enable authors to specify that all level-one heads should appear in bold, green text, which is one reason to use style sheets.

A style sheet gives the author more control over the presentation of a page. Style sheets can specify the font and colors being used, as well as the placement of the various elements. These changes can be assigned to an element and used throughout an HTML page. In fact, you can create a global style sheet and include it in all the HTML pages at your Web site, giving the pages a uniform feel.

Global style sheets are a great benefit when changing the design of a Web site. Instead of going through every page and changing all the elements, making a quick edit of the style sheet will change the background image, default font size, or the color of all the links throughout the entire site.

Using Styles Sheets

Currently, browsers supporting styles support the cascading style sheet (CSS) syntax. Some browsers support additional specifications, but the CSS standard is the most widely accepted standard and should be used for optimum compatibility between browsers.

ONLINE

The current specification can be found at **http://www.w3.org/pub/WWW/TR/ REC-CSS1**. This standard is quite easy to use and can be added to your HTML pages using the <style> tag, as illustrated with the following code:

```
<style type="text/css">

<!—

            style changes go here

—>

</style>
```

In the preceding example, the type element specifies the CSS style. Other types of style sheets can be used, but the CSS standard is used in this chapter. The optional comment tags force browsers not supporting the `<style>` tag to ignore all your styles. This code is normally found at the head of an HTML page just after the title.

Understanding Style Syntax

After you add the `<style>` tag to your HTML page, the next step is to define the attributes of a specific tag by listing the HTML element that you want to change, such as the paragraph <p> element. The following code tells the browser to display all the paragraphs in an HTML page using green text:

```
P{ color:green }
```

To assign multiple properties to an HTML element, separate the elements with a semicolon. The following example changes level-one headings to red and moves the heading 30 points from the left margin:

```
H1{ color:red; margin-left:30pt; }
```

Currently, more than 50 basic properties can be changed using the CSS style specification, so it is a good reference of all the properties to use. The current CSS specification recommendation found at **http://www.w3.org/pub/WWW/TR/RECCSS1** is a good start. Most of these properties are devoted to specifying fonts, colors, and positioning of HTML elements in a page.

Importing Style Sheets

To maintain consistent styles throughout all your documents, you will want to create global style sheet definitions. FrontPage themes, described in Chapter 10, use global style sheets in this fashion. A *global style sheet* is a file that contains style guidelines for an HTML page. The following example is from the coua.css file included with Internet Explorer 4.01.

```
body    { /*background: #FEFEFE; */    /*SMS yellow background*/
            background: #FFFFFF;         /*K2 and Proxy white background*/
            font-size: 75%;              /* K2 and Proxy */
            /* font-size: 70%; */
            font-family: Verdana, Arial, Helvetica, MS Sans Serif  }


a:link   { color: #0000CC; }
a:active    { color: #996699; }
a:visited      { color: #996699; }


p      { margin-top: .6em; margin-bottom: .6em    }
p.bigfix   { margin-top: -.4em; margin-bottom: 0em;}
p.K2   { margin-top: 0em; margin-left: 10pt;}


/*    HEADING TAGS    */
h1   { font-size: 145%;
            margin-bottom: .5em; }


h2   { font-size: 125%;
            margin-top: 1.5em;
            margin-bottom: .5em;  }


h3   { font-size: 110%;
            margin-top: 1.2em;
            margin-bottom: .5em;  }


h4   {font-size: 105%;
            margin-top: 1.2em;
            margin-bottom: .5em  }
```

```
h5   {font-size: 100%;
          margin-top: 1.2em;
          margin-bottom: .5em }


big  {  font-weight: bold;
          font-size: 105%;   }


p.proclabel   { font-weight: bold;
                    font-size: 100%;
                    margin-top: 1.2em }        /*procedure heading*/


/*    LIST TAGS    */
ol   { margin-top: .6em; margin-bottom: 0em; margin-left: 4em }


ul   { margin-top: .6em; margin-bottom: 0em }


ol ul    { list-style: disc; margin-top: .6em   }


li  { margin-bottom: .7em;
          margin-left: -2em }


/*    TERM AND DEFINITION TAGS    */
dl  { margin-top: 0em }


dt  { font-weight: bold;
          margin-top: 1em;
          margin-left: 1.5em   }


dd  { margin-bottom: 0em;            /*not currently working*/
          margin-left: 1.5em   }


dl li   { margin-bottom: .7em }    /*list item inside a term/def list*/


dl dl   {  margin-top: 0em;
          margin-left: 0em   }        /*term/def list inside a term/def list*/
```

```
/*    TABLE TAGS    */
table    { font-size: 100%;
            margin-top: 1em;
            margin-bottom: 1em }


th  { text-align: left;
        vertical-align: bottom;
        background: #dddddd    }


th.center    { text-align: center }


tr  { vertical-align: top }


td  { vertical-align: top;
        /*background: #eeeeee */}    /*no background for K2*/


/*    MISC. TAGS    */
pre      { font-family: Courier;
            font-size: 125%;
            margin-top: 1.2em;
            margin-bottom: 1.5em   }


code   { font-family: Courier;
            font-size: 125%;   }


pre code    { font-size: 100%; }


hr.sms    { color: black; text-align: left   }
    /*SMS specific rule used under procedure title*/


hr.iis  { color: black }
    /*IIS specific - preceding copyright*/
```

This example shows specific style information for most of the commonly used tags in HTML. There are examples of specifying font families as well as positioning properties and colors.

You can find information about using global style sheets along with several examples at Microsoft's CSS Gallery: **http://www.microsoft.com/truetype/css/gallery/entrance.htm**.

After you create the global style sheet, you must use the `link` command to include the style sheet with the HTML page:

```
<link rel="stylesheet" type="text/css"
    href="/styles/coua.css">
```

This command loads the global style definitions located in the coua.ccs file from the styles folder.

NOTE

If you place your global styles sheets in one directory, or one directory hierarchy, multiple Web sites under your control can easily share the style sheets. To use the consolidated directories in multiple Web sites, you can use virtual directories, as explained in Chapter 5.

Browser-Specific Considerations

One of your responsibilities is to make sure that your style sheets work on many different browsers. The constantly changing nature of the Internet essentially guarantees that different versions of the same browser will have different style functionality.

One way to handle compatibility issues is to adhere to the CSS style specification and to use only properties that all browsers support. Another way to handle this problem is to use a script to test which browser, or even version of a browser, is being used and to load the proper style sheet for that browser. The following code illustrates just such a script:

```
<script language="JavaScript">
    TempString = navigator.appVersion
    if (navigator.appName == "Netscape"){
        //use Netscape specific style sheet
        document.writeln('<link rel="stylesheet" type="text/css"
href="/styles/netscape/standard.css">');
    }
    else if (navigator.appName == "Microsoft Internet Explorer"){
        // Check to see if browser is Microsoft
```

```
    if (TempString.indexOf ("4.") >= 0){
        // Check to see if it is IE 4
        document.writeln('<link rel="stylesheet" type="text/css"
href="/styles/explorer/standard4.css">');
    }
    else {
        document.writeln('<link rel="stylesheet" type="text/css"
href="/styles/explorer/standard.css">');
    }
 }
 else
    //use the default style sheet
    document.writeln('<link rel="stylesheet" type="text/css" href="/styles/stan-
dard.css">');
</script>
```

This example enables you to have four separate global styles. The first style sheet is for Netscape Web browsers. The next two styles sheets are for Internet Explorer browsers. (Notice the test to determine which version of Internet Explorer is being used.) The final style sheet is a default for any other browser. The directory structure simply enables you to use a consistent naming scheme for your style sheets.

Understanding Dynamic HTML

Dynamic HTML is a special type of dynamic content and not a generic term for dynamic Web pages. It is actually a part of the HTML 4.0 specification that is partially implemented in Internet Explorer 4.0 and Netscape Navigator 4.0.

You can use Dynamic HTML to modify a document after it has been loaded in a browser, reformatting and displaying the changed HTML page. Before Dynamic HTML, changes of this nature required either communication with a server or the limited use of client-side scripting. Java and ActiveX provide something close to Dynamic HTML. However, these latter methods are more like little blocks in an HTML page; authors have control only over the content in those confines—not over the entire page.

The Dynamic HTML interface controls the entire document and does not require additional components, such as a Java VM or ActiveX controls. Dynamic HTML enables authors to use techniques such as hiding text until a mouse click or some other event signals the browser to display it. You can also revise, reshape, or reformat HTML elements in other ways; for example, you can change the color of the text.

Dynamic HTML relies heavily on an object model, a client-side script, and a browser that understands them both. The Dynamic HTML object model is language independent, allowing any language to be used with the object model, including nonscripting languages such as Java. You can even mix languages within a page. Although mixed-language pages can be confusing to debug, this feature can be useful if you want to convert the content at your Web site to a different language.

Another key component to Dynamic HTML is a style sheet. Most examples of Dynamic HTML, including the examples in this chapter, use styles and style sheets. These two programming elements work together to produce amazing effects.

Understanding the Object Model

The core of Dynamic HTML is found in the object model. An object model defines the interface between the content's author and the content. The Dynamic HTML object model is based on HTML and CSS elements. Almost every HTML element has a corresponding object in the Dynamic HTML object model. Each object can be modified or examined using its properties and methods.

The methods in the Dynamic HTML object model correspond to users' actions such as mouse clicks, mouse movements, and even key presses on the keyboard. These actions, or events, can trigger changes or run user-defined functions. Figure 12-1 shows an HTML page that uses Dynamic HTML. Figure 12-2 illustrates the change in the page when the user clicks on the question "What Is the FTP Service?"

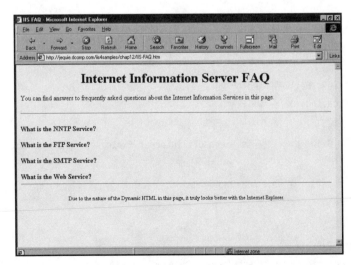

FIGURE 12-1

Dynamic HTML in the Internet Explorer.

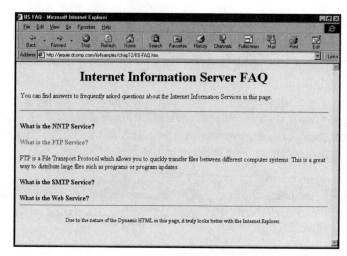

FIGURE 12-2

Clicking on a question displays some of the Dynamic HTML.

This example illustrates a few elements of Dynamic HTML that are discussed in the following sections. The code for IIS-FAQ.htm follows.

```
<!DOCTYPE HTML PUBLIC "-//IETF//DTD HTML//EN">
<html>

<head>
<title>IIS FAQ</title>

<script Language="JavaScript">
//<!—
var ver = 0;

function doInit() {
    var ua = window.navigator.userAgent;
    var msie = ua.indexOf ( "MSIE " )

    if ( msie > 0 )        // is Microsoft Internet Explorer; return version num-
ber
        ver = parseInt ( ua.substring ( msie+5, ua.indexOf ( ".", msie ) ) );
}

function DoOver(color) {
    if (ver >= 4) window.event.srcElement.style.color=color;
```

```
}

function DoOut() {
    if (ver >= 4) window.event.srcElement.style.color="black";
}

function collapseChildren(parentDiv) {
    var i;
    var div = document.all.tags("DIV");

    for (i=0; i<div.length; i++) {
        if (div(i).sourceIndex < parentDiv.sourceIndex)
            continue;
        if (parentDiv.contains(div(i)) != true)
            return;
        if (div(i).className == "Outline")
            div(i).style.display = "none";
    }
}

function ExpandCollapse()
{
    if (ver < 4) return;
    var targetElement, parentDiv;
    i = window.event.srcElement.sourceIndex;
    // is this link already nested in a DIV?
    for (parentDiv = window.event.srcElement.parentElement; parentDiv!=null;
parentDiv = parentDiv.parentElement) {
        if (parentDiv.tagName=="DIV") {
            j=1;
            break;
        }
        if (parentDiv.tagName=="BODY") {
            for (j=1; (i+j) < document.all.length &&
document.all(i+j).tagName=="BR"; j++);
            j+=2;
```

```
                break;
            }
        }
        if (parentDiv==null) {
            for (j=1; (i+j) < document.all.length && document.all(i+j).tagName=="BR";
j++);
            j+=2;
            parentDiv = document.body;
        }


        //make sure element is not off page (test for last link)
        if ( ((i+j)<document.all.length)  && (document.all(i+j).tagName == "DIV")) {


            if ( parentDiv.contains(document.all(i+j))==true
                && (document.all(i+j).className == "Outline") ) {
                targetElement = document.all(i+j);
                if (targetElement.style.display == "none")
                    targetElement.style.display = "";
                else {
                    targetElement.style.display = "none";
                    collapseChildren(targetElement);
                }
            }
        }


    window.event.cancelBubble = true;
}
//-->
</script>
</head>

<body onload="doInit()">

<h1 align="center">Internet Information Server FAQ</h1>
```

<p>You can find answers to frequently asked questions about the Internet
Information Services in this page. </p>

<hr>

<p onmouseover="DoOver('#0099FF')" onmouseout="DoOut()" onclick="if
(ver>=4){ExpandCollapse()};">
<strong>What is the NNTP Service?</strong>
<IMG SRC="whitespot.gif" WIDTH="7" HEIGHT="4">
<div class="Outline" style="DISPLAY: none">

<p>NNTP, or the Network News Transport Protocol, is the protocol
used for Usenet news.This is a popular method for communicating ideas,
and works similar to an electronic bulletin board where you post a message
for everyone to see.</p>

<p>The NNTP Service allows you to set up and control discussions. Visitors
to yournewsgroups will be able to ask questions about your products and services
and getresponses from people within your organization as well as people
that use your products and services.</p>
</div>

<p onmouseover="DoOver('#0099FF')" onmouseout="DoOut()" onclick="if
(ver>=4){ExpandCollapse()};">
<strong>What is the FTP Service?</strong>
<IMG SRC="whitespot.gif" WIDTH="7" HEIGHT="4">
<div class="Outline" style="DISPLAY: none">

<p>FTP is a File Transport Protocol which allows you to quickly transfer files
between different computer systems. This is a great way to distribute large files
such as programs or program updates.</p>
</div>

```
<p onmouseover="DoOver('#0099FF')" onmouseout="DoOut()" onclick="if
(ver&gt;=4){ExpandCollapse()};">
<strong>What is the SMTP Service?</strong>
<IMG SRC="whitespot.gif" WIDTH="7" HEIGHT="4"><br>
<div class="Outline" style="DISPLAY: none">

<p>SMTP is the Simple Mail Transport Protocol which is the
basis of E-mail. IIS includes a really simple SMTP, or E-mail,
service which can be used to help your company communicate with
virtually everyone in the world including visitors to your site
and others within you company.</p>
</div>

<p onmouseover="DoOver('#0099FF')" onmouseout="DoOut()" onclick="if
(ver&gt;=4){ExpandCollapse()};">
<strong>What is the Web Service?</strong>
<IMG SRC="whitespot.gif" WIDTH="7" HEIGHT="4"><br>
<div class="Outline" style="DISPLAY: none">

<p>What do you mean you don't know what a Web Service is?
The Web is everything. It is all inclusive. To many people, the
Web is the Internet.In reality, it is something much simpler it is
a collection of documents which are available for perusal using
the HTTP protocol. Many of these pages are connected using links
which allow client software to quickly navigate to other pages
of information which may include additional information or related
information.</p>
</div>

<hr>
<p align="center"><font size="2">Due to the nature of the Dynamic HTML in this
page, it
truly looks better with the Internet Explorer.</font></p>
</body>
</html>
```

Using Styles with Dynamic HTML

When the IIS-FAQ is first loaded, there isn't a whole lot to see. The browser only shows four questions. However, the HTML page includes answers for the questions. The answers are not displayed because of the style properties that are set to none.

Using styles can make it easier to use Dynamic HTML. In this case, style properties are used with the `<DIV>` element to hide the text that answers a question until the user clicks on the question. The following line changes the style used by the `<DIV>` element:

```
<div class="Outline" style="DISPLAY: none">
```

The display property of the `<DIV>` element is set to none, hiding all the HTML between the `<DIV>` and `</DIV>` tags. JavaScript functions are then called to clear this display property, changing it to "". This default setting displays text normally in the browser, thus enabling the programmer to hide and display text.

The `<DIV>` element is also given a class name: the Outline class. This class name can then be used in the Dynamic HTML code. The `ExpandCollapse` and `CollapseChildren` functions used in this page check to see whether a particular element is an outline. If it is, the function knows that it should change the property of this element.

The class name is a style property, and using multiple classes makes programming Dynamic HTML much easier. For example, the following code defines two classes:

```
<style type="text/css">
    .bluetext {color:Blue; letter-spacing:10px;}
    .yellowtext {color:Yellow}
</style>
```

Using the new classes, you can quickly change any element to use the properties assigned in the class. For example, the following code changes the color of the text between the `<p>` and `</p>` tags to blue when the mouse is over it and then to yellow when the mouse leaves:

```
<p onmouseover="this.classname='bluetext'"
    onmouseout="this.classname='whitetext'">
This text changes color when the mouse passes over it. </p>
```

Using Dynamic HTML Methods

Each question in the IIS-FAQ example is enclosed in <p> tags, but these are defined to use three methods available in Dynamic HTML. These methods appear in the following code:

```
<p onmouseover="DoOver('#0099FF')" onmouseout="DoOut()" onclick="if
(ver&gt;=4){ExpandCollapse()};">
```

Internet Explorer 4.0 is the only browser that currently supports the onmouseover and onmouseout methods. These methods are triggered by the user passing the mouse over the element. When the mouse first comes in contact with an HTML element, the onmouseover method is called if it is available. When the mouse leaves that element, the onmouseout method is called. In the sample, the text in the paragraph will change color when the mouse moves over the text and returns to the original color when the mouse leaves.

The onmouseover method is triggered when the user passes the mouse over the element. In this instance, the DoOver function is called. This function changes the color of whatever element has been assigned the onmouseover method, as shown in the following code:

```
function DoOver(color) {
    if (ver >= 4) window.event.srcElement.style.color=color;
}
```

The onmouseout method is called when the mouse moves away from an element. In this instance, the DoOut function is called; it returns the color of an element to the default text color, as shown in the following code:

```
function DoOut() {
    if (ver >= 4) window.event.srcElement.style.color="black";
}
```

The final method is the onclick method. When the user clicks on the element, this method is called. The onclick method in turn calls the ExpandCollapse function, which goes through a list of HTML elements to determine if they should be shown or hidden.

Creating Browser-Independent Dynamic HTML

Getting your documents to display properly on different browsers is especially difficult with Dynamic HTML. Currently, very few browsers use Dynamic HTML, and those that do, do not have the same capabilities. For example, the onmouseover and onmouseout methods are available only with Internet Explorer.

Several techniques enable you to customize an HTML page to work properly on multiple browsers. In this example, the doInit function is called when the body is loaded. This function tests the browser to see whether it is Internet Explorer 4.0. Dynamic HTML functions and methods use this information to determine whether they should be run. This approach keeps errors from appearing on browsers that don't support specific Dynamic HTML extensions.

Another way to handle different HTML versions is to use an ASP page. This approach allows the server to change the HTML sent to a browser so that the page displays correctly. This solution may be the best one because you can use ASP to strip all the Dynamic HTML from a page going to a browser that doesn't support this feature.

Chapter 13

Working with
CGI Scripts

In This Chapter

◆ Understanding CGI

◆ Creating Your Scripts

◆ Transferring to and from the Server

◆ Writing the Script

◆ Allowing Your Script to Run

Using scripts in Web pages is one way to make your Web site more dynamic. Another way to interact with the visitors to your Web site is through server-side scripting, also referred to as CGI scripts. The user can provide information that's sent by their browser to your server and then processed by the script. The response returned to the user is based on the user's input.

This chapter introduces scripting as implemented on the IIS server. Here you learn the essentials to help you get started. This chapter isn't meant to be the final word in scripting, however. Indeed, entire books have been written on how you can use scripts effectively in Web documents. By the end of this chapter you will know the basics, which can get you up and running right away.

Understanding CGI

The previous chapters have discussed scripts and scripting language as it applies to using the Web browser to work with your content. Before browsers started to handle scripts, Web sites had to rely on the server to handle all interactivity with the visitor. Early Web servers created a standard for enabling a browser to run programs, or scripts, on the server.

The standard developed for writing scripts is called *CGI*, which stands for *Common Gateway Interface*. CGI isn't a programming language; it's a specification for how scripts should be developed. Scripts that conform to this standard are referred to as *CGI scripts*. The actual programming language used to implement the script is irrelevant.

TIP

For more information about the latest version of the CGI specification, check out the information at **http://hoohoo.ncsa.uiuc.edu/cgi/overview.htm**.

ONLINE

Figure 13-1 depicts the relationship between the script, the server, and the browser. Notice that distinct steps occur in these interactions.

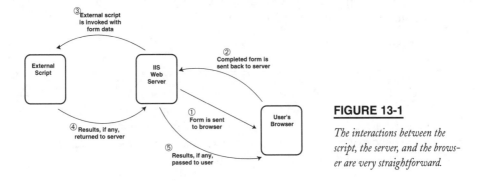

FIGURE 13-1

The interactions between the script, the server, and the browser are very straightforward.

NOTE

Although a form is the most common way to gather information for use with a script, it is not the only way. As long as information passed back to the server follows set guidelines (discussed later in this chapter), the information can come from any source. Chapter 15 contains a sample e-mail ASP that demonstrates passing information without a form.

Creating Your Scripts

What happens after a user submits input from a form? The response is sent from the browser to the server, which then acts on that response. Exactly what the server does with the information depends on the submission method used in your form, as discussed in the following section.

Submission Methods

Data can be passed from a form back to the script at the server in two ways. The submission method is actually a directive to your Web browser as to how it should formulate the response to your server. The server then acts on that response.

If you do not specify a submission method in your HTML code, then the browser assumes that you want to use the GET method. In this method, information passed back to the Web server is stuffed into an environment variable, where it can then be accessed by your script. The other method is the POST method. When your form uses this method, the server passes the information to the script as command-line parameters.

You specify the submission method to be used through the METHOD attribute, which is used with the <FORM> tag. For example, the following single line of HTML code could appear at the beginning of your form:

```
<FORM METHOD="GET">
```

> **TIP**
>
> Even if you want to use the default submission method (GET), you should still explicitly specify the submission method. The reason is that the submission method is up to the browser. You never know when you may run across a browser that doesn't follow the standard.

If you are using an HTML editor, such as FrontPage Editor, then the submission method is generally hidden. That way, you don't need to be concerned with the nitty-gritty detail of HTML code. When you create a form in FrontPage Editor, it defaults to the POST submission method. Thus, FrontPage Editor creates the following line at the beginning of the form:

```
<form method="POST">
```

In most cases, this method is just fine. If you want to use the GET method, however, you need to jump through a few hoops. To change the submission method for a FrontPage Editor form, follow these steps:

1. Right-click anywhere within your form to display a context menu.
2. Choose Form Properties from the context menu to open the Form Properties dialog box.
3. Click on the Options button. The Options for Custom Form Handler dialog box, shown in Figure 13-2, opens.
4. Use the Method pull-down list to change the submission method.
5. Close all the dialog boxes by repeatedly clicking on the OK button.

> **CAUTION**
>
> If you use the <TEXTAREA> tag (which creates scrolling text boxes) in your forms, you shouldn't use the GET method. Remember that this type of form control enables the user to input infinite amounts of text. The GET method then tries to stuff all that data into an environment variable. This approach is a sure recipe for disaster and a way to crash your server. When using a scrolling text box, you should definitely use the POST method.

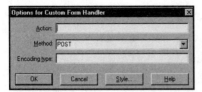

FIGURE 13-2

You can change the submission method used in a FrontPage Editor form.

The submission method being used by your form is always available to your script in the REQUEST METHOD environment variable. The contents of this environment variable will be either GET or POST, depending on your specification. Your program can then check for the method being used and use the necessary means to extract the information desired.

The ACTION Attribute

For your server to know what to do with information received from a form, you need to specify the name of the script it should use. You provide this information with the ACTION attribute, which appears in the <FORM> tag. For example, a fully specified <FORM> tag would appear this way:

```
<FORM METHOD="GET" ACTION="/Scripts/domail.pl">
```

The value assigned to the ACTION attribute is the URL of the executable script file. In this example, the URL is a relative path, which means it's on your server. The program is called domail.pl, which is a Perl script. (Perl is discussed later in this chapter.) You should provide a complete specification for the program name. Thus, if your program has an exe extension, you should include it in the specification; don't assume that the server will use a default extension.

CAUTION

The majority of scripts you execute will reside on your server. You also can specify a fully qualified URL on a different server. Unless you have established a relationship with the Webmaster at the remote server, however, pointing to a different server isn't a good idea. Scripts have a tendency to change periodically, and whatever is passed from the form to the script needs to match what the script expects. If it doesn't, errors can occur. To visitors at your site, the errors appear to be problems with your site, not with the remote script.

Choosing a Scripting Language

In broad terms, you can use almost any programming language you want for your scripts. The programming language should include the following capabilities, however:

- Capacity to access information in environment variables
- Capacity to access parameters on the command line
- Capacity to create 32-bit programs
- Propensity toward linear execution of program code

The first two items are the ways in which information can be passed to your script based on the submission method specified in the form's METHOD attribute. If your language can't handle these items easily, choose another language instead.

The third item refers to the fact that the IIS Web server works only with 32-bit CGI programs. This restriction has to do with memory usage in Windows NT. Sixteen-bit programs are stored in their own virtual machine, separate from 32-bit programs. Thus you need to use a compiler that produces 32-bit executable files for them to work with your forms.

The final capability refers to the design intent of the language. The language you select should be designed for linear execution of your program code. This concept can best be explained with an example. Suppose that your favorite language is Visual Basic. You could use this language for your scripting, but that goes against the original purpose of the language and the way in which scripts are executed. In the first place, Visual Basic's primary use is meant to be just that—visual—using forms and the like. But scripts aren't meant to be visual; they do their work behind the scenes and interface only with your Web server.

Visual Basic is also an event-driven language. When an event happens while the program is running, the code associated with that event is executed. Scripts used in an HTML environment aren't event driven. Instead, they are typically very short and are executed sequentially—in a linear manner. They typically accomplish a specific task (such as processing a few pieces of data) and return information to the server; the information is then passed to the remote browser. For these reasons, a language such as Visual Basic isn't a good choice for your scripting needs.

CAUTION

When choosing an interpreted language, such as Perl, you will need to beware of special permissions to run the scripts. Besides needing to set permissions for visitors to read and run the actual script, you will also need to set up permissions for running the interpreter. Compiled scripts, such as CGI programs written in C, need permission only to run the scripts. Setting permissions is covered later in this chapter.

The two most common languages used for scripting are C (not C++) and Perl. Perl is an acronym for *Practical Extraction and Reporting Language* and was developed primarily for use in scripting. Some of Perl's constructs are reminiscent of C; in addition, Perl has some similarities to the old DOS batch files. The examples in this chapter use the Perl programming language.

ONLINE You can obtain various versions of Perl from several Internet sites. For example, you can find a 32-bit version of Perl designed specifically for use with IIS at **http://www. activestate.com/.** Another place to look is the Windows NT Resource Kit.

NOTE

Don't assume that this chapter or this book provides everything you need to know about Perl. Other books are on the market for that. You can find online information at **http://bones.eandm.co.il/perl/pl-exp-io.html** or at any number of other locations. As you become more adept at writing scripts and your needs become more complex, you will want to invest in a good Perl reference.

Transferring Information to and from the Server

Before you write your script, it's helpful to understand exactly what your script sees when it receives information from the server, as well as how the script should return information to the server. (These are steps 3 and 4 in Figure 13-1.) The following sections explain this process.

What the Script Sees

Regardless of the type of METHOD you designated for use in your forms, your script receives a single string that contains the user input from the form. The length of the string depends on the type of information requested in the form.

 Suppose your form consists of a mailing list sign-up page. This page, which is in the file \Chap13\mail.htm from the support files, appears in 13-3.

When the user clicks on the Join List button, the user's browser compiles the information from the form and sends it as a string to the server. The server then places the string, without change, into an environment variable (QUERY_STRING) that is available to your script. When your script retrieves this environment variable, it may appear as follows:

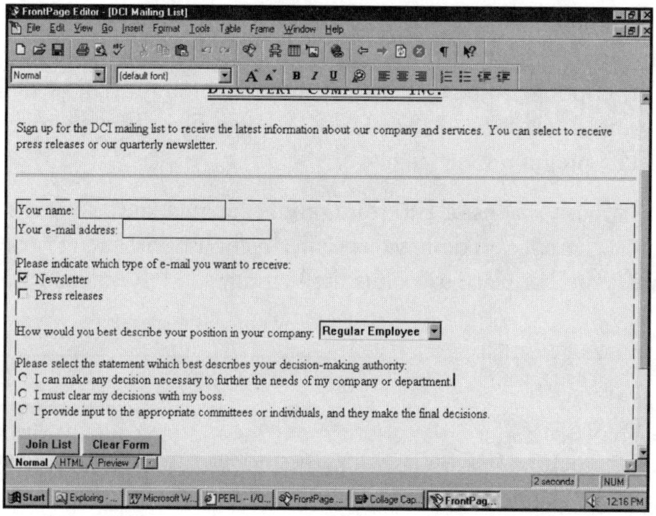

FIGURE 13-3

This form contains several standard controls that accept user input.

```
UserName=John+Doe&UserAddress=jdoe@widget.com&Newsletter=on&Position=Employee&Power
=Partial
```

Notice that I said *may* appear—the exact contents of the string depend on the user's actual input. However, the structure of the information is always the same. The information your script has to work with follows these general guidelines, as defined in CGI guidelines:

♦ The responses are separated by ampersands (&).

♦ The responses appear in the same order in which they appear in your form.

♦ The variable name you specified in your form is the first part of any response.

♦ The second part of any response is an equal sign.

♦ The final part of any response is the value specified by the user.

♦ When you use any on/off form control, such as check boxes or radio buttons, only variables associated with turned-on controls are returned to the script. (Therefore, the default setting for all controls is off.)

♦ All spaces are replaced by plus signs (+).

♦ The responses include escape codes.

These guidelines are pretty straightforward, except perhaps the last one. *Escape codes* are a standard way of treating nonstandard characters. The server, when it detects certain nonstandard characters in a response string, replaces them with escape sequences that define the hexadecimal value of the character. Escape codes come into play predominantly when the user is entering input directly into your form. For instance, if the user types an ampersand into a text field, the server can't pass that ampersand directly in the response string. If it did, your script would think that the end of the response had been reached. Instead, the server replaces the ampersand with a percent sign (%) followed by a two-digit hexadecimal value for the character, as in the following:

```
UserName=John+%26+Mary+Doe&UserAddress=jdoe@widget.com&Newsletter=on&Position=Emplo
yee&Power=Partial
```

Notice the `UserName` response. The user entered `John & Mary Doe`, but the ampersand was passed to your script as %26. Thus, your script must allow for this conversion and return the escape codes to their regular values.

Returning Information to the Server

You can also cause your program to return dynamic information from your script to the user. Thus your program can create HTML pages on-the-fly and feed them back to the user through the IIS Web server. For example, if you used the form presented in the preceding section, you might want to create a confirmation page for the user.

You create dynamic HTML pages by adding `PRINT` statements to your program. The IIS server captures any printed output and passes it along to your user. The only requirement is that you preface the output with two lines. The first contains the following code:

```
Content-type: text/html
```

This line is referred to as the MIME header, which indicates the type of information being transmitted to the remote browser. The server normally adds the MIME header (in the case of your normal HTML documents). However, the information created by your script program is passed directly to the remote browser, without interference by the server. The second line of the header is a blank line. Then you send information exactly as it would appear in a regular Web page.

Writing the Script

After you understand what you receive from the server and how you can create output to send back to the server, you are ready to put your script program together. The following sample program, written in Perl, processes the mailing list request form presented earlier in this chapter:

```perl
# Get the input from the server

if ($ENV{'REQUEST_METHOD'} eq "POST") {
    $Length = $ENV{'CONTENT_LENGTH'};                   # Environment variable con-
tains length of input
    while ($Length) {
        $FORM_DATA .= getc(STDIN);                      # Get characters from
standard input
        $Length--;
    }
} else {
    $FORM_DATA = $ENV{'QUERY_STRING'};
}


# Set initial values for array elements

$MailData{'Newsletter'} = "off";
$MailData{'PressRelease'} = "off";

# Parse the data, saving it into an array

foreach (split(/&/, $FORM_DATA)) {                      # Responses separated by
ampersands
    ($VarName, $Value) = split(/=/, $_);                # Divide at equal signs
    $VarName =~ s/\+/ /g;                               # Replace plus signs with
spaces
    $VarName =~ s/%([0-9|A-F]{2})/pack(C,hex($1))/eg;   # Replace escape codes
    $Value =~ s/\+/ /g;                                 # Replace plus signs with
spaces
    $Value =~ s/%([0-9|A-F]{2})/pack(C,hex($1))/eg;     # Replace escape codes
    $MailData{$VarName} = $Value;
}


# Append parsed data to a text file
# Text file needs to be later processed for inclusion
# in e-mail distribution lists
```

```
$Flag = "yes";
if ($MailData{'UserName'} eq "") {$Flag = "no"}
if ($MailData{'UserAddress'} eq "") {$Flag = "no"}
if ($Flag eq "yes") {
    open(OutFile, '>>/maillist.raw');
    print OutFile "$MailData{'UserName'}\n";
    print OutFile "$MailData{'UserAddress'}\n";
    print OutFile "$MailData{'Newsletter'}\n";
    print OutFile "$MailData{'PressRelease'}\n";
    print OutFile "$MailData{'Position'}\n";
    print OutFile "$MailData{'Power'}\n";
    print OutFile "\n";
    close(OutFile);
}


# Create confirmation page

print "Content-type: text/html\n\n";
print "<HTML>";
print "<HEAD>";
print "<TITLE>Mailing List Confirmation</TITLE>";
print "<HEAD>";
print "<BODY>";


print "<CENTER>";
print "<IMG SRC = \"dcilogo.gif\">";
print "<H1>DCI Mailing List</H1>";
print "</CENTER>";


if ($Flag eq "no") {
    print "We're sorry; your request cannot be processed because";
    print "you have not supplied both a name and an e-mail";
    print "address. Please return to the previous page and try";
    print "again.";
} else {
    print "Name: $MailData{'UserName'}<BR>";
```

```
print "E-mail address: $MailData{'UserAddress'}<P>";
print "<HR>";
print "<P>Thank you for registering for the DCI mailing list.";
print "This is to confirm that you have requested ";
$Getting = "";
if ($MailData{'Newsletter'} eq "on") {$Getting = "newsletters "}


if ($MailData{'PressRelease'} eq "on") {
    if ($Getting ne "") {$Getting = "both " & $Getting & "and "}
    $Getting = $Getting & "press releases ";
}
if ($Getting eq "") {$Getting = "none of our information "}
print $Getting;
print "to be sent to you.";
print "<P>";
print "Thank you for your interest in DCI, and watch your upcoming";
print "mail for more information.";
}
print "<P>";
print "<HR>";
print "<CENTER>";
print "<P>";
print "Send comments to: <A HREF =
\"mailto:Webmaster\@dcomp.com\"><EM>Webmaster\@dcomp.com</EM></A><BR>";
print "Copyright &copy 1997 <A HREF=\"http://www.dcomp.com/DCI/DCI.Htm\">Discovery
Computing Inc.</A> All rights reserved.";
print "</CENTER>";


print "</BODY>";
print "</HTML>";
```

SUPPORT FILE

This Perl program is included in the support files as \Chap13\domail.pl. If you have programmed before, you may notice some similarities between Perl and C. They aren't the same, however, and if you are well-versed in C, you need to take care to watch out for the differences.

This sample program is quite straightforward. Basically, it parses the information passed from the server, writes the information to a text file, and then creates a response to the user. At some later point, a different program will process the text file created by your script program. The reason for using a separate program to process the file is to save time. Remember that you want to provide the response to the user as quickly as possible, and processing the information may take time.

Although this chapter doesn't really explain how to use Perl, you can gather a few pieces of information just from examining this sample program:

♦ Comments begin with the pound sign (#).

♦ Program variables begin with a dollar sign ($).

♦ Variable arrays (such as $MailData) are associative in nature, meaning that the elements of the array can be referenced with text or variable names between the braces ({}).

♦ Information following a print statement is returned to the server (and passed on to the remote browser).

In other respects, programming in Perl is fairly similar to programming in any of the other popular programming languages. You may want to study the program as presented here to get a good idea of what it does and then try to make your own script program.

Allowing Your Script to Run

To run scripts on your IIS system, you first need to set the proper permissions on your /Scripts directory. If you've spent much time configuring your Web server, you may already be aware that the /Scripts directory doesn't really exist—it's a virtual directory.

You need to set permissions in two places—in the Internet Service Manager and in the Windows NT file system. The following sections explain the configuration process.

Configuring IIS for Your Script

As you already know, you configure IIS from the Internet Service Manager. The goal is to configure the directory you use for your scripts to allow execution of your scripts. If the configuration is not correct, an error is generated every time the Web server tries to run a script.

To configure IIS for directory permissions, follow these steps:

1. Open the Internet Service Manager.

2. Click on the box with a plus sign next to the computer name of your Web server to display a list of servers running on that computer.

3. Click on the Default Web Site. A list of directories used by that site appears in the results pane, as shown in Figure 13-4.

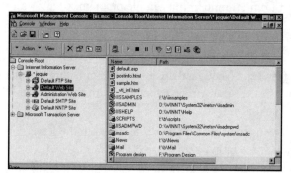

FIGURE 13-4

You can use the Internet Service Manager to control who has access to your directories.

4. In the results pane, right-click on the Scripts directory and select Properties from the shortcut menu to open the Scripts Properties dialog box (see Figure 13-5).

FIGURE 13-5

You change permissions from the Application Settings area of the Virtual Directory tab.

5. Make note of the directory used for your /Scripts directory. (It is located at the top of the box in the Properties sheet.)

6. In the Applications Settings area at the bottom of the dialog box, make sure that only the Execute check box is selected.

7. Click on OK to save your changes.

8. Close the Internet Service Manager.

Configuring Windows NT for Your Script

The second step is to make sure that the security permissions within the operating system are set properly for the directory in which your scripts are located. To configure Windows NT for directory permissions, follow these steps:

1. Browse through your desktop or use Windows NT Explorer to locate the actual directory you are using for your /Scripts directory. (You noted this directory in step 5 in the previous section.)

2. Right-click on the directory and choose Properties from the context menu. The Properties dialog box for the directory opens.

3. Click on the Security tab. The Properties dialog box now appears as shown in Figure 13-6.

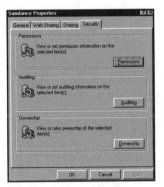

FIGURE 13-6

The Security tab of a directory Properties dialog box controls all aspects of access to the directory.

> **NOTE**
>
> If a Security tab is not available, then the drive is not an NTFS drive. You should convert the drive to NTFS to improve security. See online help for the **CONVERT** command for more information.

4. Click on Permissions. The Directory Permissions dialog box appears, as shown in Figure 13-7.

At this point, you can see the permissions that have been granted for this directory. By default, the only user with permissions is the Everyone group, which has full access to the directory. You *must* change this permission level to secure your site. Use the controls in the dialog box to change the permissions for the directory, its files, and all subdirectories so that the Everyone group has only Read and Execute permissions.

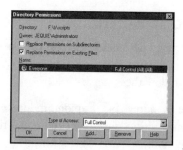

FIGURE 13-7

You have complete control over who has access to folders on your server.

Also, you can add the Administrators group and give that group Full Control permission.

When you're finished, click on the OK button to save your changes, and then close the Properties dialog box for the directory.

Chapter 14

Understanding Active
Server Pages

In This Chapter

♦ What Is ASP?

♦ Writing an ASP Page

♦ The ASP Object Model

♦ The ASP Server Components

One of the primary features of IIS is *Active Server Pages*, or *ASP*. This technology is an exciting feature that opens all sorts of possibilities for producing dynamic Web content in the shortest time possible. This chapter focuses on how you can use ASP to develop content at your site.

What Is ASP?

Active Server Pages is the result of a different way of viewing how servers and browsers should interact, and a response to the proliferation of different scripting languages available on the Web. Essentially, when you utilize ASP, you write scripts in either VBScript or JScript, and then the server takes care to serve only HTML to the browser. (Chapter 11, "Working with Client-Side Scripts," discusses both VBScript and JScript.)

When you include a script in a Web page, the script is normally served to the browser, which then compiles and runs the script. The problem with this scenario is that not all browsers understand all scripting languages, and not all browsers understand the same scripting languages in the same way. ASP removes the uncertainty by using the server to examine both the script and the browser with which it is communicating and then by passing information to the browser in a way that it can understand. The result is that you, as a content developer, can focus on the message that you are trying to convey, rather than on the means used to convey your content.

The ASP technology relies quite heavily on ActiveX controls. Occasionally, you may find reference to ActiveX Server Pages instead of Active Server Pages. Rest assured, however, that they are both the same. The reliance on ActiveX is virtually transparent to you, as a content developer, and to the user. IIS takes care of everything it can behind the scenes so that you don't need to be as concerned with details.

Writing an ASP Page

Creating ASP pages is really quite simple. The only thing that you need to do is save your files using an asp filename extension. Thus, if you would normally save a file as

MyFile.htm, you would now save it as MyFile.asp. The extension tells IIS to process the contents of the ASP file before sending it to the remote browser.

If you want, you can simply rename all your existing HTML files as ASP files; they will be processed just fine. The full functionality of ASP is not apparent, however, until you start to add scripting statements to your ASP files. After you learn the convention by which ASP scripting is added, it is very easy to use. The scripting language itself is, by default, VBScript, although you can use several other scripting languages as well.

Understanding ASP Syntax

When you are creating regular HTML pages, the HTML tags are enclosed with universally understood delimiters that indicate, to the browser, where the tag begins and ends. Consider the following HTML statement:

```
<BODY>
```

The delimiters in this statement are the < and > symbols. They tell the browser, or other application processing the HTML page, to intercept and interpret, but not display, everything between them. The tag itself, **BODY**, is contained within the delimiters.

ASP uses delimiters just as regular HTML does. These delimiters are <% and %>. Everything between these delimiters is interpreted and processed by the server; it is not passed on to the browser, although the output of the statements between the delimiters may be passed to the browser. Consider the following, which is taken from an ASP script:

```
<%For lp = 1 to 5%>
    Pass <%=lp%><br>
<%Next%>
```

This script includes both ASP delimiters and an HTML tag. Everything within the ASP delimiters consists of VBScript statements. This code implements a very simple loop structure. When IIS 4.0 processes this code, it generates the following HTML and passes it to the browser:

```
Pass 1<br>
    Pass 2<br>
    Pass 3<br>
    Pass 4<br>
    Pass 5<br>
```

Whereas a browser could not understand the original ASP file, the same browser has no trouble with the newly generated HTML file. ASP syntax is simple: you decide what processing should be done by your server and then create the code that IIS 4.0 will use to generate the pages it passes to the browser.

Picking an ASP Scripting Language

By default, ASP relies on VBScript as a scripting language. You can, however, use any of a number of other scripting languages, including the following:

- ◆ JScript (JavaScript)
- ◆ Perl
- ◆ REXX
- ◆ Python

Support for both VBScript and JScript is built into ASP, whereas support for the other scripting languages is implemented through Active Scripting plug-ins, which are available from third-party developers.

Changing Scripting Languages within a File

You can use a single scripting language in each file, or you can mix scripting languages. As an example, suppose that you want to include both VBScript and JScript in an ASP file. In this case, you would use the following construct in the ASP file:

```
<html>
<head>
<title>Example of Server-Side Scripting</title>
</head>
<body>

<script language="JScript" runat="Server">
    Response.Write("<p>Now running in JScript</p>")
</script>

<p>Now we are back at regular HTML</p>

<script language="VBScript" runat="Server">
    Response.Write "<p>Currently (" & Time() & ") running VBScript</p>"
</script>
```

```
</body>

</html>
```

Notice the use of the familiar <SCRIPT> tag along with the RUNAT attribute. The LANGUAGE attribute specifies the scripting language to be used, and the RUNAT attribute tells IIS (rather than the browser) to actually run the code. If you run this code (it is included in the support files as \Chap14\mixed.asp) on your IIS server, the server does not pass the scripts on to the browser. Instead, the browser is served the following:

```
<html>

<head>

<title>Example of Server-Side Scripting</title>

</head>

<body>


<p>Now running in JScript</p>


<p>Now we are back at regular HTML</p>


<p>Currently (10:48:17 AM) running VBScript</p>


</body>

</html>
```

Notice that this code is straight HTML; it contains no scripting language. IIS took care of the translation. Therefore, all browsers, not only those that understand the scripting languages used, can view the page. Figure 14-1 shows what the page looks like in a browser.

NOTE

The original ASP file did not use Document.Write to create output for the user. Instead, it used the Response.Write method. The reason is simple: At the time the server is translating the script, no document exists; the document object exists in the browser, not at the server. Thus to create user output, you must rely on the Response object, as described later in this chapter.

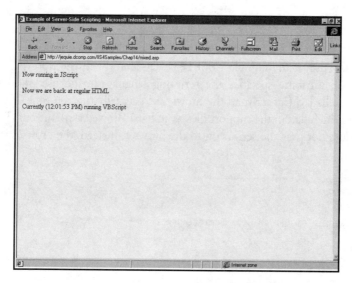

FIGURE 14-1

You can mix different scripting languages in the same ASP file.

Changing the Scripting Language for an Entire File

Rather than specify individual scripts to be processed at the server, you can also change the primary scripting language used in an entire file. (ASP uses the primary scripting language to parse anything between the <% and %> delimiters.) Exactly how you change the language depends, however, on the nature of the language to which you are changing. ASP relies on using an object, method, and property syntax, as described later in this chapter. If the scripting language that you want to use also uses this same type of syntax, then you can specify a different scripting language for the file by including a statement at the beginning of your file that indicates your preference. The following example tells IIS that you want to use JScript:

```
<%@ language = JScript %>
```

Remember that the scripting language change applies only to the current ASP file. You can mix and match scripting languages across your files, thereby leveraging any investment that you may have in your current script files without having to rewrite or translate them to another language.

When you are changing the primary language for the file, you need to keep a few things in mind. First, you should make the change on the first line of the file, and the change should be the only thing done on the line. (In other words, don't put any other statements between the <% and %> delimiters.) You should also adhere to the exact syntax shown in the example; make sure to add a space between the @ symbol and the `language` keyword.

Universally Changing the Scripting Language

As you already know, VBScript is the default language for ASP files. If you are dead-set against using VBScript, you can universally change the default scripting language used by a Web site or virtual directory. To make a universal change, follow these steps:

1. Open the Internet Service Manager.

2. Select the Web site or virtual directory that you want to change.

3. Right-click on the site or directory and select properties to open the Properties dialog box.

4. Select either the Home Directory tab for a Web site or the Virtual Directory tab for a virtual directory. The dialog box will look similar to Figure 14-2.

FIGURE 14-2

Directory information such as the default scripting language for ASP.

5. In the Application Settings section, click on the Configuration button to open the Application Configuration dialog box.

6. Select the App Options tab to access ASP configuration information, as shown in Figure 14-3.

7. In the Default ASP language field, enter the name of the scripting language that you want to be the default for your directory or Web site.

8. Click on OK to close the Application Configuration dialog box.

9. Click on OK to close the Directory or Web site properties dialog box.

10. Close the Internet Service Manager.

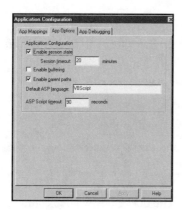

FIGURE 14-3

App Options settings determine the default scripting language used by ASP.

The ASP Object Model

To use some of the advanced features of ASP, such as the ASP server components discussed later in this chapter, you need to understand the ASP object model. If you know how to program in Visual Basic, in any of its various forms, you are probably already familiar with this object model.

Basically, you do your work using a series of objects. These objects are typically files or logical devices, but they can also be logical objects created by DLL files loaded on your server. Most objects need to be created by using the `Server.CreateObject` function. For example, the following command line creates an object used with the Advertisement Rotator component described later in this chapter:

```
Set MyAd = Server.CreateObject("MSWC.AdRotator")
```

In this case, the object that is created is named `MyAd`, and the `Server.Create Object` function relies on the `MSWC.AdRotator` DLL to create the object. After an object is created, you can use the properties and methods ascribed to the object. *Properties* are attributes or data belonging to the object, and *methods* are built-in functions that enable you to perform some action on or with the object. Different objects have different properties and methods, and trying to describe the universe of what is available would easily fill several volumes.

TIP

For more in-depth information on objects and their uses, you should refer to a good programming reference. Pick a book on Visual Basic, and you can find much of the information that you can apply to your work with ASP.

IIS 4.0 also includes a number of built-in objects that are unique to the environment created with ASP. These objects are *intrinsic,* meaning that they don't need to be created in order to be used; they exist automatically, waiting to be used in your scripts. The following sections describe the six built-in objects.

The Application Object

In the ASP environment, an application is defined as all the ASP files in a virtual directory or its subdirectories. Thus, if you create an IIS virtual directory to contain a group of ASP files, then those files constitute an application. The Application object enables you to communicate and share information among the various elements of the application. (The elements are the individual ASP files.)

The Application object uses only two methods: Lock and Unlock. These methods ensure singular access to the Application object by the current element. In this way, the data space maintained by the Application object is not corrupted by multiple elements trying to update the data space at the same time.

You can store values in the Application object in the following manner:

```
<% Application.Lock
    Application{"MyValue") = "This is my value."
    Application.Unlock %>
```

Notice the use of the Lock and Unlock methods in conjunction with actually setting the value. In this instance, you created a variable named MyValue, which now contains the value This is my value. You can then use MyValue in any other element (ASP file) in the application area. Consider the following example:

```
<% Application.Lock
    Application{"TotalVisits") = Application{"TotalVisits") + 1
    Application.Unlock %>
```

Each time the server executes this code, the TotalVisits variable is incremented by one. You can then use the following code, in any element of the application, to tell the user how many visits have been made to the ASP application:

```
<p>You are visitor <%=Application{"TotalVisits")%> to this site!</p>
```

The Lock and Unlock methods are not used here because the variable is not being changed, it is simply being read. You need to use Lock and Unlock only when you are changing the data, which is when the potential of data corruption creeps into the picture.

The Request **Object**

When a browser communicates with a server, the browser frequently passes information to the server. This information is stored in a collection of data, and that collection can be accessed by using the **Request** object. The syntax is as follows:

```
Request.Collection(varname)
```

in which *Collection* is the name of the data collection and **varname** is the variable name that you want to access. The **Request** object enables you to access variables in the following collections:

- ◆ **ClientCertificate** Contains information returned in a secure sockets layer transaction. This collection is filled out only when the browser accesses a page using the https (not http) protocol.
- ◆ **Cookies** Contains the information retrieved from the cookies files on the user's machine by the browser.
- ◆ **Form** Contains the information passed from a form when the user clicks on the Submit button in the form.
- ◆ **QueryString** Contains the information passed in an HTTP query. This information appears after the question mark in a query request.
- ◆ **ServerVariables** Contains the settings of environment variables on the server.

Different collections enable you to access different variables, which depend not only on the nature of the data being accessed but also the type of remote browser and what the user has done.

> **NOTE**
>
> The usage of collections and variables can be quite extensive. The information here should be considered a general guide only. For additional information on variables, refer to the online ASP help files.

The Response **Object**

Just as the **Request** object enables you to access information passed from the browser, the **Response** object enables you to send information to the browser. Primarily, you can use it in this version for setting the value of a cookie on the machine on which the browser is running.

NOTE

A *cookie* is a data file, stored on the user's machine, that contains configuration information. As a content developer, you decide which information is stored in the file. When the user visits your site at a later date, you can then access the cookie and retrieve the configuration information. Possible uses include user-configured home pages at your site and a list of user preferences.

If you want to use the Response object to set cookie values, you use the Cookies collection with the object. (Cookies is the only collection currently defined for the object.) These may be set for all kinds of information, but only if the browser supports cookies. For example, suppose that you want the cookie to contain the date on which the user visited your site. You could use the following:

```
<%Response.Cookies(MySite) = Now()%>
```

In this case, the name of the cookie file at the browser is MySite, and you can use this name to check for a cookie file elsewhere in your program (using the Request object, as described in the previous section).

Using different properties of the Response object (instead of the Cookies collection), you can also set different attributes of the HTML output that you are creating with the object. You can use the following properties with the Response object:

- ◆ Buffer Specifies whether the output is to be buffered or sent without buffering.
- ◆ ContentType Indicates the HTTP content type of the information being created.
- ◆ Expires Indicates the length of time before a page cached on the user's browser should be discarded.
- ◆ ExpiresAbsolute Indicates the date and time after which a page cached on a user's browser should be discarded.
- ◆ Status Specifies the value of the status line to be returned by the server.

In addition, you can use several different methods with the Response object. These include the following:

- ◆ AddHeader Specifies the HTML header value to use.
- ◆ AppendToLog Appends information to the end of the Web server log entry for this HTTP request.

♦ `BinaryWrite` Sends information to the HTTP channel without any translation.

♦ `Clear` Dumps any information contained in the output buffer.

♦ `End` Stops processing of the current ASP file and returns a result.

♦ `Flush` Sends any buffered information to the HTTP channel immediately.

♦ `Redirect` Sends a redirect message to the browser, which should cause it to connect to a different URL. (Not all browsers support redirect messages.)

♦ `Write` Sends the value of a variable, as a string, to the current HTTP channel.

The `Server` Object

The `Server` object enables you to access properties and methods that the server itself maintains. You learned about the most common `Server` object method, `Server.CreateObject`, earlier in this chapter. Other available methods include the following:

♦ `HTMLEncode` Applies HTML encoding to a specified string.

♦ `MapPath` Converts a virtual path to a physical path on the server.

♦ `URLEncode` Applies URL encoding to a specified string.

You can also set the `ScriptTimeout` property, which specifies the amount of time, in seconds, that a script can run before it times out. (The default timeout value is 90 seconds.)

The `Session` Object

When a user establishes a connection to the IIS server, a session is established. As long as that user remains connected and a timeout does not occur, then the session remains active. The `Session` object enables you to store information about the current user session. The information remains available for the entire session but is discarded when the session ends.

One of the most common uses for the `Session` object is to store configuration information unique to the current session. For instance, suppose that you read a cookie from the user. The information in the cookie can then be stored in the `Session` object, and you can access it at any time in any application page that the user may open or reload.

NOTE

`Session` object information is maintained only for sessions in which the browser supports cookies.

You store information in the `Session` object in virtually the same way as you do with the `Application` object. For example, to create a session variable that contains the country or state in which the user is located, you could use the following:

```
<%Session("Location") = "CO"%>
```

Of course, if you were loading the information from a cookie, you would use the proper `Request` object methods to retrieve the information and then set the session variable.

Several `Session` object properties are available. The first, `SessionID`, determines the identification number assigned by the server to this particular session. Another, `Timeout,` changes the default session timeout. The default value is 20 minutes, but if you wanted to change the timeout value to 10 minutes, you could use the following code:

```
<%Session.Timeout = 10%>
```

The `ObjectContext` **Object**

The `ObjectContext` object was added to IIS 4.0 to work with the Microsoft Transaction Server (MTS). This simple object has only two methods and two events.

When an ASP page uses the `Transaction` directive to run a database transaction using MTS, you can use the `ObjectContext`'s `SetComplete` and `SetAbort` methods to control the transaction. These methods generate the events `onTransactionCommit` or `onTransactionAbort`, which tells IIS to look for corresponding functions in your ASP.

A good example is an order-taking ASP file. The file has an order form that the user fills in. When the order is processed, the information is sent to the server. The server checks the inventory on hand. If the database reports that the item is out of stock, you can use the `SetAbort` method to cancel the order, which triggers the `onTransactionAbort` event. Your ASP file may include an `onTransactionAbort` function that tells users the item is out of stock and asks whether they want to place a back order.

The ASP Server Components

IIS also includes a group of ASP server components, which you can use to extend what you can do with your ASP pages. These components enable you to create dynamic, interactive Web pages without the need for complex programming. IIS features the following server components that you can use in your scripts:

- ◆ Advertisement Rotator component
- ◆ Browser Capabilities component
- ◆ Collaboration Data Objects for Windows NT Server
- ◆ Content Linking component
- ◆ Database Access component
- ◆ File Access component

These components are discussed in some detail in the following sections. A few other components are available and mentioned in Microsoft's documentation. For the most part, these components are more applicable to running the Personal Web Server. You can find more components for downloading, including a hit counter component, at Microsoft's Web site:

ONLINE ▶ **http://backoffice.microsoft.com/downtrial/moreinfo/iissamples.asp**

The Advertisement Rotator Component

This ASP component is very helpful for Web sites that rent advertisement space on a page. The component automatically rotates between a series of advertisements every time the page is opened or reloaded. The actual advertisement information is stored in a text file (called a *Rotator Schedule file*), which can be updated on-the-fly. Consequently, as your advertisements change, you need to change only the Rotator Schedule file, not the actual ASP file used to generate the Web page. Optionally, you can use a Redirection file to record clicks on the advertisement. (This feature is very helpful in billing the advertiser according to the number of hits taken.)

To use the Advertisement Rotator component, you must first create an object that represents the component. For example, the following line of code creates the `MyAd` object:

```
<%Set MyAd = Server.CreateObject("MSWC.AdRotator")"
```

After the object is created, you can use the `GetAdvertisement` method to return the full HTML information for the ad:

```
<%= MyAd.GetAdvertisement("/adverts/current.txt")%>
```

In this case, the /adverts/current.txt file is the Rotator Schedule file. When IIS 4.0 encounters this line, it replaces it with a full HTML statement that represents the ad to be displayed.

The Rotator Schedule File

The Rotator Schedule file indicates the ads to be displayed by the Advertisement Rotator component. The file is specified in the `GetAdvertisement` method, as described in the previous section. The file is nothing but an ASCII text file, which you can create with any text editor, such as NotePad.

The Rotator Schedule file contains two sections, separated by a line consisting of nothing but an asterisk. Although each element of the first file section is optional, the line with the asterisk is required. The following code is an example of a Rotator Schedule file:

```
REDIRECT /source/redirect.asp
WIDTH 440
HEIGHT 60
BORDER 0
*
/ads/gravy.gif
http://www.bigcorp.com/sauce/gravy.htm
Let us do the gravy work
2
/ads/bignews.gif
http://www.newscorp.com/
Check out today's headlines as they happen
5
/ads/dciad.gif
http://www.dcomp.com/
We provide help when you need it
3
```

The first part of the file, before the line with asterisk, contains four optional parameters. The first, `REDIRECT`, indicates the URL of the DLL or ASP file that will handle redirection for the ad; this parameter is the address of the Redirection file, as discussed in the following section.

The second line, WIDTH, indicates how many pixels wide the ads will be. If you omit WIDTH, the default is 440 pixels. The third line specifies the height of the ad, again in pixels. If you omit this parameter, the default height of 60 pixels is used.

The final line in the first section specifies a border width for the graphic. If you don't include the BORDER specification, then a border of 1 pixel is assumed.

The second part of the Rotator Schedule file contains the records, each four lines long, that specify the ads to be used. The first line of each record is the URL for the graphic to be used in the ad; the second is the URL to which the graphic is to be linked. If there is no linking URL, then you should replace the URL with a dash.

The third line of each record is the text to use as an alternative to the graphic. This feature is particularly useful for site visitors who don't use a graphic browser or who have their graphics turned off.

The final line of the advertisement record indicates the percentage of the time that the ad should be played. The Advertisement Rotator component examines the Rotator Schedule file, finds out the total of all these indicator lines, and then determines a percentage based on the number noted for this particular record. The preceding sample file has three advertisement records, and the indicator lines are 2, 5, and 3. Therefore, the first add is played 2/10, or 20 percent of the time; the second ad is played 5/10, or 50 percent of the time; and the third ad is played 3/10, or 30 percent of the time.

The Redirection File

The Redirection file is an optional file that you can use to process a jump to the URL associated with an advertisement. The Redirection file is indicated in the Rotator Schedule file, as discussed in the previous section. The file can either be a DLL or an ASP file. Unless you feel very proficient programming DLL files, you should consider creating a simple ASP file to process redirection.

NOTE

You need to include a Redirection file only if you want to process the URL jump in some way. Normally, you would redirect only if you want to track which ads were clicked and how often.

The following very simple Redirection file is saved as an ASP file:

```
<%Response.Redirect(Request.QueryString("url"))%>
```

This code simply grabs the URL from the query string and redirects the browser to that location. Normally, the preceding example would be the final line of the Redirection file, following other script lines that examine the query URL and then save it or some other value in a text file. You could then use the text files to bill your advertisers according to the number of clicks on their ads.

The Browser Capabilities Component

This ASP component is invaluable in determining how you can interact with a remote browser. Under regular scripting methods (as described in Chapter 13, "Working with CGI Scripts"), you must plan for the worst-case scenario and include all types of code in your Web pages—especially if you want all the browsers that may access your site to understand your pages.

The ASP Browser Capabilities component makes your task much easier. You can use this component to directly test the capabilities of the remote browser and then make decisions based on those capabilities. The component compares the information automatically passed by the browser in the User Agent HTTP header to a list of browser names stored in the BROWSCAP.INI file. If the component finds a match, it sets the object properties to the values contained in the INI file. If it doesn't find a match, then it uses the default values in the INI file. Finally, if no default values are specified in the INI file, then the values are set to the string "UNKNOWN".

To use the Browser Capabilities component, you use code similar to the following:

```
<%Set browser = Server.CreateObject("MSWC.BrowserType")%>
```

You can then use the following properties of the browser object in your scripting:

- ◆ `browser` The name of the browser as determined from the User Agent HTTP header.
- ◆ `version` The browser version.
- ◆ `frames` TRUE if the browser supports frames.
- ◆ `tables` TRUE if the browser supports tables.
- ◆ `backgroundsounds` TRUE if the browser supports background playing of sounds.
- ◆ `vbscript` TRUE if the browser understands VBScript.
- ◆ `jscript` TRUE if the browser understand JavaScript or JScript.

The values assigned to these properties come from the file BROWSCAP.INI, which is stored at \winnt\system32\inetsrv\. This file can also contain other values; its contents are entirely up to you. The following code is a portion of the default BROWS-CAP.INI file included with IIS 4.0:

```
;;;;;;;;;;;;;;;;;;;;;;;;;;
;;; Microsoft Browsers ;;;
;;;;;;;;;;;;;;;;;;;;;;;;;;


;;;;;;;;;;;;;;;;;;;;;;;;;;;;;;;;;;;;;;;;;;; IE 1.x
[IE 1.5]
browser=IE
version=1.5
majorver=1
minorver=5
frames=FALSE
tables=TRUE
cookies=TRUE
backgroundsounds=FALSE
vbscript=FALSE
javascript=FALSE
javaapplets=FALSE
beta=False
Win16=False


[Mozilla/1.22 (compatible; MSIE 1.5; Windows NT)]
parent=IE 1.5
platform=WinNT


[Mozilla/1.22 (compatible; MSIE 1.5; Windows 95)]
parent=IE 1.5
platform=Win95
```

Remember that this code segment is only the first part of the BROWSCAP.INI file; the entire file is approximately 24 pages long. Each browser record begins with the User Agent HTTP header information, followed by property and value pairs, which the Browser Capabilities component uses for that browser.

You can use any regular text editor to change the contents of the BROWSCAP.INI file. The only tricky part of the file is the User Agent HTTP header, which is the part within brackets at the beginning of each browser definition. If you have questions about how to put these together, check your log files to see what is captured there and then compare the header information to the HTTP specification at **http://www.w3.org**.

ONLINE

Collaboration Data Objects for Windows NT Server

The Collaboration Data Objects (CDO) for Windows NT Server is a collection of objects that you can use in ASP files to send and receive messages. A complete list of the objects follows:

◆ `AddressEntry` Holds information about the sender of a message.

◆ `Attachment` Enables you to add an object, such as a file to a message.

◆ `Attachments` Holds a collection of Attachment objects.

◆ `Folder` Accesses an Inbox or Outbox where messages are stored.

◆ `Message` Manages the actual e-mail document.

◆ `Messages` Holds a collection of Message objects.

◆ `NewMail` Creates a message without creating a new Session object.

◆ `Recipient` Contains information such as an e-mail address for the intended receiver of the message.

◆ `Recipients` Holds a collection of Recipient objects.

◆ `Sessions` Connects your application to the e-mail system; the main CDO object.

These rather generic objects work together to create e-mail messages. Basically, you create a **Session** object to start the e-mail services and log on to an e-mail server. Then you create `Messages` that have an `AddressEntry` and Recipients. The newly created `Messages` are turned over to the e-mail server for delivery. An example ASP program using CDO appears in the next chapter.

The Content Linking Component

The Content Linking component creates an automatic table of contents for a series of Web pages. The pages are then linked together, much like the pages of a physical book. This feature enables a user to click on a Next or Previous button, automatically placed on an ASP page, to view other pages in the series.

The Content Linking component relies on the contents of a Content Linking List file, which contains URLs and descriptions of pages for use in the table of contents. To use the component, you would use the following code:

```
<%Set toc = Server.CreateObject("MSWC.Nextlink")%>
```

After the `toc` object (in this example) has been created, you can use a wide variety of methods to return the URLs or descriptions stored in the Content Linking List file. The methods that you can use include the following:

- `GetListCount` Counts the number of entries in the Content Linking List file.

- `GetListIndex` Returns the index of the current page in the Content Linking List file.

- `GetPreviousURL` Returns the URL of the previous page in the Content Linking List file.

- `GetNextURL` Returns the URL of the next page in the Content Linking List file.

- `GetNthURL` Returns the URL of the nth page in the Content Linking List file.

- `GetPreviousDescription` Returns the description of the previous page in the Content Linking List file.

- `GetNextDescription` Returns the description of the next page in the Content Linking List file.

- `GetNthDescription` Returns the description of the nth page in the Content Linking List file.

The information in the Content Linking List file is stored as regular ASCII text, and the file can be named anything you like. Each line in the file represents a Web page and can hold up to three tab-separated fields. The first field, which is mandatory, is the relative URL of the page. The second field is the description of the page, and the third field is any comments that you want to note about the page. The following code is an example of a Content Linking List file:

```
page1.htm [^t] Overview of services

page2.htm [^t] Description of personnel[tab]Includes latest roster

page3.htm [^t] References[tab]Updated by John

page4.htm [^t] Testimonial letters

page5.htm [^t] Ordering information
```

In this example, the [^t] symbol represents the presence of a tab character. When you are creating the Content Linking List file, press the Tab key to indicate that you are starting a new field.

To use the Content Linking component methods in your ASP file, you may want to do something like the following:

```
<% If (toc.GetListIndex("content.txt") > 1) Then %>

    <a href = "<%=toc.GetPreviousURL("content.txt")%>">

    <img src = "/pictures/previous.gif"></a>

<% Else %>

    <img src = "/pictures/placeholder.gif">

<% End If %>

<a href = "\default.htm"><img src = "/pictures/mainmenu.gif"></a>

<% If (toc.GetListIndex("content.txt") < toc.GetListCount("content.txt")) Then %>

    <a href = "<%=toc.GetNextURL("content.txt")%>">

    <img src = "/pictures/next.gif"></a>

<% End If %>
```

In this example, the Content Linking List file is content.txt, which is stored in the same directory as the page containing this code. The example does nothing more than display active graphics for Previous, Main Menu, and Next. The Previous and Next graphics are displayed only if they are appropriate for the location of the current page in the Content Linking List file.

The Database Access Component

The Database Access component provides access to databases external to your server through *ActiveX Data Objects* (ADO) technology. You can use the component to access simple text-based databases, such as delimited text files.

> **NOTE**
>
> To access other types of databases, such as Access or SQL databases, you should use the Internet Database Connector (IDC) as described in Chapter 18.

A complete description of how to use ADO in relation to the Database Access component is beyond the scope of this chapter. For more information on the many ADO methods and properties, refer to the ASP online help for the ActiveX Data Objects reference.

The File Access Component

The File Access component provides access to file input and output functions through the `FileSystemObject`. The object provides the normal functions to open, close, read, and write files. This component is useful if you need to store state information but don't want the overhead associated with a database. The component works with text files (plain ASCII files), which you use the same as you would in any programming language. Because you can use the File Access component to read any ordinary text file, you may use it to create a "tip of the day" or some such rotating information garnered from a text file stored on disk.

Chapter 15

Putting Active Server
Pages to Work

———

In This Chapter

♦ Designing the ASP

♦ Working with Server Components

♦ Using ASP for Browser-Specific Content

♦ Debugging ASP

Chapter 14 explained the use of ASP. This chapter covers the implementation of ASP by describing how to use ASP to meet the needs of one particular Web site. This sample ASP uses components supplied with IIS to handle e-mail.

Designing the ASP

The most critical step in any type of programming or content creation is the design process. Spending a little bit of time concentrating on design issues can save a lot of time down the road. The basics to designing an ASP can be applied to any programming problem. This section goes through the process of designing a very simple, yet useful, ASP.

Determining Prerequisites

Even before beginning to design the ASP, you need to consider the following four steps: defining the problem, deciding on requirements, determining the platform, and deciding on a language.

Defining the programming problem is always quite easy for the author of a book. The problem is that the author needs an example to use and generally borrows a solution that has worked in real life. In this case, I've chosen to create an ASP that enables a visitor to the Web site to fill out a survey and subscribe to a newsletter.

In real life, defining the problem can take a lot of thought. The main purpose of defining the problem is to determine requirements. The *requirements* are a set of specifications that describe what you want to do. When all the requirements are met, the project is finished and you can go home. In this example, the requirements are that the results of a survey need to be e-mailed to Joe over in the survey-taking department.

The next step is to determine the platform. I've decided that all the examples in this chapter will be ASP examples, but you may want to consider the other avenues available before creating an ASP. This book describes several alternatives, including CGI scripting, ISAPI DLLs, and even client-side scripting.

When you take a look at the requirements for this project, it is easy to see that one could decide on using a CGI script. CGI scripts have been used for years to meet the main requirement of sending an e-mail message. In fact, an appropriate sample PERL script is described in Chapter 13.

However, using ASP may be a much better solution than the alternatives. The rationale is that the PERL script requires finding and installing a copy of PERL as well as an e-mail program. IIS includes an SMTP server, which may or may not have been installed, and some ASP components make it a snap to use this SMTP server to send e-mail. Other factors you need to consider include security and performance issues.

The final prerequisite is to decide on a language. Almost all programming tasks can be undertaken in various languages. Using ASP is no different. The two main choices are VBScript and JScript, but other scripting languages can be used as well. The example in this chapter uses VBScript.

Designing a Form

Designing a form can be quite easy. The best way to start is with a list of items that need to be on the form. In this example, the form is for a simple survey. The information being requested is the favorite type of widget and where widgets are being purchased.

While designing the form, I decided to use the form to ask the person being surveyed to sign up for the company's mailing list. This adds a few requirements that were originally unforeseen, but dealing with change is part of the design process. You can never tell when a new feature is going to be requested. Incorporating changes is usually easy early in the design phase. After you design the form, you can create it quickly with an HTML editor such as FrontPage. The final form appears in Figure 15-1.

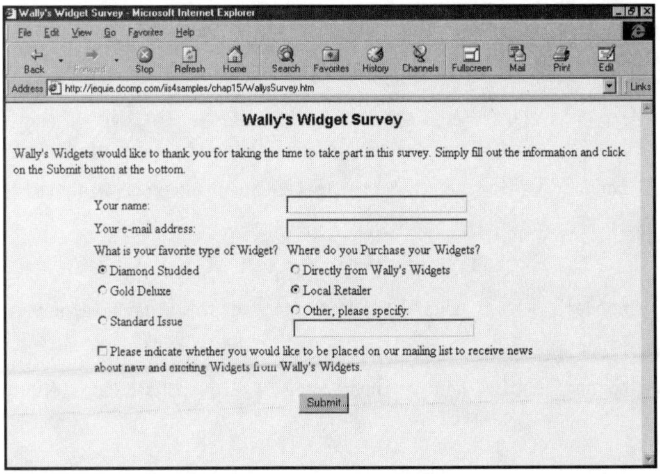

FIGURE 15-1

Wally's Widget Survey form is created for use with ASP.

The actual mechanics for creating a form are described in Chapter 9 and aren't repeated here. The code follows.

```
<html>
<head>
<title>Wally's Widget Survey</title>
</head>

<body bgcolor="white" topmargin="10" leftmargin="10">
<!— Display Header —>
<font size="4" face="Arial, Helvetica"><b>
<p align="center">Wally's Widget Survey</b></font></p>

<p>Wally's Widgets would like to thank you for taking the time to take part in
this survey. Simply fill out the information and click on the Submit button at the
bottom.</p>

<form method="POST" action="widgettally.asp">
  <table width="75%" align="center">
    <tr>
      <td>Your name:</td>
      <td><input type="text" name="Name" size="30"></td>
    </tr>
    <tr>
      <td>Your e-mail address: </td>
      <td><input type="text" name="EmailAddress" size="30"></td>
    </tr>
    <tr>
      <td style="border: medium none">What is your favorite type of Widget? </td>
      <td style="border: medium none">Where do you purchase your Widgets?</td>
    </tr>
    <tr>
      <td style="border: medium none"><input type="radio" value="diamond" checked
      name="WidgetType">Diamond Studded </td>
      <td style="border: medium none"><input type="radio" name="Supplier"
```

```
value="direct">Directly
      from Wally's Widgets</td>
    </tr>
    <tr>
      <td style="border: medium none"><input type="radio" value="gold"
name="WidgetType">Gold
      Deluxe </td>
      <td style="border: medium none"><input type="radio" name="Supplier"
value="retailer"
      checked>Local Retailer</td>
    </tr>
    <tr>
      <td align="top" style="border: medium none"><input type="radio"
name="WidgetType"
      value="standard">Standard Issue </td>
      <td style="border: medium none"><input type="radio" name="Supplier"
value="other">Other,
      please specify:<br>
        <input type="text" name="OtherSupplier" size="30"> </td>
    </tr>
    <tr>
      <td colspan="2"><input type="checkbox" name="MailingList" value="ON">Please
indicate
      whether you would like to be placed on our mailing list to receive news
about new and
      exciting Widgets from Wally's Widgets. </td>
    </tr>
  </table>
  <div align="center"><center><p><input type="submit" value="Submit"
name="Submit"></p>
  </center></div>
</form>
</body>
</html>
```

Defining an ASP

The final step is to create an ASP to process the form and create an e-mail message to Joe, who is going to tally the survey.

The first step in processing the form is to verify the information being sent from the form. For example, if the user selects to receive e-mail but doesn't include an e-mail address, the form isn't complete and needs more information.

The second step is to decide on the format of the message being sent to Joe. These specifications would have been decided in the prerequisites stage.

The ASP can now be created quite quickly. The following is the listing of the widgettally.asp:

```
<%
'get variables
Name = Request.Form("Name")
EmailAddress = Request.Form("EmailAddress")
WidgetType = Request.Form("WidgetType")
Supplier = Request.Form("Supplier")
OtherSupplier = Request.Form("OtherSupplier")
MailingList = Request.Form("MailingList")


Sub SendMail()
  message = ""


  Dim myMail
  Set myMail = Server.CreateObject("CDONTS.NewMail")


  myMail.From = EmailAddress
  myMail.To = "gpease@dcomp.com"
  myMail.Subject = "Widget Survey"


  message = Name & " likes to use " & WidgetType & " widgets which"
  message = message & " are purchased from "
  If Supplier = "other" then
    message = message & OtherSupplier & "."
  else
    message = message & Supplier & "."
```

```
      end if
      If MailingList = "ON" Then
        message = message & " " & Name & " wants to be on the mailing list."
      End If
      myMail.Body = message

      myMail.Send
End Sub
%>
<html>

<head>
<title>Survey Confirmation</title>
</head>

<body bgcolor="white" topmargin="10" leftmargin="10">
<!—  Display Header —>
<font size="4" face="Arial, Helvetica"><b>

<p align="center">Wally's Widget Survey</b></font></p>
<%
If (MailingList = "ON" and EmailAddress = "") Then
   Response.Write("We're sorry; your request cannot be processed because ")
   Response.Write("you need to supply an e-mail address to be on the mailing ")
   Response.Write("list. Please return to the previous page and try again.")
Elseif (Supplier = "other" and OtherSupplier = "") Then
   Response.Write("We're sorry; your request cannot be processed because ")
   Response.Write("you did not specify the other supplier that you use to ")
   Response.Write("purchase your widgets. Please return to the previous page ")
   Response.Write("and fill in the blank for the other supplier.")
Else
   SendMail()
   Response.Write("<P>" & Name)
   Response.Write(", thank you for participating in our survey.")
   If MailingList = "ON" Then
      Response.Write("We will keep you informed of new developments as you ")
```

```
        Response.Write("have requested with e-mail sent to " & EmailAddress)
    End If

    Response.Write("</P>")
End If


%>


<hr>
```

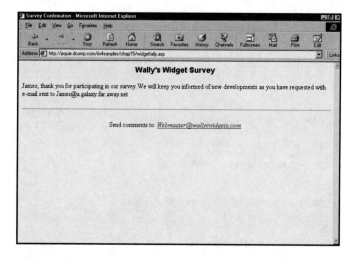

FIGURE 15-2

The ASP displays a confirmation page when done.

```
<p align="center">Send comments to: <a href="mailto:Webmaster@wallyswidgets.com">
<em>Webmaster@wallyswidgets.com</em></a><br>
</p>
</body>
</html>
```

This script uses the `NewMail` component of the Collaboration Data Object (CDO) included with IIS 4.0. This component is quite different from the other CDO components, which are described in the next section. The `NewMail` object is designed for creating a quick and easy message with very few lines of code. Unlike the other objects, most of the properties can only be written. You cannot look up, or read, the values assigned to the different `NewMail` properties.

The sample ASP shows several `NewMail` object properties that are familiar to anyone with experience using e-mail. These include properties such as `Name`, `To`, `From`, and `Subject`. These properties can be assigned values that may or may not be received from a Web browser and the message sent. In the sample program, the `Subject` is set by the ASP and not by the user of the browser.

Working with Server Components

The previous section described some of the process behind designing an ASP. One of the purposes of describing the design process is to point out that creating an ASP is more involved than creating an HTML page. ASPs provide an excellent way to create applications. Server components were included with IIS to facilitate the creation of ASP applications. This section describes how to use some of the server components to create an ASP application.

Chapter 14 describes the server components that currently ship with IIS. You can find newly developed components at Microsoft's Web site:

ONLINE ▶   **http://www.microsoft.com/iis/**

NOTE

The examples in this section assume that the SMTP server is installed and running.

This section explains how to use CDO to access the IIS SMTP server through ASP. As distributed, the SMTP server does not include any client software to access e-mail messages. However, CDO enables you to easily access e-mail messages using IIS and a couple of ASPs.

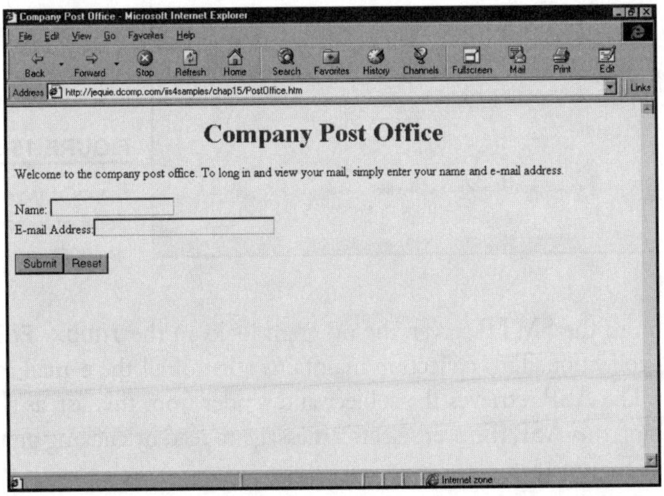

FIGURE 15-3

A simple form to access e-mail.

Using the SMTP.ASP Example

The smtp.asp file uses the CDO components included with IIS to access the SMTP server. Before a connection can be made, the program needs to get a display name and e-mail address from the user. It does so with the very simple form shown in Figure 15-3.

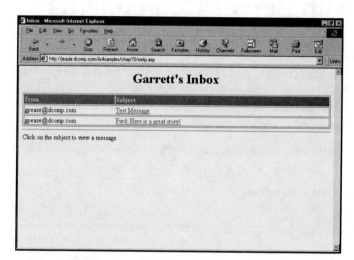

FIGURE 15-4

A user can click on a message's subject to see the message.

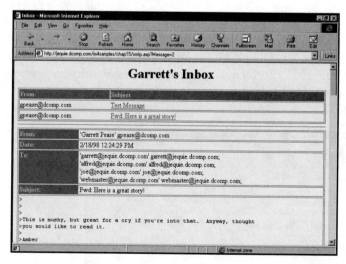

FIGURE 15-5

E-mail messages are shown on the same page as the Inbox list.

After logging on to the SMTP server, the program looks in the `Inbox Folder` at the `Messages` collection. This collection maintains a list of all the e-mail messages for the address. The ASP retrieves the subject and sender from this list, as shown in Figure 15-4. Using this ASP, the user selects a message to read by clicking on the subject, as shown in Figure 15-5.

The code for the application listed here is described in the following sections.

```
<%
'initialize a session
Dim mailSession
Dim mailInBox
Dim mailMessages

If (Session("SessionUserName") = "") Then
  If Request.Form("Name") > "" Then
    Session("SessionUserName") = Request.Form("Name")
    Session("SessionUserAddress") = Request.Form("Address")
    BeginMailSession
  End If
Else
  BeginMailSession
End If

Sub BeginMailSession()
  Set mailSession = Server.CreateObject("CDONTS.Session")
  mailSession.LogonSMTP Session("SessionUserName"), Session("SessionUserAddress")
  Set mailInbox = mailSession.Inbox
  Set mailMessages = mailInbox.Messages
end Sub
%>

<html>
<head>
<title>Inbox</title>
<style type="text/css">
<!--
th  { text-align:left; vertical-align:top;
      background:#008080; color=#00FFFF;}
-->
</style>

</head>
```

```
<body bgcolor="white" topmargin="10" leftmargin="10">
<h1 align="center"><%=mailSession.Name%>'s Inbox</h1>


<%
  Dim i

  If mailMessages Is Nothing Then
    Response.Write("There is an error with the mail server.")
  ElseIf 0 = mailMessages.Count Then
    Response.Write("You don't have any messages.")
  Else
    Response.Write("<table border=1 width=100% bordercolor=#008080 frame=box
rules=rows>")
    Response.Write("<col width=30% ><col width=70% >")
    Response.Write("<thead><tr><th>From</th>")
    Response.Write("<th>Subject</th></tr></thead><tbody>")
    For i = 1 to mailMessages.Count Step 1
      Response.Write("<tr><td>" & mailMessages.Item(i).Sender.Address & "</td>")
      Response.Write("<td><a href='smtp.asp?Message=" & i & "'>")
      Response.Write(mailMessages.Item(i).Subject)
      Response.Write("</a></td></tr>")
    Next
    Response.Write("</tbody></table>")
  End If
%>


<hr>
<%
If Request.QueryString("Message") > "" Then
  msgNumber = CInt(Request.QueryString("Message"))
  Response.Write("<table border=1 width=100% bordercolor=#008080 frame=box
rules=rows>")
  Response.Write("<col width=20% ><col width=80% >")
  Response.Write("<tr><th>From:</th>")
```

```
Response.Write("<td>")

Response.Write("'" & mailMessages.Item(msgNumber).Sender.Name & "' ")

Response.Write(mailMessages.Item(msgNumber).Sender.Address)

Response.Write("</td></tr>")

Response.Write("<tr><th>Date:</th>")

Response.Write("<td>")

Response.Write(mailMessages.Item(msgNumber).TimeReceived)

Response.Write("</td></tr>")

Response.Write("<tr><th>To:</th>")

Response.Write("<td>")

Set msgRecipients = mailMessages.Item(msgNumber).Recipients

For i = 1 to msgRecipients.Count

   Response.Write("'" & msgRecipients.Item(i).Name & "' ")

   Response.Write(msgRecipients.Item(i).Address & "; ")

   if i < msgRecipients.Count then Response.Write("<br>")

Next

Response.Write("</td></tr>")

Response.Write("<tr><th>Subject:</th>")

Response.Write("<td>")

Response.Write(mailMessages(msgNumber).Subject)

Response.Write("</td></tr>")

Response.Write("<tr><td colspan=2 leftmargin=10><pre>")

Response.Write(mailMessages(msgNumber).Text)

Response.Write("</pre></td></tr>")

Response.Write("</table>")

Else

  Response.Write("Click on the subject to view a message.")

End If


%>


</body>
</html>
```

Logging on to the SMTP Server

As described earlier, the first step to creating a CDO-based application is to log on to the e-mail server by retrieving logon information from the client. The information is provided from a form: the `Request.Form`. This object enables you to quickly retrieve information that was sent from a form with the `POST` method.

In this example, the information is stored in an `IIS Session` object, which should not be confused with its CDO counterpart. The `IIS Session` object is created when a client first connects with IIS. This object enables you to maintain information while the client goes to another Web page. The SMTP session could be stored in the `IIS Session` object, but that can be a bit confusing.

After retrieving the display name and e-mail address from the form, the `BeginMailSession` procedure is called. This procedure creates the `CDO Session`, or connection with the SMTP server, with the following code:

```
Set mailSession = Server.CreateObject("CDONTS.Session")

mailSession.LogonSMTP Session("SessionUserName"), Session("SessionUserAddress")
```

The first line creates the `Session` object. The second line uses the `LogonSMTP` method to log on with the display name and e-mail address provided by the user.

In addition, two variables are initialized to make it easier to handle the CDO objects. The CDO objects used in this example belong to a hierarchical relationship, or object model. The root of the objects is the `Session` object, in this case the `mailSession` variable.

To access the Inbox, you can simply refer to it in terms of the `mailSession`— `mailSession.Inbox`. This step doesn't require too much typing, but it soon gets out of control, because the syntax to access the messages in the Inbox is `mailSession.Inbox.Messages`. Therefore, object variables are used to represent the Inbox, `mailInbox`, and the `Messages` collection, `mailMessages`.

Displaying Available Messages

All e-mail messages sent to the SMTP server are stored in one physical location. However, the `Session` object can access only messages that are sent to its logon address. These messages are available to the programmer through the `Folder` object. The `Session` object has an `Inbox` property that can be used to quickly access the messages stored by SMTP.

All messages for the user are stored in the `Inbox.Messages` collection. In the sample code, the messages are available through the `mailMessages` variable. When the ASP first loads, the script checks `mailMessages` variable to see whether it is

`Nothing` or it failed to find any messages. Next, the script checks for messages. If messages are waiting, the script goes through the collection and displays the sender and subject.

Understanding the Message Object

The `Message` object is perhaps the most important object in the CDO collection. This object contains the message text as well as address information to get the message to its destination. A complete list of the `Message` object's unique properties follows.

- ◆ `Attachments` A collection of Attachment objects that can be sent with a message.
- ◆ `ContentBase` A string describing the type of content, used for MIME HTML, or MHTML support.
- ◆ `ContentID` Another string used for MHTML support. This string inspects Content-ID headers of incoming messages.
- ◆ `ContentLocation` A string used for MHTML support. This string describes the Content-Location header for the MIME body part.
- ◆ `HTMLText` A string that stores the text of an e-mail message with HTML formatting.
- ◆ `Importance` A value between 0 and 2; 0 represents low importance, and 2 is for high importance.
- ◆ `MessageFormat` A number that is either 0 for a MIME message or 1 for uninterrupted plain text.
- ◆ `Recipients` A collection of Recipient objects describing who the message was sent to.
- ◆ `Sender` An AddressEntry object describing the message's sender, including the sender's name and e-mail address.
- ◆ `Size` A long type value representing an approximate size of the message in bytes.
- ◆ `Subject` A string storing the subject of the message.
- ◆ `Text` A string that stores the text of an e-mail message without formatting.
- ◆ `TimeRecieved` A variable set to the time and date the message was received.
- ◆ `TimeSent` A variable set to the time and date the message was sent.

This particular script uses only a few of the `Message` properties. To start, the script uses the `Sender` and `Subject` properties to retrieve the name and e-mail address of the sender, as well as the subject of the message. These strings are displayed in a client-side form. You can easily add other fields to the form to display when the message was received or the message's size.

Sending Information to an ASP without a Form

One of the purposes of the ASP is to enable the user to read the messages in the Inbox. The script turns the `Subject` of the message into a hyperlink that points back to the ASP, as shown in the following code snippet:

```
Response.Write("<td><a href='smtp.asp?Message=" & i & "'>")
Response.Write(mailMessages.Item(i).Subject)
Response.Write("</a></td></tr>")
```

In this bit of code, `i` represents the index of the message. This value is sent to the server using the CGI GET syntax: `filename?Variable=value`. This is the same as using a form with a `GET` method. In this case, the string is created manually so that a form with its associated buttons is not required.

At the start of the script, the `Response.Form` object retrieves information sent from a form with the `POST` method. When the message value is sent, the `Response.QueryString` object retrieves the index value of the message.

Reading a Message

The server-side script at the bottom of the ASP displays the requested message. The first task is to see whether a message index was sent to the form. If a message has not yet been requested, the script displays instructions on how to read messages. (Refer to Figure 15-4.)

When a message has been requested from the user, the script uses various `Message` properties to display the message in a form on the Web page. The `Sender` property retrieves information such as the display name and e-mail address of the sender. The script even goes through the list of recipients and displays the name and address of everyone else receiving the message.

NOTE

When displaying the straight text message, you must use a tag, such as the `<pre>` tag, to tell the browser to display the text with its formatting intact. Otherwise, the text will all run together on the browser and be hard to read.

As a final note, text of the message can be displayed in a couple of ways. When the SMTP server stores a message, it is accessible in both HTML and plain text formats. If the message was sent in one format, the server still makes it available in both formats. This example retrieves the straight text of the message. This approach increases performance for the browsers' of slower computers.

Using ASP for Browser-Specific Content

One of the more useful things that as ASP can do is to serve up only HTML that a client's browser can understand. Several examples in this book use HTML comments and client-side scripting to provide the developer with better control over what HTML the browser sees. As an alternative, the developer can control what the browser sees by using ASP, which runs on the server.

One of the built-in server components that ASP can use is the `Request` component. This component enables the ASP programmer to access all server variables, including the `HTTP_USER_AGENT`, through the `ServerVariables` collection. This variable describes the client being used to access the Web site.

The following code examines the `HTTP_USER_AGENT` variable to determine which Web browser is being used. The script then adds the proper HTML to load an appropriate style sheet for that browser.

```
<%
    TempString = Request.ServerVariables("HTTP_USER_AGENT")
    If Left(TempString,9) = "Mozilla/4" Then
        'the browser supports style sheets
        Response.Write("<link rel='stylesheet' type='text/css' ")
        If InStr(TempString,"MSIE 4") > 0 Then
          'the browser is the Internet Explorer
          Response.Write("href='/styles/ie/standard.css'>")
        Else
          Response.Write("href='/styles/standard.css'>")
        End If
    End If
%>
```

One thing to be wary of when dealing with this variable is the values that are reported by the different browsers. For example, Netscape Navigator 4.0 reports that it is

"Mozilla/4.02 – (WinNT; I)," whereas Internet Explorer 4.01 is listed as "Mozilla/4.0 (compatible; MSIE 4.01; Windows NT)".

You can also use this test with Web search engine robots and spiders. (Search engines are described in Chapter 8.) Different robots report HTTP_USER_AGENTS that can be used to determine what HTML is sent using code similar to the preceding sample. For example, a search robot may report that it is "URLSeeker/1.01b."

Debugging ASP

One step that is often overlooked when creating Web content is the debugging process. ASPs are a bit more complicated than standard HTML and may require some work to get them to work properly. Even the best programs have typing errors and other bugs; ASPs are no different. IIS 4.0 includes a script debugger that you can use to debug ASPs.

IIS ships with the script debugger, but it may not have been installed. The debugger is a stand-alone program that is listed in the Program menu. Appendix A includes information for installing IIS components.

To debug an ASP, simply start the debugger on your IIS machine and select Running Documents from the View menu. This allows you to select any of the currently running ASPs to debug. If the ASP that you wish to debug is not listed, you can open the file in a Web browser.

You can then use the debugger to display variables and run code one line at a time to determine what is happening behind the scenes. However, the debugger only reports information and cannot be used on its own to fix your scripts; several other programs are required to work with it.

The first two required programs are fairly obvious. IIS is required to run the script and send information to a Web browser. The Web browser is another required program that is used to request the ASP to be debugged.

The other required program is an editor such as Notepad or FrontPage. The debugger does not allow you to change the code; you must use a separate editing program. When you discover a bug, you load the file into the editor, edit the file, and save it. Then the file can be loaded from the Web server again and tested some more.

Chapter 16

Working with ISAPI

In This Chapter

◆ What Is ISAPI?

◆ Creating Your Own ISAPI DLLs

◆ A Sample Extension DLL

◆ A Sample ISAPI Filter

◆ Using Microsoft Visual C++

In the past several chapters, you have learned how to extend the capabilities of your server by using dynamic content at your site. CGI scripts and scripting languages enable you to go beyond the "static content" that is so prevalent on the Web. This chapter introduces another programming feature that can extend the capabilities of your server—ISAPI.

What Is ISAPI?

ISAPI (pronounced "eye-zappy") is essentially a programmer's interface for IIS. ISAPI is an acronym for *Internet Services Application Programming Interface*, and it was developed jointly by Process Software Corporation and Microsoft. The primary purpose of ISAPI is to provide a high-performance alternative to CGI scripts, which tend to run fairly slowly. The primary reasons for CGI's low speed are that:

◆ Each CGI request spawns a new process, which can be both slow and resource intensive.

◆ Scripting programs are interpretive; that is, the source code for the script is parsed and executed every time it's loaded.

If you have a low-volume Web site and a fast computer, the delays associated with CGI scripts won't be that noticeable. However, if you're running a medium- or high-volume site, the delays accumulate over a number of users and can seriously degrade overall performance. This condition is particularly true when the users are sending multiple simultaneous requests to the same CGI scripts.

ISAPI was developed to overcome these problems. The Internet server API enables you to create two types of programs:

◆ Extension DLLs

◆ ISAPI filters

Even though the names don't explicitly indicate it, both types of programs are created as DLLs. *DLL* is an acronym for *dynamic link library*, and it provides a way to make common program code available to a number of programs. In the case of ISAPI DLLs, however, the program code is made available only to the IIS Web server.

Both types of ISAPI programs have specific characteristics and purposes, as discussed in the following sections.

Extension DLLs

ISAPI programs that are created as extension DLLs are designed to handle requests from the IIS Web server (see Figure 16-1). Indeed, the DLL capabilities provide extensions to the base IIS Web server, thus the name *extension DLL*. In most cases, extension DLLs are essentially equivalent to fast CGI scripts.

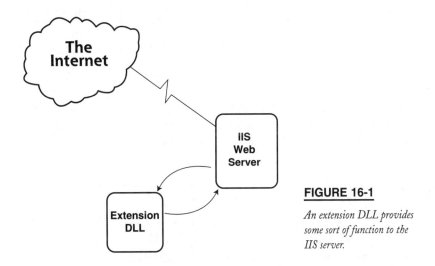

FIGURE 16-1

An extension DLL provides some sort of function to the IIS server.

An extension DLL has several advantages over a traditional CGI script program. The biggest advantage is that the DLL is loaded into memory when it is first accessed and remains in memory where it can be accessed over and over. Therefore, your DLL can be called quite quickly by the server. This approach eliminates the need to spawn another process and then translate a script program. The result is faster overall performance for medium- to heavy-load Web sites.

One possible disadvantage exists to using the DLL approach, however. If you create an extension DLL and it crashes (for whatever reason), the address space in which the DLL is operating often becomes corrupted and unstable. Because the DLL can operate in the same address space as the Web server, the potential exists for the Web server to crash also. For this reason, you should always test your extension DLLs quite thoroughly before using them.

ISAPI Filters

You can also use ISAPI to create a special type of DLL called an *ISAPI filter*. This DLL goes beyond a traditional CGI script in that an ISAPI filter actually sits between the Internet (or intranet) connection and the Web server, quietly acting as an intermediary (see Figure 16-2).

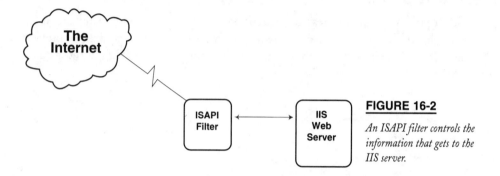

FIGURE 16-2

An ISAPI filter controls the information that gets to the IIS server.

You typically create an ISAPI filter if you want to provide some sort of encryption, decryption, or authentication on messages received for the Web server or if you want to process the information sent to the log files.

Creating Your Own ISAPI DLLs

Creating your own DLL—extension or filter—is no small task. Indeed, you need to be fairly proficient at programming to undertake such a project. It isn't the purpose of this section to describe in detail how to code a DLL. Instead, you should refer to detailed programming texts that can help you out in this area. When you know how to program a DLL (in general), you can use the information in this section to make your DLL ISAPI compliant.

TIP

If you decide to create your own DLLs, you can get some help from Microsoft SDKs (Software Developer's Kits) that contain pertinent source code files. Microsoft has recently placed its platform SDKs in one location so that they are easier to find. You can download the Microsoft SDKs you need, such as the Internet SDK, from **http://www.microsoft.com/msdn/sdk/bldenv.htm**.

Most DLLs are written using C or C++, and to create a DLL, you must have a compiler that uses the Win32 API. Good examples of acceptable compilers are those marketed by Microsoft, Watcom, or Borland. The DLL sample code provided in this chapter should work with any of these compilers.

A Sample Extension DLL

When you create an extension DLL, you are creating a function or series of functions that you can then call from the IIS Web server. Consequently, you can do almost anything your heart desires through the use of extension DLLs.

The sample extension DLL that you create in this section will help you understand how DLLs work. This DLL returns a fully formatted Web page to the browser; the page provides information about the system on which the Web server is running. For instance, you may have a Web page that has an About This Server button or link. When the user selects the option, the extension DLL is invoked and the system information is automatically sent to the user's browser.

The sample source code for this extension DLL is available in the support files. The directory (on the FTP site) is \Chap16, and the files that you need are as follows:

- **Info.c** The source code for the sample extension DLL
- **Info.def** The definitions file for the DLL
- **Info.dll** The compiled, ready-to-run version of the DLL
- **Makefile.mak** The MAK file you can use to compile Info.c yourself
- **Infotest.htm** A sample Web page that shows how to call the extension DLL

Understanding the DLL

If you load the Info.c file from the support files, you can take a look at the source code for the DLL:

```
/////////////////////////////////////////
// Info.c
// Internet Information Server 4 Administrator's Guide
// Discovery Computing Inc.
//
// This extension DLL sends information about the server to a client
```

```c
#include <windows.h>
#include <winnt.h>
#include <stdio.h>
#include <httpext.h>


/////////////////////////////////////
// Function prototypes
// These functions are used to turn some system information
// into a more intelligible formation.
CHAR *ProcessorType(DWORD);
CHAR *ProcessorArchitecture(DWORD);


/////////////////////////////////////
// GetFilterVersion
//
// Required function. This sets the DLL up so it works with
// IIS by registering for the PREPROC_HEADERS events
BOOL WINAPI GetExtensionVersion( HSE_VERSION_INFO * pVer)
{
    pVer->dwExtensionVersion = MAKELONG( 1, 0 );
    strcpy( pVer->lpszExtensionDesc,
        "Server Information" );

    return TRUE;
}



/////////////////////////////////////
// HttpFilterProc
//
// This is the main function that gets information about the
// server and sends the information to the calling client
//
// There aren't any line feeds so the information is readable
// here, but if you view the source of the HTML output
// from your browser, it is all on one line and hard to read.
```

```
//
DWORD WINAPI HttpExtensionProc( EXTENSION_CONTROL_BLOCK * pECB)
{
    CHAR achBuffer[2000];      // can add several more rows
    CHAR achCurrentRow[250]; // largest line is currently < 150
    OSVERSIONINFO osVersion;
    SYSTEMTIME stTime;
    SYSTEM_INFO siSysInfo;
    CHAR achServerBuffer[4096];
    DWORD dwServerBufferSize;
    BOOL bResult;

    //start the buffer with the header and title of the table
    sprintf(achBuffer,
            "Content-Type: text/html\r\n\r\n"
            "<html>"
            "<header>"
            "<title>Server Information</title>"
            "</header>"
            "<body>"
            "<center>"
            "<h1>Server Information</h1>"
            "<table width=\"75%%\">");

    //Add rows for the version of NT running
    osVersion.dwOSVersionInfoSize = sizeof(OSVERSIONINFO);

    if (GetVersionEx(&osVersion)){
        sprintf(achCurrentRow, //Verision
                "<tr>"
                "<th align=left>Windows NT Version</th>"
                "<td align=right>%u.%u</td>"
                "</tr>",
                osVersion.dwMajorVersion,
                osVersion.dwMinorVersion);
        strcat(achBuffer,achCurrentRow);
```

```
    sprintf(achCurrentRow, //Build information
            "<tr>"
            "<th align=left>  Build</th>"
            "<td align=right>%u</td>"
            "</tr>",
            osVersion.dwBuildNumber);
    strcat(achBuffer,achCurrentRow);
    sprintf(achCurrentRow, //Miscellaneous version info
            "<tr>"
            "<th align=left>  Miscellaneous</th>"
            "<td align=right>%.128s</td>"
            "</tr>",
            osVersion.szCSDVersion);
    strcat(achBuffer,achCurrentRow);
}


//Add a row for the server version
dwServerBufferSize = sizeof(achServerBuffer);
bResult = pECB->GetServerVariable(pECB->ConnID, (LPTSTR) "SERVER_SOFTWARE",
                achServerBuffer, &dwServerBufferSize);
if (bResult && achServerBuffer[0]){
    sprintf(achCurrentRow,
            "<tr>"
            "<th align=left>Server:</th>"
            "<td align=right>%s</td>"
            "</tr>",
            achServerBuffer);
    strcat(achBuffer,achCurrentRow);
}

//Get system information
GetSystemInfo(&siSysInfo);

//Add a row for the system architecture
sprintf(achCurrentRow,
        "<tr>"
```

```
        "<th align=left>Processor Architecture:</th>"
        "<td align=right>%s</td>"
        "</tr>",
            ProcessorArchitecture(siSysInfo.dwOemId));
strcat(achBuffer,achCurrentRow);


//Add a row for the number of processors and type
sprintf(achCurrentRow,
        "<tr>"
        "<th align=left>%u Processor(s)</th>"
        "<td align=right>%s</td>"
        "</tr>",
            siSysInfo.dwNumberOfProcessors,
            ProcessorType(siSysInfo.dwProcessorType));
strcat(achBuffer,achCurrentRow);


//get time
GetSystemTime(&stTime);
//Add rows for the time and date
sprintf(achCurrentRow,
        "<tr>"
        "<th align=left>Local Time</th>"
        "<td align=right>%02u:%02u</td>"
        "</tr>"
        "<tr>"
        "<th align=left>Local Date</th>"
        "<td align=right>%02u/%02u/%02u</td>"
        "</tr>",
            stTime.wHour, stTime.wMinute,
            stTime.wMonth, stTime.wDay, stTime.wYear);
strcat(achBuffer,achCurrentRow);


//Add end of page
sprintf(achCurrentRow,
        "</table>"
```

```
                "<hr>"
                "<address>For more information contact "
                //Change e-mail address here
                "<a href=\"mailto:webmaster@mydomain.com\">"
                "webmaster@mydomain.com</address>"
                "</center>"
                "</body>"
                "</html>");
        strcat(achBuffer,achCurrentRow);


        if ( !pECB->ServerSupportFunction( pECB->ConnID,
                        HSE_REQ_SEND_RESPONSE_HEADER,
                        "200 OK", NULL,
                        (LPDWORD) achBuffer)
            ) return HSE_STATUS_ERROR;


        return HSE_STATUS_SUCCESS;
}



/////////////////////////////////////////
// ProcessorType
// Takes the DWORD for the processor type and translates
// it into a string for output.
//
CHAR *ProcessorType(DWORD dwProcessorType)
{
    switch (dwProcessorType){
    case PROCESSOR_INTEL_386:
        return "386";
    case PROCESSOR_INTEL_486:
        return "486";
    case PROCESSOR_INTEL_PENTIUM:
        return "Pentium or 586";
    case PROCESSOR_MIPS_R4000:
        return "MIPS";
```

```
        case PROCESSOR_ALPHA_21064:

            return "ALPHA";

    default:

            return "Unknown";

    }

}



///////////////////////////////////////

// ProcessorArchitecture

// Takes the word for the architecture and translates

// it into a string for output.

//

CHAR *ProcessorArchitecture(DWORD dwOemId)

{

    //WORD wArchitecture;

    //wArchitecture = dwOemId.wProcessorArchitecture;



    switch (dwOemId){

    case PROCESSOR_ARCHITECTURE_INTEL:

        return "Intel";

    case PROCESSOR_ARCHITECTURE_MIPS:

        return "MIPS";

    case PROCESSOR_ARCHITECTURE_ALPHA:

        return "ALPHA";

    case PROCESSOR_ARCHITECTURE_PPC:

        return "Power PC";

    case PROCESSOR_ARCHITECTURE_UNKNOWN:

        return "unknown";

    default:

        return "unknown";

    }

}
```

Notice that the DLL code includes two primary functions: GetExtension-Version and HttpExtensionProc. These two functions are the minimum that are expected by the IIS Web server. Without them, the DLL won't function or an error will be generated. A third "required" function for the ISAPI standard is `TerminateExtension`. Although your DLL will work just fine without `TerminateExtension`, you may want to include it to handle unloading the DLL from memory. This function allows the DLL complete any unfinished business before being unloaded.

The IIS Web server calls the `GetExtensionVersion` function when your extension DLL is first loaded. This function returns a version number for your DLL, as well as some optional text information about the DLL. For this reason, `GetExtensionVersion` is very, very short. If you forget to include the function, however, your DLL will not function at all with the Web server.

The `HttpExtensionProc` function is the main entry point for processing done by your DLL. In the Info.dll example, this function creates the HTML output. If you omit this function from your DLL, then the Web server will not know how to invoke your program.

An extension control block facilitates communication between your DLL and the server. This data area, which is described later in this chapter, is defined in the HTTPEXT.H, as described in the following section.

The Header Files

The beginning of the sample DLL presented in the previous section uses four header files:

```
#include <windows.h>
#include <winnt.h>
#include <stdio.h>
#include <httpext.h>
```

If you have programmed in C for the Windows environment before, most of these should look familiar. The first three header files are provided with your C compiler. The one header file that may not be familiar is HTTPEXT.H. This file, which is included with Visual C++, is a standard header file that you should use when creating any extension DLL. The main body of the header file, as developed by Process Software Corporation and Microsoft, is as follows:

```
#ifndef _HTTPEXT_H_
#define _HTTPEXT_H_

#include <windows.h>
#include <wincrypt.h>
```

```
#ifdef __cplusplus
extern "C" {
#endif



/**************************************************************
 *    Manifest Constants
 **************************************************************/


#define    HSE_VERSION_MAJOR            4       // major version of this spec
#define    HSE_VERSION_MINOR            0       // minor version of this spec
#define    HSE_LOG_BUFFER_LEN          80
#define    HSE_MAX_EXT_DLL_NAME_LEN    256


#define    HSE_VERSION      MAKELONG( HSE_VERSION_MINOR, HSE_VERSION_MAJOR )

//
// the following are the status codes returned by the Extension DLL
//

#define    HSE_STATUS_SUCCESS                       1
#define    HSE_STATUS_SUCCESS_AND_KEEP_CONN         2
#define    HSE_STATUS_PENDING                       3
#define    HSE_STATUS_ERROR                         4


//
// The following are the values to request services with the
//    ServerSupportFunction().
//    Values from 0 to 1000 are reserved for future versions of the interface

#define    HSE_REQ_BASE                             0
#define    HSE_REQ_SEND_URL_REDIRECT_RESP        ( HSE_REQ_BASE + 1 )
#define    HSE_REQ_SEND_URL                      ( HSE_REQ_BASE + 2 )
#define    HSE_REQ_SEND_RESPONSE_HEADER          ( HSE_REQ_BASE + 3 )
#define    HSE_REQ_DONE_WITH_SESSION             ( HSE_REQ_BASE + 4 )
#define    HSE_REQ_END_RESERVED                     1000
```

```
//
//   These are Microsoft specific extensions
//


#define    HSE_REQ_MAP_URL_TO_PATH                (HSE_REQ_END_RESERVED+1)

#define    HSE_REQ_GET_SSPI_INFO                  (HSE_REQ_END_RESERVED+2)

#define    HSE_APPEND_LOG_PARAMETER               (HSE_REQ_END_RESERVED+3)

#define    HSE_REQ_IO_COMPLETION                  (HSE_REQ_END_RESERVED+5)

#define    HSE_REQ_TRANSMIT_FILE                  (HSE_REQ_END_RESERVED+6)

#define    HSE_REQ_REFRESH_ISAPI_ACL              (HSE_REQ_END_RESERVED+7)

#define    HSE_REQ_IS_KEEP_CONN                   (HSE_REQ_END_RESERVED+8)

#define    HSE_REQ_ASYNC_READ_CLIENT              (HSE_REQ_END_RESERVED+10)

#define    HSE_REQ_GET_IMPERSONATION_TOKEN        (HSE_REQ_END_RESERVED+11)

#define    HSE_REQ_MAP_URL_TO_PATH_EX             (HSE_REQ_END_RESERVED+12)

#define    HSE_REQ_ABORTIVE_CLOSE                 (HSE_REQ_END_RESERVED+14)

#define    HSE_REQ_GET_CERT_INFO_EX               (HSE_REQ_END_RESERVED+15)

#define    HSE_REQ_SEND_RESPONSE_HEADER_EX        (HSE_REQ_END_RESERVED+16)


//
//   Bit Flags for TerminateExtension
//
//     HSE_TERM_ADVISORY_UNLOAD - Server wants to unload the extension,
//           extension can return TRUE if OK, FALSE if the server should not
//           unload the extension
//
//     HSE_TERM_MUST_UNLOAD - Server indicating the extension is about to be
//           unloaded, the extension cannot refuse.
//


#define HSE_TERM_ADVISORY_UNLOAD                  0x00000001
#define HSE_TERM_MUST_UNLOAD                      0x00000002


//
// Flags for IO Functions, supported for IO Funcs.
//  TF means ServerSupportFunction( HSE_REQ_TRANSMIT_FILE)
//
```

```
# define HSE_IO_SYNC                    0x00000001    // for WriteClient
# define HSE_IO_ASYNC                   0x00000002    // for WriteClient/TF
# define HSE_IO_DISCONNECT_AFTER_SEND   0x00000004    // for TF
# define HSE_IO_SEND_HEADERS            0x00000008    // for TF


/************************************************************
 *   Type Definitions
 ************************************************************/


typedef   LPVOID          HCONN;

//
// structure passed to GetExtensionVersion()
//

typedef struct   _HSE_VERSION_INFO {

    DWORD   dwExtensionVersion;
    CHAR    lpszExtensionDesc[HSE_MAX_EXT_DLL_NAME_LEN];

} HSE_VERSION_INFO, *LPHSE_VERSION_INFO;



//
// structure passed to extension procedure on a new request
//
typedef struct _EXTENSION_CONTROL_BLOCK {

    DWORD    cbSize;                 // size of this struct.
    DWORD    dwVersion;              // version info of this spec
    HCONN    ConnID;                 // Context number not to be modified!
    DWORD    dwHttpStatusCode;       // HTTP Status code
    CHAR     lpszLogData[HSE_LOG_BUFFER_LEN];
                     // null terminated log info specific to this Extension DLL
```

```
    LPSTR      lpszMethod;                 // REQUEST_METHOD
    LPSTR      lpszQueryString;            // QUERY_STRING
    LPSTR      lpszPathInfo;               // PATH_INFO
    LPSTR      lpszPathTranslated;         // PATH_TRANSLATED


    DWORD      cbTotalBytes;               // Total bytes indicated from client
    DWORD      cbAvailable;                // Available number of bytes
    LPBYTE     lpbData;                    // pointer to cbAvailable bytes


    LPSTR      lpszContentType;            // Content type of client data

    BOOL (WINAPI * GetServerVariable) ( HCONN      hConn,
                                        LPSTR      lpszVariableName,
                                        LPVOID     lpvBuffer,
                                        LPDWORD    lpdwSize );


    BOOL (WINAPI * WriteClient)  ( HCONN      ConnID,
                                   LPVOID     Buffer,
                                   LPDWORD    lpdwBytes,
                                   DWORD      dwReserved );


    BOOL (WINAPI * ReadClient)  ( HCONN      ConnID,
                                  LPVOID     lpvBuffer,
                                  LPDWORD    lpdwSize );


    BOOL (WINAPI * ServerSupportFunction)( HCONN      hConn,
                                           DWORD      dwHSERRequest,
                                           LPVOID     lpvBuffer,
                                           LPDWORD    lpdwSize,
                                           LPDWORD    lpdwDataType );


} EXTENSION_CONTROL_BLOCK, *LPEXTENSION_CONTROL_BLOCK;


//
// Bit field of flags that can be on a virtual directory
//
```

```
#define HSE_URL_FLAGS_READ            0x00000001    // Allow for Read
#define HSE_URL_FLAGS_WRITE           0x00000002    // Allow for Write
#define HSE_URL_FLAGS_EXECUTE         0x00000004    // Allow for Execute
#define HSE_URL_FLAGS_SSL             0x00000008    // Require SSL
#define HSE_URL_FLAGS_DONT_CACHE      0x00000010    // Don't cache (vroot only)
#define HSE_URL_FLAGS_NEGO_CERT       0x00000020    // Allow client SSL certs
#define HSE_URL_FLAGS_REQUIRE_CERT    0x00000040    // Require client SSL certs
#define HSE_URL_FLAGS_MAP_CERT        0x00000080    // Map SSL cert to NT account
#define HSE_URL_FLAGS_SSL128          0x00000100    // Require 128 bit SSL
#define HSE_URL_FLAGS_SCRIPT          0x00000200    // Allow for Script execution


#define HSE_URL_FLAGS_MASK            0x000003ff


//
//   Structure for extended information on a URL mapping
//


typedef struct _HSE_URL_MAPEX_INFO {

    CHAR    lpszPath[MAX_PATH]; // Physical path root mapped to
    DWORD   dwFlags;                // Flags associated with this URL path
    DWORD   cchMatchingPath;    // Number of matching characters in physical path
    DWORD   cchMatchingURL;     // Number of matching characters in URL


    DWORD   dwReserved1;
    DWORD   dwReserved2;


} HSE_URL_MAPEX_INFO, * LPHSE_URL_MAPEX_INFO;




//
// PFN_HSE_IO_COMPLETION - callback function for the Async I/O Completion.
//

typedef VOID
```

```
(WINAPI * PFN_HSE_IO_COMPLETION)(

                            IN EXTENSION_CONTROL_BLOCK * pECB,
                            IN PVOID      pContext,
                            IN DWORD      cbIO,
                            IN DWORD      dwError
                            );


//
// HSE_TF_INFO defines the type for HTTP SERVER EXTENSION support for
//  ISAPI applications to send files using TransmitFile.
// A pointer to this object should be used with ServerSupportFunction()
//  for HSE_REQ_TRANSMIT_FILE.
//

typedef struct _HSE_TF_INFO {

    //
    // callback and context information
    // the callback function will be called when IO is completed.
    // the context specified will be used during such callback.
    //
    // These values (if non-NULL) will override the one set by calling
    //  ServerSupportFunction() with HSE_REQ_IO_COMPLETION
    //
    PFN_HSE_IO_COMPLETION    pfnHseIO;
    PVOID  pContext;

    // file should have been opened with FILE_FLAG_SEQUENTIAL_SCAN
    HANDLE hFile;

    //
    // HTTP header and status code
    // These fields are used only if HSE_IO_SEND_HEADERS is present in dwFlags
    //
```

```
       LPCSTR pszStatusCode; // HTTP Status Code  eg: "200 OK"


       DWORD   BytesToWrite;  // special value of "0" means write entire file.
       DWORD   Offset;        // offset value within the file to start from


       PVOID   pHead;         // Head buffer to be sent before file data
       DWORD   HeadLength;    // header length
       PVOID   pTail;         // Tail buffer to be sent after file data
       DWORD   TailLength;    // tail length


       DWORD   dwFlags;       // includes HSE_IO_DISCONNECT_AFTER_SEND, ...

} HSE_TF_INFO, * LPHSE_TF_INFO;



//
//   HSE_SEND_HEADER_EX_INFO allows an ISAPI application to send headers
//   and specify keep-alive behavior in the same call.
//

typedef struct _HSE_SEND_HEADER_EX_INFO  {

    //
    // HTTP status code and header
    //

    LPCSTR   pszStatus; // HTTP status code  eg: "200 OK"
    LPCSTR   pszHeader; // HTTP header

    DWORD    cchStatus; // number of characters in status code
    DWORD    cchHeader; // number of characters in header

    BOOL     fKeepConn; // keep client connection alive?

} HSE_SEND_HEADER_EX_INFO, * LPHSE_SEND_HEADER_EX_INFO;
```

```
//
//   CERT_CONTEXT_EX is passed as an argument to
//  ServerSupportFunction( HSE_REQ_GET_CERT_INFO_EX )
//

typedef struct _CERT_CONTEXT_EX {
    CERT_CONTEXT    CertContext;
    DWORD           cbAllocated;
    DWORD           dwCertificateFlags;
} CERT_CONTEXT_EX;



/***********************************************************
 *    Function Prototypes
 *    o  for functions exported from the ISAPI Application DLL
 ***********************************************************/

BOOL  WINAPI    GetExtensionVersion( HSE_VERSION_INFO  *pVer );
DWORD WINAPI    HttpExtensionProc(  EXTENSION_CONTROL_BLOCK *pECB );
BOOL  WINAPI    TerminateExtension( DWORD dwFlags );

// the following type declarations is for use in the server side

typedef BOOL
    (WINAPI * PFN_GETEXTENSIONVERSION)( HSE_VERSION_INFO  *pVer );

typedef DWORD
    (WINAPI * PFN_HTTPEXTENSIONPROC )( EXTENSION_CONTROL_BLOCK * pECB );

typedef BOOL  (WINAPI * PFN_TERMINATEEXTENSION )( DWORD dwFlags );


#ifdef __cplusplus
}
#endif


#endif  // end definition _HTTPEXT_H_
```

The Extension Control Block

The IIS Web server communicates with your extension DLL through an *extension control block,* or ECB. One ECB is created for each access of the DLL. This data area has a very specific layout and is used for passing information to the DLL, as well as for passing information back to the server. The ECB should have the structure specified in the `EXTENSION_CONTROL_BLOCK` section of the header file (see the preceding section). Table 16-1 shows the meanings of each member of the ECB.

Table 16-1   Fields for the Extension Control Block

Field	Direction	Meaning
cbSize	To DLL	Size of the ECB, in bytes. This value should not be changed.
dwVersion	To DLL	Version for this ISAPI specification. The high word (first two bytes) is the major version number, and the low word (last two bytes) is the minor version.
ConnID	To DLL	Unique number assigned by the IIS server. This number tracks multiple ISAPI instances and should not be changed.
dwHttpStatusCode	From DLL	Status of the current transaction.
lpszLogData	From DLL	Log-file message for your DLL. This message should be null terminated. The IIS server writes the message to the log file.
lpszMethod	To DLL	Request method used to initiate the call to the DLL. Equivalent to the `REQUEST_METHOD CGI` variable.
lpszQueryString	To DLL	Query passed from the HTML form. The query is null terminated. Equivalent to the `QUERY_STRING CGI` variable.
lpszPathInfo	To DLL	Null-terminated path provided by the server. Equivalent to the `PATH_INFO CGI` variable.
lpszPathTranslated	To DLL	Null-terminated translated path provided by the server. Equivalent to the `PATH_TRANSLATED CGI` variable, which indicates the virtual-to-physical path mapping.
cbTotalBytes	To DLL	Total number of bytes sent from the remote client. Equivalent to the `CONTENT_LENGTH CGI` variable.
cbAvailable	To DLL	Number of bytes (out of `cbTotalBytes`) available in the buffer pointed to by `lpbData`.
lpbData	To DLL	Pointer to client data of `cbAvailable` number of bytes.
lpszContentType	To DLL	Null-terminated string indicating the content type of the client data. Equivalent to the `CONTENT_TYPE CGI` variable.

When your DLL is called, the IIS server allocates a client data buffer of at least 48KB, unless cbTotalBytes is smaller. If IIS is unable to allocate the minimum size, it generates an error. If your DLL is processing information passed from a user form, then you need to pay attention to the client data buffer; it contains the information that you need.

If cbTotalBytes is equal to cbAvailable, the client data buffer pointed to by lpbData holds all available data. If cbAvailable is less than cbTotalBytes, the buffer at lpbData contains only a portion of the client data. In this case, your DLL must use the ReadClient function to read the next buffer full of data. ReadClient is one of four functions included in the ECB definition. These functions are the following:

- ◆ GetServerVariable Copies information about an HTTP connection, including CGI variables, into a buffer.
- ◆ WriteClient Uses a buffer to send information to the client.
- ◆ ReadClient Reads information from an HTTP request into a buffer.
- ◆ ServerSupportFunction Accesses some predefined server functions.

NOTE

The ECB functions can be quite useful in your extension DLL. For more information on these functions, refer to an ISAPI programming book or to the online documentation for ISAPI.

Compiling the DLL

If you want to compile the source code file for the sample DLL, you may need to install a platform SDK on your system. Microsoft's Visual C++ 5.0 includes all the header files that you need. For older compilers, or compilers from other companies, you may need to download an updated Win32 platform SDK and the Internet SDK. These SDKs make the HTTPEXT.H header file (described earlier in the chapter) available to you.

The Info.dll file was created using MSVC 5.0. The easiest way to compile it is to go to the command prompt, change to the directory into which you have copied the sample files, and then enter the following at the command prompt:

```
nmake /f makefile.mak
```

Installation and Use

After you compile Info.c into Info.dll, or if you use Info.dll from the support files, you can install and use the DLL by simply copying it to your /Scripts directory and then calling it from an HTML file. The support files include the following HTML file, which calls the DLL:

```
<html>
<title>Extension DLL Sample</title>
<body>
<center><h1>Whiz-Bang Web Site</h1></center>

<hr>
Welcome to our Web site. We are sure you will like what you find
here. If you would like to know more about the server on which
this site is operating,
<a href="/scripts/info.dll" NOCACHE>click here</A>.
<hr>

<p>Please come again soon!
</body>
</html>
```

This page, when viewed in a browser, appears as shown in Figure 16-3. Notice that the sample page contains only a single link to another area. However, your page can contain as much other information as desired.

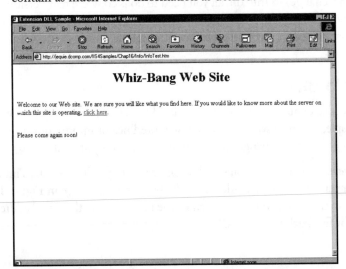

FIGURE 16-3

You can create a link from a Web page to an extension DLL.

When the user clicks on the link, it calls the Info.dll file, not another page. If the DLL has not been called before, the IIS server loads and initializes the DLL (by the server calling the `GetExtensionVersion` that function that you have defined). The IIS server then calls the main part of the DLL, which is defined by the `HttpExtension -Proc` function. At this point, the server does nothing except wait until your DLL returns control to it. From a user's perspective, this DLL displays information about the server on which it is running. Figure 16-4 shows the Web page that appears on the user's screen. (Again, remember that this Web page was created by the Info.dll extension, not by an HTML file.)

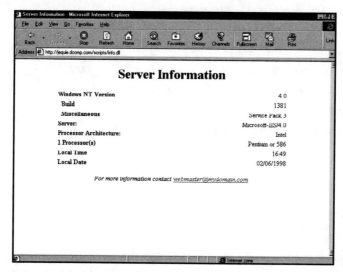

FIGURE 16-4

The Info.dll extension DLL returns information about your server.

If you make any changes to Info.dll, all you need to do is copy the new version to your /Scripts directory. You will need to stop and restart IIS, however, because the DLL is loaded and maintained in memory when you first call it.

Modifying Info.dll

If you like the idea behind the Info.dll extension DLL, you can modify it to your liking. For example, you may want to add a few more lines of information to the output, or you might want to change the appearance of the output a bit.

There is, however, one line that you should change before putting the DLL into actual use on your server. The e-mail address at the bottom of the page in Figure 16-4 is hard-coded into the DLL; you should change the text to reflect the actual address you want to use for feedback from users.

A Sample ISAPI Filter

An ISAPI filter is a special type of DLL that logically sits between the TCP/IP connection and your IIS Web server. The DLL is called every time an HTTP message is received, so you can process the incoming message in any way desired before the Web server ever sees it.

When you create an ISAPI filter, you can specify which type of HTTP notifications the filter will handle, and you can also assign a priority to your filter. Thus multiple filters can be installed, each handling different types of HTTP notifications. If multiple filters are designed for the same notifications, the priority assigned to the filters determines which filter sees the notification first. If both filters have the same priority level, the filter that is loaded first receives top priority.

The sample ISAPI filter in this section will help you understand how these filters work. Although most ISAPI filters are designed for encryption or some other security purpose, this particular sample is a bit different. It intercepts the URL being requested by the user and substitutes a different URL based on information contained within a redirection text file. You would use such a filter, for instance, to note URLs that are no longer valid at your site. You could then redirect users to an error page at your site, which would prevent them from getting an HTTP error when they request a page that no longer exists.

Understanding the DLL

If you load the Redirect.c file from the support files, you can take a look at the source code for the DLL:

```
/////////////////////////////////////
// redirect.dll
// Internet Information Server Master's Handbook
// Discovery Computing Inc.
//
// This ISAPI filter looks at all file requests and compares
// the URL to the contents of a text file (REDIRECT.TXT) to
// see if the URL should be redirected. If so, the filter
// substitutes the redirected URL for the original URL.

#include <windows.h>
#include <stdio.h>
```

```
#include <httpfilt.h>


/////////////////////////////////////
//GetFilterVersion
//
//   Required function. This sets the DLL up so it works with
//   IIS by registering for the PREPROC_HEADERS events
BOOL WINAPI GetFilterVersion (PHTTP_FILTER_VERSION pFilterVersion)
{
    pFilterVersion->dwFilterVersion = HTTP_FILTER_REVISION;
    strcpy (pFilterVersion->lpszFilterDesc,
        "REDIRECT - Redirects client to another page.");

    pFilterVersion->dwFlags= ( SF_NOTIFY_ORDER_HIGH ¦ // high priority
                                SF_NOTIFY_SECURE_PORT ¦
                                SF_NOTIFY_NONSECURE_PORT ¦
                                SF_NOTIFY_PREPROC_HEADERS
                          );

    return TRUE;
}



/////////////////////////////////////
//HttpFilterProc
//
// This is the function that gets information from IIS when
// there is an SF_NOTIFY_PREPROC_HEADERS and checks the
// REDIRECT.TXT file to see if anything needs to be redirected
//
DWORD WINAPI HttpFilterProc (PHTTP_FILTER_CONTEXT pFC,DWORD
dwNotificationType,LPVOID pvNotification)
{
    if (dwNotificationType==SF_NOTIFY_PREPROC_HEADERS){
        HTTP_FILTER_PREPROC_HEADERS *pHeaders=(HTTP_FILTER_PREPROC_HEADERS
*)pvNotification;
```

```
        FILE *pRedirectionFile;
        CHAR achMovedFile[256];   // File listed as missing in REDIRECT.TXT
        CHAR achNewURL[256];      // New location of missing file
        CHAR achURL[2048];        // Current URL that is being tested
        BOOL done = FALSE;

        // This is needed for the GetHeader call
        DWORD cb;
        cb = sizeof( achURL);

        // Get the URL using ISAPI
        if (pHeaders->GetHeader( pFC, "url", achURL, &cb)){
            // Now open the file and check the URL
            // The file location will need to be changed
            pRedirectionFile = fopen( "c:\\REDIRECT.TXT","r");
            while (!done && !feof( pRedirectionFile)){
                // Read in information from file
                fscanf( pRedirectionFile, "%s\t%s", achMovedFile, achNewURL);

                // See if the requested URL has been moved
                if (!stricmp( achURL, achMovedFile)){
                    // Change the URL
                    if (!pHeaders->SetHeader( pFC, "url", achNewURL))
                        return SF_STATUS_REQ_ERROR; // when unable to change URL
                    done = TRUE;
                }
            }
            fclose( pRedirectionFile);

            return SF_STATUS_REQ_HANDLED_NOTIFICATION;
        } else return SF_STATUS_REQ_ERROR;

    }
    // nothing to redirect
    return SF_STATUS_REQ_NEXT_NOTIFICATION;

}
```

Notice that the structure of this ISAPI filter is similar to the structure of the extension DLL discussed earlier in the chapter. Two functions, `GetFilterVersion` and `HttpFilterProc`, must be integrated into the DLL. As with an extension DLL, `GetFilterVersion` is called when the DLL is first loaded; it should return not only the version information of the DLL but also the notification types the DLL was designed for and the priority that should be assigned to the DLL. The Web server notes the information, and when HTTP messages with those notification types occur, the server passes the messages to the `HttpFilterProc` function of the filter.

IIS 4.0 contains a function that you may want to include in your filters. Before unloading the filter from memory, IIS will try to call a `TerminateFilter` function. You can use this function to return any system resources back to the computer or to close any connections before the filter is stopped.

The Header Files

Notice that the source code for the filter does not use the same header files as the extension DLL uses. In this instance, three header files are used:

```
#include <windows.h>
#include <stdio.h>
#include <httpfilt.h>
```

The biggest difference is the use of the HTTPFILT.H header file, which is a standard header file you should use when creating ISAPI filters. The header file defines the structures used by both IIS and your filter. You can study the header file to understand what is required when you create your own filters. The main body of the header file, as developed by Microsoft, is as follows:

```
#ifndef _HTTPFILT_H_
#define _HTTPFILT_H_


#ifdef __cplusplus
extern "C" {
#endif



//
//  Current version of the filter spec is 4.0
//
```

```
#define HTTP_FILTER_REVISION     MAKELONG( 0, 4);


#define SF_MAX_USERNAME          (256+1)
#define SF_MAX_PASSWORD          (256+1)
#define SF_MAX_AUTH_TYPE         (32+1)


#define SF_MAX_FILTER_DESC_LEN   (256+1)



//
// These values can be used with the pfnSFCallback function supplied in
// the filter context structure
//


enum SF_REQ_TYPE
{
    //
    // Sends a complete HTTP server response header including
    // the status, server version, message time and MIME version.
    //
    // Server extensions should append other information at the end,
    // such as Content-type, Content-length etc followed by an extra
    // '\r\n'.
    //
    // pData - Zero terminated string pointing to optional
    //      status string (i.e., "401 Access Denied") or NULL for
    //      the default response of "200 OK".
    //
    // ul1 - Zero terminated string pointing to optional data to be
    //      appended and set with the header.  If NULL, the header will
    //      be terminated with an empty line.
    //

    SF_REQ_SEND_RESPONSE_HEADER,

    //
```

```
//  If the server denies the HTTP request, add the specified headers
//  to the server error response.
//
//  This allows an authentication filter to advertise its services
//  w/o filtering every request.  Generally the headers will be
//  WWW-Authenticate headers with custom authentication schemes but
//  no restriction is placed on what headers may be specified.
//
//  pData - Zero terminated string pointing to one or more header lines
//      with terminating '\r\n'.
//


SF_REQ_ADD_HEADERS_ON_DENIAL,


//
//  Only used by raw data filters that return SF_STATUS_READ_NEXT
//
//  ul1 - size in bytes for the next read
//


SF_REQ_SET_NEXT_READ_SIZE,


//
//  Used to indicate this request is a proxy request
//
//  ul1 - The proxy flags to set
//      0x00000001 - This is a HTTP proxy request
//
//


SF_REQ_SET_PROXY_INFO,


//
//  Returns the connection ID contained in the ConnID field of an
//  ISAPI Application's Extension Control Block.  This value can be used
//  as a key to coordinate shared data between Filters and Applications.
```

```
//
//   pData - Pointer to DWORD that receives the connection ID.
//

SF_REQ_GET_CONNID,


//
// Used to set a SSPI security context + impersonation token
// derived from a client certificate.
//
// pData - certificate info ( PHTTP_FILTER_CERTIFICATE_INFO )
// ul1 - CtxtHandle*
// ul2 - impersonation handle
//

SF_REQ_SET_CERTIFICATE_INFO,


//
// Used to get an IIS property
// as defined in SF_PROPERTY_IIS
//
// ul1 - Property ID
//

SF_REQ_GET_PROPERTY,


//
// Used to normalize an URL
//
// pData - URL to normalize
//

SF_REQ_NORMALIZE_URL,


//
// Disable Notifications
```

```
        //
        // ul1 - notifications to disable
        //

            SF_REQ_DISABLE_NOTIFICATIONS,
    } ;



enum SF_PROPERTY_IIS
{
        SF_PROPERTY_SSL_CTXT,
        SF_PROPERTY_INSTANCE_NUM_ID
    } ;



    //
    // These values are returned by the filter entry point when a new request is
    // received indicating their interest in this particular request
    //

enum SF_STATUS_TYPE
{
        //
        // The filter has handled the HTTP request.  The server should disconnect
        // the session.
        //

            SF_STATUS_REQ_FINISHED = 0x8000000,


        //
        // Same as SF_STATUS_FINISHED except the server should keep the TCP
        // session open if the option was negotiated
        //

            SF_STATUS_REQ_FINISHED_KEEP_CONN,
```

```
//
// The next filter in the notification chain should be called
//

SF_STATUS_REQ_NEXT_NOTIFICATION,

//
// This filter handled the notification.  No other handles should be
// called for this particular notification type
//

SF_STATUS_REQ_HANDLED_NOTIFICATION,

//
// An error occurred.  The server should use GetLastError() and indicate
// the error to the client
//

SF_STATUS_REQ_ERROR,

//
// The filter is an opaque stream filter and we're negotiating the
// session parameters.  Only valid for raw read notification.
//

SF_STATUS_REQ_READ_NEXT
};


//
// pvNotification points to this structure for all request notification types
//

typedef struct _HTTP_FILTER_CONTEXT
{
    DWORD           cbSize;
```

```
//
//  This is the structure revision level.
//

DWORD            Revision;

//
//  Private context information for the server.
//

PVOID            ServerContext;
DWORD            ulReserved;

//
//  TRUE if this request is coming over a secure port
//

BOOL             fIsSecurePort;

//
//  A context that can be used by the filter
//

PVOID            pFilterContext;

//
//  Server callbacks
//

BOOL (WINAPI * GetServerVariable) (
    struct _HTTP_FILTER_CONTEXT * pfc,
    LPSTR                        lpszVariableName,
    LPVOID                       lpvBuffer,
    LPDWORD                      lpdwSize
    );
```

```
BOOL (WINAPI * AddResponseHeaders) (
    struct _HTTP_FILTER_CONTEXT * pfc,
    LPSTR                         lpszHeaders,
    DWORD                         dwReserved
    );


BOOL (WINAPI * WriteClient) (
    struct _HTTP_FILTER_CONTEXT * pfc,
    LPVOID                        Buffer,
    LPDWORD                       lpdwBytes,
    DWORD                         dwReserved
    );


VOID * (WINAPI * AllocMem) (
    struct _HTTP_FILTER_CONTEXT * pfc,
    DWORD                         cbSize,
    DWORD                         dwReserved
    );


BOOL (WINAPI * ServerSupportFunction) (
    struct _HTTP_FILTER_CONTEXT * pfc,
    enum SF_REQ_TYPE              sfReq,
    PVOID                         pData,
    DWORD                         ul1,
    DWORD                         ul2
    );


} HTTP_FILTER_CONTEXT, *PHTTP_FILTER_CONTEXT;


//
// This structure is the notification info for the read and send raw data
// notification types
//


typedef struct _HTTP_FILTER_RAW_DATA
```

```
{
    //
    //  This is a pointer to the data for the filter to process.
    //

    PVOID         pvInData;
    DWORD         cbInData;        // Number of valid data bytes
    DWORD         cbInBuffer;      // Total size of buffer

    DWORD         dwReserved;

} HTTP_FILTER_RAW_DATA, *PHTTP_FILTER_RAW_DATA;


//
//  This structure is the notification info for when the server is about to
//  process the client headers
//

typedef struct _HTTP_FILTER_PREPROC_HEADERS
{
    //
    //  For SF_NOTIFY_PREPROC_HEADERS, retrieves the specified header value.
    //  Header names should include the trailing ':'.  The special values
    //  'method', 'url' and 'version' can be used to retrieve the individual
    //  portions of the request line
    //

    BOOL (WINAPI * GetHeader) (
        struct _HTTP_FILTER_CONTEXT * pfc,
        LPSTR                      lpszName,
        LPVOID                     lpvBuffer,
        LPDWORD                    lpdwSize
        );

    //
    //  Replaces this header value to the specified value.  To delete a header,
```

```
//   specified a value of '\0'.
//

BOOL (WINAPI * SetHeader) (
    struct _HTTP_FILTER_CONTEXT * pfc,
    LPSTR                          lpszName,
    LPSTR                          lpszValue
    );

//
//   Adds the specified header and value
//

BOOL (WINAPI * AddHeader) (
    struct _HTTP_FILTER_CONTEXT * pfc,
    LPSTR                          lpszName,
    LPSTR                          lpszValue
    );

    DWORD HttpStatus;               // New in 4.0, status for SEND_RESPONSE
    DWORD dwReserved;               // New in 4.0

} HTTP_FILTER_PREPROC_HEADERS, *PHTTP_FILTER_PREPROC_HEADERS;

typedef HTTP_FILTER_PREPROC_HEADERS HTTP_FILTER_SEND_RESPONSE;
typedef HTTP_FILTER_PREPROC_HEADERS *PHTTP_FILTER_SEND_RESPONSE;

//
//   Authentication information for this request.
//

typedef struct _HTTP_FILTER_AUTHENT
{
    //
    //   Pointer to username and password, empty strings for the anonymous user
```

```
    //
    //  Client's can overwrite these buffers which are guaranteed to be at
    //  least SF_MAX_USERNAME and SF_MAX_PASSWORD bytes large.
    //

    CHAR * pszUser;
    DWORD  cbUserBuff;

    CHAR * pszPassword;
    DWORD  cbPasswordBuff;

} HTTP_FILTER_AUTHENT, *PHTTP_FILTER_AUTHENT;


//
//  Indicates the server is going to use the specific physical mapping for
//  the specified URL.  Filters can modify the physical path in place.
//

typedef struct _HTTP_FILTER_URL_MAP
{
    const CHAR * pszURL;

    CHAR *      pszPhysicalPath;
    DWORD       cbPathBuff;

} HTTP_FILTER_URL_MAP, *PHTTP_FILTER_URL_MAP;



//
//  Bitfield indicating the requested resource has been denied by the server due
//  to a logon failure, an ACL on a resource, an ISAPI Filter or an
//  ISAPI Application/CGI Application.
//
//  SF_DENIED_BY_CONFIG can appear with SF_DENIED_LOGON if the server
//  configuration did not allow the user to logon.
//
```

```
#define SF_DENIED_LOGON            0x00000001
#define SF_DENIED_RESOURCE         0x00000002
#define SF_DENIED_FILTER           0x00000004
#define SF_DENIED_APPLICATION      0x00000008


#define SF_DENIED_BY_CONFIG        0x00010000


typedef struct _HTTP_FILTER_ACCESS_DENIED
{
    const CHAR * pszURL;              // Requesting URL
    const CHAR * pszPhysicalPath;     // Physical path of resource
    DWORD        dwReason;            // Bitfield of SF_DENIED flags

} HTTP_FILTER_ACCESS_DENIED, *PHTTP_FILTER_ACCESS_DENIED;


//
//   The log information about to be written to the server log file.  The
//   string pointers can be replaced but the memory must remain valid until
//   the next notification
//

typedef struct _HTTP_FILTER_LOG
{
    const CHAR * pszClientHostName;
    const CHAR * pszClientUserName;
    const CHAR * pszServerName;
    const CHAR * pszOperation;
    const CHAR * pszTarget;
    const CHAR * pszParameters;

    DWORD   dwHttpStatus;
    DWORD   dwWin32Status;

    DWORD   dwBytesSent;              // IIS 4.0 and later
    DWORD   dwBytesRecvd;             // IIS 4.0 and later
    DWORD   msTimeForProcessing;      // IIS 4.0 and later
```

```
} HTTP_FILTER_LOG, *PHTTP_FILTER_LOG;


//
//   Notification Flags
//
//   SF_NOTIFY_SECURE_PORT
//   SF_NOTIFY_NONSECURE_PORT
//
//       Indicates whether the application wants to be notified for transactions
//       that are happening on the server port(s) that support data encryption
//       (such as PCT and SSL), on only the non-secure port(s) or both.
//
//   SF_NOTIFY_READ_RAW_DATA
//
//       Applications are notified after the server reads a block of memory
//       from the client but before the server does any processing on the
//       block.  The data block may contain HTTP headers and entity data.
//

#define SF_NOTIFY_SECURE_PORT              0x00000001
#define SF_NOTIFY_NONSECURE_PORT           0x00000002

#define SF_NOTIFY_READ_RAW_DATA            0x00008000
#define SF_NOTIFY_PREPROC_HEADERS          0x00004000
#define SF_NOTIFY_AUTHENTICATION           0x00002000
#define SF_NOTIFY_URL_MAP                  0x00001000
#define SF_NOTIFY_ACCESS_DENIED            0x00000800
#define SF_NOTIFY_SEND_RESPONSE            0x00000040
#define SF_NOTIFY_SEND_RAW_DATA            0x00000400
#define SF_NOTIFY_LOG                      0x00000200
#define SF_NOTIFY_END_OF_REQUEST           0x00000080
#define SF_NOTIFY_END_OF_NET_SESSION       0x00000100



//
//   Filter ordering flags
```

```
//
// Filters will tend to be notified by their specified
// ordering.  For ties, notification order is determined by load order.
//
// SF_NOTIFY_ORDER_HIGH - Authentication or data transformation filters
// SF_NOTIFY_ORDER_MEDIUM
// SF_NOTIFY_ORDER_LOW  - Logging filters that want the results of any other
//                        filters might specify this order.
//

#define SF_NOTIFY_ORDER_HIGH            0x00080000
#define SF_NOTIFY_ORDER_MEDIUM          0x00040000
#define SF_NOTIFY_ORDER_LOW             0x00020000
#define SF_NOTIFY_ORDER_DEFAULT         SF_NOTIFY_ORDER_LOW

#define SF_NOTIFY_ORDER_MASK            (SF_NOTIFY_ORDER_HIGH   |   \
                                         SF_NOTIFY_ORDER_MEDIUM |   \
                                         SF_NOTIFY_ORDER_LOW)

//
// Filter version information, passed to GetFilterVersion
//

typedef struct _HTTP_FILTER_VERSION
{
    //
    // Version of the spec the server is using
    //

    DWORD  dwServerFilterVersion;

    //
    // Fields specified by the client
    //

    DWORD  dwFilterVersion;
```

```
        CHAR    lpszFilterDesc[SF_MAX_FILTER_DESC_LEN];
        DWORD   dwFlags;



    } HTTP_FILTER_VERSION, *PHTTP_FILTER_VERSION;



    //
    // A filter DLL's entry point looks like this.  The return code should be
    // an SF_STATUS_TYPE
    //
    // NotificationType - Type of notification
    // pvNotification - Pointer to notification specific data
    //

    DWORD
    WINAPI
    HttpFilterProc(
        HTTP_FILTER_CONTEXT *       pfc,
        DWORD                       NotificationType,
        VOID *                      pvNotification
        );

    BOOL
    WINAPI
    GetFilterVersion(
        HTTP_FILTER_VERSION * pVer
        );

    BOOL
    WINAPI
    TerminateFilter(
        DWORD dwFlags
        );

    #ifdef __cplusplus
```

```
}
#endif


#endif // _HTTPFILT_H_
```

Notification Types

The Web server classifies incoming HTTP sessions or messages according to type. These classifications are called *notifications*, and your filter can register for specific notifications. When a session or message is received that matches the specified notification, the filter is called into action. Table 16-2 describes the various notification types.

Table 16-2   ISAPI Filter Notification Types

Notification Value	Notifies Filter For
SF_NOTIFY_ACCESS_DENIED	Notifies the filter when an access denied error message is going to be sent. The filter can then return a custom message to the client.
SF_NOTIFY_AUTHENTICATION	Provides authentication of the client.
SF_NOTIFY_END_OF_NET_SESSION	Initiates termination of a session with the client.
SF_NOTIFY_END_OF_REQUEST	Calls the filter at the end of every request and keeps a network connection open while the notification is called.
SF_NOTIFY_NONSECURE_PORT	Initiates sessions over a nonsecure port.
SF_NOTIFY_LOG	Writes information to the server log.
SF_NOTIFY_PREPROC_HEADERS	Notifies the filter for all preprocessed headers.
SF_NOTIFY_SEND_RESPONSE	Enables filter to process headers being sent to the client for a particular request.
SF_NOTIFY_READ_RAW_DATA	Provides notification of all messages received. The filter is passed all raw data, both headers and data.
SF_NOTIFY_SECURE_PORT	Initiates sessions over a secure port.
SF_NOTIFY_SEND_RAW_DATA	Provides notification of all messages sent; this value is the opposite of the SF_NOTIFY_READ_RAW_DATA value.
SF_NOTIFY_URL_MAP	Maps a logical URL to a physical path.

The GetFilterVersion function in your DLL uses notification values from Table 16-2 to specify which notifications are to be handled by your filter. These notifications are actually defined in the ISAPI filter header and should be logically ORed with each other to derive a final notification value that GetFilterVersion passes back to the IIS server.

In addition, you can also OR the priority values shown in Table 16-3 into the same notification value. Remember, however, that only a single priority value can be set, regardless of how many notifications you register for.

Table 16-3 ISAPI Filter Priority Values

Priority Value	Meaning
SF_NOTIFY_ORDER_DEFAULT	Function at the default priority
SF_NOTIFY_ORDER_LOW	Function at a low priority
SF_NOTIFY_ORDER_MEDIUM	Function at a medium priority
SF_NOTIFY_ORDER_HIGH	Function at a high priority

In the GetExtensionVersion function of the Redirect.dll filter shown in the previous section, the code that specified notifications and priority is as follows:

```
pFilterVersion->dwFlags= ( SF_NOTIFY_ORDER_HIGH ¦ // high priority
                           SF_NOTIFY_SECURE_PORT ¦
                           SF_NOTIFY_NONSECURE_PORT ¦
                           SF_NOTIFY_PREPROC_HEADERS
                         );
```

This code registers a high priority for both secure and nonsecure ports for preprocessed headers.

CAUTION

Your ISAPI filter should register only for those notifications it absolutely needs. Remember that every notification you intercept and process adds more overhead to the processing of your messages and can have a negative impact on the overall performance of your Web site.

Compiling the Filter

If you want to compile the source code file for the sample DLL, you may need to install a platform SDK on your system. Check and see whether your compiler has the

HTTPFILT.H file; it is included with Microsoft's Visual C++ 5.0. If you can't find the header, go to **http://www.microsoft.com/msdn/sdk/bldenv.htm**; you can download the updated build environment, and perhaps the sample applications as well.

The Redirect.dll file was created using Microsoft Visual C++ 5.0. The easiest way to compile this file is to go to the command prompt, change to the directory into which you have copied the sample files, and then type the following at the command prompt:

```
nmake /f makefile.mak
```

Installing the Filter

To use the filter, you should move the compiled DLL to the /Scripts directory on your server. You then need to accomplish two tasks: create your redirection file and add the filter to the list of filters used at your site.

The Redirection File

The text file on which the filter relies is called a redirection file. This file, which is called Redirect.txt, contains pairs of URLs. The first URL on a line is the one for which the filter looks. The second URL on a line (separated from the other by a tab) is the one with which it should be replaced. The sample Redirect.txt file, provided as part of the support files for this book, looks like this:

```
/dci/johnson.htm      /dci/error.htm
/booklist/books.htm   /books.htm
```

Although this example is very short, you can make the redirection file as long as you want. Remember to separate the URL pairs with a tab and that the URL on the right (the one being substituted) should be located on your current site. You should also make sure that the URL on the right does not appear on the left in some other line. If this duplication occurs, your filter could end up in an infinite loop, forever replacing the same URL.

NOTE

The Redirect.txt file should be stored in the root directory of drive C. This location is hard-coded into the filter; if you want to store the redirection file in a different location, you will need to change the source code and recompile.

Adding the Filter

To use the filter, you need to add it to a list of ISAPI filters that IIS will load when it starts. You can add the filter to the list by following these steps:

1. Open the Internet Service Manager.
2. Right-click on the Web site that will use your filter and select Properties from the pop-up menu.
3. Select the ISAPI Filters tab in the Web Site Properties dialog box, as shown in Figure 16-5.
4. Select the Add button to display the Filter Properties dialog box, as shown in Figure 16-6.

FIGURE 16-5

IIS maintains a list of filters being used at your Web sites.

FIGURE 16-6

You can easily add an ISAPI filter to your Web site.

5. Enter the name in the Filter Name field.
6. Enter the path to the DLL file or use the browse button to find the DLL.
7. Click on OK to close the Filter Properties dialog box. Your filter will now appear in the list of filters on the Web Site Properties dialog box. The priority of your filter is listed as unknown until it loads and signals its priority to IIS.

8. Click on OK to close the Web Site Properties dialog box.

9. Close the Internet Service Manager.

Running the Filter

After you have installed your filter DLL and you restart IIS, the filter is loaded and initialized. This initialization, as discussed earlier, registers with IIS to indicate which notifications it wants to receive. When an appropriate notification is received, the HttpFilterProc function is called into action. This function is the main entry point for your DLL. When called by the server, the HttpFilterProc function receives the following variables:

◆ pfc Points to the HTTP_FILTER_CONTEXT structure (defined shortly).

◆ notificationType Indicates the type of event being processed, as specified earlier in the section "Notification Types." This variable is meaningful only if your filter is designed to handle more than a single notification type and you want each to be handled differently by the filter.

◆ pvNotification Points to a structure that contains the information associated with the notification type.

The HttpFilterProc function uses quite a few different structures. In addition to the HTTP_FILTER_CONTEXT structure pointed to by the pfc variable, the pvNotification variable can point to any number of structures, depending on the notificationType (as shown in Table 16-4).

Table 16-4 Structures Pointed to by the pvNotification **Variable**

Notification Type	Structure
SF_NOTIFY_ACCESS_DENIED	HTTP_FILTER_ACCESS_DENIED
SF_NOTIFY_AUTHENTICATION	HTTP_FILTER_AUTHENT
SF_NOTIFY_LOG	HTTP_FILTER_LOG
SF_NOTIFY_PREPROC_HEADERS	HTTP_FILTER_PREPROC_HEADERS
SF_NOTIFY_READ_RAW_DATA	HTTP_FILTER_RAW_DATA
SF_NOTIFY_SEND_RAW_DATA	HTTP_FILTER_RAW_DATA
SF_NOTIFY_SEND_RESPONSE	HTTP_FILTER_SEND_RESPONSE
SF_NOTIFY_URL_MAP	HTTP_FILTER_URL_MAP

In the case of the Redirect filter, the notification type is SF_NOTIFY_PREPROC _HEADERS, so the HTTP_FILTER_PREPROC_HEADERS structure is used. Consequently,

two structures are used for this single notification type: HTTP_FILTER
_CONTEXT and HTTP_FILTER_PREPROC_HEADERS. The six potential data structures used by HttpFilterProc are described in the following sections.

HTTP_FILTER_ACCESS_DENIED

This structure is used when a filter is notified of a 401 Access Denied error. The HTTP_FILTER_ACCESS_DENIED structure can produce a different error message for the client. The organization of this structure is defined in the HTTPFILT.H file as follows:

```
typedef struct _HTTP_FILTER_ACCESS_DENIED
{
    const CHAR * pszURL;
    const CHAR * pszPhysicalPath;    // Physical path of resource
    DWORD        dwReason;           // Bitfield of SF_DENIED flags


} HTTP_FILTER_ACCESS_DENIED, *PHTTP_FILTER_ACCESS_DENIED;
```

These are the members of the structure:

- ◆ pszURL The URL to the denied resource
- ◆ pszPhysicalPath The physical path to the resource being denied
- ◆ dwReason A bit field explaining the reasons for denying the resource

The possible reasons for denying the resource are as follows:

- ◆ SF_DENIED_LOGON The client couldn't be logged in.
- ◆ SF_DENIED_RESOURCE The resource is denied to the client using the Windows NT's access-control list.
- ◆ SF_DENIED_FILTER A filter denied the request.
- ◆ SF_DENIED_APPLICATION Either a CGI or ISAPI application denied the request.
- ◆ SF_DENIED_BY_CONFIG The server's configuration denied the request. This reason may also appear as SF_DENIED_LOGON.

HTTP_FILTER_AUTHENT

This structure is used when the notification type is SF_NOTIFY_AUTHENTICATION, which means that the server is about to authenticate a client attempting to establish a connection. You use this notification type to replace the server's authentication routines with your own. One reason for doing so is to customize the security features of your Web site or to limit who can have access to your site.

If you look back at the HTTPFILT.H file, you can see that the HTTP_FILTER_ AUTHENT structure has the following organization:

```
typedef struct _HTTP_FILTER_AUTHENT
{
    CHAR *      pszUser;
    DWORD       cbUserBuff;
    CHAR *      pszPassword;
    DWORD       cbPasswordBuff;
} HTTP_FILTER_AUTHENT, *PHTTP_FILTER_AUTHENT;
```

The members used in the structure are as follows:

- ◆ pszUser A pointer to a string containing the user name of the client. If the string is empty, the client is attempting to connect anonymously.
- ◆ cbUserBuff The size of the pszUser buffer.
- ◆ pszPassword A pointer to a string containing the password of the client.
- ◆ cbPasswordBuff The size of the pszPassword buffer.

HTTP_FILTER_CONTEXT

The HTTP_FILTER_CONTEXT structure pointed to by the pfc variable contains context information used to communicate between the server and your filter. The filter can use the pFilterContext member to associate any context information with the HTTP request. The SF_NOTIFY_END_OF_NET_SESSION notification can be used to release any such context information. As defined in the HTTPFILT.H file, the HTTP_FILTER_CONTEXT structure appears as follows:

```
typedef struct _HTTP_FILTER_CONTEXT
{
    DWORD       cbSize;
    DWORD       Revision;
    PVOID       ServerContext;
    DWORD       ulReserved;
    BOOL        fIsSecurePort;
    PVOID       pFilterContext;
```

```
BOOL    (WINAPI * GetServerVariable) (
    struct _HTTP_FILTER_CONTEXT * pfc,
    LPSTR       lpszVariableName,
    LPVOID      lpvBuffer,
    LPDWORD     lpdwSize
    );

BOOL    (WINAPI * AddResponseHeaders) (
    struct _HTTP_FILTER_CONTEXT *    pfc,
    LPSTR     lpszHeaders,
    DWORD     dwReserved
    );

BOOL    (WINAPI * WriteClient)  (
    struct _HTTP_FILTER_CONTEXT *    pfc,
    LPVOID      Buffer,
    LPDWORD     lpdwBytes,
    DWORD       dwReserved
    );

VOID *    (WINAPI * AllocMem) (
    struct _HTTP_FILTER_CONTEXT *    pfc,
    DWORD       cbSize,
    DWORD       dwReserved
    );

BOOL    (WINAPI * ServerSupportFunction) (
    struct _HTTP_FILTER_CONTEXT *    pfc,
    enum SF_REQ_TYPE     sfReq,
    PVOID       pData,
    DWORD       ul1,
    DWORD       ul2
    );
} HTTP_FILTER_CONTEXT, *PHTTP_FILTER_CONTEXT;
```

The structure contains quite a few members, including pointers to five callback functions that can be used in your filter. The first group of members contains the following functions:

- ◆ cbSize The size of the HTTP_FILTER_CONTEXT structure, in bytes.
- ◆ Revision The revision level of the structure.
- ◆ ServerContext Reserved for server use (do not change).
- ◆ ulReserved Reserved for server use (do not change).
- ◆ fIsSecurePort If TRUE, this event is being conducted over a secure port.
- ◆ pFilterContext A pointer your filter can use for any context information you want to associate with this request. Any memory your context information uses can be safely freed during the SF_NOTIFY_END_OF_NET_SESSION notification.

The following callback functions are included in the structure:

- ◆ GetServerVariable Points to a function that retrieves information about the IIS server and the connection between IIS and your filter.
- ◆ AddResponseHeaders Points to a function that adds a header to the HTTP response.
- ◆ WriteClient Sends raw data back through IIS to the remote client.
- ◆ AllocMem Allocates memory for use by your filter. Memory allocated with this function will automatically be freed when the request is completed.
- ◆ ServerSupportFunction Extends the ISAPI filter functions. The parameters used with the function vary depending on the extension being used.

For more information on using the callback functions, you should refer to either an in-depth programming text for ISAPI or to the ISAPI documentation available with your SDK.

HTTP_FILTER_LOG

This structure is used when the notification type is SF_NOTIFY_LOG, which means that IIS is about to send information to the server log file. You intercept this notification type if you want to modify what is sent to the log file or if you want to build your own analysis of what IIS is doing.

You can't change the strings pointed to in this structure, but you can change the pointers themselves. If you change the pointers, the memory into which they point must have been allocated with the AllocMem callback function in the HTTP_FILTER_CONTEXT structure. (Allocating memory in this way allows IIS to manage the memory and deallocate it when appropriate.)

From the HTTPFILT.H file, you can determine that the organization of the `HTTP_FILTER_LOG` structure is as follows:

```
typedef struct _HTTP_FILTER_LOG
{
    const CHAR *    pszClientHostName;
    const CHAR *    pszClientUserName;
    const CHAR *    pszServerName;
    const CHAR *    pszOperation;
    const CHAR *    pszTarget;
    const CHAR *    pszParameters;
    DWORD           dwHttpStatus;
    DWORD           dwWin32Status;
    DWORD           dwBytesSent;
    DWORD           dwBytesRecvd;
    DWORD           msTimeForProcessing;
} HTTP_FILTER_LOG, *PHTTP_FILTER_LOG;
```

IIS 4.0 has added three new members (to the eight that were available in IIS 3.0) to this structure. These are the members of the structure:

- ◆ `pszClientHostName` A pointer to the host name of the client.
- ◆ `pszClientUserName` A pointer to the username of the client. If this string is empty, the user is anonymous.
- ◆ `pszServerName` A pointer to the name of the server to which the client is connected.
- ◆ `pszOperation` A pointer to the HTTP command being logged.
- ◆ `pszTarget` A pointer to the target of the HTTP command.
- ◆ `pszParameters` A pointer to the parameters passed to the HTTP command.
- ◆ `dwHttpStatus` The HTTP status code.
- ◆ `dwWin32Status` The Win32 error code. (Additional information can be gleaned with the Win32 `GetLastError` function.)
- ◆ `dwBytesSent` The number of bytes sent to the client. (New with IIS 4.0.)
- ◆ `dwBytesRecvd` The number of bytes received from the client. (New with IIS 4.0.)

◆ `msTimeForProcessing` The time required to process the client's request, in milliseconds. (New with IIS 4.0.)

HTTP_FILTER_PREPROC_HEADERS

This structure is used when IIS is about to process the client HTTP headers (when the notification type is SF_NOTIFY_PREPROC_HEADERS). You use this notification type if you want to analyze the client headers for some reason; this notification type is used in the sample Redirect filter.

The organization of the HTTP_FILTER_PREPROC_HEADERS structure, as defined in HTTPFILT.H, is as follows:

```
typedef struct _HTTP_FILTER_PREPROC_HEADERS
{
BOOL    (WINAPI * GetHeader) (
    struct _HTTP_FILTER_CONTEXT * pfc,
    LPSTR    lpszName,
    LPVOID   lpvBuffer,
    LPDWORD  lpdwSize
    );

BOOL    (WINAPI * SetHeader) (
    struct _HTTP_FILTER_CONTEXT * pfc,
    LPSTR    lpszName,
    LPSTR    lpszValue
    );

BOOL    (WINAPI * AddHeader) (
    struct _HTTP_FILTER_CONTEXT * pfc,
    LPSTR    lpszName,
    LPSTR    lpszValue
    );

DWORD    HttpStatus;
DWORD    dwReserved;
} HTTP_FILTER_PREPROC_HEADERS, *PHTTP_FILTER_PREPROC_HEADERS;
```

The members of the structure include three pointers to functions, as well as a reserved member (dwReserved) and an HttpStatus, which is a new member for IIS 4.0 and stores the current HTTP status. The first member is a pointer to the GetHeader function, which retrieves the header value. Header names should contain the trailing colon, and you can also use the special values of method, url, and version. The GetHeader function uses the following parameters:

- ◆ pfc The filter context for this request from the pfc passed to the HttpFilterProc.
- ◆ lpszName A pointer to the name of the header to retrieve.
- ◆ lpvBuffer A pointer to a buffer where the value of the header will be stored.
- ◆ lpdwSize The buffer size, which must be set before making the call. (If you don't set the size before making the call, your DLL will crash without an explanation.) After the call, lpdwSize contains the number of bytes retrieved, including the null terminator.

The second member is a pointer to the SetHeader function, which is used to change or delete the value of a header. This function uses the following parameters:

- ◆ pfc The filter context for this request from the pfc passed to the HttpFilterProc.
- ◆ lpszName A pointer to the name of the header to change or delete.
- ◆ lpszValue A pointer to the new name for the header (null terminated). If the new name is an empty string, the header is deleted.

The third member is a pointer to the AddHeader function, which adds a header. The variables used for this function are the same as those used for the SetHeader function.

HTTP_FILTER_RAW_DATA

This structure is used for both the sending and receiving notification types for raw data. The structure is organized as follows in the HTTPFILT.H file:

```
typedef struct _HTTP_FILTER_RAW_DATA
{
    PVOID pvInData;
    DWORD cbInData;
    DWORD cbInBuffer;
    DWORD dwReserved;
} HTTP_FILTER_RAW_DATA, *PHTTP_FILTER_RAW_DATA;
```

The members of the structure are as follows:

- ◆ pvInData A pointer to the data buffer.
- ◆ cbInData The amount of data in the buffer.
- ◆ cbInBuffer The size of the buffer, in bytes.
- ◆ dwReserved Reserved for future use.

HTTP_FILTER_SEND_RESPONSE

The HTTP_FILTER_SEND_RESPONSE is the same as the HTTP_FILTER_PRE-PROC_HEADERS structure. The only difference is in the way in which they are used. The SF_NOTIFY_SEND_REPONSE notification occurs prior to sending headers to the client. The GetHeader, SetHeader and AddHeader functions can be used to look at, change, or add to the headers being sent. See the section about HTTP_FIL-TER_PREPROC_HEADERS for more detailed information.

HTTP_FILTER_URL_MAP

This structure is used when the notification type is SF_NOTIFY_URL_MAP. This notification type is used when IIS is about to map a URL to a physical path. You use this notification type if you want to modify the mapping of the URL. The HTTP_FILTER_URL_MAP structure is organized as follows in the HTTPFILT.H file:

```
typedef struct _HTTP_FILTER_URL_MAP
{
    const CHAR *    pszURL;
    CHAR *          pszPhysicalPath;
    DWORD           cbPathBuff;
} HTTP_FILTER_URL_MAP, *PHTTP_FILTER_URL_MAP;
```

The members of the structure are as follows:

- ◆ pszURL A pointer to the URL that's being mapped.
- ◆ pszPhysicalPath A pointer to a buffer where the physical path is located. (You modify this path if you want to do your own mapping.)
- ◆ cbPathBuff The size of the buffer, in bytes.

Using Microsoft Visual C++

The examples so far in this chapter show you how to create an IIS extension from scratch. These examples should work with any compiler that will create DLLs for

Windows NT. However, when developing a product, such as an ISAPI extension DLL, using Microsoft technologies, you can expect to find a Microsoft tool that will help do the job. This final part of the chapter describes how to use Microsoft's Visual C++ 5.0 to create ISAPI DLLs. This compiler includes an ISAPI Extension Wizard to help create ISAPI DLLs.

Using the ISAPI Extension Wizard

The ISAPI Extension Wizard is similar to other wizards included with Visual C++ in that it gives you a quick start to a program using the Microsoft Foundation Classes, or MFC. The MFC is a collection of C++ classes that encapsulate, or hide, C functions. MFC version 4.21 includes a few Internet Server classes that you can use when creating extension DLLs. These functions are described in the AFXISAPI.H header file.

The ISAPI Extension Wizard creates a skeleton extension with everything that you need to get started with an ISAPI extension. This skeleton is made by creating source files and classes derived from the appropriate MFC Internet Server API. To use the ISAPI Extension Wizard, follow these steps:

1. Open Microsoft's Visual C++.

2. Select New from the File menu. The New dialog box, shown in Figure 16-7, opens.

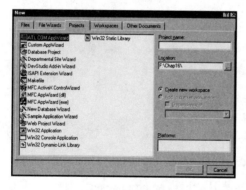

FIGURE 16-7

You must select the wizard you want to use.

3. Select ISAPI Extension Wizard from the list in the Projects Tab.

4. Enter a Project Name. You may also want to change the location of the project.

5. Select OK to start the ISAPI Extension Wizard, as shown in Figure 16-8.

6. Select either the Generate a Filter Object option or Generate a Server Extension Object option, depending on whether you are creating an ISAPI filter or an ISAPI extension. You can also change the Wizard-created default class name and description.

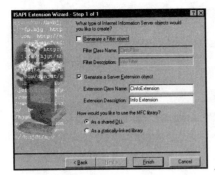

FIGURE 16-8

The ISAPI Extension Wizard offers help for both extension DLLs and filter DLLs.

7. Determine whether you want to use the shared MFC DLLs or not.

8. Select Finish. The ISAPI Extension Wizard will create some files for your extension and return you to Visual C++.

Developing the DLL

Microsoft's ISAPI Extension Wizard only lays the groundwork for creating your extension. You still have to complete three more steps to turn the Wizard-created project into a working extension.

This section works through the additional steps, using InfoWiz.dll as an example. InfoWiz.dll is similar to the Info.dll but allows the user to send his or her name and browser's name to the server using a simple form, as shown in Figure 16-9. The extension DLL is called and returns information about the server to the browser, as shown in Figure 16-10.

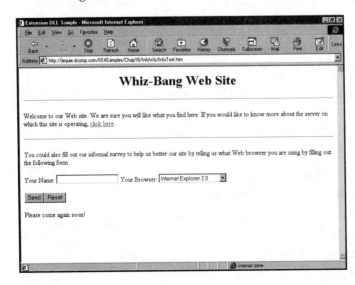

FIGURE 16-9

The new InfoWiz.dll accepts information from a form.

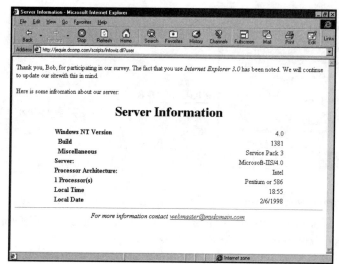

FIGURE 16-10

InfoWiz.dll returns information based on the input received from the form.

The final code from this example can be found in the directory (on the FTP site) \Chap16\InfoWiz.

Parsing Requests

The first step in developing your DLL is to set up a parse map. A parse map takes the string passed to the server from the browser and decides what function should be used from the DLL. Take, for example, the form that calls the InfoWiz.dll. When Bob, who is using Internet Explorer 4.0, requests information about the server, the form data that is sent to IIS looks like this:

```
POST InfoWiz.dll?User? HTTP/1.0
```

```
. . .
```

```
UserName=Bob&Browser=Internet+Explorer+4
```

IIS sends this data to the InfoWiz.dll, which must try to make sense of, or parse, the information. Parsing occurs in the command-parsing map section of the InfoWiz.cpp file. This section determines which DLL function will be called when a user sends a request to IIS. The following code appears in the InfoWiz.cpp:

```
BEGIN_PARSE_MAP(CInfoWizExtension, CHttpServer)
    // TODO: insert your ON_PARSE_COMMAND() and
    // ON_PARSE_COMMAND_PARAMS() here to hook up your commands.
    // For example:
    ON_PARSE_COMMAND(Default, CInfoWizExtension, ITS_EMPTY)
```

```
    DEFAULT_PARSE_COMMAND(Default, CInfoWizExtension)
END_PARSE_MAP(CInfoWizExtension)
```

An extension DLL may include several functions. The ISAPI Extension Wizard automatically created a default function, which is adequate when you want your DLL to do only one thing. This example adds another function, User, which personalizes the server information just a bit. The following lines were added to the command-parsing map:

```
    ON_PARSE_COMMAND(User, CInfoWizExtension, ITS_PSTR ITS_PSTR)
    ON_PARSE_COMMAND_PARAMS("UserName BrowserType")
```

The first line of code uses the ON_PARSE_COMMAND macro to tell the DLL which function, User, to call when a browser sends the User request. The macro also determines what type of parameters to send the function. The other line of code uses the ON_PARSE_COMMAND_PARAMS macro to determine which parameters to use.

Adding Functionality

The next step is to create your function. First take a look at the default function created by the ISAPI Extension Wizard in the following code:

```
void CInfoWizExtension::Default(CHttpServerContext* pCtxt)
{
    StartContent(pCtxt);
    WriteTitle(pCtxt);

    *pCtxt << _T("This default message was produced by the Internet");
    *pCtxt << _T(" Server DLL Wizard. Edit your CInfoWizExtension::Default()");
    *pCtxt << _T(" implementation to change it.\r\n");

    EndContent(pCtxt);
}
```

The default function includes a few member function calls that help to create the HTML page being returned to the browser. The first function called is StartContent(). This function sends information describing the type of information being returned to the server. The information corresponds to the "Content-Type: text/html\r\n\r\n" string used in previous examples. If you aren't sending an HTML-type document, you must override this function. The second function,

`WriteTitle()` creates a header. It calls `GetTitle()` to get the title of the HTML page being created. However, you need to override `GetTitle()`, as described later. The third function, `EndContent()`, creates the rest of the HTML page including the `</BODY>` and `</HTML>` tags.

As you can see, the `<<` operator has been overloaded so that you can easily add a string to the HTML page being created. Looking at the source code in AFXISAPI.H, you can see that this operator has been overloaded for LPCTSTR, long int, short int, CHtmlStream, double, and float types.

The example in this chapter changes the default function and adds the new `User` function. When adding new functions, you also need to add declarations to the header file. The new functions are listed in the following code:

```
void CInfoWizExtension::Default(CHttpServerContext* pCtxt)
{
    StartContent(pCtxt);
    WriteTitle(pCtxt);


    CreateServerInfoTable(pCtxt);


    EndContent(pCtxt);
}


// The User function returns a more personalized version of
// the server's information
void CInfoWizExtension::User(CHttpServerContext* pCtxt,
        LPCTSTR pstrUserName, LPCTSTR pstrBrowserType)
{
    StartContent(pCtxt);
    WriteTitle(pCtxt);

    *pCtxt << "<p>Thank you, "
        << pstrUserName
        << ", for participating in our survey. "
        << "The fact that you use <em>"
        << pstrBrowserType
        << "</em> has been noted. We will continue to update our site"
        << "with this in mind.</p>"
```

```
        << "<p>Here is some information about our server:</p>";
    CreateServerInfoTable(pCtxt);


    EndContent(pCtxt);
}
```

Both functions display the same server information using the new `CreateServerInfoTable` function. This function is basically the same function used in the Info.dll example, though it has been changed to take advantage of the `CHttpServerContext` variable.

The final step to creating a working DLL is to override the existing the `GetTitle()` function. This function can be quite simple as the following sample illustrates:

```
LPCTSTR CInfoWizExtension::GetTitle() const
{
    return "Server Information";
}
```

There ISAPI Extension Wizard also includes a few comments that can be quite helpful. One is found at the bottom of the main Wizard-generated CPP file. This comment describes how to change your extension so that it no longer uses the MFCs. You may want to follow these instructions if you want to get rid of the little bit of additional overhead included with MFC.

Creating Corresponding HTML Pages

The final step is to create the HTML pages that will access the DLL. In this example, I have simply taken the HTML page that was used with the Info.dll extension and changed it to use Infowiz.dll. I also added a form to take advantage of the new `User` function. Here is the complete HTML listing:

```
<html>
<title>Extension DLL Sample</title>
<body>
<center><h1>Whiz-Bang Web Site</h1></center>

<hr>
```

```
<p>Welcome to our Web site. We are sure you will like what you find
here. If you would like to know more about the server on which
this site is operating, <a href="/scripts/infowiz.dll" NOCACHE>click here</A>.</p>
<hr>
<p>You could also fill out our informal survey to help us better our
site by telling us what Web browser you are using by filling out
the following form.</p>
<form action="/scripts/infowiz.dll?user" method=POST>
  <p>Your Name: <input type="text" name="UserName" value="">
    Your Browser: <select name="BrowserType" size="1">
      <option value="Internet Explorer 2.0">Internet Explorer 2.0</option>
      <option value="Internet Explorer 3.0">Internet Explorer 3.0</option>
      <option value="Internet Explorer 4.0">Internet Explorer 4.0</option>
      <option value="Netscape Navigator 3.0">Netscape Navigator 3.0</option>
      <option value="Netscape Navigator 4.0">Netscape Navigator 4.0</option>
      <option value="Other">Other</option>
    </select></p>
  <p><input type="submit" value="Send"><input type="reset"></p>
</Form>
<p>Please come again soon!</p>
</body>
</html>
```

The code that calls the extension DLL in the form contains a question mark followed by the name of the function you will be using. To call the default function, simply call the extension DLL directly as shown in the first call to Infowiz.dll.

Chapter 17

Creating Content with
Visual InterDev

———

In This Chapter

◆ What Is Visual InterDev?

◆ Using Projects

◆ Using Image Composer

◆ Using Media Manager

The preceding chapters in this part explained how to create dynamic Web content. This chapter shows you how to use one of Microsoft's new tools for creating and managing this content. Microsoft Visual InterDev is part of the Developer Studio suite of programs and can be tightly integrated with IIS to create dynamic content.

Visual InterDev ships with several programs that can be quite helpful when you are creating multimedia content for your Web site. These additional applications (Image Composer, Microsoft Music Producer, and Multimedia Manager) are covered at the end of this chapter.

What Is Visual InterDev?

Visual InterDev is a program that helps Web content creators develop Web applications. It goes a long way beyond a simple text editor, such as Notepad, for example, where you enter HTML and scripts into a Web page. Here is a list of some of the most important features of InterDev:

◆ Visual InterDev accesses pages on your Web server. This feature enables multiple authors to work on the same pages using either Visual InterDev, for your programmers, or FrontPage, for everyone else.

◆ Using extensions for IIS, Visual InterDev will properly configure the Web server to run and test applications.

◆ Visual InterDev automatically updates the pages on the Web server when it saves files. This feature enables other users to test the Web pages and applications with their favorite Web browsers.

◆ Local project files are used to help one developer access files on his or her computer while another developer works on the same files at another location. In addition, a source control program such as Microsoft SourceSafe enables multiple developers to work on the same project simultaneously.

◆ Visual InterDev includes several sample applications that you can use as starting points for creating your own Web applications.

◆ Visual InterDev's online help system includes useful references including HTML, VBScript, JScript, and ADO references.

♦ Visual InterDev uses standard HTTP to connect with the Web server, allowing you to configure and create Web applications without having physical access to the server.

These features are explained in more depth throughout this chapter as they are used to illustrate how to create dynamic content using Visual InterDev.

NOTE

Visual InterDev uses two sets of server extensions. The FrontPage extensions are used to access the Web files. In addition, you can install separate Visual InterDev extensions on IIS that enable developers to modify application settings. Because these extensions can be a security risk on your Web server, however, you should install them only on a development or test installation of IIS.

Microsoft Visual SourceSafe

Microsoft's Visual SourceSafe is a version control program; that is, it sits in the background and helps track revisions being made on a program. This program enables individual developers to see where changes have been made and to even undo some of those changes. Visual SourceSafe also enables a user to lock a file when he or she is working on it so that no one else works on the same file at the same time.

When trying to manage a Web site that is being modified by a team of developers, Visual SourceSafe can be a lifesaver. Using FrontPage or Visual InterDev, all the developers can modify every file at the site. What happens when two developers want to work on the same file? Visual SourceSafe, running on the Web server, can track who wants to access a file and control who gets to work on the file at any given time.

For more information about using Visual SourceSafe to manage a Web site, check out **http://www.microsoft.com/ssafe/views/web.htm**.

Using Projects

Visual InterDev is quite similar to other Microsoft developer tools and uses the same interface as Visual C++ and Visual J++. One of the similarities is that Visual InterDev combines related files into a project. A project file is a local file that manages a project with a list, or link, of the various related files. Developers choose files to work on from this list, and a local copy is made. The local copy maintains the same basic directory structure that is used at the Web site, which facilitates project management.

The first step to working with Visual InterDev is to create a project file. You can use any one of the four project wizards provided with Visual InterDev and described in Table 17-1 or create your own wizards for creating projects.

Table 17-1 Visual InterDev Project Wizards

Wizard	Description
Web Project Wizard	Creates or connects to an existing FrontPage Web located on a server, allowing you to edit and add files to a Web site.
Sample Application Wizard	Installs and configures sample applications onto a Web server.
Departmental Site Wizard	Creates a basic site with customizable navigation bars and default What's New, People, and Feedback pages.
New Database Wizard	Begins the process of creating a database application by specifying an SQL source and creating a data source project.

Creating a Web Project

The Web Project Wizard is the quickest way to get a project up and running with Visual InterDev. In this example, I assume that you simply want to access an existing Web site with Visual InterDev. The FrontPage server extensions must be installed and running for this example to work. Setting up a Web to use FrontPage is described in Chapter 7. Follow these steps to access a Web with Visual InterDev.

1. Open Visual InterDev.

2. Select New from the File menu. The Projects tab should be selected as shown in Figure 17-1.

3. Enter a path in the Location field for the local path used to store the project files.

4. Enter a Project Name for the project.

5. Select Web Project Wizard from the list of available projects. The list of available projects depends on the Visual Studio programs installed on your computer.

6. Select OK to begin the Web Project Wizard. The first step of this wizard is shown in Figure 17-2.

7. Enter the Web server's name in the field. A list will be maintained so the next time that you use this wizard, you can simply select the server from the list.

8. Select Next to move on to the second step of the Web Project wizard, shown in Figure 17-3.

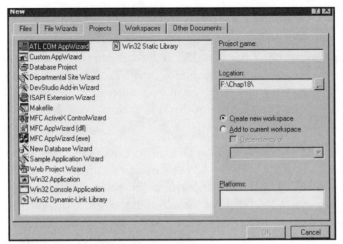

FIGURE 17-1

You must select a Project Wizard.

FIGURE 17-2

Connecting to a Web server with the Web Project Wizard.

FIGURE 17-3

Connecting to a FrontPage Web with the Web Project Wizard.

9. Select an existing FrontPage Web to connect to. You connect to the files at your Web site through an existing FrontPage Web. Alternatively, you can create a new Web.

10. Select Finish. The Wizard will now process the information and collect a list of files currently in the Web.

Editing Files in a Web Project

After a Web project is created, accessing the files in the Web and editing them is quite easy. The main work area of Visual InterDev is divided into two window panes. You use the pane on the left to browse the Web project with the FileView tab. You use the InfoView tab to access the online help system that comes with Visual InterDev. You use the right pane for editing files from the Web project or displaying help topics from InfoView.

The Web files are listed in a hierarchical arrangement in the FileView that matches the directory structure of the Web site. Clicking on a plus sign displays subdirectories and files, whereas clicking on a minus hides subdirectories and files. Double-clicking on a filename retrieves a local copy of the file and opens it in an edit window, as shown in Figure 17-4.

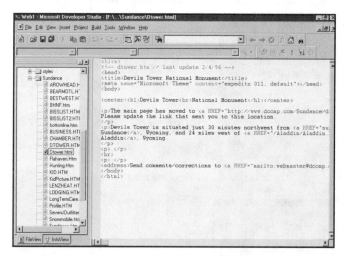

FIGURE 17-4

Editing a file with Visual InterDev.

Visual InterDev edit windows display HTML files as straight text. This product is quite different from the nearly WYSIWYG HTML editor FrontPage. However, compared to other plain text editors such as Notepad, Visual InterDev has a lot of advantages. These advantages include:

- ◆ **Advanced editing features**. Visual InterDev has several advanced editing features that are part of the Developer Studio interface. These features include advanced search and replace options as well as the capability to do a text search through all the files in a directory.

- ◆ **Color coding**. The Visual InterDev editor displays text using special color codes that help to find and read the HTML codes.

- ◆ **Project files**. Visual InterDev's projects give you quick access to other files at the Web site.

◆ **Multiple document interface.** Visual InterDev enables you to have several HTML files open at once. Simply using the Window menu, you can move from one document to another.

◆ **Quick help reference.** Visual InterDev includes an HTML quick reference. To access the quick reference, select the HTML tag you want help with and press the F1 key.

◆ **Script wizards.** Visual InterDev includes wizards to quickly add scripts and ActiveX controls to HTML pages.

Creating Files in a Project

After creating a project, you will eventually add files to that project. This step is quite easy with Visual Interdev. Depending on the type of file you will be adding, you may even want to use one of the file wizards to create the new page.

Visual InterDev includes two file wizards for adding new files. The Data Form Wizard is useful for creating Active Server Pages that add, change, and delete records in a selected database. The Template Page Wizard creates a default page based upon a selected template or theme.

Using the Template Page Wizard

A template is simply a basic framework for a new page. This tool can be especially helpful when you want to maintain a similar appearance throughout a Web site. Another way to achieve a unified look is to use a theme. A *theme* is a collection of graphics, such as background and bullet images, as well as styles that can be included in a Web page or an entire Web site.

Themes and templates are great to use, provided that you can find some that suit your purposes. You can check out Web sites such as the Microsoft Visual InterDev Web site at **http://www.microsoft.com/vinterdev** to find more templates and other Visual InterDev add-ons to use. A final alternative is to create your own templates and themes for use with the Template Page Wizard.

Using Image Composer

Microsoft Image Composer is a graphics program that you can use to compose graphics for your Web site. The term *compose* is used instead of *draw* or *paint* because the Image Composer is an excellent application for combining various graphical images or adding effects to create a new image. This program is not meant to replace full-featured paint or drawing programs, but it does give a content developer a great tool to enhance existing images.

The program can use several different images formats, including the standard Web graphic formats of GIF and JPEG files. This flexibility enables you to create images in other programs and to use images created by other people. The program can also use the Windows TWAIN interface to connect to a scanner.

An image loaded into the Image Composer is treated as an object called a *sprite*. Sprites can be moved around in relation to other objects and modified using different tools and plug-ins. The InterDev CD-ROM contains many sample images that you can use. The best way to start is to load a few images and experiment with the program.

Composing Images

Image Composer includes several tools for manipulating images, and each tool includes many options for fine-tuning the effects you are applying to an image. Follow these steps to prepare a background image, which is one of the effects available in Image Composer.

1. Start the Image Composer program from the Start menu. The program initially appears to look like Figure 17-5.

FIGURE 17-5

Image Composer is ready to manipulate images.

2. Click on the Insert Image File button on the toolbar. This action opens an Insert from File dialog box that uses the standard Open File dialog box.

3. Select an image to load. The example loads the Torus.mic file included on the InterDev CD-ROM.

4. Click on OK to insert the image.

5. Click on the Warps and Filters tools to display the Warps and Filters dialog box.

6. Select Color Enhancement from the list, and the dialog box appears (see Figure 17-6) with the Wash filter selected.

FIGURE 17-6

Color enhancements change the way an image appears.

7. Select the torus image and then click on Apply. This step applies a Wash filter to the torus, giving it a ghostly appearance. Applying a Wash filter is a great way to fade an image for use as the background of a Web page.

8. Select a different image and a different effect to experiment with. The Undo button comes in handy when you don't like a particular effect.

Creating Text Images

The Image Composer includes a text tool for adding text to an image. Text that is added to an image is treated as a separate object, or sprite. Consequently, the effects that are available for editing images can be used with text objects as well. The following steps illustrate how to manipulate text to create a rainbow colored banner.

1. Start the Image Composer program from the Start menu.

2. Click on the Text tool on the left side. This action opens the Text dialog box shown in Figure 17-7.

FIGURE 17-7

The Text tool enables you to insert text.

3. Enter your text into the Text field.

4. Change the font, if desired, by clicking on the Select Font button and selecting a font from the standard Font dialog box.

5. Click on the Apply button to create the text object.

6. Select the Patterns and Fills tool to open the Patterns and Fills dialog box, shown in Figure 17-8.

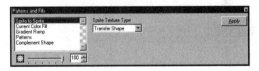

FIGURE 17-8

Patterns and Fills create interesting effects.

7. Select the Color Ramp fill from the list. This option displays a graduated change in color that can be applied to the text.

8. Double-click on one of the four corner colors to change the colors used in the color ramp.

9. Select Apply, and the text will be filled with the color ramp from the dialog box.

10. Experiment with other patterns and fills. The Undo button enables you to undo the last change.

Using Media Manager

Media Manager is useful for keeping track of and organizing the multimedia elements (that is, graphic, audio, or video files) stored on a computer or on the network. The chief use of this program is to quickly search through a collection of graphics, sound, and other media files that will be used in Web pages.

Media Manager stores files in special Media Manager folders, which simplifies the process of creating an index of filenames, sizes, locations, and other basic information about the files. Media Manager also maintains annotations for the different files in a database. The main annotation database may be stored on a networked computer and shared by many developers.

Managing Media Manager Folders

One of the first things that you will notice about Media Manager is that a Media Manger icon wasn't added to the Start menu. The reason is that Media Manager is used inside Windows NT Explorer. You create Media Manager folders in the same way as you create normal file folders, and these folders appear to be standard folders with an additional view, called Thumbnail view. Figure 17-9 illustrates the new Thumbnail view in Windows NT Explorer.

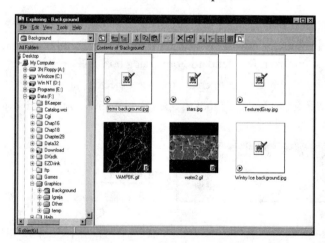

FIGURE 17-9

Windows NT Explorer displays Media Manager folders.

When Media Manager is first installed, you have the option of converting the Media folder in your Windows NT directory to a Media Manager folder. You can create Media Manger folders either by creating new folders or by converting existing folders.

Media Manager adds an option to Windows NT Explorer that enables you to create a new Media Manager folder. Simply right-click wherever you want to create the folder, such as a disk drive, an existing folder, or the Desktop. Then select the

New menu option and Media Manager folder. This menu option can be seen in Figure 17-10.

The other way to create a Media Manager folder is to convert an existing folder, which is the best approach when your media is already organized. Find the folder you wish to convert to a Media Manager folder. Converting a folder also converts all of its subfolders. Right-click on the folder and select Convert to a Media Manager Folder.

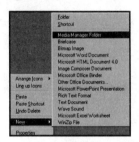

FIGURE 17-10

You can use the Shortcut option to create a new Media Manager folder.

When your media files are organized into Media Manager folders, you can use the special properties of these folders. Two of the more useful things that you can do are to preview the file and to create annotations.

Previewing a Media File

Depending on the type of media file you have, several options are available for previewing it. One option is to create a small thumbnail that is displayed in the Media folder. The other is to play the file in place.

Creating a thumbnail is quite easy. Simply right-click on a file and select the Create Thumbnail option. Some files, such as audio files, do not allow you to create thumbnails. Figure 17-9 shows a mixture of files, some of which have thumbnails.

Some media types, including audio and video files, can be played in place. Media Manager uses the Media Player program to handle this process, so only those files supported by the Media Player can be played. When you select a supported file, VCR-like controls appear at the bottom of the file; these controls enable you to play the file, as shown in Figure 17-11.

NOTE

The file's Property sheet also contains a Preview tab, which you can use to preview a file. Simply open the Preview tab on the file's Property sheet and use the controls to preview the file.

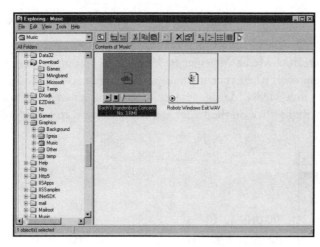

FIGURE 17-11

Media Manager folders enable you to play a file in place.

Creating Annotations

You can create annotations for your media files. Annotations are helpful when you are searching for media files because you can search through the annotations to quickly find the files that you want. To make annotations for a media file, follow these steps:

1. Select the file that you want to annotate.

2. Open the file's Properties dialog box by right-clicking on the file and selecting Properties from the pop-up menu.

3. Click on the Annotations tab and the dialog box should look similar to Figure 17-12.

4. Select an annotation property from the Property list.

5. Enter a note in the Value field.

6. Repeat steps 4 and 5 until you have made all the notes you want.

7. Click on OK to close the Property sheet.

NOTE

If you do not find an appropriate field, you can use the Modify button (see Figure 17-12) to add other fields. This button opens a dialog box that accepts additional annotation fields.

Finding Media Files

Media Manager includes a search engine that can be used to find specific files from Media Manager folders. This search engine is quite similar to the Windows NT Find

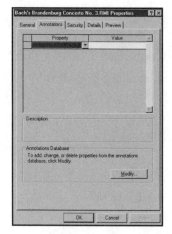

FIGURE 17-12

A media file's Property sheet includes an Annotations tab.

Files capability and can search for files by annotation fields or other file properties. The following steps describe how to search for a media file.

1. Click on the Start button and select Files or Folders in Media Manager from the Find option. The dialog box is shown in Figure 17-13.

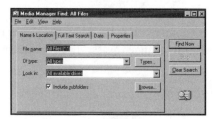

FIGURE 17-13

Find files by name or by type.

2. Enter part of the filename, if known, in the File Name field.

3. Click on the Types button to select a type of file using the Browse For File Type dialog box shown in Figure 17-14. Changing the file type may add a tab to the find dialog box.

FIGURE 17-14

File types are grouped for easy reference.

4. Click on the Full Text Search tab to search for a text file containing specific text.

5. Enter any text in the Look for Text or Annotations Matching field.

6. Select a date range when the file was last modified or created (use the Date tab).

7. Click on the Properties tab to search by any property or annotation.

8. Select an appropriate property from the Property list. This list includes file properties and annotation field names.

9. Select a search condition from the Condition list.

10. Enter a value for the property in the Value field.

11. Select Find Now to get a list of matching files. If the list is too large, you can change any of the values in steps 2 through 10 to limit the search.

12. Click on the close button to close the dialog box when you are done searching for files.

Controlling Media Manager

Media Manager is a service that is always running behind the scenes. From time to time, this service will run its indexer to update the index of all your media files. The default setting is to update the index every hour. Because the Media Manager Indexer can use up a lot of resources, you may want to change this setting. To take control of Media Manager, follow these steps:

1. Open the Control Panel by clicking on the Start menu and selecting Control Panel from the Settings option.

2. Double-click on the Media Manager icon to open the Media Manager applet shown in Figure 17-15

3. Select an option for when the Media Manager Indexer should run to update the index.

4. Optionally, stop the Media Manager Indexer using the Stop Indexer button. The only time that you need to stop the Media Manager Indexer is to rename the root Media Manager folder.

5. Click on OK to close the Media Manager applet.

The Media Manager applet includes a tab for the annotation database. This tab enables you to set the location of the annotation database. Changing the file location is useful when it is stored on a network for use by several people.

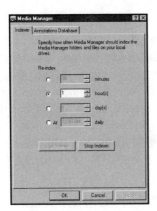

FIGURE 17-15

The Media Manager applet controls the Media Manager Indexer.

Using Music Producer

The Music Producer program is for creating original music files. Even people without a musical background, myself included, can create interesting music files that can be added to Web pages.

Music Producer creates two types of files. One is a work file used only by Music Producer. This file type has the mpp extension and can be loaded to edit sounds at a later time. Music Producer can also save your work in a MIDI file. MIDI stands for Musical Instrument Digital Interface. This type of file is quite small and is easy to add to a Web page.

The main Music Producer program appears in Figure 17-16. To experiment with the program, simply click on the Preview button. The program will then begin playing music. You can then change any of the elements, such as Style and Band. The changes are reflected immediately in the sound you hear. After creating a desirable sound, select a Length and click on Compose to create the file. Use the Play button in the lower-right corner to check out the final results. To save the file for use at your

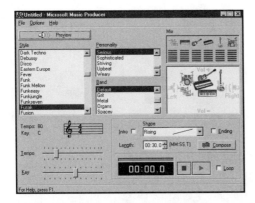

FIGURE 17-16

Even the musically challenged can use Music Producer.

Web site, select Save as MIDI from the File menu. You will have your own MIDI file to add to a Web page or play elsewhere to your heart's content. The Media Manager applet controls the Media Manager Indexerview button. The program will then begin playing music. You can then change any of the elements, such as Style and Band. The changes are reflected immediately in the sound you hear. After creating a desirable sound, select a Length and click on Compose to create the file. Use the Play button in the lower-right corner to check out the final results. To save the file for use at your Web site, select Save as MIDI from the File menu. You will have your own MIDI file to add to a Web page or play elsewhere to your heart's content.

Creating a MIDI file is straightforward. For the most part, the controls such as Style and Tempo are self-explanatory. Others are quick to reveal themselves; for example, changing the Band setting changes the instruments used in playing the music. Another feature enables you to move the instruments around in the Mix area to change the sound effects. A final note is that the Shape setting really applies only when you are using the Play button.

After you create the file, you can add the following code to an HTML page to play the MIDI file in the background:

```
<bgsound src="CoolMusic.mid" loop="-1">
```

This tag will play the CoolMusic.mid file. The Loop property determines how many times the file will be played. To continually loop the file, set the Loop property to -1.

PART IV

Database Publishing with IIS

Chapter 18

Using the Internet
Database Connector

In This Chapter

◆ What Is ODBC?

◆ Creating an IDC Connection

If you work with quite a bit of information that is stored in databases, you can use that information to help make your Web site more dynamic. The key to doing this task quickly and easily is using the Internet Database Connector, or IDC, which is built into IIS. This tool enables you to utilize the ODBC capabilities of Windows to communicate with an ODBC-compliant database to request and subsequently display information.

IDC is not used to create new databases or to add information to existing databases. Instead, IDC enables you to access information in an existing database. The examples in this chapter create the various files that IDC needs to tap into information contained in an Access database.

What Is ODBC?

ODBC, an acronym for *open database connectivity*, is a specification that allows an application to access information from a database program. Essentially, ODBC provides a way to use OLE technology to access information using SQL queries. As an example, you might have a database that utilizes ODBC. A program, external to the database, can pass SQL queries to the database using ODBC. The database then returns the results of the SQL query, via ODBC, to your program.

Since ODBC's general introduction in late 1992, many database vendors have adopted the specification as a way to share information in the Windows environment. In fact, if you purchased or updated a full-featured relational database in the last few years, it probably supports ODBC.

NOTE

Some vendors may not support ODBC as part of their base product, but they may offer ODBC add-ons that provide the ODBC connectivity you need to take advantage of IDC.

As you learned in Chapter 16, ISAPI is a programming specification that facilitates communication between an Internet server (IIS) and an application program. Technically, ODBC is also an interface specification used by programmers. After it's implemented in a product, however, you can take advantage of ODBC without worrying about the specifics of how it works behind the scenes.

Creating an IDC Connection

IDC is an acronym for *Internet Database Connector.* This feature of IIS provides a way for you to extend the capabilities of standard HTML, in conjunction with ODBC, so that you can access information in an ODBC database. To implement an IDC link, you need only the following five items:

- ◆ A database table
- ◆ An ODBC data source name (DSN)
- ◆ An IDC file
- ◆ An HTX file
- ◆ An HTML file

The best way to show how to create these items is within the context of an example. Each of the following sections shows how to develop an item necessary for an IDC link. In this case, the example is an HTML form that enables users to access a database of computer hardware manufacturers and to search by any of several criteria.

Your Database Table

With IDC, you can access information stored in a ODBC-compliant database. Most modern databases, including Microsoft SQL Server, Microsoft Access, and Paradox for Windows, offer some sort of ODBC compliance. Exactly how you put your database together doesn't really matter; you can create any fields you want. The important thing is the availability of ODBC in your database.

For this example, you can use an Access database provided as a support file, \Chap18\Hardware.mdb. Within the database is a table called Manufacturer. Table 18-1 shows the layout of the Manufacturer table.

Setting Up an ODBC Data Source Name

The second step in establishing your IDC link is to establish a data source name (DSN) for your database. ODBC requires that you establish a DSN for each data source that you use. In the sample Access database, the DSN is the Access database filename, which is Hardware.mdb.

You can use the ODBC applet in the Control Panel to establish your DSN. As an example, the following steps create a DSN for the Hardware.mdb database:

Table 18-1 **Table Layout for** `Manufacturer`

Field Name	Type	Length
ManufacturerID	AutoNumber	Long Integer
ManufacturerName	Text	50
Address1	Text	50
Address2	Text	50
City	Text	25
State	Text	2
ZIP	Text	12
TollFree	Text	30
MainNumber	Text	30
FaxNumber	Text	30
URL	Text	50

NOTE

If you don't have a copy of Access, you won't be able to directly load or view the database provided as a support file. If you have a different ODBC-compliant database, then you may want to try opening the database file anyway. Some programs convert from one format (Access) to another (your database) automatically. You do not, however, need a copy of Access to use an Access database with IDC. Indeed, all you need is the ODBC driver for Access, which should already be loaded on your system and which you learn about in the next section.

1. Open the Control Panel.

2. Double-click on the ODBC icon. The ODBC Data Source Administrator dialog box appears, as shown in Figure 18-1.

NOTE

If the ODBC icon isn't visible in your Control Panel, the proper ODBC drivers aren't installed on your system. See your database documentation for information on installing the proper drivers.

3. Click on the System DSN tab. (This tab shows the DSNs already defined for your system.)

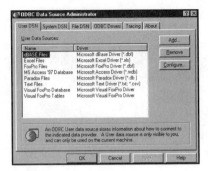

FIGURE 18-1

To use IDC, you must define data source names for your ODBC objects.

NOTE

Although ODBC enables you to create types of DSNs other than System DSNs, IDC works only with System DSNs. Using any other type of DSN results in IDC not working properly or at all.

---

4. Click on the A̲dd button. This action starts the Create New Data Source dialog box, as shown in Figure 18-2.

5. Highlight the Microsoft Access Driver and click on the Finish button. The ODBC Microsoft Access Setup dialog box appears, as shown in Figure 18-3.

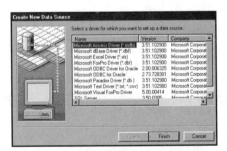

FIGURE 18-2

The Create New Data Source dialog box displays the currently installed ODBC drivers.

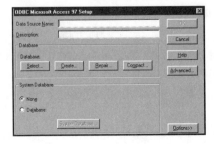

FIGURE 18-3

You use the ODBC Microsoft Access Setup dialog box to define the location and type of data source.

> **NOTE**
>
> The contents of the ODBC Setup dialog box may differ if you are not using the same version of Access (97) used in this example or if you are using a different database program entirely.

6. Enter the name that you want to use for your DSN in the Data Source Name field. This entry should be a descriptive name, such as **Mfg Database**.

7. Enter a description for this DSN in the Description field. This step is optional but may help you remember the purpose of this DSN later.

8. Click on the Select button. This action opens a standard file selection dialog box. Select the Access database you want to use. (For this example, the file is Hardware.mdb.)

9. Click on OK to accept your choice. The database name now appears in the ODBC Microsoft Access Setup dialog box.

10. Click on OK to close the ODBC Microsoft Access Setup dialog box. The newly defined DSN should appear in the list of system DSNs.

11. Click on OK to close the ODBC Data Source Administrator dialog box.

Your IDC File

IDC requires you to establish a file that indicates the name of the database file and table you're planning to access. This information and some additional housekeeping items are stored in what is called an "IDC file." (Bet you can't figure out where the name came from.) The IDC file holds one field per line, followed by a colon, a space, and then the value to be assigned to the field. For instance, the following line is a single field from an IDC file:

```
Datasource: Mfg Database
```

Table 18-2 lists the fields that you can use in your IDC file.

Notice that only three fields are really required in the IDC file: `Datasource`, `SQLStatement`, and `Template`. Most of the time, you won't need to use the additional fields unless you have a specific need, as dictated by your database program.

A Simple IDC File

The easiest way to establish an IDC file is to create one that returns the same information each time it's accessed. The IDC file is nothing but an ASCII text file. You can easily create an IDC file using any text editor, such as Notepad.

Table 18-2 IDC File Fields

Field	Meaning
Content Type	A valid MIME type, indicating what will be returned to the client.
Datasource	The name that you assigned to your ODBC data source (step 6 in the preceding section). This field is mandatory in the IDC file.
Expires	The number of seconds to wait before refreshing a cached output page.
MaxFieldSize	The maximum buffer space allocated by the ODBC driver for each field in your query. (The default value is 8,192 bytes per field.)
MaxRecords	The maximum number of records the driver will return from a query.
ODBCConnection	The type of ODBC connection to establish. If set to *pool*, the connection is left open pending future ODBC requests. If set to *nopool* (the default), connections are closed after each use. Pooling provides faster throughput but ties up resources longer.
Password	The password used to access the database table. If you supply a password, you must supply a username. (See the Username field.)
RequiredParameters	The parameter names, separated by commas, that you want the ODBC query to return. Typically this field isn't used for simple queries.
SQLStatement	The SQL statement on one or more lines. If the statement occupies multiple lines, each line after the first must begin with a plus sign (+). This field is mandatory in the IDC file.
Template	The name of the HTX file that you created (covered later in this chapter). This field is mandatory in the IDC file.
Translationfile	The path and filename of a character-mapping file used for publishing information in non-English languages.
Username	The username required to access the database table.

As an example, suppose that you want to access the sample computer manufacturer's database and have it return a list of the various manufacturers sorted by company name. This task is very easy when you know the SQL query that you want to use to extract the information. The following SQL query extracts the desired information from the sample database:

```
SELECT * FROM [Manufacturer] ORDER BY ManufacturerName
```

> **NOTE**
>
> For help with SQL, refer to either the online help for Access or a good SQL reference book, such as *Microsoft SQL Server 7 Administrator's Guide* by Ron Talmage, published by Prima Publishing.

This simple SQL SELECT statement uses only two keywords (FROM and ORDER BY). In this example, you are selecting the entire table (Manufacturer) and sorting it by the ManufacturerName field.

With your SELECT statement in hand, you are ready to put together the IDC file. The following sample file is included as the support file \Chap18\Mfg.idc:

```
Datasource: Mfg Database
Template: MfgList.htx
SQLStatement:
+SELECT * FROM [Manufacturer] ORDER BY ManufacturerName
```

This IDC file contains only the three mandatory fields. These fields indicate the ODBC data source to use to get information, the HTX file to use as a template for the output, and the SQL statement to use to retrieve the required information. Each of the first two fields occupy a single line in the IDC file; the SQLStatement field occupies two lines. In this case, the continuation line begins with the plus sign (+) to signify that it's part of the same SQL query. In a multiple-line query, each line would begin with the plus sign, as well.

Parameters in an IDC File

You can also use parameters in the SQL statement defined in your IDC file. These parameters tie into the field names that you specify in an HTML form. (You learned about forms in Chapter 9.) You then use the same field name, surrounded by percent signs (%), and include it in your IDC file. This technique enables you to request information from the user, which is then used to modify the information extracted from the database.

For example, suppose that you created an HTML form that enables the user to specify the state for which they want to see a list of manufacturers. The file \Chap18\State.idc, from the support files, is an example of such an IDC file:

```
Datasource: Mfg Database
Template: MfgList.htx
SQLStatement:
```

```
+SELECT * FROM [Manufacturer]
+WHERE State = '%State%'
+ORDER BY ManufacturerName
```

In this case, the SQLStatement field is much longer than a statement without parameters, because it contains a single replaceable parameter—%State%. The percent signs tell IIS that this field is a parameter. The server then looks for the State field in the HTML form from which this IDC file was called and replaces the %State% parameter with the value of that variable. Thus, if the user selects CO (for Colorado), the query is automatically translated as follows:

```
Datasource: Mfg Database
Template: MfgList.htx
SQLStatement:
+SELECT * FROM [Manufacturer]
+WHERE State = 'CO'
+ORDER BY ManufacturerName
```

If the SQL statement needs an asterisk, such as when using the LIKE operator in a WHERE clause, you need to modify the proper line in the IDC file just a bit. Suppose that you want to search for all manufacturers beginning with a certain group of letters. You might think that the following line would work:

```
+WHERE ManufacturerName LIKE '%MfgStart%*'
```

This line doesn't provide the desired results, however. Instead, you need to remove the asterisk and include two more percent signs in the clause, as in the following line:

```
+WHERE ManufacturerName LIKE '%MfgStart%%%'
```

This usage translates to the desired result just fine.

Your HTX File

An HTX file defines how you want to display the output from your query. The name *HTX file* comes from the accepted filename extension, htx, which identifies the file as an extended HTML file. HTX files can be used only with IDC.

For the most part, HTX files look just like regular HTML files. However, you can use a few additional tags to define how to display the ODBC data returned by your IDC query. For instance, the <%begindetail%> and <%enddetail%> tags indicate the beginning and end of your format section. Notice the use of the angle brackets and percent signs. In this case, the combination defines the tag as an extended HTML tag.

> **NOTE**
>
> You may recognize the <% and %> delimiters as the same delimiters used in ASP files. Don't confuse HTX with ASP files, however; they are definitely not the same. (For more information on ASP files, refer to Chapter 14.)

Within the format section (which actually defines the beginning and end of a database record), you use the <% and %> markers around column names to define where your output should appear. For example, the file \Chap18\MfgList.htx, one of the support files, represents a very simple HTX file:

```
<html>
<head>
<title>Computer Hardware Manufacturer List (Complete)</title>
</head>
<body>

<center><h1>Computer Hardware Manufacturers</h1></center>
<p>The following list represents the entire database, in
manufacturer order.
<p>
<table>
<tr><th>Manufacturer</th><th colspan="2">Address</th><th>City</th>
<th>State</th><th>ZIP Code</th><th>Main Phone</th>
<th>Toll-free Number</th><th>Fax Number</th><th>URL</th></tr>
<%begindetail%>
<tr><td><%ManufacturerName%></td><td><%Address1%></td>
<td><%Address2%></td><td><%City%></td><td><%State%></td>
<td><%ZIP%></td><td><%MainNumber%></td><td><%TollFree%></td>
<td><%FaxNumber%></td><td><%URL%></td></tr>
<%enddetail%>
</table>

</body>
</html>
```

Notice that the <%begindetail%> and <%enddetail%> tags enclose a single table row. Because these tags define the limits of a database record, each record in the database appears in its own table row. Column names are then used, again with <% and %> delimiters, to indicate the contents of the cells within a row.

Conditional Tags

Your HTX file can contain tags that implement conditional logic. If you're already familiar with programming concepts, you may intuitively know how to use the <%if%>, <%else%>, and <%endif%> tags. Basically, the conditional statement following the <%if%> tag is evaluated. If it is true, then everything between the statement and the <%else%> or <%endif%> tags is executed. If it is not true and if you include the optional <%else%> tag, then everything between the <%else%> tag and the <%endif%> tag is executed.

SUPPORT FILE

As an example, load the file \Chap18\NewList.htx from the support files. This file is an expansion of the HTX file presented in the preceding section:

```
<html>
<head>
<title>Computer Hardware Manufacturer List (Complete)</title>
</head>
<body>

<center><h1>Computer Hardware Manufacturers</h1></center>
<p>The following list represents the entire database, in
manufacturer order. (Company names shown in <b>bold</b>
have toll-free numbers you can use to contact them.)
<p>
<table>
<tr><th>Manufacturer</th><th colspan="2">Address</th><th>City</th>
<th>State</th><th>ZIP Code</th><th>Main Phone</th>
<th>Toll-free Number</th><th>Fax Number</th><th>URL</th></tr>
<%begindetail%>
<tr><%if TollFree GT "100"%>
<td><b><%ManufacturerName%></b></td>
<%else%>
<td><%ManufacturerName%></td>
<%endif%>
<td><%Address1%></td>
```

```
<td><%Address2%></td><td><%City%></td><td><%State%></td>
<td><%ZIP%></td><td><%MainNumber%></td><td><%TollFree%></td>
<td><%FaxNumber%></td><td><%URL%></td></tr>
<%enddetail%>
</table>


</body>
</html>
```

Here the conditional tags determine whether the database contains a toll-free number for the manufacturer. If a toll-free number is available, the company name is shown in bold. If not, the company name is not bold. The general format of the `<%if%>` tag is as follows:

```
<%if value1 operator value2%>
```

You can replace *value1* and *value2* with any values you want, and you can replace *operator* with one of the following operators:

EQ	Equals
LT	Less than
GT	Greater than
CONTAINS	Returns TRUE if *value2* is contained anywhere in *value1*

Values used in a conditional statement can be any column name, any built-in variable (described in the next section), or any constant. Notice from the sample file, however, that when you use column names in an `<%if%>` tag, the column name isn't surrounded by the `<%` and `%>` delimiters.

Built-in Variables

Your conditional statements can use either of two built-in variables if desired. The `CurrentRecord` variable indicates the iteration through a `<%begindetail>` and `<%enddetail%>` section. The first time through, `CurrentRecord` is zero. It's incremented once for each additional time through the section.

The `MaxRecords` variable indicates the setting that you made for `MaxRecords` in the IDC file. As such, it isn't particularly helpful in determining the number of records returned in a query. But it is useful for determining whether you've reached the maximum number—a limit that you may have set for your query.

Unfortunately, the built-in variables can be used only in an <%if%> tag; they can't be used elsewhere in the HTX file. Thus, the following code lines will not produce the desired results:

```
<%begindetail%>
<tr><td>CurrentRecord</td><td><%ManufacturerName%></td>
<td><%Address1%></td><td><%Address2%></td><td><%City%></td>
<td><%State%></td><td><%ZIP%></td><td><%MainNumber%></td>
<td><%TollFree%></td><td><%FaxNumber%></td><td><%URL%></td></tr>
<%enddetail%>
```

Instead of providing a record counter, as you might hope, this code simply prints the word CurrentRecord in the first cell of each record in the table.

IDC Parameters

You can include parameters from your IDC file in your HTX file. Remember that these parameters are nothing more than the variables provided by someone in an original HTML form. You include these parameters by prefacing the parameter name with the letters idc and a period (.) and then surrounding the entire parameter with the <% and %> tags. (This construct may look very familiar to readers comfortable with the object model described in Chapter 14.)

SUPPORT FILE

This modified version of the preceding HTX file includes parameters from an IDC file. This file is contained in the support files as \Chap18\StateList.htx:

```
<html>
<head>
<title>Computer Hardware Manufacturer List (For a State)</title>
</head>
<body>

<center><h1>Computer Hardware Manufacturers</h1></center>
<p>You requested a list of all hardware manufacturers within
<emp><%idc.State%></emp>. Using this specification, the following
companies are currently included in our database. (Company names shown in
<b>bold</b>
have toll-free numbers you can use to contact them.)
<p>
<table>
```

```
<tr><th>Manufacturer</th><th colspan="2">Address</th><th>City</th>
<th>State</th><th>ZIP Code</th><th>Main Phone</th>
<th>Toll-free Number</th><th>Fax Number</th><th>URL</th></tr>
<%begindetail%>
<tr><%if TollFree GT "100"%>
<td><b><%ManufacturerName%></b></td>
<%else%>
<td><%ManufacturerName%></td>
<%endif%>
<td><%Address1%></td>
<td><%Address2%></td><td><%City%></td><td><%State%></td>
<td><%ZIP%></td><td><%MainNumber%></td><td><%TollFree%></td>
<td><%FaxNumber%></td><td><%URL%></TD></tr>
<%enddetail%>
</table>


</body>
</html>
```

Notice the difference in the beginning text, before the table starts. This example uses the `<%idc.State%>` tag. Because of the `idc.` preface, the IIS server understands that you're referring to an IDC file parameter, not to a column name.

Your HTML File

The easiest way to access the information in a database from a Web page is to create a simple link between the document and the IDC file. This very simple HTML document, included in the support files as \Chap18\Simple.htm, does just that:

```
<html>
<head>
<title>Computer Hardware Manufacturers</title>
</head>
<body>

<center><h1>Computer Hardware Manufacturers</h1></center>

Welcome to the computer hardware manufacturer finder page.
```

This page allows you to access a large database of vendor names
and contact information. You can use this information to determine
how to get in touch with a particular computer hardware company.

<p><hr><p>

To see a list of manufacturers, sorted by company name,

<a href="/scripts/hardware/mfg.idc">click here</a>.

<p><hr><p>

</body>

</html>

Notice that the link points to the `Mfg.idc` file, which is located in a subdirectory of the `/Scripts` area (where you should place your IDC files). To the user, this file looks like a regular Web page, as shown in Figure 18-4.

FIGURE 18-4

You can establish a link to an IDC file as a normal anchor in a Web document.

When the user clicks on the link, IDC displays the information defined in the IDC file according to the format shown in the HTX file. The IDC file used with this page is the Mfg.idc file, which was developed earlier in the chapter. The HTX file, MfgList.htx, was also discussed earlier in the chapter.

The result, when executed, is shown in Figure 18-5. Notice that the file displays the information in table form, just as desired when putting together the HTX file.

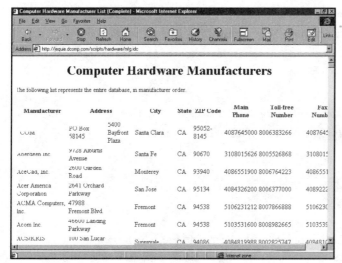

FIGURE 18-5

IDC enables you to quickly create dynamic Web documents.

NOTE

Notice that the ZIP codes and phone numbers in the table are not formatted. The reason is that the fields are stored unformatted in the Access database, and IDC returns information in the same format in which it is stored in the database. If you want to view formatted information, you must either save it as formatted or create scripts to format the text for you. (From a Web perspective, the former method is much faster than the latter.)

SUPPORT FILE

As mentioned earlier in this chapter, you can also use HTML forms to pass parameters to your IDC file. The following is a modified version of the HTML file, stored in the support files as \Chap18\PickState.htm. This version of the file enables the user to select a specific state by which to limit the database output.

```
<html>

<head>

<title>Computer Hardware Manufacturers</title>

</head>

<body>


<center><h1>Computer Hardware Manufacturers</h1></center>


Welcome to the computer hardware manufacturer finder page.
This page allows you to access a large database of vendor names
```

and contact information. You can use this information to determine how to get in touch with a particular computer hardware company.

```
<p><hr><p>
```
To see a list of manufacturers, sorted by company name,
```
<a href="/scripts/hardware/mfg.idc">click here</a>.
<p><hr><p>

<form method="post" action="/scripts/hardware/state.idc">
```
To limit the output to those companies in a specific state, pick the state here
```
<select name="State">
<option value="AL">Alabama
<option value="AK">Alaska
<option value="AZ">Arizona
<option value="AR">Arkansas
<option value="CA">California
<option value="CO">Colorado
<option value="CT">Connecticut
<option value="DE">Delaware
<option value="FL">Florida
<option value="GA">Georgia
<option value="HI">Hawaii
<option value="ID">Idaho
<option value="IL">Illinois
<option value="IN">Indiana
<option value="IA">Iowa
<option value="KS">Kansas
<option value="KY">Kentucky
<option value="LA">Louisiana
<option value="ME">Maine
<option value="MD">Maryland
<option value="MA">Massachusetts
<option value="MI">Michigan
<option value="MN">Minnisota
<option value="MS">Mississippi
<option value="MO">Missouri
```

```
<option value="MT">Montana
<option value="NE">Nebraska
<option value="NV">Nevada
<option value="NH">New Hampshire
<option value="NJ">New Jersey
<option value="NM">New Mexico
<option value="NY">New York
<option value="NC">North Carolina
<option value="ND">North Dakota
<option value="OH">Ohio
<option value="OK">Oklahoma
<option value="OR">Oregon
<option value="PA">Pennsylvania
<option value="RI">Rhode Island
<option value="SC">South Carolina
<option value="SD">South Dakota
<option value="TN">Tennessee
<option value="TX">Texas
<option value="UT">Utah
<option value="VT">Vermont
<option value="VA">Virginia
<option value="WA">Washington
<option value="WV">West Virginia
<option value="WI">Wisconsin
<option value="WY">Wyoming
</select>
and then click on the <input type="submit"> button.
</form>
<p><hr><p>

</body>
</html>
```

Figure 18-6 shows the result of this HTML code.

Notice that the HTML <FORM> tag points to a different IDC file. The reason is that the IDC file must take the form variables into account. In this case, the IDC file is the \Chap18\State2.idc file from the support files. This file is essentially the same as

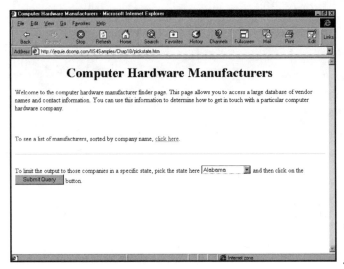

FIGURE 18-6

The variables in an HTML form can be used in IDC.

the State.idc file discussed earlier in the chapter, with one minor difference:

```
Datasource: Mfg Database
Template: StateList.htx
SQLStatement:
+SELECT * FROM [Manufacturer]
+WHERE State = '%State%'
+ORDER BY ManufacturerName
```

As you can tell by looking at the IDC file, the `Datasource` is the same as the previous IDC file and as in the original State.idc file, but the `Template` (HTX file) is different. The HTX file in this instance is the StateList.htx file, which was also discussed earlier in the chapter:

```
<html>
<head>
<title>Computer Hardware Manufacturer List (For a State)</title>
</head>
<body>

<center><h1>Computer Hardware Manufacturers</h1></center>
<p>You requested a list of all hardware manufacturers within
<emp><%idc.State%></emp>. Using this specification, the following
companies are currently included in our database. (Company names shown in
<b>bold</b>
```

```
have toll-free numbers you can use to contact them.)
<p>
<table>
<tr><th>Manufacturer</th><th colspan="2">Address</th><th>City</th>
<th>State</th><th>ZIP Code</th><th>Main Phone</th>
<th>Toll-free Number</th><th>Fax Number</th></tr>
<%begindetail%>
<tr><%if TollFree GT "100"%>
<td><b><%ManufacturerName%></b></td>
<%else%>
<td><%ManufacturerName%></td>
<%endif%>
<td><%Address1%></td>
<td><%Address2%></td><td><%City%></td><td><%State%></td>
<td><%ZIP%></td><td><%MainNumber%></td><td><%TollFree%></td>
<td><%FaxNumber%></td></tr>
<%enddetail%>
</table>

</body>
</html>
```

Here the parameter from the IDC file is used, as discussed earlier in the chapter. Figure 18-7 shows the result of a search for companies in Illinois.

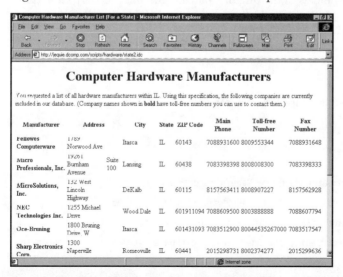

FIGURE 18-7

An IDC Web document can display IDC file parameters and the results from your SQL query.

Chapter 19

Microsoft Transaction
Server

———

In This Chapter

◆ Understanding MTS

◆ Controlling MTS

◆ Configuring MTS Security

◆ Using MTS with ASP

◆ Registering Components

◆ Creating Components

Microsoft Transaction Server, or MTS, is one of the technologies included with IIS to assist with using databases. This server monitors *transactions,* which are simply a collection of database activities that should either succeed or fail together, even if the activities require many steps. An example of a transaction is creating an order. When placing the order, you may need to update inventory and billing information as well as place the order.

Understanding MTS

MTS is a vital component of IIS, and IIS cannot be installed without MTS, although it is a separate component. One reason for this arrangement is that MTS is used to manage IIS Web applications. Web applications can be run as separate packages under MTS. This approach allows the program to be isolated and maintains IIS integrity should the Web application crash.

For example, you could have created a buggy ISAPI application to provide feedback to site visitors. In this example, assume that more visitors try to access this application than the original developer planned. The ISAPI application fails. Because MTS is managing the application, it can stop your application and the visitors will simply get an error message. Without MTS, the failing ISAPI application might bring your Web server to a halt.

This same technology is available for monitoring database transactions that are taking place at your Web site. MTS tracks any changes that are being made to a database. All the changes tied to a transaction must pass or fail together, even if the transaction includes several steps normally viewed as separate transactions. In order to use MTS for database transactions at your Web site, you will need to configure MTS to watch the database and use ASP scripts. This configuration is described later in the chapter.

MTS manages transactions through a collection of packages that are installed on a computer. These packages are collections of components that can be used by MTS. The packages are classified as library or server packages. *Library packages* are collections of general purpose tools, or components. *Server packages* are more versatile and may be used to manage different programs on the server; they may also require additional security.

> **NOTE**
>
> A minimum IIS installation also does a minimum MTS installation. You may need to run the Windows NT 4.0 Option Pack setup program again to install other MTS components such as the MTS development samples and documentation.

Controlling MTS

You manage MTS in much the same way that you manage IIS using Microsoft Management Console (MMC) tools. Two preconfigured tools control MTS. One is the MTS snap-in included in the Internet Service Manager. The other tool is Server Explorer, or MTS Explorer, shown in Figure 19-1. The only noticeable difference between them is that Transaction Server Explorer includes links to documentation at Microsoft's Web site.

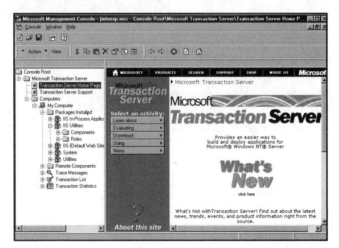

FIGURE 19-1

Transaction Server Explorer controls the MTS settings and connects to Microsoft's Web site.

MTS Explorer can be started from the Programs menu on the Start menu. Transaction Server Explorer is a program in the Microsoft Transaction Server submenu of the Windows NT 4.0 Option Pack menu.

Configuring MTS Security

From the IIS administrator's perspective, the main function of Microsoft Transaction Server is to control database operations from ASP pages. To use this feature, you will have to add packages and components to the basic MTS configuration, or use pre-configured packages. MTS includes security features that enable you to limit who can add, remove, and change package information.

MTS security is based on roles and the type of package. A *role* is similar to a Windows NT group. The role describes different things that a user can do. A role is created and users are *mapped*, or assigned, to that role. The user can then do anything that is allowed by the role.

One of the basic packages included with MTS is the System package, which controls different aspects of MTS. The default installation of MTS creates two roles for the System package. The Administrator role enables a user to access all the functions in MTS Explorer. The Reader role enables a user to view the objects in MTS Explorer, but not to access any of the other functions, such as exporting packages, shutting down server processes, or installing new objects.

NOTE

If MTS is installed on a Window NT Server machine being used as a primary or backup domain controller, only users who are in the domain administrator's group can manage packages in MTS Explorer.

Some of the other packages, namely, the IIS In-Process Applications and the Utilities packages, do not have roles assigned to them, because they are library packages instead of server packages. For a library package to use the available security features, you must add roles to these packages (see the section "Creating MTS Roles" later in this chapter). The packages must then be changed from library to server packages. There is also one package without roles, the IIS Utilities package, to which you cannot assign any roles.

Assigning Users to MTS Roles

When you first install MTS, the service needs to be mapped to a username. Until MTS roles are mapped to users, MTS does not do any security checks. Therefore, anyone who can access MTS Explorer can also control MTS. The following steps describe how to map a Windows NT user to an MTS role:

1. Open MTS Explorer or the Internet Service Manager.
2. Display the packages installed in the scope pane. You may need to click on the plus sign next to the Computers folder, the My Computer icon, and the Packages Installed folder before you can see these packages.

3. Select a package containing the controls where you want to assign roles. Unless you have assigned roles to the other packages, only the System package has roles that can be assigned.

4 Double-click on the Roles folder to display the available roles. The program should look similar to Figure 19-2, depending on the package you are working with.

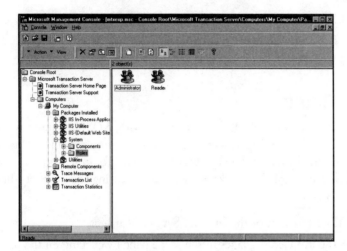

FIGURE 19-2

MTS roles are assigned using MTS Explorer.

5.. Double-click on the icon of the role you wish to assign. This action opens the Users folder.

6. Double-click on the Users folder to open it. The folder is initially empty because no users have been assigned.

7. Select New from the Action menu and then choose User. This action opens the Add Users and Groups to Role dialog box shown in Figure 19-3.

FIGURE 19-3

MTS can use any of the groups or users from your Windows NT Domain.

8. Select the Groups and Users to add to this role. You may need to use the Show Users button to locate user accounts.

9. Select Add to assign the selected group or user to the list at the bottom of the dialog box.

10. Repeat steps 8 and 9 until you have selected all the users and groups for this role.

11. Select OK to make the changes and return to MTS Explorer.

12. Repeat steps 3 through 11 for other packages.

13. Close MTS Explorer.

Creating MTS Roles

You may find that the two default roles included with MTS are quite limiting. Perhaps you want to give developers a chance to add and run new objects, but don't want them to accidentally delete the objects already there. To do so, you can create a new role to which you assign all your developers. The following steps describe how to create a new MTS role:

1. Open MTS Explorer or the Internet Service Manager.

2. Display the installed packages in the scope pane by clicking on the plus sign next to the Computers folder, the My Computer icon, and the Packages Installed folder as necessary.

3. Select a package that will be getting a new role.

4. Double-click on the Roles folder to display the available roles. The program should look similar to Figure 19-2, depending on the package you are working with.

5. Make sure that the Roles folder is selected.

6. Select New from the Action menu and then choose Role. This action opens the New Role dialog box, shown in Figure 19-4. If you are adding a role to a library package, a warning dialog box appears before this New Role dialog box. The warning states that security can't be set to a library package.

7. Enter a name for the new role in the dialog box. This action activates the OK button.

8. Select OK to add the new role to the package.

9. Repeat steps 3 through 8 to add roles to other packages.

10. Close MTS Explorer.

FIGURE 19-4

Assign a name for your new role.

Enabling MTS Security

After you create the roles and assign users to them, you can enable security on the various packages. In MTS, you can enable security at many levels. Security can be enabled on a particular package, a component in the package, or even at the interface level for the component. To enable security on MTS, follow these basic steps:

1. Open MTS Explorer or the Internet Service Manager.
2. Display the installed packages in the scope pane by clicking on the plus sign next to the Computers folder, the My Computer icon, and the Packages Installed folder as necessary.
3. Select a package that will have security enabled. Optionally, you can select a component of a package or an interface of one of the components.
4. Right-click on the package, or other object, and select Properties from the pop-up menu. This action displays the package's Properties dialog box.
5. Select the Security tab and the property sheet appears, as shown in Figure 19-5.
6. Select Enable Authorization Checking. If this check box is not grayed out, it could be because you are working with a library package. If you really want to change the security, you will have to change the package to a server package by going to the Activation tab and selecting the Server Package option.
7. Select the level of authorization from the Authentication Level of Calls drop-down list.

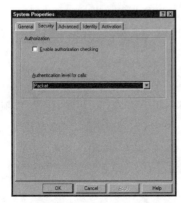

FIGURE 19-5

Security features are located in the Properties dialog box.

8. Select OK to close the Properties dialog box to apply the changes.

9. Close MTS Explorer.

Using MTS with ASP

One of the best uses for MTS is to handle any database transactions at your Web site through ASPs. These ASPs require several server objects, which are described in Chapter 14, "Understanding Active Server Pages."

As mentioned earlier in this chapter, MTS can be used to manage database transactions. A *transaction* is an operation that succeeds or fails as a whole, even though it may involve many steps. An example is creating an order: you create an order, check inventory, and prepare a bill. Transactions enable you to easily cancel all the steps if any one of the steps fails. The process of undoing any changes made when a transaction fails is called *rolling back*.

Without the benefit of MTS, reliable database updates are difficult to implement. You would have to keep track of all the changes that were being made throughout the entire order-taking process, or whatever else you were doing. This type of tracking would require several scripts to handle all the changes, as well as all the scripts and forms used to get the input from the client.

Transaction objects are not intended to span more than one ASP. If you want to manage an order and have one component for creating an order and one component for creating a bill, both components must be included on the same page. Using the same logic, you should not store transaction objects in ASP Application or Session objects. Transaction objects are automatically deactivated when a transaction is completed. Calls to transaction objects after that time cause errors.

Creating a Transactional Script

The first step to using transactions within an ASP application is to declare that the script uses transactions by placing the following `@transaction` directive at the top of a page:

```
<%@ transaction = Some_Value %>
```

`Some_Value` represents the type of transaction that will be used in the ASP. This value can be one of the following:

- ◆ `Not_Supported` Does not support, or start, a transaction
- ◆ `Required` Begins a new transaction

♦ `Requires_New` Begins a new transaction

♦ `Supported` Does not begin a transaction

One thing to remember is that not all the scripts in your application need to be transaction scripts. Only use transaction scripts where transaction processing takes place. One place that you cannot put transaction scripts is in the global.asa file that stores scripts used by an entire application.

NOTE

The global.asa file is a special script file that can be placed in the root directory of a Web application. This file is used to store information across several ASPs.

Completing Transactions

The main purpose of MTS is to determine whether a transaction completes successfully or fails. However, you may also want to abort a transaction manually, such as when an operation not monitored by MTS fails.

For example, MTS cannot roll back file changes or variable changes. Currently, the only resources that support full rolling back are databases. Because MTS cannot roll back these events, it does not monitor them. It is possible that your transaction must access a nondatabase file. If this action fails, you will need to call the `SetAbort` method and manually abort the transaction. You will also have to create your own scripts to restore any files or variables.

Using Transaction Events

When a transaction is completed, successfully or not, you can create `OnTransactionCommit` and `OnTransactionAbort` events to notify a user and control any additional processing that may be required. Using the `OnTransactionAbort` event, you can manually roll back things such as file updates or variable changes that MTS doesn't currently support.

The following code uses the `OnTransactionCommit` and `OnTranscationAbort` events to notify a user that an order was processed.

```
<%@ TRANSACTION = Required %>

<%

'use buffered output to display different pages

Response.Buffer = True

%>
```

```
<html><body>
<h1>Welcome to our online ordering system</h1>

<%
Set OrderAction = Server.CreateObject("Company.OrderComponent")
OrderAction.Place(Request("OrderNumber"))
%>

<p>Thank you for your order. It is being processed.</p>
</body></html>

<%
'display following page on success
Sub OnTransactionCommit()
    Response.Clear()
    Response.Write "<html><body>"
    Response.Write "<h3>Thank you for your order.</h3>"
    Response.Write "It will be sent to you shortly."
    Response.Write "</body></html>"
    Response.Flush()
End Sub
%>

<%
'display following page on failure
Sub OnTransactionAbort()
    Response.Clear()
    Response.Write "<html><body>"
    Response.Write "<h3>Order Error</h3>"
    Response.Write "Your order could not be processed."
    Response.Write "</body></html>"
    Response.Flush()
End Sub
%>
```

Registering Components

MTS can handle rolling back information only on installed components. Therefore, before a component (including all the components that handle your database updates) can be used in a transaction, that component must be registered in an MTS package and be properly configured.

You can use the Internet Service Manager or MTS Explorer to register components in MTS. You should create a new library package and include all your components in this new package, rather than put the components in an existing package. Optionally, you can use server packages to use MTS role-based security on your transactions or to make your components accessible to applications on remote servers.

Creating a Package

Creating a new package sets boundaries for a process running on your server. All the components included in a package will run in the same process. By separating components into packages, you can have components from multiple packages working at the same time.

This feature is one of the main reasons for placing your own components in your own packages. Because each package runs in its own process, if your application should fail for any reason, the rest of the processes being used by IIS will continue to work. Similarly, should any of the components used by IIS fail, your processes will continue.

MTS Explorer includes a Package Wizard that you can use to create a package based on prebuilt package files or to create an empty package. Prebuilt packages are stored in files with a pak extension. The packages can be installed by dragging and dropping the pak files into MTS Explorer or with the Package Wizard. The following steps describe how to create a new package for MTS:

1. Open MTS Explorer or the Internet Service Manager.
2. Display the installed packages in the scope pane by clicking on the plus sign next to the Computers folder, the My Computer icon, and the Packages Installed folder as necessary.
3. Select the Packages Installed folder.
4. Select New from the Action menu and then choose Package. The Package Wizard dialog box opens.
5. Select Create an Empty Package. This action moves you to the first step of the Wizard.
6. Enter a name for your package in the field provided.

7. Select Next to move to the final dialog box, shown in Figure 19-6.

8. Specify a user account for the package to use. The default option uses the currently logged on user. This option is fine unless you want to use role-based security or have some other purpose in mind.

9. Select Finish. The new package is added to MTS.

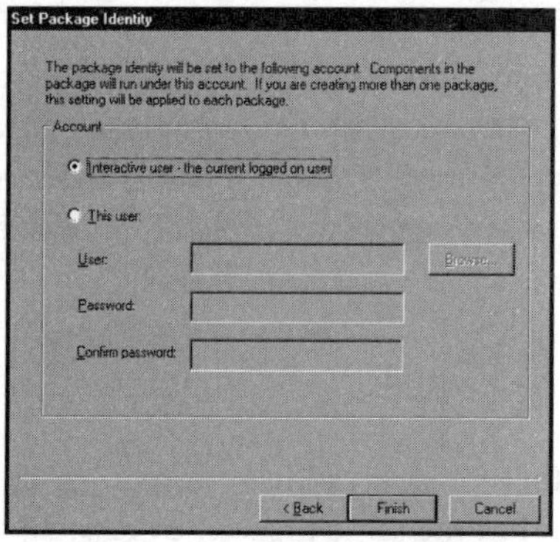

FIGURE 19-6

Packages are assigned user accounts.

Adding Components to a Package

After creating your new package, you will need to add components. *Components* are little bits of programs that are built to the Component Object Model, or COM, specification. This concept basically means that the component was designed to be accessed through another program.

To add components to a package, you use MTS Explorer or the Internet Service Manager. You can use either program's Component Wizard, or you can simply drag and drop a DLL onto the package.

The following steps describe how to add a component to a package:

1. Open MTS Explorer or the Internet Service Manager.

2. Display the installed packages in the scope pane by clicking on the plus sign next to the Computers folder, the My Computer icon, and the Packages Installed folder as necessary.

NOTE

When dealing with components, remember that the same component can be installed in several packages. Also remember that because components are only small bits of code, it is possible to store several components in one DLL. Therefore, different components from the same DLL can be installed in different packages.

Creating Components

To take full advantage of MTS, you will need to find the necessary components for your applications. These components are COM in-process server components, which means that they can run inside MTS. These files are
stored in DLLs created using programs such as Visual Basic, Visual C++,
or Visual J++ (to list the Microsoft products available). Any development
tool that creates ActiveX compatible objects will work.

The exact nature of creating COM components that will work with MTS is
beyond the scope of this book. However, this chapter provides the information that you need to get the components up and running after they have
been created.

3. Select the Package that will get the new component.

4. Open the Components folder for the package. This action starts the
   Component Wizard, shown in Figure 19-7.

5. Select Install New Component(s). This action displays the dialog box
   shown in Figure 19-8.

FIGURE 19-7

*The Component Wizard
installs new components as
well as already registered
components.*

FIGURE 19-8

*The Component Wizard dis-
plays files and the components
to add.*

6. Click on Add Files to add files to the list on the top. Because DLL files are system files, you will need to make sure that the Hidden Files option in Windows NT Explorer is set to Show All Files, or you won't be able to see any files in the subsequent Select Files to Install dialog box.

7. Select a file using the Select Files to Install dialog box. To limit the files displayed in the dialog box, change the Files of Type list to display DLLs.

8. Click on OK to return to the Component Wizard. The selected DLL appears in the Files to Install list, and the available components appear in the Components Found list, as shown in Figure 19-9.

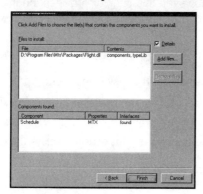

FIGURE 19-9

The Component Wizard automatically finds components to add.

9. Select a component from the Components Found list. To select multiple components, hold down the Ctrl key while you select components.

10. Select Finish. This action adds the components and their interfaces to the package, as shown in Figure 19-10.

11. Close MTS Explorer.

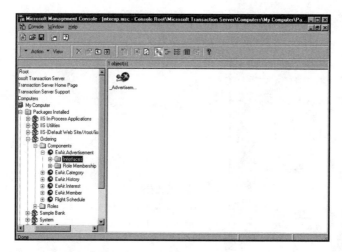

FIGURE 19-10

Click on a few plus symbols to see the newly installed components and their interfaces.

Chapter 20

Communicating with
Database Servers

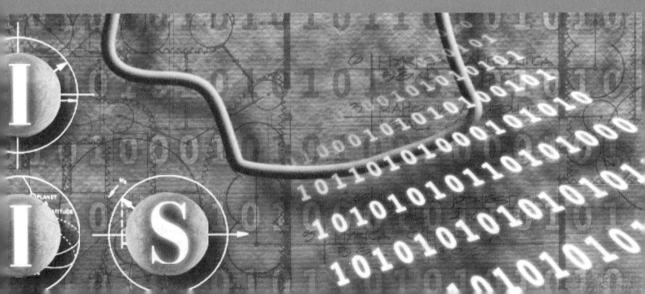

In This Chapter

◆ Developing Distributed Servers

◆ Access through a Query

◆ Accessing Databases Directly

In the previous two chapters, you learned how to use databases on your server to create dynamic Web pages. This chapter explains how you can extend that knowledge to take advantage of databases that may be stored at other sites on the Internet or on different servers on your intranet.

In practice, accessing a local database is very similar to accessing a remote database. In creating the database access tools available to you, the distributed nature of the network was taken into account. You can use either of the two primary methods to access remote databases:

◆ Through an HTML query

◆ Through direct access

Both of these access methods are explored a little later in this chapter.

The uses to which databases can be put on the Internet or an intranet are astounding and quite diverse. The examples in this chapter rely on connecting with perhaps the most-accessed and available databases on the Net: those maintained by the various search sites such as Yahoo, Alta Vista, and HotBot.

Developing Distributed Servers

As your Web site becomes larger and busier, it is not uncommon for the traffic to start "bogging down" your server. Although you can use several methods to improve the performance of your server (see Chapter 27), one of the techniques you might want to consider is off-loading your database processing to a different server. This approach enables you to fine-tune your hardware and your network configuration to match the needs of your users.

Databases are a natural item to consider placing on their own server. All you need to do is move a few elements to the secondary server:

◆ The database itself

◆ The ODBC configuration

◆ The DLLs and executable files that you use for access (if any)

In addition, you may need to change your DLLs to look for the database in the proper location on the network. For example, if you developed a DLL that looks for the database on a physical drive on your local server, you may need to change the DLL so that it uses a UNC path or a mapped drive to access the remote information.

By moving your databases to another server, you allow the back-end processing (which involves processing the SQL queries) to take place on a different server. This technique frees your primary server to do more work with other users.

> **NOTE**
>
> Moving databases from one server to another can be a time-consuming and daunting task, particularly if you have many users who currently access and use the database. You should not move a database without carefully considering how your action will affect the current users of that database. In the long run, moving the Web server to another computer may be the best course of action.

Access through a Query

One method you can use to access information on a remote database server is to access the database by using a query. Typically, this method involves developing a form on your site that gathers the information you need to place in the query. You then send the query to the remote site and allow that site to respond with the necessary HTML code.

This approach generally requires a Web server to be operating at both sites. On some occasions, however, the remote system may not be using a Web server, but rather a full-blown application that simply responds using HTML. For example, the network administrator at the remote site may be using a program that is not a traditional Web server, but still receives HTTP commands (as a Web server would do), processes them, and then responds with HTML output that a Web client can use.

The Pros and Cons

As with any computing solution, using a query to access remote information has pros and cons. On the plus side, you can develop links between your site and the remote database rather quickly. In addition, you don't necessarily need to tell the Webmaster for the remote site that you are establishing the link; you are simply accessing the remote data in the form developed and accepted by that site.

On the negative side, if you are accessing a database at a site managed by someone else, you have little control over the content or format of that data. In addition, the remote site may periodically change the rules by which information is accessed. The upshot of both of these factors is that you must spend a fair amount of time periodically testing your connections with the remote site. After all, you need to discover any problems before your users complain that they cannot use the links that access the information.

Finding Query Requirements

To establish a link with a remote database, you need to discover the requirements of that database. You can get this information in a couple of ways:

◆ Look for the query requirements at the site

◆ Contact the Webmaster and request the requirements

◆ Figure them out on your own

The following sections discuss these methods.

Checking the Site

Some sites, but definitely not all, list their query requirements at their Web site. For instance, suppose you want to connect with the database maintained by Yahoo. For some reason, you want to send a query directly to the site, rather than work through the forms found at those sites. You can visit Yahoo and find the information you need to initiate a search directly from your site. This information is found at **http://www.yahoo.com/docs/yahootogo/search**, as shown in Figure 20-1.

ONLINE ▶

Other sites may include similar information on the proper way to connect to their database.

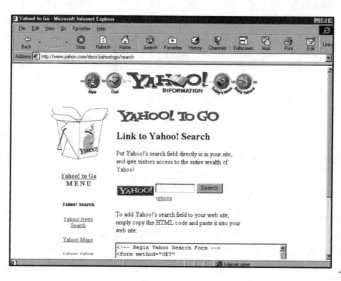

FIGURE 20-1

Some Web sites include instructions on how to link from your site to theirs.

Contacting the Webmaster

If you cannot find the proper information by examining the site itself, you might want to try contacting the Webmaster. Most sites include a contact list or an e-mail link that you can use to send e-mail to the proper person.

When you contact the Webmaster, your message should contain the following information:

- Who you are
- Where your site is located
- What you want to do
- What you need from the Webmaster

Most Webmasters are very pleased when people want to connect to their site, and if you develop a form that enables your users to directly access the database at the remote site, you are actually removing some of the burden from the remote site's server.

Don't be surprised if you have to wait for the Webmaster's response. Not all Webmasters check their e-mail every day, and they may not have the proper information available right away. If you haven't heard in about a week, however, you may want to send another message or find a different way to get the information you need.

Doing Your Own Work

You can easily find the information you need to establish a remote link by simply looking at the forms developed at the remote site. After all, you are developing forms that provide the same functionality as the forms at the remote site.

As an example, suppose you want to develop a form that enables you to search the database at HotBot. This task is simple enough; all you need to do is display the search page maintained by the site (**http://www.hotbot.com/index.html**) and then use your browser to view the source HTML for the page. Here is the source code for what I was viewing on a recent visit to the site:

```
<!— these two calls load the environment with variables —>
<!— using the name=value pairs in the URL —>
<!— for each name like 'BAR', a variable appears call 'form_BAR' —>
<!— FOO is just a temp var to pass the query string to the parse function —>
<!— UISTATE: NORMAL QUERY PAGE —>
<HTML>
<HEAD>
<!— define some variables for use in the browser match —>
<!— LIBRARY DEFINED ITEMS —>
```

```
<!— DEFAULTS —>
<!— #set var="INFOBOX"                    value="33" —>
<!— BROWSER TARGETING (overrides defaults) —>
            <!— IE3 Win only —>
            <!— #set var="INFOBOX"              value="44" —>
            <!— accept defaults —>
<TITLE>HotBot</TITLE>
</HEAD>
<BODY bgcolor="#00cc33"
background="http://static.hotbot.com/images/bg_base_green.gif" text="#000000"
link="#ff0000" vlink="#ff0000" alink="#0000ff">
<FORM ACTION="/" NAME="form">
<a href="http://www.hotbot.com/meta/logobar3.map"><img
src="http://static.hotbot.com/images/logobar3.gif" border=0 width=600
height=18 USEMAP="#logobar3map" alt="Wired Digital Navigation"></a>
<MAP NAME="logobar3map">
 <AREA SHAPE=RECT COORDS="0,0,125,18"   HREF="http://help.hotbot.com/">
 <AREA SHAPE=RECT COORDS="126,0,209,18" HREF="http://www.wired.com/news/">
 <AREA SHAPE=RECT COORDS="210,0,279,18" HREF="http://www.hotwired.com/">
 <AREA SHAPE=RECT COORDS="280,0,355,18" HREF="http://www.wired.com/wired/">
 <AREA SHAPE=RECT COORDS="356,0,425,18" HREF="http://www.livewired.com/">
 <AREA SHAPE=RECT COORDS="426,0,505,18" HREF="http://www.suck.com/">
 <AREA SHAPE=RECT COORDS="582,0,600,18" HREF="http://www.wired.com/home/">
</MAP>
<!— table number 1 —>
<TABLE CELLPADDING=0 CELLSPACING=0 BORDER=0 WIDTH=606 HEIGHT=45> <!— this table
has 3 columns and 1 row —>
 <TR>
  <TD WIDTH=195 HEIGHT=45 ALIGN=RIGHT VALIGN=MIDDLE>                  <!— 1, 1 —
>
   <IMG SRC="http://static.hotbot.com/images/logo_hb1_green.gif"
    BORDER=0 ALT="· H o t B o t ·" width=195 height=45 border=0>
  </TD>
  <TD WIDTH=286 HEIGHT=45 ALIGN=LEFT VALIGN=MIDDLE>                   <!—
1, 2 —>
   <font face="geneva, arial" size=2><i><b>The WIRED Search Center</b></i></font>
```

```
 </TD>
 <TD WIDTH=125 HEIGHT=45 ALIGN=RIGHT VALIGN=MIDDLE>              <!— 1, 3 —>
<a
href="http://nsads.hotwired.com/event.ng/Type=click&ProfileID=240&RunID=1087&AdID=2
184&GroupID=1&FamilyID=129&TagValues=2.5.6.25.256.317.322.389.411&Redirect=http:%2F
%2Fwww.hotwired.com%2Fcgi-
bin%2Fredirect%2F591%2Fhttp:%2F%2Fwww.hotwired.com%2Fdreamjobs%2F"
TARGET="_top"><img
src="http://static.wired.com/advertising/blipverts/houseads/djanim.gif" BORDER=1
height=35 width=125 alt="Click here for Dream Jobs"></a>
 </TD>
  </TR>
</TABLE>
<!— table number 2 —>
<TABLE cellpadding=0 cellspacing=0 border=0 width=601>
<TR>
<TD width=118 align=right valign=middle><img
src="http://static.hotbot.com/images/spacer.gif" width=118 height=1></TD>
<TD width=12><img src="http://static.hotbot.com/images/spacer.gif" width=12
height=1></TD>
<TD colspan=14><img src="http://static.hotbot.com/images/spacer.gif" width=350
height=1></TD>
<TD rowspan=1 valign=top align=middle width=120></TD>
</TR>
<TR>
<TD width=118 align=right valign=middle><FONT FACE="geneva, arial"
SIZE=1><b><i></i></b></font></TD>
<TD width=12><img src="http://static.hotbot.com/images/spacer.gif" width=12
height=1></TD>
<TD align=right valign=middle colspan=1>
<FONT FACE="geneva, arial" SIZE=1>look for </font><SELECT NAME="SM" >
 <OPTION VALUE="MC"     >all the words
 <OPTION VALUE="SC"     >any of the words
 <OPTION VALUE="phrase" >exact phrase
 <OPTION VALUE="title"  >the page title
```

```
<OPTION VALUE="name"    >the person
<OPTION VALUE="url"     >links to this URL
<OPTION VALUE="B"       >Boolean phrase
    </SELECT>
</TD>
<TD width=67 valign=middle></TD>
<TD> </TD>
<TD> </TD>
<TD> </TD>
<TD> </TD>
<TD> </TD>
<TD> </TD>
<TD> </TD>
<TD> </TD>
<TD> </TD>
<TD> </TD>
<TD> </TD>
<TD> </TD>
<TD rowspan=1 valign=top align=middle width=125> </TD>
</TR>
<TR>
<TD width=120 align=right valign=middle colspan=1><font face="geneva, arial"
color=#ffffff size=2><b><i>Search : <nobr>The Web</nobr></i></b></font><BR>
<img src="http://static.hotbot.com/images/spacer.gif" width=120 height=1></TD>
            <TD width=6><img src="http://static.hotbot.com/images/spacer.gif"
width=6 height=1></TD>
            <TD align=right valign=top colspan=1><INPUT TYPE=text VALUE="" SIZE=35
name="MT" maxlength="300"><br><input TYPE=image
            src="http://static.hotbot.com/images/super.gif" name="super" border=0
            width=195 height=16 alt="Super Search"></TD>
            <TD width=67 valign=top><input TYPE=image
            src="http://static.hotbot.com/images/btn_search.gif" name="search"
border=0 width=67 height=21 alt="Search"></TD>
            <TD align=right valign=top colspan=13>
<a href="/vendors/merchants.html"><img src="http://static.hotbot.com/images/shop-
wired1.gif" height=24 width=125 border=0 ALT="Shop Wired"></a></TD>
```

```
</TR>
</table>
<!— table number 3 —>
<TABLE CELLPADDING=0 CELLSPACING=0 BORDER=0> <!— this table has 8 columns and 17
rows —>
  <TR>
  <TD WIDTH=114 HEIGHT=0></TD>
  <TD WIDTH=16 HEIGHT=0></TD>
  <TD WIDTH=37 HEIGHT=0></TD>
  <TD WIDTH=73 HEIGHT=0></TD>
  <TD WIDTH=110 HEIGHT=0></TD>
  <TD WIDTH=110 HEIGHT=0></TD>
  <TD WIDTH=20 HEIGHT=0></TD>
  <TD WIDTH=125 HEIGHT=0></TD>
  </TR>
  <TR>
  <TD WIDTH=114 ALIGN=RIGHT VALIGN=TOP ROWSPAN=12>   <!— 1-12, 1 —>
   <!— begin partner links here the link is relative because of the memoryleak —
>

<!— Begin partner link insertion below —>
<a href="/meta/search_partners2.map"><img
src="http://static.hotbot.com/images/search_partners2.gif" width=114 height=236
USEMAP="#search_partners2_map" ISMAP border=0></a>
<MAP NAME="search_partners2_map">
<AREA SHAPE=RECT COORDS="0,0,114,21" HREF="/usenet.html">
<AREA SHAPE=RECT COORDS="0,22,114,40" HREF="/newsbot/index.html">
<AREA SHAPE=RECT COORDS="0,41,114,59" HREF="/partners/business.html">
<AREA SHAPE=RECT COORDS="0,60,114,78" HREF="/partners/people.html">
<AREA SHAPE=RECT COORDS="0,79,114,96" HREF="/partners/email.html">
<AREA SHAPE=RECT COORDS="0,97,114,116" HREF="http://www.classifieds2000.com/cgi-
cls/display.exe?hotbot+class">
<AREA SHAPE=RECT COORDS="0,117,114,135" HREF="/partners/websitez.html">
<AREA SHAPE=RECT COORDS="0,136,114,155" HREF="http://stocks.hotbot.com/">
<AREA SHAPE=RECT COORDS="0,156,114,173" HREF="/partners/forumone.html">
<AREA SHAPE=RECT COORDS="0,174,114,210" HREF="/partners/filez.html">
```

```
</MAP>
<!- end partners insertion ->
  </TD>
  <TD WIDTH=16 ALIGN=LEFT VALIGN=TOP ROWSPAN=12>     <!- 1-12, 2 ->
    <img src="http://static.hotbot.com/images/spacer.gif" width=16 height=1 bor-
der=0>
  </TD>
  <TD WIDTH=330 ALIGN=LEFT VALIGN=TOP COLSPAN=4>     <!- 1, 3-6 ->


    <IMG SRC="http://static.hotbot.com/images/spacer.gif" width=330 height=1 bor-
der=0>
  </TD>
  <TD WIDTH=20   ALIGN=LEFT VALIGN=MIDDLE COLSPAN=1 ROWSPAN=17><!- 1-17, 7 ->
     
    <!-<img src="http://static.hotbot.com/images/spacer.gif" WIDTH=15 HEIGHT=50
BORDER=0>->
  </TD>
  <TD WIDTH=125 VALIGN=top ALIGN=RIGHT ROWSPAN=17>          <!- 1-17, 8 ->
    <img src="http://static.hotbot.com/images/spacer.gif" height=8 width=1 bor-
der=0><BR>
    <!- below is 120x60 commerce image ->
    <a
href="http://nsads.hotwired.com/event.ng/Type=click&ProfileID=89&RunID=173&AdID=2070
&GroupID=1&FamilyID=118&TagValues=2.5.6.25.158.174.229.233.241.389.411&Redirect=http
:%2F%2Fwww.1800flowers.com%2Fcgi-bin%2F800f%2Fcollection.pl%2FhotbotVDF%2F4%2F0%2F0"
TARGET="_top"><img
src="http://static.wired.com/advertising/blipverts/1800flowers/if120.gif" BORDER=1
height=60 width=120 alt="Click here for 1-800-Flowers"></a>
    <BR>
    <center>
    <a href="/vendors/merchants.html"><font color=#00ffff face="geneva, arial"
size=1><b>Find more deals</a>
    </center>
    <BR>
    <BR>
    <!- insert gif of commerce partners, and image map ->
```

```
    <!— start commerce include —>
<img src="http://static.hotbot.com/images/list5.gif" width=125 height=434 border=0
USEMAP="#shopmap" border=0>
<MAP NAME="shopmap">
<AREA SHAPE=RECT COORDS="0,0,125,28" HREF="http://www.hotwired.com/cgi-bin/redi-
rect/418/http://www.gap.com/onlinestore/Storefront.asp">
<AREA SHAPE=RECT COORDS="0,29,125,63" HREF="http://www.hotwired.com/cgi-bin/redi-
rect/423/http://barnesandnoble.bfast.com/booklink/click?sourceid=10164&categoryid=h
omepage">
<AREA SHAPE=RECT COORDS="0,64,125,98" HREF="http://www.hotwired.com/cgi-bin/redi-
rect/424/http://www.outpost.com">
<AREA SHAPE=RECT COORDS="0,99,125,134" HREF="http://www.hotwired.com/cgi-bin/redi-
rect/343/http://expedia.msn.com/pub/eap.asp?eapid=2-1">
<AREA SHAPE=RECT COORDS="0,135,125,170" HREF="http://www.hotwired.com/cgi-bin/redi-
rect/420/http://www.onsale.com">
<AREA SHAPE=RECT COORDS="0,171,125,205" HREF="http://www.hotwired.com/cgi-bin/redi-
rect/425/http://www.1800flowers.com/cgi-bin/800f/collection.pl/hotbotbirth/0/0/1">
<AREA SHAPE=RECT COORDS="0,206,125,241" HREF="http://www.hotwired.com/cgi-bin/redi-
rect/419/http://www.getsmart.com/hotbotmalla">
<AREA SHAPE=RECT COORDS="0,242,125,267" HREF="http://www.hotwired.com/cgi-bin/redi-
rect/442/http://www.kodak.com/go/shop">
<AREA SHAPE=RECT COORDS="0,268,125,304" HREF="http://www.hotwired.com/cgi-bin/redi-
rect/426/http://www.musicblvd.com/cgi-bin/tw/1155_0_/mb2/live/mrkt/specials.txt">
<AREA SHAPE=RECT COORDS="0,305,125,338" HREF="http://www.hotwired.com/cgi-bin/redi-
rect/344/http://carpoint.msn.com/route/?dest=%2F&src=hotbot">
<AREA SHAPE=RECT COORDS="0,339,125,372" HREF="http://www.hotwired.com/cgi-bin/redi-
rect/427/http://speedserve.com/speedsrv/alliance/Wired.html">
<AREA SHAPE=RECT COORDS="0,373,125,406" HREF="http://www.hotwired.com/cgi-bin/redi-
rect/429/http://www.virtualvin.com/vlinks/hotbot/index.html">
<AREA SHAPE=RECT COORDS="0,407,125,434" HREF="http://www.hotwired.com/cgi-bin/redi-
rect/428/http://www.wired.com/wired/subscribe/shopwired/">
</MAP>
<!— end commerce include —>
    <!— end —>
    <BR>
```

```
   <center>
   <a href="/vendors/longlist.html"><font color=#00ffff>More
merchants</font></a></b></font>
   </center>
   <BR>
  </TD>
 </TR>
 <TR>
  <TD WIDTH=37>                <!— 2, 3 —>
   <img src="http://static.hotbot.com/images/date.gif" width=37 height=7 border=0
ALT="Date">
  </TD>
  <TD WIDTH=293 ALIGN=LEFT COLSPAN=3>        <!— 2, 4-6 —>
   <INPUT TYPE=checkbox NAME="date" VALUE="within"  >
   <SELECT NAME="DV">
    <OPTION VALUE="7"     >in the last week
    <OPTION VALUE="14"    >in the last 2 weeks
    <OPTION VALUE="30"    >in the last month
    <OPTION VALUE="90"    >in the last 3 months
    <OPTION VALUE="180"   >in the last 6 months
    <OPTION VALUE="365"   >in the last year
    <OPTION VALUE="730"   >in the last 2 years
   </SELECT>
  </TD>
 </TR>
 <TR>
  <TD WIDTH=37>              <!— 3, 3 —>
   <!— <img src="/images/domain.gif" width=37 border=0 ALT="Domain"> —>
  </TD>
  <TD WIDTH=293 ALIGN=LEFT COLSPAN=3></TD>          <!— 3, 4-6 —>
 </TR>
 <TR>
  <TD WIDTH=37>              <!— 4, 3 —>
   <IMG SRC="http://static.hotbot.com/images/continent.gif" WIDTH=37 HEIGHT=7
ALT="Continent">
```

```
</TD>
<TD WIDTH=293 COLSPAN=3>                        <!— 4, 4-6 —>
 <INPUT TYPE=checkbox NAME="RD" VALUE="RG"  >
 <SELECT NAME="RG">
  <OPTION VALUE=".com"  >North America (.com)
  <OPTION VALUE=".net"  >North America (.net)
  <OPTION VALUE=".edu"  >North America (.edu)
  <OPTION VALUE=".org"  >North America (.org)
  <OPTION VALUE=".gov"  >North America (.gov)
  <OPTION VALUE="NA"    >North America (all)
  <OPTION VALUE="EU"    >Europe
  <OPTION VALUE="SE"    >Southeast Asia
  <OPTION VALUE="AS"    >India & Asia
  <OPTION VALUE="SA"    >South America
  <OPTION VALUE="DU"    >Oceania
  <OPTION VALUE="AF"    >Africa
  <OPTION VALUE="ME"    >Middle East
  <OPTION VALUE="CA"    >Central America
 </SELECT>
</TD>
</TR>
<TR>
 <TD WIDTH=37></TD>                              <!— 5, 3 —>
 <TD WIDTH=293 COLSPAN=3 ALIGN=LEFT VALIGN=MIDDLE>        <!— 5, 4-6 —>
  <FONT FACE="geneva, arial" SIZE=1 COLOR=#003300><img
src="http://static.hotbot.com/images/spacer.gif" height=6 width=10>
  <br>Include media type:</font><br>
  <FONT FACE="geneva, arial" SIZE=1 COLOR=#003300>
  <INPUT TYPE=checkbox NAME="FVI"  >Image
  <INPUT TYPE=checkbox NAME="FRA"  >Audio
  <INPUT TYPE=checkbox NAME="FVV"  >Video
  <INPUT TYPE=checkbox NAME="FSW"  >Shockwave
  </FONT>
 </TD>
</TR>
<TR>
```

```
  <TD WIDTH=37 ></TD>                          <!— 6, 3 —>
  <TD WIDTH=293 VALIGN=BOTTOM COLSPAN=3>              <!— 6, 4-6 —>
   <img src="http://static.hotbot.com/images/spacer.gif" width=1 height=8 bor-
der=0><BR>
   <FONT FACE="geneva, arial" SIZE=1>Return Results:</FONT><BR>
   <img src="http://static.hotbot.com/images/spacer.gif" width=1 height=2 bor-
der=0></TD>
 </TR>
 <TR>
  <TD WIDTH=37 ></TD>                          <!— 7, 3 —>
  <TD WIDTH=293 COLSPAN=3>                    <!— 7, 4-6 —>
   <SELECT NAME="DC" >
    <OPTION VALUE="10"  >10
    <OPTION VALUE="25"  >25
    <OPTION VALUE="50"  >50
    <OPTION VALUE="100"  >100
   </SELECT>
   <SELECT NAME="DE">
    <OPTION VALUE="2"  >full descriptions
    <OPTION VALUE="1"  >brief descriptions
    <OPTION VALUE="0"  >URLs only
   </SELECT>
  </TD>
 </TR>
 <TR>
  <TD WIDTH=37 ></TD>                          <!— 8, 3 —>
  <TD WIDTH=293 VALIGN=TOP COLSPAN=3>                <!— 8, 4-6 —>
<!— Super Button *was* here —>
  </TD>
 </TR>
 <TR>
  <TD WIDTH=37 ></TD>                          <!— 9, 3 —>
  <TD WIDTH=293 ALIGN=LEFT VALIGN=BOTTOM COLSPAN=3> </TD> <!— 9, 4-6 —>
 </TR>
 <TR>
```

```
   <TD WIDTH=37 ></TD>                                        <!— 10, 3 —>
   <TD WIDTH=293 ALIGN=LEFT VALIGN=BOTTOM COLSPAN=3></TD>      <!— 10, 4-6 —>
  </TR>
  <TR>
   <TD WIDTH=330 ALIGN=LEFT VALIGN=BOTTOM COLSPAN=4>          <!— 11, 3-6 —>
    <a href="index.html"><img src="http://static.hotbot.com/images/clear.gif" bor-
der=0 ALT="Clear Form"></a>
   </TD>
  </TR>
  <TR>
   <TD WIDTH=330 COLSPAN=4> </TD>                        <!— 12, 3-6 —>
  </TR>
  <TR>
   <TD WIDTH=460 COLSPAN=6>                     <!— 13, 1-6 —>
    <BR><IMG SRC="http://static.hotbot.com/images/label_cybrarian_green.gif"
WIDTH=439 HEIGHT=23 BORDER=0>
   </TD>
  </TR>
  <TR>
   <TD WIDTH=130 ROWSPAN=4 COLSPAN=2></TD>   <!— 14-17, 1-2 —>
<!— CYBRARIAN TABLE: each col is 110 wide, each row is 110 high —>
   <TD WIDTH=330 HEIGHT=1 COLSPAN=4>                  <!— 14, 3-6 —>
    <img src="http://static.hotbot.com/images/spacer.gif" width=330 height=1 border=0>
   </TD>
  </TR>
  <TR>
   <TD WIDTH=110 HEIGHT=110 VALIGN=TOP COLSPAN=2>    <!— 15, 3-4 —>
    <FONT FACE="geneva, arial" SIZE=1 COLOR=#ffffcc>REFERENCE<BR>
    <A HREF= "http://www.wired.com/cybrarian/frame/reference/stats.html">
    <FONT COLOR=#666600>Statistics</FONT></A><BR>
    <A HREF= "http://www.wired.com/cybrarian/frame/reference/people.html">
    <FONT COLOR=#666600>People finder</FONT></A><BR>
    <A HREF= "http://www.wired.com/cybrarian/frame/reference/words.html">
    <FONT COLOR=#666600>Dictionaries</FONT></A><BR>
```

```
 <A HREF= "http://www.wired.com/cybrarian/frame/reference/words.html">
 <FONT COLOR=#666600>Style guides</FONT></A><BR>
 <A HREF= "http://www.wired.com/cybrarian/frame/reference/maps.html">
 <FONT COLOR=#666600>Atlases</FONT></A><BR>
 <A HREF= "http://www.wired.com/cybrarian/frame/reference/maps.html">
 <FONT COLOR=#666600>Maps</FONT></A><BR>
 </FONT>
</TD>
<TD WIDTH=110 HEIGHT=110 VALIGN=TOP>               <!— 15, 5 —>
 <FONT FACE="geneva, arial" SIZE=1 COLOR=#ffffcc>TECHNOLOGY<BR>
 <A HREF= "http://www.wired.com/cybrarian/frame/tech/news.html">
 <FONT COLOR=#9933ff>News</FONT></A><BR>
 <A HREF= "http://www.wired.com/cybrarian/frame/tech/comp.html">
 <FONT COLOR=#9933ff>Computing</FONT></A><BR>
 <A HREF= "http://www.wired.com/cybrarian/frame/tech/download.html">
 <FONT COLOR=#9933ff>Downloads</FONT></A><BR>
 <A HREF= "http://www.wired.com/cybrarian/frame/tech/web.html">
 <FONT COLOR=#9933ff>Web tools</FONT></A><BR>
 <A HREF= "http://www.wired.com/cybrarian/frame/tech/tutorials.html">
 <FONT COLOR=#9933ff>Programming</FONT></A><BR>
 <A HREF= "http://www.wired.com/cybrarian/frame/tech/techorgs.html">
 <FONT COLOR=#9933ff>Organizations</FONT></A><BR>
 </FONT>
</TD>
<TD WIDTH=110 HEIGHT=110 VALIGN=TOP>               <!— 15, 6 —>
 <FONT FACE="geneva, arial" SIZE=1 COLOR=#ffffcc>CURRENT<BR> AFFAIRS<BR>
 <A HREF= "http://www.wired.com/cybrarian/frame/politics/news.html">
 <FONT COLOR=#cc0099>News</FONT></A><BR>
 <A HREF= "http://www.wired.com/cybrarian/frame/politics/commentary.html">
 <FONT COLOR=#cc0099>Commentary</FONT></A><BR>
 <A HREF= "http://www.wired.com/cybrarian/frame/politics/cyber.html">
 <FONT COLOR=#cc0099>Cyber rights</FONT></A><BR>
 <A HREF= "http://www.wired.com/cybrarian/frame/politics/us_gov.html">
 <FONT COLOR=#cc0099>US government</FONT></A><BR>
 <A HREF= "http://www.wired.com/cybrarian/frame/politics/world.html">
```

```
  <FONT COLOR=#cc0099>World</FONT></A><BR>

  </FONT>

 </TD>

</TR>

<TR>

 <TD WIDTH=110 HEIGHT=110 VALIGN=TOP COLSPAN=2>      <!— 16, 3-4 —>

  <FONT FACE="geneva, arial" SIZE=1 COLOR=#ffffcc>BUSINESS<BR>

  <A HREF= "http://www.wired.com/cybrarian/frame/business/news.html">

  <FONT COLOR=#666600>News</FONT></A><BR>

  <A HREF= "http://www.wired.com/cybrarian/frame/business/ad.html">

  <FONT COLOR=#666600>Advertising</FONT></A><BR>

  <A HREF= "http://www.wired.com/cybrarian/frame/business/ad.html">

  <FONT COLOR=#666600>Marketing</FONT></A><BR>

  <A HREF= "http://www.wired.com/cybrarian/frame/business/company.html">

  <FONT COLOR=#666600>Yellow pages</FONT></A><BR>

  <A HREF= "http://www.wired.com/cybrarian/frame/business/orgs.html">

  <FONT COLOR=#666600>Organizations</FONT></A><BR>

  <A HREF= "http://www.wired.com/cybrarian/frame/business/jobs.html">

  <FONT COLOR=#666600>Careers</FONT></A><BR>

  </FONT>

 </TD>

 <TD WIDTH=110 HEIGHT=110 VALIGN=TOP>               <!— 16, 5 —>

  <FONT FACE="geneva, arial" SIZE=1 COLOR=#ffffcc>INVESTING/<BR> FINANCE<BR>

  <A HREF= "http://www.wired.com/cybrarian/frame/invest/stocks.html">

  <FONT COLOR=#9933ff>Stocks</FONT></A><BR>

  <A HREF= "http://www.wired.com/cybrarian/frame/invest/indices.html">

  <FONT COLOR=#9933ff>Indices</FONT></A><BR>

  <A HREF= "http://www.wired.com/cybrarian/frame/invest/sec.html">

  <FONT COLOR=#9933ff>SEC filings</FONT></A><BR>

  <A HREF= "http://www.wired.com/cybrarian/frame/invest/sec.html">

  <FONT COLOR=#9933ff>IPOs</FONT></A><BR>

  <A HREF= "http://www.wired.com/cybrarian/frame/invest/research.html">

  <FONT COLOR=#9933ff>Research</FONT></A><BR>

  </FONT>
```

```
    </TD>
    <TD WIDTH=110 HEIGHT=110 VALIGN=TOP>                <!— 16, 6 —>
      <FONT FACE="geneva, arial" SIZE=1 COLOR=#ffffcc> HEALTH/<BR>  SCI-
ENCE<BR>
        <A HREF= "http://www.wired.com/cybrarian/frame/health/wellness.html">
        <FONT COLOR=#cc0099>Wellness</FONT></A><BR>
        <A HREF= "http://www.wired.com/cybrarian/frame/health/resources.html">
        <FONT COLOR=#cc0099>Resources</FONT></A><BR>
        <A HREF= "http://www.wired.com/cybrarian/frame/health/sci_orgs.html">
        <FONT COLOR=#cc0099>Organizations</FONT></A><BR>
        <A HREF= "http://www.wired.com/cybrarian/frame/health/sci_research.html">
        <FONT COLOR=#cc0099>Research</FONT></A><BR>
      </FONT>
    </TD>
  </TR>
  <TR>
    <TD WIDTH=110 HEIGHT=110 VALIGN=TOP COLSPAN=2>     <!— 17, 3-4 —>
      <FONT FACE="geneva, arial" SIZE=1 COLOR=#ffffcc>CULTURE<BR>
        <A HREF="http://www.wired.com/cybrarian/frame/culture/art.html">
        <FONT COLOR=#666600>Art</FONT></A><BR>
        <A HREF="http://www.wired.com/cybrarian/frame/culture/books.html">
        <FONT COLOR=#666600>Books</FONT></A><BR>
        <A HREF="http://www.wired.com/cybrarian/frame/culture/film.html">
        <FONT COLOR=#666600>Film</FONT></A><BR>
        <A HREF="http://www.wired.com/cybrarian/frame/culture/music.html">
        <FONT COLOR=#666600>Music</FONT></A><BR>
      </FONT>
    </TD>
    <TD WIDTH=110 HEIGHT=110 VALIGN=TOP>                <!— 17, 5 —>
      <FONT FACE="geneva, arial" SIZE=1 COLOR=#ffffcc>MEDIA<BR>
        <A HREF="http://www.wired.com/cybrarian/frame/media/newspapers.html">
        <FONT COLOR=#9933ff>Newspapers</FONT></A><BR>
        <A HREF="http://www.wired.com/cybrarian/frame/media/magazines.html">
        <FONT COLOR=#9933ff>Magazines</FONT></A><BR>
        <A HREF="http://www.wired.com/cybrarian/frame/media/radiotv.html">
        <FONT COLOR=#9933ff>TV</FONT></A><BR>
```

```
  <A HREF="http://www.wired.com/cybrarian/frame/media/radiotv.html">
  <FONT COLOR=#9933ff>Radio</FONT></A><BR>
  <A HREF="http://www.wired.com/cybrarian/frame/media/zines.html">
  <FONT COLOR=#9933ff>Internet</FONT></A><BR>
  </FONT>
 </TD>
 <TD WIDTH=110 HEIGHT=110 VALIGN=TOP>              <!— 17, 6 —>
  <FONT FACE="geneva, arial" SIZE=1 COLOR=#ffffcc>REC<BR>
  <A HREF="http://www.wired.com/cybrarian/frame/rec/auto.html">
  <FONT COLOR=#cc0099>Auto</FONT></A><BR>
  <A HREF="http://www.wired.com/cybrarian/frame/rec/travel.html">
  <FONT COLOR=#cc0099>Travel</FONT></A><BR>
  <A HREF="http://www.wired.com/cybrarian/frame/rec/sports.html">
  <FONT COLOR=#cc0099>Sports</FONT></A><BR>
  <A HREF="http://www.wired.com/cybrarian/frame/rec/games.html">
  <FONT COLOR=#cc0099>Games</FONT></A><BR>
  <A HREF="http://www.wired.com/cybrarian/frame/rec/vice.html">
  <FONT COLOR=#cc0099>Vice</FONT></A><BR>
  </FONT>
 </TD>
 </TR>
</TABLE>
<font face="Arial, Helvetica" size=1 color="#FFFFFF">
<a href="http://help.hotbot.com/tidbits.html">Sign up</a> for<br> search tips
and<br> news about HotBot.
</font>
<INPUT TYPE="hidden" NAME="OPs" VALUE="MDRTP">
<INPUT TYPE="hidden" NAME="_v" VALUE="2">
<INPUT TYPE="hidden" NAME="DU" VALUE="days">
<INPUT TYPE="hidden" NAME="SW" VALUE="web">
</FORM>
<br>
<A HREF="http://www.inktomi.com/"><IMG
src="http://static.hotbot.com/images/imap_ads.gif"
USEMAP="#admap" BORDER=0 ALT="powered by INKTOMI" width=478 height=50></A>
```

```
<br>
<MAP NAME="admap">
 <AREA coords="0,0,126,50"    href="http://www.inktomi.com/"></AREA>
 <AREA coords="300,3,384,33"
href="http://home.netscape.com/comprod/mirror/index.html"></AREA>
 <AREA coords="390,3,477,33" href="http://www.microsoft.com/ie/"></AREA>
</MAP>
<font face="Arial, Helvetica" size=1>
<img src="http://static.hotbot.com/images/spacer.gif" height=1 width=130 border=0">
Copyright &#169; 1996-97 Wired Digital, Inc. All rights reserved.
</font>
</body>
</html>
```

Most of the code on this page will do you little good; sites like HotBot are designed to change every time you visit them. Although the window dressing may change, however, the core of the page (the form that results in a search) does not change. Examine the code and look for everything between the <FORM> and </FORM> tags. You can pull this code directly from the page and then adapt it to the page you are developing.

If for some reason you cannot view the source code for a page, you can always examine the URL generated by a form. As an example, suppose you are visiting Alta Vista and you do a simple search for pages containing the keywords *particle* and *theory*. When you click on the Submit button, the URL in your browser changes to the following:

```
http://www.altavista.digital.com/cgi-bin/query?pg=q&what=web&fmt=.&q=particle+theory
```

This URL, obviously, is the output from the form used by Alta Vista. If you refer to Chapters 9 and 13, you can figure out what is being passed to the database at Alta Vista. By knowing this information and the options provided on Alta Vista's form page, you can construct your own form to fulfill the same query requirements.

Developing the HTML Page

After you know how the database query should be put together, you can create an HTML page that contains the form necessary to generate the query. If desired, you can also create a static page that simply has buttons that perform the query. This second option is the simplest and is the one examined in the following section.

Creating Static Links

Static links can come in handy if you have a highly focused page and you want your users to be able to access data at a different site. For example, suppose you have a Web page that focuses on Missouri history during the Civil War. In this type of page, you may be publishing several of your own resources, but you may want to include links to search engine results as well. Figure 20-2 shows an example of this type of Web page.

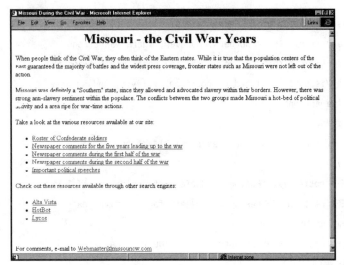

FIGURE 20-2

You can create static links to database information at other sites.

Nothing very fancy happens on this Web page. The bottom of the page offers three links to other sites—search engines on the Web. If these links simply displayed the search pages at the sites, they would be of little value to the users of the Missouri page. Instead, the links can include the code necessary to actually search the databases at the sites and then return the information.

The benefits to this approach are that your users can find the information they need quickly and you don't need to worry about updating the Missouri page that often. The following example shows the coding used in the Missouri Web page, which is available in the support files for this book as \Chap20\Missouri.htm:

```
<HTML>

<HEAD>

<TITLE>Missouri During the Civil War</TITLE>

</HEAD>
```

```
<BODY>
<CENTER><H1>Missouri - the Civil War Years</H1></CENTER>

When people think of the Civil War, they often think of the Eastern
states. While it is true that the population centers of the East
guaranteed the majority of battles and the widest press coverage,
frontier states such as Missouri were not left out of the action.

<P>Missouri was definitely a "Southern" state, since they allowed and
advocated slavery within their borders. However, there was strong
anti-slavery sentiment within the populace. The conflicts between the
two groups made Missouri a hot-bed of political activity and an area
ripe for war-time actions.

<P>Take a look at the various resources available at our site:
<UL>
    <LI><A HREF="roster.txt">Roster of Confederate soldiers</A></LI>
    <LI><A HREF="news1.htm">Newspaper comments for the five years
        leading up to the war</A></LI>
    <LI><A HREF="news2.htm">Newspaper comments during the first half
        of the war</A></LI>
    <LI><A HREF="news3.htm">Newspaper comments during the second half
        of the war</A></LI>
    <LI><A HREF="speeches.htm">Important political speeches</A></LI>
</UL>

<P>Check out these resources available through other search engines:
<UL>
    <LI><A HREF="http://www.altavista.digital.com/cgi-bin/query
        ?pg=aq&what=web&fmt=.&q=missouri+and+%22civil+war%22&r=
        %22civil+war%22&d0=&d1=">Alta Vista</A></LI>
    <LI><A HREF=" http://www.search.hotbot.com/hResult.html?
        SM=MC&MT=missouri+%22civil+war%22&DV=7&RG=.com
        &DC=10&DE=2&OPs=MDRTP&_v=2&DU=days&SW=web&search.x
        =32&search.y=8 ">HotBot</A></LI>
    <LI><A HREF=" http://www.lycos.com/cgi-bin/pursuit
```

```
            ?query=missouri+%22civil+war%22&matchmode=and&cat=lycos

            &x=13&y=17 ">

            Lycos</A></LI>

    </UL>


    <P><HR><P>


    For comments, e-mail to <A HREF="Webmaster@missouricw.com">
    Webmaster@missouricw.com</A>


    </BODY>
    </HTML>
```

Notice the code for the search-site links. The HREF attribute is set to the entire query string, which can be sent to the remote server. This link leads directly to the results page returned by that server; the user does not have to deal with an intervening search page.

Creating the links for this page was easy. The only requirement was to define the search needed for the desired results at each site. Then, while viewing the results page at the site, the URL was copied from the browser. This URL was then pasted into the code for the Missouri HTML page.

NOTE

It was impossible to show the entire URL for each query on a single line in the preceding listing. However, the URL should appear on a single line.

Developing a Dynamic Form

In Chapter 9, you learned how to create forms that enable you to work with external programs such as CGI scripts. If you understand the information required by a database access program at a remote server, you can access the information in that server by using a form. You learned how to get the information for using a form earlier in this chapter.

Suppose you want to create a form that enables visitors to your site to search an index at a remote site. You want the users to be able to type in a keyword or phrase and then pass that information on to the remote server, which would then return the results of the query. The following code enables your visitors to search WebCrawler (a Web index), using a form at your site. (This file is included in the support files as

\Chap20\Web.htm.)

```
<HTML>
<HEAD>
<TITLE>Search WebCrawler</TITLE>
</HEAD>

<BODY>
<CENTER><H1>Search for Information</H1></CENTER>


You can find information through WebCrawler by filling out the
following and clicking on the Search button.


<FORM NAME="wcsearchform" ACTION="http://www.webcrawler.com/cgi-bin/WebQuery"
METHOD="GET">
<P>
Display
<SELECT NAME="mode">
<OPTION value="compact" SELECTED>titles
<OPTION value="summaries">summaries
</SELECT>
for
<SELECT NAME="maxHits">
<OPTION>10
<OPTION SELECTED>25
<OPTION>50
<OPTION>75
<OPTION>100
</SELECT>
sites

<P>Keywords:
<INPUT NAME="searchText" SIZE=45> <INPUT TYPE="submit" value="Search">
</FORM>


<P><HR><P>
```

```
For comments, e-mail to <A HREF="Webmaster@dcomp.com">
Webmaster@dcomp.com</A>


</BODY>
</HTML>
```

This page displays a very simple form (see Figure 20-3). The user simply needs to fill in the blank and make a couple of selections to retrieve information from WebCrawler.

FIGURE 20-3

You can use forms to tie your site to remote databases.

SUPPORT
FILE

Using this same approach, you can develop links to a number of remote databases from your site. For instance, you can develop a page that gives the user access not only to WebCrawler but also to several other indexes. The following code implements such a scenario and is included in the support files as \Chap20\Multi.htm.

```
<HTML>
<HEAD>
<TITLE>Search Indexes</TITLE>
</HEAD>


<BODY>
<CENTER><H1>Search for Information</H1></CENTER>


You can find information through various indexes by entering your
keywords and clicking on the index button of your choice.
```

```
<P><HR><H3>HotBot</H3>
<FORM action="http://www.hotbot.com/" name="HSQ">
Search where?
<SELECT NAME="SW" >
    <OPTION VALUE="web" selected>the Web
    <OPTION VALUE="usenet">Usenet News
</SELECT>
for
<SELECT NAME="SM" >
    <OPTION VALUE="MC" selected>all the words
    <OPTION VALUE="SC">any of the words
    <OPTION VALUE="phrase">the exact phrase
    <OPTION VALUE="name">the person
    <OPTION VALUE="url">links to this URL
    <OPTION VALUE="B">the Boolean expression
</SELECT>
returning
<SELECT NAME="DC">
    <OPTION VALUE="10">10
    <OPTION VALUE="25" selected>25
    <OPTION VALUE="50">50
    <OPTION VALUE="75">75
    <OPTION VALUE="100">100
</SELECT>
results with
<SELECT NAME="DE">
    <OPTION VALUE="2" selected>full descriptions
    <OPTION VALUE="1">brief descriptions
    <OPTION VALUE="0">URLs only
</SELECT><BR>
Keywords:
<INPUT TYPE="text" VALUE="" SIZE=40 name="MT" maxlength="100">
<INPUT TYPE="submit" VALUE="Search HotBot">
</FORM>
```

```
<P><HR><H3>Lycos</H3>
<FORM ACTION="http://www.lycos.com/cgi-bin/pursuit" METHOD="GET">
Search where?
<SELECT NAME="cat">
    <OPTION SELECTED value="lycos">the Web
    <OPTION value="sounds">Sounds
    <OPTION value="graphics">Pictures
    <OPTION value="a2z">By Subject
</SELECT>
Keywords:
<INPUT TYPE="text" NAME="query" VALUE="" SIZE=40>
<INPUT TYPE="submit" VALUE="Search Lycos">
</FORM>



<P><HR><H3>WebCrawler</H3>
<FORM NAME="wcsearchform" ACTION="http://www.webcrawler.com/cgi-bin/WebQuery"
METHOD="GET">
<P>
Display
<SELECT NAME="mode">
<OPTION value="compact" SELECTED>titles
<OPTION value="summaries">summaries
</SELECT>
for
<SELECT NAME="maxHits">
<OPTION>10
<OPTION SELECTED>25
<OPTION>50
<OPTION>75
<OPTION>100
</SELECT>
sites<BR>
Keywords:
<INPUT TYPE="text" NAME="searchText" SIZE=40>
```

```
<INPUT TYPE="submit" VALUE="Search WebCrawler">
</FORM>



<P><HR><H3>Yahoo</H3>
<FORM METHOD="GET" ACTION="http://search.yahoo.com/bin/search">
Keywords:
<INPUT TYPE="text" NAME="p" VALUE="" SIZE=40>
<INPUT TYPE="submit" VALUE="Search Yahoo">
</FORM>



<P><HR><P>



For comments, e-mail to <A HREF="Webmaster@dcomp.com">
Webmaster@dcomp.com</A>



</BODY>
</HTML>
```

This code uses four forms, one for each index (HotBot, Lycos, WebCrawler, and Yahoo). You need four forms because each form is directed to a different target database at four different sites, and each database requires its own particular parameters to work properly. The main body of the page, when displayed, appears as shown in Figure 20-4.

Testing Your Form

Web documents that create links to databases at other servers are just like any other Web page. When you are done creating your documents and your links, you will want to take the time to check your work. If you run into problems, you should inspect the following items:

- ◆ **URL.** Does the ACTION method of the form use the proper URL? Is it a full URL? If you suspect an addressing problem, check the URL used when you submit a form at the site itself.

- ◆ **Variables.** Does your form include all the variables required by the database?

- ◆ **Query.** Is the query being submitted properly? Is the syntax what is expected by the database?

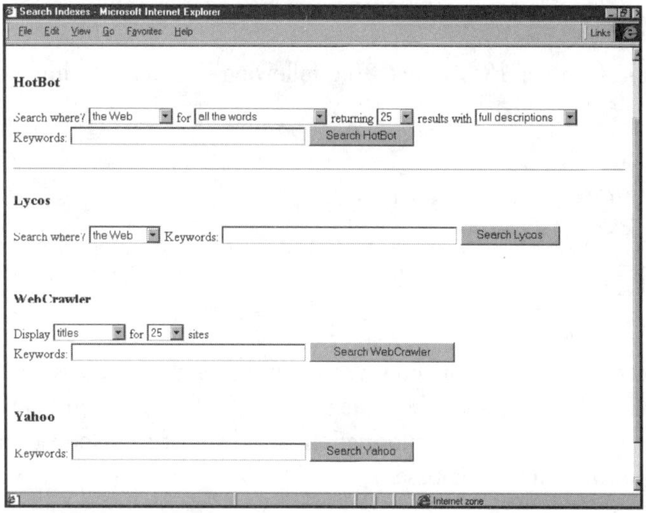

FIGURE 20-4

You can combine multiple forms into a single Web page.

Most problems can be directly attributed to one of these items. If you are still having problems, you should contact the Webmaster at the site to enlist his or her help.

TIP

If you create a form that is tied to a remote database over which you have no control, chances are good that you also do not have control over the script or program that is accessing the database at the remote site. In this instance, you will want to check your connection at least weekly. If the interface (including the script) at the remote site changes, you will need to change your access page right away.

Accessing Databases Directly

The other method of accessing remote databases is to access them directly. This is an unwieldy way of saying that you have control over the remote database; typically, the database is on a different server within your own local area network. The two common reasons for the database being on another server are (1) to share the burden of serving information to the public and (2) to prevent internal users who are updating the database from placing a burden on the primary Web server itself. For whatever reason the database is on the other server, you want to be able to access the data from your Web site.

You access the information stored on the server simply by using the same methods that you learned about in previous chapters. The only difference is that the database is not stored on the same system as the Web server.

### Part IV

LAN Databases

As you learned in Chapter 18, you need the following five items to implement an IDC link:

- ◆ A database table
- ◆ An ODBC data source name (DSN)
- ◆ An IDC file
- ◆ An HTX file
- ◆ An HTML file

How do you access the information, however, when the database table is on a remote system? In practice, the process can be quite simple. The first two items are the key. Thus, the focus of accessing remote information directly must be to look at the DSN that you set up for the remote database.

If the database is located on another system accessible through your local area network, you can set up a system DSN for the database the same as you did for a local database. The only difference is that when you specify the database, you use a mapped drive or a UNC as the path for the database.

For example, Figure 20-5 shows the ODBC Access Setup dialog box that should look familiar by now. (The use of this dialog box was covered in Chapter 20.)

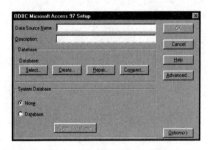

FIGURE 20-5

The ODBC Access Setup dialog box enables you to define a system DSN.

When using this dialog box, you click on the Select button to choose the actual database to be associated with this DSN. This action displays a standard Windows file selection dialog box. If the database is on a mapped drive, you can access it as you would a database on a local drive. If the database is accessible through your network but not on a mapped drive, you can simply enter the full UNC path as the filename. As far as IDC is concerned, the link to the remote database is transparent and works the same wherever the database may be.

Internet Databases

What happens, however, if the remote database is not accessible through a local area network? What if the database is accessible only through the Internet? The easiest solution is to follow these steps:

- ◆ Set up a Web server on the remote system
- ◆ Create system DSNs on the remote system
- ◆ Move your applications (IDC) to the remote system

Although this solution may sound like overkill, it enables you to use the procedures discussed earlier in this chapter to access any data on the remote system. The user accesses a Web page at server A and then clicks on a link or enters information in a form on that page, which then hands off the request to server B. Server B then serves up the information to the user. This relationship is depicted in Figure 20-6.

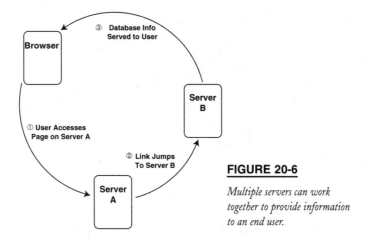

FIGURE 20-6

Multiple servers can work together to provide information to an end user.

Remember that the purpose of off-loading your database to another system is to distribute the burden of serving up the database among several computers. By applying the concepts discussed here, you can off-load quite a bit of the database-related processing, freeing up your original server to deal with requests for your main Web pages.

PART

V

Establishing and
Maintaining Security

Chapter 21

Securing Your Internet
Services

In This Chapter

◆ The Basis of IIS Security

◆ Security Issues for Your Site

If you were to open up a retail store or an office to the public, you would automatically become concerned about security. You want to make sure that your inventory or your equipment does not walk away on its own. In addition, you want to protect your store or office from after-hours intruders.

When you open an intranet or Internet site, you also need to be concerned about security. Essentially, you are opening your doors (even though they are virtual doors) to the public. This chapter discusses how security concerns relate to the services you offer at your site. Here you learn some essential security concepts, as well as some of the particulars you should pay attention to based on the services you offer.

The Basis of IIS Security

The security system in Internet Information Server is patterned after and takes advantage of the security system offered by Windows NT. Thus it is helpful for you to understand at least the basics of Windows NT security in order to understand how to secure your site. It is not the purpose of this chapter to provide everything you need to know to implement a secure site. In fact, it would be virtually impossible to do so.

This statement may seem somewhat strange. It is not, however, if you understand two concepts. First, security is not a condition; it is a process. Second, security is implemented through the application of small bits and parts that together make up a whole. Security is therefore implemented through various components.

> **NOTE**
>
> If you need to brush up on Windows NT security, you should refer to a good general-purpose Windows NT book (such as Prima's *Windows NT Server 5 Administrator's Guide* by Paul E. Robichaux) or to a book specifically dedicated to Windows NT security.

Security as a Process

Several hundred years ago, people in European civilizations secured their castles by surrounding them with a large stone wall and a perhaps a moat. Elsewhere, people implemented security by moving far from their enemies and building their homes into a cliff or on top of a mountain. Later, attackers became more adept at circumventing these attempts at security.

As cities became larger and more complex, security consisted of using locks and putting valuables in special safes. Unfortunately, attackers often overcame these security precautions as well.

In the global virtual community made possible by the Internet, large stone walls, moats, cliffs, and physical locks or safes do not provide security. We live in a world where attackers do not have to present themselves physically at our computers. The attackers could be in the same room, but more often they are across town or somewhere else in the world. In addition, attackers are not easily identified as such. They don't need to look like the Mongol hordes; an attacker may be a disgruntled employee, a challenge-seeking teenager, or an overzealous competitor.

It seems that every advance made in security (from cliffs to stone walls to moats and on to locks and safes) is matched by another advance that makes it easy to circumvent the first advance. For instance, ladders and ropes overcame cliffs; ladders, battering rams, and explosives overcame stone walls; boats and bridges overcame moats; and skeleton keys and picks overcame locks and safes. The same is true in the virtual world of networking. As new advances promise greater security, other discoveries highlight ways around the advances.

The upshot is that you *must* view security as a process. What is considered secure today is not considered secure tomorrow, as ways are found to circumvent today's security. The only answer, it seems, is to keep abreast of security technology and always attempt to stay one step ahead of the modern attackers.

Keeping Up with Security Issues

When you start viewing security as a process, one of the first things that you will do is to try to keep informed as new security issues arise. This approach will help you implement new security features when they become available. Your views of the importance of security will determine how much time you spend keeping up with security issues. The carefree administrator will wait until the site comes crashing down before looking into the latest news about securing a Windows NT Internet site.

Here are a couple examples of online resources that will help keep up with news about online security:

ONLINE ➡️

   ◆ **http://register.microsoft.com/regwiz/forms/pic.asp** Sign-up site for e-mail newsletters from Microsoft. Although they are not necessarily good for learning about the latest security development, newsletters such as the *Microsoft BackOffice News* will let you know when service packs and patches are available. These products are often created in response to security issues.

- **http://techweb.cmp.com/nc/forms/newsletter.html**   Subscription page to the *Network Computing Newsletter*. This newsletter is put together by the staff at *Network Computing Magazine* and has up-to-date information about networks, including security issues.

- **news://comp.os.ms-windows.nt.admin.security/**   A newsgroup devoted to Windows NT security issues.

- **http://www.microsoft.com/security/**   Microsoft Security Advisor Program that has information on security issues in Microsoft's products.

- **http://www-ns.rutgers.edu/www-security/reference.html**   A source of links to more information about Web and Internet security.

The Components of Security

One of the great truths of technological security is that you can't find it at one-stop shop. Indeed, the only way to build a security net (for today, at least) is to combine various tactics, policies, and tools. This process is analogous to a bank, which, to secure its building, combines a series of perimeter alarms, video cameras, locks, and construction techniques. Although each individual item may be surmountable by an attacker, the cumulative effect of all the items can present a barrier so intimidating that no attacker would take the actions necessary to breach the security measures.

In the computing world, you can implement many little things to increase your security. Items such as creating a written security policy, limiting user permissions, physically securing your systems, automatically logging inactive systems off, enforcing good password policies, and using NTFS file and directory permissions can go a long way toward making your site secure. When combined with commercial security products and management tools, the net effect is a site that is secure against all but the most knowledgeable attackers.

Security Issues for Your Site

As you work with IIS, you will find that various security issues crop up from time to time. You should address some of these issues as you are first starting your site; others become more critical as your site grows or the popularity of your site increases. The following sections describe issues you need to understand to improve the security of your site.

The User Account

When you install IIS, it creates a special user account that is used for all subsequent access to your system. This account, called the *user account*, is created using the following name:

IUSR_*server*

The *server* part of the account name is determined by the server on which IIS is installed. Thus, if the server name is moskee, the user account has the following name:

IUSR_MOSKEE

You can use the User Manager for Domains to view the details on this account. (If you are not running IIS on the main domain server, you may need to use the User Manager that handles users for that computer.) Figure 21-1 shows an example of a

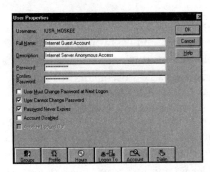

FIGURE 21-1

IIS creates a user account for all Internet access.

user account set up by IIS, as viewed in the User Manager.

The IIS setup program randomly generates the password for the user account. The account is set up so that it belongs only to the GUESTS group.

The IIS user account has no special features; to Windows NT, it's just another valid user account. All anonymous access through the Web server, FTP server, or Gopher server is logged into your computer using this account. You should keep the following issues in mind about the user account:

◆ You can change the password as needed. In fact, you may want to change it to some difficult password that only you know. If you change it, you need to change it using the User Manager.

◆ You should make sure that the security privileges assigned to the user account and to the GUESTS group are appropriate for the level of access that you want untrusted users to have. (By definition, all anonymous users fall into the category of untrusted users.)

- You should make sure that file and directory permissions are set properly for this account or for the GUESTS group as a whole.
- Any changes that you make to the GUESTS group also affect the user account.
- You may want to set up individual user accounts for individual Internet services. To do so, set up three new user accounts, one for each of your IIS servers. You can then change the username and password information in the Internet Service Manager to match the new accounts.

FTP Logons

You are already aware that FTP is one of the oldest protocols on the Internet. In the days when FTP was created, Internet users weren't as concerned about security as they are in today. Thus, the FTP program doesn't encrypt user IDs and passwords transmitted over the network.

What does this information mean to you? Primarily, it means a large security risk if you allow FTP users to log on using their names and passwords. Remember that the IIS server accepts two types of FTP access: anonymous and credentialed. The anonymous access is no big deal; because anonymous access occurs under the user account discussed earlier, you can limit the access that this user has to your system.

Credentialed access is another matter, however. Under this approach, someone logging on to your site needs to provide a valid Windows NT user ID and password. After that information is provided, the user has access to your site commensurate with his or her security privileges. Thus, you as an administrator could log on with your administrator ID and password and go about your work. Because FTP doesn't encrypt information, your administrator ID and password are *transmitted over the network;* someone could intercept that information and use it. That person then has a master key into your network.

To protect against this situation, you have several choices:

- **Disable FTP access completely.** This strategy seems rather drastic, but it would solve the problem.
- **Set up different, limited accounts for FTP access.** This method is fine, but nothing prevents the user from accessing by using the more comprehensive password (his or her regular one).
- **Allow only anonymous logons.** This approach satisfies most people. If you need to provide greater access to your site to some users, you can set up RAS dial-in accounts, which can use encrypted passwords.

To permit only anonymous logons, follow these steps:

1. Start the Internet Service Manager program, shown in Figure 21-2.
2. Right-click on your FTP site and select Properties. (Figure 21-2 shows the Default FTP Site.) This action displays the Default FTP Site Properties dialog box, as shown in Figure 21-3.

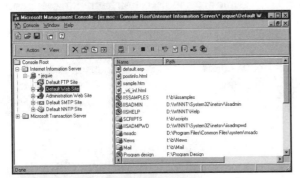

FIGURE 21-2

The Internet Service Manager enables you to control Internet services.

FIGURE 21-3

The FTP Site Properties dialog box contains the various configuration settings for the IIS FTP server.

3. Select the Security Accounts tab.
4. Make sure that the Allow Anonymous Connections check box is selected (at the top of the dialog box).
5. Select the Allow Only Anonymous Connections check box if necessary.
6. Click on OK to save your changes.
7. Stop and restart the FTP server.
8. Close the Internet Service Manager.

NOTE

It is important to restart the FTP server (or IIS as a whole) because anyone currently logged on under a nonanonymous mode continues to remain connected. Stopping and restarting the server breaks all existing FTP connections and means that everyone needs to again log on.

Document Files

Documents is a loose term that applies to everything you publish on your Internet servers. To secure the information in your server, you should keep all content directories separate from executable files (as discussed in the following section). In addition, you should make sure that the directories containing your documents have only the Read permission set. This scheme prevents users from corrupting your documents.

> **NOTE**
>
> You can set permissions only on directories stored on a drive using the NTFS format. A good rule of thumb is to store all your Internet data on an NTFS drive.

Setting Read permissions on a directory is fairly easy, but as far as IIS is concerned, you must follow two phases. First, you must set the permissions within IIS itself, and then you must set them within Windows NT.

Setting Permissions in IIS

If a particular directory is a virtual directory or a home directory for IIS, then you must specify, within IIS, what type of access is allowed to that directory. Two basic sets of permissions can be changed. The first set determines whether a browser can read and write files to your Web site. Writing, or uploading, a page to your site is available only in browsers that support the HTTP 1.1 protocol's PUT feature. The other set of permissions determines whether scripts, or programs, can be run in the directory on the server. You can set access permissions in IIS by following these steps:

1. Start the Internet Service Manager program. (Refer to Figure 21-2.)
2. Select the name of the site that uses the directory whose access you want to change. This action displays a list of directories in the result pane.
3. Locate the directory whose permissions you want to modify.
4. Right-click and select Properties from the shortcut menu to display the directory's Properties dialog box, as shown in Figure 21-4. (The dialog box reflects the directory's name.)
5. In the Access Permissions area in the middle of the dialog box, select the Read check box and clear the Write check box.
6. In the Permissions area at the bottom, select None to prevent the server from running any scripts or programs in this directory. The Script option is for ASP or IDC scripts, whereas the Execute option allows the server to run DLL or EXE files in the directory.

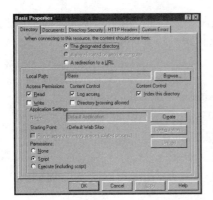

FIGURE 21-4

The directory's Properties dialog box specifies how a server accesses a directory.

7. Click on OK to save your changes.

8. Repeat steps 4 through 7 for any other directories whose access you want to change.

9. Click on OK to close the directory's properties dialog box.

10. Restart the server whose directories you changed and then close the Internet Service Manager.

Setting Permissions Using Windows NT

After making sure the access permissions are set properly in IIS, you can set them in Windows NT itself. To set the permissions used in a directory, follow these steps:

1. Use Windows NT Explorer or browse your desktop to locate the directory for which you want to set permissions.

2. Right-click on the icon for the directory to display a context menu.

3. Choose the Properties option from the context menu. The Properties dialog box for the directory opens.

4. Click on the Security tab. (If a Security tab isn't visible, then the directory does not reside on an NTFS drive.)

5. Click on the Permissions button. The Directory Permissions dialog box, shown in Figure 21-5, opens.

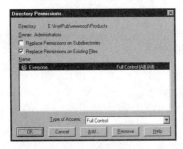

FIGURE 21-5

You can set a wide range of permissions for a directory.

6. Make sure that the Replace Permissions on Subdirectories check box is selected, as well as the Replace Permissions on Existing Files check box.

7. If multiple users have access to the directory, click on the name of the user whose access you want to change. (In Figure 21-5, the only user is Everyone, a special user indicating all user accounts.)

8. Select the Read option in the Type of Access pull-down list.

9. Click on OK. Windows NT asks you to confirm that you want to replace permissions on all existing subdirectories.

10. Click on Yes. Windows NT changes the permissions and again displays the Properties dialog box for the directory.

11. Click on OK to close the Properties dialog box.

Executable Files

Consider very carefully whether you want users to execute files on your system, including, of course, any CGI, ISAPI, ASP, and IDC programs (as covered in earlier chapters of this book). Any time you allow an untrusted person to run a program, you make your system vulnerable.

Remember that IIS allows for various classifications of executable files. Files that are basically scripts, such as ASP and IDC, can run in a directory that won't accept an EXE file called by a CGI script. Being able to classify executable files gives you control over the types of files that a user can run on your server.

Nevertheless, you might not want to completely ban executable files from your server. On the contrary, it is quite common—and often desirable—to have executable files on your system. The point is that you should not place them on your system willy-nilly. Doing so is akin to opening the door to your home and inviting anyone off the street into your living room. Think carefully about whether you need to offer executable programs.

If your service needs require you to allow at least some executable files, keep the following points in mind:

◆ Make sure that the executable file runs in a directory that has limited access to the rest of your system.

◆ Make sure that only Script permission is given when you don't need to run the EXE files.

◆ Make sure that the directory containing the executable file has only the Execute access set in the Internet Service Manager and only the Execute privilege set in Windows NT. (Follow virtually the same steps described the preceding section.)

◆ Make sure that information uploaded by an executable is benign. (You don't want someone uploading a Trojan horse program, for example.)

In addition, if your FTP or Web sites permit users to upload files, you should make sure that no way exists for the remote user to then execute those files. You can protect yourself by giving the upload directory only the Add permission within Windows NT.

IP Address Checks

The Internet Service Manager enables you to limit access to your servers by IP address. This feature is a great boon, particularly for intranet users. You can specify that only requests from specific IP addresses can access your system or, conversely, you can deny requests from specific addresses.

Use of this feature is the same for Web and FTP servers. IIS enables you to either limit access by specific IP address or grant access based on IP address. Both approaches use similar steps but are discussed individually in the following sections. You can change the access for a complete site or for only a directory.

Limiting Access by IP Address

When you limit access by IP address, you start from the basis that everyone initially has access to your server. Then you specify who does not have access. To limit access by IP address, in this case, the Web server's address) follow these steps:

1. Start the Internet Service Manager program, shown earlier in Figure 21-2.

2. Right-click on the name of the Web site you want to change and select Properties from the context menu. This action displays the Properties dialog box for the site.

3. Click on the Directory Security tab. The dialog box now appears as shown in Figure 21-6.

FIGURE 21-6

You can limit access to your server on the Directory Security tab.

4. Click on the Edit button in the IP Address and Domain Name Restrictions area of the dialog box. This action opens the IP Address and Domain Name Restriction dialog box, shown in Figure 21-7.

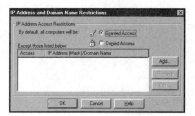

FIGURE 21-7

Limiting access based on IP address is one of the security schemes available.

5. Select the Granted Access radio button at the top of the dialog box if necessary.

6. Click on the Add button to specify an IP address that should be denied access to your server. The Deny Access On dialog box, shown in Figure 21-8, opens.

FIGURE 21-8

You can deny access to a single IP address, a group of addresses, or a domain name.

7. To deny access to your site to a single IP address, select the Single Computer radio button.

8. To deny access to computers from an entire range of IP addresses (such as an entire domain), select the Group of Computers radio button.

9 To deny access to a domain, select the Domain Name radio button. A warning box may tell you that this option forces a reverse DNS lookup on every call to your Web site (which can cause a performance drop at your site). A better option would be to deny access to a range of IP addresses.

10. In the IP Address field, specify the address of the computer or one of the computers in the group. If you know the computer or domain name, but not the IP address, you can use the DNS lookup button to find the IP address. If you selected the Domain Name option in step 9, enter a domain name rather than an IP address.

11. If you selected the Group of Computers radio button (step 8), then specify a subnet mask in the Subnet Mask field.

12. Click on OK, and the IP address (and possibly subnet mask) or domain name appears in the list of excluded addresses.

13. Repeat steps 6 through 12 until you have specified all the addresses and domains that you want to exclude.

14. Click on OK to save your changes.

15. Restart the Web server and close the Internet Service Manager. Restarting the Web server logs off anyone who may be connected from your newly excluded domains.

Granting Access by IP Address

Granting access by IP address means that you run a very limited site. Under this view, you start from the assumption that only users to whom you explicitly give access should have access to your site. This approach is typically used on intranets, where you know the IP addresses of members.

To limit access to a particular IP address (in this case, the FTP server's address), follow these steps:

1. Start the Internet Service Manager program, shown earlier in Figure 21-2.

2. Right-click on the name of your FTP site and select the Properties option from the context menu. This action displays the Service Properties dialog box for the server.

3. Click on the Directory Security tab. The dialog box that appears is similar to that shown earlier in Figure 21-7.

4. Select the Denied Access radio button at the top of the dialog box. (You have now closed your site to everyone.)

5. Click on the Add button to specify an IP address that should be granted access to your server. This action displays the Grant Access On dialog box, shown in Figure 21-9.

6. To grant access to a single IP address, select the Single Computer radio button.

FIGURE 21-9

You can grant access to a single IP address, group of addresses, or domain name.

7. To grant access to computers from an entire range of IP addresses (such as an entire domain—perhaps your intranet), select the Group of Computers radio button.

8. To grant access to a domain, select the Domain Name radio button. This option may cause a small performance penalty, but one that is not nearly as bad as for a Web site, because a reverse DNS lookup will be performed whenever someone tries to connect to your FTP site.

9. In the IP Address field, specify the address of the computer or one of the computers in the group. You can use the DNS lookup to find the IP Address of a computer. If you selected the Domain Name radio option in step 8, then you have to enter a domain name instead of an IP address.

10. If you selected the Group of Computers radio button (step 7), then specify a subnet mask in the Subnet Mask field.

11. Click on OK, and the IP address (and possibly subnet mask) or domain name appears in the list of those granted access.

12. Repeat steps 5 through 11 until you have specified all the addresses you want to have access to your site.

13. Click on OK to save your changes.

14. Restart the FTP server, disconnecting everyone connected, and close the Internet Service Manager.

Chapter 22

Creating a Secure IIS
Environment

———

In This Chapter

- ◆ Procedural Security
- ◆ Logical Security
- ◆ Physical Security
- ◆ Firewall Security
- ◆ Intranet Security

In the preceding chapter, you learned how to use IIS features to increase the security at your site. In most situations, however, you also need to consider other security elements. Although the server does not implement these elements, they are, nonetheless, just as important to the overall well-being of your site.

This chapter describes the basics of how you can secure the environment in which IIS operates. This chapter does not claim to be the definitive guide on site security, but it does provide some good general information and guidance. When you have mastered all the information in this chapter, you will want to move on to books dedicated to securing computer installations. As is pointed out throughout this chapter, many of those types of documents can be found on the Internet itself.

ONLINE You can find helpful security-related links at online at **http://somarsoft.com/sec-sites.htm.**

Procedural Security

An essential part of any security you might implement at your site is the procedures you follow for your day-to-day operations. Quite honestly, effective security affects everything you do, every day, in relation to your computer systems. However, you must pay particular attention to several procedural areas when implementing security. The following sections cover these issues.

Developing a Written Plan

The first procedural issue you must address is to develop a *written* security plan. A wise person once said that a plan not written is not really a plan. This statement is true because plans are easy to forget. If you have it in writing, however, your plan becomes a set of written guidelines on which you can base all your subsequent actions.

To create an effective security plan, you need to understand how your system currently works, as well as how you want it to work. This knowledge isn't as easy to acquire as it sounds. Much of the information in this book can help you to understand how your system works, but only you can decide how you *want* it to work. How you want your system to work becomes, in effect, your vision of your service.

This knowledge enables you to figure out the best way to turn the vision a reality. But don't expect to get there overnight; you must make sure that each step you take along the way does not decrease your current security level or make your system harder for others to access or use.

When you start to write your plan, you should include these two items:

- ◆ An indication of what you are doing for security
- ◆ An indication of what you will do if your security doesn't work

These items might seem odd, but if you don't know what you are doing for security, it's doubtful that you have any security at all. In fact, your security might be just an illusion. Next, you need to know what you are going to do if your security is breached. Will you change passwords? Will you secure your system with SSL? Or will you cut off all outside connections until the security hole is plugged?

Exactly what you do is up to you, but you basically must set some checkpoints, along with a threshold that will trigger some remedial action on your part. If the checkpoints are breached and the threshold is reached, you need to be prepared to carry out your remedial actions.

Making Backups

Most people don't think about backups as part of a security plan. Instead, they think of them as insurance in case of mechanical failure or human error. This view is good, but perhaps not the best.

Suppose that you are running an Internet site and find out that someone has broken into your system. Maybe the intruder found an unprotected directory or a way to execute a Trojan horse program on your system. If you detect the breach early enough, you can simply restore your earlier system from the backup, plug the security leaks, and continue business as usual. Without the backups, you couldn't take this approach. Thus, backups become critical not only from an insurance standpoint but also from a security perspective.

When you make backups, you need to make two types: a day-zero backup and routine backups. Routine backups are those that you make as a matter of course. Most people back up their server every day or two, with a complete backup every week. The only problem with this system is that you may not detect a security problem for a week or a month. By that time, all your backups may also be compromised. What do you do then?

That's where the day-zero backup comes into play. This level of backup earns its name from the fact that it's made when you first get your system up and running. At this point (day zero), you know that the security of your system hasn't been compromised because no one other than you has accessed the system.

Using your day-zero backup is a serious decision, because it erases all your password files and perhaps destroys your "evolutionary system configuration." It can take quite a bit of work to bring your system back up to its current status. More often than not, however, security problems are limited to a particular part of your server, and you can restore just that part from the day-zero backup. For example, if you think the server programs themselves have been corrupted, you can simply reload those programs.

TIP

When you make backups, make sure to store a set at your site and another set away from your site. This advise is particularly important with your day-zero backup. Having dual backups means that you should always have access to a backup set, regardless of the crisis.

Enforcing Passwords

You already know that Windows NT gives you quite a bit of latitude in setting up your password system. Passwords are the primary security feature for user accounts under Windows NT. To make your system secure, you should follow these guidelines:

- ◆ **Password expiration.** Always make sure that your passwords expire after a reasonable period, such as every two weeks. If you want even greater security, have your passwords expire more often.
- ◆ **Password length.** In practice, the longer the password, the more difficult it is to break. Unfortunately, users will also have more difficulty setting and remembering longer passwords. You should require passwords to be at least five characters long. Never allow blank passwords.
- ◆ **Password uniqueness.** Turn on password history tracking. Users should not be able to reuse the same password. You should instruct the system to remember at least the last three or four passwords for each user.
- ◆ **Password changing.** Make sure that users can change their passwords right away (no minimum password age) and that they must log on to make the change.
- ◆ **Account lockout** Turn on account lockout so that an account is locked for at least 15 minutes if three unsuccessful logon attempts occur.

If you apply these guidelines, as a minimum, you will have a secure password system. Ultimately, however, the effectiveness of your security depends on your willingness to enforce your policies for everyone.

You can easily establish password policies that require all users to change their password every two weeks. But what if John, your closest and dearest friend, comes to you and says that he's tired of changing his password all the time? If you make an exception in his case and change his account so that his password never expires, you are starting to dismantle your security procedures. You might not think it's a big deal, but if someone else gets hold of John's password, that person will have a permanent passkey into your system.

> **TIP**
>
> Take time to educate users on the importance of passwords. When users understand what someone else can do with their password, or by guessing their password, they will often become more cooperative with you. You can also take the time to help your users come up with creative passwords that are harder to guess.

Another good idea is to get rid of default passwords in your system. A prime candidate is the Guest account that is included by default with Windows NT. Everyone knows that the Guest account is there, and that knowledge provides half the information needed to log on under that account. If you don't need Guest access, get rid of the account. Even if you need Guest access, get rid of the default Guest account and create a different account for your guests—one that uses a different, unique name and password.

 You can find out more about changing passwords at **http://joda.cis.temple.edu /~stauffer/NTdocs/NTchangepass.html.**

Using Log Files

If you are using the NTFS filing system, you can take advantage of one of the most powerful security options offered by Windows NT—the capability to enable auditing and use log files. Log files enable you to determine what has happened on your system. The files can be very extensive, or they can be very limited in nature. At a minimum, your log files should enable you to determine who had access to your system, and particularly who had access to critical or sensitive areas of your system.

Because managing log files takes additional time, you may be tempted to not keep them. Regardless, you should still take advantage of the log file capability of Windows NT. Why? Because figuring out how someone breached your security or compromised your system is virtually impossible if you can't follow some tracks. The best tracks you have are those contained in your log files.

To use log files effectively, you need to understand the concept of auditing and how to then access and manage the log files.

Understanding Auditing

Auditing is an NTFS security feature that tracks access to a file or directory by a user or group of users. Auditing is a very powerful feature, and you can control exactly what types of access are audited.

In some ways, setting up auditing is similar to setting permissions for a file or directory. All you need to do is display the Properties dialog box for the file or directory for which you want to create an audit trail, click on the Security tab, and then click on the Auditing button. The Directory Auditing dialog box then appears, as shown in Figure 22-1.

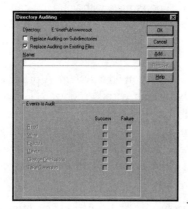

FIGURE 22-1

The Directory Auditing dialog box controls exactly what auditing is done on a file or directory.

This example shows the dialog box for setting up auditing on a directory. If you had selected a file instead, a slightly different dialog box would be displayed. The title bar would be different, and the first two check boxes in the dialog box would be missing (they don't have any meaning for files). If you are setting up auditing for a directory, the first two check boxes control whether the audit should apply to files in the directory, as well as to subdirectories in the directory.

The Directory Auditing dialog box contains two major areas. The first area, in the center of the dialog box, is where you specify the users or groups whose actions you want to audit. You use the Add and Remove buttons to control the list of accounts you want audited. If you want to audit all activity on a directory or file, select the Everyone group. (Realize, however, that this setting can make your audit trail quite large.)

At the bottom of the dialog box, you specify the actions you want to audit. Notice that you can audit both the success and failure of a wide range of actions. The failure side is particularly helpful because you can easily track who has tried to get into a file or directory and failed in their efforts.

Consider carefully what you are trying to achieve through auditing. When auditing is turned on and a recordable event occurs, the Security log file generates a record. Therefore, you need to actively manage the log file, as discussed in the next section. On a busy system, the Security log file can overflow rather quickly. Keep in mind that judicious use of file and directory auditing also enables you to detect security problems.

Managing Log Files

As Figure 22-2 shows, Windows NT enables you to track almost everything that happens on your server. This information is logged in one of three log files and can be reviewed with the Event Viewer. You start the Event Viewer by following these steps:

1. Choose the Programs option from the Start menu to display the Programs menu.

2. Choose Administrative Tools (Common) from the Programs menu to display a menu of administrative tools.

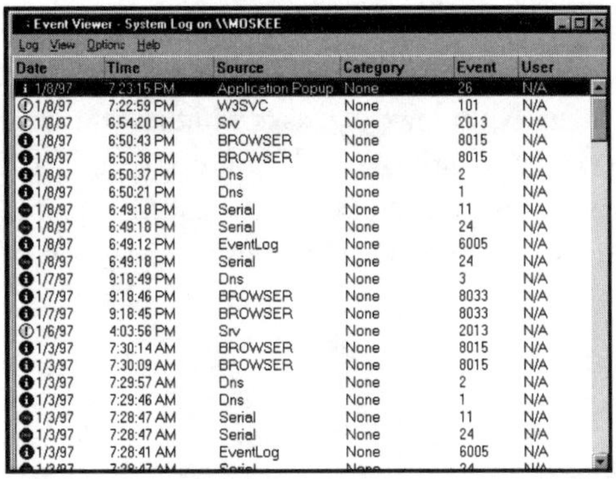

FIGURE 22-2

The Event Viewer enables you to manage the Windows NT audit logs.

3. Click on the Event Viewer option. The Event Viewer window opens.

Windows NT maintains three types of logs: system, security, and application. Specify the log you want to view by selecting any of the following options from the Log menu:

◆ **System** Tracks events generated by Windows NT, for example, device drivers not loading or messages about system memory usage.

◆ **Security** Tracks security violations, including all Windows NT permissions logging.

◆ **Application** Lists events generated by your application programs. The exact types of events logged can differ from program to program.

Obviously, the log most pertinent to the topic of this chapter is the security log. You should review the security log at least daily. Pay particular attention to the contents of the Category and User fields. Look for events that appear out of line with what you know should be happening. Pay special attention to repetitive events. For instance, you might notice several unsuccessful attempts at logging on to your system. This pattern indicates either that someone is having difficulty (and perhaps needs some training) or that someone is trying to break into your system.

NOTE

Depending on the activity on your site, the process of analyzing your log files may take a while. Over time, however, you will be able to tell if something is wrong in the log files simply by glancing over them quickly.

If you want additional information about an event, double-click on the event to open the Event Detail dialog box, as shown in Figure 22-3.

With the Event Viewer, you can manage your log files easily. For example, after reviewing your log file for a particular day, you might want to get rid of it. Just choose Clear All Events from the Log menu. Windows NT asks whether you want to save the events in an archive before clearing the log file. If you do, specify a filename. Archive files use the extension evt. Thus, you can save the event log in a file such as April.evt. You can review the events in the archive file by using the Open command from the Log menu.

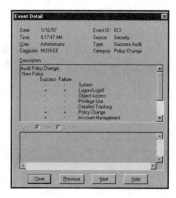

FIGURE 22-3

The security log keeps detailed information on each event.

Using Third-Party Analyzers

Many third-party software products are available to assist you in analyzing the use of your Internet site. Most of these programs are designed to run and track hits to your Web site or to analyze your log files and generate reports that show which areas are the most popular. These tools are generally used to create marketing analysis reports; however, these tools also provide some useful security information.

From a security standpoint, the analysis reports can help you track down the location of your visitors. If you find a security problem coming from a particular domain or IP address, you can use the techniques explained in Chapter 21 to block those visitors. The log analyzers also help you filter through the log files to find specific information, which can save a lot of time at a really busy site. Log-analyzing software is covered again in Chapter 26.

Logical Security

The term *logical security* refers to ways in which you can configure your Windows NT system to improve security. This concept includes setting up a meaningful, security-friendly directory structure and watching the programs used on your system. Both of these topics are discussed in the following sections.

Creating Your Directory Structure

Your directory structure should help implement your security plans. I know of a company that installed a server with a 2GB drive because the designers wanted to have plenty of room for data files shared among all the nodes on their network. The problem was that the company then configured the entire 2GB as one large drive. A much better approach would have been to partition the drive into three or four smaller drives. That way, the company could keep its operating system on one drive and secure it against intruders. The data could be kept on the other drives, which could be made available to the general network population.

After your directory structure becomes manageable, you should learn what's in your directories. Unfortunately, very few people give much thought to what's in their directories—particularly the critical directories. For example, you should have a working knowledge of everything in your Windows NT system directories. Why? Because this information gives you a reference point for determining whether someone has been tampering with your critical files.

A good way to keep track of your files is to create a file (on paper if desired) that lists the files in each critical directory. You can do so from the command prompt by typing either of the following commands from within the critical directory:

> **dir > prn**

> **dir > a:dirlist.txt**

The first command sends the directory listing to the printer; the second sends it to a disk file named `dirlist.txt` on drive A. Keep this printout or file in a safe place, and you can compare it to your current directory contents if a question ever arises.

TIP

If you have a very active site, you might want to take the added precaution of examining your directories daily. This job is easy enough if you use **DIR /OD /TW** at the command line, which sorts files in the order in which they were last written to. You then can examine the files to make sure that you agree that any new files should be there.

Watching Program Use

Have you installed Internet services in the past that you no longer need or use? For instance, when you first installed IIS, did you install the FTP server, but now no longer use it? If so, remove the server and any other components you no longer use. Every component you leave running is one more door into your system. If the component is a door you never check, it represents a grave security risk.

Because most Internet services—regardless of the vendor—are run as Windows NT services, you must at least stop the service using the Services applet in the Control Panel. To stop a service and disable it in the Control Panel, follow these steps:

1. Open the Control Panel.

2. Double-click on the Services applet to display the Services dialog box shown in Figure 22-4.

3. Scroll through the list of installed services and select the one you want to stop.

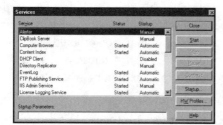

FIGURE 22-4

The Services dialog box tracks all the services installed on your system.

4. Click on the Stop button to stop the service.

5. Click on the Startup button to display the Service dialog box, shown in Figure 22-5.

FIGURE 22-5

You can modify the way in which any service is started.

6. Choose the Disabled radio button to disable the service so it cannot be started.

7. Click on OK to save your change and close the Service dialog box.

8. Click on Close to close the Services dialog box.

9. Close the Control Panel.

After stopping and disabling the service, if the software provides an uninstall program, you can remove the programs for the Internet service. If you do not have an uninstall program, you need to seek out the documentation provided with the software, contact the vendor, or "strong arm" your way through removing the software by deleting it and searching the Registry for any related entries.

You can find out more about Internet security at the World Wide Web Security FAQ. This site is available online at **http://www-genome.wi.mit.edu/WWW/faqs/www-security-faq.html**.

Physical Security

So far in this chapter, you have learned various ways to implement security by using the machine in different ways or by changing your internal procedures. Another aspect of any security plan is the actual physical security of your computer system. The two facets to physical security are using gateway machines and securing your hardware.

Adding Gateway Machines

Whenever you are connected to the rest of the world, you need to be concerned with who comes knocking at your computer's door (so to speak). With the speed at which electronic transactions occur in today's world, it is humanly impossible for you to monitor every message, every file, and every transaction that comes from the outside world to your computer.

Gateways are dedicated hardware devices that can be configured as stopping points between the outside world and the "inner sanctum" of your network. The primary purposes of a gateway include:

♦ Authenticating messages
♦ Authenticating users

If a message or a user doesn't meet the requirements for entry into your network, the gateway blocks that message or user. In this way, the gateway protects your critical data and system programs from intrusion.

In addition, if a potential intruder mounts an attack against your network, that attack theoretically affects only the gateway machine. Even if it is compromised, the systems behind the gateway (your internal systems) are protected from the attacker.

Gateways often work through a process called *packet filtering*. This term simply means that the gateway examines incoming message packets to determine their validity. For example, the gateway may look at the destination IP address of the packet or at the sender's IP address. The system then compares these addresses to lists or criteria maintained by the gateway. If the message is destined for an IP address not on the network, it is deleted and not passed through the gateway. Likewise, if the message originated at an IP address that is not on an "allowed list" or that is included on a "prohibit list," then the message is again deleted and not passed through. The filtering process is transparent to those within your network, of course.

Limiting Physical Access

Clearly, the only way you can ensure the effectiveness of the security measures that you have already implemented is to limit access to the physical server. In a perfect world, your network servers should be in a locked room, and only a handful of people should have the key.

Imagine, if you will, a scenario in which a disgruntled employee determines that he or she has the "right" to seek retribution against your company. One of the most sensitive areas to seek redress is in the network servers. If the person can get to the servers, he or she can do all sorts of things:

- Log on by trial and error
- Find a system that is still logged on and open for use
- Turn off one or more servers
- Physically disconnect and take a server
- Reboot to a floppy, bypass security, and directly access information on the server's hard drive
- Reboot to a floppy and copy a Trojan horse or damaging program to the server's hard drive

Do these scenarios sound too far out to believe? These things, and many more, have all happened. The shame of the matter is that they could have been averted if the companies had simply limited the physical access to the servers.

Another closely related matter is that you weaken the security of your overall network if your users leave their machines logged on and unattended for any length of time. If John, who is a manager and has fairly high security clearance, leaves his computer on over the lunch hour, it is an open invitation to tamper with the network and the data to which John has access. Leaving a logged-on machine unattended is akin to leaving your house unlocked and the front door open for an hour or two.

The solution to this potential problem is twofold. First, you need to inform all employees of their responsibility to log off their systems whenever they step away from their computers. Second, you can use screen savers that start running after 60 seconds or so and require passwords to stop.

Using Secure Machines

The final stage in a security plan—and the one offering the best security possible— is to use physically separate machines for the services you offer. In the case of IIS, this plan means arranging for a single Windows NT Server machine, running IIS, to be connected to the Internet. This machine doesn't serve as your LAN server at all; it's strictly for Internet access. Although this setup might seem extreme, it provides optimal security because those outside your organization cannot get to the machines on your internal LAN. Instead, outsiders are limited to the server attached to the Internet.

The drawback to this approach is that you must use the physical server for all published information. For example, if you want to create a new Web document, you must create it on the server. Or you must create it on a different system, save it to floppy disk, and then transfer the floppy to the server. You can't create the document on another workstation and then upload it because your workstations aren't connected to the Internet server. Thus, using a secure machine often involves changing some of your internal work habits. If this strategy is acceptable in light of the security gained, you should plan accordingly.

Securing against Nature

As a final note on physical security, you should be prepared for the worst that nature can throw at you. Physical security should include protection against such things as earthquakes, fire, and electrical outages as well as protection against malicious, or even naïve, attacks by other people.

For the most part, the best protection against nature is a good backup procedure, which will enable you to recover all the data on your system. Always store this backup set away from your site; a fireproof safe in your office may not protect the backup media from an earthquake.

Another form of protection is to not put all your eggs in one basket. Putting all of your servers in one place is asking for problems. You never now when the next earthquake will hit or when the next backhoe will sever your phone line. When possible, have a backup system at another location, maybe even a branch office at the other end of the country. This solution may be the only way to keep the system running until repairs can be made.

Along the same lines as natural disasters is the fact that mechanical components can break down or become damaged. Many protective devices, such as hot-swappable hard disk drives and even power supplies, are available for large networks. For smaller sites, a spare computer that can be used as a server and even a spare hard disk drive or two can be lifesavers.

Firewall Security

The term *firewall* is very popular these days. Unfortunately, this term has two uses. In the strictest sense of the word, a firewall is any set of tools and procedures that, when carried out, shield your system from unwanted intrusion. Thus, if you apply many of the ideas you have gleaned from this chapter, you will have erected a firewall for your network.

The other use of the term, however, is what I refer to as a "marketing use." If you read the popular press or look through network magazines, you can find reference to and advertisements for "firewalls." This usage implies that you can call a toll-free number, order a firewall, and install it next week. (You can obtain more information about firewall providers at **http://www.ncsa.com/hotlinks/firewall.html.**)

To a degree, this meaning is true. Some commercial products can serve as a firewall. Remember, however, the definition of a firewall as provided earlier in this section. Any tool that helps protect you from unwanted intrusion can be considered a firewall. This broad definition means that a wide disparity can exist between the capabilities, features, and approaches of various commercial products. The issue of firewalls is a particularly "fuzzy" area of computing and one in which the buyer should definitely beware.

Most commercial firewalls include some sort of gateway implementation, as discussed earlier. They may also include special router hardware or additional software to use on each of your network nodes. Because the commercial firewall market is so broad, what you get from one product will definitely differ from what is offered by another. From a conceptual standpoint, firewalls are very simple (see Figure 22-6).

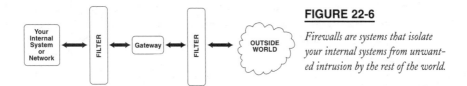

FIGURE 22-6

Firewalls are systems that isolate your internal systems from unwanted intrusion by the rest of the world.

Using a Proxy Server as a Firewall

Another product that can be used as a firewall is a *proxy server*. One such proxy server is Microsoft Proxy Server 2.0. This program acts as a selective gateway to your network, because all information passes through it.

The proxy server sits between your local network and the Internet. It is assigned one IP address, recognizable by the Internet. All of the machines, or clients, in your organization are then given bogus IP addresses. This disallows any direct connection between a client and an Internet server. The proxy server analyzes all network traffic and routes information to the proper client.

While the proxy server is analyzing network traffic, it can also be used to deny certain types of connections, such as FTP or HTTP. Even when you allow a protocol, such as HTTP, to be used, you can use the proxy server to deny access to specific sites.

You should note that the concept of a firewall is not limited to use on the Internet. Indeed, the concept applies just as well to an intranet. If you are making your system available to others outside your organization (company or department) in some fashion, you need to be concerned with the security of that system. Your concerns, when analyzed, acted upon, and implemented, become your firewall.

Intranet Security

You already know that an intranet is an internal network that uses Internet tools within a finite configuration. In most respects, an intranet is no different than the Internet as a whole; after all, the same tools are used, so the difference is simply a matter of scale.

In most organizations, you probably trust the people within the organization more than you do those in the outside world. One advantage of an intranet is that you don't need to worry that much about people outside your organization mounting an attack against your intranet. After all, nothing connects that intranet and the outside world, right?

> **NOTE**
>
> Many intranets are, in fact, connected to the Internet. In these instances, the intranet is the main stomping ground for company employees, but it also provides ultimate access to the Internet. These environments require a firewall and one or more gateways between the intranet and the Internet, as discussed briefly in the preceding section.

However, even intranets face security risks. Most of the issues revolve around securing the network itself. If you, as network administrator, apply the ideas already discussed in this chapter, you will go a long way toward solving any potential security problems.

As you are implementing your intranet, one security area you are bound to face is how to deal with multiple departments. Larger organizations are naturally divided into specialized departments, such as sales, marketing, and production. When you deploy an intranet to tie all these groups together, you will undoubtedly make quite a bit of information available on that intranet.

The problem is that some of the information may be appropriate for use in just one department. For example, some of the information maintained by the Human Resources department would not necessarily be appropriate for general release to the rest of the company.

You can approach this problem in various ways. The solution lies in ensuring that you compartmentalize the information for each department: place it in its own directory or even on its own server. You can then limit access to the directories or servers according to the IP address or username of the person accessing the intranet.

Chapter 23

Utilizing the Secure
Sockets Layer

In This Chapter

◆ What Is SSL?

◆ Implementing SSL

◆ Usage Differences

◆ Using the Key Manager

If you are interested in commerce on the Internet, you may have heard of a protocol known as *Secure Sockets Layer*, or *SSL*. This chapter focuses on what SSL is and how you can use it at your site to provide the security you need.

What Is SSL?

The Secure Sockets Layer is a security protocol developed by Netscape and RSA Data Security, Inc. The goal of the protocol is to assure that data transferred between the browser and your server remains private. Quite a few browsers support at least one version of SSL, which means that by implementing a secure site with SSL, you have the greatest chance of the largest number of users being able to conduct business with you. Effectively, SSL provides three functions for Web communications:

◆ **Authentication** Ensures that the intended server (your SSL-enabled server) actually receives and uses the information you send it.

◆ **Encryption** Ensures that no other party can intercept and use the data intended for your server. (RSA encryption is very secure.)

◆ **Integrity** Ensures that the data contained in the transmission has not been altered from the time it left the sender until it arrived at the destination.

Regular versus Secure Connections

SSL was developed in response to fears of credit card information becoming public knowledge through transmission over the Internet. In real life, much of this response has been a form of mass hysteria. Granted, normal Internet transmissions are not secure, and someone could tap into the information you transmit. The reality, however, the risk is infinitesimal. Indeed, someone is much more likely to learn your credit card number when you give the card to a waiter, waitress, or telephone operator.

Sockets are another name for a TCP communication channel. The Secure Sockets Layer is a protocol that is positioned between the TCP/IP protocol and the communications protocol used by the client and server (see Figure 23-1). Because of the way in which SSL is implemented, security is attached to the entire communications channel, not to individual documents or files transferred over the channel.

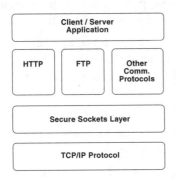

FIGURE 23-1

The Secure Sockets Layer is positioned between the TCP/IP protocol and your communications protocol.

This last statement may require a bit more explanation. It is possible to implement security on a file-by-file basis. Under this approach, you might secure your transmission by encrypting a file before sending it. When the file is received at the other end, the user must decrypt the file before using it. Someone intercepting the file cannot decode it without the proper decryption algorithm.

When you secure a communications channel, you automatically secure all information transmitted over the channel. In addition, the encryption /decryption cycle is normally performed transparently, without the need for user intervention. This approach (securing the channel, not individual documents) is the approach used by the SSL protocol.

Different Versions of SSL

The SSL protocol was first introduced in late 1994 and slightly revised in early 1995. This first version of SSL was, believe it or not, referred to as SSL 2.0. (I have not been able to determine what happened to 1.0.) The current version of SSL is version 3.0, which was last updated in November, 1996.

ONLINE If you are interested in technical information on SSL 2.0, you can find it documented at **http://home.netscape.com/newsref/std/SSL_old.html**. The newer version, SSL 3.0, is documented at **http://home.netscape.com/eng/ssl3/index.html**.

When IIS was first released, it supported SSL 2.0. Currently, IIS supports SSL 3.0. SSL 3.0 introduced several improvements, including the following:

◆ **Improved security.** SSL 3.0 is less vulnerable to certain types of aggressive intruder attacks than SSL 2.0.

◆ **Improved functionality.** SSL 3.0 allows both server and client to change, on demand, the encryption algorithms and keys used in a communication session. SSL 3.0 also supports record compression and can handle a wider range of certificates than SSL 2.0 handled.

◆ **Improved flexibility.** SSL 3.0 supports various message packet formats, which allow a record to contain part of a message, a whole message, or several messages. This new flexibility is transparent to the user.

◆ **Backward compatibility.** Under SSL 3.0, both client and server can fall back to SSL 2.0 if either devise detects that the client or server it is communicating with cannot understand SSL 3.0.

Requirements for a Secure Connection

For a secure connection to occur, both the server and the browser must be capable of supporting the same version of SSL. If you are running a secure site, meaning that you have implemented SSL on your Web server, the user's browser can detect this information from the URL used to connect to your site. (This procedure is explained a bit later in the chapter.) The browser then knows that, to establish a communications channel, it must procure the information necessary to decrypt transmissions that it receives from the server and encrypt whatever it sends. This information is provided in the form of *keys* that lock and unlock the transmitted messages.

When the browser is in the process of establishing a communications channel with your Web site, it requests from the server a public key. Messages sent by the browser to the server are then encrypted with this public key. The server can then decrypt them using its private key. From the standpoint of the server, the opposite happens. It requests, from the browser, a public key. The server uses this key to encrypt everything it sends to the browser. The browser, in turn, uses the private key to decode the message.

Thus, for SSL communications, two sets of keys come into play. Both the server and the browser possess their own public and private keys, which enable the machines to encrypt and decrypt messages securely.

Understanding Certification Authorities

In today's world, knowing who you can and cannot trust is growing increasingly difficult. In normal human relations, we tend to trust only people who have proven to be trustworthy. The world of electronic commerce offers very few clues to help establish the trustworthiness of someone who is across the country or around the world.

After all, you won't necessarily be dealing with the person on a daily basis to be able to make a judgment.

Even the value of the encrypted data is reduced if you are not sure about the party with whom you are exchanging data. One solution, which many people now use, is to rely on special *Certification Authorities*. These companies do nothing but check out and verify the right of an organization to conduct electronic commerce. The Certification Authority (CA) then issues the registered key pair that IIS uses to conduct secure communications. This key pair is often referred to as a *digital certificate*.

The authority chosen by Microsoft for use with the IIS Web server is VeriSign, Inc. If you want to learn more about either CAs or digital certificates, you can visit its Web site at **http://www.verisign.com**.

Implementing SSL

From the server side of the fence, to implement SSL you need to accomplish several tasks. These include the following steps:

1. Generate a key pair file and a request file.
2. Request an SSL certificate.
3. Install the certificate in IIS.
4. Enable SSL in the server itself.

The following sections explain these steps in detail.

Generating Files

To set up SSL on your system, you need a digital certificate, as discussed earlier in this chapter. To get the certificate, you need to generate two files: one for your use and the other to put in your request. Together, these two files are known as a *key pair*. With IIS, key pairs are generated through the Key Manager program.

Regardless of which method you use, you will need some standard information to generate your key pair. This information includes the following:

♦ An encryption password.

♦ The two-character designation for the country where you are located. For the United States, use US. For other countries, use the two-character code that is also your highest-level domain identifier (for example, MX in Mexico).

♦ The state in which your server is located.

♦ The city in which your server is located.

♦ Your company name.

♦ Your department name (Marketing, Sales, and so on).

♦ The domain name of your server.

This information goes into creating the files necessary for SSL registration and certification. All of the items should be self-explanatory, except perhaps the first item. When you generate key files, the generation routines rely on the presence of an encryption password. You can use any password you desire, but it should be one you won't forget.

Using the Key Manager

IIS includes a special program called Key Manager that generates and manages the various keys you may need for different parts of your secure site. To use the Key Manager to generate a key pair, follow these steps:

1. Start the Internet Service Manager.

2. Choose the Key Manager icon on the toolbar. This action runs the Key Manager program, and shortly you see the program window shown in Figure 23-2.

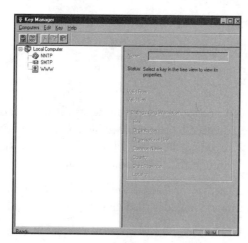

FIGURE 23-2

The Key Manager enables you to manage your various digital keys.

3. Click on the WWW server icon for your machine. (If more than one version of IIS is installed on your single machine, you may need to select among the various servers to indicate which server is to receive the new key.)

4. Choose Create New Key from the Key menu. The Create New Key Wizard, shown in Figure 23-3, starts. This Wizard creates a text file that can be sent a request to a CA for a digital certificate.

5. Click on Next to begin the process of creating a request for a digital certificate. This action opens the first dialog box requesting information about your key, as shown in Figure 23-4.

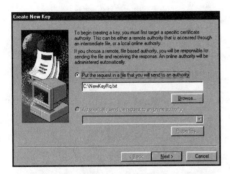

FIGURE 23-3

The Create New Key Wizard helps to create your key pair.

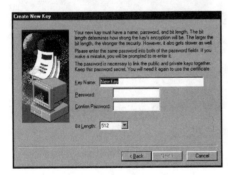

FIGURE 23-4

Creating a public key begins with a name, a password, and a size.

6. Enter the name you want to use for this key in the Key Name field. If you will be using multiple keys with your system, you should use a descriptive key name.

7. Enter your encryption password in the Password and Confirm Password fields.

8. Select a Bit Length for your key. The size of the key determines the strength or quality of your encryption. The larger the key, the harder it is to crack the encryption. Of course, your computer must also encrypt and decrypt messages, so a large key can cause performance to slow down. The default of 512 is good for most uses.

9. Click on Next to begin entering information about your organization. This step is shown in Figure 23-5.

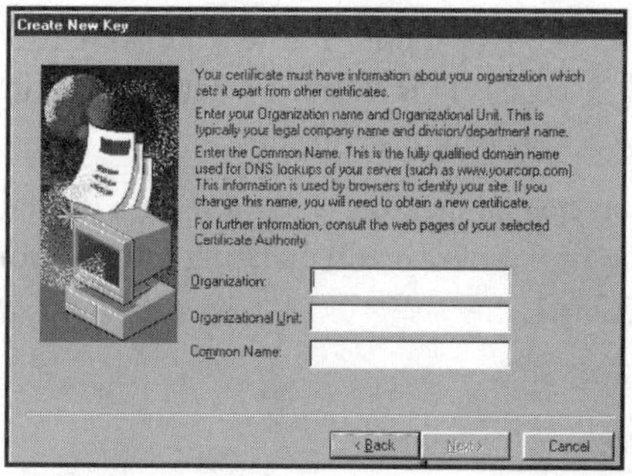

FIGURE 23-5

To create a public key, you will need to describe your organization.

10. Enter your company's name in the Organization field.

11. Enter your department name in the Organizational Unit field.

12. Enter the domain name (www.mydomain.com) in the Common Name field.

13. Click on Next to move on to the next step, where you are asked to enter information about your location, as shown in Figure 23-6.

FIGURE 23-6

The certificate request needs information about your location.

14. Select your country code from the Country drop-down list; enter your state and city in the State/Province and City/Locality fields.

15. Click on Next to move to the next step, shown in Figure 23-7, which requires information about yourself so that the CA can contact you.

16. Enter contact information in the dialog box. Your name may have been retrieved for you; otherwise, you can enter it in the Your Name field. Put your e-mail address in the E-mail address field and a phone number in the Phone Number field.

17. Click on Next to view some information about the Key that you are about to create.

18. Click on Finish, and the Key Manager creates your Key request for you. A new key appears in the Key Manager window when the process is finished.

FIGURE 23-7

You need to include contact information with the certificate request.

The Key Manager, in creating your key pair, creates a request file to be sent to the Certification Authority that you will be using. If you type the request file, it appears similar to the following:

```
Webmaster: gpease@dcomp.com
Phone: 3072832717
Server: Microsoft Key Manager for IIS Version 4.0


Common-name: www.dcomp.com
Organization Unit: Software
Organization: Discovery Computing Inc.
Locality: Sundance
State: Wyoming
Country: US


— —-BEGIN NEW CERTIFICATE REQUEST— —-
MIIBPTCB6AIBADCBgjELMAkGA1UEBhMCVVMxEDAOBgNVBAgTB1d5b21pbmcxETAP
BgNVBAcTCFN1bmRhbmNlMSAwHgYDVQQKExdEaXNjb3ZlcnkgQ29tcHV0aW5nIElu
YzERMA8GA1UECxMIU29mdHdhcmUxGTAXBgNVBAMTEGplcXVpcS5kY29tcC5jb20w
XDANBgkqhkiG9w0BAQEFAANLADBIAkEApTT9ISIJeQPW1m+ZRbNuWIa73Qdxcc/B
QW7VfcQpca+vaI4oSLeY6SToRZBtDWXmDh8AgACkOHcOSVl77TREhQIDAQABoAAw
DQYJKoZIhvcNAQEEBQADQQCeSNGOFXgc2wc9AUkGXIXm5b3LrZb0toktaYdmPd75
JYUHBrKXNZZLkMNV9I784GA55bvPoGnXiGMbVBYQAbSG
— —-END NEW CERTIFICATE REQUEST— —-
```

This request file is nothing more than a plain ASCII text file. At this point, you are ready to request your certificate.

Requesting the Certificate

You already know that you request a digital certificate from a CA. Before you can request your certificate (or at least before VeriSign will issue your certificate), you must register your site online. To start the certification process, connect to the Certificate Signing Request page at the VeriSign site at **https://digitalid.verisign. com/ss_getCSR.html.** This page appears in Figure 23-8.

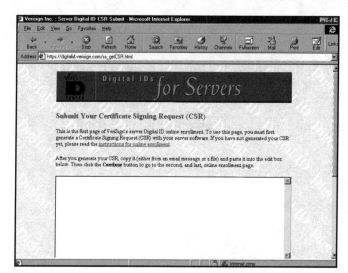

FIGURE 23-8

To obtain a digital certificate, you need to register with VeriSign.

If you scroll down the page, near the bottom you find a large text box where you are required to enter your request. This information was generated by the Key Manager program and saved in the NewKeyRq.txt file. Load that file in a program such as Notepad, copy it to the Clipboard, and paste it in the text box on the Web page.

When you are done pasting your request information, click on the Continue button at the bottom of the Web page. You'll see the verification page, where all your site information is displayed. This information is derived from the request information that you pasted in the previous page. Figure 23-9 shows an example of the verification page for Discovery Computing Inc..

Scroll through the page to make sure that the information is correct. If you need to change anything, you need to use the Key Manager program again with the proper command-line parameters. You can then paste the request information, again, into the previous Web page.

If everything on the page is correct (and it should be if you used Key Manager properly), then near the bottom of the page you can specify that you are using a Microsoft server and provide a "challenge phrase" that will verify your identity at a later time.

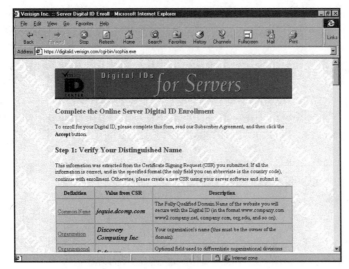

FIGURE 23-9

VeriSign derives information about your site from your digital request.

Now you are ready to continue down the page. You need to supply contact information about three people:

◆ **Technical contact** The person in charge of the server

◆ **Administrative contact** The head of the company or the manager responsible for the server

◆ **Billing contact** The person who pays the company's bills

If you are running a small company, you might not have three people for these positions; you may have only one or two. Use the check boxes on the page to indicate this fact.

Near the bottom of the page, you can specify a payment option (credit card, check, or PO). If you are providing a PO, you must fax it to VeriSign immediately; if you are paying by check, you must send it to VeriSign at the same time that you provide your registration request. As of this writing, certification costs $349 for the first certificate and $249 for additional certificates for the first year, and $75 for each additional year.

To complete the enrollment, you must also provide some way for VeriSign to verify the reality of your company or organization. If you are listed with Dun & Bradstreet, you can provide a DUNS number on the form. If your company does not have a DUNS number (which is often true for small or new companies), you must fax VeriSign a copy of your business license or your Articles of Incorporation.

After VeriSign receives your online request, it can proceed to process your certificate request. From this point, it can take anywhere from three to five working days to receive your certificate. The reason for the delay is not just the workload at VeriSign, but also to allow time to process your documentation and payment. VeriSign sends your certificate via e-mail to the technical contact noted in your registration request.

Installing the Certificate

When you receive your certificate from VeriSign, you need to install it. The certificate itself looks very similar to the certificate request that you originally transferred to VeriSign. A typical certificate may look like this:

```
From:     microsoft-request-id@verisign.com
To:       jsmith@harryshats.com
Subject:  Certificate Request


- --BEGIN CERTIFICATE- -·

IBCAFooCAQAB1YwXDQYJKoZIhvcNAECBQAJwczELMAkGA1UEMCVVNBMxIDAeBgNV
BAMTIDSX0QIQER1NA3VyDwzaQXR5LCBQbmMuMRwGgYDdVQQLExhQZXJzbhIENx21
cnRpZm1TJXCjSYhYFRYxNVNdPgVuINOXE01hcmtlwCBUZXNIFNlcFnZciA5M1TAw
MB4cA1UEChUlNBaMIER1GEhUiYdGpEjAIy9MwxW1D7aBgNV0VFBAsTlBlcnNvbmE
gQ2VydG1mXWNhdGUDAhBDxgNVjMTJ0AskW4Tu4j2HAlyrRlcN0NTTQU2VyAdpmVy
HEOGwzDMBEc5MjMygIMwWcQEwtc2DVBdTOGEwZEHBYDzMswCQY6DVQQGEwJVUzEg
IDExUThNMAsGSGSxINbJ3JQEBAQU0sAMFAEgCQQWU/gaygQvV0BhB3IqgGd4LSqA
GkD1iN3sEPfST0CqGXY5X3oZB4QnArA7mIfvpNi1tAgaYimvRbkP4XYeNy1MBmHL
AwD8QYJ+KoZIhvcNAQE8HJCDQQByps9EahjKKAefP+z+8NYNCqNfkhckggP2oL6s
pwhvEiP8m+bFy6HNDUlFz8ZrVOu3WQapgLPV90kIskNKX3au
- --END CERTIFICATE- -·
```

You need to copy only the certificate part of this message to a text file. The certificate portion starts with the line **BEGIN CERTIFICATE** and concludes with the line **END CERTIFICATE**. You can use Notepad to copy the certificate; copy the message to the Clipboard and then paste it in a Notepad file. Save the file as a text file; for example, you could use the name mycert.txt for your file.

TIP

Make sure that your e-mail program has not corrupted your certificate in any way. Some e-mail programs add extra spaces to the beginning or end of each line. If yours does this, or if you change even one character in the certificate, you will not be able to use it. A valid certificate has 64 (and only 64) characters per line except for the last line.

Now you are ready to install the certificate. You do this by using the Key Manager. Earlier versions also included a command-line utility, but it is no longer included with IIS.

When you have the mycert.txt file in hand, you are ready to install your key. To use the Key Manager to install the certificate, follow these steps:

1. Start the Internet Service Manager.

2. Choose the Key Manager icon from the toolbar. This action runs the Key Manager program, and shortly you see the program window.

3. Select the key you want to install in the list of systems, servers, and keys.

4. Choose Install Key Certificate from the Key menu to display a standard Open dialog box.

5. Select the file that contains your certificate (mycert.txt).

7. Click on Open. The Open dialog box closes, and you are asked to enter your key file password.

8. Enter the password you used when you created the key file pair. Click on OK to close the dialog box. The Server Bindings dialog box appears, as shown in Figure 23-10.

9. Click on OK to close this dialog box unless you want to use a specific IP address or port number. The default value allows IIS to handle the IP addresses and ports that are assigned.

10. Close the Key Manager and choose Yes to commit your changes. The certificate is now installed and ready to use.

FIGURE 23-10

SSL may be configured for specific IP addresses and ports.

TIP

Always make a backup copy of your certificate and key files. You will need these items if you ever need to reinstall IIS or if (for some reason) your key file becomes corrupted.

At this point, you are just about ready to start using SSL at your site. The only thing left to accomplish is to configure IIS to use the SSL protocol. This topic is covered just a bit later in this chapter.

Enabling SSL

The final step is to enable SSL in the Web server itself, using the Internet Service Manager. To configure IIS for SSL, follow these steps:

1. Open the Internet Service Manager to display the Internet Service Manager window, shown in Figure 23-11.

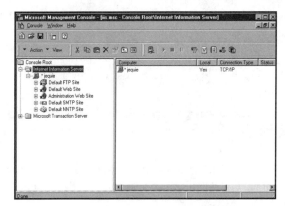

FIGURE 23-11

Configuring Internet services with the Internet Service Manager.

2. Select the name of your Web server. This action displays the directories in the results pane of the window.

3. Right-click on the directory you want to make secure and select Properties from the shortcut menu. (If you make your home directory secure, then your whole site will require SSL connections to be accessed.) This action displays the Properties dialog box for the directory.

4. Select the Directory Security tab. From this tab, you determine all the security features of this directory.

5. Click on the Edit button in the Secure Communications area in the middle of the dialog box. The Secure Communications dialog box, shown in Figure 23-12, opens.

6. Select the Require Secure Channel When Accessing This Resource check box.

7. Click on OK to save your changes.

8. Click on OK to close the Properties dialog box for your directory.

9. Click on the Stop icon to stop your Web server service.

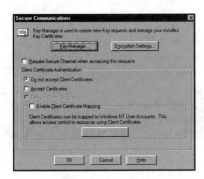

FIGURE 23-12

Making a directory secure with SSL.

10. Click on the Start icon to restart your Web server.

11. Exit the Internet Services Manager.

Usage Differences

From a Webmaster's perspective, setting up SSL in your server doesn't really affect the operation of your site. You can continue to make files available in the secure directories as you normally would. The only operational difference is in creating links to pages. If you establish a link to a document in a secure directory, you must preface the URL with **https://** instead of with **http://**. The additional *s* stands for "secure."

When users try to access your secure documents, they also need to use the **https://** specification. If they don't, they can't access the documents; instead, they'll see an error message.

Using the Key Manager

Earlier in this chapter, you learned how to use the Key Manager to create key pair files and to install certificates. Believe it or not, those two uses are the primary purpose of the Key Manager. In fact, many Webmasters use the Key Manager once or twice (to install keys) and then forget about the program.

You can, however, do a few other things with the Key Manager. For example, you can review the status of the keys you have installed. This feature comes in handy because you need to renew your certificates on a yearly basis.

To view a certificate, simply open the Key Manager and select it on the left side of the program window. When you do, the information in the left side of the window changes to reflect the properties of the selected key. Of particular importance are the Valid From and Valid Until fields. If your Web site relies heavily on your secure status, you will want to mark these dates as important milestones on your calendar. In that way, you can remember to renew your certificates at the appropriate time.

> **NOTE**
>
> You can renew your certificates by simply following the directions at the CA's Web site. For example, VeriSign's site has several pages that walk you through the renewal process.

The Key Manager does not automatically save your changes to disk. Instead, they are retained in memory and stored on disk only when you explicitly instruct the program to do so. In this respect, the Key Manager is similar to some of the other Windows NT "manager" programs. (The Disk Administrator, which falls into this category, does not write changes to disk until you explicitly instruct it to do so.)

The upshot is that you should always remember to commit your changes to disk if you want to keep them. If you try to exit the program without saving your changes, the Key Manager alerts you to the fact. To save the changes (which is a good idea from time to time), choose the Commit Changes Now option from the Servers menu.

PART VI

Issues for Serious Site Management

Chapter 24

Implementing Remote Administration

In This Chapter

◆ Understanding Remote Administration

◆ Installing Remote Administration Support

◆ Using Remote Administration

◆ Remote Administration and Security

Throughout this book, you have used the Internet Service Manager to configure various sections of IIS. (In Chapter 3, you learned specifically how to use this tool.) By now, you may have the impression that you must use Internet Service Manager to configure IIS. If so, you have a mistaken impression.

The Internet Service Manager is used primarily for controlling servers that are on the local server or that are accessible through a local area network. But what if you want to control a server that is located elsewhere on the Web? This chapter describes the Remote Administration tool for IIS and explains how you can use it to manage your servers anywhere in the world.

Understanding Remote Administration

IIS 4.0 enables you to administer your server from anywhere on the Internet. The most frequent use of this capability is to administer the server from somewhere else on your own local or wide area network. Either way, you use your Web browser to connect to your server and perform the administration functions you need. After starting up your Web browser, connect to the following URL:

http://*yourserver*/iisadmin

In this example, you should replace *yourserver* with your host and domain name. For instance, to connect to my server (www.dcomp.com), I would use the following URL:

http://www.dcomp.com/iisadmin

The iisadmin directory is a virtual directory that was set up when you first installed IIS. When you connect to the URL, you see the Web page displayed in Figure 24-1.

Notice that you cannot use remote administration until you set up IIS to make it available. If you did not get a screen that looks like Figure 24-1, you are already set up to use remote administration properly. In this case, you can safely skip the next section.

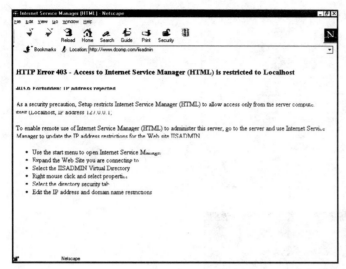

FIGURE 24-1

Remote administration support has not been installed on this server.

Installing Remote Administration Support

You cannot administer your site from a remote system unless you first install remote administration and then configure IIS to allow it to be used. Both steps in this two-step process are done at the server console. Start by logging on with Administrator privileges.

Making Sure That the Proper Files Are Installed

The first task is to make sure that you have the proper remote administration files installed. To install the necessary files, follow these steps:

1. Choose the Programs option from the Start menu. The Programs menu appears.

2. Choose the Windows NT 4.0 Option Pack option from the Programs menu.

3. Choose the Windows NT 4.0 Option Pack Setup option to start the Setup program, as shown in Figure 24-2.

4. Click on Next to enter the Setup program.

5. Click on the Add/Remove button to display the dialog box shown in Figure 24-3.

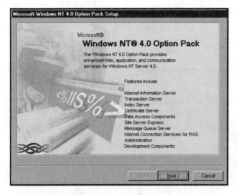

FIGURE 24-2

The Setup program enables you to add new Option Pack components.

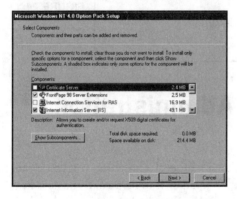

FIGURE 24-3

Setup shows which components are currently installed.

7. Select the Internet Information Server (IIS) component.

8. Click on Show Subcomponents to display the dialog box shown in Figure 24-4.

9. Select the check box beside the Internet Service Manager (HTML) option if necessary.

10. Click on OK to continue.

11. Click on Next. The necessary files are copied to your system.

12. Click on Finish to close the Setup program.

Configuring IIS to Allow Remote Administration

The next step in setting up remote administration is to configure IIS so that an administrator at a remote terminal can access the proper files. This process is done through the regular IP security features of IIS. To configure IIS for remote administration, follow these steps from the server console:

1. Start the Internet Service Manager provided with IIS.

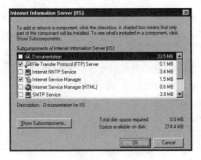

FIGURE 24-4

IIS uses many different components.

2. Look for a new Web site on your server called IISADMIN or Administration Web Site. (This site was created when you installed the remote administration files, as discussed in the previous section.)

3. Right-click on the Web site located in step 2. A context menu appears.

4. Choose Properties from the context menu. The Properties dialog box for the new Web opens.

5. Click on the Directory Security tab.

6. Click on the Edit button (the third one—near the bottom of the dialog box). This displays the IP Address and Domain Name Restrictions dialog box, as shown in Figure 24-5.

FIGURE 24-5

You can control which other computers have access to your site.

7. If the default access method, as shown at the top of the dialog box, is for all computers to be granted access, skip to step 11.

8. Click on the Add button. The Grant Access On dialog box opens.

9. Specify the IP address of the computer from which you will be doing remote administration.

10. Click on OK.

11. Click on OK again to close the IP Address and Domain Name Restrictions dialog box.

12. Click on OK to close the Properties dialog box.

13. Close Internet Service Manager.

Now you need to get the port number assigned by IIS for remote administration. This port number will vary from installation to installation; it is randomly selected when the remote administration files are installed. To find the number, simply look at the Web Site tab of the Properties dialog box for the administration Web site. (This dialog box was displayed in step 4 of the preceding steps.) The port number noted in the TCP Port field is the one you need; mark it down. You can then close the Internet Service Manager.

You can now use remote administration, but only from the computer system you specified in these steps. If you want to use it from another computer, you must go through the same steps and give rights to the other computers to access your site.

Using Remote Administration

After you install and configure remote administration support on your server, you are ready to use it to configure and maintain your servers. The only way in which using local administration (using Internet Service Manager) differs from using the HTML version is the layout of the interface. You can even use remote administration to start and stop the servers, which was not possible with earlier versions of IIS.

To start remote administration, simply use your browser to connect to the iisadmin directory on the remote server, using the port number that you wrote down in the last section. For example, if you are controlling the www.dcomp.com server and the port number was 9213, then you will use the following URL in your browser:

> **http://www.dcomp.com:9213/iisadmin**

If you do not have administrator rights on the computer that you are seeking to connect with, you are asked to provide a username and password. Then you can view the remote administration screen, which is shown in Figure 24-6.

Here you are asked to specify the type of font that IIS should use in displaying information. Note that this screen comes up only the first time you use remote administration. After you select a font size, the main administration page is displayed, as shown in Figure 24-7.

The interface used in remote administration is very similar to the interface used in the Internet Service Manager at the server console. Each choice shown in the center of the page represents a service you can configure. To see what is available under each service, click on the plus sign to the left of the service name; when you are done, click on the minus sign to again collapse the display.

If you want to start, stop, or otherwise control a server, all you need to do is select it in the main portion of the page and then click on the appropriate command on the

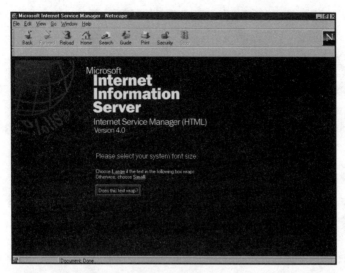

FIGURE 24-6

The opening remote administration screen.

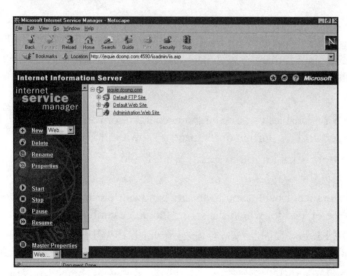

FIGURE 24-7

The main remote administration page is similar to the Internet Service Manager.

left side of the screen. For example, if you want to stop the server, you would first select the server that you want to stop and then click on Stop.

The following section covers each service that you can configure.

Configuring the Web Server

To configure your Web server, click on the server you want to affect and then click on the Properties command on the left side of the screen. This action contacts your IIS server and displays the page shown in Figure 24-8.

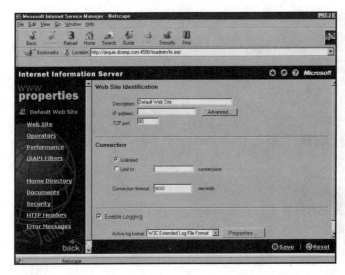

The layout of the main portion of this Web page is very similar to the Properties dialog box you use when working with the Internet Service Manager locally at the server. The only difference is that the Web page does not use tabs. Instead, the major categories, which would normally be represented by tabs, are displayed on the left side of the screen.

- ◆ **Web Site** Enables you to configure general information about the Web server. This portion of the page is shown in Figure 24-8.

- ◆ **Operators** Enables you to specify who should have administrative rights on the server.

- ◆ **Performance** Enables you to specify bandwidth restraints and adjust the type of load for which the server should be configured.

- ◆ **ISAPI Filters** Enables you to specify which ISAPI filters are installed on the server, as well as the order in which they are executed.

- ◆ **Home Directory** Enables you to indicate the main content directory for the Web site.

- ◆ **Documents** Enables you to set up the default documents displayed by the server, along with an optional document footer.

- ◆ **Security** Enables you to configure who has access to your site.

- ◆ **HTTP Headers** Enables you to change the way the Web server constructs headers on information it sends.

- ◆ **Error Messages** Enables you to customize the way the Web server responds to error conditions.

These categories generally function in the same way as the corresponding tabs in the Properties dialog box function. However, because of differences in the way information in Web pages is constructed, some administration pages differ a little more from their Properties dialog box counterparts than others. Nevertheless, even though the Web page interface is slightly different than the Internet Service Manager, you can still accomplish the same tasks.

Configuring the FTP Server

To configure your FTP server remotely, simply return to the main remote administration page (by clicking on Back if necessary) and then click on the name of the desired FTP server in the center of the page. You can then click on the Properties command on the left side of the page. When you do, the page shown in Figure 24-9 appears.

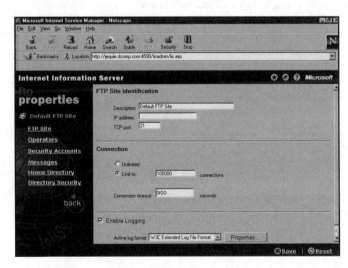

FIGURE 24-9

You can configure your FTP server remotely.

Six choices are available near the top of the page:

- ◆ **FTP Site** Enables you to configure general information about the FTP server. This area is shown when you first click on Properties, as illustrated in Figure 24-9.

- ◆ **Operators** Enables you to specify who should have administrative rights on the server.

- ◆ **Security Accounts** Enables you to configure who has nonanonymous log-on access to your FTP site.

- ◆ **Messages** Enables you to change the messages that appear when people connect with and exit from your site.

◆ **Home Directory** Enables you to indicate the main content directory for the FTP site.

◆ **Directory Security** Enables you to configure who has access to your site as a whole.

Many of these choices accomplish the same tasks as the corresponding choices for the Web server. You can view or change current settings simply by clicking on the button that represents what you want to change.

TIP

When you make a change in the information displayed on the screen, it is only updated on the server if you click on the Save button at the bottom of the page. If you instead click on any other button (which results in a different page being displayed), the changes you made are discarded.

Chapter 25

Wide Area Intranets

In This Chapter

- ◆ A Quick Introduction to PPTP
- ◆ Implementing a VPN
- ◆ Implementation Considerations
- ◆ Adding PPTP Support at the Server
- ◆ Connecting When the Internet Provider Does Not Support PPTP

Although much of the recent interest in networking has focused on the Internet, a closely related concept is the corporate intranet. Basically, the only difference between the Internet and an intranet is the size and number of connections; technologically, the two are very similar. Intranets are geographically less diverse and obviously entail fewer people than the Internet as a whole.

As an example, suppose that Amalgamated Industries wants to set up its own internal network to tie together its departments. If Amalgamated is located in a single site, then setting up such a network becomes a relatively easy task. As the number of branch offices increases, eventually Amalgamated will desire a way to tie the networks at the individual offices together. This model of combining different networks via standard communications links (that is, phone lines) is the same model used to develop the Internet. Unfortunately for Amalgamated Industries, as the number and geographic diversity of its sites increase, the cost associated with simply establishing the infrastructure for its intranet also increases.

The cost and complexity increases even more if Amalgamated wants its on-the-road people to have access to the network. All of a sudden, it must establish a remote access server (RAS) and use dial-up networking on the remote computers. The long distance or toll-free costs associated with establishing these connections can mount very quickly.

This chapter focuses on how companies in the same situation as Amalgamated can reduce their communication costs by using the regular Internet along with Windows NT Server 4.0 and IIS.

A Quick Introduction to PPTP

Windows NT Server 4.0 supports a new communications protocol referred to as *PPTP*, or Point-to-Point Tunneling Protocol. This protocol enables users to effectively establish intranets over a wide area at a low cost. In order to understand PPTP, you must first understand a bit about normal connection protocols.

Standard Connection Protocols

A regular dial-up connection established with the Internet uses several standard protocols to communicate with the network. You already know about TCP/IP, which is the protocol at the heart of tools used on both the Internet and an intranet. SLIP and PPP are the two protocols that have historically been used to facilitate TCP/IP communication over a dial-up connection.

SLIP stands for Serial Line Internet Protocol, and it was developed in the early 1980s to allow UNIX systems to communicate with other UNIX systems over modems. Versions of SLIP were introduced for UNIX systems as early as 1984. Several products on the market implement SLIP for Windows systems. Perhaps one of the most popular is Trumpet WinSock by Peter Tattam, a program for Windows 3.1 that includes not only the SLIP protocol implementation but also a built-in dialer for connecting with an Internet provider.

The problem with SLIP is that the industry never accepted it as an Internet standard. It is widely viewed as a "nonstandard solution," and support for the protocol is giving way to *PPP* (or Point-to-Point Protocol). PPP accomplishes the same purposes as SLIP but in a much more robust manner. A PPP connection includes error detection and correction, as well as packet authentication. These features provide a relatively secure connection over ordinary phone lines. In addition, PPP is a recognized Internet standard protocol, so it is receiving the widest share of development efforts today.

The Need for Tunneling

When a corporation is trying to deploy an intranet, it must establish the internal standards for the network. For example, it may settle on using IPX/SPX (which is rooted in Novell networks) or NetBEUI (which is grounded in Windows networks). If a salesperson on the road wants to connect to the network in the home office, both systems must use the same protocol (either IPX/SPX or NetBEUI in this example) to establish a connection.

Traditionally, remote connections have been made over expensive dial-up lines. For example, the salesperson would use his modem to dial an 800 number, which rings at the home office. The phone connection enables the salesperson's computer to behave as if it is a part of the network. Besides the obvious speed issues (a modem is slower than a local network connection), the only downside is scalability and cost, both of which are related.

Scalability refers to the fact that while the salesperson is connected, no one else can establish a connection on that line. Why? Because the connection is defined by a single modem at both ends of the phone line. If the company wants to scale this environment for additional salespeople, it must add more modems and phone lines, one for each potential simultaneous connection. This approach adds to the cost of the operation, besides the per-minute cost of the 800 lines and monthly cost of the terminating local lines.

The answer to these problems is to use a low-cost solution such as the Internet to transport information that would otherwise travel on a private network. The terminology for this concept is a *virtual private network*, or *VPN*. Using a VPN, the salesperson can dial into a local Internet provider and connect to the home office through the Internet lines. Additional salespeople could be doing the same thing, and together these connections are channeled over a single Internet connection at the home office. The result is lower costs all around—the home office does not need individual modems, company-sponsored 800 lines, or local terminating numbers. In addition, in-house support personnel can be pared down because the burden for support of the network (the Internet) has been shifted to the Internet provider.

NOTE

In theory, a VPN can replace a corporate WAN entirely, although this changeover may not occur for some time because WANs are so pervasive in the industry.

The only downside to this arrangement is the use of communication protocols and security. The Internet, as a network, has standardized on a single communication protocol: TCP/IP. In addition, the Internet is not known as a completely secure environment. This is where tunneling, or encapsulation, comes into play. *Tunneling* simply means that a secure channel can be established between a client (the salesperson) and a server (the home office) using whatever protocol the parties desire. Tunneling technology encloses the original packets (IPX/SPX or NetBEUI in this example) inside temporary TCP/IP packets that travel over the Internet. The outer packet can be stripped off at either end of the connection.

The Emergence of PPTP

In 1995 and early 1996, the PPTP forum developed the PPTP specification. The forum was an ad hoc group made up of Microsoft and remote-access vendors including Ascend Communications, ECI-Telematics, 3Com/Primary Access, and US Robotics. The protocol supports remote access over the Internet to Windows NT servers. PPTP, an extension of PPP, permits remote access to private corporate networks transparently via local access to an Internet provider—exactly the scenario described in the preceding section. However, in PPTP the native packets used by the VPN are encrypted before they are encapsulated in the TCP/IP wrapper. When the packets are received at the other end of the connection, the wrapper is stripped off and the encrypted packet is decrypted. This process is illustrated in Figure 25-1.

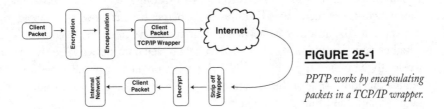

FIGURE 25-1

PPTP works by encapsulating packets in a TCP/IP wrapper.

In addition to encryption and encapsulation, PPTP employs packet authentication for security purposes. Each packet, as it is received at the server, is verified to make sure that it is authentic and that access is permitted for the packet.

PPTP is implemented as a native protocol in all the current and future versions of Windows, including Windows NT Server 4.0, Windows NT Workstation 4.0, and Windows 95.

PPTP is an open standard that can be implemented by anyone in the computing field. For more technical details of the standard, check out the information at **ftp://ftp.microsoft.com/developr/drg/PPTP/**.

Implementing a VPN

The following sections discuss how implementing a VPN affects the client, the Internet provider, and your site.

What the Client Needs

As far as clients are concerned, they can continue to operate their network applications as they always have. All clients need to do is make sure that they connect with the Internet provider using the PPP protocol. Implementing a PPTP VPN is transparent to the user; no additional training or expense is necessary.

Clients can also use their regular network applications. These applications are not forced to use a single network protocol. Any of the following are compatible with PPTP:

◆ TCP/IP

◆ IPX

◆ NetBIOS

◆ NetBEUI

Network applications that rely on a different protocol will not work with PPTP. Notice that TCP/IP is supported within PPTP. Encrypting a TCP/IP packet inside another TCP/IP packet may seem a little strange. After all, couldn't the packet just be sent in its original form? The reason for this seeming redundancy is that many private networks use their own IP addressing scheme. If your network is closed, that is, not open to the Internet as a whole, then you don't need to be concerned about whether your IP addresses clash with a totally separate network elsewhere in the world. By wrapping the original TCP/IP packet in another packet, the inner packet retains the addressing of the private network while the outer packet routes the message through the Internet as a whole.

What the Internet Provider Needs

The Internet provider is perhaps one of the most critical links in the concept of implementing a PPTP VPN. Remember that the client is connecting to the provider using regular PPP. In order to make PPTP work, the Internet provider must be using equipment that converts the regular PPP packets to PPTP packets. These packets are then transported to your site for processing.

The equipment used by the provider is referred to in the PPTP specification as a *front-end processor*. In reality, it is simply an answering device for the dial-up lines. The PPTP processing information is built into the firmware that manages these devices. Thus, the Internet provider's communications equipment vendors must supply a product that can convert incoming information into the necessary PPTP format.

Consequently, you must make sure that people dialing into your VPN go through an Internet provider that has upgraded its equipment to use PPTP. Many communications equipment providers have announced that their equipment will soon (or does now) support PPTP, and some have even said that their upgrades to PPTP will be provided free of charge. These announcements provide an incentive for Internet providers to start implementing PPTP as soon as possible.

What Your Site Needs

To implement a PPTP VPN, you need two items: a gateway server and a communications server. The communications server acts as the interface to the network, and these types of servers are available from any number of vendors. Your Windows NT Server 4.0 system, which is running IIS, can serve as your gateway server. The gateway server must implement the PPTP protocol, which can be done under Windows NT Server 4.0. In addition, you must set up RAS for use with your PPTP communications channels. Later in this chapter, you learn how you can set up Windows NT Server 4.0 to use PPTP.

Implementation Considerations

As you consider developing your own VPN, you need to be concerned with two particular issues: performance and security. Compromises in either area definitely affects your ability to achieve your network goals.

Performance Issues

You may be wondering whether the extra steps of encryption and encapsulation that are inherent in PPTP can have a negative impact on the performance of your VPN when compared with an existing WAN. This performance issue has two sides: the performance hit from the overhead of PPTP and the performance of the Internet as a whole.

When you are using your own WAN, you are responsible for the overall performance of the network. As a rule, WAN performance can be more than acceptable. In most instances, the only hit on performance is the quality of the connection between the remote client and the server at the home office. In this respect, a PPTP VPN can operate at a higher performance level than the WAN, but only because the quality of local connections (between the client, server, and Internet providers) is typically higher than the quality of long-distance connections. Higher-quality connections transfer information closer to the rated speed of the modem.

On the flip side of the coin, the Internet itself may add some delays to your VPN traffic. The Internet is notoriously slow at times, depending on the route followed by the packets destined for your server. Obviously, this routing delay is not present in a WAN. For all but the most time-critical applications, any slight transmission delays through the Internet are more than offset by the cost savings realized.

Security Issues

As you are no doubt aware, security is always a great concern on the Internet. The network administrator, who is ultimately responsible for the deployment of corporate data on an intranet, must be sure that the security implemented on the VPN is adequate and will keep attackers out of the network.

Clearly, the most secure type of intranet is one implemented through private connections, whether you string your own cable or lease dedicated data lines. However, the cost of this approach is prohibitive for many companies and for many uses.

PPTP addresses security concerns by utilizing native Windows NT security algorithms and methods. The security level that results from incorporating Windows NT security measures and forcing RAS servers on the Internet to accept only PPTP clients who utilize data encryption is usually acceptable for many applications and particularly for smaller, private networks.

Adding PPTP Support at the Server

You can add PPTP to Windows NT Server 4 in almost the same way that you add any other network protocol. The primary difference is that the protocol ties directly to RAS instead of to a physical network adapter. This process requires a certain amount of RAS configuration during the installation of PPTP. Because RAS is required to implement PPTP, you should install and configure RAS before attempting to install the PPTP protocol.

Adding the PPTP Protocol

To add the PPTP protocol to the server at your site, insert your Windows NT Server CD-ROM in the server and follow these steps:

1. Open the Control Panel.
2. Double-click on the Network applet in the Control Panel. This action displays the Network dialog box.
3. Click on the Protocols tab. The Network dialog box appears, as shown in Figure 25-2.

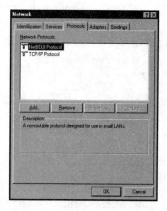

FIGURE 25-2

You add protocols, such as PPTP, using the Protocols tab.

4. Click on the Add button. The Select Network Protocol dialog box appears.
5. Scroll through the list of available protocols and select the Point To Point Tunneling Protocol option.
6. Click on OK to begin the installation of the protocol. You are asked how many VPNs you want to enable, as shown in Figure 25-3.

FIGURE 25-3

You can determine how many VPNs you want.

7. Enter the number of simultaneous PPTP channels that you may have open on your system. You can select any number from 1 to 256. It is a good idea to select a minimum of 3, even if you anticipate only a single PPTP connection at any given time.

8. Click on OK to finish the installation of the PPTP protocol. The necessary files are copied from the CD to your system.

You have now completed the first part of the PPTP installation, and the protocol itself has been installed on your system. You must now configure RAS for the new protocol.

Setting Up RAS for PPTP

After you installed PPTP, you were automatically asked questions about how you wanted to configure RAS for your PPTP connections. To set up RAS, follow these steps:

1. Specify which device you want to use for RAS at the Add RAS Device dialog box (see Figure 27-4).

FIGURE 25-4

PPTP works in conjunction with RAS.

2. Click on the OK button. The Remote Access Setup dialog box lists the devices that you are configuring for RAS.

3. Click on the Add button to add more VPN ports to RAS. Repeat steps 1 and 2 to add each of your VPN ports to RAS. If you specified three VPNs in the preceding section, the completed Remote Access Setup dialog box appears as shown in Figure 25-5.

4. Click on the Continue button. If you have NetBEUI installed as a protocol and you are installing RAS for the first time, a dialog box asks whether NetBEUI clients should have access to the entire network or to the server only.

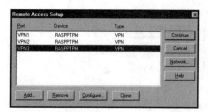

FIGURE 25-5

You can configure RAS to work with each of your VPN ports.

5. Make your selection and click on OK to continue. If you are installing RAS for the first time, the RAS Server TCP/IP Configuration dialog box is displayed. This dialog box is very similar to other TCP/IP configuration dialog boxes that you have used in Windows NT.

6. Assuming that you know how you are using TCP/IP on your network, you can change the settings in this dialog box to reflect how a client should be connected to your network using TCP/IP.

7. Click on OK to continue. The balance of the RAS files are copied to your system.

8. Close the Network dialog box and restart your system.

Setting Up User Accounts

As you may have surmised by now, using PPTP is very similar to using regular RAS under Windows NT. A person establishes the network connection by "dialing" into your network. Once connected, he or she has any access to the network that you have decided on.

Therefore, you must set up a Windows NT user account for each person who will be using one of your VPN channels. This account is set up the same as any other account from the User Manager for Domains. When you are setting up a user account, click on the Dialin button at the bottom of the New User dialog box to display the Dialin Information dialog box shown in Figure 25-6.

Make sure that you select the Grant Dialin Permission to User check box. For an account coming in over a VPN PPTP connection, you should not use the Call Back option, however.

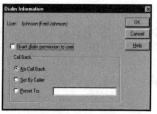

FIGURE 25-6

You can configure RAS to work with each of your VPN ports.

Testing a Connection

With your PPTP protocol installed, RAS enabled, and the various dial-in user accounts set up, you are ready to test your VPN. As described earlier in this chapter, establishing a client connection is actually a two-step process. First, your clients establish a regular PPP protocol connection with an Internet provider, and then they dial into your VPN to establish a PPTP connection. In general, these are the steps to be followed:

1. Make sure that the Internet providers being used by your clients support the PPTP protocol.
2. Discuss with the Internet provider what steps it requires to initiate a PPTP connection. (The exact steps to follow can vary from provider to provider.)
3. Have one of your users dial in to the Internet provider and establish a regular PPP connection.
4. Follow the instructions that you received in step 2 for establishing the PPTP connection.
5. Use your client network applications as you normally would.

NOTE

If the Internet provider your clients are using does not support PPTP, then they cannot establish a PPTP connection with your server. In this instance, you may be able to use client-side PPTP, as discussed in the following section.

Connecting When the Internet Provider Does Not Support PPTP

Earlier in this chapter, you learned that the best way for PPTP to be implemented is through an Internet provider that supports PPTP. In this instance, the client does not need to do anything else. Unfortunately in this imperfect world not every Internet provider can be counted on to support PPTP. When one doesn't, you can sidestep the provider and still implement PPTP by installing both Dial-Up Networking (DUN) and the PPTP protocol at the client and then changing the way in which you log on to a remote server.

Installing Dial-Up Networking

Dial-Up Networking is the name of the client portion of Remote Access Server. In essence, RAS is installed on the server (the one receiving the call), and DUN is used on the client (the one initiating the call). You start DUN by following these steps:

1. Double-click on the My Computer icon on your desktop. This action opens a window showing the various drives and resources on your system.

2. Double-click on the Dial-Up Networking icon. If you are using DUN for the first time, a dialog box informs you that DUN is currently uninstalled and asks whether you want to install it. If DUN is already installed, you can skip these steps.

3. To install DUN, click on the Install button on the dialog box. You are then prompted for the location from which DUN should be installed.

4. Specify the location of the install directory for Windows NT, which is typically the path to your Windows NT Workstation CD-ROM. The files for DUN are then installed, and you should see the dialog box shown in Figure 25-7.

FIGURE 25-7

You must specify which modem DUN should use.

5. Use the pull-down list to select the modem for your dial-up connection.

6. Click on the OK button. The Remote Access Setup dialog box, shown in Figure 25-8, opens.

7. Because you want to use a single modem for DUN, click on the Continue button. The files for DUN are copied to your system.

8. Restart your system when prompted.

At this point, DUN is installed on your system. You can now add the PPTP protocol, as described in the next section.

FIGURE 25-8

You may use multiple devices for DUN.

Implementing Client-Side PPTP

Adding the PPTP protocol to a client is relatively simple; the process is the same as adding any other protocol. Earlier in this chapter, you learned how to add PPTP to the server. Adding it to a client is very similar, but there are one or two differences.

If you are in a networking environment that uses Windows NT and Windows 95, only Windows NT 4.0 includes the PPTP protocol as part of the native operating system. If you want it for Windows 95, you can download this protocol from Microsoft at **http://www.microsoft.com/communications/pptp.htm**. Windows 98 will include the protocol on the installation CD and won't require a separate download. The following steps add PPTP to Windows NT Workstation 4.0, but the process for adding PPTP to Windows 95 (after downloading) is very similar.

ONLINE

1. Open the Control Panel.
2. Double-click on the Network applet in the Control Panel. The Network dialog box appears.
3. Click on the Protocols tab.
4. Click on the <u>A</u>dd button. The Select Network Protocol dialog box appears, as shown in Figure 25-9.

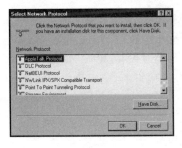

FIGURE 25-9

You can install several different protocols on your client.

5. Select the Point To Point Tunneling Protocol option from the list of available protocols.
6. Click on OK to begin the installation of the protocol. You are asked how many VPNs you want to enable.
7. Select the default value of 1 because your client needs to call only a single network.
8. Click on OK to finish the installation of the PPTP protocol. The necessary files are copied from the CD to your system.
9. DUN (RAS) setup starts automatically, and you should see the Remote Access Setup dialog box (refer to Figure 25-8). Your modem should be the only device listed in the dialog box.

10. Click on the <u>A</u>dd button. The Add RAS Device dialog box opens.

11. Select the VPN channel that you just created as your new device, and then click on OK. The Remote Access Setup dialog box now lists both your modem and the VPN channel.

12. Click on the Continue button. The PPTP protocol is now installed on your system.

13. Close the Network dialog box and restart your system.

Setting Up Phonebook Entries

DUN works by setting up *phonebook entries*, which define how a connection is made with a remote network. To use PPTP from a client, you actually need to define two phonebook entries. The first entry establishes a PPP connection with your Internet provider. Chances are good that you already have such a phonebook entry defined for your client. If not, then you need to contact your Internet provider.

The second required entry connects to the PPTP host (the remote server) after you are connected with your Internet provider. Setting up this entry is similar to setting up any other phonebook entry, but there are some differences. Follow these steps to create and add the proper PPTP phonebook entry:

1. Double-click on the My Computer icon on your desktop.

2. Double-click on the Dial-Up Networking icon. This action opens the Dial-Up Networking dialog box, as shown in Figure 25-10.

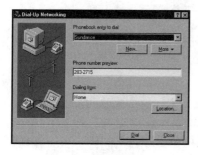

FIGURE 25-10

Dial-Up Networking uses phonebook entries.

3. Click on the <u>N</u>ew button. This action starts the New Phonebook Entry Wizard, as shown in Figure 25-11.

4. Enter a name for this entry. For the sake of this example, enter the name **Corporate PPTP.**

5. Click on the <u>N</u>ext button to continue to the Wizard's next screen, shown in Figure 25-12.

6. At this point, you can leave all the check boxes blank. Even though you

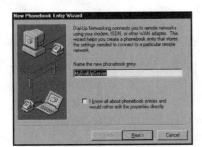

FIGURE 25-11

Windows NT uses a wizard to create phone-book entries.

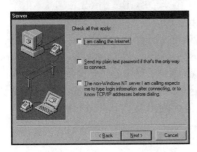

FIGURE 25-12

You need to indicate the type of connection being made.

are calling through the Internet, this particular phonebook entry is not to connect to the Internet. Instead, it is used to connect to your remote PPTP host.

7. Click on the Next button to continue to the Modem or Adapter screen, shown in Figure 25-13.

8. Select the VPN channel as the device that you are using for this connection.

9. Click on the Next button to continue. This screen asks for the phone number to be used to dial this connection.

10. As the phone number, enter the IP address of the PPTP host that you are connecting with. For instance, if the IP address is 206.144.95.2, then that is how you would enter the phone number.

11. Click on the Next button to continue. You are informed that your phone-book entry has been created.

12. Click on Finish to end the Wizard.

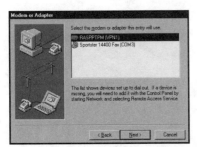

FIGURE 25-13

You can select the modem or adapter that you are using for the connection.

Logon Changes

With DUN, PPTP, and your phonebook entries set up, you can now use your VPN. (How was that for a lot of abbreviations in a single sentence?) Connecting to the remote PPTP host is very simple and involves only a single extra step from what you would normally do when connecting to your Internet provider.

Using the phonebook entry that you already created for your Internet provider (not the PPTP entry), establish a connection with the Internet provider. At this point, a PPP connection is established, and you can access the Internet as you normally would. When you are ready to connect to the PPTP host, use DUN again, but without disconnecting from your Internet provider. This time, you use the PPTP phonebook entry to dial the IP address. In the steps covered in the previous section, you would use the Corporate PPTP phonebook entry. Windows NT then establishes a PPTP connection with the remote host, and you should see a logon dialog box, as if you were connected to the host with a regular network connection.

Chapter 26

Utilizing Log Files

In This Chapter

◆ Log File Formats

◆ Logging Options

◆ Using Log Files

When you install IIS, you have the opportunity to create log files. These log files provide a certain amount of security for your site because they provide a trail of every event that has occurred. All three IIS servers enable you to create log files. This chapter focuses on how those log files are put together and how you can use them to help manage your site.

Log File Formats

It seems there are almost as many log file formats on the market as there are servers. Unfortunately, different servers save their log information in different formats; IIS is no exception.

Trying to examine every possible log format would be an impossible (and impractical) task. However, a few log file formats are worth examining: two are so-called common log formats, and the third is the W3C extended log format.

NCSA Common Log Format

The National Center for Supercomputing Applications (NCSA) has devised a standard way of saving access information to a log file. The purpose of this standard is to set the stage so that programs using the log file data can work on any number of products. This standard, appropriately enough, is called the *common log format*.

Many of the Web servers on the market understand and use the common log format. Although not as comprehensive as the standard logging information saved by IIS, the information in a common log format file is more than adequate for tracking what's happening at a site.

IIS allows you to save your logging information in NCSA format if desired. Information is saved as a series of records, with each field separated by a space. If no data is available for a particular field, then a dash is used as a placeholder. If you were to type a common log format file, the information contained in it would look like this:

```
205.163.44.5 - - [12/Feb/1998:11:08:03 -0700] "GET /program design/overview.shtm
HTTP/1.1" 200 7876
205.163.44.5 - - [12/Feb/1998:11:08:23 -0700] "GET /Default.asp HTTP/1.1" 200 2149
```

```
205.163.44.5 · · [12/Feb/1998:11:08:38 -0700] "GET /Garrett/G_home/ HTTP/1.1" 404 623
205.163.44.5 · · [12/Feb/1998:11:08:53 -0700] "GET /bhsui/ HTTP/1.1" 302 290
205.163.44.5 · · [12/Feb/1998:11:08:54 -0700] "GET /bhsui/Default.htm HTTP/1.1" 200 6811
```

Even if you don't save your log files in common log format, you can always convert them from standard IIS format to NCSA format, as discussed later in this chapter.

Microsoft IIS Log Format

Another log file format used by IIS is referred to as *IIS format*. As with the NCSA files, IIS format files are saved as regular ASCII text files. Each line within the file represents a single record, and each record reflects an event to which your server responded. Fields in each record are separated by commas, and a carriage return/line feed combination terminates a record. The maximum record length is 1,200 bytes, which is more than adequate. If a longer record is generated for some reason, it's truncated to the proper length.

Within a record, individual fields can be up to 150 bytes long. Because of the nature of the data being recorded, this maximum is unlikely to be exceeded. If it were, however, the field would be truncated to stay within the limit.

The following code lines are a portion of an IIS log file:

```
205.163.44.5, ·, 2/12/98, 11:04:09, W3SVC1, ALAGOINHAS, 205.163.44.8, 5148, 290,
1520, 200, 0, GET, /program design/hierarchy.htm, ·,
205.163.44.5, ·, 2/12/98, 11:04:13, W3SVC1, ALAGOINHAS, 205.163.44.8, 4376, 289,
3484, 200, 0, GET, /program design/objects.htm, ·,
205.163.44.5, ·, 2/12/98, 11:04:13, W3SVC1, ALAGOINHAS, 205.163.44.8, 1733, 291,
3471, 200, 0, GET, /program design/creatures.htm, ·,
205.163.44.5, ·, 2/12/98, 11:04:17, W3SVC1, ALAGOINHAS, 205.163.44.8, 1712, 290,
2747, 200, 0, GET, /program design/monsters.htm, ·,
205.163.44.5, ·, 2/12/98, 11:04:30, W3SVC1, ALAGOINHAS, 205.163.44.8, 13390, 292,
3175, 200, 0, GET, /program design/characters.htm, ·,
205.163.44.5, ·, 2/12/98, 11:04:30, W3SVC1, ALAGOINHAS, 205.163.44.8, 340, 290,
7876, 200, 0, GET, /program design/overview.shtm, ·,
```

This excerpt represents only a few records from the file. Notice that each record can be quite long, and the plain-text approach to record formatting makes them difficult to interpret just by looking. Each record consists of 15 fields, separated by commas. If no data exists for a particular field, a hyphen appears as a placeholder. Table 26-1 details the meaning of the fields in each record.

Table 26-1 IIS File Format Record Fields

Field	Meaning	Comment
1	Client's IP address	
2	User name	Valid only for FTP or for nonanonymous logon for other services
3	Date	
4	Time	
5	Service	W3SVC (Web), MSFTPSVC (ftp)
6	Server name	
7	Server's IP address	
8	Processing time	How long it took, in milliseconds, to process the request
9	Bytes received	
10	Bytes transmitted	
11	Service status code	See below
12	Windows NT status code	See below
13	Operation name	Command received by the server
14	Operation target	Document or file accessed by the operation
15	Parameters	Optional, based on operation

Notice that two status code fields are generated for each record. The service status code indicates the code returned by the service itself. Different services (Web, FTP, and Gopher) generate different status codes. For instance, the Web server generates a code 200 when an operation is completed successfully. The Windows NT status code is the system-level status code returned by the operating system.

W3C Extended Log Format

The W3C Extended Log Format is the default logging format used by IIS and is derived from recommendations of the World Wide Web Consortium, hence the W3C acronym. This log format is also stored as an ASCII file, and the default settings display less information than the other file formats, as the following sample shows:

```
#Software: Microsoft Internet Information Server 4.0
#Version: 1.0
#Date: 1998-02-12 18:19:36
#Fields: time c-ip cs-method cs-uri-stem sc-status
18:19:36 205.163.44.5 GET /rex/ 404
18:19:52 205.163.44.5 GET /rexes/Default.htm 200
```

```
18:20:11 205.163.44.5 GET /_themes/expeditn/exptextb.jpg 304

18:20:11 205.163.44.5 GET /IIS4Samples/ 200

18:20:15 205.163.44.5 GET /IIS4Samples/Chap11/ 200

18:20:26 205.163.44.5 GET /IIS4Samples/Chap11/JSExample.htm 200

18:20:37 205.163.44.5 GET /IIS4Samples/Chap11/JSExample2.HTM 200

18:20:37 205.163.44.5 GET /IIS4Samples/Chap22/ 200

18:21:01 205.163.44.5 GET /IIS4Samples/Chap22/Missouri.htm 200

18:21:01 205.163.44.5 GET /Sundance/ 403

18:21:29 205.163.44.5 GET /Garrett/Family/ 403

18:21:46 205.163.44.5 GET /Garrett/Family/PhotoAlbum.htm 200

18:21:46 205.163.44.5 GET /Garrett/Family/Photos/Family.jpg 200

18:21:46 205.163.44.5 GET /Garrett/Family/Photos/WarrensFamily.jpg 200

18:22:19 205.163.44.5 GET /Garrett/Family/Photos/MnR1.jpg 200
```

This file format differs in many ways from the other file formats that have been illustrated. For example, the comments at the top of the file begin with a # sign and describe some basic information about the files, such as the server version and the time that the file was created. The last comment is the most noteworthy because it describes the contents of the rest of the file.

In this example, the final comment gives an abbreviated clue as to the contents of the log file. The possible abbreviations are explained in Table 26-2. This log file format is the easiest to customize, and you can select any of the fields from Table 26-2 to be in the log file.

IIS provides several ways to create log files. This characteristic makes it unique among Internet servers. You can configure logging for each of your IIS services by using the Properties dialog box for each service in the Internet Service Manager. To enable or disable logging, follow these steps:

1. Open Internet Service Manager.
2. Right-click on the service for which you want to set logging and select Properties from the shortcut menu. This action displays the Properties dialog box for that service.
3. Click on the Site tab. The Properties dialog box now appears, as shown in Figure 26-1.
4. Select the Enable Logging check box.

With logging enabled, you are ready to determine how that logging should occur. The balance of this section of the dialog box is where you indicate your logging preferences. Notice that this dialog box contains two other controls.

Table 26-2 W3C Extended Log File Fields

Field Abbreviation	Name	Explanation
date	Date	Date the action was taken.
time	Time	Time that the event occurred.
c-ip	Client IP Address	IP address requesting the event.
cs-username	User Name	If a client logs on with a user name, that information appears here.
s-sitename	Service Name	A numbered service name such as W3SVC# (Web), MSFTPSVC# (ftp), NNTPSVC# (nntp), or SMTPSVC# (smtp).
s-computername	Server Name	Name of the computer running the service.
s-ip	Server IP	IP address of the server.
cs-method	Method	The method causing the event is generally a GET or POST.
cs-uri-stem	URI Stem	The URI stem represents the logical location of the item being requested.
cs-uri-query	URI Query	Logs the query part of the event's URI.
sc-status	HTTP Status	Reports the HTTP status code.
sc-win32-status	Win32 Status	Reports any Win32 status codes.
sc-bytes	Bytes Sent	Reports bytes sent by server during event.
cs-bytes	Bytes Received	Reports bytes received by client from the server.
time-taken	Time Taken	How long it took, in milliseconds, to process the request.
s-port	Server Port	Port the server is communicating on.
cs-version	Protocol Version	Version of HTTP being used.
cs(User-Agent)	User Agent	Description of client being used.
cs(Cookie)	Cookie	Stores any cookie information being used, usually a value used to track an ASP session.
cs(Referer)	Referrer	May include information about a previous page.

CAUTION

Even though you can turn off logging, creating log files is a good idea. Properly using log files helps you manage your overall Internet site. If you don't have the log files, you won't be able to manage as effectively.

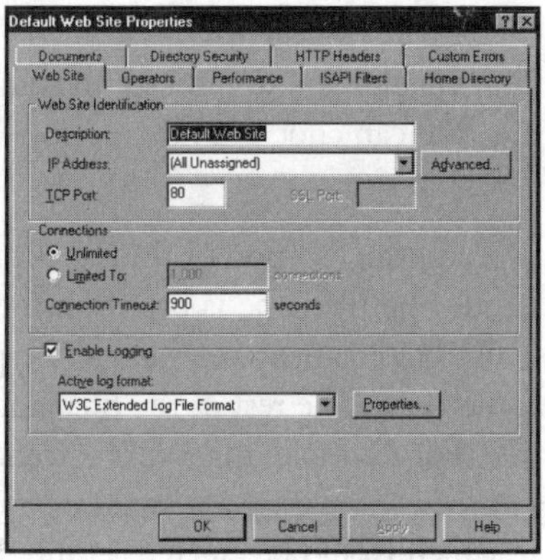

FIGURE 26-1

Internet Service Manager enables you to control logging for each of your Internet services.

NOTE

After you have changed logging configuration information for a service, you should stop and restart the service. Your log file changes don't take effect until the server is restarted.

Logging to a File

The easiest way to create your log is to store the information in a text file, which IIS will handle if you choose one of the options that logs to a file. To choose such an option, specify the format in which you want IIS to save the log files. If you click on the Active log format pull-down list, you can see that you can save files in the Microsoft IIS Log File Format, the NCSA Common Log File Format, or the default W3C Extended Log File Format. All of these log file formats were discussed earlier in this chapter.

After you settle on a file format, you can instruct IIS to open a new log file based on one of the following criteria:

- ◆ **Daily.** This option causes a new log file to be created every day. The old log file is closed and the new one opened when the first loggable event occurs after midnight.

- ◆ **Weekly.** This option causes a new log file to be created every week. The old log file is closed and the new one opened when the first loggable event occurs after midnight on Sunday morning.

- ◆ **Monthly.** This option causes a new log file to be created every month. The old log file is closed and the new one opened when the first loggable event occurs on the first day of the month.

- ◆ **Unlimited file size.** This option uses only one log file.
- ◆ **When file size reaches.** This option enables you to indicate the largest file size that you want IIS to create. You can choose a file size anywhere from 1MB to 4,094MB (4GB) in size.

At the bottom of the dialog box, you can specify the location of the log files. Notice that you can't specify the filename to be used. The filename is based on the type of log file being created and the criteria being used to create a new file. Each type of log file format uses a specific prefix to create a filename. The rest of the filename reflects the criteria being used to create the new file. For example, the W3C Extended Log File Format uses the prefix EX. A logging criteria of creating a new file every day will result in a filename such as EX980705.log, which would be created on July 5, 1998.

Logging to a Database

If you select ODBC logging from the Active log format list, you can direct IIS to store log entries in a database. Notice that the database must be ODBC compliant and must be installed on the server. If this option is not available, the server does not have the appropriate type of database program installed. In many ways, logging to a file is very similar to working with the IDC, as discussed in Chapter 18, "The Internet Database Connector."

To log information to a database, you need four pieces of information. Click on the Properties button to find the dialog box where each piece of information is stored in the appropriate fields:

- ◆ ODBC Data Source Name (DSN)
- ◆ Table
- ◆ User Name
- ◆ Password

These items are covered in the following sections.

The Data Source Name

Whenever you work with ODBC, you need to set up what is called a *data source name* (*DSN*) for each data source that you use from different programs. For a Microsoft Access database, the DSN is the Access database filename; for SQL Server, you can assign a name to your database tables.

To set up a DSN, you use the ODBC applet in the Control Panel. This step occurs, of course, outside of IIS or Internet Service Manager. As an example, suppose that you want to save your log entries in an Access database named InetLogs.mdb. Follow these steps to create a log file DSN:

1. Minimize Internet Service Manager if you have it open.

2. Create your Access database (`InetLogs.mdb`), making sure that a table in it contains the fields indicated in the next section.

3. Open the Control Panel.

4. Double-click on the ODBC applet. The ODBC Data Source Administrator dialog box appears, as shown in Figure 26-2.

NOTE

If the ODBC applet isn't visible in the Control Panel, the proper ODBC drivers aren't installed on your system.

FIGURE 26-2

You define data source names for your ODBC objects in the ODBC Data Source Administrator dialog box.

5. Click on the System DSN tab. This tab shows the DSNs already defined for your system.

6. Click on the Add button to start the Create New Data Source Wizard, as shown in Figure 26-3.

7. Highlight the Microsoft Access Driver and click on the Finish button. The ODBC Microsoft Access Setup dialog box appears, as in Figure 26-4.

NOTE

The contents of your ODBC Setup dialog box will not be the same as shown in Figure 26-4 if you are not using the same version of Access used here or if you are using a different database program entirely.

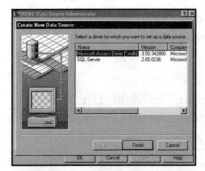

FIGURE 26-3

The ODBC applet uses a wizard to help you create a DSN.

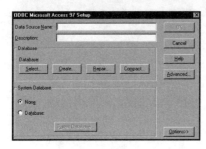

FIGURE 26-4

You use the ODBC Microsoft Access Setup dialog box to define the location and type of data source.

8. In the Data Source Name field, enter the name that you want to use for your DSN. This name should be descriptive, such as *Log Files*.

9. In the Description field, enter a description for this DSN. This step is optional, but it may help you to remember the purpose of this DSN later.

10. Click on the Select button to see a standard file selection dialog box. Select the Access database that you set up in step 2.

11. After you find your database file in the dialog box, click on OK to accept your choice. The database name now appears in the ODBC Microsoft Access Setup dialog box.

12. Click on OK to close the ODBC Microsoft Access Setup dialog box. The newly defined DSN should appear in the list of system DSNs.

13. Click on OK to close the ODBC Data Source Administrator dialog box.

After the DSN is defined, you can return to the Internet Service Manager and indicate the DSN name in the Properties dialog box. This name must match exactly the name that you entered in step 8.

The Table Name

Modern relational databases enable you to store several types of objects in a database. With products such as Access, you can define tables, reports, queries, and program modules. In the Table field in the Properties dialog box, you specify the name of the table in the database in which to save the log file records.

The database table should be constructed to receive the same information that is placed in a text log file. Exactly how you put the table together depends on the database that you are using. Regardless of the database, however, the fields in the table should have the names and characteristics shown in Table 26-3.

Table 26-3 Table Organization for an IIS Log

Field Name	Use	Type	Size
ClientHost	Client's IP address	Text	255
Username	User name	Text	255
LogTime	Date and Time	Date	Long
Service	Service	Text	255
Machine	Server name	Text	255
ServerIP	Server's IP address	Text	50
Processingtime	Processing time	Integer	Short
Bytesrecvd	Bytes received	Integer	Short
Bytessent	Bytes transmitted	Integer	Short
Servicestatus	Service status code	Integer	Short
Win32status	Windows NT status code	Integer	Short
Operation	Operation name	Text	255
Target	Operation target	Text	255
Parameters	Parameters	Text	255

When you put your table together, you should use the exact field names shown in Table 26-3; *these are mandatory*. The capitalization doesn't matter, but the spelling matters quite a bit. If you are off by even one character, your log file won't work properly. IIS includes an SQL template file that can be run in an SQL database program to create the necessary table. This file, logtemp.sql, is found in the \WINNT\SYSTEM32\InetSrv directory or in a similar directory, depending on the installation on your computer.

User Name and Password

If your database is set up to use security features such as user names and passwords, you need to specify those items in the proper fields of the Properties dialog box. These should be valid user names and passwords, exactly as they are used in your database program. If you haven't defined these elements for the database, you can leave them blank in the Properties dialog box.

If you use user names and passwords, don't use the administrator or superuser information in the Properties dialog box. To maintain security, you may want to create a special user (with the associated password) in your database program. Give this user just the minimum privileges necessary to write to the database table. This way, you get the maximum security with the least risk of giving away your user name and password.

How Log Files Affect Performance

You should know that the logging choices you make can affect the performance of your site. Each method of storing a log file has its own performance trade-offs.

If you are writing your log file to disk, IIS needs to maintain the log file by continually writing information to the file. This process happens quickly and shouldn't be much of a performance trade-off. However, as the site becomes busier, writing log file information requires more work. IIS also maintains separate log files for every site that you are running. Running several busy sites on one machine will use up a noticeable amount of resources when logging information to a disk.

Writing your log file to a database has a different type of effect on performance. When you write to a database, each record is committed as it's created; there is no buffer to worry about. However, because every record is being stored as it's created, an overall slowdown can occur in your site response. The degree to which this delay is felt depends on several factors:

♦ **Disk speed.** Saving information to disk will take longer on a disk with a slow access rate.

♦ **Location of the database.** Transferring the information over the network can take longer if the database is on a remote server rather than on the local server.

♦ **Implementation of the database.** A poorly implemented ODBC database can have a negative effect on the performance of your system.

♦ **Size of the database.** The larger the database, the more time necessary to process the database and add a record.

Using Log Files

After you have instructed IIS to create log files, you need to worry about what to do with them. Exactly how you use log files may depend on your site needs, as well as the method that you are using to save the log files. The following sections should give you some ideas on how you can use the log files created by IIS.

Custom Programs

Many programs that you can use to analyze your log files are available. Most of these programs are generic and work with only a limited number of log file formats. You can also create your own custom programs. Because log files are written in plain ASCII text, writing a custom program to extract needed information shouldn't be that tough. You can use any programming language that you want; if you save your log information to a database, you can use the programming features of the database.

As an example, at Discovery Computing Inc, we use Access to process our log files. The log files can then be compiled into reports that provide the information we need to manage our site. The log file in Figure 26-5 shows page-by-page activity on our Web site for the previous week. We use special filtering routines to weed out "bogus" activity events. For instance, we don't count visits from within our own network, and we have filtered out visits by robots from around the Web. The result is a nice, clean snapshot of how our site is doing. Another way that you can use log files saved in

Web Site Hits - Weekly/Monthly/Life to Date Summary

	1/27/97	1/28/97	1/29/97	1/30/97	1/31/97	2/1/97	2/2/97	Past 7 Days	Month to Date	Life to Date
Aladdin	19	15	14	1	8	16	10	83	197	2,844
Arrowhead Motel	5 2	7 3	5 3	1	14 1			31 10	89 19	2,131 582
Avalon Writing Center			1			1		1	3 2	209
Bear Lodge Motel	5 2	7 1	5 2		14 1			31 6	89 15	2,131 596
Bear Lodge Outfitters	21 12	22 14	30 14	3 7	15 13	11 9	10 13	112 82	27 28	3,706 3,750
Bell Pourche Chamber of Commerce		7 12	7		5	6	4	41	10	1,260
Best Western in Sundance	5 4	7	5 2	1	14 4			31 11	89 12	2,131 502
Business Climate	12 3	21	15 1	1	17			66 8	299 40	4,258 584
CanAm SD		2			2	1		5	1	127
Crook County		7 16	17	2	3	8	16	69	24	1,982
DCI - Authoring	8	3	7	1	1	9	4	33	51	2,917
DCI - Bear Lodge	15 18	19 6	3 11	4 3	9 13	8 9	12 12	70 72	47 43	1,683 2,076
DCI - Building		3	1		2	2		8	2	171
DCI - Consulting	1				2			3	22	298
DCI - Fulfillment	14		4					18	71	1,236
DCI - Internet Advertising	3	3		1	1	4		12	4	271
DCI - Manufacturing	6		1			10	13	30	92	914
DCI - Publishing	4	3	1		2	1		11	27	604
DCI - Search Engines			1			2		3	2	96
Devils Tower	49	45	40	6	38	29	33	240	552	8,176
Devils Tower Trading Post	4	6	4	1	3	5	8	31	13	941
Discovery Computing Inc.	15 174	19 146	3 138	4 43	9 118	8 125	12 147	70 891	47 406	1,683 26,690
Garbage Notice										13
higbee's	5	7	5		14			31	89	2,131
Hulett										1
Hurd's Sundance Texaco	5	7	5		14			31	89	2,131
IMA Lodging	171	94	135	19	122	101	114	756	215	18,198
Joining	1		2	1				5	1	65
JR Myhre	15 1	19 1	3 1	4	9	8	12	70 3	20	1,608 339
Just Kids Doll Shop	15 8	19 2	3 9	4 5	9 6	8 13	12 4	70 47	20 17	1,515 1,911
Lenz Distributing	15 7	19 4	3 3	4	9 4	8 4	12 4	70 26	20 8	1,581 832
Little River Water									115	447
Mark Hughes	15	19	3	4	9			50	27	1,663
Moorcroft										5
Mountain View Campground	5	7	5		14			31	89	2,131
Officers		1	1		1 1	1	1	5	2	72
Other Web		1	3	3	1		1	9	1	111
Sagebrush Realty		2						2		517
SD Can-Am		4	12	4		6	8	2	36	10	945

2/3/97   1

FIGURE 26-5

A sample report created from log file entries in a database.

databases is to create custom programs that allow the database tables to be used with the Internet Database Connector (covered in Chapter 18). In this way, you can use your Web browser to view statistics about your site. This feature is extremely useful if you need to administer your site remotely or if you want to make the information available on the Web.

Converting Log File Formats

IIS includes a program that enables you to convert your text-based log files from the IIS format to a different format. You can use the convlog.exe program to convert IIS log files to EMWAC format or common log file format. This program is installed at the same time that you install IIS. By default, the program is located in the \WINNT\system32\ directory.

> **NOTE**
>
> It is possible for the `convlog.exe` file to be buried within several layers of directories. Use the Find Files feature of Windows NT to help locate the file's exact location.

To convert your IIS log files to EMWAC format, follow these steps:

1. Choose the <u>P</u>rograms option from the Start menu.
2. Choose the Command Prompt option to open a command-prompt window in which you can perform the remaining steps.
3. Create a directory in which to do your work; then, change to that directory.
4. Copy the IIS log files to the directory.
5. Enter the following command at the command prompt, replacing *inlog* with the name of the log file that you want to convert:

   ```
   convlog inlog
   ```

After a few moments, the conversion process is complete, and you can use the file in its new format. If you want to convert to the common log file format instead of EMWAC format, substitute the following command in step 5:

```
convlog -t ncsa inlog
```

Many more options are available to use with `convlog`, but most are for use in special circumstances that you probably won't encounter. To see the complete syntax for the command, you can simply enter `convlog` at the command prompt without any parameters.

Managing the Log Files

Eventually, you'll reach a point where you need to make some decisions about log files. Making those decisions early in the game can save you both time and hassle later on.

Perhaps the biggest decision is how long you're going to keep the log files generated by IIS. If you have an active site, the log files (text or database) can mount up very quickly. Unless you have unlimited hard disk space, you probably need to set a time frame after which the log files are deleted or moved to an archive media.

Another option is to periodically toss out the information you no longer need from individual log file records. In the 15 fields generated for each log file record, you receive quite a bit of information—and not all of it is useful. At our site, we tend to throw out the fields indicating the server name, server IP address, processing time, bytes sent and received, and status codes. Most of this information (almost half of each record) is unnecessary for the management decisions that we make at our site.

You can also filter your records to pull out events that you don't need. For example, most people connected to the Internet are interested only in events generated by users outside their organization. You can use your IP address or subnet mask to filter out events generated by your own computers. Depending on the number of people on your network, this step could decrease your log file size quite a bit.

If you are running an intranet, you obviously can't filter out an entire subnet. Instead, you may want to filter specific client IP addresses—those used by your intranet content development staff, for example.

TIP

If you are running an exclusive intranet, sort your log files by IP address to make sure that no unauthorized access from outside your organization is occurring. Looking through IP addresses for those that don't belong to your assigned IP address ranges makes this process easy.

Chapter 27

Monitoring and
Improving Performance

In This Chapter

◆ Performance and the Task Manager

◆ The Performance Monitor

◆ IIS and the Performance Monitor

◆ Improving Performance

As you undoubtedly know by now, implementing an Internet or intranet site can place a tremendous burden on your hardware. In many cases, you are running not only Web, FTP, and Gopher servers but also a DNS server, mail server, and database program—all on the same system. The result is many, many services all running at the same time, vying for a share of the system resources.

Unfortunately, adding more services can cause slower response times for all the services on the system. Thus, you shouldn't be surprised to learn that one of the challenges an administrator faces is to find ways to improve the performance of the computers assigned to the Internet or intranet site.

Windows NT includes two tools that you can use to measure and thereby improve your system performance: the Task Manager and the Performance Monitor. This chapter teaches you to use these two tools to make your systems the best they can be.

Performance and the Task Manager

The Task Manager included with Windows NT 4.0 provides features that you can use to help measure the performance of your system. To display the Task Manager, right-click on the Taskbar and then choose the Task Manager option from the context menu. When the Task Manager is displayed, click on the Performance tab. The Task Manager window then appears, as shown in Figure 27-1.

The Task Manager displays information about how your system is doing in relation to its two primary resources: the CPU and system memory. If you double-click anywhere within the Performance tab, a larger representation of your CPU and memory usage is displayed, as shown in Figure 27-2. To return the Task Manager to normal, simply double-click on the graph.

If you examine the Taskbar while the Task Manager is running, you will notice a small green square at the right side, near the system time. This block represents a "gas gauge" that indicates how much of your CPU's capacity is being used. You can minimize the Task Manager and keep an eye on the gas gauge, or you can choose Hide When Minimized from the Options menu and then minimize the Task Manager. (If you do the latter, the Task Manager won't even show up on the Taskbar.) To redisplay the Task Manager, double-click on the gas gauge.

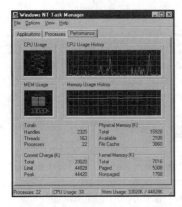

FIGURE 27-1

The Performance tab of the Task Manager displays general performance information about your system.

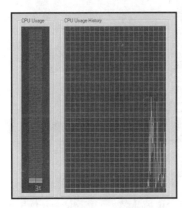

FIGURE 27-2

The Task Manager can also display an enlarged version of your performance information.

By keeping an eye on the Task Manager while you're in the middle of a normal day at your site, you can get a general idea of how your resources are holding up. If you need more in-depth information, you need to use the Performance Monitor, as discussed in the next section.

The Performance Monitor

The Performance Monitor is the one tool built into Windows NT that can help you make your system outstanding. Unfortunately, it's also one of the tools that system administrators commonly overlook. If you know how to use the Performance Monitor already, then you can safely skip this section and proceed to the section, titled "IIS and the Performance Monitor."

To start the Performance Monitor, choose Programs from the Start menu, choose Administrative Tools (Common), and then choose Performance Monitor. The Performance Monitor program window opens, as shown in Figure 27-3.

MENU

TOOLBAR

DISPLAY AREA

STATUS BAR

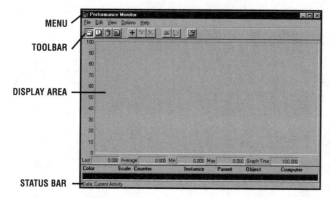

FIGURE 27-3

The Performance Monitor uses a familiar Windows interface.

At first glance, the Performance Monitor window looks very nondescript. As you will shortly learn, appearances can be deceiving, and you can use this plain-looking window to gather information on a host of system functions.

The User Interface

The Performance Monitor uses a typical Windows interface. The program window is divided into several areas. At the top of the program window is the menu bar, just above the toolbar. Most of the program window is occupied by the display area. At the bottom of the program window is the status bar. These areas of the user interface are discussed in the following sections.

The Menus

At the top of the program window is a menu bar with menus named File, Edit, View, Options, and Help. Most of the options available from the menus are also available from the toolbar, as described in the next section.

The choices available from the File menu depend on which Performance Monitor window you're viewing. All the options have the same purpose; just the wording of the choices varies. The following list describes the major purpose of each File menu option:

◆ **New** Eliminates all your current window settings and opens a new window of the type you're currently using.

◆ **Open** Enables you to load from disk any settings that you have previously saved.

◆ **Save Settings** Saves your current settings to disk, using a previously defined filename.

◆ **Save Settings As** Saves your current settings to disk under a new filename.

◆ **Save Workspace** Saves settings from all your Performance Monitor windows.

◆ **Export** Enables you to save your settings in a format other than the native Performance Monitor format.

◆ **Exit** Exits the program.

Like the choices in the File menu, the wording of those in the Edit menu also changes depending on which Performance Monitor window you're viewing. The Edit menu includes the following options:

◆ **Add To** Enables you to add an object to the current Performance Monitor window.

◆ **Edit** Enables you to change a chart line (in the Chart window) or an alert item (in the Alert window).

◆ **Time Window** Enables you to modify the amount of detail displayed along the horizontal axis in the display area.

◆ **Clear Display** Clears the information shown in the display area.

◆ **Delete From** Removes an object from the current Performance Monitor window.

Use the View menu to choose the Performance Monitor window that you want to show in the display area. The four options are as follows:

◆ **Chart** Shows a graphic representation of object performance over time.

◆ **Alert** Shows alerts generated when the performance of an object passes a threshold that you define; you also can choose the action to be performed when the threshold is passed.

- ◆ **Log** Enables you to specify the objects whose actions you want to monitor; the activity of those objects is then recorded in a log file for later analysis.
- ◆ **Report** Enables you to create reports based on the performance of objects in your system.

With the **O**ptions menu, you can control how the Performance Monitor derives, stores, and displays information. Choices in the **O**ptions menu are fairly standard, but the first choice always varies depending on the Performance Monitor window being viewed. (The first four items in the following list represent options that are displayed in the first menu position, based on which window is selected.) Here are the choices on this menu:

- ◆ **C**hart Appears when working with the Chart window. It enables you to change display properties of the chart.
- ◆ **A**lert Appears when working with the Alert window. It enables you to change how alerts are generated.
- ◆ **L**og Appears when working with the Log window. It allows you to change how the log file is created and where it's saved.
- ◆ **R**eport Appears when working with the Report window. It allows you to change how often the report is updated.
- ◆ **Menu and Title** Displays the menu bar and title bar.
- ◆ **T**oolbar Displays the toolbar.
- ◆ **S**tatus Bar Displays the status bar.
- ◆ **Always on Top** Displays the Performance Monitor window on top of whatever other program windows are open on-screen.
- ◆ **Data F**rom Enables you to specify where Performance Monitor should obtain its information. Your choices are from current activity (real time) or from a prerecorded log file.
- ◆ **U**pdate Now Forces the information in the display area to be updated.
- ◆ **B**ookmark Enables you to save text information with your log file. The bookmark is designed so that you can make notes about the log file.

The Toolbar

The Performance Monitor includes a toolbar at the top of the program window. You can turn on this toolbar, if it's not visible on your system, by choosing **T**oolbar from the **O**ptions menu. The various tools on the toolbar perform many of the same functions that you can select from the menus.

Notice that the tools are divided into four groups. The left-most group, consisting of four tools, controls which window is currently shown in the display area; these four tools correspond to the four choices in the Uiew menu. The first tool displays the Chart window, the second the Alert window, the third the Log window, and the fourth the Report window.

The second group of tools provides a way to quickly modify items added to the windows. The first option is for adding an object, the second for editing an object, and the third for deleting an object. These tools correspond to choices available on the Edit menu.

The third group of tools corresponds to the last two choices on the Options menu. The first tool updates the information in the display window, and the second sets a bookmark in a log file.

The fourth group consists of a single tool. This tool serves the same purpose as the first choice on the Options menu—displaying the options for the window that you are viewing.

The Display Area

The display area of the Performance Monitor changes depending on which window you have selected from the Uiew menu or from the toolbar. When you select the Chart window, the display area shows a chart. This chart displays the performance of selected objects over time. The vertical axis is a scale appropriate to the objects, and the horizontal axis represents time.

When you select the Alert window, the display area shows the alert log. The legend at the bottom of the display area represents the objects about which you want to be alerted. The main part of the display area is the log of when those alerts have been triggered.

When you select the Log window, the display area shows a list of the objects you're logging, as well as the status of the log file itself. When you select the Report window, the display area shows the objects that you have added to the report.

The Status Bar

At the bottom of the Performance Monitor program window is a status bar. It functions like the status bar for any other Windows program. Its primary purpose is informational, but it doesn't provide much information. If you select a menu item, a quick reminder of what the item is used for appears in the status bar. When you are working in the display area, however, the status bar merely tells you the origin of the information in the window (current activity or log file).

To turn the status bar on or off, choose <u>S</u>tatus Bar from the <u>O</u>ptions menu. If a check mark appears next to the option, the status bar is on; if no check mark appears, the status bar is off.

Monitoring Objects

You can monitor objects in any window that makes the most sense for your purposes. To add an object, click on the Add tool on the toolbar to display the Add To dialog box. The exact appearance of this dialog box depends on the window currently displayed. For example, if you're working in the Chart window and you choose to add an object, the dialog box appears as shown in Figure 27-4.

FIGURE 27-4

Use the Add To dialog box to add an object to a window.

Notice that the dialog box enables you to select a <u>C</u>omputer, an Ob<u>j</u>ect, a Coun<u>t</u>er, and an <u>I</u>nstance. These items are hierarchical. For example, selecting a computer determines the objects that are available. Likewise, selecting an object affects the counters that are available, and the counter affects the instances that are available.

The objects available on a particular computer system are, to a degree, dependent on what's installed on that system. Different system components provide different Performance Monitor objects. Common objects include processors, memory, cache, threads, and processes. In addition, different application programs may add their own objects that the Performance Monitor can access.

Within objects, you can monitor different counters or instances of counters. The counters vary, depending on the object you've selected. For example, if you select the processor object, you can monitor counters such as processor time and interrupt usage. If you select threads, you can monitor counters such as thread state and thread wait reason.

TIP

To find out what a specific instance within an object represents, click on the <u>E</u>xplain button in the Add To dialog box. An explanation appears at the bottom of the dialog box.

Refresh Rate

One of the items changed most often when using the Performance Monitor is the refresh time. This value determines how often the Performance Monitor samples the values necessary to update the display. The default refresh time depends on which window you are viewing. To change the refresh rate, click on the Options tool on the toolbar, or choose the first option under the Options menu. Doing so with the Chart window selected, for example, displays the Options dialog box shown in Figure 27-5.

FIGURE 27-5

In the Options dialog box, you can change display and acquisition properties of the selected window.

To change the refresh rate, select the Periodic Update radio button and then change the value in the Interval field. If you want, you also can select the Manual Update radio button. If you select this button, however, you get updated information in the Performance Monitor only when you click on the Update tool on the toolbar or choose Update Now from the Options menu.

> **TIP**
>
> You can use the other selections in the Options dialog box, as desired, to change display properties of the current window.

Printing Reports

Unfortunately, the Performance Monitor doesn't allow you to print results. When you need a hard copy of your performance results, you have two options. First, you can capture the contents of the screen and then use a graphics editing program to print the screen. (This approach is particularly effective when displaying the Chart window.) For example, you can use the Paint accessory to print a report by following these steps:

1. In the Performance Monitor, display the window that you want to print.

2. Maximize the Performance Monitor program window.

3. Press the PrintScreen key. This action copies a "snapshot" of your desktop to the Windows Clipboard.

4. Minimize the Performance Monitor program window.

5. Open the Paint accessory.

6. Choose Paste from the Edit menu. A copy of the Performance Monitor program window should appear in Paint.

7. Choose File, Print to open the Print dialog box.

8. Click on OK to send your printout to the printer.

9. Close the Paint accessory.

The other option for printing Performance Monitor information is to export the raw data generated by Performance Monitor to another program, for example, a database program or a spreadsheet program, and then use that program to print the information. This method of printing Performance Monitor data enables you to include additional information necessary to your report. This way, you also can change the format or appearance of the information using the capabilities of your spreadsheet or database program. To export the Performance Monitor information and print a report, follow these steps:

1. In the Performance Monitor, display the window containing the information that you want to export.

2. Choose File, Export to open the Export As dialog box shown in Figure 27-6.

FIGURE 27-6

Use the Export As dialog box to create an export file from the Performance Monitor.

3. In the Save as Type pull-down list (lower-left corner), select TSV or CSV. (TSV stands for *tab-separated values*; CSV means *comma-separated values*.)

4. In the File Name field, specify the name to be used for this file.

5. Select the drive and directory in which to store the file.

6. Click on Save to save the export file.

After the information is saved to a disk file, you can use your spreadsheet or database program to load the data and manipulate it. You then can print the information with that program.

IIS and the Performance Monitor

When you install IIS on your system, a group of new Performance Monitor objects is added. You can use these objects to monitor how your IIS server is performing based on the components that you have installed at your site.

How valuable the IIS objects are to you depends on how busy your site is. If you're running a couple of hundred connections per day, you may not have enough activity to monitor. However, if you're running a couple of hundred connections per hour, you're getting into the range where you might be able to really benefit from a good analysis of how your site is being used.

The Performance Monitor objects installed are best discussed according to the server for which they are applicable. One object, however, applies to IIS as a whole. This object is called *Internet Information Services Global*. Table 27-1 details the counters that are available for this object.

The most useful counters in the IIS Global object are undoubtedly those concerned with the bandwidth limit. As you learned earlier in the book, when you configure your IIS services, you can limit the bandwidth used by external requests for your services. If you impose a limit, you may want to use the Total Blocked Async I/O Requests counter to make sure that you aren't turning away too many people. If this counter is high, look at loosening your bandwidth limit. If the counter is quite high, you may need to look at getting a larger Internet service connection for your site.

Web Performance

If you're interested in measuring performance for your Web server, the Performance Monitor includes an object that you can use. The *Web Service* contains quite a few counters you can monitor, as described in Table 27-2.

If your Web site becomes very busy, some of these counters can help you to determine where to direct your development or implementation efforts. For example, if you have a high number of Not Found Errors, you need to examine your Web log files and see where the problem lies. If it's a page that you removed from your site, you may need to reinstate it or provide a link page that informs people of the new URL for the page.

When you use the counters, you can specify what instance you want to use for it. The instance can either be for your entire server or for specific Web sites that you have installed.

Table 27-1 **Counters for the Internet Information Services Global Object**

Counter	Description
Cache Flushes	Number of times the memory cache has been flushed (thrown away) due to file or directory changes in an IIS directory tree.
Cache Hits	Number of times a requested object was found in the cache.
Cache Hits %	Ratio of cache hits to cache requests.
Cache Misses	Opposite of the Cache Hits counter; represents the number of times a requested object wasn't found in the cache.
Cached File Handles	Number of open file handles cached by all IIS services.
Current Blocked Async I/O Requests	Number of I/O requests currently blocked by the bandwidth limit imposed in IIS.
Directory Listings	Number of directory listings cached by all IIS services.
Measured Async I/O Bandwidth Usage	Average amount of bandwidth used each minute.
Objects	Number of objects cached by all IIS services.
Total Allowed Async I/O Requests	Number of I/O requests permitted by the bandwidth limit imposed by IIS.
Total Blocked Async I/O Requests	Number of I/O requests blocked by the bandwidth limit imposed by IIS.
Total Rejected Async I/O Requests	Number of I/O requests rejected by the bandwidth limit imposed by IIS.

Table 27-2 **Counters for the Web Service Object**

Counter	Description
Anonymous Users/sec	Rate at which users are making anonymous connections to the Web server.
Bytes Received/sec	Rate at which information is received by the Web server.
Bytes Sent/sec	Rate at which information is transmitted by the Web server.
Bytes Total/sec	Total of Bytes Received/Sec and Bytes Sent/Sec.
CGI Requests/sec	Rate at which CGI (common gateway interface) requests received.
Connection Attempts/sec	Rate at which connection attempts are made to the Web server.
Current Anonymous Users	Number of anonymous users currently connected to the server.
Current Blocked Async I/O Requests	Number of I/O requests currently blocked by the bandwidth limit imposed in IIS.
Current CGI Requests	Number of CGI requests currently being processed.

Table 27-2 Counters for the Web Service Object (continued)

Counter	Description
Current Connections	Number of current connections to the server (sum of Current Anonymous Users and Current NonAnonymous Users).
Current ISAPI Extension Requests	Number of ISAPI requests currently being processed.
Current NonAnonymous Users	Number of nonanonymous users currently connected.
Delete Requests/sec	Rate at which requests using the DELETE method are received.
Files Received/sec	Rate at which files are received by the Web server.
Files Sent/sec	Rate at which files are sent by the Web server.
Files/sec	Total of Files Received/sec and Files Sent/sec.
Get Requests/sec	Rate at which requests using the GET method are received.
Head Requests/sec	Rate at which requests using the HEAD method are received.
ISAPI Extension Requests/sec	Rate at which ISAPI requests are received.
Logon Attempts/sec	Rate at which logon attempts are made.
Maximum Anonymous Users	Maximum number of anonymous users simultaneously connected.
Maximum CGI Requests	Maximum number of CGI requests simultaneously processed by the server.
Maximum Connections	Maximum number of simultaneous connections (sum of Maximum Anonymous Users and Maximum NonAnonymous Users).
Maximum ISAPI Extension Requests	Maximum number of ISAPI requests simultaneously processed by the server.
Maximum NonAnonymous Users	Maximum number of nonanonymous users simultaneously connected.
Measured Async I/O Bandwidth Usage	Average measured bandwidth of asynchronous I/O per minute.
NonAnonymous Users/sec	Rate at which users are making nonanonymous connections to the server.
Not Found Errors/sec	Rate at which requests couldn't be satisfied because the requested document couldn't be found.
Other Request Methods/sec	Reception rate for requests that don't use the PUT, GET, POST, HEAD, TRACE, or DELETE methods.
Post Requests/sec	Rate at which requests using the POST method are received.
Put Requests/sec	Rate at which requests using the PUT method are received.
System Code Resident Bytes	Bytes set aside for use by system code.

Table 27-2 Counters for the Web Service Object (continued)

Counter	Description
Total Allowed Async I/O Requests	Number of requests allowed by bandwidth limit settings since startup.
Total Anonymous Users	Total number of anonymous users who have connected to the server.
Total Blocked Async I/O Requests	Number of requests denied based on bandwidth limit settings since startup.
Total CGI Requests	Number of CGI requests received by the server.
Total Connection Attempts	Number of connection attempts made to the Web server.
Total Delete Requests	Number of requests using the DELETE method.
Total Files Received	Total number of files received by the Web server.
Total Files Sent	Total number of files sent by the Web server.
Total Files Transferred	Total of Files Received and Files Sent.
Total Get Requests	Number of requests using the GET method.
Total Head Requests	Number of requests using the HEAD method.
Total ISAPI Extension Requests	Number of ISAPI requests received.
Total Logon Attempts	Number of logon attempts that have been made to the server.
Total Method Requests	Number of HTTP requests using the PUT, GET, POST, HEAD, TRACE, or DELETE methods.
Total Method Requests/sec	Rate at which requests are received that use the PUT, GET, POST, HEAD, TRACE, or DELETE methods.
Total NonAnonymous Users	Total number of nonanonymous users who have connected to the server.
Total Not Found Errors	Number of requests that couldn't be satisfied because the requested document couldn't be found.
Total Other Request Methods	Number of HTTP requests that don't use the PUT, GET, POST, HEAD, TRACE, or DELETE methods.
Total Post Requests	Number of requests using the POST method.
Total Put Requests	Number of requests using the PUT method.
Total Rejected Async I/O Requests	Number of asynchronous requests rejected.
Total Trace Requests	Number of requests using the TRACE method.

FTP Performance

The FTP server provided with IIS also includes some counters that you can use to measure site performance. These counters are contained within the FTP Server object, as described in Table 27-3.

Table 27- Counters for the FTP Server Object

Counter	Description
Bytes Received/sec	Rate at which information is received by the FTP server.
Bytes Sent/sec	Rate at which information is transmitted by the FTP server.
Bytes Total/sec	Sum of Bytes Received/Sec and Bytes Sent/Sec.
Current Anonymous Users	Number of anonymous users currently connected.
Current Connections	Number of current connections (sum of Current Anonymous Users and Current NonAnonymous Users).
Current NonAnonymous Users	Number of nonanonymous users currently connected.
Maximum Anonymous Users	Maximum number of anonymous users simultaneously connected.
Maximum Connections	Maximum number of simultaneous connections (not necessarily the total of Maximum Anonymous Users and Maximum NonAnonymous Users).
Maximum NonAnonymous Users	Maximum number of nonanonymous users simultaneously connected.
Total Anonymous Users	Total number of anonymous users who have connected.
Total Connection Attempts (all instances)	Number of attempted connections to the FTP server.
Total Files Received	Total number of files received by the server.
Total Files Sent	Total number of files sent by the server.
Total Files Transferred	Total of Files Received and Files Sent.
Total Logon Attempts	Number of logon attempts made at the server.
Total NonAnonymous Users	Total number of nonanonymous users who have connected.

If you are trying to figure out whether to make your FTP site an "anonymous only" site, you can use the performance counters in this object. Monitor the nonanonymous counters, and you can determine whether the number of connections justifies the security risk posed by allowing nonanonymous logons. .

Instances used for your counters can be for individual FTP sites that you host at your server or for all FTP sites. Note, however, that the Total Connection Attempts (all instances) counter works only for the total server, not for individual FTP sites.

Active Server Pages Performance

The server used to service ASP files can be monitored by using the Active Server Pages object. This object includes a fair number of counters, as detailed in Table 27-4.

Improving Performance

The major benefit of Performance Monitor is that you can examine your system under load and determination where performance is substandard or lacking. When you know where performance is lacking, you can take actions to correct the deficiency.

When should you start to monitor your system performance? Typically, you should do so at the first sign that your system is running slowly. If your server seems sluggish when you do work on it or if your visitors are complaining that your site is slow, then you need to find out why. That is where the Performance Monitor comes into play. You can apply the information provided in this chapter to monitor virtually every facet of the work done by IIS. On the hardware front, either of two items is the most likely cause of a sluggish server: the amount of memory in your system or the type of CPU that you are using.

Before you run out and add more memory, upgrade your CPU, or add another CPU to your system, you should use the Performance Monitor to check out the problem and verify your suspicions. You do this by applying the information that is covered in this chapter, along with the guidelines in the following sections. If you monitor the proper system counters, you can make sure that a decision to spend additional money is a good one.

Overall Performance

IIS is a high-needs program that runs around the clock on your server. The more visitors you have at your site and the more components you have installed, the higher the resource needs of the system. By actively monitoring how your system performs with IIS running, you can come up with ways to make your system run even better. The key advantage of improving overall performance is faster access time for people visiting your site.

Chances are good that the hardware on which you're running IIS is also running other servers. For example, you may also be running a DNS server and a mail server on the same system as IIS. As you analyze the performance of your various servers, you might not see any real problems in an individual server, but you might detect problems in your entire site. These problems can manifest themselves in an individual server, but they are likely to crop up in the other servers as well.

Table 27-4 Counters for the Active Server Pages Object

Counter	Description
Debugging Requests	Number of debugging document requests received by the server.
Errors During Script Runtime	Number or errors generated while running a script.
Errors From ASP Preprocessor	Number of errors generated just prior to the script running.
Errors From Script Compilers	Number of errors generated while compiling scripts.
Errors/Sec	Rate at which the server detects errors.
Memory Allocated	Total memory allocated by the ASP server.
Request Bytes In Total	Total number of bytes added to the ASP queue.
Request Bytes Out Total	Total numbers of bytes processed and removed from the ASP queue.
Request Execution Time	Time (in milliseconds) to fulfill most recent ASP request.
Request Wait Time	Time (in milliseconds) since the most recent ASP request was processed.
Requests Disconnected	Number of requests not fulfilled due to communications failure.
Requests Executing	Number of requests currently executing.
Requests Failed Total	Number of requests in which errors were encountered.
Requests Not Authorized	Number of requests not fulfilled because of insufficient access rights.
Requests Not Found	Number of requests not fulfilled because files weren't available.
Requests Queued	Number of requests pending in the processing queue.
Requests Rejected	Number of requests refused because of lack of queue space or resources.
Requests Succeeded	Number of requests successfully completed.
Requests Timed Out	Number of requests that timed out.
Requests Total	Number of requests added to the queue since ASP server was started.
Requests/Sec	Number of client connections per second.
Script Engines Cached	Number of script engines pending execution in the queue.
Session Duration	Time required, in milliseconds, to complete the most recent request.
Sessions Current	Number of sessions currently being processed.
Sessions Timed Out	Number of sessions that have timed out.
Sessions Total	Number of sessions completed.
Template Cache Hit Rate	Percent of requests found in the template cache.
Template Notifications	Number of templates invalidated in cache because of change notification.
Templates Cached	Number of templates queued up at the current time.
Transactions Aborted	Number of transactions completed prematurely.
Transactions Committed	Number of transactions completely finished.
Transactions Pending	Number of transactions awaiting completion.
Transactions Total	Number of transactions processed since startup.
Transactions/Sec	Rate at which transactions are being processed.

These types of problems typically can be boiled down to the amount of memory in your server or the type of CPU you're using. You can use the Performance Monitor to diagnose the problem.

Evaluating Memory Usage

From information that is provided in various places in this book, you already know that Windows NT uses a concept called *virtual memory*. That is, your system uses as much RAM as it can; when it runs out, it swaps information to and from the hard disk in a page file. With this concept in mind, you can monitor the performance of two counters to see how they relate to each other. This information will give you a better understanding of how your system's memory is functioning.

First, examine the Pages/Sec counter of the Memory object. This counter indicates how many pages are being swapped to disk every second by Windows NT. The Pages/Sec counter is the primary way that you can determine whether your server is paging information to disk excessively. (In technical terms, excessive paging is sometimes referred to as *thrashing*.) As the value of the Pages/Sec counter increases, your server responsiveness is reduced. The reason is that your server must spend a greater percentage of its time reading and writing the page files from disk instead of using the faster access RAM memory.

The highest acceptable value for the Pages/Sec counter can vary from system to system. One way to determine whether your server is spending too much time paging is to observe whether processor activity (as evidenced by the % Total Processor Time counter of the System object) drops significantly as the Pages/Sec counter increases. Such a drop indicates that your system is more occupied with swapping pages than with processing instructions. You can also compare the Pages/Sec counter to the Avg. Disk Sec/Transfer counter of the Logical Disk object. If both counts are high, your system is spending quite a bit of time swapping information to and from the disk.

If analysis of the counters indicates that your system is spending excessive time paging information to and from disk, then memory is acting as a bottleneck to your system. In such a situation, adding more memory can help increase system performance dramatically.

TIP

As you add more memory to your system, you may also consider replacing your hard drive with a faster model. The faster the hard drive, the shorter the time your system must wait when page file swaps are necessary.

Evaluating CPU Performance

You already know that the CPU is the heart of your system. The Performance Monitor enables you to perform a checkup on the CPU to determine whether it is slowing your overall performance. You can examine several pertinent counters.

First, take a look at the % Processor Time counter of the Processor object. Add this to the Chart window and then add the % Disk Time counter from the Physical Disk object. If the processor time is consistently high (over 75%) and your disk time is low (under 10%), you would probably benefit from an upgraded or additional CPU.

On the other hand, if your disk time is high, you may benefit from a faster hard drive more than an upgrade to your CPU. If your hard drive has an access time of 10ms or greater and your disk time is high, then start considering a faster hard drive (8ms or less). You can also consider a faster hard drive controller or a different drive interface type, all of which can improve performance. After you replace the hard drive, repeat the monitoring to see whether the CPU performance improves.

If you really want to confirm a suspected CPU bottleneck, take a look at the Processor Queue Length counter of the System object. If the queue length is greater than 2 for extended periods, the rest of your system is waiting inordinately long on your CPU. In a situation like this, you definitely need to add another CPU or upgrade the one you have.

Evaluating Your Network Connection

If you are running an Internet or intranet site, you are in the business of communicating with others over a network connection. The connection may be a dedicated digital link with the network, or it may be the wiring and network interface cards that you use for your intranet.

In either case, if you have examined both the memory and CPU and found them to be satisfactory, then you need to start looking at your network connection. Each of the Performance Monitor objects for individual servers includes some sort of counter that enables you to measure the bandwidth being used by the server. In addition, you can use the Total Blocked Async I/O Requests counter of the IIS Global object to determine whether the bandwidth is acting as a bottleneck to your users. Monitor the counter over a period of time—perhaps a week or a month—to see whether it is going up, down, or staying the same. When you have this information, you need to figure out whether the cost of a faster connection (and they are costly) is acceptable for the type of information that you are publishing and the number of users that you want to serve.

Chapter 28

Customizing IIS

In This Chapter

◆ The Metabase

◆ The Registry Structure

◆ Editing the Registry

◆ The Registry Entries

Microsoft maintains system settings in the Windows NT Registry. The Registry is a database that stores settings in an easy-to-access method. However, using the Registry to change the settings of system services requires rebooting the server before the settings can take effect. To overcome this limitation, IIS stores settings in the Metabase. System settings are also maintained in the Registry to maintain compatibility with earlier releases of IIS.

This chapter shows you how to customize IIS using both the Metabase and the Registry. Topics include how the databases are structured, how you can change the information in them, and how information about IIS and the various IIS components is stored.

The Metabase

Most of the server settings have been moved from the Registry to the more efficient Metabase. This special file stores information so that IIS can reference it quickly. The only ways to access the Metabase are by using the Internet Service Manager or by creating programs that can access the IIS Admin Objects user interface or the IIS Admin Base Object.

Most system administrators will use the Internet Service Manager (see Chapter 4), which provides an easy-to-use interface for the various IIS settings. The settings are found in a property sheet and organized on the various tabs that appear there.

Creating programs to access the Metabase requires a programmer who can use the Microsoft Active Directory Services Interface to access the IIS Admin Objects user interface or knows how to program DCOM (Distributed Component Object Model) objects such as the IIS Admin Base Object. These two subjects are beyond the scope of this book. However, if you feel comfortable with this type of programming, the IIS documentation includes a reference on the different entries available in the Metabase, and you can create a program to directly change these entries.

One of the most useful aspects of the Metabase is that settings can be inherited, or passed on to lower levels. For example, several settings that are set at the server level are passed on to each of the services running on that server. When a new service is installed, such as an additional Web server, these settings are automatically inherited. The same type of inheritance occurs when a directory or file is added to a server.

The Registry Structure

Information in the Registry is stored in a hierarchical fashion, which is not dissimilar to the way that other structures work within Windows NT. For instance, the directory structure used on a disk drive is hierarchical. The concepts behind the Registry may seem confusing at first, but its organization is very logical. The Registry consists of four distinct parts:

◆ **Trees** Major divisions of the Registry

◆ **Hives** Major divisions of trees

◆ **Keys** Groups of related settings within a hive

◆ **Values** Data stored within a key

As changes are made to system settings, the changes are stored in the Registry in the form of values, which are placed in keys that are determined by the nature of the program doing the placing.

Registry Trees

The Registry consists of five major trees. These trees comprise all aspects of the Windows NT operating system:

◆ **HKEY_CLASSES_ROOT.** OLE-related information, including shortcuts. Also includes information on file associations.

◆ **HKEY_CURRENT_USER.** Specific profile settings for the user that is currently logged on to the system.

◆ **HKEY_LOCAL_MACHINE.** Machine-related specifics, such as installed hardware and software, swap file settings, startup settings, and so on. (Virtually all IIS information is stored in this tree.)

◆ **HKEY_USERS.** User-specific settings for all user profiles that are defined for the system.

◆ **HKEY_CURRENT_CONFIG.** Configuration information about the current hardware settings.

Even though five trees are in the Registry, this structure can be deceiving. Windows NT uses pointers for several of the keys. For instance, the HKEY_CLASSES _ROOT is nothing but a pointer to the HKEY_LOCAL_MACHINE\SOFT-WARE\CLASSES subkey. Likewise, HKEY_CURRENT_USER is a pointer to a subkey within the HKEY_USERS key. Thus, of the five trees, only three (HKEY_LOCAL_MACHINE, HKEY_CURRENT_CONFIG, and HKEY_USERS) actually represent information stored on disk.

Registry Hives

The first major divisions under each of the Registry trees are known as hives. According to Microsoft information, a *hive* is a discrete body of keys, subkeys, and values that is rooted at the top of the Registry hierarchy. For instance, the HKEY_LOCAL_MACHINE tree contains the following hives:

- ◆ HARDWARE
- ◆ SAM
- ◆ SECURITY
- ◆ SOFTWARE
- ◆ SYSTEM

Hives are the part of the Registry either stored on disk or constructed in memory. Of the five hives in the HKEY_LOCAL_MACHINE tree, only the first (HARDWARE) is constructed in memory when your system is first started. The other four hives represent information stored on disk.

Registry Keys

Registry hives are broken down into *keys*, which are organizational units for Registry information. Keys are analogous to folders on your hard drive in that both are designed to contain information.

Each key within the Registry can contain values and subkeys. In turn, the subkeys can contain additional values and subkeys. Just as disk-drive folders can contain files and additional folders, the keys under each hive can contain values and subkeys. This structure is the basis of the hierarchical organization of information in the Registry.

Registry Values

Values within a key (or subkey) contain data. This data consists of the current setting (or settings) for the value. For example, a value may contain the TCP/IP port used by IIS or the IP addresses that you don't want accessing your system.

Data can be of five basic types:

- ◆ **REG_BINARY.** Numeric information that can be of any length.

- ◆ **REG_DWORD.** Numeric information that is limited to a length of 32 bits.
- ◆ **REG_EXPAND_SZ.** String information that can be any length and whose length can change over time. Normally, this data type is used for system and program variables.
- ◆ **REG_MULTI_SZ.** A series of string values, each separated by a NULL character. This data type is typically used for information lists, such as those displayed in drop-down lists. It is also used for multiline messages.
- ◆ **REG_SZ.** A string value that can be of any length but is static; its value does not change.

In addition, applications can define their own special types of data. The exact type of data maintained for a value is determined by that value's use.

Editing the Registry

There are many ways in which the information in the Registry can be changed. First, many of the programs that you use every day (including IIS) change the information stored in the Registry. Second, you can use configuration programs to change Registry information. For example, when you use a Control Panel applet or the Internet Services Manager, you change information stored in the Registry.

The final way to change the Registry is with a special program known as a Registry Editor. Many places in this book have directed you to change Registry entries in order to modify specific features of IIS. Consequently, you probably already know how to use the Registry Editor. What you may not know is that Windows NT typically installs two different Registry Editors on your system, out of three possible choices:

- ◆ Windows NT Registry Editor
- ◆ Windows 3.*x* Registry Editor
- ◆ Windows 95 Registry Editor

These Registry Editor names do not refer to the actual Registries that they edit; instead, they refer to the interface that is used in the Registry Editor. All three Registry Editors enable you to make changes to the same Windows NT Registry.

The Windows NT Registry Editor is installed on all Windows NT systems. The other Registry Editor that is installed depends on how your system was configured when you installed NT. If either of the following conditions are met, then the Setup program installs the Windows 3.*x* version of the editor:

- ◆ You install Windows NT in a directory that already contains Windows 3.*x*.
- ◆ You are upgrading an earlier version of Windows NT, and that earlier version was originally an upgrade to Windows 3.x.

Thus the way to make sure that the Windows 95 Registry Editor is installed is to upgrade your Windows 95 system to Windows NT—or to start with a fresh install of the operating system (not an upgrade).

Because the Registry Editors are fundamentally different, they are discussed individually in the following sections. The steps used elsewhere in this book for editing the Registry reflect using the Windows 95 Registry Editor interface; it is the cleanest and easiest interface to use. The usage information in the following sections is provided so that you can at least know how to use the two major Registry Editor interfaces provided on your system.

The Windows NT Registry Editor

The Windows NT Registry Editor is installed on all systems and is patterned after the program that has been available since Windows NT was first released. This editor is provided for users with a Windows NT background who may be comfortable with the interface. To run the Windows NT Registry Editor, follow these steps:

1. Choose the <u>R</u>un option from the Start menu. This action displays the Run dialog box.
2. Type **regedt32** in the <u>O</u>pen field. (Regedt32 is the name of the Registry Editor program.)
3. Click on the OK button to display the Registry Editor, as shown in Figure 28-1.

The interface used in the Windows NT Registry Editor is similar to other Windows NT tools, although it does not take full advantage of the slick Windows NT 4.0 interface. The program window contains five other windows, one for each Registry tree. Within a tree window, the display is divided. At the left side of the window, you can see the keys of the Registry tree. In the right side, you can see any data that are stored in a key.

Finding Information

The sheer size of the Registry and the amount of information it contains means that you must know what you want to edit before you begin poking around, especially if you are using the Windows NT Registry Editor. Despite the amount of information

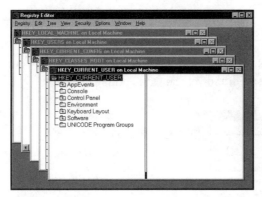

FIGURE 28-1

The Windows NT Registry Editor displays each tree in its own window.

in the Registry, the program does not have a good find feature. Although you can search for information, you can do so only at a key level; you cannot search the contents of the keys. To search for something, choose the Find Key option from the View menu. This action displays the Find dialog box, shown in Figure 28-2.

FIGURE 28-2

You can search the Registry for different keys.

In the Find What field, you enter exactly what you want to find. At the bottom of the dialog box, you can specify whether the Find should be case sensitive and whether only whole words matches should be returned.

You can also search forward or backward through the current tree. When you click on the Find Next button, the Registry Editor attempts to find a key matching the string that you entered. If a match is found, it is highlighted in the tree windows.

Editing Values

You change Registry settings by changing the contents of a value. Use one of these methods to edit a value:

◆ Double-click on the value name in the right side of the tree window.

◆ Click on the value name and press Enter.

Both methods produce the same results; you are shown a dialog box that allows you to edit the information in the value. The type of dialog box you see depends on the type of data contained in the value you are editing. As an example, if you are editing a value that contains string data, the editing dialog box appears, as shown in Figure 28-3.

When you are finished making changes in the value, click on the OK button. The information is immediately saved, and you can edit additional values.

FIGURE 28-3

The dialog box used to edit values depends on the type of data being edited.

Creating Keys or Values

Depending on the needs of your system, you can add new values to the Registry or even add new keys. (You cannot add new hives; these are set in stone by the operating system.) The Registry Editor enables you to quickly and easily add values or keys.

To add a key, select the existing hive or key under which the new key should appear. You should select the hive or key in the left side of a tree window. (This concept is the same as using the Explorer to add a new folder.)

As an example, suppose that you want to add a new key to the HKEY_LOCAL_MACHINE\SYSTEM\CurrentControlSet\Services\InetInfo key. Just follow these steps:

1. Make sure that the HKEY_LOCAL_MACHINE tree window is selected.
2. Move to the left side of the window; then, locate and select the \SYSTEM\CurrentControlSet\Services\InetInfo key.
3. Choose the Add Key option from the Edit menu. This action displays the Add Key dialog box, shown in Figure 28-4.

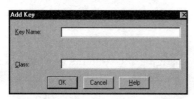

FIGURE 28-4

The Add Key dialog box is where you define the name of a new key.

4. Enter the name for your new key in the Key Name field. (You can ignore the Class field; it is not really used in the Windows NT Registry Editor.)
5. Click on the OK button. The new key is added within the currently selected hive or key.

At this point, you have created a new key. You can then add values to the new key following much the same process (only you select the Add Value option from the Edit menu). The information that you add to the Registry remains there until it is either changed by you or by a program you may be using.

The Windows 95 Registry Editor

Chances are good that the Windows 95 Registry Editor is installed on your system. If not (if the Windows 3.*x* Registry Editor was installed instead), you can install this version by copying the following files from your Windows NT Workstation 4.0 CD-ROM:

◆ REGEDIT.EXE

◆ REGEDIT.HLP

◆ REGEDIT.CNT

You can install these files to any directory that you want. However, if the Windows 3.*x* Registry Editor is installed on your system, Microsoft recommends that you do not copy the Windows 95 Registry Editor to your system directory (typically, c:\winnt). The reason is that you may overwrite the Windows 3.*x* Registry Editor.

When you are ready to run the Windows 95 Registry Editor, follow these steps:

1. Choose the Run option from the Start menu. This action displays the Run dialog box.

2. Type **regedit** in the Open field. (Regedit is the name of the Windows 95 Registry Editor program.)

3. Click on the OK button to display the Registry Editor, as shown in Figure 28-5.

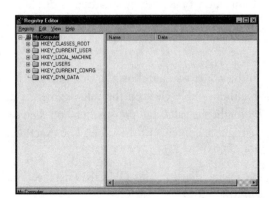

FIGURE 28-5

The Windows 95 Registry Editor uses a tree organization to represent the entire Registry.

The interface used in the Windows 95 Registry Editor is much simpler than the interface of the Windows NT Registry Editor. The Registry Editor window has two parts: the left part displays the different trees, hives, and keys of the Registry, and the right part displays the values.

Finding Information

Because the Registry varies from system to system and is so large, it is often difficult to locate exactly what you want to edit. Later in this chapter, you learn of the different places where IIS stores information in the Registry, but the Windows 95 Registry Editor includes a handy search command that makes finding detailed information a breeze. You start this command by choosing Find from the Edit menu. The Find dialog box is shown in Figure 28-6.

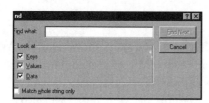

FIGURE 28-6

The Windows 95 Registry Editor allows you to search every part of the Registry.

In the Find What field, you enter exactly what you want to find. In the middle of the dialog box, you specify where the Registry Editor should look for the information: Keys, Values, or Data. When you click on the Find Next button, the Registry Editor attempts to find the string that you entered.

If the Registry Editor finds a match, it is highlighted in one of the editor windows, depending on where the information was found. For example, if the match was found in a key name, the information is displayed in the left portion of the editor window. Conversely, if the match was found in a value, the information is displayed in the right portion.

Editing Values

Most editing tasks take place in the values that are shown in the right portion of the editor window. To edit a value, either double-click on the value name (in the right side of the editor window) or highlight the value and press Enter. You then see a dialog box that prompts you to change the contents of the value. The exact dialog box that you see depends on the data type of the value.

For example, if you are changing a value that contains DWORD data, you see a dialog box similar to the one shown in Figure 28-7.

When you are done making changes, click on OK to change the Registry value.

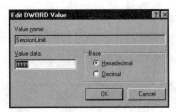

FIGURE 28-7

You can edit any values contained in the Registry.

Adding Keys or Values

The Windows 95 Registry Editor enables you to quickly and easily add new keys or values to the Registry. To add a key, select the existing hive or key under which the new key should appear. You should select the hive or key that is in the left side of the editor window. Then choose the New option from the Edit menu and select the Key option. The new key is added, and you can change its name as desired.

You can add a value to an existing key in much the same way. To add a value, follow these steps:

1. Look in the left side of the editor window for the key in which you want to place the new value.

2. Choose the New option from the Edit menu. This action displays a submenu of items you can create.

3. Click on the choice that represents the type of value you want to create. (You have three choices: String Value, Binary Value, or DWORD Value.) When you make your choice, a new value appears in the right side of the editor window.

4. Change the name of the new value to the name you want to use.

5. Edit the value (as described in the previous section) so that it contains the information desired.

The Registry Entries

When you install IIS on your system, a great number of keys and entries are added to the Registry. Sometimes, keeping track of all the changes can be frustrating. In most instances, however, the various IIS configuration programs are all you ever need to make changes to the Registry.

The following sections detail the various Registry entries that have meaning for IIS. Note that, on your system, some of these entries may not exist. If you have a need for the entry, you can create it using the Registry Editor of your choice.

CAUTION

Editing the Registry, although doing so is quick and easy, can be fraught with unseen danger. Simply misspelling a word or inadvertently deleting an entry can disable your entire system. Whenever possible, make your changes using a tool other than the Registry Editor. If you must edit the Registry directly, make sure that you have a complete system backup or a Registry backup before making your changes.

Global Registry Entries

The Registry entries that affect all portions of IIS are contained in the HKEY_ LOCAL_MACHINE\SYSTEM\CurrentControlSet\Services\InetInfo\Parameter s key. The various entries are detailed in Table 28-1.

Web Server Registry Entries

The Web server is arguably the most-used portion of IIS. When the Web server is installed, quite a few entries are automatically added to the Registry. The entries shown in Table 28-2 are placed in the HKEY_LOCAL_MACHINE|\SYSTEM \|CurrentControlSet\Services\W3SVC\Parameters key.

FTP Service Registry Entries

The FTP service utilizes many different Registry entries to control how the service functions. Most of the entries shown in Table 28-3 are controlled through the Internet Service Manager. These values are available in the HKEY_LOCAL_ MACHINE\SYSTEM\CurrentControlSet\Services\FTPSVC\Parameters key.

ASP Server Registry Entries

The ASP Registry entries are an adjunct to the Web server entries. The ASP entries are stored in HKEY_LOCAL_MACHINE\SYSTEM\CurrentControlSet\ Services\ W3SVC\ASP\Parameters and are described in Table 28-4.

Table 28-1 Global Registry Entries

Value	Data Type	Range	Default Value	Meaning
CacheSecurity Descriptor	DWORD	0–1	0	Specifies whether security descriptors are cached for file objects. The default is disabled (0).
CheckCert Revocation	DWORD	0–1	0	Specifies whether IIS checks client certificates for revocation. The default is disabled (0).
Disable MemoryCache	DWORD	0–1	0	Specifies whether server caching is enabled. The default is disabled (0) and can not be changed with the Internet Service Manger.
ListenBackLog	DWORD	1–unlimited	25	Specifies the maximum number of active connections to hold in the queue.
MaxConcurrency	DWORD	0–0xFFFFFFFF	0	Specifies the number of threads that IIS can exe cute per processor installed in the server. The default value of 0 allows IIS to make the determination.
MaxPoolThreads	DWORD	0–0xFFFFFFFF	10	Specifies the number of pool threads to be created per processor.
MinFileKbSec	DWORD	1–8192	1000	Specifies a divisor rate used to calculate a timeout for a connection. Note that the value is specified in bytes per second, not Kb per second, as the name implies.
ObjectCacheTTL	DWORD	0–0x7FFFFFFF	30	Specifies the Time To Live (TTL) setting, which defines the length of time (in seconds) that objects are held in cached memory. Setting the value to 0xFFFFFFFF turns off TTL, which means objects to remain in the cache until they are overwritten.

Table 28-1 Global Registry Entries (continued)

Value	Data Type	Range	Default Value	Meaning
PoolThread Limit	DWORD	0–0xFFFFFFFF		Specifies the maximum number of pool threads that can be created in the system. The default is 2 for every megabyte of RAM in your system.
ThreadTimeout	DWORD	0–0xFFFFFFFF	0x00015180 (24 hours)	Specifies the amount of time (in seconds) an input-output processing thread should be maintained even if there is no I/O activity on the system.
UserTokenTTL	DWORD	0–0x7FFFFFFF	0x00000384 (15 minutes)	Specifies the time (in seconds) that user security tokens are allowed to remain alive in the cache.

Table 28-2 Web Server Registry Entries

Value	Data Type	Range	Default Value	Meaning
AcceptByteRanges	DWORD	0, 1	1	Specifies whether the server can process the "Range" header for type "bytes:", according to the Internet specification for such request types. The default is enabled (1).
AllowGuestAccess	DWORD	0, 1	1	Specifies whether Guest logons are permitted. The default is allowed (1).
AllowSpecial CharsInShell	DWORD	0, 1	0	Specifies whether the Cmd.exe special characters (such as &) are allowed on the command line when running batch files (bat and cmd files). The default is disabled (0). Because these special characters can pose a security risk, you should not enable this capability.

Table 28-2 Web Server Registry Entries (continued)

Value	Data Type	Range	Default Value	Meaning
DLCCookieMenu DocumentString	String			Specifies the name of the host menu for clients that support cookies, but not HOST headers.
DLCCookieName STring	String			Specifies the name of a cookie sent to down-level clients, allowing the server to route an HTTP request to the proper Web site.
DLCHostNameSTring	String			Specifies the name of a Web site containing the down-level host menu. The menu is stored in `DLCCookeie MenuDocumentString` and is a document listing all the Web sites sharing a single IP address. The user selects a server from this menu.
DLCMenuString	String			Specifies the string used by the server to check all down-level requests by a client.
DLCMungeMenu DocumentString	String			Specifies the file used with down-level clients that do not support cookies to request the proper URL.
DLCSupport	DWORD	0, 1	0	Specifies whether down-level clients will be supported. This entry is useful only when a site needs to support older clients that don't support the use of the HOST headers to access multiple Web sites using a single IP address.
EnableSvcLoc	DWORD	0, 1	1	Specifies whether IIS services can register with the Windows NT service locator, which allows the Internet Service Manager to find the services. The default is enabled (1).

Table 28-2 Web Server Registry Entries (continued)

Value	Data Type	Range	Default Value	Meaning
LogErrorRequests	DWORD	0, 1	1	Specifies whether to record errors in the log file. The default is enabled (1).
LogSuccessful Requests	DWORD	0, 1	1	Specifies whether successful activities should be recorded in the log file. The default is enabled (1).
SSIEnableCmd Directive	DWORD	0, 1	1	Specifies whether the `#exec cmd` directive is enabled. This value is not created by default and must be created to allow IIS to use the `#exec cmd` directive in server-side includes.
TryExceptDisable	DWORD	0, 1	0	Specifies whether exception caching is enabled when calling the `HttpExtension proc()` of an ISAPI application. This entry should be enabled only for debugging ISAPI applications.
UploadReadAhead	DWORD	0 - 0x800 00000	0x0000C000	Specifies the default amount the server will read ahead when a client posts data to the server before passing control to the application.
UsePoolThreadForCGI	DWORD	0, 1	1	Specifies whether to use a server pool thread to do CGI processing.

Table 28-3 Ftp Service Registry Entries

Value	Data Type	Range	Default Value	Meaning
AllowGuestAccess	DWORD	0, 1	1	Specifies whether guest logons are permitted.
AnnotateDirectories	DWORD	0, 1	0	Specifies whether directory annotation is enabled. The default (0) is for directory annotation to be disabled.

Table 28-3 Ftp Service Registry Entries (continued)

Value	Data Type	Range	Default Value	Meaning
EnablePortAttack	DWORD	0, 1	0	Specifies whether ports other than the default ftp port (20) are allowed to be used. By default, no other ports can be used. If you set this value to 1, then other ports can be used and the security at your site is compromised.
EnableSvcLoc	DWORD	0, 1	1	Specifies whether IIS services can register with the Windows NT service locator, which allows the Internet Service Manager to find the services. The default is enabled (1).
LowercaseFiles	DWORD	0, 1	0	Specifies whether directory listings are considered all lowercase for doing comparisons and searches.

Table 28-4 ASP Server Registry Entries

Value	Data Type	Range	Default Value	Meaning
ProcessorThreadMax	DWORD	1 - 200	10	Specifies the number of threads to create per processor.
RequestQueueMax	DWORD	1 - 0xFFFFFFFF	0x0000001F4	Specifies the maximum number of script requests maintained in the request queue, available for each thread.

Index Server Registry Entries

The Microsoft Index Server places a good number or entries in the Registry. The entries detailed in Table 28-5 are contained in the HKEY_LOCAL_MACHINE\SYSTEM\CurrentControlSet\Control\contentindex key.

Table 28-5 Index Server Registry Entries

Value	Data Type	Range	Default Value	Meaning
CiCatalogFlags	DWORD	0 - 2	0	Controls how Index Server handles notifications. If set to 0 (the default), then notifications are handled normally. If set to 1, then notifications for remote UNC paths are turned off. If set to 2, then local path notifications are turned off.
DaemonResponse Timeout	DWORD	1 - 120	5	Timeout value (in minutes) to determine whether the CiDaemon process is looping because of a corrupted file.
EventLogFlags	DWORD	0 - 7	2	Controls the generation of specific event log messages.
FilterContents	DWORD	0, 1	1	Specifies filtering to take place. The default (1) means contents and properties are filtered. If set to 0, only properties are filtered.
FilterDelay Interval	DWORD	0 - 600	20	Specifies the length of time to wait when the number of documents to filter equals the FilterRemainingThreshold setting in seconds.
Filter Directories	DWORD	0, 1	0	Specifies whether directories are filtered. The default (0) does not filter directories; 1 does.
FilterFiles WithUnknown Extensions	DWORD	0, 1	1	Specifies whether only files with registered extensions are filtered. The default (1) means that any files are filtered, whereas 0 means that only registered file types are filtered.
FilterRemaining Threshold	DWORD	0 - 320	2	Specifies a value that determines whether a delay should be allowed when the number of documents to be filtered is less than the value of this entry.
FilterRetries	DWORD	1 - 10	4	Specifies the maximum number of times a file is retried if failures occur while trying to filter it.

Table 28-5 Index Server Registry Entries (continued)

Value	Data Type	Range	Default Value	Meaning
FilterRetry Interval	DWORD	2 - 240	30	Specifies the number of seconds between attempts to filter the contents of a file being used by another process.
ForcedNetPath ScanInterval	DWORD	10 - unlimited	120	Specifies the interval, in minutes, between forced scans on directories.
Generate Characterization	DWORD	0, 1	1	Specifies whether automatic generation of abstracts is done. The default (1) enables automatic generation.
IsapiDefault CatalogDirectory	String			Specifies the default content index catalog directory.
IsapiMaxEntries InQueryCache	DWORD	0 - 100	10	Specifies the maximum number of cached queries.
IsapiQueryCache PurgeInterval	DWORD	1 - 120	5	Specifies the time interval (in minutes) a query cache item will remain alive.
IsapiRequest QueueSize	DWORD	1 - 100000	16	Specifies the maximum number of Web query requests to queue when busy with other queries.
IsapiRequest ThresholdFactor	DWORD	1 - 100000	3	Specifies the number of threads per processor beyond which query requests are queued.
IsIndexing NNTPSvc	DWORD	0 - 1	1	Specifies whether the index catalog should be configured to work with the NNTP service.
IsIndexing W3SVC	DWORD	0 - 1	1	Specifies whether the index catalog should be configured to work with IIS.
MasterMerge CheckpointInterval	DWORD	256 - 4096	256	Specifies how much work (data written to the new master index, in kilobytes) to redo in case a master merge is paused and restarted.
MasterMergeTime	DWORD	0 - 1439	0	Specifies the time at which master merge will occur. This entry is stored as the number of minutes after midnight.

Table 28-5 Index Server Registry Entries (continued)

Value	Data Type	Range	Default Value	Meaning
MaxActiveQuery Threads	DWORD	1 - 1000	2	Specifies the maximum number of query threads. This entry establishes the maximum number of concurrently processed asynchronous queries.
MaxActive RequestThreads	DWORD	1 - 1000	2	Specifies the maximum number of threads to process requests such as queries and query result retrieval to the Content Index service.
MaxCachedPipes	DWORD	0-1000	3	Specifies the maximum number of unconnected pipes cached by the Content Index service.
Max Characterization	DWORD	20 - 500	320	Specifies the number of characters in the automatically generated characterization (abstract).
MaxFilesize Filtered	DWORD	0 - unlimited	256	Maximum size (in kilobytes) of a single file to be filtered using the default filter. If the default filter is used for a nonregistered file bigger than this number, only properties will be filtered.
MaxFilesize Multiplier	DWORD	4 - 0x FFFFFFFF	8	Specifies the maximum amount of data that can be generated from a single file, based on its size. This value is a multiplier. The default value of 4 means a file can generate up to four times its size in content index data.
MaxFreshCount	DWORD	1000 - 40000	5000	Specifies the maximum number of files whose latest indexed data is not in the master index. When this limit is reached, a master merge will be started.
MaxIdeal Indexes	DWORD	2 - 100	5	Specifies the maximum number of indexes considered acceptable in your system. When the number of indexes climbs above this number and the system is idle, then an annealing merge will take place to bring the total count of indexes to this number.

Table 28-5 Index Server Registry Entries (continued)

Value	Data Type	Range	Default Value	Meaning
MaxIndexes of	DWORD	10 - 150	50	Specifies the maximum number persistent indexes in the catalog. If this number is exceeded, a shadow merge will be performed to bring the total below this number.
MaxMerge Interval	DWORD	1 - 60	10	Sleep time (in minutes) between merges.
MaxPending Documents	DWORD	1 - 50000	32	The number of pending documents to be filtered before considering CI out-of-date for property queries.
MaxQuery ExecutionTime	DWORD	50 - infinite	10000	Maximum execution time of a query, in milliseconds. If a query takes more than this amount of CPU time, processing of it will be stopped and an error generated.
MaxQuery Timeslice	DWORD	1 - 1000	50	Maximum amount of time (in milliseconds) to execute a query in a single time slice. If more asynchronous queries are active than allowed query threads, then a query is put back on the pending queue after this time interval.
MaxQueueChunks	DWORD	10 - 30	20	Maximum number of chunks (memory blocks) in the buffer for keeping track of pending documents.
MaxRestriction Nodes	DWORD	1-4 billion	250	Specifies the number of nodes that can be processed in a single query. This entry is a direct reflection of the complexity of the query.
MaxRunning Webhits	DWORD	1 - 200	20	Specifies how many concurrent users can access the Index Server at any given point.

Table 28-5 Index Server Registry Entries (continued)

Value	Data Type	Range	Default Value	Meaning
MaxShadowFree ForceMerge	DWORD	5 - 25	15	Specifies a maximum percentage of the disk space that can be occupied by the shadow indexes. If the free space falls below the percentage in MinDiskFree ForceMerge and the shadow indexes occupy more space than specified in MaxShadow FreeForceMerge, a master merge is started.
MaxShadow IndexSize	DWORD	5 - unlimited	20	Specifies the percentage of disk space that can be occupied by the shadow indexes before a master merge is started.
MaxSimmultaneous Requests	DWORD	1-20000	100	Specifies the maximum number of simultaneous connections to support. This value should be at least as large as IsapiMax EntriesInQueryCache.
MaxWebhits CpuTime	DWORD	5 - 7200	10	Specifies the timeout value for the Webhits process, in seconds. If a document is not processed within the noted time, an error is generated.
MaxWordLists	DWORD	10 - 30	20	Maximum number of word lists that can exist at one time.
MaxWordlistSize	DWORD	10 - unlimited	14	Maximum amount of memory, in 128KB blocks, that can be consumed by an individual word list.
MinDiskFree ForceMerge	DWORD	5 - 25	15	Specifies the percentage of free disk space that acts as a threshold for starting a master merge. If the free space falls below this specification and the shadow indexes occupy more space than specified in MaxShadowFreeForceMerge, a master merge is started.
MinIdleQuery Threads	DWORD	0 - 1000	1	Minimum number of idle threads kept alive to process incoming queries.
MinIdleRequest Threads	DWORD	0 - 1000	1	Specifies the minimum number of threads kept alive to await processing incoming requests to the Content Index service.

Table 28-5 Index Server Registry Entries (continued)

Value	Data Type	Range	Default Value	Meaning
MinMergeIdleTime Threads	DWORD	10 - 100	90	Specifies the average percentage of free CPU time that must exist before an annealing merge can be performed.
MinSizeMerge bined	DWORD Wordlists	1024 - 10240		1024Specifies the minimum com- size of word lists (in kilobytes) that will force a shadow merge.
MinWordlist Memory	DWORD	1 - 10	5	Minimum free memory (in megabytes) for word list creation.
NNTPSvcInstance	DWORD	1 - 0xffffffff	1	Identifies the instance of the NNTP server being indexed by the catalog. Each virtual server is identified by a unique number.
PropertyStore memory	DWORD BackupSize	32 - 5000000		1024Specifies the amount of used to back up the property cache, using system pages. Intel based machines use 4K pages, whereas Alpha machines use 8K pages.
PropertyStore buffers MappedCache	DWORD	0 - unlimited		16Maximum size of memory (in 64-KB pages) for the property cache.
RequestTimeout	DWORD	0 - 1000000000	10000	Specifies the amount of time in milliseconds a query client should wait before failing to connect to an instance of the Content Index service. A client will fail immed- iately if the service is not running.
ThreadClass Filter	DWORD	20, 40, 80, 100	Idle Priority Class	Specifies the priority class of the CiDaemon process. The value 20 is Normal Priority Class, 40 is Idle Priority Class, 80 is High Priority Class, and 100 is Real-Time Priority Class.
ThreadPriority Filter	DWORD			Specifies the priority of the filtering thread within the CiDaemon process.
ThreadPriority Merge	DWORD			Specifies the priority of the merge thread within the CiDaemon process.
W3SvcInstance	DWORD	1 - 0xffffffff	1	Identifies the instance of the Web server being indexed by the catalog. Each virtual server is identified by a unique number.

Table 28-5 Index Server Registry Entries (continued)

Value	Data Type	Range	Default Value	Meaning
Webhits DisplayScript	DWORD	0 - 2	1	Determines whether scripting code is displayed in results when the virtual directory being searched contains script files. 0 specifies no script highlights. 1 returns script highlights for ASP files, but not for Perl files. A value of 2 returns hit highlights for all scripts.

SMTP Service Registry Entries

The SMTP Server Registry entries are to control the e-mails service included with IIS. The SMTP entries are stored in HKEY_LOCAL_MACHINE\ SYSTEM\CurrentControlSet\Services\SmtpSvc\Parameters and are described in Table 28-6.

Table 28-6 SMTP Server Registry Entries

Value	Data Type	Default Value	Meaning
Directory BuffSize	DWORD	1000	Specifies the maximum memory buffer used while processing messages from the Pickup directory.
DnsSocket Timeout	DWORD	60000	Specifies the maximum amount of time, in milliseconds, to wait for a response from the DNS server before retrying.
MaxAddress Objects	DWORD	100000	Specifies the maximum number of address objects that represent addresses in memory.
MaxDirectory Buffers	DWORD	2000	Specifies the maximum number of buffers used during processing to store messages from the Pickup directory.
MaxMail Objects	DWORD	100000	Specifies the maximum number of mail objects that represent messages in memory.
NumDns ResolverSockets	DWORD	10	Specifies the number of sockets the SMTP service opens to communicate with a DNS server.

NNTP Service Registry Entries

The NNTP Server also includes a few Registry entries to control the way your news server works. These NNTP entries are stored in HKEY_LOCAL_ MACHINE\ SYSTEM\CurrentControlSet\Services\NntpSvc\Parameters and are described in Table 28-7.

Table 28-7 SMTP Server Registry Entries

Value	Data Type	Range	Default Value	Meaning
Article TimeLimit	DWORD		4 (weeks)	Specifies the age limit for an article to be accepted from a client. All articles older than this time are rejected.
EnableNntp	DWORD		1	A nonzero value specifies that all postings will be stamped with the NNTP Posting Host header. This value includes the news client's domain name, which is useful in tracking posts.
Generate ErrFiles	DWORD		0	A zero value specifies that err files are not generated. Changing this value will generate err files for all failed postings.
History Expiration	DWORD		4	Specifies the interval in seconds for storing an article's Message Id in the History table using the formula HistoryExpiration*60*60*24.
HonorApproved Header	DWORD		1	A nonzero value requires the name of the newsgroup moderator in the Approved header on moderated postings. A zero value allows all Approved headers on moderated postings.
HonorClient MessageID	BOOL	True or False	True	Specifies whether the NNTP server should use available client provided Message Ids.
MailFromHeader t	DWORD	0 — 2	0	For moderated postings, configures the From header of a message mailed to the moderator. The values are 0 for blank, 1 for the news server administrator's address, and 2 uses the contents of the message.

Table 28-7 SMTP Server Registry Entries (continued)

Value	Data Type	Range	Default Value	Meaning
NewsCrawler Time	DWORD		30	Specifies the interval (in minutes) used to search for expired articles. Outdated articles are then discarded.
NumExpire Threads	DWORD		4	Specifies the number of threads used to expire messages.
Shutdown Latency	DWORD		2	Specifies, in minutes, the maximum time used by NNTP for cleaning up during shutdown.
StartupLatency	DWORD		2	Specifies, in minutes, the maximum time used by NNTP to wait for an instance of the service to start.

PART VII

Additional Content Considerations

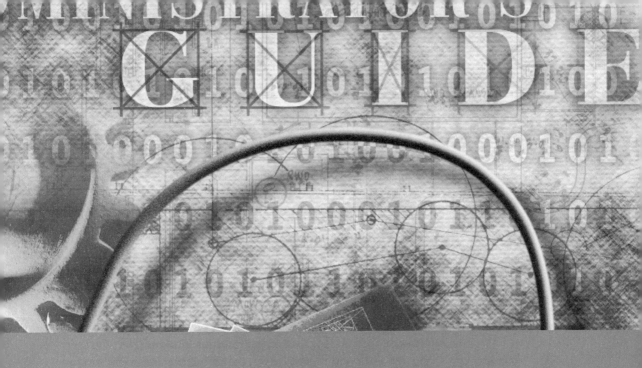

Chapter 29

Indexing Your Content

In This Chapter

◆ Understanding Index Server

◆ Indexing Documents

◆ Creating Your Query Interface

◆ Searching Indexed Documents

◆ Maintaining Your Indexes

In Part IV, three chapters explained how you can publish dynamic database information at your Web site. What happens, however, when the Web site itself is the database? What if you want people to be able to find information in existing Web pages or in documents you make available over the Web?

This chapter focuses on the tool that enables you to handle this problem: Microsoft Index Server. Here you learn how to manage this tool and how to create the support files that make it useful.

Understanding the Index Server

Microsoft Index Server is an IIS component that enables you to index a wide variety of documents and to make those indexes available on the Web. The user can then query the indexes to discover which documents meet their criteria. Index Server enables you to index not only plain-text documents but also documents in HTML, Word, PowerPoint, and Excel format. You can also install filters that enable you to include documents stored in other file formats. The new Index Server 2.0 will also index your news and e-mail servers, if you are using these IIS components.

To understand how Index Server works, and indeed to understand the balance of this chapter, you must know a few terms:

◆ **Corpus.** The entire body of documents indexed by Index Server.

◆ **Query.** The actual collection of words and phrases that define the characteristics of what is being looked for.

◆ **Scope.** The specification, determined by a user, that identifies where to conduct a search.

◆ **Restriction.** A combination of keywords or specifications used to narrow the result set returned from a query.

◆ **Result set.** The subset of documents within the scope that meets the demands of the query.

◆ **Catalog.** A directory (Catalog.wci) that contains all the files used by Index Server.

One other thing to understand about Index Server is that just like all the other components of IIS, there are multiple ways to control the service. Index Server can be controlled using the MMC or an HTML interface.

Using the MMC Interface

Index Server includes a snap-in for use with MMC. The snap-in gives you full access for controlling Index Server. When you installed Index Server, a tool was included for use with MMC in which the snap-in is preinstalled.

You can run this tool from the Start menu by selecting Programs, Windows NT 4.0 Option Pack, Microsoft Index Server and Index Server Manager. This action starts MMC with the predefined Index Server tool, as shown in Figure 29-1.

FIGURE 29-1

MMC uses a snap-in to control Index Server.

Using the Internet Service Manager

The Index Server snap-in can also be added to the Internet Service Manager. This feature enables you to control Index Server as well as all other aspects of your Web site from a central location. After the snap-in is installed, simply find the Index Server folder to access its properties. The following steps describe how to install the Index Server snap-in:

1. Choose the Programs option from the Start menu. This action displays the Programs menu.

2. Choose Windows NT 4.0 Option Pack, Microsoft Internet Information Server and then Internet Service Manager. This starts the Internet Service Manager.

3. Choose Add/Remove Snap-in from the Console menu. This action displays the Add/Remove Snap-in dialog box, shown in Figure 29-2.

4. Click on the Add button at the bottom of the dialog box. This action displays the Add Snap-in dialog box, shown in Figure 29-3.

FIGURE 29-2

The Internet Service Manager can be customized with snap-ins.

FIGURE 29-3

MMC maintains a list of available snap-ins.

5. Double-click on the Index Server icon. A new Connect to Computer dialog box opens; it looks like Figure 29-4.

6. Select the Another Computer option and specify a networked computer with an Index Server installation. Otherwise, use the default Local Computer option to control a local Index Server installation.

7. Click on the Finish button to return to the Add/Remove Snap-in dialog box, shown in Figure 29-3.

8. Click on OK to add the snap-in and return to the Internet Service Manager.

9. Close the Internet Service Manager when done.

10. Select Yes when prompted to save the console settings.

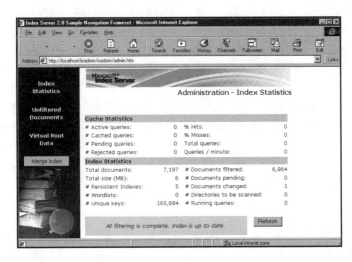

FIGURE 29-4

The Index Server snap-in connects to a local or networked computer.

Using the HTML Interface

Index Server can also be controlled through an HTML interface. By default, this interface is usable only on the local machine. This interface is stored with the IIS HTML interface; see Chapter 24 for information on changing the security of this directory.

You can run this tool from the Start menu by selecting Programs, Windows NT 4.0 Option Pack, Microsoft Index Server and Index Server Manager. This action starts the Index Server HTML interface in your default Web browser, as shown in Figure 29-5.

FIGURE 29-5

The Index Server HTML interface.

Indexing Documents

Index Server does its work by processing information stored in virtual directories. You already know about virtual directories and how to create them, so covering that process again, at this point, would be redundant. However, you should know that Index Server can work only with documents stored in virtual directories. Thus, to include documents in the index, you must include those documents in a virtual index or a subdirectory to a virtual index.

From the time that Index Server is first installed, it will constantly run in the background, indexing all of your virtual directories. This program is meant to be a totally automatic tool. However, to use it effectively, you still have to understand how it works. You will find more on selecting the directories to index in the section "Maintaining Your Indexes" at the end of this chapter.

How Indexing Is Done

Index Server creates an index in a way that does not disturb your other system operations. Indexing is done when files in the directories being indexed are changed, but only when the CPU is not busy. All indexing operations are done in the background while your other services complete other tasks.

The actual process that Index Server follows is fairly simple in concept. In practice, the indexing process goes through three main phases: filtering, word breaking, and normalization.

Filtering

The first step in indexing a document is filtering the source materials. Documents can be stored on a system in a variety of formats, including HTML format (Web documents), Microsoft Word format (your word processing documents), and Excel format (your spreadsheet documents). There may be many other document formats on your system, as well.

Index Server uses *content filters* to access information stored in different formats. These filters can read the source documents and extract the information necessary for later steps in the indexing process. By default, Index Server includes content filters for the following formats:

- ◆ Text files
- ◆ HTML files
- ◆ Microsoft Word files
- ◆ Microsoft Excel files
- ◆ Microsoft PowerPoint files

In addition, you can add various third-party filters. For example, Adobe has a filter for its popular PDF files. You can download the PDF filter from Adobe's Web site at **http://www.adobe.com**.

ONLINE ▶

Content filters are responsible for three primary functions:

- ◆ Extracting text
- ◆ Detecting language changes
- ◆ Processing objects

The first task simply means that the content filter converts information from the source format to a format that the later phases of the indexing process can use. The second function of the filtering stage is recognizing language shifts in the source document. This step occurs automatically as long as the language information is stored with the source document. The filter then passes this information, along with the text it has extracted, to the later phases of the indexing process. Index Server uses the language information to make sure that the proper word breakers and normalizers are loaded.

The content filter's final task is to process objects as they appear in the source documents. Using OLE, it is very possible for a source document to contain pieces and parts of other documents. For example, a Word document may include a portion of an Excel spreadsheet. The filter can recognize the source format of these objects and then switch to the proper secondary filter to process the object.

Word Breaking

Even though the content filters produce output that is different from the original source format, it is still not in a condition to be indexed. The next phase of indexing is called *word breaking,* which simply means examining the stream of words from the filter to determine which words go into the index.

Identifying words may sound like an easy task. After all, all you need to do is look for spaces and punctuation, right? To a degree, this answer is correct. However, Index Server works with many different languages, and each language handles words in a slightly different manner. In fact, some languages (such as Japanese) don't use spaces and punctuation to signal word breaks at all.

Index Server uses language-specific word breakers that understand how to convert the output of the content filters into valid words. The word breakers analyze text to identify words based on the language's structure and syntax. Index Server includes word breakers for the following languages:

- ◆ Dutch
- ◆ English (International)
- ◆ English (U.S.)
- ◆ French
- ◆ German
- ◆ Italian
- ◆ Japanese
- ◆ Spanish
- ◆ Swedish

Normalizing

When the word breakers are through, a module called a *text normalizer* takes over for the final stage of indexing. Basically, normalizers make the words uniform in their representation. Normalizing minimizes the amount of storage necessary for words in the index. These modules are responsible for performing the following tasks:

- ◆ Standardizing capitalization
- ◆ Removing unnecessary punctuation
- ◆ Removing noise words

Although the first two tasks of the normalizers are self-explanatory, the third function may not be. *Noise words* are words that are necessary to the syntax and grammar of the language, but don't have much meaning outside of their context. For instance, in English the common articles (a, an, the, at, and so on) and pronouns (he, she, you, I, and so on) are considered noise words. Every language has its own group of noise words that the normalizers strip from the word lists.

The noise word list maintained by Index Server for the English language comprises about 100 words. These words account for about half of the bulk of regular written text. Thus when the noise words are stripped out, the resulting text is about half its original size.

When the normalization phase is complete, the remaining words are added to the index.

Controlling Individual Web Documents

You can control the way in which individual Web documents are indexed by including special META tags in the header section of the HTML document.

You already know that HTML documents are divided into two sections: the header and the body. The header section is used to define global information that is not displayed, but that is used to manage the document. If you include the following META statement in the header of your document, Index Server ignores the document while indexing:

```
<META NAME="robots" CONTENT="noindex">
```

Remember that this technique applies only to HTML documents. Unfortunately, you cannot tag other types of documents (Word, Excel, or text) to prevent them from being indexed.

You can also use the META statement to control the language resources used when indexing. If you set the META statement's NAME property to ms.locale, you can use the

CONTENT field to determine which language Index Server will use. The following META statement tells Index Server to use the English language:

```
<META NAME="ms.locale" CONTENT="EN">
```

The CONTENT field can use either the text abbreviation or a decimal number to describe the language.

Creating Your Query Interface

In Chapter 18, you learned how to use IDC to access information in an ODBC data source. Index Server enables you to access information that it maintains in much the same manner. Instead of using IDC and HTX files, however, you use IDQ and HTX files. You then pull both files together using an HTML file for your query. The following sections describe exactly how to develop each type of interface file that Index Server uses.

Your IDQ file

Index Server requires that you create an IDQ file that specifies the index that you want to access and the parameters governing that access. An IDQ file is nothing but a normal ASCII text file with a filename extension of idq. It consists of two major parts: the Names section and the Query section.

The Names Section

The Names section of an IDQ file is optional, meaning that you do not have to include it in the file. The purpose of the section is to enable you to reference non-standard information in your Index Server query. Nonstandard information includes information such as the property summaries available in Microsoft Office documents. These can be accessed using a *globally unique identifier* (GUID).

NOTE

Constructing the Names section looks like a very confusing job, especially to nonprogrammers. Fortunately, you need to include the Names section only if you want to use some nonstandard information.

The structure of the Names section is as follows:

```
[Names]
DocTitle                                 = F29F85E0-4FF9-1068-AB91-08002B27B3D9 2
DocSubject( DBTYPE_STR¦DBTYPE_BYREF )     = F29F85E0-4FF9-1068-AB91-08002B27B3D9 3
DocAuthor( DBTYPE_STR¦DBTYPE_BYREF )      = F29F85E0-4FF9-1068-AB91-08002B27B3D9 4
```

This short example shows how you should put your Names section together. Each Names section entry has four possible columns—two to the left of the equal sign and two to the right. The first column is the name by which you want this information known. For example, the first item in this sample Names section uses the name DocTitle. Later, when you want to refer to the information, you simply use this name as you would any other variable or column name.

The second column in each entry is optional; it specifies the data type of the information. This column is enclosed within parentheses. Table 29-1 lists the various data types that you can use. If you omit the data type, then Index Server assumes that it is DBTYPE_WSTR¦DBTYPE_BYREF (a string passed by reference).

Notice that Table 29-1 includes several data types that seem redundant. For example, eight data types are integers. This repetition allows the data types to correspond to different ActiveX requirements for those pieces of information. Another value that you will often see, DBTYPE_BYREF, is not a data type at all; it controls the way that data is sent.

If you look back at the sample of the Names section, you can see that some items have a compound data type. For example, the second item uses a data type of (DBTYPE_STR¦DBTYPE_BYREF). The first part of this data type is the actual definition of how the data is to be treated (as a string), and the second part indicates that the data should be passed not as a value, but by reference. In this way, a pointer to the data is passed, not the data itself.

The first column to the right of the equal sign (the third column in each item) is the GUID for the application that is responsible for the information. In this example, the GUID refers to Microsoft Word. Different applications from different vendors have different GUIDs.

The final column is the PROPID, or property ID, of the property that you want to access within the application. This value is based on the property in question. You can also use a string for the PROPID, as long as you enclose the string in quotation marks.

Table 29-1 Data Types Used in the Names Section of an IDQ File

Data Type	Meaning
DBTYPE_I1	Integer
DBTYPE_UI1	Integer
DBTYPE_I2	Integer
DBTYPE_UI2	Integer
DBTYPE_I4	Integer
DBTYPE_UI4	Integer
DBTYPE_I8	Integer
DBTYPE_UI8	Integer
DBTYPE_R4	Real number
DBTYPE_R8	Real number
DBTYPE_CY	Currency
DBTYPE_DATE	Date
DBTYPE_BOOL	Boolean (TRUE or FALSE)
DBTYPE_STR	String
DBTYPE_WSTR	Unicode string
DBTYPE_BSTR	Basic string
DBTYPE_GUID	GUID
DBTYPE_VECTOR	Vector
VT_FILETIME	File date and time

So, how do you find out which information to use in the Names section? How can you know which data types, GUIDs, and properties to use? No definitive guide is available, but the best sources are in the software developer's kits (SDKs) for each product whose information Index Server can read. For example, if you want to know which information is permissible to use for Microsoft Word, then you need to refer to the Word SDK.

The Query Section

The Query section of the IDQ file is where you define the parameters of your actual query. The section consists of system variables, followed by an equal sign, and then the setting that you want to make for the variable. The following Query section is about as simple as you can get:

```
[Query]
CiScope=\
```

```
CiColumns=filename
CiRestriction=%CiRestriction%
CiTemplate=/Scripts/output.htx
```

Each of the four variables shown here is required in any IDQ file. They define the scope, columns returned, restrictions, and HTX file template to use. Table 29-2 lists the most common system variables you can use in the Query section of an IDQ file.

Table 29-2 System Variables Used in the Query Section of an IDQ File

Variable	Meaning
CiCatalog	Location of the index catalog.
CiColumns	List of columns available in the HTX file. Column names are separated by commas.
CiDeferNonIndexedTrimming	Can be **TRUE** or **FALSE**. Used to specify how much post-processing is done on a list of matches. You should set this variable to **TRUE** if the scope of your query is set to the virtual root (`CiScope=\`) and the query does not examine properties.
CiFlags	Specification of the depth of search. **DEEP** means the directory given in CiScope and all directories below it; **SHALLOW** means only the directory specified in CiScope.
CiForceUseCi	If **TRUE**, the query is forced to use the content index, even if it is out-of-date.
CiLocale	Defines the locale (language) used to issue the query.
CiMaxRecordsInResultSet	Maximum number of query results to return from a query.
CiMaxRecordsPerPage	Maximum number of records to display on a page.
CiRestriction	Query restriction.
CiScope	Query scope, which is the starting directory for the search as either a virtual or physical path name.
CiSort	Sort specification consisting of a series of columns followed by either [a] for ascending or [d] for descending order. Column specifications are separated by commas, as in CiSort=City[a], Phone[d].
CiTemplate	HTX file to use for query output.

You can find other variables (quite a few of them) in your online documentation.

The sample Query section also contains the following line:

```
CiRestriction=%CiRestriction%
```

In this case, the information on the right side of the equal sign is surrounded by percent (%) signs. This convention indicates that the name represents a parameter passed from the HTML file that is calling the IDQ file. IDQ files frequently use passable parameters.

Your HTX File

The HTX file you use with Index Server is very similar to the HTX files used with IDC. For the most part, HTX files look just like regular HTML files except that you can add some additional tags that define how the information returned by Index Server should be formatted. For example, the `<%begindetail%>` and `<%enddetail%>` tags indicate the beginning and end of your format section. (A format section is analogous to a single database record.) The use of the angle brackets and percent signs as delimiters identify the tag as an extended HTML tag instead of a regular HTML tag.

Within the format section, you use the `<%` and `%>` markers around column names to define where your output should appear. The column names are the same names you specified earlier in the Query section of the IDQ file.

As an example, consider the following HTX file. This simple file displays the query results for products that match a user's specific search specification. This file is contained in the support files as \Chap29\prod1.htx.

```
<html>
<head>
<title>Query Results</title>
</head>
<body>

<center><h1>Johnson Widget Co.</h1></center>
<p>The following items represent those which match your
specifications. All information is current as of today.

<%begindetail%>
<p>Document: <%DocTitle%>
```

```
<%ProdNum%>: <%ProdName%><br>
<%ListPrice%>
<%enddetail%>


</body>
</html>
```

Notice that the `<%begindetail%>` and `<%enddetail%>` tags enclose relatively few commands. These commands display a single record returned by the query. Column names are then used, again with `<%` and `%>` delimiters, to indicate what information is displayed for each record. If desired, your HTX file can also contain the same conditional tags that you can use with IDC.

The HTX implementation used for Index Server includes a rich selection of built-in variables. You can use these variables either in conditional statements or within the body of your HTX file. Table 29-3 lists the read-only variables that Index Server supports.

You can use these built-in variables to improve the appearance of the information returned by your HTX file. The following example (which is in the support files as \Chap29\prod2.htx) uses these variables.

```
<html>
<head>
<title>Query Results</title>
</head>
<body>


<center><h1>Johnson Widget Co.</h1></center>
<p>The following items represent those which match your
specifications. All information is current as of <%CiQueryDate%>.</p>


<%if CiMatchedRecordCount eq 0%>
    <p>No documents matched your specifications. </p>
<%else%>
    <h4>Documents <%CiFirstRecordNumber%> to <%CiLastRecordNumber%></h4>
<%endif%>
<%begindetail%>
<p>Document: <%DocTitle%>
<%ProdNum%>: <%ProdName%><br>
```

```
<%ListPrice%></p>
<%enddetail%>


</body>
</html>
```

Notice the use of the `CiMatchedRecordCount` variable in the `IF` statement. This variable enables you to determine, on-the-fly, whether any records satisfied the user's query. If not (as in this case), the variable tells you that no matching records were found. If matching records are found, then additional built-in variables indicate the record numbers being displayed.

Table 29-3 Read-Only Variables Available in Your HTX File

Variable Name	Meaning
CiBookmark	Reference to the first row on the page.
CiContainsFirstRecord	Contains 1 if this page contains the first record of the query results; 0 otherwise.
CiContainsLastRecord	Contains 1 if this page contain the last record of the query results; 0 otherwise.
CiCurrentPageNumber	Current page number of the query results.
CiCurrentRecordNumber	Current record number.
CiFirstRecordNumber	Record number of first record on the current page.
CiLastRecordNumber	Record number of last record on the current page.
CiMatchedRecordCount	Total number of records matching a query.
CiOutOfDate	Contains 1 if the content index is out of date; 0 otherwise.
CiQueryIncomplete	Contains 1 if the query could not be resolved using the content index and `CiForceUseCI` was set; 0 otherwise.
CiQueryTimedOut	Contains 1 if the query exceeded the time limit for execution; 0 otherwise.
CiQueryDate	Date the query was executed on the Web server.
CiQueryTime	Time the query was executed on the Web server.
CiQueryTimeZone	Time zone of the Web server.
CiRecordsNextPage	Number of records on the next page.
CiTotalNumberPages	Total number of pages used to contain query results.
CiVersionMajor	The major version number of Index Server.
CiVersionMinor	The minor version number of Index Server.

> **NOTE**
>
> The <%begindetail%> and <%enddetail%> block is outside the IF...THEN loop (rather than inside) because no detail will ever be displayed if no records are returned by the query.

Your HTML File

To create a query that works, you need to provide an HTML file (a regular Web document) that contains a link to the IDQ file that is used to define your query. The easiest solution is to simply include the IDQ file as the target of a form. The following HTML file, which is available in the support files as \Chap29\Widget.htm, illustrates this technique.

```
<html>
<head>
<title>Johnson Widget Company</title>
</head>
<body>


<center><h1>Search for Widget Answers</h1></center>


Welcome to Johnson Widget Company. We have many solutions
available for all your widget needs. If you would like to
search our database of widget-related documents, enter the
words or phrases that you want to search for, and then click
on the Submit Query button.


<br><hr><br>
<form method="post" action="/scripts/widget.idq">
    Enter words or phrases:
<input type="text" name="CiRestriction" size="50" maxlength="75">
<input type="submit" value="Submit Query">
</form>
<br><hr><br>


</body>
</html>
```

Notice that the `ACTION` attribute of the form points to an IDQ file. When the user clicks on the Submit Query button, the IDQ file is loaded and processed. The IDQ file then uses the HTX file to create output that displays the results of the query.

Searching Indexed Documents

After you install Index Server and create the three pieces necessary to use it (the IDQ, HTX, and HTML files), you are ready to do some searching. With this in mind, you can create the following IDQ file and place it in your Scripts directory. This file is stored in the support files as \Chap29\Sample.idq.

```
[Query]
CiScope=\
CiColumns=filename
CiRestriction=%CiRestriction%
CiTemplate=/Scripts/sample.htx
```

This IDQ file also points to an HTX file, which should also be located in your Scripts directory. You can create the following file from scratch, or you can find it as part of the support files as \Chap29\Sample.htx.

```
<html>
<head>
<title>Sample HTX file</title>
</head>
<body>

<h1>Query results</h1>

<%if CiLastRecordNumber eq 0%>
    <p>No documents matched your specifications. </p>

<%else%>
<ul>
<%begindetail%>
<li>Document: <%filename%>
<%enddetail%>
</ul>
<%endif%>
```

```
</body>
</html>
```

Finally, you need an HTML file to access your sample. The following sample HTML file can be stored in any directory that is accessible at your Web site. This file is stored in the support files as \Chap29\Sample.htm.

```
<html>
<head>
<title>Index Server Test</title>
</head>
<body>

<center><h1>Search for Site Information</h1></center>

<p><hr><p>
<form method="post" action="/scripts/sample.idq">
    Enter words or phrases:
<input type="text" name="CiRestriction" size="50" maxlength="75">
<input type="submit" value="Submit Query">
</form>
<p><hr><p>

</body>
</html>
```

When you view this HTML file in your Web browser, it is very simple indeed. Figure 29-6 shows what the user sees.

All the user needs to do is to enter a word or phrase that Index Server should look for. To see some results from your search, make sure that you enter a phrase that has a high probability of success. I entered the word *computer* as my search word, and the results are shown in Figure 29-7.

Notice that the output from this HTX file is very plain; there are no links or other devices to enable the user to actually access the information returned in the query. Nevertheless, the example illustrates how to use HTX files with Index Server and how the user views the returned information.

FIGURE 29-6

You can access Index Server through a regular Web form.

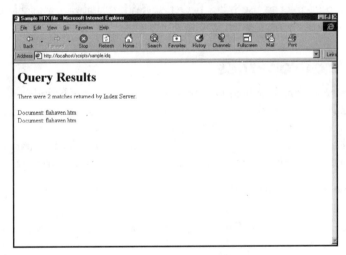

FIGURE 29-7

The results of an Index Server query are displayed using an HTX file.

Maintaining Your Indexes

Index Server is almost maintenance free. The server automatically indexes documents that change, updating information as necessary. However, you may need to specify the directories that Index Server should include in the index. When a file in one of these directories is changed, Windows NT actually notifies Index Server of the change. Notice that Index Server does not need to scan files to determine whether a change occurred. Instead, the operating system takes care of all the necessary notifications. Consequently, Index Server does not affect performance by periodically scanning for file changes.

When Index Server knows there has been a change, it simply makes note of the fact and then waits. The changed file may not be indexed right away; in fact, Index Server typically waits until a number of changes have been made, and then it looks for an opportunity to index the files. Indexing does not happen in preference to other activities on the server. Instead, Index Server works in the background, using CPU time as it becomes available. This approach makes perfect sense because you normally prefer to give priority to servicing other activities, such as answering requests across the Web.

The only time you should ever need to actively do something with Index Server is when one of the following events occurs:

♦ You need to add or delete a directory from those indexed by Index Server.

♦ You want to force Index Server to reindex your site.

In day-to-day management, these events occur very infrequently. The upshot is that you don't need to do a lot to use Index Server. Instead, it is always available in the background, awaiting the time when you need to use it.

Changing Index Properties

When Index Server is first installed, all virtual directories are set to be indexed. There are probably only two times when you would not want Index Server to index your directories. If you aren't going to use the search capabilities, you may as well turn them off. You may also decide to tell Index Server not to index the IIS documentation. You can specify whether a directory will be indexed or not using the following steps:

1. Choose the Programs option from the Start menu. This action displays the Programs menu.

2. Choose the Windows NT 4.0 Option Pack option from the Programs menu.

3. Choose the Internet Service Manager option from the Microsoft Internet Information Server submenu.

4. Double-click on the computer name in the scope pane that has the server you are configuring to open a list of directories.

5. Double-click on the site location, probably Default Web Site, to see a list similar to that in Figure 29-8.

6. Right-click on a directory, such as the IISHelp directory, and select Properties from the pop-up menu.

7. Make sure that you are looking at the Virtual Directories tab, as shown in Figure 29-9.

8. Uncheck the Index This Directory option in the middle of the property sheet. Index Server will no longer update information about this directory.

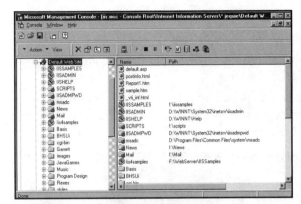

FIGURE 29-8

The Microsoft Management Console enables you to change your directories properties.

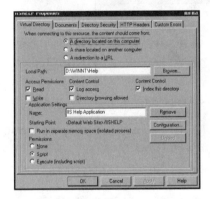

FIGURE 29-9

The property sheet gives full control over your virtual directories.

9. Click on OK to close the Properties dialog box.

10. Close the Internet Service Manager and save your changes when prompted.

Forcing an Indexing Pass

Index Server normally updates indexes during system "free time" to avoid disrupting routine system operations. However, you may want to force an indexing pass of your source documents to make sure that the indexes are as up-to-date as possible. Follow these steps to force an indexing pass:

1. Choose the Programs option from the Start menu. This action displays the Programs menu.

2. Choose the Windows NT 4.0 Option Pack option from the Programs menu. This action displays a list of submenus for the various services installed with IIS.

3. Choose the Index Server Manager option from the Microsoft Index Server submenu. This action starts your MMC and loads the Index Server Manager tool, as shown earlier in Figure 29-1.

4. Click on the plus next to Index Server on Local Machine folder to display the catalog's location in the scope pane.

5. Click on the plus next to the catalog to display the Directories and Properties folders in the scope pane.

6. Select the Directories folder. This action displays a list of directories to index in the results pane, shown in Figure 29-10. You may want to resize the amount of space used to display the directory's names.

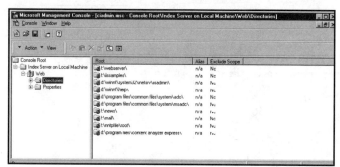

FIGURE 29-10

You can pick the directories that you want to index.

7. Right-click on a directory and choose Rescan from the pop-up menu. A dialog box asks whether you want a Full rescan.

8. Click on Yes to rescan the directory, or No to scan only those documents that have yet to be scanned.

9. Close the Index Server Manager when done.

At this point, Index Server processes the virtual directories you specified. You won't see any overt indication that the indexes are being updated because Index Server works in the background. If you open the Task Manager and look at the Processes tab, you can tell that Index Server is doing its work (see Figure 29-11). The length of time it takes to update your indexes depends on how much information you are indexing at your site.

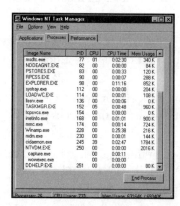

FIGURE 29-11

Index Server updates your indexes in the background.

Chapter 30

FTP Site Content

In This Chapter

◆ Setting Up a Directory Structure

◆ Files at Your Site

◆ Friendly Messages

◆ Directory Annotation

If you installed the FTP component of IIS, you have probably given some thought as to exactly what you want to offer at your site. FTP is a wonderfully universal way to make files available on the Internet. Even a person without access to a Web browser might have access to FTP. If the content of your site is of value, then people will have an interest in visiting and downloading information to their computers.

This chapter describes some techniques for building an FTP site. Here you learn not just how to structure your directories but also what to put in those directories to make your site easy to use.

Setting Up a Directory Structure

The directory structure you use on your FTP site can be very flexible. When you first installed your FTP server, you needed to specify a home directory. However, you may not have given the structure much thought. Before your FTP server has been operational very long, you should think about organization. Your directory structure affects how users access information at your site. The next several sections can assist you in determining how to structure your site.

Public Directories

Most people set up an FTP site because they want to make some type of files available to the public. In this case, you need to determine how you want those files to be accessed. Historically, most sites have stored public FTP files in a subdirectory called *pub.* This directory name has no special significance; it is simply a shorthand name for "public." Public files reside in or under the pub directory at most sites.

Within your public directory, you should plan the organization of your directories. If your site contains graphics or sound files, for example, you might organize the directories according to topic. Here is an example of a directory structure for such a site:

NOTE

Public directories are typically used for anonymous FTP connections. They contain the files you want others to access, download (hopefully), and use. Whether you include a pub directory is, obviously, up to you. If you are counting on people from a UNIX environment visiting your site, it doesn't hurt to include the directory. If you place it at the highest level in your site—right off the home directory—then well-behaved visitors will know that they should look through files only in the pub directory, not in other directories at the site.

```
pub
    graphics
        animals
        celebrities
        local
        products
            turbo
                gif
                jpeg
            excel
    sounds
        movies
        television
        products
            training
            descriptions
        radio
            midi
            wav
```

As with the hard drive on your computer system, the directory structure you use at your FTP site is entirely up to you. In general, however, you should make the structure general enough to not be overbearing (too many directories), but specific enough to provide a moderate degree of organization to the files. You can tread this fine line if you simply think about how site visitors will want to access the information you publish.

User Directories

When you specify a home directory for your FTP site, that directory is presented to a visitor as the root directory for your site. In this context, the root directory has the same meaning as the root directory on a disk drive connected to your computer; it's the directory from which all other subdirectories at the site originate.

The IIS FTP server enables you to specify special subdirectories that can be used to differentiate the home directory from the root directory presented to a user. Suppose that you will have different users logging on to your site, each using his or her user ID and password. If the home directory for your site contains a subdirectory with the same name as the user ID, that subdirectory becomes the root directory for that user. For example, if someone logs on under FTP using a user ID of BobJones and you have a subdirectory with the name BobJones, then that subdirectory becomes the root directory for that FTP session. In this scheme, the user never even knows that your site includes other directories; the user sees only the directory with his or her name on it.

The upshot of this strategy from a site-management perspective is that you can control who sees what at your FTP site. You can store files intended for different users in their specific directories, and others won't have access to those files. This feature can be a great boon to your FTP site if you allow different types of users to log on. This statement is particularly true if you do not allow anonymous FTP, wherein each FTP user *must* have a user ID and password for your site.

Even if you allow anonymous FTP at your site, setting up user directories can be advantageous. If you create an Anonymous subdirectory within the home directory, then Anonymous becomes the root directory for anybody logging on by using anonymous FTP. As an example, suppose that you allow anonymous FTP at your site and you also have two employees, Bob Jones and Carol Thomas, who log on for FTP access. The directory structure could be the following:

```
Home
    BobJones
    CarolThomas
    Anonymous
        pub
            graphics
            sounds
```

Notice that pub, the public directory described earlier, is now placed under the Anonymous subdirectory. Remember, too, that anonymous FTP users would never see the BobJones or CarolThomas directories; the Anonymous directory would be their home directory, and they would see the pub directory when they examine the contents of their home directory.

CAUTION

If someone successfully logs on with a user ID for which you haven't created a directory (including Anonymous), the IIS FTP server home directory is his or her root directory. This means that the user can see and access other directories off the home directory, including any directories belonging to other users.

Upload Directories

Unlike many Internet tools, FTP has always allowed a two-way interchange of information. You can set up areas on your site where people can upload, rather than just download, information. If you decide to allow this, you may want to set up special directories for uploading. With this plan, all uploaded files will be in one area, so you can review them before making them available to other users for downloading.

By default, IIS is installed to allow only publishing of information on the FTP site. Thus visitors can read and retrieve information, but they cannot upload it. If you want to create an upload area, you must do the following:

♦ Make sure that the upload directory has the permissions set so that members of the user group to which the FTP account belongs have Write permissions.

♦ Configure IIS so that your site has Write permissions enabled. (To do so, edit the properties of the FTP home directory in the Internet Service Manager for the FTP server.)

TIP

If you want to create an upload directory that has limited access, make it a virtual directory. You can then give Write permissions, within IIS, for that directory. In addition, the upload directory will not be visible from any normal directory listing command by a casual user. Therefore, to upload something, the user must explicitly know the name of the directory to which the upload is to be made.

Files at Your Site

If you have ever visited a busy FTP site, you have probably noticed that hundreds, if not thousands, of files were available for download. Your FTP site can easily start amassing huge numbers of files. To manage them, you need an understanding of both your site and your files.

In some respects, many of the same content issues that apply to a Web site also apply to an FTP site. For instance, you should be aware of the following issues when adding files:

♦ **Focus.** Your files can be much more manageable if you focus your content around a given topic or interest area. Focus also helps people to remember the special nature of your site, which can mean repeat visits.

♦ **Copyright issues.** Many files are copyrighted, and infringing on the copyrights of others can lead to legal liabilities. Make sure that you know who owns the copyright on files you post. Conversely, if you are providing original files, make sure that you include a copyright notice that indicates who has the rights to your information.

♦ **Compressed files.** Use compressed files when your source files are large or involve quite a few related files; this method facilitates downloading. Make sure that you match the compression methods used with the types of systems your visitors are likely to use.

♦ **Virus issues.** If you allow uploads to your FTP site, you need to make sure that they do not contain a virus before you make them available to other people. Numerous virus-checking programs are available.

These items, in addition to liability for content, are covered in Chapter 6. You may want to review the contents of that chapter with an eye toward applying the concepts to your FTP site. The following few sections detail some matters that are of particular concern to managers of FTP sites.

Filenames and Directory Names

Different operating systems, of course, offer vastly different ways in which you can name a file. If you have ever connected to a UNIX FTP site, you can typically tell because the filenames tend to be quite long. Although these names may not cause a problem for people who know UNIX, they can be troublesome for people downloading files to foreign systems.

The solution is to use a little common sense in naming your files. For instance, Windows NT has no problem with the following filename:

```
This file contains a narrative of my summer vacation.doc
```

Just because you can use this name, though, doesn't mean you should. If someone connects from a system with a more limited file-naming system, you could cause problems for them when they download to their system.

The operating system is not the only consideration, however. If you use long filenames, you could cause frustration on the part of your users. Think how tiresome it is to waste valuable online time to type long filenames in preparation for a file transfer. Add to that the fact that some people may misspell the long names and need to do it all again. Frustrated users—for any reason—are users who aren't likely to return to your site. You should use some conservative judgment when putting together your filenames.

A final consideration is to not put spaces in the file or directory names. Spaces work well in filenames for Windows NT and Windows 95, but many tools and operating systems can't handle spaces.

Informational Files

You are probably intimately aware of the contents of your FTP site. Unfortunately, not everyone who visits your site will be as familiar with it as you are. For this reason, you need to make some information available to your users. Although you cannot always post signs that explain where things are or what is in each file, you can take some steps to improve the accessibility of your site.

The easiest way to make your site accessible is to include a text file in each directory that explains the contents of that directory. This file should have a common descriptive name, such as ReadMe.txt or Index.txt. You could then place information in that file to help the user decide which of your other files are interesting enough to download.

For example, the following is a possible ReadMe.txt file for a fictitious FTP site for an electronics company:

```
Johnson & Davis Electronics


Welcome to our ftp site. This document has been prepared to give you
an idea of what is available here.


File Name        Contents
=====================================================================
Benchmark.txt    Benchmark results from the June tests of the
                 Independent Testing Labs. Includes not only info
                 on J&D products, but how we stack up to the
                 competition.


CarrionSS.ps     Product specifications for the Carrion 25
                 commercial molten widget heater. Postscript output
                 format; simply copy to a printer port.
```

```
UltimaSS.ps        Product specification sheet for the Ultima 5000
                   personal widget magnetizer. Postscript output
                   format; simply copy to a printer port.


NL9801.doc         &D newsletter for January, 1998. MS Word format.
NL9802.doc         J&D newsletter for February, 1998. MS Word format.
NL9803.doc         J&D newsletter for March, 1998. MS Word format.
NL9804.doc         J&D newsletter for April, 1998. MS Word format.
NL9805.doc         J&D newsletter for May, 1998. MS Word format.
NL9806.doc         J&D newsletter for June, 1998. MS Word format.
NL9807.doc         J&D newsletter for July, 1998. MS Word format.
NL9808.doc         J&D newsletter for August, 1998. MS Word format.


Fiscal97.ps        J&D 1997 fiscal report. Postscript output format.
Employment.doc     J&D employment application


If there are other files you would like to see made available, send
us an e-mail at ftp@jd.com.


Last update: 7/31/98
```

The idea behind the informational files is that users will view them or download them and then read through them before downloading any other files.

Friendly Messages

Another way to improve the professionalism of your FTP site is to include a welcome message when people first connect. This welcome message can be friendly and informative, or it can be matter-of-fact; the content is up to you. The IIS FTP server enables you to set three different kinds of messages:

♦ **Welcome.** This message can be quite long; it is displayed when people first connect to the site. Typically, it is a friendly greeting, along with general information about the site or its content. This message is a great place to describe your informational files. You can also use it to tell about any mirror FTP sites you may have established.

♦ **Exit.** This short message is displayed when a user leaves your FTP site.

◆ **Maximum Connections.** This message is displayed when you have set a limit on the number of simultaneous connections to your site and the maximum has been reached.

To change any (or all) of the FTP server messages, follow these steps:

1. Open the Microsoft Management Console.
2. Double-click on the Internet Information Server folder and computer name of the FTP server you want to change. A list of sites on the server appears.
3. Right-click on the Default FTP site icon and select the Properties option.
4. Click on the Messages tab. The Properties dialog box appears, as shown in Figure 30-1.
4. Enter your messages into the appropriate fields.
5. Click on OK to save your changes.
6. Close the Microsoft Management Console.

FIGURE 30-1

IIS enables you to specify up to three messages, which are shown to users at your site.

Directory Annotation

Many FTP clients include a feature called *directory annotation*. With this feature enabled, people will see a help file (if you have created it) every time they change to a directory for the first time.

NOTE

Annotation files are useful only to users who understand their FTP client software well enough to know how to turn it on. You should not use annotation files in strict preference to the informational files discussed earlier in the chapter. Instead, use them both to support novice and advanced users.

If you use directory annotation at your site, you may be tempted to use the same informational files that you learned about earlier in this chapter as your annotation files. Although this approach is possible, it is not always the best policy. Your informational files can be rather long, and annotation files are displayed when first entering a directory. Consequently, the file can scroll off the screen before the user has a chance to pause it. A better solution might be to create an annotation file that directs the user to read the informational file. This method of annotating creates short files and maximizes your use of informational files.

To support directory annotation at your FTP site, you need to learn how to create the annotation files and then enable directory annotation on your server. These tasks are covered in the following sections.

Creating Annotation Files

Creating annotation files is rather easy because annotation files are nothing but ASCII text. Therefore, you can create the file with your favorite text editor (such as Notepad). When you are done with the file, you must name it ~ftpsvc~.ckm. Note that the filename is very specific (and very arcane), and no other filename will do.

TIP

If you create an annotation file with Notepad, the file automatically has the filename extension txt. If you rename the file to the proper name using the desktop or the Explorer, the file may still have the txt extension, as in ~ftpsvc~.ckm.txt. This filename will not work. The only sure-fire workaround that I have found is to open a command-prompt window and use the **REN** command to do the actual renaming. Alternatively, make sure that the filename has quotes around it when you first save it.

Remember that annotation files are designed to be one per directory, so every directory you want to annotate should have its own ~ftpsvc~.ckm file. You may also want to hide the file so that it does not show up in regular directory listings. To create a hidden file, follow these steps:

1. Use the desktop or Explorer to display the contents of the directory that contains the ~ftpsvc~.ckm file.
2. Right-click on the ~ftpsvc~.ckm file. A context menu for the file appears.
3. Choose the Properties option from the context menu. The Properties dialog box for the file, shown in Figure 30-2, opens.

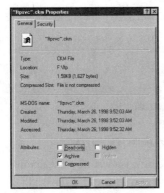

FIGURE 30-2

*The Properties dialog box gives
you complete control over the
attributes of a file.*

4. Select the Hidden check box in the Attributes section at the bottom of the
   dialog box.
5. Click on the OK button. (The file may disappear from the file listing; it
   should because it is now a hidden file.)
6. Close the folder window or Explorer.

TIP

Hidden files are not normally displayed in Explorer or from the desktop. If you
decide to list hidden files, then choose Options from the View menu, click on
the View tab, and then choose Show All Files.

Enabling Directory Annotation

The two ways in which you can enable directory annotation are temporarily and permanently. Your choice depends on whether you want to place the decision in the
hands of the visitor to your site or you want to enable it yourself. The two methods
are discussed in the following sections.

Temporarily Enabling Directory Annotation

If you don't want directory annotation on by default, then all you need to do is create
the annotation files and place them in your directories. It is then up to the visitor to
your site to try directory annotation to see whether it is available.

TIP

If you want the visitor to decide whether to turn on directory annotation, you
may want to mention that fact in your site's welcome message. (The welcome
message was discussed earlier in this chapter.)

After a visitor has established a connection with your FTP site, all he or she needs to do is enter the following at the FTP prompt:

```
literal site ckm
```

This statement turns on directory annotation for the duration of the person's visit. Other simultaneous or subsequent visitors are not affected.

Permanently Enabling Directory Annotation

Unfortunately, the IIS FTP server does not have an easy way to permanently enable directory annotation. Instead, you need to add an entry in the Windows NT Registry. (Why this feature wasn't added to the FTP service properties accessible through the Internet Service Manager is a mystery.) To change the Registry, follow these steps:

1. Choose the Run command from the Start menu.

2. Enter **regedit** in the Open field.

3. Click on the OK button. This action runs the Registry Editor, as shown in Figure 30-3.

4. Open the HKEY_LOCAL_MACHINE\SYSTEM\Current ControlSet\Services\MSFTPSVC\Parameters key.

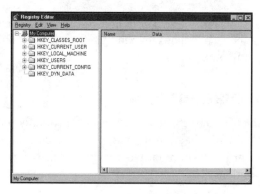

FIGURE 30-3

The Registry Editor enables you to modify the contents of the Windows NT configuration Registry.

5. Choose New from the Edit menu and then choose DWORD Value. This action adds a new value to the right side of the Registry Editor, and you are prompted to rename it.

6. Rename the new value to **AnnotateDirectories** (one word).

CAUTION

Be very careful as you are editing the Registry. Entering the wrong information or inadvertently deleting a key or value could render your system unstable or unusable.

7. Double-click on the newly added value. The Edit DWORD Value dialog box appears, as shown in Figure 30-4.

8. Enter the value **1** in the Value Data field. (This entry is the same as TRUE, indicating that directory annotation is on; 0 is FALSE, meaning it is off.)

9. Click on OK. The data value is updated.

10. Close the Registry Editor.

FIGURE 30-4

You can easily edit a value in the Registry Editor.

11. Stop and restart the FTP server.

Testing Directory Annotation

If you turn on directory annotation to make it the default at your site, you can easily test to see that the change took place. The best way to test is to access your site using an FTP client program and then make sure that your annotation files are displayed. To test directory annotation, follow these steps:

1. Locate a computer with access to the Internet or to your local area network (if you are using an intranet). This computer should be running Windows NT or Windows 95; it should not be the server on which IIS is running.

2. Choose Programs from the Start menu and then choose Command Prompt. This action opens a command-prompt window.

3. At the command prompt, enter the command **ftp**, followed by the DNS address or IP address of your FTP server.

4. When prompted, log on to your site as you normally would.

5. When the FTP prompt appears, use the **cd** command to change to a directory that has an annotation file within it.

At this point, you should see the contents of the annotation file on the screen. If you don't, recheck your actions from the last two sections to make sure that everything is set up properly.

Chapter 31

Understanding Additional
Content

In This Chapter

♦ Understanding NNTP

♦ Understanding SMTP

♦ Understanding VRML

♦ Understanding XML

Many other types of content distributed on the Internet don't readily fall into the category of either Web pages or FTP content. This chapter discusses a few of these additional forms of content, such as e-mail and Usenet news, and how they apply to an IIS installation.

Understanding NNTP

IIS includes an NNTP service with IIS. As described in Chapter 2, NNTP is a very simple service that enables clients to post messages and read them. Newsgroups can be a good way to maintain an open forum and are much easier to set up using the NNTP service than trying to create a similar service with a Web server.

Maintaining a Newsgroup

One of the issues that should be first and foremost in the mind of any Newsgroup administrator is the storage of newsgroup messages on the server. Of all the types of content described in this book, these messages will cause the administrator's largest storage headache. Overnight, a hot discussion topic can generate hundreds of posting. And they all need to be stored someplace for others to view.

Another issue to decide is whether the messages will be simple text messages, or whether the messages will include attachments. Attachments can take up a huge amount of space. Examples of Usenet newsgroups that have thousands of messages and take up quite a bit of space are any group in the alt.binaries hierarchy, especially groups such as alt.binaries.sounds.mp3 and alt.binaries.games. Although you aren't likely to be hosting sites like this with your IIS NNTP server, the same management concerns apply.

Organizing a Newsgroup Hierarchy

One of the main concerns with newsgroup is to create a reasonable hierarchy for finding information. For a few ideas on creating a hierarchy for your newsgroups, you may want to take a look at existing newsgroups. Here are three sample hierarchies that may appear in a newsgroup reader. The first group includes a simple hierarchy to divide the discussion areas into subgroup after subgroup. The geometry group is divided into groups that cover the most popular areas of discussion. The last hierarchy includes an announce and events group for four different countries, as well as a couple of general purpose groups.

```
3dfx.d3d.drivers

3dfx.events

3dfx.game.discussion

3dfx.game.requests

3dfx.game.support

3dfx.game.upcoming

3dfx.games.glquake

3dfx.glide

3dfx.glide.linux

3dfx.oem.products.canopus.pure3d

3dfx.oem.products.diamond.monster3d

3dfx.oem.products.hercules.stingray128-3d

3dfx.oem.products.intergraph.i3dv

3dfx.oem.products.jazz.adrenaline_rush

3dfx.oem.products.orchid.righteous3d

3dfx.oem.products.quantum3d.obsidian

3dfx.oem.products.realvision.flash3d

3dfx.oem.products.skywell.magic3d

3dfx.oem.products.techworks.power3d

3dfx.opengl

3dfx.products

3dfx.products.voodoo2

3dfx.test

geometry.announcements

geometry.college

geometry.forum

geometry.institutes

geometry.pre-college

geometry.puzzles

geometry.research

geometry.software.dynamic

mensa.au.announce

mensa.au.events
```

```
mensa.config

mensa.de.announce

mensa.de.events

mensa.sigs.giftedchildren

mensa.talk.misc

mensa.uk.announce

mensa.uk.events

mensa.us.announce

mensa.us.events
```

While you are creating a newsgroup hierarchy, there are two major points to remember. The first is the base group name, such as 3dfx or geometry in the preceding list. Although anyone connecting to your server should know who you are, the possibility always exists that your group could be added to another server or propagated to the Usenet community. Another area of concern is that people will send messages that don't easily fit into any of the groups that you have created. For example, someone may want to post a message about warranty information. However, if your only groups are for announcements and events, they may not know where to post the message. For this reason, you may want to create a miscellaneous group.

Creating Newsgroups

After you design the hierarchy, you can begin to create the hierarchy for your users to visit. Follow these steps to create a newsgroup:

1. Open the Internet Service Manager.
2. Click on the plus next to the server in the scope pane with the NNTP server installed.
3. Click on the plus next to the NNTP server. The Internet Service Manager will display the main NNTP components, as shown in Figure 31-1.
4. Select the Directories icon to show all the newsgroups currently available; this pane should be empty.
5. Click on Action and select Virtual Directory from the New submenu. This action starts the New Virtual Directory Wizard, shown in Figure 31-2
6. Enter the newsgroup name in the space provided. This action enables the Next button.
7. Click on Next to continue.
8. Enter a directory name to store the newsgroup messages or use the Browse button to find a directory to use.

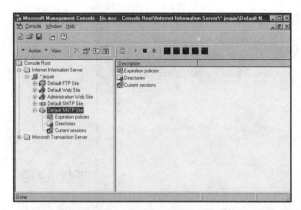

FIGURE 31-1

The Internet Service Manager displays NNTP settings.

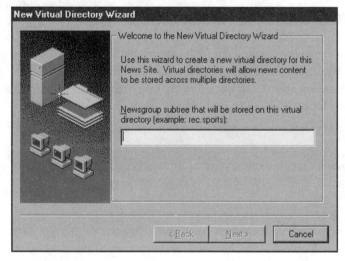

FIGURE 31-2

The New Virtual Directory Wizard makes it easy to create a newsgroup.

9. Select Finish. If you entered a new directory name, a dialog box asks you to confirm the creation of the new directory before creating the directory. The new newsgroup appears in the Internet Service Manager's results pane, as shown in Figure 31-3.

10. Continue adding new newsgroups using steps 5 through 9 until all the newsgroups of your hierarchy are created.

11. Close the Internet Service Manager.

Setting Expiration Limits on Messages

One of the major concerns that goes along with newsgroups is storage. The beauty of newsgroups is that the information comes from several people and is stored in a central location. However, the messages eventually begin to take up more and more space, especially when the newsgroups are popular or active.

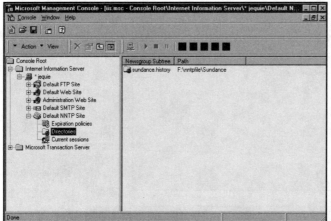

FIGURE 31-3

The New Virtual Directory Wizard makes it easy to create a newsgroup.

To properly manage a newsgroup, you must keep track of the number of messages coming in. After a while, you should be able to get a feel for the amount of traffic at your site. Determine the amount of disk space that can safely be used for the newsgroup and determine a time for messages to be kept before they expire and are deleted.

NOTE

The NNTP server uses two main types of expiration policies: time and disk space. You can choose to use both if you can't decide on one that works best.

When setting up an expiration policy, remember that parts of message threads will begin to disappear. Depending on the type of message threads that develop on at your site, you may want to extend the expiration time for messages of some newsgroups.

TIP

Sometimes the same questions just pop up over and over in a newsgroup. For this reason, you may want to create a FAQ, or frequently asked questions, message that is constantly updated and sent to the newsgroup about the time the old FAQ expires.

When you first set up your newsgroups, you should add a general expiration policy that applies to all of the newsgroups at your site. You can later add policies for specific newsgroups as the need arises. The following steps describe how to create an expiration policy:

1. Open the Internet Service Manager.

2. Click on the plus next to the server in the scope pane with the NNTP server installed.

3. Click on the plus next to the NNTP server. The Internet Service Manager will display the main NNTP components, as shown earlier in Figure 31-1.

4. Select the Expiration Policies icon to show all the newsgroups currently available; this pane should be empty.

5. Click on Action and select Expiration Policy from the New submenu. This action starts the New Expiration Policy Wizard, shown in Figure 31-4.

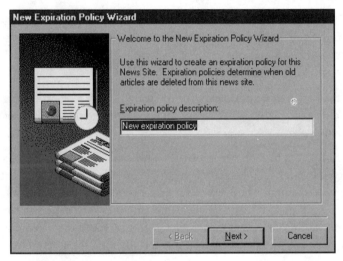

FIGURE 31-4

The New Expiration Policy Wizard helps you create an expiration policy.

6. Select an option to determine whether the policy will be used for all newsgroups or only for selected newsgroups. Selecting the Only Selected Newsgroups on This Site option adds an extra step to selecting newsgroups.

7. Select Next to move to the step shown in Figure 31-5.

8. Select the When Articles Become Older Than option and specify a time to make old messages expire.

9. Select When the Combined Group Size Exceeds option and specify the maximum disk space to be used for the newsgroup.

10. Select Finish to add the new policy your NNTP server.

11. Close the Internet Service Manager.

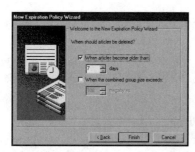

FIGURE 31-5

The New Expiration Policy Wizard includes several options for removing messages.

Using NNTP Client Programs

For the NNTP server to be useful, people will need to be using an NNTP client. This requirement really isn't a big deal for people who use the latest and greatest Web browsers, because the full versions of both Netscape Communicator and Internet Explorer ship with NNTP client components.

However, for the best results, you may want to create a Web page explaining where to get NNTP client programs, as well as including information on how to set up the different programs to visit your site.

There are several places to look for information about NNTP client software. For starters, you could check out **http://www.yahoo.com/Computers_and_Internet/Software/Internet/Usenet/**. Another good starting location is Jim Buyen's Windows NT Web Server Tools page at **http://www.primenet.com/~buyensj/ntwebsrv.html**. This page includes NNTP client and server software specific to Windows NT. However, many of client programs are available for other platforms as well.

Indexing NNTP information

One of the really useful features of the NNTP server's tight integration with IIS is the capability to use the Index Server with NNTP. Using the Index Server is described in Chapter 29. To specify whether a newsgroup is indexed, simply use the following steps:

1. Open the Internet Service Manager.
2. Click on the plus next to the server in the scope pane with the NNTP server installed.
3. Click on the plus next to the NNTP server. The Internet Service Manager will display the main NNTP components, as shown earlier in Figure 31-1.
4. Select the Directories icon to show all the newsgroups currently available.
5. Right-click on the newsgroup you want to edit and select Properties from the pop-up menu. This action displays the newsgroup's property sheet, shown in Figure 31-6.

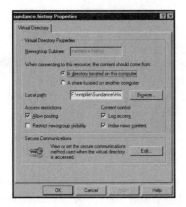

FIGURE 31-6

The property sheet enables you to change the indexing status of a newsgroup.

6. Make sure that the Index News <u>C</u>ontent option is selected or deselected, depending on whether you want the information included in the searches available from your site. The default is to index the content.

7. Close the Internet Service Manager.

Understanding SMTP

The SMTP server included with IIS is really a very simple service. It provides the minimum functionality that is needed to get the mail going. Its simplicity makes it an ideal service for sending and receiving mail via Web pages. Chapter 15 explains how to use the SMTP server for handling e-mail needs at a Web site.

However, the server is not something that you would want to use for handling a large corporation's e-mail activity where privacy is needed. For one thing, the messages are not very well protected from snooping. If you want to read an e-mail message, go to the Drop directory in your mailroot directory. The default location is C:\InetSrv\ MailRoot\Drop\. Simply double-click on any of the messages to read them, or drop them into Notepad.

The only real concerns when dealing with this e-mail server are disk space and handling errors.

Cleaning Up the Mail

Mail has a tendency to accumulate on a server, especially with e-mail programs, such as the example in Chapter 15, that do not delete mail after the message is read. Most e-mail clients, however, delete mail or have the option of deleting mail when it is read. Of course, there aren't any e-mail clients that delete the message if the user doesn't log on. You may want to periodically check the Drop folder to make sure that it isn't getting filled with old e-mail messages.

Undeliverable mail is another story. When a message cannot be delivered, a copy of the message is sent to the user with a nondelivery report, or NDR. You can also have a copy of the NDR sent to an administrator. An NDR is treated just like any other mail message, and if undeliverable, it will be moved to the Badmail directory.

Managing Domains

The SMTP server enables you to create and manage two types of domains: local and remote. A *local domain* stores messages in the Drop folder. A *remote domain* is one that the SMTP server really doesn't control. Messages are sent to this domain, which is located through a DNS server, or an NDR message is sent to the sender.

The real use of a remote domain is to control the way in which messages are sent to another domain. For example, you could install the SMTP server on a computer in the shipping department named shipping.company.com. This server will handle the e-mail for the shipping department. The corporate e-mail server could be on a computer named mail.company.com. Because this server is a remote computer, you can create a remote domain on the shipping computer to handle the way e-mail is sent out to the main company e-mail server.

After you create a remote domain, three settings enable you to control how mail is sent there. You can set a delivery route, set authentication, and require that the receiver use Transport Layer Security, or TLS.

Creating a Remote Domain

The first step to controlling the way that e-mail is sent to a remote location is to create the domain. The following steps describe how to create a remote domain for your SMTP server:

1. Open the Internet Service Manager.
2. Click on the plus next to the server in the scope pane with the SMTP server installed.
3. Click on the plus next to the SMTP server. The Internet Service Manager will display the main SMTP components.
4. Select the Domains icon to see a list of domain icons, as shown in Figure 31-7. By default, there will only be one domain, which is the default local domain.

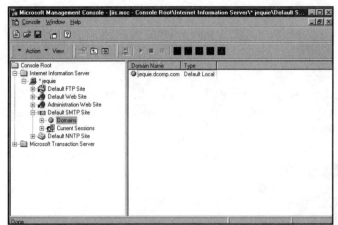

FIGURE 31-7

The Internet Service Manager displays domain information.

5. Select New and then select Domain from the Action menu. This action starts the New Domain Wizard, shown in Figure 31-8.

6. Select the Remote option to create a new remote domain.

7. Select Next to continue.

8. Enter the name of the remote domain. This action enables the Finish button.

9. Select Finish. This action creates the new remote domain and returns you to the Internet Service Manager.

10. Close the Internet Service Manager.

FIGURE 31-8

The New Domain Wizard creates new remote and local domains.

Configuring a Remote Domain

After the remote domain is created, you can use the domain's properties to change the various settings. Follow these steps to configure a remote domain:

1. Open the Internet Service Manager.

2. Click on the plus next to the server in the scope pane with the SMTP server installed.

3. Click on the plus next to the SMTP server. The Internet Service Manager will display the main SMTP components.

4. Select the Domains icon to see a list of domain icons, as shown earlier in Figure 31-7.

5. Right-click on the remote domain that will be configured, and select Properties from the pop-up menu. This action opens the domain's property sheet, shown in Figure 31-9.

FIGURE 31-9

The remote domain's property sheet controls routing options.

6. Enter a domain name or IP address in the Route Domain field to specify a server to send messages through. If you are entering an IP address, place the address in brackets.

7. Select Outbound Security to change the security information. This action displays the Outbound Security dialog box, shown in Figure 31-10.

8. Select one of the three authentication schemes for use with the remote domain. Some of the options require you to specify account information.

9. Optionally, select the TLS encryption option if the remote mail server uses Transport Layer Security

10. Click on OK to return to the property sheet; click on OK again to apply the changes and return to the Internet Service Manager.

11. Close the Internet Service Manager.

Understanding VRML

VRML stands for Virtual Reality Modeling Language. It is a way to present virtual images to the world. You can create an image using 3-D shapes to represent your office building or the town in which you live.

FIGURE 31-10

The Outbound Security dialog box displays security options.

Adding VRML to a Web site is easy to do. You don't need any additional software. IIS can serve up VRML pages just as easily as it can serve HTML pages. In fact, you can combine the two by using the `<embed>` tag. Use the following code to include a file containing a 3-D representation of an office in an HTML document:

```
<embed src="office.wrl">
```

Although adding VRML to a Web site is quite easy, you should be aware of a few potential problem areas. First, VRML files can be quite big; because their size can cause a problem with bandwidth, VRML files are often compressed. In addition, you have to be aware of creation and display issues.

Creating a 3-D world can be a chore. It is a very good idea to let someone else do it, or at least look for a good 3-D design program that will create VRML for you. Although you can code VRML by hand (just as you can code HTML by hand), coding VRML is a lot more complicated.

There is also the issue of browsing VRML. VRML is cool, imaginative, and lets you do things you never thought of doing with a Web page. However, it can also be hard to navigate, and you need the right tools. Luckily for you, Internet Explorer, which is required to install IIS, includes VRML, so you can take a look at VRML examples and see how they work. Here are a few places you may want to check out for additional information:

ONLINE

◆ Mesh Mart's VRML update page includes links to find information about creating VRML worlds and finding VRML browsers. You can find Mesh Mart's VRML page at **http://www.meshmart.org/vrmlup.htm.**

◆ Refraction.com has put together a site with a lot of good documentation that can answer your questions. This site also contains a few VRML examples. Refraction's site is at **http://www.refraction.com/vrml/.**

◆ The VRML Repository is perhaps the best source of information relating to VRML. The repository is found at **http://www.sdsc.edu/vrml/.**

Understanding XML

Extensible Markup Language (XML) is another markup language that is designed to help in the creation of more dynamic Web content and Web applications. XML is still a new development in the World Wide Web and isn't fully implemented yet. At the time this book went to press, the only available implementation of XML for use on the Web was included in Internet Explorer using the Channel Definition Format (CDF).

CDF is a sample use of XML that enables content developers to offer automatic information through the use of channels. On the surface, CDF looks a lot like HTML because of the similarities between the two markup languages. However, they are not the same, and currently only Internet Explorer supports this technology.

Watch for XML to pop up in many different forms and locations as the popular browsers begin to support it. In the meantime, you can use CDF if you limit your content to visitors using Internet Explorer. Check out the following sites for additional information:

- ◆ The W3C maintains the working draft for XML at **http://www.w3.org/pub/WWW/TR/WD-xml.html**.
- ◆ Microsoft is also getting into the act with XML. To see what Microsoft has to say about XML, check out **http://www.microsoft.com/standards/xml/**.

Appendix A

Installing Internet
Information Server

———

Installing IIS

If you do not already have IIS installed on your server, you will find the information in this appendix invaluable. If IIS is already installed, then you can safely skip the information provided here.

Assuming that Windows NT Server 4.0 is already installed on your system, you can easily tell whether an early version of IIS is installed. First, click on the Start button and then choose Programs. If the resulting Programs menu includes an Internet Information Server option, then an earlier version of IIS has been installed. If the resulting Programs menu includes a Windows NT 4.0 Option Pack option, click on it. If the submenu contains a Microsoft Internet Information Server option, then IIS 4.0 has been installed. If neither of these options is available on your Programs menu, then you need to install the software.

Setting up IIS 4.0 isn't particularly difficult, but you need to go through specific steps in the proper order. One preliminary step that really isn't necessary can be quite helpful. This step is to acquire a CD-ROM containing the Windows NT 4.0 Option Pack, referred to simply as the Option Pack in the rest of this appendix. IIS 4.0 is part of the Option Pack, and using the CD-ROM can ease installation—especially downloading and storing the nearly 80MB of required files. The necessary steps are as follows:

- ◆ Installing the service pack
- ◆ Making sure that Internet Explorer 4.01 is installed
- ◆ Installing the IIS software and other upgrades included with the Windows NT Option Pack

The following sections explain the details.

Installing the Service Pack

Before you can use any components within IIS 4.0, you must install at least Windows NT 4.0 service pack 3. This service pack is available on the Option Pack CD-ROM, or you can check Microsoft's Web site to see whether a more recent service pack is available. Refer to Chapter 2 for more information about service packs.

The downloaded service pack (and the version on some CD-ROMs as well) is stored in a compressed format. Previous service packs required separate steps to decompress the files and install them. Service pack 3 has to be one of the easiest to install service packs that Microsoft has created for Windows NT. The following instructions explain the easiest way to install service pack 3, using the Option Pack CD-ROM:

1. Place the CD-ROM in the computer. If Autoplay is enabled on your installation of Windows NT, you will see a Web page with several links to follow to install the service pack.

2. Click on the Install link to open a page describing the steps to install the Option Pack.

3. Scroll down the page to the section on installing the Windows NT 4.0 service pack 3 and click on the link to install either the Alpha or X86 service pack on your computer. A warning appears with a dialog box asking to open or download the file.

4. Select the Open option to run the service pack installation program.

5. Select Next on the Welcome screen. This screen displays one selected option to install the service pack.

6. Select Next to see a screen that enables you to create an uninstall directory. The default option backs up the files that service pack is going to replace on your hard disk.

7. Select the No option and click on Next. The default option is useful only if the service pack doesn't work properly or you plan to uninstall IIS at a later time.

8. Select Next. The program installs the service pack on your computer. After the files are copied, you need to reboot the computer.

This method is by far the easiest way to install the service pack. Of course, if Autoplay is not be enabled on your server, you will have to find the installation program on the CD-ROM. Using the Windows NT Explorer or My Computer, open the file \Winntsp3\i386\nt4sp3_i.exe or \Winntsp3\i386\nt4sp3_i.exe on your CD-ROM drive, depending on whether you have an Alpha or X86 machine. This file starts the program listed in step 4 of the preceding instructions.

Before Installing IIS 4.0

IIS 4.0 is distributed as part of the Windows NT 4.0 Option Pack, an update to Windows NT. However, some of the updated technology that is used with IIS 4.0 is included in Internet Explorer (IE) 4.01. If you do not have IE 4.01 installed on your system, you must install it before you can install the Option Pack. If you already have IE 4.01 running on your system, then you can skip this section.

One thing to note is that the Option Pack CD-ROM includes a copy of the basic IE browser. This version does not include some of the IE 4.0 features, such as Microsoft NetMeeting and NetShow. However, most of these features won't be used on your server, anyway. If you already have IE 4.0 installed, you might want to download the 4.01 upgrade. You can find information for downloading this upgrade at **http://www.microsoft.com/ie4/**.

ONLINE

Installing the Servers

With IE 4.01 installed, you are ready to upgrade your server by installing the IIS 4.0 and other Option Pack components. These components are stored in a collection of compressed files but are installed using one installation program. You can locate these files either on the Option Pack CD-ROM or from the Microsoft Web site (**http://backoffice.microsoft.com/downtrial/optionpack.asp**). Here is a short list of the main components of the Microsoft Windows NT 4.0 Option Pack:

ONLINE

- ◆ **Internet Information Server.** Includes services for handling FTP and Web sites as well as NNTP and SMTP servers.

- ◆ **Transaction Server.** Handles transactions, such as database transactions, allowing you to undo transactions or cancel them. (This essential component of IIS is covered in Chapter 19.)

- ◆ **Index Server.** Indexes your site. (See Chapter 29 for details.)

- ◆ **Microsoft Management Console.** Configures and controls IIS. This technology will probably be included in Windows NT 5.0. (See Chapter 3 For details.)

- ◆ **Data Access Components.** Installs various drivers and files necessary for ODBC and database access. (Databases are covered in Part IV.)

To install IIS 4.0, follow these steps:

1. Start the Setup program by double-clicking on the Setup Program icon found on the Option Pack CD-ROM or in the directory containing the files that you downloaded. The opening dialog box shows some of the Option Pack features.

2. Click on <u>N</u>ext to see the Software License Agreement. You must agree to abide by the terms of this agreement before installing and running the software.

3. Click on Accept to find a list of installation options, as shown in Figure A-1 and described in steps 4 through 6.

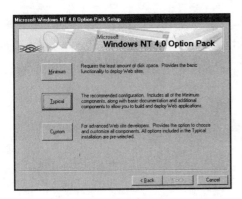

FIGURE A-1

IIS has three basic configurations: minimum, typical, and custom.

4. Select <u>M</u>inimum installation to install the minimum IIS 4.0 components. This configuration includes the Web Publishing service and tools needed to manage it.

5. Select <u>T</u>ypical installation to install both a Web site and an FTP site and have the documentation to go with them.

6. Select C<u>u</u>stom installation to select the components that you want to use. This option opens the dialog box shown in Figure A-2, which is also used when you add or remove components at a later time. Some of the options listed in Figure A-2 require other components to work, so deselecting one option may deselect many options.

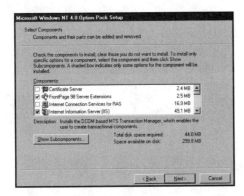

FIGURE A-2

The custom installation enables you to select your own combination of components.

7. Select the directories to be used for the services that you will be installing. Your selection depends on the type of installation that you are doing. With the minimum installation, you will be asked for the physical location of your Web site.

8. Select <u>N</u>ext to select a location for Microsoft Transaction Server. The default location for MTS will generally be fine, so you don't need to make any changes.

9. Select <u>N</u>ext again to open the dialog box shown in Figure A-3.

10. Select either <u>L</u>ocal or <u>R</u>emote administration of your server. If you select the Remote option, you will need to enter an account with administrative rights.

11. Select <u>N</u>ext; you will have to wait while the files are installed for your server.

12. Reboot the computer after IIS 4.0 is installed.

You can also use this Setup program to add or remove IIS components after the initial installation. For example, if you get a full-featured e-mail server, you may want to remove the SMTP server.

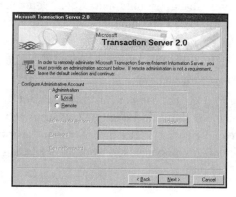

FIGURE A-3

Remote administration requires administrative rights.

Appendix B

Troubleshooting
Your Site

———

After IIS is installed at your site, you need to test your installation to make sure that everything is working as it should. This appendix focuses on testing different aspects of your site and troubleshooting any problems you may discover. If you are lucky, you may never need the information in this appendix. On the other hand, understanding the principles and information covered here doesn't hurt.

Testing Your Installation

When you install IIS, three components can be installed: the Web server, the FTP server, and the Gopher server. These components should be tested individually to ensure that they are functioning properly and that people can access your site. The following sections explain how to test each service.

> **NOTE**
>
> If you run into problems testing any component of your installation, follow the applicable troubleshooting steps covered later in this appendix.

Testing the Web Server

Before you can go through the testing steps for your Web server, you must have HTML files in your home directory.

> **NOTE**
>
> When you install IIS, a default HTML page is automatically installed. This page is provided for example use only; it contains links to other Microsoft sites. This page is more than adequate for testing purposes.

When you are ready to test your Web server, follow these steps:

1. Locate another computer that has access to your system either through the Internet or through your local intranet.

2. Start a Web browser program on the testing computer.

3. Enter the URL for your new server in the URL field of the browser. (Be sure to include the http:// specification at the front of the URL, along with any port specification if you installed the Web server to use a nonstandard port.)

The default page for your server should appear on the browser's screen.

Notice that the testing steps are really quite simple. When you are done (and if your server is accessible through the Internet), you may want to contact one or more friends across the country and ask them to follow the same steps. If all is working right, they should be able to see your information just as easily as you did.

Testing the FTP Server

When you are ready to test your FTP site installation, you can use Windows NT to make sure that a character-based FTP client can access your FTP server. Follow these steps:

1. Locate another computer that has access either to the Internet or to your intranet. This computer should be running Windows NT and will be used for all subsequent testing steps.

2. Choose the Programs option from the Start menu. The Programs menu appears.

3. Choose the Command Prompt option from the Programs menu. A command prompt window opens.

At the command prompt, enter the command **ftp**, followed by the DNS address of your FTP server. For example, the following command starts the FTP program and connects to a remote host:

```
ftp ftp.dcomp.com
```

5. When the FTP prompt appears, try to display a directory of the remote server by using the **DIR** command. (Figure B-1 shows an example of an FTP directory listing.)

```
Command Prompt - ftp dcomp.com                          _ □ X
Microsoft(R) Windows NT(TM)
(C) Copyright 1985-1996 Microsoft Corp.

C:\>ftp dcomp.com
Connected to dcomp.com.
220 dci-server Microsoft FTP Service (Version 3.0).
User (dcomp.com:(none)): anonymous
331 Anonymous access allowed, send identity (e-mail name) as password.
Password:
230 Anonymous user logged in.
ftp> dir
200 PORT command successful.
150 Opening ASCII mode data connection for /bin/ls.
d--------    1 owner    group          0 Jun 10  1996 Marketing
d--------    1 owner    group          0 Apr 24  1996 pub
d--------    1 owner    group          0 Oct 28  1996 Upload
226 Transfer complete.
201 bytes received in 0.24 seconds (0.84 Kbytes/sec)
ftp>
```

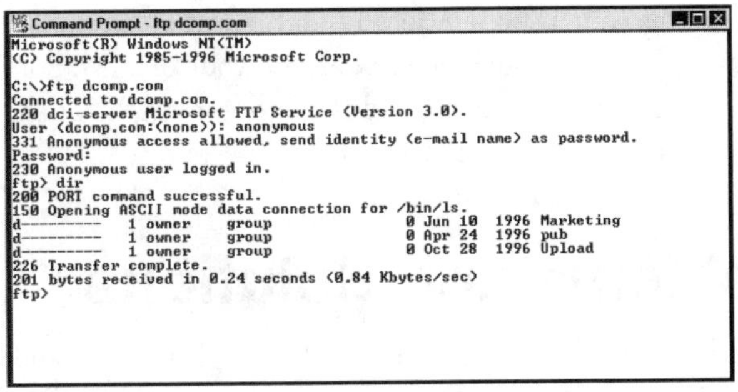

FIGURE B-1

An FTP directory listing looks very much like a DOS or UNIX directory listing.

You can also use a Web browser to test the availability of your FTP site. To ensure that the FTP client in a Web browser can reach your FTP server, follow these steps:

1. Start a Web browser on a computer connected to the Internet or your intranet.

2. Enter the URL for your new FTP server in the URL field of the browser. (Be sure to include the `ftp://` specification at the beginning of the URL, along with any port specification if you installed your FTP server to use a nonstandard port.)

3. A directory of files from your FTP site should appear on the browser's screen. (Figure B-2 shows an example of an FTP directory as displayed by a Web browser.)

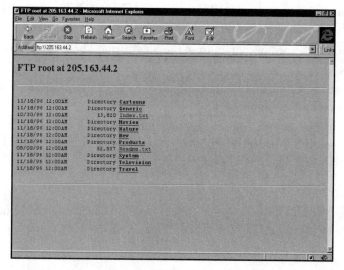

FIGURE B-2

Web browsers can access FTP sites.

When you are done testing your FTP site locally, and if you are connected to the Internet, you may want to contact someone else outside your organization and ask that person to follow the same testing steps. If all is working right, he or she should be able to see your information just as easily as you did.

Common Problems and Solutions

By and large, using IIS to publish information is fairly straightforward and easy. At times, however, you may bump into something that puzzles you. The following sections provide some guidance for common problems you may encounter.

General Problems

Many types of problems apply to all IIS services. These problems typically have to do not with IIS, but with other "pieces of the puzzle" that must be in place for IIS to function as expected. The following sections detail a few of these general problems.

Clients Can't Locate the Server

This problem is a common one for new Internet sites. To narrow down the problem, determine the IP address of your server. Then go to another computer (preferably outside of your organization) and try to connect to your server using the IP address. For instance, if your IP address is 205.163.44.2 and you want to connect to your Web server, you could use the following URL in a browser:

```
http://205.163.44.2
```

Likewise, if you are testing your FTP server, you could use the following at the Windows NT command prompt to attempt to connect to your FTP server:

```
ftp 205.163.44.2
```

If the connection works when you are using the IP address, but not when you are using the domain name, the problem lies with your DNS server or the DNS entry for your site. If the connection doesn't work either way, the problem is in your IIS server.

DNS Problem

If the problem is your DNS server, try the following solutions:

◆ Check the Services area of the Control Panel to see that your DNS server is functioning. If the DNS service hasn't been started, start it.

◆ Check your DNS configuration files to make sure that your spelling and syntax are correct. DNS configuration files can be tricky, so look for small things such as missing periods or misspelled server names.

◆ If your DNS server seems to be functioning, contact the Internet provider for the computer from which you did the original checking. Its DNS server may not be providing a correct resolution to your domain name. Talk over your problem with the tech support personnel.

If you still cannot determine the solution to the problem, then you may need to do some troubleshooting specific to your DNS server. For some good guidance in this area, refer to the book *DNS and BIND* by Paul Albitz and Cricket Liu, published by

O'Reilly and Associates. If you have access to the Internet, you can try the following sites for more information on DNS theory and management:

ONLINE

- ♦ **ftp://ftp.njit.edu/pub/dns/Comp.protocols.tcp-ip.domains.FAQ**
- ♦ **http://www.telemark.net/~randallg/ntdns.htm**

Server Problem

If the problem is related to your IIS server, try these potential solutions:

- ♦ Use the Internet Service Manager to make sure that your server is actually running. The Internet Service Manager indicates in its program window whether each of your servers is running.

- ♦ Use the Network applet in the Control Panel to make sure that your TCP/IP configuration is correct.

- ♦ Make sure that you have a valid Internet connection to the server. The best way to test the connection is to use the `Ping` command from the server to verify the existence of an outside server. (I always try the command **`ping internic.net`** at the command prompt.) If you get a response, you have an active connection; if you don't, you have a connection problem.

Reinstalling IIS in a Different Directory

If, for some bizarre reason, you need to reinstall IIS in a directory different from where it was first installed, you can do so with a minimum of trouble. The Windows NT 4.0 Option Pack Setup program used to install IIS and its components enables you to remove your installation. To effectively remove and reinstall your IIS site, follow these steps:

1. Remove any IIS components outside of the base components. For instance, remove the NetShow server or dbWeb.

2. Start the Setup program (the one you used to install IIS) and use the Remove All button. Follow any instructions presented on the screen. Removing IIS does not affect the directory structure you installed for your documents.

3. Reinstall IIS, ensuring that you use the directories you want to use.

4. Configure IIS for any necessary home directories or virtual directories.

5. Transfer any content from your old directories to your new directories.

6. Remove the old directories, as appropriate.

Problems in Accessing Files and Directories on the System

Problems in accessing files and directories have several causes, but all of them should be relatively easy to fix.

First, check to make sure that the documents and directories are within the home directory you created for your server. As an alternative, you could make a directory on another drive accessible as a virtual directory, as discussed in Chapter 5.

Next, make sure that none of the filenames or directory names contain spaces. Even though Windows NT allows spaces in names, some client software (including Web browsers and FTP clients) tend to have problems with such conventions.

The Root Directory Isn't Visible

If you try to use the root directory of a drive as your target for a home or virtual directory, you may not get the expected results because the naming for targets doesn't follow traditional path usage. Suppose that you want to use the root of drive E as your home directory. You might be tempted to use the following as the target:

```
E:\
```

Doing so generates an error, however. Instead, you need to use the following identification:

```
E:
```

Notice that the only difference is the deletion of the backslash, which historically indicates the root directory. (Go figure!)

Virtual Directories Aren't Visible

Chapter 5 explains how you can set up virtual directories to be used by IIS. If you have directory browsing turned on for your Web browser or if your visitors are using FTP or Gopher, users may comment that they can't see your virtual directory. Unfortunately, although an IIS virtual directory is accessible, it isn't visible. Thus a virtual directory is of use only when you are explicitly linking to a resource in the virtual directory or if the user explicitly knows the directory name and enters that as the target.

By way of example, say that you have a Web page containing several links. One or more of the links point explicitly to documents or other files in the virtual directory. When the user clicks on the link, the information in the virtual directory is loaded with no problem. However, if you have directory browsing turned on, the user doesn't see the virtual directory in any directory list.

In the FTP realm, suppose that you have a virtual directory off the root directory and that the virtual directory is named MyFiles. Even though you can't see the virtual directory in the directory listing, you could enter the following command at the FTP prompt to access the directory:

```
cd MyFiles
```

Problems with the Web Server

Various problems can crop up when you are managing your Web server. The following sections highlight a few of the more common problems relating to Web servers.

Users Receive a URL Error When Connecting to the Server

This problem is caused most often by the user not specifying a file to load when entering a URL. For example, the user may enter the following as a URL:

```
http://www.dcomp.com/sundance
```

Because no filename is indicated here, the browser and server assume that the URL is a directory. If the sundance directory contains no default document and directory browsing is disabled, an error is generated. Three possible solutions exist for this problem:

◆ Create a default document for the sundance directory.

◆ Ignore the problem. (You may want to force the user to specify a document name.)

◆ Enable directory browsing, as discussed in Chapter 4.

When Connecting to the Server, Only a Directory Is Visible

This problem occurs when two conditions are met. First, you have enabled directory browsing. Second, you don't have a default document file available. Both topics are covered in some detail in Chapter 5.

Problems with the FTP Server

Running an FTP server is not very demanding. In fact, because you are simply making files available to other people, you can manage those files (and the directories they are in) as part of your normal daily operations. Once in a while, you may run into problems. The following sections provide some guidance for common problems you may encounter.

FTP Files and Directories Are Not Accessible

If users connected to your FTP site can't see the files and directories you intended, you can check several items.

First, make sure that the documents and directories are within the home directory you specified for your FTP server or in one of the actual subdirectories to the home directory. As an alternative, you could make a directory on another drive accessible as a virtual directory, as discussed in Chapter 5.

Next, make sure that the directories have the Read permission set. You can set the FTP Read permission within Internet Services Manager by following these steps:

1. Start the Internet Service Manager.

2. Double-click on the computer name of your FTP server to display the FTP Service Properties dialog box.

3. Click on the Directories tab. The FTP Service Properties dialog box displays a list of directories defined for your FTP site.

4. Double-click on the directory with which you are having problems. You should see the Directory Properties dialog box, as shown in Figure B-3.

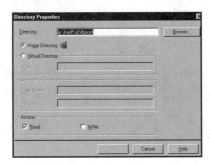

FIGURE B-3

The Directory Properties dialog box controls availability and access to FTP directories.

5. Select the Read Access Permission check box at the bottom of the dialog box.

6. Click on OK to save your changes.

7. Close the FTP Service Properties dialog box.

8. Stop and restart your FTP server.

9. Close the Internet Services Manager.

In addition to making sure that the FTP access permissions are set, you need to make sure that the proper Windows NT security permissions are set for the directory. To set the Windows NT Read permission, follow these steps:

1. Use Windows NT Explorer or your desktop to display the folder for the directory with which you are having problems.

2. Right-click on the folder. A context menu for the directory appears.

3. Choose the Properties option from the context menu. The Properties dialog box for the directory opens.

4. Click on the Security tab.

5. Click on the Permissions button. The Directory Permissions dialog box, shown in Figure B-4, opens.

FIGURE B-4

You can change permissions for a directory or file.

6. Make sure that the user group to which your FTP guests belong has the Read permission set.

7. Click on OK to save your changes.

8. Close the Properties dialog box.

Some Web Browsers Display an Error when Connecting to My FTP Site

A common cause of browser errors is the listing style used at the FTP site. (Listing styles are discussed in Chapter 4.) Switching to UNIX directory listings can help minimize browser errors. To change the directory listing style, follow these steps:

1. Start the Internet Service Manager.

2. Double-click on the computer name of your FTP server to display the FTP Service Properties dialog box.

3. Click on the Directories tab. The FTP Service Properties dialog box now appears, as shown in Figure B-5.

FIGURE B-5

The Internet Service Manager controls how FTP directory listings are displayed.

4. Select the UNIX radio button at the bottom of the dialog box.

5. Click on OK to save your changes.

6. Close the Internet Service Manager.

Another possible cause of browser errors is your use of annotation files, as described in Chapter 30. The only effective way to guard against this problem is to disable annotation files. Unfortunately, not using annotation files may seriously hinder effective character-based FTP access to your site.

Information Cannot Be Uploaded to the FTP Site

This problem occurs because you haven't set the proper permissions on your FTP directories. By default, all directories at your site have only the Read permission set. To upload files, the Write permission must also be set. To set the FTP Write permission, follow these steps:

1. Start the Internet Service Manager.

2. Double-click on the computer name of your FTP server to display the FTP Service Properties dialog box.

3. Click on the Directories tab. The FTP Service Properties dialog box displays a list of directories defined for your FTP site.

4. Double-click on the directory with which you are having problems. You should see the Directory Properties dialog box, as shown earlier in Figure B-3.

5. Select the Write Access Permission check box at the bottom of the dialog box.

6. Click on OK to save your changes.

7. Close the FTP Service Properties dialog box.

8. Stop and restart your FTP server.

9. Close the Internet Services Manager.

Before a user can actually upload information, you must also change the Windows NT security permissions for the directory. To set the Windows NT Add permission, follow these steps:

1. Use Windows NT Explorer or your desktop to display the folder for the directory with which you are having problems.

2. Right-click on the folder. A context menu for the directory appears.

3. Choose the Properties option from the Context menu. The Properties dialog box for the directory opens.

4. Click on the Security tab.

5. Click on the Permissions button to display the Directory Permissions dialog box, as shown earlier in Figure B-4.

6. Make sure that the user group to which your FTP guests belong has the Add permission set.

7. Click on OK to save your changes.

8. Close the Properties dialog box.

I Want To Restrict New File Downloads Until They Have Been Viewed

Because many site managers feel responsible for whatever is offered at their site, you probably want to review uploaded files before making them available for download. If you provide a single upload directory, you can prohibit information from being downloaded immediately by doing the following:

◆ Within the Internet Service Manager, disable the Read permission on the upload directory, but make sure that the Write permission is set.

◆ Within Windows NT, make sure that only the Add permission is set.

With these permissions set in this manner, information can be written to the directory, but not read. To change the permissions as required, follow the steps outlined in the preceding section.

Index Server Won't Return a Match for a File That Exists on My System

This problem typically happens with a recently added file or when Index Server has not yet indexed a file. One solution is to force an indexing pass as described in Chapter 29. You may also want to double-check to make sure that the file in question is in a directory that Index Server is indexing.

Other, less-common events could also cause such a problem. For example, the user could have issued a query that was too complex for Index Server to process, or the CPU was very busy and could not allocate enough time to process the query. If you suspect one of these reasons, you can restate your query or try again later.

Appendix C

Frequently Asked
Questions

There are perhaps a million and one questions that could be asked about IIS and the myriad of ways you can use it. This appendix focuses on the most common questions that crop up in relation to IIS. You can use this information with the information in Appendix B to improve and enhance your IIS site.

> **NOTE**
>
> Although you can find some quick general answers here, this appendix is not a substitute for the main text. Where appropriate, answers to the following questions direct you to the relevant chapter(s).

General IIS Questions

The following questions apply to IIS in general, or to all IIS components.

What is IIS?

IIS is an acronym for Microsoft's Internet Information Server. This server provides HTTP (Web) and FTP services (plus a few ancillary services) for systems running Windows NT Server. The latest version, IIS 4.0, is the subject of this book and is available for free download from Microsoft as an upgrade to earlier versions of IIS (**http://www.microsoft.com/iis/default.asp**).

Can IIS 4.0 be used on Windows NT workstation?

No, IIS is designed to run only on Windows NT Server. Windows NT Workstation will run the Personal Web Server, but not IIS 4.0.

What are the minimum system requirements for IIS?

According to Microsoft information, you can run IIS on any system capable of running Windows NT Server 4.0. For satisfactory performance, however, you will want at least a Pentium system with 32MB of memory, a fast hard drive, and a network connection. Detailed system requirements, including those for other Windows NT platforms, can be found in Chapter 2.

What online resources are available for IIS information?

Some of the many on-line resources for IIS follow.

ONLINE

♦ **http://www.microsoft.com/iis/default.asp**. The home page for IIS 4.0, with links to more Microsoft-sponsored information.

♦ **http://www.15Seconds.com/**. The site for a very comprehensive FAQ document for IIS. The document includes information for all versions of IIS, not just 4.0.

♦ **http://www.dsi.org/dsi/IIS.htm**. This site includes information on how to use IDC effectively at your site.

You can use these sites as jumping-off points to other sites of interest, or you can use your favorite search engine to search for information about IIS or one of its components.

Is there a huge difference between IIS 3.0 and 4.0?

Microsoft has made quite a few changes in the move from IIS 3.0 to IIS 4.0. Perhaps the biggest change is in the way that IIS 4.0 stores its configuration information. In previous versions of IIS, information was stored in the regular Windows NT Registry. IIS 4.0 stores configuration information in a *metabase*. With IIS 3.0, the server would need to be stopped and restarted to read the Registry. Configuration changes in IIS 4.0 that use the metabase do not require the server to be stopped and restarted.

Do I need to install all the servers when I install IIS?

No, IIS allows you to pick and choose which services you want to install. If you plan on using remote administration, however, you must install the Web server. And a few servers require additional services. For example, you cannot install the Web server with the Microsoft Transaction Server or the Internet Service Manager.

Is Internet Service Manager the only way to manage my IIS services?

No, you can also use an HTML interface, which enables you to manage your services with any Web browser and a TCP/IP connection to the server. The Internet Service Manager can be used remotely only on computers connected to the same domain as the IIS machines.

How do I change the TCP/IP ports that IIS uses?

Different IIS services use different TCP/IP ports by default. When you first install IIS, it assumes that you want to use the generally accepted ports for Web and FTP service. To change the ports, use the Internet Service Manager. Display the Site tab of the Properties dialog box for a server. On this tab, change the value in the TCP Port field. Selecting OK or Apply to change the Port. Anyone connected to the previous port will be disconnected.

Is it possible to use virtual servers with IIS?

Yes, but you need an individual IP address and/or port assigned to each virtual server. You must also configure your DNS server to recognize the IP addresses and configure Windows NT to receive each IP address. Information on virtual servers is covered in Chapter 5.

Do I need to have a DNS server installed at my site to use IIS?

In a word, no. That being said, you will probably be happier if you get your own DNS server up and running. Doing so enables you to make changes quickly, particularly if you have developed numerous virtual sites. Make sure to work closely with your Internet provider to set up your DNS server properly.

Will IIS perform DNS name lookups for those connecting to my site?

Generally, it will not. When changing the security settings for your site, you can lock out a domain. This approach forces IIS to do a DNS lookup on all the connections being made, but it will not display this information in the log file. You can, however, use log analysis programs to do DNS lookups on IP addresses stored in a log file.

Can IIS create separate log files for each service?

Yes. This option is the default setting for IIS. All services have their own directory where log files are stored. In fact, not only every server but also every virtual server has its own directory.

Does IIS support simultaneous use of multiple IP ports?

No, the servers in IIS support the use of only single IP ports. You can assign many sites to a single IP address by using a different port number for each site. However, each site will send and receive information on only one port.

Web Server Questions

The following questions apply to only the Web server component of IIS.

Does IIS allow me to specify multiple default documents for my Web server?

Yes. You need to use the Web server's Properties dialog box within the Internet Service Manager. Click the Documents tab and make sure the Enable Default Document check box is selected. You can use the Add and Remove buttons to change the default documents in the list. Close the dialog box, and the Web server will start using the new settings.

Does the Web server support imagemaps?

Yes. You can use both server- and client-side imagemaps. See Chapter 8 for more information on how to implement and use imagemaps.

Does the IIS Web server support server-side includes?

Yes, through the use of the `#include` statement. This statement, which is covered in Chapter 10, enables you to include external text files in the HTML file that contains the `#include` statement. HTML files that use the `#include` statement must use the filename extension stm instead of htm. Chapter 10 also describes several other server-side directives.

Can the HTTP 401 Access Denied error message be changed?

All error messages are stored as files in the C:\WINNT\help\common\ directory. You can either edit the files that are in that directory or create your own HTML files for displaying error messages. To use different HTML files, open the Web site's

Properties dialog box, using the Internet Service Manager. The Custom Errors tab enables you to assign HTML pages to the different errors.

Does the IIS Web server support Java applets?

Yes. Java applets are sent to the client in the same way that graphics images are sent. It is up to the client to then process the applet correctly.

How can I add MIME types for my site?

One of the benefits of the Web is that you can publish files in many different formats. Although IIS supports quite a few file formats, at some point you may want to publish a file type that was not available or was not anticipated when IIS was designed. In these instances, you must add Multipurpose Internet Mail Extension (MIME) mapping for the file.

To add MIME mapping, open the Internet Service Manager and right-click on the server's name. Select Properties from the pop-up menu to get the properties sheet for your server. Click on File Types in the Computer MIME Map section of the dialog box. The File Types dialog box appears.

The File Types dialog box is used to control all of the MIME maps on your system. You can scroll through the list to see all of the file types that are already mapped. To add another file mapping, click on New Type. This opens a File Type dialog box.

This dialog box is where you set the new mapping. Enter the file's extension in the Associated Extension field and the MIME setting in the Content Type (MIME) field. Close the dialog boxes and your new mapping is added to the server.

FTP Server Questions

The following questions apply only to the FTP component of IIS.

What is FTP?

FTP is an acronym for *File Transfer Protocol*. More than just a protocol, however, FTP describes a program that uses the client-server paradigm to transfer files from one computer to another. The client program connects with an FTP server running on a network server. The client can then issue commands that enable the user to transfer or manage files. For more information on FTP, refer to Chapter 1.

Will the IIS FTP server allow both anonymous and nonanonymous logons?

Yes, it supports both. Anonymous FTP is a very common method of transferring information on the Internet. Nonanonymous FTP is helpful when you want a person to have more access to your server. The downside of using nonanonymous access is that you open a potential security hole because the FTP protocol does not encrypt information sent across a communications channel. Therefore, your user ID and password are sent as plain text.

How can I tell who is connected to my FTP server?

The Internet Service Manager enables you to quickly view who is currently connected to your server. Once the Internet Service Manager is open, open the FTP server's Properties dialog box. From the Site tab, click the Current Sessions button to display information about the users logged on to your server.

If you want to know who has logged on to your server in the past, examine the IIS log files stored in the FTP server directory, MSFTPSVC1.

Gopher Server Questions

The following questions apply only to the Gopher component of IIS.

What is Gopher?

Gopher is a program developed at the University of Minnesota. Gopher defines a communications protocol used by both a client and a server. The client connects with the server and allows a user to transfer information published on the server. In many ways, Gopher can be considered a cross between the World Wide Web and FTP. Although it lacks all the bells and whistles of the Web, Gopher is more than adequate for finding or disseminating information, particularly in a nongraphical environment.

What happened to the Gopher server?

A Gopher server was included in earlier versions of IIS. Beginning with IIS 4.0, the Gopher server was dropped completely.

IIS Add-on Questions

Besides the basic IIS services, many add-ons are provided as part of IIS 4.0. The following sections address questions related to many of these add-ons.

ASP

The following questions are related to the ASP server provided with IIS 4.0.

What is ASP?

ASP is an acronym for *Active Server Pages*. This technology, introduced with IIS 3.0, enables you to create server-side programs that are translated to plain HTML when they are served to the client browser. ASP is based on Microsoft's ActiveX platform.

After the ASP portion of IIS is installed, how do I begin using it?

Basically, all you need to do is start renaming your content pages with the ASP filename extension (instead of htm). Using this extension does little good, however, unless the pages contain information or scripting that the ASP server can parse and serve.

What scripting language does ASP use?

By default, ASP relies on VBScript as the scripting language. You can use other scripting languages by changing the settings in the Web site's Properties dialog box. Open the dialog box to the Home Directory tab. Click on the Configuration button to access the Application Configuration dialog box. The App Options tab includes a Default ASP language field, where you enter the default scripting language's name. See Chapter 14 for more information on changing the scripting language.

FrontPage 98

The following questions are related to FrontPage 98, which is designed to work with IIS 4.0.

What is FrontPage 98?

FrontPage 98 is a combination HTML editor and Web site manager. Using the tools provided in FrontPage 98, you can easily develop content for your Web site without the need to learn HTML or be a programmer. In addition, you can quickly organize the content of your site based on your needs.

How do I add raw HTML information when I am using FrontPage Editor?

You can add HTML code directly into a document by clicking the HTML tab at the bottom of the Editor page. This action displays the HTML source code used by FrontPage, and you can make changes directly to the code.

Why can't I change URLs within FrontPage Editor?

Changing URLs or doing other high-level actions (such as adding directories) is considered part of managing your Web, not a single document. Therefore, FrontPage expects you to use FrontPage Explorer to make these Web-wide changes.

Index Server

The following questions concern the Index Server component.

Does IIS include any text search engines?

IIS includes the Index Server, a text search engine for use with the Web server (see Chapter 29). In addition, numerous search engines that work with IIS are available from third parties.

Do I need to do anything to manage Index Server after it is installed?

No, Index Server is designed to be as maintenance free as possible. Indexing of information is handled automatically, and the only changes you may need to make are to identify additional directories that you want to index, or directories that you no longer want to index. Most of your development efforts for Index Server are associated with creating Web pages that link to the server and enable your site visitors to access the information stored there.

ISAPI

The following questions concern general (nonprogramming) ISAPI issues.

What is ISAPI?

ISAPI is an acronym for *Internet Server Application Programming Interface*. It is a specification, developed by Microsoft, for programmers to use when writing applications and tools that work as part of the IIS environment.

What is the difference between ISAPI extensions and filters?

Both ISAPI filters and extensions run as DLLs on your system. A filter is loaded and sits between the incoming communications channel and IIS. There it can filter any information, as the designer programs it to do. An ISAPI extension provides an add-on to IIS that is available whenever a user clicks on a link that points to the DLL. In essence, filters are available at all times, whereas extensions are available on demand.

Can I install more than one ISAPI filter for use with IIS?

Yes, you can do so by using the Web site's Properties dialog box. Use the Internet Service Manager to open the Properties dialog box for the site that will be using the filter. (Right-click on the site and select Properties from the shortcut menu.) Click on the ISAPI Filters tab. This tab includes buttons that add or remove filters to your site and change the priority of the filters. See Chapter 16 for additional information on installing and using ISAPI filters.

Security Questions

Security is always an issue with IIS. The following questions are related to different aspects of security.

Are there any security problems with IIS?

As with most computing tools, most security problems that crop up can be attributed to a misunderstanding of how to apply or use the existing security features of the software or operating system. Earlier versions of IIS had known security problems, but these have all been corrected in IIS 4.0. However, IIS 4.0 is not necessarily problem free; indeed, additional security problems may be discovered over time. The best way to keep abreast of these issues is to join security or IIS mailing lists or newsgroups.

For more information on security and IIS, refer to Section V.

How does IIS security relate to Windows NT security?

The security features implemented in IIS are closely related to and rely on the security features of Windows NT. You need to understand both views of security to effectively secure your site.

Is the security of my site compromised if I have FAT drives in my system?

That depends on how your site is set up. If you have nothing but FAT drives, then the answer is definitely yes—your site security has been compromised. If you are running IIS on an NTFS drive and you have other drives that are set up as FAT, then your security may not be compromised. In this case, make sure that no user (including any scripts you have at your site) has access to the FAT drive.

Which user authentication protocols does the IIS Web server support?

IIS uses both Basic and Challenge/Response authentication. If both are enabled in the Internet Service Manager, then Challenge/Response (the more secure protocol) is always attempted before reverting to the Basic protocol.

Does IIS support SSL?

The IIS Web server supports SSL 3.0. To use SSL, you need to obtain a digital certificate. One place to get a certificate is from VeriSign at **http://www.verisign.com**. You can find out more about SSL in Chapter 23.

Scripting Questions

IIS supports many different types of scripting. The following questions address a few issues related to this area.

What browser-dependent languages does IIS support?

IIS supports the most popular languages, including JavaScript and VBScript. The real trick is to get your visitors to use browsers that support the scripting languages you use on your HTML pages. In addition, you can use Web-distributed languages such as Java and ActiveX.

Where can I get Perl for IIS?

The best source online is Hip Communications at **http://www.ActiveState.com/**. This version of Perl is designed to work as an ISAPI add-on for IIS and fully supports the 32-bit processing necessary to work with IIS.

Does IIS support WinCGI?

WinCGI is an interface specification for running CGI on Windows platforms. This specification is supported in other Web servers, notably those from Netscape and O'Reilly. Unfortunately, IIS does not support WinCGI. WinCGI is a 16-bit specification, and IIS requires all applications to conform to a 32-bit processing model.

Why do I get an Access Denied error when executing my CGI script?

In order for a CGI script to work properly, you must have the permissions set properly on the directory in which the CGI script is executing—normally, the /Scripts directory. Use the Internet Service Manager to make sure the permissions on the /Scripts directory are set to allow execution (on the Directories tab); then, use Windows NT to set the permissions on the physical directory to allow your service users to execute programs in that directory.

Database Questions

IIS enables you to dynamically publish information stored in databases. The following questions address this area.

What is IDC?

IDC is an acronym for *Internet Database Connector*. This feature of IIS enables you to define and use a simple interface to dynamically retrieve information from ODBC-compliant databases. IDC is covered in Chapter 18.

Can I use nonsystem DSNs with IDC or other IIS features that use ODBC?

IDC and other parts of IIS enable you to interface with an ODBC-compliant database. Before doing so, however, you must set up a data source name (DSN) for the data source. Because IIS runs as a service on your system, it requires all DSNs to be system DSNs. If you have already defined other types, they cannot be used with IIS.

I get an error every time I try to access an ODBC database through IIS.

The error is probably an Attempt to Create ODBC Datasource Failed error, which means that IIS cannot find the DSN for your data source. Typical causes are that you either forgot to define the DSN or that you did not define it as a system DSN. See Chapter 18 for more information.

Index